emerging concepts in management

edited by

Max S. Wortman, Jr.

University of Massachusetts

Fred Luthans

University of Nebraska

emerging concepts in management
second edition

process, behavioral, quantitative, and systems

macmillan publishing co., inc.
New York

collier macmillan publishers
London

Macmillan Publishing Co., Inc.
866 Third Avenue, New York, New York 10022

Collier-Macmillan Canada, Ltd.

Library of Congress Cataloging in Publication Data

Wortman, Max Sidones   comp.
    Emerging concepts in management.

    Includes bibliographical references.
    1. Management—Addresses, essays, lectures.
I. Luthans, Fred, joint comp. II. Title.
HD31.W66   1975   658'.008   73-22624
ISBN 0-02-430040-3

Printing: 1 2 3 4 5 6 7 8   Year: 5 6 7 8 9 0

preface

The field of management has changed significantly during the past decade. Not only have new concepts and approaches been developed in the field, but the interest of decision makers in fields other than business administration has deepened considerably. Problems in hospitals, public agencies, urban structures of many types, voluntary associations, educational institutions, and military institutions have cried for adequate administration during the past decade. As a result of these new problem areas, the scope of management has widened considerably.

Today the development of concepts and theories to carry the field of management into the 1980s and 1990s is more important than the development of specific techniques. Managers and academicians are intensely interested in conceptual frameworks of the subject, the breakthroughs in the traditional process approaches, the strengthening of behavioral approaches, the continuing evolution of quantitative frameworks that improve organizational operations, the development of integrated systems approaches enveloping management as a total system or a cohesive set of subsystems, and the formulation of solutions to new managerial problems that are just beginning to emerge.

Throughout the book, the major emphases are on concepts and research, rather than specific techniques, because we feel that these conceptual frameworks and empirical findings will benefit both the management student and the practitioner more in the long run. Unfortunately, techniques today are frequently outdated in a very short time. This book also attempts to integrate the four major types of approaches to management with the new orientation to management in such fields as public administration, educational administration, urban administration, military administration, sports administration, and environmental administration. Utilizing an interdisciplinary approach, the book presents the newest contributions to management in an orderly, readable sequence.

Several criteria were used in the editing of this book. First, was the issue truly critical in one of the four major approaches to management today? Or was the issue one that would lay a major foundation for the study of management by a student or practitioner? Second, was it an issue that would excite a person to explore further the field of management, in his or her academic studies and later as a practitioner? Third, was the issue oriented toward the future or toward the solution of future problems? Fourth, was the article understandable? Was it clear? Did it truly delineate the concept or problem? On the basis of these criteria, the articles were selected.

This book is an attempt to integrate the recent contributions of faculty and practitioners into a cohesive whole for undergraduate and graduate students and for practitioners. Its primary purpose is to present new journal articles to the beginning student in management as both primary and supplementary materials in basic management courses in undergraduate and junior college courses and in the management foundation course in master's programs. The materials can be used in such diverse fields as business administration, hospital administration, health care administration, educational administration, public administration, hotel and restaurant administration, urban administration, and military administration. This book can also be used for management-training programs for neophyte managers and for executives who wish to have current information on the state of management in the United States. The materials have been selected from the 1970–1973 period.

The six major parts of the book provide a strong conceptual framework for management today. Part I presents concepts and theories in management, the social responsibilities of management, and the expanding scope of management. Part II discusses the major new thrusts in the ongoing development of the process approach to management. In Part III, the behavioral approaches to management are examined. Included are selections on individual and group behavior in the organization, the dynamics of the formal organization, the continuing development of behavioral concepts in management, and the evolving field of organization development. Part IV provides a positive view of the continuing development of the quantitative approaches to management, including analytical techniques and simulation methods used in decision making in the modern organization. Part V examines the continuing evolution of systems concepts employed by management. Illustrations of these concepts are provided in articles on developing systems analyses and management information systems. In the last part, the future of management and some of the challenges facing management in the next twenty-five years are discussed.

Each part of the book is preceded by an integrative statement on the edited materials. At the end of each part, questions are provided to stimulate discussion of the issues and to improve individual study. Following the questions, a selected reference list is provided to encourage the reader to undertake additional study in the area.

We would like to thank all of the researchers and scholars whose contributions are reprinted in this book, and the publishers and authors who granted permission to reprint these articles. Specific acknowledgment of the authors and publishers is noted at the beginning of each selection. We would also like to thank Kirk, Sara, and Cora Wortman for their assistance in preparing the materials for publication. We sincerely appreciate the assistance of Ms. Carol P. Mizaur in the typing of the manuscript.

M. S. W.
F. L.

Correlation Matrix

Emerging Concepts in Management Second Edition — Table of Contents	Albers 4th ed.	Dale 3rd ed.	Donnelly Gibson Ivancevich	Fulmer	Haiman & Scott	Hellriegel & Slocum
			Chapter Numbers			
I. Foundations of Management						
A. Conceptual Frameworks for Management	1, 2, 3	1, 2	1	3, 4	1, 3	1, 3
B. Changing Values and Social Responsibility	14, 23			20	6	2
C. Expanding Scope of Management	13	4, 21, 22, 23		21		2
II. Process Approaches						
A. Planning	15, 16	13	4	8	7	8
B. Organizing	4, 5, 6	3, 8, 10	3, 5	10	10, 11, 13, 14	4
C. Directing	12, 17, 18, 22	16	10	14, 15	5	12
D. Controlling	19	17	6	12	29, 30, 31, 32	9
E. Staffing	11	14		11, 18	19	
III. Behavioral Approaches						
A. Organization Theory	8, 9	11	11	5, 6, 7, 16	28	5
B. Organizational Behavior	21	6	7, 8, 9	19	25, 26, 27	10, 11, 13
C. Organization Development	10	12	12		14, 22	14, 15
IV. Quantitative Approaches						
A. Operations Management	16, 19	20, 26	13, 15, 16, 17	9	4, 8	6
B. Analytical Techniques	16	26	14			
C. Simulation Methods	16					
V. Systems Approaches						
A. Systems Concepts	20					3
B. Systems Analyses		25	18		9	
C. Management Information Systems	19, 20	24	19			
VI. Management in the Future		27		22, 23	33	16

Management Textbooks

Chapter Numbers

Emerging Concepts in Management Second Edition — Table of Contents	Hicks 2nd ed.	Kast & Rosenzweig 2nd ed.	Koontz & O'Donnell 5th ed.	McFarland 4th ed.	Miner	Sisk 2nd ed.	Terry 6th ed.
I. Foundations of Management							
A. Conceptual Frameworks for Management	12, 24	1, 3, 4, 5	1, 2	1, 2	1, 2, 3	1, 2	1, 4, 5
B. Changing Values and Social Responsibility	5	2, 6	4	3, 26	16	3	2
C. Expanding Scope of Management		7, 8, 19, 20, 21	5	27			
II. Process Approaches							
A. Planning	4, 16, 25, 26	17	6, 7, 8, 10, 11	14, 16	4, 5	4, 5	10, 11, 12, 13
B. Organizing	2, 17	9	12, 13, 14, 16, 18	4, 5, 6, 7	7, 8	10, 11, 12	14, 16, 17
C. Directing	21, 22, 28	13	25, 27, 28	21, 24	11, 12	16, 17, 19	9, 20
D. Controlling	23	18	29, 30, 31	15, 17	14	20, 21, 22	3, 23, 24, 25, 26
E. Staffing			21, 22, 23	20	15	6	22
III. Behavioral Approaches							
A. Organization Theory	1, 19	3, 7	26	7, 8		9, 11	15, 18
B. Organizational Behavior	3, 7, 8, 9, 10, 11, 18	10, 11, 12, 16		18, 19, 23	10	15, 18	19
C. Organization Development	6, 14, 20, 27, 31	16, 22	20, 24	9, 10, 11, 15, 22	9, 13	14	3
IV. Quantitative Approaches							
A. Operations Management	29			6			
B. Analytical Techniques	29	15	9	13		8	7, 8
C. Simulation Methods							
V. Systems Approaches							
A. Systems Concepts	30	5		4			
B. Systems Analyses	30	14, 15					
C. Management Information Systems	30	14, 15				7	
VI. Management in the Future	32	23	32		23	23	27

contents

part I   foundations of management

1

a. conceptual frameworks for management

1. technology and environment

4

Herbert Simon

2. contingency theory of management: a path out of the jungle

16

Fred Luthans

b. changing values and social responsibility in management

3. is business the source of new social values?

22

Otto A. Bremer

4. how to put corporate responsibility into practice

29

Terry McAdam

c. expanding scope of management: public, health, and international

5. the emerging public corporation

40

John Kenneth Galbraith

6. the politics of public–private management   **43**
Frank H. Cassell

7. a more rational approach to health care delivery   **58**
John T. Gentry

8. international management of tomorrow: a new frontier of administrative
thought   **72**
Narendra K. Sethi

part II   process approaches   **81**

a. planning

9. improving essential facets of planning integration   **84**
Bruce N. Baker

10. corporate strategic planning—some perspectives for the future   **89**
William K. Hall

b. organizing

11. organizational metamorphosis: a dynamic model   **96**
Joseph M. Pastore

12. hospital organization in the post-industrial society   **106**
Gordon L. Lippitt

c. directing

13. a new look at managerial decision making   **121**
Victor H. Vroom

14. communication revisited   **135**
Jay Hall

d. controlling

15. the many dimensions of control   **149**
Leonard Sayles

16. managing through feedforward control   **158**
Harold Koontz and Robert W. Bradspies

e. staffing

17. manpower administration: a new role in corporate management 169
Frank H. Cassell

18. affirmative action program: its realities and challenges 174
Gopal C. Pati and Patrick E. Fahey

part III behavioral approaches 189

a. organization theory

19. a contingency model of organization design 192
Y. K. Shetty and H. M. Carlisle

20. organization and management techniques in the federal government 201
Forest W. Horton, Jr.

b. organizational behavior

21. a behavioral model of the organization 213
Ralph M. Stogdill

22. the management of work 220
Dorothy A. Seese

23. motivation versus learning approaches to organization behavior 228
Fred Luthans and Robert Ottemann

c. organization development

24. organization development 236
Alan D. Bauerschmidt and Richard W. Brunson

25. job enrichment lessons from AT&T 241
Robert M. Ford

part IV quantitative approaches 257

a. operations management

26. the nature of operations research 260
ORSA Committee on Professional Standards

27. operations research: recent changes and future expectations in business
organizations   268
Elmer Burack and Robert B. D. Batlivala

b. analytical techniques

28. organization decision theory: a synthesis   282
Richard Tersine

29. forecasting the future   295
Robert M. Fulmer

c. simulation methods

30. a systems approach to corporate modeling   301
James B. Boulden

31. a computerized simulation model for colleges and universities   309
Vincent R. LoCascio

part V   systems approaches   319

a. systems concepts

32. general systems theory: applications for organization and management   322
Fremont E. Kast and James E. Rosenzweig

33. models for examining organizations   337
Richard J. Tersine and Max B. Jones

b. systems analyses

34. systems analysis: a decision process   348
Richard de Neufville

35. model-based systems analysis: a methodology and case study   355
John F. Rockart

36. urban planning: ripe for systems analysis   366
Jerry L. Pollack and Martin I. Taft

c. management information systems

37. management information system planning for the executive   373
Paul Siegel

38. tailoring the information system   388
John G. Burch and Felix R. Strater

part VI   management in the future   399

39. the third sector and domestic missions   401
Amitai Etzioni

40. society's frontiers for organizing activities   413
James D. Thompson

index   427

emerging concepts in management

foundations of management

part I

For many years, academicians and practitioners have called for the improvement of the foundations upon which management is based.[1] Most of these calls have been directed toward the development of the philosophy of management, theories of management, and management as a profession. However, these pleas to improve the conceptual foundations of management have gone largely unheard. Before World War II, the major contributions in the field of management were dedicated to the establishment of principles of management. Few of these principles were tested by empirical research. Only a handful of managers, such as Frederick W. Taylor, Henri Fayol, and Frank Gilbreth, began to experiment with managerial techniques and to conceptualize new foundations for the field of management. Just before World War II, Chester I. Barnard began to introduce some of the behavioral components of modern organizations.

During the decades of the 1950s and 1960s, the calls for firmer conceptual foundations of management continued. Several systematic attempts to establish a unified philosophical basis for the entire field of management rather than the

---

[1] For an early statement on attempts to professionalize management, see Mary P. Follett, "How Must Business Management Develop in Order to Possess the Essentials of a Profession?" and "How Must Business Management Develop in Order to Become a Profession?" in *Business Management As a Profession*, ed. Henry C. Metcalf (Chicago: A. W. Shaw Co., 1927), pp. 73–102.

separate philosophies of individual managers have been initiated.[2] These philosophical attempts have not always been related to the continuing evolution of a science of management. Some of these efforts have led to the analysis of management theory,[3] the examination of managerial ethics and values,[4] and new frameworks for the professionalization of management.

However in the past few years, there have been new manifestations of these areas of philosophy, theory, and values. In examining the philosophy and theory of management, the impact of technology, the internal environment, and the external environment upon organizations have become major areas of study.[5] The effects of changing values in the society upon modern organizations have become increasingly evident through the demands for socially responsible managements in these organizations.[6] Throughout many different disciplines, administrative components have been formulated including public administration, educational administration, hospital administration, manpower administration, military administration, and sport administration. These expanding areas within management have led to the study of administration in older forms such as hospitals, universities, public agencies, and religious organizations, as well as new forms such as public corporations including the U.S. Postal Service and COMSAT and many nonprofit corporations such as the Rand Corporation and the Rockefeller Foundation.

The readings in this part attempt to provide an understanding of these new attempts to conceptualize innovative management frameworks, to explain the impact of changing managerial and societal values upon organizations, and to delineate some of the new frontiers in the expanding scope of management.

The first section is a discussion of the shifts in emphasis in analyzing conceptual

[2] For example, see Max S. Wortman, Jr., "A Philosophy of Management," *Advanced Management*, 26, No. 10 (October 1961), pp. 11–15; William D. Litzinger and Thomas E. Schaefer, "Management Philosophy Enigma," *Academy of Management Journal*, 9, No. 4 (December 1966), pp. 337–343; and Robert F. Pethia, "Values in Positive and Normative Administrative Theory: A Conceptual Framework and Logical Analysis," *Proceedings of the 10th Annual Midwest Management Conference* (Carbondale, Ill.: Business Research Bureau, Southern Illinois University, 1967), pp. 1–19.

[3] See Harold Koontz (ed.), *Toward a Unified Theory of Management* (New York: McGraw-Hill Book Company, 1964); Orlando Behling, "Unification of Management Theory: A Pessimistic View," *Business Perspectives*, 3, No. 4 (Summer 1967), pp. 4–9; and Edwin B. Flippo, "Integrative Schemes in Management Theory," *Academy of Management Journal*, 11, No. 1 (March 1968), pp. 91–98.

[4] Joseph W. Towle (ed.), *Ethics and Standards in American Business* (Boston: Houghton Mifflin Co., 1964); and George W. England, *Ethics and Employment* (Minneapolis: Graduate School of Business Administration, University of Minnesota, May 1967).

[5] Stahrl Edmunds and John Letey, *Environmental Administration* (New York: McGraw-Hill Book Company, 1973); S. Prakash Sethi, *Up Against the Corporate Wall* (Englewood Cliffs, N.J.: Prentice-Hall, Inc., 1971); Dow Votaw and S. Prakash Sethi, *The Corporate Dilemma* (Englewood Cliffs, N.J.: Prentice-Hall, Inc., 1973); and George A. Steiner, *Business and Society* (New York: Random House, 1971).

[6] For discussion of these changing values, see Fred Massarik, "Changing Social Values and Their Impact on Future Management Organization and Picture," *Academy of Management Proceedings, 30th Annual Meeting* (San Diego: San Diego State College, 1970), pp. 63–76; Robert M. Fulmer, "Business Ethics: Present and Future," *Personnel Administration*, 34, No. 5 (September–October 1971), pp. 48–56; and Daniel Yankelovich, "Business in the '70's: Decade of Crisis," *Michigan Business Review*, 24, No. 5 (November 1972), pp. 27–31.

frameworks for management. Herbert A. Simon stresses the need for a more profound understanding of Man himself and indicates that the major problems of today's society will be solved through the development of more and better technology rather than less. In the second selection, Fred Luthans attempts to utilize the contingency theory of management to integrate past approaches of management into a unitary whole.

Otto Bremer then examines the values of today's society; he maintains that business values are becoming societal values and that managers have a major responsibility to the society in terms of the types of decisions made and the priorities reached. Terry McAdam describes the ways in which executives can integrate social considerations into the operations of their organizations. In a series of steps, he shows the way in which a social responsibility review can be implemented.

In expanding the scope of management in the past few years, many new types of organizations have evolved. In the third section, John K. Galbraith examines the concept that extremely large firms in the society are basically public institutions. In turn, Frank H. Cassell discusses the increasing interrelationship between public and private organizations and notes that this new world of management has significant implications for business education. In the third selection, one of these organizational efforts is analyzed—the health care delivery system. Through a series of assessment methods, John T. Gentry provides a conceptual model utilizing system output criteria including comprehensiveness, quality, continuity, and economy. In still another expanding field of management, Narendra K. Sethi discusses the new frontiers for management in the international arena.

conceptual frameworks for management

1. technology and environment   Herbert Simon

The word "technology" usually brings to mind Man's artifacts. It brings to mind machines: steel mills and power stations, bulldozers and oil refineries. It brings to mind synthetic materials—nylon and plastics—and powerful substances—DDT and polio vaccine. It brings to mind production processes: continuous strip mills and hybridization of corn. It brings to mind transportation and communication devices: the automobile and jet plane, telephone and television. It brings to mind nuclear weapons and the ABM. It brings to mind the consequences, good and bad, that these machines, materials, and processes have had and are having for the human condition and for Man's environment.

But to view technology in terms of machines and tangible substances is to mistake the shell for the snail, or the web

Reprinted from *Management Science*, 19, No. 10 (June 1973), pp. 1110–1121, with the permission of the publisher and the author.

for the spider. Technology is not things; it is knowledge—knowledge that is stored in hundreds of millions of books, in hundreds of millions or billions of human heads, and, to an important extent, in the artifacts themselves. Technology is knowledge of how to do things, how to accomplish human goals. When the artifacts that technology permits Man to produce are destroyed by fire or flood or war, he uses his knowledge, his technology, to replace and improve them. So the technology stored in Western European minds and in the minds of the Japanese permitted those peoples to reconstruct their physical environment in a tiny fraction of the time it required Mankind to create similar environments for the first time.

Technology is knowledge of how to do things, and not all of the things it teaches us to do are done. We know how to build an SST, more or less, but at present we are not building it. It is sometimes said that once technology has taught us how to do something, we are unable to resist doing it. That, of course, is an exaggeration.

The decision to apply technology is made in the matrix of our social institutions. It may be a decision of consumers that they wish to enjoy a new product discovered and developed by technology; it may be a business decision that a particular exploitation of new technology will be profitable; it may be a political decision to spend public funds to exploit a particular technological opportunity. Most often, in important cases, it is a whole host of decisions made through all of these institutional structures.

Thus, we have television because consumers want to view it, and will pay for sets; because companies can make a profit manufacturing and distributing it; and because the government has seen fit to allocate broadcasting channels to it. We *do not*, in most communities, have viable mass transit, also a consequence of series of decisions by consumers, by business concerns and investors, and by governments. Technology may be, and sometimes is, overused or abused "because it is there," but mostly its application or non-application results from the same apparatus that makes the other decisions in our society. If we are pleased with the contribution that has been made to the quality of our lives by the applications of technology, the credit should go to the social institutions that made those applications possible; if we are distressed by undesirable uses of technology, the blame should be placed on those same institutions. But in either event, it is less important that we assign praise or blame than that we learn how to improve our decision-making institutions, and, by improving them, to make a continually wiser use of our growing body of technological knowledge. I assume it to be the main function of these lectures to examine the paths we may follow toward improving our procedures for deciding when and how particular technologies shall receive application.

impacts of technology on society

Technology, as stored knowledge, has major impacts on society along at least seven dimensions:

1. It enhances our abilities to accomplish individual and collective goals (e.g., to produce an adequate supply of food);

2. It often produces unintended and unwanted side effects, typically proportional in magnitude to its intended effects (e.g., the amount of sulfur oxides vented to the atmosphere grows proportionally with the production of energy);

3. It provides *knowledge* about these same side effects, which might otherwise go undetected, so that we can take account of them in our decisions to use or eschew the use of particular technologies (e.g., chromatography, an example of advanced technology, enables us to detect trace quantities of possibly noxious substances in air or water or food);

4. It provides alternative routes among which we may choose in pursuing our goals (e.g., planes, trains, and cars as alternative modes of transportation);

5. It makes us aware of new needs, and sets new goals (e.g., technology taught us that we need adequate quantities of vitamins in our diets);

6. It provides tools for analysing and understanding complex systems (e.g., the standard tools of management science which may be applied to the decision process for selecting technologies);

7. It provides knowledge of ourselves, helping to define the terms of the human condition (e.g., it instructs us about how human aspiration levels are determined, and how human beings manage frequently to redefine the situations in which they find themselves as zero-sum games).

Perhaps we should divide this list into two parts, reserving the term "technology" for the first two items (the ones we focus upon in typical discussions of the blessings and threats of technology). Then, in this fanciful terminology, the last five items become "metatechnology": the knowledge that influences and determines the way in which we decide to apply "technology." Metatechnology widens our range of technological alternatives, enhances our power to trace actual or potential consequences and their interconnections, and changes our views of our environment, our goals, and ourselves.

I hope you will not take my label, "metatechnology," too seriously. Perhaps you can substitute a more descriptive and less pretentious term for it. Or perhaps, after you read what I have to say about metatechnology, you will decide that it is synonymous with management science.

In the rest of my remarks, I will have more to say, perhaps, about metatechnology than about technology. My excuse for this emphasis is that we exist in an age of metatechnology. Historians, I venture to predict, will see the Second World War as a dividing point: the preceding period characterized by an exceedingly rapid growth of technology, the following period by a growth of metatechnology at an even more rapid pace. Prometheus, who stole fire from the gods, was the patron of the Age of Technology. The Age of Metatechnology will need a new patron, a child of Prometheus, who will kindle the wraths of the gods anew by stealing from them their decision procedures: their linear programming algorithms and their simulation techniques.

Now I have been talking exclusively about technology, and its offspring, metatechnology. It is time that I introduce the *environment* into the picture. I shall do this by means of three examples, which serve to illustrate the role or roles of technology and its applications both in creating environmental problems and in finding remedies for them. My examples will refer to three of the four primordial elements: water, air, and fire. Perhaps I will have a little to say later, also, about the fourth element, land.

water: eutrophication and phosphates

Some rhetorical phrases are so striking as to make their truth or falsity irrelevant. The slogan "Lake Erie is dead!" is such a phrase. Lake Erie may die, but the slogan is surely immortal.

By now we have all become knowledgeable about the broad principles of water pollution. We know that when organic substances in water decay, they extract oxygen from the water; and that if the dissolved oxygen is extracted more rapidly than it is replenished, the water becomes deficient in oxygen, is unable to support fish life and, at more severe levels of depletion, begins to stink.

Apart from the total oxygen demand placed upon water by organic substances, when water is rich in certain such substances, periodic and undesired blooms of algae occur—if not a greening of America, at least a greening of its waters. This is the process that has been curiously (from the human standpoint) named eutrophication. What is good for algae is not always good for us. There are other problems of pollution of water by particular substances— mercury being a recent item of concern— and by heat; but I will stick to oxygen depletion and eutrophication.

Oxygen depletion is the "classical" problem of water pollution. Technology for handling it has been available for some time, and has, in fact, been sufficiently widely applied that many streams in the United States are in better condition today than they were thirty years ago. So-called secondary treatment of sewage reduces the oxygen demand imposed on water by a combination of rapid, controlled decomposition of organic wastes and removal of solids in the form of sludge. Disposal of the sludge becomes a new, but relatively minor, solid waste problem, which may now be on its way to solution through current experiments in Illinois on piping sludge to farmlands where it can be applied as fertilizer.

Since several technologies are available for handling it, oxygen depletion has long since passed from the realm of technological to that of economic and political problems. If the current Federal program, which contemplates expenditure of several billion dollars a year for a decade, is carried through vigorously, most of our streams promise to be in relatively good shape from the standpoint of oxygen supply: fish will live, and Lake Erie will breathe again. Technology will have offered us satisfactory and economical solutions for this particular unwanted consequence of our activities.

Eutrophication exhibits technology in a somewhat different stance. Science has not yet finished its homework on the subject. I think the experts will not challenge the statement that the basic chemical and biological mechanisms of eutrophication are not sufficiently understood, qualitatively or quantitatively, to allow for confident prescription of remedies or confident prediction of their effects. Dissolved phosphates are the most commonly accused culprits in triggering algal bloom (although probably only in inland waters, nitrogen being regarded as the more likely limiting factor in estuaries), but even this is not known with any assurance. Nor is it known to what level phosphates must be limited to prevent the condition from occurring, nor how these limits vary with the presence or absence of other substances.

If basic science about eutrophication is deficient, engineering techniques for dealing with it are equally lacking. Most of us do not want the doctor to stand idle simply because he is not confident of the nature of the disease. Sometimes, especially *in extremis*, it is a good idea just to try something. In a couple of cases, something has been tried and has apparently succeeded. In both Lake Menona, near Madison, and Lake Washington, near Seattle, eutrophication has been halted by the simple, but costly, experiment of building sewers that conduct wastes around these lakes that formerly were dumped into them.

So if we do not know what nutrients cause eutrophication, we know that eliminating all of them will stop it. Moreover, we know that at least some lakes will improve their condition very rapidly over a span of just three or four years, or even less; although we are warned that this last finding may not extrapolate to all lakes, but may depend on size, depth, and many other factors. But diversion of wastes only works, of course, if an alternative body of water stands ready to receive those wastes, and will not be as badly damaged by them as the body of water we are trying to restore. We need additional technological alternatives for dealing with eutrophication.

When the experts are silent or divided, the amateurs take over. And we have had a very lively amateur hour on eutrophication. It has been based on the logic: phosphates cause eutrophication, detergents contain phosphates, hence we should remove phosphates from detergents. Never mind, as I have already pointed out, that the validity of the major premise is in doubt. There are worse things to be said about the minor premise and the conclusion. To be sure, detergents contain phosphates. So do the other components of municipal wastes; so does the runoff from farmland that has been fertilized with phosphates. Detergent phosphates account for perhaps one-third of all of the phosphates deposited in lakes, streams, and estuaries, more in some parts of the country, less in others. Our present knowledge of the chemistry of eutrophication provides no assurance that elimination of all phosphates from detergents will solve the problem in even a single lake. On this point one can hear violent disagreement among experts.

But the most serious question of all is this: if we remove phosphates from detergents what will replace them? Few of us are prepared to give up washing ourselves or our clothes to prevent eutrophication. In recent months, we of the general public have become pretty knowledgeable about some of the alternatives. We know that there is a substance called NTA, which, on the basis of its general chemical structure as well as a trickle of experimental data, should be treated with extreme caution until proved harmless. We know —because it has been done—that a variety of substances can replace phosphates in detergents. Some of them are highly corrosive to human skin and flesh, others are apparently harmless, some even have a little washing power. We have absolutely no assurance that even the apparently harmless among them will cause fewer or less serious problems than are caused by the phosphates.

I do not want to deprive any housewife of the feeling of civic virtue she experiences when she takes a box of low-phosphate detergent from the supermarket shelf. But I do want to disabuse her of the notion that she is con..:ibuting much to solving the eutrophication problem. She is contributing to removing one-half the phosphate from municipal wastes which may or may not change the prospects for eutrophication, and she is substituting for phosphates other substances that may or may not be less harmful.

Even with our present comparative ignorance of the mechanisms of eutrophication, there is a sensible and feasible alternative that goes much further toward a remedy than would the elimination of phosphates from detergents: the incorporation of processes for phosphate removal in present and planned sewage treatment works. Several quite cheap processes exist for removing 90% or more of the phosphates from municipal wastes. Using one of these processes in conjunction with secondary treatment removes, of course, not only the detergent phosphate, but also the other, approximately equal, phosphate component in sewage. I believe that the EPA has already taken steps to see that phosphate removal is incorporated in appropriate cases in plans for treatment plants financed under the Federal program. If one feels the urge to apply political pressure on the eutrophication problem, I would suggest as one appropriate pressure point the surveillance of this program to make sure that it is carried out vigorously.

Perhaps I have carried this particular example far enough. It illustrates what happens when we have too little technology—too little knowledge of the fundamental processes governing the phenomena of interest; too little knowledge of alternative remedial actions and their consequences. A knowledge vacuum is most often filled by demagoguery, by brief, frenetic public rhetoric and symbolic action followed by disillusionment and distraction of attention to other matters.

This example illustrates also that, even in the absence of full scientific understanding of a problem, courses of action may be available which, while undramatic and relatively costly, will keep the problem within manageable proportions until we can find more fundamental solutions.

Eutrophication is a technological problem. It is also an economic and political problem. It will be solved by the application of more technology, not less. It will be solved sooner and better if we do the science necessary to understand the biochemical phenomena involved in it. And it will be solved sooner and more economically if we employ sensible decision procedures to its solution—a sophisticated metatechnology—than if we leave it to public oratory, scapegoating and legalizing of the sort that we have been hearing over the past couple of years.

air: autos and air pollution

I turn now from water to the second element, air, and in order to be concrete, I will focus on a single source of pollution, the automobile. Again, this is a topic on which every newspaper reader and television viewer has become knowledgeable; and, again, this example will show that the antidote for inadequate and inaccurate knowledge is more and more accurate knowledge.

At a basic scientific level, auto emissions are not much better understood than eutrophication. "Emissions" covers a heterogeneous mixture of noxious substances, notably hydrocarbons, carbon monoxide, and oxides of nitrogen, along with tetraethyl lead and carcinogenic aromatic hydrocarbons. In particular, two things are imperfectly known. First, what level of exposure to each of these substances is harmful to human health? The difficulties in assessing the effects of long-term low-level exposure are especially formidable. Second, how do the several substances interact; in particular, what is the interaction in the atmosphere of the oxides of nitrogen with the other components, with sulfur oxides, and with ozone? Some recent experiences in Los Angeles and New York, and some laboratory data *suggest* that reducing carbon monoxide, sulfur oxides and hydrocarbon levels without reducing the oxides of nitrogen correspondingly may actually aggravate smog. "Suggest" is quite different from "prove," and solid facts and verified theories are still hard to come by.

If our understanding of the effects of emissions leaves something to be desired, there are certain things about the current technology of internal combustion engines that we know all too well. In particular, most of the obvious things one would do to decrease hydrocarbon and carbon monoxide emissions lead to an increase in the production of oxides of nitrogen. At a crude level, the reason is this: to decrease hydrocarbons and carbon monoxide, one wants more complete combustion, and higher combustion temperatures help to achieve that. But high temperatures are exactly what Nature calls for in order to fix atmospheric nitrogen—that is, to produce oxides of nitrogen.

Until about 1970, we solved this problem by ignoring it. We pretended that we were going to deal with auto pollution by setting limits on hydrocarbon and carbon monoxide emissions, and waved away the oxides of nitrogen. When the ghost refused to go away, we (meaning, in this case the auto manufacturers) told ourselves how difficult and costly it would be to remove it forcibly, and proceeded to develop elaborate schemes for catalytic treatment of the exhaust gases. That led to new problems—the "poisoning" of the catalysts by tetraethyl lead, and the danger that leadless gas would have a higher content of carcinogenic aromatic hydrocarbons. All of these problems are solvable, and are being solved to a moderate degree of satisfaction though not well enough to satisfy the 1975 air standards that Congress established.

As we also are beginning to learn, the solutions are not costless—not at all. They are going to add perhaps as much as $500 to the cost of every automobile that is sold. That is only a few billion dollars a year for the nation—roughly the same amount we are prepared to invest in new waste treatment plants—and certainly not too high a price to pay for pure air. Not too high a price, that is, if pure air is what we get for it. But there is no assurance today that NOx emissions from the conventional internal combustion engine can be brought down, at any tolerable price, to levels that will be acceptable in the long run. The auto manufacturers are eloquent, and quite believable, in their testimony on the unreasonableness of the 1975 emission standards—unreasonableness from the standpoint of current technological feasibility.

So we are engaged in a great national gamble that the internal combustion engine can be cleaned up. To my mind, Pennsylvania State Lottery tickets are a better investment than that gamble. Moreover, it is a gamble that we need not take. There are a host of conceivable, but unproven, alternatives to the conventional internal combustion engine. The amount of research and development effort that has been devoted, by private industry or anyone else, to exploring these alternatives is minuscule in comparison with the R & D effort that has been devoted to bringing the conventional auto engine to its present level of performance.

The current legal and political pressure on auto manufacturers to meet the 1975 emission standards, which will not be met, has led to an actual decrease in effort to design unconventional power plants for cars, as all available engineers are drawn off by the crash program. Meanwhile, the Federal government funds its own program (inhouse and contract) for R & D on unconventional auto engines at the munificent level of about $10 million per year. Attempts to get that figure raised to $25 million and gradually to $100 have thus far met with no success whatsoever and with precious little support even from within the lawyer-managed EPA. All this at a time when skilled human resources in the aerospace industry, which has strong technical capabilities of just the kind that would be needed, are severely underemployed.

If this situation appears to make no

sense to you, perhaps it is because it is in fact senseless. If it is, we should not lay the trouble at the door of a faulty technology, but at the door of a faulty metatechnology: a faulty decision process. It is an elementary principle of economics that a society's basic research and development cannot be left entirely to private industry, because then there will always be underinvestment in R & D. Many of the economic benefits of R & D cannot be captured fully by the developer, and he will not take account of these valuable public goods that flow from his efforts in his investment decisions. It is good economics, as well as good public policy, to provide substantial public subsidy for research and development.

In the second place, it is ridiculous for a society that is prepared to spend billions of dollars each year in order to produce nonpolluting auto engines not to hedge its bets, since the prospects of success are "iffy" at best, by spending a few hundred millions to expand its inventory of alternatives in case the conventional one does not pan out. Yet it is in precisely this un-hedged, unprotected posture that we stand today. The question is not whether the conventional or the unconventional engine is the "right" solution. The question is whether it is sensible to pretend certainty in the face of complete uncertainty, and to refuse to buy cheap insurance.[1]

Again, I have not exhausted the lessons that could be learned by examining the question of auto emissions. I hope that I have demonstrated that here too we need more technology, not less. In particular,

[1] Most of the arguments to "prove" that we should stick with the conventional engine compare the pre-pollution-control costs of that engine with the supposed costs of nonconventional engines. When we add $500 in cleanup devices to the conventional engine, the terms of the comparison are changed radically. This thought has not yet penetrated very deeply into the policy planning process.

we need to stop gambling unnecessarily on a single proposed course of action. We need to hedge our bets by resolute explorations of alternatives to the internal combustion engine. And we need to make sure that these explorations are funded at an appropriate level by government.

fire: environment and energy

If you will humor me in continuing my metaphor, I would like now to talk about fire: specifically, about Man's needs for energy, and how he can meet these needs in ways that are consistent with protection of the environment.

The environmental issues relating to energy are not unlike those we have already encountered in discussing water pollution and auto emissions. But what most strongly characterizes the situation in energy is the interconnectedness of things. A sound energy policy must reconcile the availabilities of fuels with Man's demands for energy and with the environmental consequences of disposing of the products of energy production. It must take account of consequences for the atmosphere, especially the consequences of venting enormous quantities of oxides of nitrogen and sulfur, in the case of fossil fuels, and radiation in the case of nuclear energy.[2] It must take equal account of consequences for water quality, especially the consequences of disposing of large quantities of waste heat into lakes and streams.

[2] Radiation must be considered in the case of fossil fuels as well as nuclear energy, because the small amounts of radioactive material found in coal, multiplied by the large quantities of coal that are burned to produce energy, contribute amounts of radioactivity to the atmosphere that are not small compared with those produced by nuclear generation of energy. I am not aware that any full-scale evaluations have been made of the relative magnitudes of the radiation problems with fossil and nuclear generation, respectively.

Thus, we must discover and develop technologies that will remove sulfur from fuels or stack gases; technologies for securing the fuel and other efficiencies that go with high temperatures, but without generating large quantities of oxides of nitrogen; technologies to prevent the escape of harmful radiation from nuclear and fossil plants; nuclear technologies (breeder reactors and/or fusion processes) that will conserve limited supplies of natural nuclear fuels, technologies for disposing of waste heat harmlessly, or better yet, recovering some of it for useful purposes to the extent that the Second Law of Thermodynamics permits us to do so. We must, in short, act strongly to expand the whole range of energy technologies available to us in order to enable us to exercise essential policy choices.

In the energy realm, the Federal government is pursuing a more vigorous program of support for research and development than in the realm of auto emissions. We might point to deficiencies in the program. For example, there is perhaps too much reliance on private enterprise for spontaneously finding solutions to the sulfur oxides problem. But, speaking generally, the Federal support appears to be aimed at the right targets and to be funded at an acceptable level.

To apply wisely the energy technologies that R & D provides us with, we must also create an effective metatechnology: tools of systems analysis that will enable us to assess tradeoffs, identify bottlenecks, detect unsolved problems, set R & D priorities. No one has yet created adequate tools for planning a national energy system or the components within that system.

In building this metatechnology, there are several booby traps to be avoided. One of these booby traps, into which we have fallen frequently in the past, is to dump our planning resources down the rat hole of prediction studies. There already exists a five foot shelf of books containing predictions of U.S. energy use and fuel availability for various periods of time into the future. The predictions in these volumes are probably mostly wrong, as predictions about such matters almost always are; but that does not mean that we should now undertake a whole host of new predictions, which will almost certainly be equally wrong. It means that we must learn how to plan in the face of genuine uncertainty, that is, in the face of the unpredictable or only slightly predictable.

Planning without prediction (or with only a *little* prediction) is neither paradoxical nor impossible. Let us pick a large number: a zillion, say. At some date in the future, perhaps 1990, perhaps 2000, perhaps 2010, we will produce and consume a zillion KWH of energy per year. That is true for any scenario of the future you can generate; changing the scenario may change the date at which the zillion level will be reached, but won't change the fact that it will be reached in a generation or so. Moreover, it is not at all important to know just when we will reach the zillion-KWH level. What is important is to know how we will sustain that level without exhausting our resources, our environment and ourselves.[3]

There is little point, therefore, in devoting our efforts to spinning out scenarios of the sort recently made notorious by "world dynamics" or the Club of Rome report.[4]

Instead, what is needed are models that can be used to examine alternative steady states of an energy system at a zillion-KWH level and other levels. One such model, and to the best of my knowledge, the only such model, has already been constructed by Kenneth Hoffman at Brookhaven (personal communication), employing a linear programming framework.

How would we use such a steady-state model? We could, for example, ask how much SO_x would be vented to the atmosphere in producing our zillion KWH of energy with various combinations of nuclear and fossil plants, assuming current technology; and how much if we assumed various changes in technology. Conversely, if we set standards for allowable SO_x, we could ask what changes in technology would be required to meet these standards. We could estimate rates of substitution between the production of radiation, on the one hand, and the production of SO_x and other noxious gases, on the other. A steady-state planning model of the energy system could help guide both our choice among alternative routes for expanding our energy-generating capacity and our selection of priorities for R & D in the energy field.

It may be a matter of surprise to you that the only energy-planning model of this sort that exists today was the product of a one-man self-initiated effort. If you are not astonished at this state of affairs, I must confess that I am—astonished and appalled. We drown in detailed statistical

---

[3] I hope it will not be thought that I am contemplating—much less advocating—exponential growth into the indefinite future. Sooner or later, the increase in energy use must come to a halt. But long before that happens, we will have to find out how to live comfortably and safely in a world with substantially higher rates of energy production and consumption than now prevail. This is the essential middle-run energy planning task.

[4] The deficiencies of these kinds of speculative dynamic models have been adequately explored by reviews of the Club of Rome

report in recent issues of *Science* and the *New York Times* book review section. My strictures on the use of dynamic models for analysis of the energy system should not be interpreted as a general condemnation of dynamic modeling or dynamic programming. Indeed, in other contexts where it has seemed to me appropriate (e.g., inventory control and production smoothing) I have been an enthusiastic practitioner of dynamic programming.

and predictive reports on energy, in studies of innumerable special aspects of energy problems, but we lack the elementary analytic and planning capabilities needed for sensible design of the energy system; capabilities which we know perfectly well how to create. I can only hope that my remarks, addressed to the group of people technically best equipped to design and construct such planning models, will have more effect than my cries in the wilderness of Washington have had over the past several years.

The job needs to be done. It can, and should, be done as a series of successive approximations, and an expenditure of $100 thousand would be more than enough to produce the first-approximation model. For a problem as important as designing the energy system, we need not just a single model, but several competing models to bring to light the consequences of the alternative sets of explicit and implicit assumptions built into each of them. We can easily afford the cost of such "duplication."

In addition to the obvious uses of such systems models, already mentioned, they will be invaluable in guiding the engineering design of components of the energy system. Without such guidance, environmental considerations will almost certainly not be incorporated appropriately in the technology. DDT, an example borrowed from another realm of technology, is a case in point. I do not wish to argue here whether DDT has been, on balance, a boon or a bane. The point is simply that DDT does exactly what it was designed to do: the chemists who discovered it were searching for a long-lived, broad-band insecticide, and that is just what they found. If they had been asked to look for a less persistent insecticide, or one more selective in its action, they would have found that too; indeed, a number of substances fitting that description already exist.

Magnetohydrodynamics provides another example of the same phenomenon, this one directly relevant to the energy system. Until about two years ago, it appears that no consideration was given in R & D on MHD, to oxides of nitrogen, Because of the temperatures used, and the resulting high temperatures of stack gases, the technology of MHD is particularly conducive to the production of NOx. Now it may be that we will find ways of using MHD to produce the energy we do want without producing the NOx we do not want. That remains to be seen. We are likely to achieve this goal, however, only if we include limitations on NOx levels among the design criteria for the R & D effort. The side effects of technologies will receive consideration only to the extent that the designers of the technologies are given appropriate systems guidelines to direct their design efforts. And such systems guidelines can only come from planning models of the general sort I am proposing.

lessons from the three examples

Before taking up my final topic, the technology of Man, I would like to summarize briefly the lessons that were drawn from my three examples of eutrophication, auto emissions, and energy.

We have seen the importance of deepening our scientific understanding of the phenomena at the base of important environmental problems: the importance of understanding, for example, the chemical and biological processes of eutrophication.

We have seen the importance of broadening the range of technological alternatives open to us, of avoiding unnecessary risks from gambling on specific uncertain technologies: the importance, for example, of a vigorous R & D effort directed at the development and perfection of nonconventional auto engines.

We have seen the importance of developing the metatechnology, of improving our decision-making tools: the importance, for example, of constructing steady-state models of the energy system.

All of these things—deepening our scientific knowledge, broadening our repertory of alternatives, building an effective metatechnology—call for more technology, not less. Environmental problems will not be solved by slogans; they will not be solved by romantic visions of returning to a simpler pre-technological past. In the absence of viable technological alternatives, they will not be solved by legislation and regulation. They may be solved by a more vigorous pursuit of basic science, imaginative engineering and sophisticated management science.

a technology of man

It is fashionable nowadays to counterpose humanity to technology: to posit a fundamental antithesis between the demands of technology and the demands of Man's true nature. But surely that is nonsense. Technology is knowledge, and Mankind's hopes rest on knowledge, not on ignorance.

There is every reason to be optimistic about the rate at which we are finding solutions to the problems Man faces in his interactions with his environment: the problems of hunger, sickness, poverty, the quality of the environment—and even the population problem. We have less reason to be confident that we are finding solutions to the problems that are built into the innermost nature of Man himself. As the external problems yield to the applications of technology and become less pressing, the internal ones will become prominent and urgent. Let me give two examples of what I mean by "internal problems."

Man has been variously defined as a featherless biped, a rational animal, and an animal endowed with a soul. Let me propose yet another definition: Man is the insatiable animal. No matter what he has, he can conceive of having more. In the face of Man's insatiability, how do we limit, as ultimately we must, the demands he places on Nature? It has been suggested that the excessive demands on Nature are the result of Man's producing, and that if we substitute leisure for work, we will limit production, hence the demands also.

The claim that leisure necessarily makes smaller demands on the environment than work seems to me to be suspect. Let me describe, by way of illustration, the N-Book Problem. I used to think that a man who owned more than about 3,000 books, was just being ostentatious, since that is about as many as he would be likely to read in a lifetime. I now understand the fallacy of my argument. If a man did not know in advance exactly what book he would sometime want to consult, he might wish to have many more than 3,000 books —he might want the whole Library of Congress available to him. During his lifetime, he would use only a tiny fraction of it, but any fraction he happened to need at a given moment would be there.

Now along with the N-Book Problem there is an N-House Problem and an N-Golf Problem, and so on. There is no limit to the possessions with which we might want to surround ourselves, even though each one of them was used only a small fraction of the time. (I wrote this sitting at the computer terminal in the study of my home!)

How do we design a world in which each man can have a rich variety of experiences and activities without making unacceptable demands upon resources? What is the per-hour resource demand of a chessplayer (including the air-conditioned room in which he is playing), of a golfer (including the land on which the links are built)? And how do we avoid creating an enormous under-utilized capacity of chess sets, and golfing equipment?

This is perhaps the place to emphasize the fourth primordial element, land, that I neglected earlier. Activities vary widely in the demands they make on land, and land will in many cases be the resource that they exhaust first. Leisure and transportation begin to replace food, lumber and fiber production as the major users of land. How many golfers will an acre of land support; how many cross-country skiers; how many skimobiles, how many hikers?

I do not mean to imply that there are unsolvable problems here. But there is an important and difficult task of systems design; a task that will have to be undertaken in a world of *either* work or leisure. It is a task that can be tackled with the tools of management science and economics, and I commend it to you as an important and interesting undertaking.

Closely related to Man's apparent insatiability is the way in which demands adjust to expectations. The precise meaning of human insatiability is that aspirations adapt to the environment—if the environment does not change too rapidly—in such a way that what one wants is just a little more than what one has, and perhaps a little more than one can reasonably expect to have. Expectations are formed by comparison, comparison with what one has had, and comparison with what others have.

From a Darwinian standpoint, the survival value of this adjustable aspiration level is obvious. But it has an unfortunate consequence. It tends to turn life into a zero-sum game. If we only know that we are well off when we are better off than others, then there must be as many losers as winners.

A couple of centuries ago, Malthus reminded us of a fundamental, difficult problem, the population problem. We now have the technology to solve it, even if we have not yet applied that technology to the extent necessary to stabilize the world's population. Today, our research on aspiration levels makes us aware of a problem that is at least equally fundamental and difficult: our prospensity to turn every situation into a zero-sum game. Any hope in the possibility of human progress must rest on a belief that this problem, too, can be solved. Can we invent a new game for Mankind—for ourselves—a game in which there are prizes for all? Can we invent such a game without destroying the competitive striving that we depend upon to get the world's work done? Or can we find alternative motivations to replace that striving? William James called for a moral equivalent for war. War is just one of the many zero-sum (or negative-sum) games that we play. We need a moral equivalent not only for war but for the whole mechanism of social comparison that now decides who has won the game.

If I had any inkling of the solution, you may be sure that I would share it with you. Lacking a solution, I can only propose that we add it to the agenda of new technology that we must find. Here, as with the other problems I have discussed, our hope lies in knowledge, in understanding ourselves. Here, as with the other problems, we are going to need more and better technology, not less.

2. contingency theory of management: a path out of the jungle

Fred Luthans

Over a decade ago Harold Koontz wrote about the existing management theory jungle in which he identified six different theoretical schools of thought.[1] Although Koontz wrote the article to defend the process approach, his efforts have turned out to be a losing battle. The traditional management process has failed to unify management theory.

Today a jungle of management theories still exists, but there are some clearly identifiable paths that seem to be leading out of the jungle. The purpose of this article is to identify the paths and trace them through the jungle and beyond. The figure accompanying this article can be used as a guide to the discussion; it shows that the path leading up to the current jungle was the process approach. Other names applied to this path were classical, traditional, universal, operational, and functional.

The starting point for this process approach can be traced to the work of Henri Fayol. In 1916, he identified the universal functions of management as planning, organizing, commanding, coordinating, and controlling. He also described some universal principles of management such as unity of command and equal authority and responsibility. Unfortunately, Fayol's work on the func-

tions and principles of management did not become part of the mainstream of management theory in this country until the 1950s. Since that time, there have been many other process theorists, but they have not added much to Fayol's original conception of management theory.[2]

Much of the terminology has been changed; for example, Fayol's commanding is now known as directing or leading. Also the meanings of Fayol's functions have become broader; for example, planning now incorporates decision making, and directing incorporates communication, motivation, and leadership. The principles have also changed in terminology and number. Yet, despite these changes, the universality assumption is still made, and the process approach as a theoretical base for management remains basically the same as that given by Fayol over fifty years ago.

The process approach has undoubtedly had some unjustifiable criticism over the years. However, it is also true that it was not strong enough to weather the storm of protest in recent years. This approach became overgrown and entangled by other theoretical approaches. By 1960 the process path had been completely overrun, and two separate paths emerged in opposite directions. These new paths became known as the quantitative and behavioral approaches to management.

[1] The six schools identified by Koontz were the management process, empirical, human behavior, social system, decision theory, and mathematical schools. Harold Koontz, *Academy of Management Journal* (December 1961), pp. 174–88.

[2] Probably the most widely recognized standard bearers of the process approach in modern times are Harold Koontz and Cyril O'Donnell, authors of *Principles of Management* (New York: McGraw-Hill Book Company, 1972). The book, which came out in 1955, is in its fifth edition.

the new paths

quantitative approach

The quantitative approach has its roots in the scientific management movement that actually predates the process approach. However, as a major thrust in management theory, the quantitative approach really got under way about 1960. This new approach made a clean break from the traditional process orientation of management.

During the 1960s the quantitative approach was characterized by the techniques of operations research. Various mathematical models were developed to solve decisional problems. However, it soon became apparent that, although OR techniques were effective tools for management decision making, this approach fell short of providing a theoretical base for management as a whole.

Starting in about 1970, the quantitative approach turned away from emphasis on narrow operations research techniques toward a broader perspective of management science. The management science approach incorporates quantitative decision techniques and model building as in the OR approach, but it also incorporates computerized information systems and operations management. This latter emphasis in the quantitative approach marked the return toward a more broadly based management theory.

behavioral approach

At about the same time the quantitative approach broke off from the process base, the behavioral approach struck out on its own. At first the behavioral path was characterized by human relations. Simplistic assumptions were made about human beings, and equally simplistic solutions to behavioral problems were offered. The human relations movement in the 1960s searched for ways to improve morale, which was assumed would lead to increases in productivity. This approach certainly did no harm, but it also produced few, if any results.

Around 1970, about the same time the quantitative approach moved from emphasis on narrow operations research to a broad management science perspective, the behavioral approach had a parallel development. This path veered toward a more broadly based organizational behavior approach, and now relies heavily on the behavioral sciences and makes more complex assumptions. More direct attention is devoted to organization theory and organization development. Organizational behavior is the result of the interaction between the human being and the formal organization.

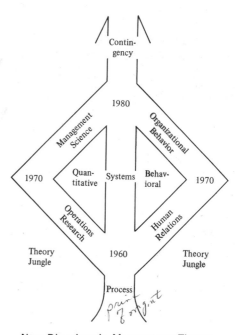

New Directions in Management Theory.

systems approach

While the quantitative and behavioral approaches were going their separate ways, a new trend appeared—the systems approach. During the 1960s to the present, it took up where the process approach left off in unifying management theory.

As a specific, theoretical approach, systems can be traced back to the natural and physical sciences nearly a quarter of a century ago. The application to management has been more recent. The systems approach—physical, biological, or managerial—stresses the interrelatedness and interdependency of the parts to the whole. Systems have served as a magnet to attract the quantitative and behavioral approaches to management.

At the present time, both the management science and organizational behavior detours are heading back toward the main path of systems. In management science, the new emphasis on computer applications and operations management techniques are systems based. The same holds true for organizational behavior. The formal organization is viewed as a system consisting of structure, processes, and technology, and the human being is conceived of as a system containing a biological-physiological structure, psychological processes, and a personality.[3]

Whether systems will actually unify the quantitative and behavioral approaches to management only time will tell. To date, the quantitative, behavioral, and systems approaches are clear but distinctly separate paths through the jungle. However, as indicated by the figure, both the behavioral and quantitative paths are headed toward the systems path. If the three approaches do come together in the next ten years, then the results may be something entirely different. This something that is deriffent

[3] Fred Luthans, *Organizational Behavior* (New York: McGraw-Hill Book Company, 1973).

from the sum of the parts is referred to in the figure as the contingency theory of management.

contingency theory

The beginning of a path called contingency or sometimes situational is just starting to emerge.[4] The figure indicates that by 1980 this path may be the one that leads management out of the existing jungle of theories. The pressure leading to a contingency theory has largely come from people who are actually practicing management.

For the past fifteen years, scholars, consultants, and practicing managers have attempted to apply either quantitative or behavioral approaches, depending on their orientation, to all situations. The performance results of this universalist assumption were generally disappointing. Certain quantitative approaches worked in some situations with some types of problems but not in others. The same was true for behavioral approaches. For example, job enrichment seemed to work well with skilled technicians but not skilled machine operators.[5]

Two of the difficulties encountered in practice were that the quantitative people could not overcome behavioral problems and the behavioral people could not overcome operations problems adaptable to quantitative solutions. In the 1970s it is becoming more and more apparent that neither the quantitative nor behavioral approaches have all the answers for all situations.

[4] For example see Robert J. Mockler, "Situational Theory of Management," *Harvard Business Review* (May–June 1971), pp. 146–55, and Fremont E. Kast and James E. Rosenzweig, *Contingency Views of Organization and Management* (Chicago: Science Research Associates, Inc., 1973).

[5] William E. Reif and Fred Luthans, "Does Job Enrichment Really Pay Off?" *California Management Review* (Fall 1972), pp. 30–37.

Many of today's management theorists believe that a systems-based theory can solve the quantitative/behavioral dilemma. The December 1972 issue of the *Academy of Management Journal* was entirely devoted to general systems theory (GST) applied to management. The authors weighed the pros and cons of whether GST can unify management. The majority concluded that the systems approach is appealing and has a great deal of future potential, but is as yet incomplete. The open, as opposed to closed, systems view is able to cope better with the increased complexity and environmental influence facing today's managers. Systems concepts such as entropy (a system will become disorganized over time) and equifinality (a system can reach the same final state from different paths of development) are quite applicable to the present managerial situation.

Despite the advances made in general systems development and the trend for both the quantitative and behavioral approaches to move toward a systems base, a contingency path seems better suited to lead management out of the present theory jungle. Kast and Rosenzweig, who are closely associated with the systems approach, support this view, at least for the present. They call for a contingency approach, a mid-range concept that falls somewhere between "simplistic, specific principles" and "complex, vague notions."

The contingency approach "recognizes the complexity involved in managing modern organizations but uses patterns of relationships and/or configurations of subsystems in order to facilitate improved practice."[6] Important breakthroughs in various subsystems of management (organization design, leadership, behavior change, and operations) have already demonstrated the value of the contingency approach.

current contingency approaches

Pigors and Myers have been associated with a situational approach to personnel management for the past twenty-five years. However, the work of Joan Woodward in the 1950s marks the beginning of a situational approach to organization and to management in general. She clearly showed in the British companies studied that organization structure and human relationships were largely a function of the existing technological situation. Armed with this and supporting follow-up evidence, some organizational theorists such as Lawrence and Lorsch began to call for contingency models of organizational structure.[7]

organization designs

The contingency approach to organization design starts with the premise that there is no single design that is the best for all situations. The classical approach was to say that a bureaucratic design would lead to maximum efficiency under any circumstances. The neoclassical theorists pushed decentralization for all conditions. It is inferred that even the modern free-form

---

[6] Fremont E. Kast and James E. Rosenzweig, "General Systems Theory: Applications for Organization and Management," *Academy of Management Journal* (December 1972), p. 463.

[7] Joan Woodward, *Industrial Organization* (London: Oxford University Press, 1965). Follow-up evidence from William L. Zwerman, *New Perspectives on Organization Theory* (Westport, Conn.: Greenwood Publishing Corporation, 1970). For examples of support for contingency models see Paul R. Lawrence and Jay W. Lorsch, "Differentiation and Integration in Complex Organizations," *Administrative Science Quarterly* (June 1967), pp. 1–47, and, more recently, Y. K. Shetty and Howard M. Carlisle, "A Contingency Model of Organization Design," *California Management Review* (Fall 1972), pp. 38–45.

systems and matrix designs have universal applicability. In practice, the classical, neo-classical, or modern structural designs did not hold under all situations.

For example, bureaucracy was not able to cope with a highly dynamic situation; decentralization did not work well in a highly cybernated situation; and the free-form, matrix designs were not adaptable to a situation demanding cutbacks and stability. Even Warren Bennis, who has been a leading advocate of discarding classical, bureaucratically organized structures and replacing them with modern free-form, behaviorally oriented structures has recently retrenched. Ironically, because of his actual experience as a practitioner, he now admits that bureaucratic structures may be appropriate in certain situations.[8]

The contingency designs are conditional in nature. The bureaucracy may work best in a stable situation and the free form in a dynamic situation. Technology, economic and social conditions, and human resources are some of the variables that must be considered in a contingent organization design.

model of leadership

More has probably been written about leadership than any other single topic. Although all this attention has been devoted to it, for years research was not able to come up with any concrete results. Most often the leader and his traits were examined. Recently, the work of Fred Fiedler, who emphasizes the importance that the situation has in leadership effectiveness, has produced a significant breakthrough. Based on years of empirical research, Fiedler was able to develop a contingency model of leadership effectiveness.

[8] Warren Bennis, "Who Sank the Yellow Submarine?" *Psychology Today* (November 1972), pp. 112–20.

In simple terms, the model states that a task-directed leader is most effective in very favorable and very unfavorable situations, but that a human relations-oriented leader is most effective in moderately favorable and moderately unfavorable situations.[9] Of special interest, however, is his ability to classify situations according to the three dimensions of position power, acceptance by subordinates, and task definition. This type of classification is the necessary goal of any contingency approach.

model of behavioral change

Although not generally recognized in a managerial context, the contingency approach has been widely applied to behavioral change in mental health and education. Based on the principles of operant conditioning, this approach assumes that behavior depends on its consequences. Therefore, to change a person's behavior, he must be able to perceive a contingent relationship between his behavior and the consequence of that behavior. This contingent relationship, once established, will affect the frequency of subsequent behavior.

The author is currently directing a major field research program that is using this contingency concept. The approach is called Organizational Behavior Modification (O.B. Mod.). It can be used to train industrial supervisors through a process method of instruction to be contingency managers of their workers. Preliminary results of this program are very encouraging.[10] The study has demonstrated that

[9] Fred Fiedler, *A Theory of Leadership Effectiveness* (New York: McGraw-Hill Book Company, 1967).

[10] Fred Luthans, Robert Ottemann, and David Lyman are currently in the process of writing the study in monograph form. Published results may be available in late 1973 or 1974.

when first-line supervisors apply O.B. techniques to their subordinates, desirable job behaviors leading to improved performance can be accelerated through the use of reinforcement and undesirable behaviors can be decelerated through the use of punishment.

However, the key to the success of the approach depends upon the worker's ability to perceive the contingency that if he behaves a certain way, then his behavior will result in a certain consequence. The if-then contingency pattern used in O.B. Mod. is similar to the contingency approaches used in organizational design and leadership style.

approaches in the quantitative area

Although the examples so far are primarily drawn from organizational behavior, the quantitative areas have also begun to use contingency approaches. Operations research itself is actually based on a situational premise. The starting point in developing any OR model is to account for the situational givens. However, as OR was applied through the years this premise was often abused. Questionable initial assumptions which were often totally divorced from reality were cranked into OR models. However, in recent years with the development of a broader management science approach, more attention is being given to situational factors. Recent books in the management science area have begun to use a situational framework. For example, Stanley Young states that:

We must know under what conditions it is advisable to move from Linear Programming to rule of thumb and then back to Linear Programming. There is an overconcern with single decision rule, and we must learn how to use different combinations of rules under a variety of operating conditions.[11]

This article suggests that a contingency approach may be the path out of the existing theoretical jungle in management. The process path was split by the behavioral and quantitative paths. However, neither of these approaches by itself seems capable of leading management out of the jungle. Currently, the systems path seems to be drawing them together toward a unified theoretical development, but by the time the juncture is reached in the future, something may emerge which differs from the sum of the parts. This outcome is predicted to be the contingency theory of management.

The successful contingency approaches in the behavioral and quantitative areas which are beginning to surface are evidence of the potential that a contingency theory may have for leading management out of the theory jungle. The overall goal of a contingency theory of management would be to match quantitative, behavioral, and systems approaches with appropriate situational factors.

Although this goal would be difficult to reach, the contingency theory could serve as an effective framework for development. Fiedler's work proves that it is possible. His contingency model could serve as a prototype. The challenge for the future is to develop a contingency theory for management as a whole.

[11] Stanley D. Young, "Organization as a Total System," in Fred Luthans, ed., *Contemporary Readings in Organizational Behavior* (New York: McGraw-Hill Book Company, 1972), p. 109. For other examples see David W. Miller, and Martin K. Starr, *Executive Decisions and Operations Research* (Englewood Cliffs, N.J.: Prentice-Hall, 1970) and Thomas R. Prince, *Information Systems for Management Planning and Control* (Homewood, Ill.: Richard D. Irwin, Inc. 1970).

changing values and social responsibility in management

3. is business the source of new social values?

Otto A. Bremer

Business is today the most significant force shaping American life and the strongest influence determining the everyday values of the average citizen; the operative values in the management of a corporate enterprise tend to become the operative values in the daily life of society.

I have been making this suggestion to groups of businessmen in recent months, and I have not been getting much agreement. Most executives react by claiming that the opposite is true: business is fighting for the survival of its way of life, and at times it seems as if all the rest of society is against it. They ask how I can support my statement when—

. . . a steady stream of newspaper and magazine articles blames business for nearly every social ill, from pollution and

Reprinted from *Harvard Business Review*, 49, No. 6 (November–December 1971), pp. 121–126, with permission of the publisher. © 1971 by the President and Fellows of Harvard College; all rights reserved.

racial tension to unemployment and the war in Vietnam;

. . . a growing percentage of college graduates are eschewing business for other occupations;

. . . a statement from Ralph Nader receives more positive public response than one from a thoughtful corporate manager.

All this surface evidence, however, may be misleading. We must be careful how we interpret it. If it is true that businessmen are being blamed for so much of what seems wrong in our society, the foregoing points could actually be supporting evidence that the influence of business is indeed greater than ever before and that some people are reacting against what they perceive to be the negative aspects. An influence can be significant in the reaction it stimulates.

Consider what is happening on the campuses. "Surely," say those who disagree with my thesis, "values are being expressed there which were not shaped by business." Perhaps, but let us look deeper. The present student generation has grown up with less value input from traditional sources than any previous one. It is also the first to have had a lifelong exposure to nontraditional values through television. My experience with these students has convinced me that, more than any older generation, they are keenly aware of the dominant influence of business on society.

Of course, they react in a variety of ways. Some are not aware of how much they have been influenced and accept rather uncritically the priority of economic values. This group is becoming smaller and smaller. More commonly, and with varying degrees of intensity, students sense the effect of business on nearly every aspect of life and are fearful of further domination in the future. The more vocal ones label the influence "oppressive"; the more active ones attempt to escape it by establishing some form of "counter-culture."

The purpose of this article is to show why I am firmly convinced that the future of our society is going to be determined more by the day-to-day decisions of corporate managers—and the values that dictate these decisions—than by any other single influence. This conclusion is reached after 25 years as a student of business, a pastor to businessmen, and a campus pastor in turbulent Isla Vista watching the Bank of America burn. I am convinced that if the business community will recognize the challenge that goes with the crucial influence it wields, we will not only insure a better future for the American people but also provide a renewed sense of meaning, purpose, and fulfillment for business executives.

supporting evidence

I first became aware of the impact of business on a person's nonbusiness attitudes and values in pastoral counseling associa-

tions with businessmen. I had always assumed that the basic values of a person—in business and in private life—were shaped from mother's knee, church, community, and so on. But I discovered the following:

- Those executives who were most confident about life, open to other persons, and able to cope with present-day ambiguities and changes often described their corporate life in ways that showed they were influenced by very positive (from my point of view) values within the organization.
- When businessmen discussed questions of religious belief, marital relations, and all kinds of interpersonal problems, their views were loaded with attitudes and opinions reflecting values operative in corporate life.

Moreover, I also discovered that corporate values were embedded in the lives of both business and nonbusiness people alike.

It is difficult to find specific illustrations that adequately support my sweeping thesis. One problem is that the influence of business decisions on social values has two aspects: (a) the cumulative effect on people's values of the business decisions themselves, and (b) the way the values which dictate these decisions tend to become the values determining non-business behavior.

Most readers will be familiar with examples of the first aspect, such as products and promotion practices that reputedly affect people's behavior and values. Each of us could supply further illustrations by reflecting on recent nonbusiness behavior that was influenced by business decisions.

Less attention, however, has been given to the way in which economic and business values supporting these decisions have been transferred from business institutions to society in general. Here are some illustrations from my own experience:

- Of all our institutions, the family is most vulnerable to the influence of business values spilling over society in general. In my marriage and family counseling I often encounter people who look upon the family as primarily a financial institution— usually without being aware this is happening. Success is judged by the amount of capital accumulation and the expansion of assets. Difficulties, such as divorce and the rejection of younger members, frequently have their roots in the charge that someone is "unproductive" or "does not contribute to family success." Unconditional love, in the traditional, religious sense, has given way in these families to the standards of accountability appropriate to business.

- Increasingly, other institutions are adopting business methods and the values that support them, such as efficiency, profitability, productivity, and quantitative criteria. There is no campaign by businessmen to bring this about, but demands to put public schools, universities, social service agencies, and churches on a "sound business basis" are receiving more and more support these days. In most cases I find myself approving, but should we not think long and hard about the future effects? For example, one group of churches is adopting Planning, Programming, Budgeting Systems (PPBS) as its basic administrative tool, and the church "executives" are attending explanatory seminars at the University of Michigan School of Industrial Relations. The present leadership is confident it can modify the assumptions of quantitatively measurable results to include the intangible aims and purposes of religion. Somehow, though, the two seem diametrically opposed.

- Think about the way an average citizen invests in a pension fund. The value message he gets from the fund manager is most likely focused at maximizing his return on the investment in financial terms; he watches the fund closely and identifies his future with it. But are there not other returns on this investment, based on other values that are being overridden by the solely economic one? The investor thinks in economic terms about his future because he has been influenced in that direction. But what about his future in terms of a clean environment, racial equality, and individual dignity? There are corporations which further these virtues and make a profit, and corporations which do not further them and make a profit. Why not invest in the former to insure a more "valuable" future? Most people don't think of this because economic values are dominating the others.

the traditional mix

I hasten to add that none of the foregoing illustrations prove that the values determining business decisions actually become the values which people in society accept as normal. Very few research instruments are available to assess the influence of business on society in the area of values. Even if the instruments were available now, only time would reveal what the actual consequences will be.

Obviously, we must do our own thinking on this elusive issue. We should probably start with a look at how the values of the average American have been formed in the past and what the roles of business and other institutions have been up to recently.

The United States has traditionally

depended on the interplay of various "value input sources"—farm life, communities, churches, business, education, and so on—to shape the values of each individual and, in sum, the values of society. The outcome, on the whole, has been very good. Each institution (or what I am calling value input source) made its contribution, but society—individually and collectively—made the final decision as to which values would prevail.

A parallel can be drawn between this process of value formation and classical economic theory. We have had a kind of laissez-faire approach to the development of our common values. The value input sources can be compared to the factors of production, each trying to maximize its own return or advantage. The community of individuals acts like the marketplace with an "unseen hand" determining the ultimate influence that each value input source is to have. In the long run, competition has perhaps not been perfect, but the resultant mix of generally accepted values has been rather good.

Classical economic theory, of course, depends on each element seeking to maximize its own return in the marketplace. U.S. institutions have tended to perform similarly. A kind of *advocacy* tradition has developed in which each institution (as a value input source for society as a whole) is expected to support the maximum expression of its value position.

Economic theory also holds that the participants in the marketplace need not be concerned about the consequences of vigorously pursuing their own advantages —the process of individual maximization will always produce the result that is best for the total society. Likewise, a societal institution has not been expected to concern itself with the consequences of maximizing its own value position. There has always been the unspoken assumption that no one source will dictate the values of the whole society, that somehow the

final mix of generally accepted values will be a balanced combination of the best from all value input sources. For example:

- The church preaches absolute charity, forgiveness, mercy, sharing, and other values that, if actually adopted by society as a whole, would result in economic chaos. When the church becomes "practical" and starts modifying its maximized position (i.e., instead of just preaching "peace," it suggests a date for withdrawal of troops from Vietnam), there is often a great outcry from parishioners that the church has betrayed its advocacy role of standing firm for its absolute value position.

- The university finds itself held to a similar self-maximizing role. If it responds to the calls of "relevance" —from either a practical public or a socially conscious student body—the university is accused of betraying the objective, purely intellectual role of an academic institution. The assumption is that if it does not advocate its own unique position, the final mix of our common values will suffer.

- Business—as a value input source for society as a whole—is the main focus of this article and will be dealt with in detail. Most readers, however, will be aware that many voices cry "betrayal" when business seems to compromise in any way the maximization of economic values.

a competitive advantage

Today, the foregoing scenario is no longer applicable. In the language of our parallel in economic theory, the competition between the various value input sources has become quite "imperfect." The influence of education, family, community, church, and so on, in forming the values that individuals live by, is greatly diminished, and the influence of business is consequently stronger than ever before.

Think for a moment about what has happened to the traditional value input sources that influenced the everyday life of Mr. John Q. Citizen a generation or two ago:

Agricultural society. Even when people were leaving the farm in large numbers, they did not do so without having internalized some "down-to-earth" values that lasted a lifetime. Farming itself is now a big business, highly mechanized with daily life influenced more by the values of nearby urban centers than by the agricultural routines of the past.

Family. The extended family of the past helped to secure the passing on of values from generation to generation. Today, few children have daily contact with grandparents who, as Margaret Mead says, "cannot conceive of any future for the children than their [the grandparents'] own past lives.[1]

Town or community. People are now more apt to experience short, rootless residential stops in innumerable, indistinguishable suburbs than to live in the town where they were born and intend to die; thus, assimilation of community mores is considerably weakened.

Religion. One does not really need the results of the many studies showing that people today look less and less to the churches and synagogues as a source of values. It is obvious that religion is not nearly the integrative and normative force that it once was.

Education. I suspect that most readers of this article can recall an elementary school experience characterized by uncritical transmittal of the values of the American way of life. To be sure, these

[1] *Culture and Commitment: A Study of the Generation Gap* (Garden City, New York, Natural History Press/Doubleday & Company, Inc., 1970), p. 1.

values were usually seen from the perspective of a white Anglo-Saxon, Protestant middle class imbued with patriotism and the puritan ethic, but the influence was strong. Today, we are more sensitive to the pluralistic nature of society and less willing to impose the values of the majority.

Direct evidence of the demise of traditional value sources is seen in the attempt of many young people to reestablish meaningful contact with contemporary substitutes for them: mystical cults take the place of organized religion; earth food, ecology action, and closeness to nature substitute for the farm; and communal living replaces the extended family.

While the sources of traditional values decline in influence, in some cases as a direct result of industrial growth, people still make choices and decisions based on some kind of substantive input—although most don't think about where this input comes from. How are these choices and decisions made and what influences them? It is hard to actually *prove* that the values dictating business decisions are gradually filling the vacuum. My earlier illustrations, however, suggest that the influence of business has not declined and that now, by default, business finds itself with far more influence on society than ever intended—or desired.

the emerging monopolist

We are all familiar with cases where single institutions have dominated the values of other societies. In fact, many immigrants to the United States from Prussia and elsewhere sought to escape what they called a "military society." Other immigrants remembered with some nostalgia an "agricultural society" in which the farm, as a living ecosystem, was the pervasive model. For some, this nostalgia almost blotted out the fact that they had left their homelands because the domination by agricultural values stifled new ideas and possibilities for industrial development.

Experience taught both the early settlers and later immigrants that one way to safeguard freedom was to be certain that checks and balances were built into the formal and informal structures of American culture. Few concepts are more deeply embedded in our understanding of what the American way of life is all about.

During the past half-century, however, the description of the United States as a "business society" has been used more and more. The designation expresses a positive and appreciative recognition of the success of the business community in contributing to the highest standard of living in the world. But could "business society" also describe a modern counterpart to the church-dominated society of the middle ages or the military societies, both past and present?

In asking this question, I do not mean to imply that business has decided it *wants* a broad influence on society. Most corporate executives have been influenced by the traditional American understanding of the relation of business to the rest of society. "Most values," they would say, "are formed by the church, the home, the school, but not by business. Business may respond to these values, but it does not supplant or create them." To suggest to executives that business is somehow heavily influencing the values of society is, in effect, like changing the rules in the middle of the game.

Nobody I talk to wants such a description to be true—but what if a realistic look at the accumulated changes in society says that it is true? What if all the mobility, urbanization, affluence, and applied technology resulting from business decisions, as well as the values dictating such

decisions, have so changed the way our lives are shaped that we have not only new rules but also a new ball game? In the old ball game, even so great an influence as the commercial control of mass media (particularly television) was not critical because the people listening and watching had had their values formed by significant input from a variety of traditional sources. The situation is drastically changed when these influences are absent.

redressing the balance

I realize that my argument is full of questions. And I am sure that the thoughtful reader has many more questions. Moreover, some readers will object that there has been a rather casual and undefined use of the terms "value," "values of business," and "values of society." My defense is twofold: *first*, the answers to the questions raised must come from the business community itself, out of its own sense of urgency and concern; *second*, it would seem unwise to get bogged down in the technical language (jargon) of sociology or philosophy, let alone of religion.

I can, however, offer a tentative answer to one question that is almost always raised when I discuss this issue: If this analysis is true, what does it mean to the businessman? Obviously, to be overly specific would deny the statement that meaningful response must come from business leaders themselves. But let me give some minimal suggestions:

1. *Face the possibility that the analysis may be true.* When it is admitted that the subject of societal values and the relation of business decisions to them is new and unfamiliar territory for most corporate managers, it must also be admitted that there is an ever-present temptation to avoid dealing with things so vague. This

implies a commitment to finding the truth, one that challenges the most competent and creative leadership.

2. *Think of "social responsibility" as an internal rather than external concern.* If the influence of business on the values of society is as great as suggested, the first social responsibility of business is to ask whether the values perceived as influencing the daily operation of the business are values that are desired for society as a whole. Attention to extra-business involvements—such as contributions to charities and education or executives volunteering for community projects—becomes secondary to a concern for the values operating behind corporate decisions.

3. *Increase your ability to discern the social consequences of management decisions.* The kind of attention being given to environmental consequences should be broadened to include the effects on society and the values of its citizens. Experimentation might be made with someone—a kind of ombudsman for corporations and trade associations—who will alert management to the effect of corporate actions on societal values.

4. *Develop a competence in setting social goals.* The management function must be enlarged to include more than the ability to achieve "predetermined goals." Managers need to develop a sensitivity to the effect of their pursuit of these goals on the configuration of society in general.

concluding note

At this point, the reader is likely to be very concerned about the issues raised, even though not necessarily in full agreement with the thesis I am presenting. Many readers are probably among those who feel most keenly the pressures which society is putting on business leaders. My hope is that what I am suggesting will not be seen as another such pressure; rather, it is meant as a way of making sense out of the changes which are taking place and providing a framework for establishing present-day corporate priorities.

Moreover, I do not mean to deny the positive influence of business values on society, such as the quality of judging people on the basis of individual competence rather than on wealth, family, or connections. There are many other similar examples, but these should not lull us into complacency about the value crisis confronting us.

As I stated at the outset of this article, the operative values in the management of a corporate enterprise tend to become the operative values of the average citizen. If this is true, it seems clear that the future will be largely shaped by the business community. The central issue then becomes whether or not businessmen are going to make the kinds of decisions and establish the necessary priorities that will channel their growing influence toward furthering a better world.

4. how to put corporate responsibility into practice

Terry McAdam

[handwritten annotations: 7 steps, categories of social resp]

Most early corporate ventures into the arena of social responsibility were reflex actions. Perceived social pressure and the threat of increasing legal pressure prompted management to react intuitively and subjectively to social responsibility issues. Today, such "knee jerk" responses to the wide array of problems and pressures are poorly received by just about everyone. The number of social responsibility issues has multiplied and their complexity has increased. Corporations are no longer regarded as purely economic institutions, but social ones as well. As more and more companies respond to the mounting pressures for corporate action, corporate managers are realizing that they must allocate their resources more systematically and rationally to achieve meaningful results and minimize unproductive and counterproductive efforts. The question is: How?

Here is one approach a company can take to tackle the social responsibility issues that confront it. It includes some basic steps familiar to most corporate managers—analyzing the issues, evaluating performance, setting priorities, allocating resources to those priorities, and implementing policies and programs that deal with the issues within resource constraints.

stimulants to action

In the past five years, more corporations than ever before have begun to grapple

Reprinted from *Business and Society Review/Innovation*, No. 6 (Summer 1973), pp. 8–16, with permission of the publisher and the author.

with the issues grouped under the rubric of "corporate social responsibility." For example, research by H. Eilbert and I. R. Parnet indicates that over 90 percent of the largest corporations in the United States have now assigned formal responsibility for such issues to either an officer or a high-level committee. Before 1965, less than $2\frac{1}{2}$ percent of these companies had such a position.

Three developments seem to be responsible for stimulating so many companies to take action:

1. *Pressures on corporations to deal with social responsibility issues have intensified.* According to Louis Harris and Associates, the proportion of the general public having "a great deal of confidence" in top business declined from 55 percent in 1966 to 27 percent in 1973. This same decline in confidence shows up in answers to more detailed questions about corporate performance in *both* business and social areas. Several reasons appear to be behind this dissatisfaction: (a) irresponsible behavior by a few corporate managers; (b) widespread and growing public disenchantment with all large institutions and their leadership; and (c) the increased popularization of social responsibility issues by the press and groups such as the Council on Economic Priorities and the Corporate Accountability Research Group. In addition, the proliferation of proxy proposals and stockholder suits indicates that the public, and public advocates, are tending more and more to hold management accountable for corporate behavior. As Ralph Nader has said, "A way to get more corporate responsibility is simply to recognize the principle that people who have power and make decisions should be

more accountable for the consequences of their decisions and not . . . insulated to the degree they are at the present time from the arm of the law through corporate shielding."

Government has added to the pressures by placing more consumer protection/social responsibility legislation on the books in the past ten years than in the prior one hundred. The number of proposed bills dealing with social responsibility issues and the corporation has skyrocketed. Local community pressures for corporate involvement also appear to be increasing. Executives across the country report a steady stream of requests for their active participation in local affairs and for corporate cash (and materials) contributions to new causes. Moreover, local regulations and laws have multiplied (e.g., local laws banning high-phosphate-content detergents).

Finally, some executives—particularly those whose plants and offices are in deteriorating urban areas—feel physically threatened by the hostile attitudes and behavior surfacing in their communities. They find themselves forced to deal with social issues to safeguard not only their corporate profit performance but, more important, their employees and property.

2. *Many of the arguments against some form of corporate involvement have, for the most part, been dismantled or refuted by persuasive counter-arguments.* Since the subject has been discussed and debated in the literature ad nauseum, this article assumes that the reader generally agrees that some form of socially responsible corporate behavior is both appropriate and beneficial to the corporation. A first cut at how to evaluate such behavior is given later on.

3. *Corporate managers are adopting new attitudes about the kinds of activities their companies should undertake.* Many businessmen and women are taking a broader interest as individuals in the work, life styles, and social fabric that surround them. At home and with friends, they are engaging in more substantive discussions of their work and its social implications. There appears to be a greater willingness to question institutional objectives, strategies and performance. While not a new phenomenon, it seems clearly on the upswing. The net result of the expanding concerns of today's business people has been a growing interest in the issues of corporate social responsibility. As economist Robert Heilbroner puts it, in *In the Name of Profit*, "I suspect that . . . businessmen themselves recoil from the implication that they are 'only' moneymakers. One of the problems of the theology of capitalism is that capitalists do not like to act like the creatures of pure self-interest that they are supposed to be." Moreover, as these attitudes develop and spread, corporations are finding it advantageous to improve their performance records on social responsibility issues in order to attract and hold high-quality personnel, many of whom are also embracing new sentiments about the social responsibilities of business.

With this background in mind, how can a company begin to evaluate its present record on social responsibility issues? How can it reflect that concern in its corporate objectives, strategy, and programs? How can it deploy its resources to strengthen performance in the future? And, should such actions prove useful and effective, how can they be integrated into the everyday management processes?

approaching the problem

Though no easy solution is conveniently at hand, some helpful ideas can be distilled from corporations' past experiences and current experiments in dealing with the wide spectrum of social responsibility issues. Businessmen we have talked to in different industries say that to make any headway with social responsibility issues inside large and complex corporations, one must be positive and flexible, adhere to several ground rules, and recognize the major pitfalls. Our own modest experience to date confirms this.

1. *Be positive and flexible.* A *positive* approach shows up in management's determination to seek progress in agreed-upon areas in an agreed-upon time. Implicit here is a common understanding of the facts and the issues in the selected areas. A *flexible* approach shows up in the organization's willingness to explore a variety of "problem" definitions, performance measures, program solutions, and other actions required to achieve the progress desired. Moreover, it means not losing heart if progress is slow or if the positive intentions of the effort are not immediately recognized as such by some corporate constituencies.

2. *Adhere to several ground rules.* From corporate experience and the literature, we find several valuable rules for getting the program off to a good start:

- Make a top management commitment to appraise corporate social responsibility performance objectively and to change corporate policy, if appropriate, on the basis of the facts and information developed. This appraisal will rest on definitions and measures of social responsibility which must be developed as part of the overall evaluative process. A clear commitment and subsequent action by the chief executive officer can enormously improve social responsibility performance—perhaps more so than any other single factor.
- Get line management to participate in this performance appraisal. Line managers and members of the cor-

poration's operating units should be encouraged to gather and evaluate facts on performance and to develop alternative proposals for changing or correcting corporate performance in their areas of responsibility. Their participation in developing new behavior patterns increases 100-fold the program's chances of success.

- Control expectations throughout the organization by setting modest goals initially, and then push hard to raise them as progress is made. In addition, it is wise to create an experimental atmosphere that encourages people to try new analytic and programmatic approaches and to accept the fact that some mistakes may be made.
- Concentrate early efforts on understanding company performance and on deciding what action to take, rather than on how and what to report to the corporation's various constituencies.
- Install a formal follow-up procedure. Developing and implementing policies to upgrade a company's overall social responsibility performance is a long-term proposition. It requires repeated efforts with correction, follow-up, and lots of hard work.

3. *Recognize major pitfalls.* Despite good intentions, sound plans, and enthusiasm, a company can still run into pitfalls in dealing with social responsibility issues. It may find, for example, that progress and performance are difficult to measure quantitatively; the complexity of some of the issues consumes "excessive" analytical time; agreement on the parameters of analysis (and even concern) is hard to reach; and addressing social responsibility issues generates internal friction at many levels of the corporation.

If the company recognizes that these pitfalls exist and that it must take them in its stride, it can soon get down to the real work of analyzing social responsibility issues.

analyze the issues

The quantitative measurement of corporate performance in most social responsibility areas is still a crude science, at best. But despite this state of the art, a corporation desiring to tackle the most crucial issues can do so. The following seven steps serve as a starting point:

1. *Identify and define performance categories relevant to a social responsibility review of the company.* This step can be completed by segregating social responsibility issues into categories of corporate action, using the following types of questions as a guide: Are the action areas measured by the same kinds of performance yardsticks? Do they tend to be managed by similar organizational units? Do they affect one specific constituency? And so on. The objective is to break down the totality of the corporation's actions and their related social impact into a manageable number of categories for analysis and evaluation. Summarized below is a set of categories recently developed by one U.S. corporation; these may serve as thought-starters.

· · ·

These categories are limited in number and are not mutually exclusive; they contain at least two issues that are relatively new—environmental control and minority/women hiring and advancement. Furthermore, they may not be comprehensive from some points of view (e.g., military production is not included). And no doubt other issues will emerge from the shifting social scene—but the point is to group issues and activities into a manageable number of categories and get started.

2. *Briefly review performance across all*

Categories of Social Responsibility Issues

---

a. Product line (e.g. dangerous products)
b. Marketing practices (e.g. misleading advertising)
c. Employee education and training
d. Corporate philanthropy
e. Environmental control
f. External relations (including community development, government relations, disclosure of information, and international operations)
g. Employee relations, benefits, and satisfaction with work
h. Minority and women employment and advancement
i. Employee safety and health

---

activity categories in order to identify areas of high vulnerability or opportunity, and to get an overview for resource allocation decisions that must be made later. A simple way to get started is to pose, and attempt to answer, a series of questions about corporate activities. For example:

- Is anyone's life, health, or safety endangered by our actions or products?
- Do we comply with all laws and regulations—federal, state, and local?
- What are the major in-house concerns regarding our social responsibility performance?
- What will be the impact of continuing a given activity—on our employees, customers, stockholders, and the public in general?
- If we change our actions, will our constituencies understand why? Will they misinterpret our motives?
- Is new legislation likely to be implemented which will regulate this activity?
- What action has our competition taken? Industry in general?
- Can we estimate the total cost of each activity area?

After attempting to answer such questions, a company should be able to assess which activity areas are most vulnerable to criticism, which are most in need of being improved either by increasing current efforts or implementing new ones, and which present opportunities to contribute to the solution of social problems while expanding the business.

Categories of Social Responsibility Issues

Product Line
Internal standards for product
- Quality, e.g., does it last?
- Safety, e.g., can it harm users or children finding it?
- Disposal, e.g., is it bio-degradable?
- Design, e.g., will its use or even "easy" misuse cause pain, injury or death?

Average product life comparisons versus
- Competition
- Substitute products
- Internal standards or state-of-the-art regular built-in obsolescence

Product performance
- Efficacy, e.g., does it do what it is supposed to do?
- Guarantees/warranties, e.g., are guarantees sufficient, reasonable?
- Service policy
- Service availability
- Service pricing
- Utility

Packaging
- Environmental impact (degree of disposability; recycleability)
- Comparisons with competition (type and extent of packaging)

Marketing Practices
Sales practices
- Legal standards
- "Undue" pressure (a qualitative judgment)

Credit practices against legal standards
Accuracy of advertising claims—specific government complaints
Consumer complaints about marketing practices
- Clear explanation of credit terms
- Clear explanation of purchase price
- Complaint answering policy
  —Answered at all

—Investigated carefully
—Grievances redressed (and cost)
—Remedial action to prevent future occurrences

Adequate consumer information on
- Product use, e.g., dosage, duration of use, etc.
- Product misuse

Fair pricing
- Between countries
- Between states
- Between locations

Packaging

Employee Education and Training
Policy on leaves of absence for
- Full-time schooling
- Courses given during working hours

Dollars spent on training
- Formal vocational training
- Training for disadvantaged worker
- OJT (very difficult to isolate)
- Tuition (job-related versus nonjob-related)
- Special upgrading and career development programs
- Compare versus competition

Special training program results (systematic evaluations)
- Number trained in each program per year
- Cost per trainee (less subsidy)
- Number or percent workers still with company

Plans for future programs
Career training and counseling
Failure rates
Extend personnel understanding
- Jobs
- Skills required later
- Incentive system now available
- Specific actions for promotion

cont.

Categories of Social Responsibility Issues—*continued*

Corporate Philanthropy

Contribution performance

- By category, for example:
  - —Art
  - —Education
  - —Poverty
  - —Health
  - —Community development
  - —Public service advertising
- Dollars (plus materials and man-hours if available)
  - —As a percent of pretax earnings
  - —Compared to competition

Selection criteria for contributions

Procedures for performance tracking of recipient institutions or groups

Programs for permitting and encouraging employee involvement in social projects

- On company time
- After hours only
- Use of company facilities and equipment
- Reimbursement of operating units for replaceable "lost" time
- Manpower support
  - —Number of people
  - —Man-hours

Extent of employee involvement in philanthropy decision-making

Environmental Control

Measurable pollution resulting from

- Acquisition of raw materials
- Production processes
- Products
- Transportation of intermediate and finished products

Violations of government (federal, state, and local) standards

Cost estimates to correct current deficiencies

Extent to which various plants exceed current legal standards, e.g., particulate matter discharged

Resources devoted to pollution control

- Capital expenditures (absolute and percent)
- R & D investments
- Personnel involved full time; part time
- Organizational "strength" of personnel involved

Competitive company performance, e.g., capital expenditures

Effort to monitor new standards as proposed

Programs to keep employees alert to spills and other pollution-related accidents

Procedures for evaluating environmental impact of new packages or products

External Relations

Community Development

Support of minority and community enterprises through

- Purchasing
- Subcontracting

Investment practices

- Ensuring equal opportunity before locating new facilities
- Identifying opportunities to serve community needs through business expansion (e.g., housing rehabilitation or teaching machines)
- Funds in minority banks

Government Relations

Specific input to public policy through research and analysis

Participation and development of business/government programs

Political contributions

Disclosure of Information/Communications

Extent of public disclosure of performance by activity category

Measure of employee understanding of programs such as:

- Pay and benefits
- Equal opportunity policies and programs
- Position on major economic or political issues (as appropriate)

Relations/communications with constituencies such as stockholders, fund managers, major customers, and so on

International

Comparisons of policy and performance between countries and versus local standards

Employee Relations, Benefits, and Satisfaction with Work

Comparisons with competition (and/or national averages)

- Salary and wage levels
- Retirement plans
- Turnover and retention by level
- Profit sharing

Categories of Social Responsibility Issues *continued*

- Day care and maternity
- Transportation
- Insurance, health programs and other fringes
- Participation in ownership of business through stock purchases

Comparisons of operating units on promotions, terminations, hires against breakdowns of

- Age
- Sex
- Race
- Education level

Performance review system and procedures for communication with employees whose performance is below average

Promotion policy—equitable and understood

Transfer policy

Termination policy (i.e., how early is "notice" given)

General working environment and conditions

- Physical surroundings
  —Heat
  —Ventilation
  —Space/person
  —Lighting
  —Air conditioning
  —Noise
- Leisure, recreation, cultural opportunities

Fringe benefits as a percent of salary for various salary levels

Evaluation of employee benefit preferences (questions can be posed as choices)

Evaluation of employee understanding of current fringe benefits

Union/industrial relations

- Grievances
- Strikes

Confidentiality and security of personnel data

Minority and Women Employment and Advancement

Current hiring policies in relation to the requirements of all affirmative action programs

Specific program of accountability for performance

Company versus local, industry and national performance

- Number and percent minority and women employees hired by various job classifications over last 5 years
- Number and percent of new minority and women employees in last 2 to 3 years by job classification
- Minority and women and nonminority turnover
- Indictments for discriminatory hiring practices

Percent minority and women employment in major facilities relative to minority labor force available locally

Number of minority group and women members in positions of high responsibility

Promotion performance of minority groups and women

Specific hiring and job upgrading goals established for minority groups and women

- Basic personnel strategy
- Nature and cost of special recruiting efforts
- Risks taken in hiring minority groups and women

Programs to ease integration of minority groups and women into company operations, e.g., awareness efforts

Specialized minority and women career counseling

Special recruiting efforts for minority groups and women

Opportunities for the physically handicapped

- Specific programs
- Numbers employed

Employee Safety and Health

Work environment measures

- OSHA requirements (and extent of compliance)
- Other measures of working conditions

Safety performance

- Accident severity—man-hours lost per million worked
- Accident frequency (number of lost time accidents per million hours)
- Disabling injuries
- Fatalities

Services provided (and cost of programs and manpower) for :

- Addictive treatment (alcohol, narcotics)

cont.

Categories of Social Responsibility Issues—*continued*

Employee Safety and Health—cont.
- Mental health

Spending for safety equipment
- Required by law/regulation
- Not required

Special safety programs (including safety instruction)

Comparisons of health and safety performance

with competition and industry in general

Developments/innovations in health and safety

Employee health measures, e.g., sick days, examinations

Food facilities
- Cost/serving to employee; to company
- Nutritional evaluation

---

3. *Select the most critical activity areas and review performance in depth.* This step can be initiated by meshing a first cut at perceived activity categories (from step 1) with the types of questions posed in step 2. It should be extended, whenever possible, by developing specific quantitative data. If quantitative measurement is not possible, either because facts are not available or reliable measures of performance have not yet been developed, one can retreat to a description of management procedures and policy to estimate qualitatively the corporation's position or performance. The [previous pages] illustrate potential areas to analyze in reviewing each activity category. They are by no means complete. New measures and analytical approaches can be added every day. Any company seriously evaluating its performance will no doubt add detailed measures in each category when tailoring this general approach to its own situation and data.

4. *Develop a basic strategy for each activity area.* This strategy should not dictate specific program responses, but should help to provide general guidelines for major resource allocation decisions, and integrate social responsibility thinking into everyday corporate planning, evaluating, and management. The [following] table summarizes various philosophies and the level of effort most likely to flow from them. A company can, of course, modify these general level-of-effort options for different activity categories. Admittedly, the strategic choices made will be in-

fluenced by the personal values of the top executives and the type of organization they and their associates would like the corporation to be in the future.

Social Responsibility Philosophy	Resulting Level of Effort
Lead the industry	Substantial experimentation and applied research; some failures should be anticipated when breaking new ground
Be progressive	Large effort to grapple with full range of issues; some breaking of new ground likely
Do only what is required	Careful investigation of all requirements, plus advance planning for likely new requirements
Fight all the way	No action other than defensive reaction to likely criticism/investigations

Having set a general level of effort, the company can define the boundaries of the major activity areas by answering questions such as, Which activities can, and must, we accept responsibility for now? In the near future? How far should our responsibility go? Should other members of the industry be involved? How?

5. *Set specific but realistic objectives for new programs or for revisions in existing activities.* The discipline of setting specific objectives is worthwhile for three reasons:

(a) It cncourages managers to think carefully about the resources allocated to each program; (b) It makes the goals clear to everyone; and (c) Most important, this is the point at which possible trade-offs between short-term "social responsibility accomplishment" and short-term profit can begin to emerge and be evaluated.

6. *Develop, implement, and monitor the new or revised programs.* If the line units have participated in the steps so far, they will likely have many practical ideas about the programs needed to improve or change activities in their areas. In addition to them, however, analytic support from some staff or other group may be needed to ensure that the analysis is objective and that effective new programs are developed. The work done in developing, implementing, and monitoring the programs should be aimed at making sure that the projects respond to the results of a specific performance review; the objectives for proposed programs are clearly defined; resource trade-off decisions are based on a "best possible" understanding of the costs and likely benefits of alternative programs: and programs that are implemented remain effective. Feedback on performance is vital to ensure that the organization sustains its commitment to action.

No matter how well one has laid the groundwork, however, operating units may still resist the changes. This resistance will decrease, it is to be hoped, as companies begin to reap the benefits of the new programs.

7. *Integrate this approach into the basic management processes.* Ultimately, if sustained attention is to be paid to social responsibility performance, this approach must be integrated into the basic processes of managing the business, from corporate planning and strategy to individual job descriptions and incentive programs. Without this integration, the approach is a meaningless exercise.

organize the effort

How a company organizes its social responsibility effort depends on many variables—the quality of personnel involved, the degree of their commitment to the social responsibility issues, their ability to secure line management input and support for policy changes, and their capacity to follow through on implementing new programs. The best organizational arrangement for one company may be quite inappropriate for another. Five possible approaches include:

1. *The Officer.* To be effective in an organization of any size, the officer must be in a reasonably high-level position, well-respected, and supported by a quality staff. If his charter embraces the full range of corporate social responsibility issues, he will have to be prepared to devote most of his time to the task. Because of the heavy time commitment, a company electing this approach generally rotates the job every two to three years to ensure that qualified managers will be receptive to such an assignment. With each change of officer, however, comes the risk that the continuity and drive of the effort will slacken. This is particularly true if the company has jumped into the task without any corporate responsibility strategy or "game plan." Thus, changeover procedures must be carefully thought out for this approach to work effectively.

2. *The Task Force.* The task force is a commonly used approach. Since it tends, however, to be crisis-oriented (as are many corporate responses to social responsibility issues), it is not very effective for mid- to long-range planning. Another drawback of the task force is that it is less able to implement changes in operating practices because few permanent lines of communication exist between it and company operating units. Finally, task force members are nearly always part-time participants in the review and develop-

ment process, and unless they have first-rate staff support, they may not acquire sufficient understanding of specific problems. On the plus side, the task force approach is a good way to get an activity started quickly. If team members are carefully selected, the task force can bring together a group knowledgeable in many key operating elements of the business. Thus, the important factors to make this option effective are good people, a focused effort, and quality staff work.

3. *The Permanent Board Committee*. A board-level committee has several arguments in its favor:

- As tangible evidence of top management's commitment to deal with social responsibility issues, it is a stimulus for the effort to gain support at key operating levels.
- With the muscle of individual board members behind the effort, the review procedure can be rigorous and thorough.
- Since most board members have a broad perspective, their approach to social responsibility issues can be more comprehensive.
- Outside board members often can bring new insights to the subject and thus can contribute significantly to the effort.

To make this approach work, however, the board committee must be supported by adequate staff and have access to objective and quantitative reviews of operating performance. Since board members are further away from daily operations, their need for good support and information is imperative if they are to fully understand the problems. With proper backup, this option can be a highly effective one. Its principal drawback is that it may be difficult to maintain a reasonable rate of progress because of the heavy time demands placed on board members.

4. *The Permanent Management Committee*. A permanent management committee has many of the attributes of the board committee. It has the same need for good staff work, sufficient time commitment of committee members, and specific background information for decision making. Though a management committee is more familiar with the business than a board committee, it may be hampered somewhat by a lack of objectivity.

5. *The Permanent Organization Group*. Having within the organization structure a permanent department or group continuously engaged in analyzing, resolving, and responding to corporate social responsibility issues may be the best option of all. Such a group can, over time, build up stronger communication lines than any of the other approaches. Through regular feedback, it can keep the company alert to issues and ensure continuity of analytic efforts. It also offers continuing evidence of top management's commitment to social responsibility. The only danger is that a permanent organizational unit risks drifting out of the mainstream of activity and becoming too narrowly focused on one pet issue. Although such specialization can be a positive influence on company performance in the chosen area, it prevents management from dealing systematically with the remaining issues.

Regardless of which organizational option, or combination of options, is chosen, the likelihood of positive results is enhanced if:

- The organizational unit reports progress regularly to top management, reaffirming top-level interest.
- Analysts working on corporate social responsibility issues have full access to company data once they have secured management's agreement to a general line of inquiry.

- The unit keeps detailed performance records and formalizes analytic procedures so that subsequent efforts can build on knowledge acquired in earlier efforts.
- Reviews of individual performance in social responsibility activities are integrated into the corporation's overall personnel or performance review system as confidence grows in which factors to measure.

In net, there is still a great deal to be learned about how to analyze and respond to corporate social responsibility issues. This article has proposed some analytic and organizational approaches that have emerged from the limited and occasionally mixed corporate experience to date.

Though progress in strengthening management techniques for dealing with social responsibility issues may be slow, the learning process seems to have begun in earnest. In one sense, this effort is just in time. The pace of change is accelerating as new issues are raised and new pressures are brought to bear. As techniques for analyzing and responding to corporate social responsibility issues are sharpened and integrated into the ongoing practices of planning and managing the business, corporate efforts in this area should become much more effective. Should corporations take the first step? As Oliver Wendell Holmes once said, "The opportunity and challenge is there to go beyond the merely profitable and take part in the action and the passion of our time. . . ."

expanding scope of management: public, health, and international

5. the emerging public corporation

John Kenneth Galbraith

There are two disparate views of the modern, large corporation—two very different views of General Electric and General Motors and General Dynamics and General Mills and General Foods. These and the other generals—something less than a battalion, about a thousand in all—contribute close to half the production of goods and services in the United States. The distinction is between what may be called the "traditional" and what may be called the "evolutionary" view of the large corporation.

the traditional approach

In the traditional view, a deep and, indeed, unbridgeable chasm divides the state from the firm. The differentiation between the government on one side and private

Reprinted from *Business and Society*, No. 1 (Spring 1972), pp. 54–56, with permission of the publisher and the author.

enterprise on the other is fully accepted. Regulation of private enterprise by the state may be necessary, but such control as there may be is subject to a heavy burden of proof. The general right that the corporation be free from interference is deeply imbedded in our history and tradition. The right is further protected by what might be called corporate privacy. You can't regulate what you don't know about. The government can ask for information only after establishing a specific need to know. It is almost as though there is a broad presumption that what one does not know about corporate behavior does not hurt anyone.

The corollary of this view is that the corporation is kept honest and its operations are kept aligned with the public interest by the fact of competition. It is the market, not the state, that serves as the ultimate regulatory force. The market is an expression of public will, manifested in everyday purchases of goods and services; and since the public cannot be in conflict with itself, the corporation must respond to public needs. This is what puts the burden of proof on state intervention and makes such intervention necessary only if, somehow or other, the orders and signals of the marketplace have failed.

Admittedly, many who hold this view concede that the market can, indeed, fail. Firms can become too large, monopoly and oligopoly can replace competition, the state can be influenced or even suborned by the great corporations. It's quite possible, to paraphrase Marx, that the state becomes, in fact, the executive committee of the corporate bureaucracy. But in this view, the solution lies not in controlling corporate power, but in dissolving it—in reviving the market and in restoring competition. The conditions under which private business can truly be private must thus be reestablished. At this point, there is always an appeal for the rigorous enforcement of the antitrust laws and the breaking up of the giants.

private enterprise becomes public

The evolutionary view of the corporation is sharply at odds with the traditional one. It says that the development of General Motors, Jersey Standard, and General Dynamics invokes, at some stage in growth and in power, a clear, clean break with the economics of the private firm in the classical market. At some point, these overwhelming large firms become, and I emphasize this term, *public institutions*. The clichés of private enterprise serve primarily, at this point, to disguise the essentially public character of the great corporation, including its private exercise of what is in fact a public power. Such a corporation fixes its prices, controls its costs, integrates backwards so as to control the supply of its raw materials, and

influences, persuades, and, on occasion, bamboozles its customers. The giant corporation has powerful enough leverage in the community that getting what it needs from the government becomes pro tanto sound public policy. It has, on frequent occasions, a hammer-lock on the Pentagon.

The most striking example of such a corporation, or the one on which one can take the strongest position, is the highly developed and fully specialized weapons firm—Lockheed, for example. Lockheed's physical plant is extensively owned by the government and leased to Lockheed. The company's working capital comes from the government in the form of progress payments. Its business comes all but exclusively from the government. Its cost overruns are socialized. Its capital needs—even those resulting from the mismanagement of its civilian business—are guaranteed by the government. Only its earnings and the salaries of its executives are in the private sector. Is such a firm private? Well, under the Constitution I am reminded that a man is entitled to believe anything!

The line between private and public enterprise in cases such as Lockheed is so exotic as to be ludicrous. This demarcation is, in fact, a device for diverting the attention of the public, the congressional committees, and the Comptroller General from what is in fact managerial error, executive perquisites, lobbying for new expenditures (including new weapons systems), profits, and political activity by executives and employees—all of which in a de jure public bureaucracy (or a full-fledged public corporation like the Tennessee Valley Authority) would be subjects of the greatest concern. Thus is public business hidden behind the cloak of corporate privacy.

But the specialized weapons firms, in this view of the corporation, are only the obvious case. General Motors, a different example, both sets the prices for its cars, and, in conjunction with the other automobile companies, foreign and domestic, does so for all cars. This has great effect on the public. General Motors negotiates wage contracts, and this likewise has great public effect—such public effect as has persuaded the President of the United States, in one of the more radical of his several recent radical moves, to place the price system in abeyance—a plank not part of the 1968 Republican platform. (I'm not criticizing the act, mind you.) General Motors also designs cars and incorporates or rejects safety features, also with public consequence. Its emphasis on engine design has public effect, as does the level of emissions therefrom. And General Motors powerfully influences highway construction. Few, if any, of our state legislatures make decisions that have greater impact on the public than are made annually by this one corporation. And its decisions as to what it will make, where it will produce, and what and from whom it will import have considerably more international impact than those of the very important men—my one-time colleagues in the State Department—who preside with no slight rancor over the affairs of, let us say, Chad or Mali.

The evolutionary view of the corporation therefore accepts its tendency to become assimilated to the state and regards this tendency as essentially irreversible. This view no longer presumes that the corporation has private affairs that should be protected from public scrutiny. It follows that while autonomy in the corporation's operations may have practical merit, there is no longer a presumption against public regulation. While there remains the danger that the firms will regulate their regulators, it is precisely such regulation—not the rehabilitation of market constraints nor, parenthetically, voluntary virtue—to which one must look for the protection and advancement of the public interest.

lifting the veils

While I have presented two opposing views of the corporation with strict impartiality, it should not come as a surprise that I believe the evolutionary view has far more going for it than the traditional view.

The antitrust laws—basic to the traditional view—are eighty years old, approaching their centenary. The last really important dissolution occurred sixty years ago. This is not prima facie an encouraging record. Each new generation of reformers has held that only the feckless ineptitude and cowardice of its predecessors has kept the market from being restored. And then each new generation, its bravery notwithstanding, has also failed. I believe we can safely and however sadly conclude that if these laws were ever going to work wonders for anyone but lawyers, they would have worked them by now. And I argue that confidence in the efficacy of these laws has provided considerable support for irresponsible corporate power, in that the laws sustain the hope and perpetuate the myth of the all-powerful marketplace. These laws keep alive the illusion that public business is private, and they keep the burden of proof on those who propose regulations or even call for disclosure. And these laws totally suppress the possibility—many would say the specter—of the ultimate development of public ownership. I suggest that no one could do more for General Motors than this.

I do not object to according autonomy to the corporation. It is necessary for effective administration and effective production. There is no doubt that the independent entity, the autonomous corporate organization, is a highly useful device for undertaking and conducting complex industrial tasks. The fact that such an organization has emerged where steel must be manufactured in megatons, automobiles made in the millions, and chemicals processed on a vast scale, added to the fact that something very like the corporate entity has appeared in societies as diverse as those of the United States and the Soviet Union, indicates the utility of the autonomous corporate device. But in the evolutionary view of the corporation, autonomy is not a right by matter of principle; it is merely a pragmatic decision.

Accordingly, where there is a clash between corporate goals and the public interest—as with the safety of products, industrial effects on the environment, the effect of price and wage settlements on the economy, the equity of profits, or the appropriateness of executive compensation—there is no natural right of the corporation to be left alone. And I come here to a very important point: There is no barrier—in the developed case of special-

ized weapons firms like Lockheed or the incompetent ones like Penn Central, for example—to stripping away the purely artificial facade of private enterprise and converting such corporations into fully publicly owned enterprises. The one thing worse than a General Motors whose public character is recognized is a General Motors whose public character is denied. And the one thing worse than a General Dynamics that is publicly owned and publicly controlled is a General Dynamics that is publicly owned but privately controlled.

There is no magic in stripping away the myth that the market controls the modern corporation, and no magic in stripping away the hope that it sometime could be made to do so. I am quite convinced that divesting the corporation of these cloaks is the very first step toward any useful program for reform.

6. the politics of public–private management

Frank H. Cassell

Who would have imagined twelve years ago that the government would be running the passenger service of the railroads, or that the government would rescue a huge aircraft firm from certain bankruptcy by lending it cash and furnishing contracts to keep the business alive? Or that a conservative American government would abandon its old theories about the free market and intervene in the economics of society to manage wages and prices? Or that the

same conservative government would propose guaranteed incomes for the poor, even for those who work but are so poorly paid by private enterprise that they would need public subsidy to meet the barest subsistence level of living? Who would have expected President Nixon to sign a general public employment law to employ 150,000 people in public service jobs for an investment of $2.25 billion?[1]

Frank H. Cassell, "The Politics of Public–Private Management," pp. 7–18, *MSU Business Topics*, Summer 1972. Reprinted by permission of the publisher, Division of Research, Graduate School of Business Administration, Michigan State University.

[1] The Emergency Employment Act was signed by President Nixon on 12 July 1972. The idea of governmentally guaranteed work dates back to 1836 when it was proposed by Louis Blanc. Prior to Karl Marx, this public employment is what Europeans thought socialism meant.

Who would have thought, even in New Deal days, that the federal government would be underwriting well over 50 percent of all the research and development work in the nation, thus providing much of the motive, power, and ideas for private enterprise?[2] Who would have foreseen that the traditional operations and values of the marketplace would be challenged so regularly and would be in conflict so often with the priorities and values arrived at through community action, or that free market operations often would be superceded by the planning of social and economic action needed to fulfill the needs and priorities demanded by the community?

Indeed, it is fair to ask whether there is any longer such a thing as a pure business problem. Or whether, instead, public and private, the needs of the people and of the economy, have become so crossed and intertwined that we have arrived, without our quite knowing it, at a time when few decisions of the private sector can be made without an expression by the public of its legitimate concern for the consequences of those decisions.

So pervasive has the trend become that proposals for its further extension—for even more intertwining of public and private enterprise—come from surprising sources. For example, Roger S. Ahlbrandt, chairman of Allegheny Ludlum Industries, Inc., is urging the government to adopt centralized economic planning, lest the steel industry slip further behind in world competition with totally managed economies. He refers to an

economic sickness that affects our whole nation and society. It is a sickness directly connected to the fact that our nation has

not had, and still lacks, a coherent international economic policy ... America's foreign policy for generations has been influenced by *military* and *political* considerations. But we now live in a world where *economic considerations* must assume first priority. ... We in this nation find ourselves now trying to compete not just with individual steel companies, for example, for both domestic and overseas markets—but with ENTIRE ECONOMIES, in which a central decision-making body determines allocation of raw materials and other resources, directs the flow of finance, determines the penetration of markets, establishes costs and prices, and—in truth—*governs* and *directs* the entire national economic entity. In those nations, government and people look upon industries as "national assets," which increase their national strength and improve their living standards. Unfortunately, this cannot be said of public and government attitudes toward business and industry in the United States. ... We must recognize that the sweep of change, inside and outside our country, is not reversible. The four great economic blocs that compete with us globally will not disappear and go away. And their policies—economic, social and political—do not come out of any of *our* textbooks.[3]

Another example of a surprising proposal for much greater involvement of the public sector in private enterprise has come from the Committee for Economic Development. It reasons that all institutions are under question because of the "sluggishness of social progress." The committee also notes that some of government's tasks are being contracted out to business, and it proposes a vast extension of that process into "new hybrid types of public–private corporations ... to combine the best attributes of government (funds, political capacity, public accountability) and of private enterprise (systems analysis, research and technology, managerial ability) in the optimum mix for

---

[2] In 1971, the federal government financed 55 percent of the $26.9 billion spent nationally for basic and applied research and for development. *Annual Report of the Council of Economic Advisers* (Washington, D.C.: U.S. Government Printing Office, 1972).

[3] Roger S. Ahlbrandt, "For Whom the Steel Bell Tolls," Speech before the Steel Industry Economics Seminar, Wayne State University, Detroit, Michigan, 12 April 1972.

dealing effectively with different kinds of socio-economic problems."[4] The CED further states: "This emerging partnership is more than a contractual relationship between a buyer and seller of services. Fundamentally, it offers a new means for developing the innate capabilities of a political democracy and a private enterprise economy into a new politico-economic system capable of managing social and technological change in the interests of a better social order. . . . The government–business relationship is likely to be the central one in the last third of the twentieth century."[5]

In a later section of this article the implications of Ahlbrandt's proposal, which is aimed at government economic planning to aid industry, and the CED's proposal, for public–private corporations to handle many aspects of our lives, will be considered. Both of the proposals certainly give impetus to the idea that there is no longer such a thing as a pure business problem and, henceforth, few private sector decisions can be made without consideration of the public's legitimate concerns. This idea even now is too little understood in its implications regarding the decision-making process. For example, what do these new facts mean for managers and administrators who are selected and trained to cope with a corporate environment they can control and influence, one characterized by a high degree of predictability rather than unpredictability, and often chaotic and conflicting pressure, brought to bear by the surrounding community over which the managers have little or no control? What do they mean to men who, accustomed to working within and conforming to a system that seems to satisfy

their needs, are confronted with community people who feel that system does not satisfy community needs and therefore want to change or replace it? What do they mean for managers and planners, long accustomed to think in terms of orderly processes for the achievement of well-defined objectives which have been fed in from the top of the typical business organization? What do they mean for educators and for those business schools who have charged themselves with educating managers for both the public and private sectors?

The implications of the new and growing public–private sector are so immense that the questions are only dimly understood and the answers are not available. The implications are particularly challenging to the business schools because of the time lag between an individual's training and his accession to power. Business schools currently are training students who will not be in management positions with real decision-making power for another fifteen to twenty years. But the new kinds of community pressures already exist and are baffling; they are producing consternation among the current crop of executives trained fifteen to twenty years ago.

the better mousetrap?

In the private sector, historically, priorities have been determined by the profit motive. If a worse mousetrap made more profit, it would be produced. In the public sector, priorities have been determined through the political process. People in government, either elected or appointed, have sought to perceive the needs of the community and plan to meet those needs. Of course, there always has been pressure from the electorate, but formerly it was largely through the established political procedure, through the election of people who thought your way and through

[4] Research and Policy Committee, Committee for Economic Development, *Social Responsibilities in Modern Corporations*, New York, June 1971, p. 59.
[5] Ibid.

political lobbying to achieve your aims. Even the inevitable conniving and sly deals operated through the established political procedure. And here too the mousetrap analogy is applicable; if a worse mousetrap would get you elected, it would be invented.

Planning was involved in both private and public sectors, but it usually was ordered from the top down; planners sought to convert objectives—determined somewhere in the board rooms, the mayor's office, or legislative halls—into an orderly and workable program.

challenges to traditional planning

Both of these traditional methods for determining priorities, by profit in the private sector and political decisions in the public, are under wide attack. One reason is that the planning system has become circular, listening to itself and responding not to the needs of people but to the demands, goals, or needs of planning itself. Challenges from everywhere are racking all of our institutions. The institutions are finding their traditional behavior and priorities are not in tune with or capable of accommodating the demands of contesting forces; each force wants the institutions to behave in a manner calculated to benefit them. Thus, for both public and private institutions, there are whole new arsenals of pressure, from the bottom up rather than the top down, and it is often expressed not through what we have thought were the normal channels but in many new ways of social protest. These new bottom-up pressures illustrate a conflict both of values and organizational methods, and in both cases the new pressures make the people subjected to them extremely uncomfortable. People are devising new ways to demand consideration in the

making of decisions that affect their lives,

Their clamor to be heard is a sufficiently recognizable phenomenon to be finding its way into our humor. Russell Baker said in *Harper's* recently: "People who have the power to make things happen don't do what people do, so they don't know what needs to happen." True enough, no doubt, and the people with power still may not do what people do, but they are certainly going to be told what needs to happen.[6]

varieties of pressure

Sometimes the new pressures serve chiefly as dramatic attention-getting devices. A community group in Chicago, distressed over the prevalence of rats in the neighborhood, summoned their alderman to a planning meeting. When the alderman did not come, the president of the group nailed a dead rat to his front door; the alderman was present at the next meeting. Another example is the Fox, an anonymous Fox River Valley (Illinois) man who is fighting pollution symbolically. He once dumped on the reception room carpet of a steel firm's local office a bucket of the foul sludge that was draining out of the company's pipelines into the once beautiful Fox River. The Fox became an instant folk hero.

Often new pressures are designed to change traditions and procedures that have proved to be unresponsive to needs. Did we ever hear of a tenants' union until a decade ago? By withholding rents until a recalcitrant landlord meets their demands, the tenants' unions are challenging what we always have thought were basic property rights of the landlord, protected through generations of common law. The

[6] Management schools are beginning to study this phenomenon. See G. Zaltman, P. Kotler, and I. Kaufman, eds., *Creating Social Change* (New York: Holt, Rinehart, Winston, forthcoming).

tenants' unions did not fare well at first, but they are beginning to win some victories in the courtrooms as some of the old beliefs about property rights are giving way.

Other examples of pressures aimed at unresponsive procedures can be seen in the struggle for more community control over schools. Recall the devastating school strikes in New York City in 1968. They had complex causes, but at their heart was an insurgent demand by neighborhood people to have some control over the kind of education their children were getting, and to determine priorities for their children, who clearly were being short-changed by traditional methods. The result was instant conflict not only with the giant school bureaucracy but also with the contractual rights of the giant teachers' union. The neighborhood people lost their battle in New York; they lost in the school board offices, in the governor's office, and in the legislative sessions in Albany. But the struggle for community control and for schools that will be answerable to the people who use them will continue.

Consider pollution, which brings other challenges to unresponsive procedures. The attacks from the new insurgents are two-pronged: against the government in demands for protection against the side effects of the industrial revolution, and against the corporations, seeking board members who will place the public interest, survival itself, against, or at least along-side, the profit motive. Louis S. B. Leakey recently warned the American Association for the Advancement of Science that man is in imminent danger of extinction, perhaps within fifty years, unless he uses "his wonderful computer brain" to ward off impending disaster.[7] Many are listening

to such messages and trying to act, some-times fumbling, sometimes winning a little. These kinds of pressures are new and must be reckoned with. The line between public and private sectors in this area of environmental control is muddled, but basically the attack is on procedures, either by government or by industry, that have turned out to be threatening to the majority. Slowly, but perhaps inevitably, some political leaders are beginning to align themselves with these causes.

who decides war or no war?

Perhaps the most wrenching of all the new public pressures are those that aim not at attracting attention to an injustice or challenging unsatisfactory and unresponsive procedures, but those that aim at fundamental policies. There is no better example than our society's agony over the Vietnam war. It has produced challenge after challenge, all of them aimed at basic policies and long accepted procedures of our society: the right of the government to collect taxes, to wage war, to conscript citizens, and the right of any industry to produce any kind of product as long as it returns a profit. There have been those who refused to pay taxes for what they felt was pointless destruction of human life and the environment. There have been those who tried to prevent private enter-prise from producing napalm and frag-mentation bombs, contending that no governmental policy and no profit motive could possibly justify such instruments of horror. The invasion of Cambodia in the spring of 1970 brought an outpouring of infuriated young people; some were killed, many went to jail. And a significant part of our young generation simply has refused to fight such a war, in many ways challenging the government's right to be in the war at all and to force any citizen to participate. To observers of society, this

[7] Speech by Louis S. B. Leakey, 27 December 1971, in Philadelphia. Reported in *Chicago Sun-Times*, 28 December 1971, p. 3.

upheaval is an object lesson in what can happen when people perceive that they are not a part of the deciding and planning processes but are, in fact, an object of the planning. These fundamental challenges may be leading to permanent changes in the society's authority system.

anyone can play

One of the important factors about the new kinds of community demands for a share in priority planning is that anyone can play. In many cases, it has not been the sophisticated and educated people in business and government who have acted to highlight the shortcomings of the system; it has been the people who experienced the consequences, people who organized outside the system because the system had entirely excluded them from power in the first place. This included young people with no power who went to prison and into exile rather than fight an unconscionable war; black people who formed their own unions or black caucuses within unions because they were denied any impact on policy; poor people who have been cheated by credit abuses long protected by law; ethnic groups who feel they have been getting the short end of the socioeconomic stick; taxpayers and recipients of public services who are seeing their own interests trampled by powerful public employee unions claiming a greater and greater share of the public funds; and women who are deciding they are people and not possessions.

The point is that everyone is demanding a share in making the decisions that affect their own lives and seeking new ways to enforce these demands. The implication of these bottom-up public pressures are tremendous. One such implication is that untrained people are telling professional managers how to do their jobs and what is expected of them. Another is the inter-

twining of private and public sectors mentioned previously. Decisions that once were made privately and regulated by the profit motive now are being profoundly affected by public policy and by the political process. And politics is not orderly in the planning sense; priorities arising out of political pressures often are not in the best order of efficiency. Politics challenges integrated systems which, to operate well, depend on mathematical or planning logic for effective use of resources. These systems fall apart when the political logic leads to apparently inefficient uses of resources or to goals which make political but not planning sense. This, in effect, is a clash of systems and even a clash of life styles of the corporation people and the community.

Wherever the influence of the public interest is extended into the private sphere, and wherever the private decision-making power is turned over to the public–political process of decision making, this kind of clash is invited. There is a crucial distinction between decision making in the private and in the public sector; different rules apply. This seems to be little understood. It is this inherent distinction that makes a steel company's advocacy of greater economic planning by government and a CED proposal for public–private partnership in business both so surprising. Both proposals open the private decision-making process to public participation with its frequent and continuing conflict among a variety of communities.

In his speech Ahlbrandt sees economic advantages for American industry in the world market if the government orders economic priorities but takes no note of the kinds of pressures that will be brought to bear on that government process. The CED talks of a method "to insulate the (public–private) corporation from political pressures."[8] It suggests that public ac-

[8] CED, *Social Responsibilities*, p. 60.

countability would be achieved through a board of directors, partially elected and partially appointed, with a tenure, perhaps of seven years, overlapping political terms. But apparently when it talks of political pressures it thinks only of those brought to bear by governmental officials. Nowhere does it mention the kinds of pressures being brought by the public, pressures to which the proposed new public–private corporations will most emphatically be opened. The CED proposal may even be a new kind of Magna Carta for those millions of people who have been frozen out of the private decision-making process, and who, whether from the right or from the left, are attempting politically to be heard.

conflicting priorities

Let us look at some of the priorities and expectations that society seems to have of its various institutions, both public and private: (1) full employment without inflation; (2) clean air and clean water at no additional cost; (3) the right of every person to adequate medical care, perhaps in the form of cradle-to-grave health insurance, at no extra cost; (4) more recreational space without harming the living space for all forms of life, including an expanding human population; (5) more economic growth and more sophisticated technology without employee dissatisfaction and unemployment; (6) extension of the good life to the have nots without inconveniencing the haves; (7) free college education for all students with motivation and ability even though not enough jobs are available for the educated; and (8) the efficiency of an automated interchangeable society without dehumanizing the individual and making him interchangeable too.

Obviously these wants bring conflicting and contradictory pressures on both public and private institutions. They involve choices which will be difficult to make. More than that, they involve costs, which also are subject to counterpressures. Most of us prefer a choice that will cost someone else something. But the costs must lodge somewhere.[9] It has been society's habit to allocate costly, economically unrewarding tasks to government. Government, in turn, subcontracts some of those tasks back to the private sector, adding greatly to the fuzziness of the line between public and private business. Put another way, in the areas where priorities are set by the community rather than the marketplace, the job is given to government, but that job and the extent of the dollars involved will, in turn, affect the marketplace. Countless private enterprises, not only those in defense-related programs, are government subcontractors. Thus they are an extension of government, and, consequently, their priorities are set politically rather than traditionally by profits. These subcontracted activities include military procurement, space exploration, research and development, and claims administration by Blue Cross.

Without seeming to recognize the implications of public priority setting for these subcontractors, the Committee for Economic Development calls this *privatizing* the public sector.[10] It also might be viewed, perhaps more accurately, as *publicizing* the private sector, since the most important element of control is priority not production. Perhaps this is why large government contractors and their unions try to influence the public ordering of priorities through their lobbies. The greater the subcontracting to private enterprise, the greater the chance and incentive for the individual citizen to influence priorities, even though it may be difficult to do so.

[9] "La Peau de Chagain," Balzac's thesis that every aspiration of the heart, brain, or will that is fulfilled must in the end be paid for.
[10] CED, *Social Responsibilities*, p. 51.

Some idea of the extent of government subcontracting to private business can be seen in federal government expenditures for goods and services. These increased 750 percent between 1930 and 1970. In 1930, federal expenditures for goods and services accounted for 1.5 percent of the gross national product; in 1970, they accounted for 10 percent. If we include state and local government expenditures as well as federal, governmental spending accounts for 22 percent of GNP.[11] Government contracting for services and supplies in fiscal 1970 amounted to $48 billion.

the regulators

Deciding, taking action, getting results, fulfilling expectations, and evaluating performance are the usual managerial functions. But it is the deciding that must come first, before action and evaluation of action. What is different today is that people in the society are saying: "These are our priorities. We want to decide. We want them fulfilled. That is what we expect of the economic system and the manager." But the manager only can bring these changes about as he manages the reallocation of resources of manpower and capital not necessarily according to where they bring their best economic return, but where they satisfy the community's needs and expectations regardless of the level of profit.

Even this is not the whole story because, in the absence of the profit regulator, a substitute must be found to enable the community to assess and evaluate the value of services rendered or products produced against the cost. Even prior to

[11] U.S. Department of Commerce, Office of Business Economics, Summary National Income and Product Series, 1929–70, *Survey of Current Business* 51, no. 7 (July 1971): 46, Table A, Gross National Product.

this step is the need to provide the planning which enables the community to decide its priorities in the first place. Planning in this case is not merely a technical process; it is a political process—the means for a community to decide at the local and national levels what it considers more important and what it considers less important. Planning and assessment of costs and benefits are essential if the community is to decide effectively among the choices open to it instead of having the choice established by the market system. It is essential if the quality of the services and efficiency with which they are rendered is to be evaluated.

A business with a government contract usually has tended to evaluate value in terms of the profit it can make on such a contract, not on the value of the good or service to society. This is where the community and private enterprise collide. If the community prevails and the profit potential is too low versus other opportunity, business will require a subsidy to make the contract attractive enough for business to eschew other opportunity. The community, through subsidies, programs private enterprise to fulfill its wishes. But it is important to note that we refer to fulfilling the community's wishes, not those of private business. This is why the steel industry, if it is looking for public planning of the economy, may be shopping for a package it does not really want.

a new social contract

There is increasing interest in considering quality of services and community priorities in the determination of gross national product, giving additional weight in the index to those products with greatest utility in filling social needs, and subtracting from the index the costs of disposing of the mountains of waste that are the by-products of production and marketing (called the *disproduct*).[12] It is an intriguing concept and one that may yet be useful in the ordering of priorities in our increasingly complex society. Willard Wirtz, former secretary of labor, recently gave a boost to the proposal for a council of social advisers by suggesting the development of a system of social accounting as efficient and comprehensive as economic accounting.[13] Joel F. Henning, program director at the Adlai E. Stevenson Institute for International Affairs, has proposed a tandem idea; he suggests a dual system of chartering large corporations, state and national, with the national charter to be issued on "a showing of fiscal and social responsibility." David Rockefeller, chairman and chief executive officer to the Chase Manhattan Bank, foresees the day when corporations may be required to publish a "social audit," but he cautions that there may have to be new laws to assure that the more socially responsive firms will not suffer a competitive disadvantage.

What is new to the generations trained in our schools of business where profit is the primary criterion of success is that priorities are going to be set increasingly by community consensus or a political decision of one form or another. These priorities will not necessarily, or even probably, be in accord with those set by the profit system. The profit regulator allows us to throw out what is unprofitable,

[12] A. A. Berle, Jr., "What GNP Doesn't Tell Us," *Saturday Review*, 31 August 1968.

[13] Willard Wirtz, in the Julius Rosenthal lecture series on "Labor and the Law," Northwestern University, 1, 2, 3 March 1972. In 1967, Senator Fred Harris introduced a full opportunities and national goals and priorities act, creating not only a council of social advisers but also, within Congress, a joint social responsibilities committee that would parallel the Joint Economic Committee. It was not passed. Senator Walter Mondale later reintroduced the bill which passed the Senate but died in the House of Representatives.

to weed out what is inefficient but not what is worthless. The profit system can decide among efficiencies, but does not decide whether or not the service or product should be provided at all. It does not distinguish, for example, between the disposal of trash and the creation of trash.

Ultimately, of course, it will be the cost relative to the benefit of the cost that will serve as the basis for decision, both for the social utility of the service or product and where its cost is best applied. In the private sector, increased social benefits will increase the cost of goods and services. In the public sector, increased social benefits will increase taxes. In the former case, profitability competes against general consumer interests; in the latter, differing segments of the electorate will compete against each other as to whether the social good is worth the price. But if the benefits are a desired priority, their costs must lodge one place or the other.

With scarce resources of money and manpower, the community will need to order its needs and values. This will require the analytical tools of the planner, the economist, the financial expert, plus the input of the social scientists, to produce the information on costs and benefits which will assist the community to decide what service should come first, second, and third, and what should be omitted.

Profit is a single criterion of performance, therefore simple and easily understood. The criteria being used by the community to measure the performance of its institutions are often multiple, interlinked, and complex.

Suppose we add one criterion to profit, for example, a guaranteed job to each employee who successfully completes a one-year probationary period. Think of the interaction of short-term profits with this new goal and the planning that has to be done in order to accommodate both long-term profits and job security. Without this requirement, the planning of manpower revolves around the cycle of business; with this requirement, business plans (and those of the economy as well) have to be built around a stable demand, which is needed to guarantee jobs. Planning shifts from anticipating cycles to controlling them. (As the national economy balance moves from the production of goods to the production of services, planning for job tenure may be substantially easier, due to the lessened effect of business cycles on employment in service occupations.)

the visible hand

The implication is clear that with a competing method for ordering priorities, there also will be divergences in values, as well as in means and ends. At its very basic level, the competing method can represent a conflict of social as against pure economic values and objectives. But it also represents an effort to have the visible hand of the citizen replace the invisible hand of competition as the regulator—at least in some decision-making areas, especially those that most affect the citizen.

a new ball game for business schools

The newer decision-making process poses a particular problem for the business schools, a problem that, for the most part, is just beginning to be faced. This decision-making process will require managers with the talent and temperament to plan and be comfortable with uncertainties and unknowns, who can find a consensus which must sometimes come through confrontation, and who can help adjust and readjust public and private systems to accommodate the new pressures and changing priorities. This is in contrast to the current goals of providing the executive and the planner with the tools to take the risk out of taking risks.[14]

[14] "The Corporation and the Community: Realities and Myths," *MSU Business Topics*, Autumn 1970, p. 18.

There is something of a tendency for business schools to assume that planning and establishing priorities according to profit somehow also will produce the plans and priorities needed to be responsive to social needs and political pressures. This reflects a gulf between those who assume that a management tool, planning, is a tool for all purposes and times and those who feel that planning to meet social needs and political realities is different, not in degree, but in kind, from profit planning.

who is responsible for whom?

There may be a tendency, too, for people to say: "What is so new about all this? Plenty of corporations have shown that they can accept social responsibility, haven't they?" It is true that many staff functions in private enterprise now exist not because they can be justified by their direct profit contribution, but because community priorities run over into the firm and become those of the firm because it cannot help itself. Many firms, some reluctantly, have discovered that they cannot live entirely apart from their environments.[15] It has been the fashion for a corporation to feel it has some responsibility for its local community and to allow some of its businessmen time to participate on boards such as Community Chests and the Urban League. The assumption is that business is helping to determine what is wise and good for society. But there appears to be a shift away from this business responsibility for the community idea toward community responsibility for business.

Citizens are learning that it was the community that gave the corporation its

[15] In the article referred to in ibid., the author argued that community involvement is largely a delegated function, to keep it from interfering with the main stream of corporate activity.

power and that it can take that power away, that the community rather than the corporation can impose standards of behavior, and that it is the community that decides what institutions are needed and how they should behave.[16] Thus, the more or less accidental (and often reluctant) involvement of business in community affairs is far from the same thing as the more fundamental ordering of priorities by community pressures, the kind of new decision making with which we are being confronted. There are conflicts in values and methods and the people involved have different needs, goals, and aspirations. These differences explain why such matters are slow to find their way into the curricula of the business schools. They simply pose difficult problems for schools; to some they are a basic challenge to the established methods. But, perhaps more importantly, few have yet understood the meaning of the changes going on about us. We still tend to think in terms of the antitrust laws and government regulation from the top.

needed: a new impulse

The last great creative impulse in the area of business education occurred about twelve years ago. That was before the government began running the passenger trains, bailing out a bankrupt aircraft industry, controlling wages and prices,

financing more research, and talking about guaranteed incomes.

This educational shake-up stemmed from two reports on higher education for business completed in 1959: the Gordon–Howell report, financed by the Ford Foundation, and the Pierson report, financed by the Carnegie Corporation.[17] These reports were sharp indictments of the general state of business education and, by extension, of all higher education. Although they found a wide variation in quality, they pinpointed the general weaknesses of the schools at that time: (1) excessive vocationalism (an overemphasis upon training for specific jobs) tended to block the individual's maximum intellectual growth and thus ultimately damage his career. At the same time it denied society the kinds of broad-gauged thinking needed to get at the roots of complex and interrelated problems. (2) Creeping intellectual obsolescence was reflected in rigid curricula, inadequate foundation courses, and poor teaching methods. (3) Low standards of most business schools attracted both low caliber students and low caliber faculty and a highly inbred faculty. (4) Poor quality and inadequate quantity of business research contributed to the absence of a stimulating intellectual atmosphere.

The reports made specific recommendations about how to correct these weaknesses, but we can see from our present vantage point that the recommendations did not (and perhaps could not) encompass all the problem areas. In neither report, for example, was there specific mention of the fields of manpower administration or labor–management relations,

---

[16] "The concept of the corporation was developed to give government a vehicle for accomplishing activities in the public interest. Originally corporate charters were rarely granted to accomplish things the government could do for itself but chose to delegate, such as building bridges or highways, or helping to administer colonies, as the British East India Co. did for the English crown. Thus it seems obvious that government has the right to ensure that corporations operate in the public interest." Joel H. Henning, "Found a Dual System of Corporate Chartering," *Chicago Sun-Times*, 30 January 1972.

[17] Robert Aaron Gordon and James Edwin Howell, *Higher Education for Business* (New York: Ford Foundation, Columbia University Press, 1959). Frank C. Pierson, *The Education of American Businessmen* (New York: Carnegie Corporation, McGraw-Hill Book Co., 1959).

although studies of executive behavior even then showed these to be primary and difficult problems taking up much of the executive's time. Urban studies were not referred to in either study except under the rubric of environment—whatever that meant. And in the knotty area of decision making, the reports seemed to rest with the assumption that the decision-making processes of business were adequate for most purposes, not having anticipated the political–social enigmas that confront business today. For that matter few could have anticipated the virtual social revolution which has occurred since that time.

The curricula recommended in the Pierson report allotted only three hours, 5 percent of the total, to public control of business, and three to six hours, 5 to 10 percent of the total, to social science courses in human behavior and management. The Gordon–Howell report recommended a requirement of six hours of study in the legal, social, and political environment; that, too, represents only about 10 percent of the total core.

What seemed to be missing from the reports' findings was the knowledge and development of insight to enable a person to understand what is going on about him in the human–social–political sense, its consequences to himself, the institution which he serves, and to people who get in the way of his decisions. The sheer immensity of these changes and complexities seems to suggest the need for an updating of the Pierson and Gordon–Howell reports to evaluate progress made and formulate new paths to follow.

updating the studies of business education

Such an updating particularly will be needed if suggestions like those for greater governmental economic planning and new kinds of public–private corporations actually are adopted. Both Ahlbrandt in his speech and the CED in its proposal refer to significant roles for the universities in the processes they advocate. Ahlbrandt, in saying that the economic, social, and political policies of the four great economic blocs that compete with the United States globally do not come out of U.S. textbooks, goes on to say: "May I suggest, finally, that our nation's educators in economics bear, within industry, a responsibility to recommend courses of action that will solve our problems? You may find that you may even have to rewrite the old textbooks—so pervasive is change in our brave new world."[18] (Parenthetically, what textbooks? Smith, Ricardo, Mill, Marshall? Or Keynes, Hansen, Galbraith, Samuelson?)

The CED, in advocating new partnerships between government and private enterprise, says: "It by no means will be an exclusive partnership, for other private institutions, especially universities, will also play very significant roles."[19] But it apparently has not sensed just how startlingly different those roles will be.

What would the updaters of the business school reports find now, twelve years later? They would find that, in general, the business schools have been strengthened. A generation of business school graduates probably has received a better education than earlier generations. Their tools in the area of quantitative analysis are infinitely more advanced than those of earlier graduates. They likely would find a growth of educational pluralism in the schools of business which, in the long run, may be the healthiest development of all. They would see substantial experimentation. The most exciting development and the most relevant, for our emphasis, is the

---

[18] Ahlbrandt, "For Whom the Steel Bell Tolls."

[19] CED, *Social Responsibilities*, p. 59.

growth in concern for the relationships of business schools to the community. Educational researchers now would find a number of schools attempting to graft on urban studies or manpower management courses. But the main thrusts continue, even here, to be quantitative and technological, seeking to solve urban problems primarily with business and system techniques.

the new hybrid

A few schools have adopted or are moving toward the generic management approach. This approach leads to teaching management to people who may be headed toward either the public or the private sectors, people who will work in public and community (urban) administration, education, and health and medical care, as well as in business and industry. This requires that the student come to understand not only what the tools are, but also whether they apply or can be adapted in different decision-making contexts as in the case of planning—the private, competitive context and the community or urban development context.

Finally, they would find a number of business and management schools currently moving beyond the mere grafting on of urban studies courses to full-fledged urban studies curricula, with at least three distinguishing orientations. These are: (1) the knowledge required to manage complex urban institutions, including the political area of decision making, and the management of the delivery of goods and services to the citizens of a community; (2) technical knowledge, including systems analysis, applied to the solving of community problems such as traffic control and highway development, pollution control, housing development, and general physical environmental improvement; and (3) development among members of the newer

urban populations of the capacity to govern, the ability to achieve self-determination and economic self-sufficiency. The updaters of the business education reports would find, as we have suggested, that there have been significant shifts in the nature of business problems, particularly those that deal with increasing interrelationships between public and private sectors and with the strident demands of once-quieter people for a share in the making of decisions about priorities.

Large corporation chief executives behave increasingly as if they were public administrators and vice versa. In a sense they are becoming more alike as they exchange expertise, jobs, and private enterprise managerial technology for public management experience with its pluralistic decision making. They are becoming more alike in another way: the managerial bureaucracies of each, the public and the private, are being challenged to share their decision making and economic and social benefits with new power groups who are seeking entrance into the system and the power needed to enforce a full sharing of the fruits of production.

The burden of this article indeed suggests a blurring of distinctions between the public and private managerial elite. But it contends that, although there are common denominators, the public and private managerial elite presently are not readily interchangeable because of the fundamental differences in the decision-making process for the setting of priorities. The emerging questions cannot yet be answered because both public and private management are in states of transition, but they must be explored by those who would devise curricula to train managers to manage in an urban society. What form of management or manager will emerge during this time of fundamental change in the society?

There have been other shifts in our

society in the past twelve years. The economy of the United States has shifted from goods producing to service producing. Former Secretary of Labor Willard Wirtz estimates that by 1980 two people will be in service industries for every one in production.[20]

Manufacturing employment is expected to have the slowest rate of growth, up only 21 percent between 1965 and 1980. In contrast, the fastest growing area is expected to be state and local government, all of it in the service area. Public employment is expected to increase 66 percent from 1965 to 1980. Other large increases are expected in finance, insurance and trade, and in all those areas concerned with services designed to improve the quality of the environment and of life itself (66 percent).[21]

opportunities and preferences for managers

New managers will be needed, but they will be largely outside the traditional career areas with which business schools have concerned themselves. They will be needed particularly in health care delivery, education, public and urban administration and finance, environmental administration, and manpower intensive industries, and they will be heavily concentrated at state and local government levels.

The people of the nation in the 1960s and 1970s have expressed their concern for improving the quality of life in the society. Whether or not this is a transitory movement remains to be seen because we do not know yet whether man will use what Leakey called his "wonderful computer brain" to work for his own survival.

We are learning that many of the best students in our society are selecting job options where they feel they have a chance to do something about man's condition. This can range from making community institutions work effectively, to providing services for the sick, poor, unemployed, and persecuted, to defending man against his efforts to destroy his environment, to eliciting a higher quality of performance from the various levels of government. Many of these careers are in the political-sociological-educational areas not usually found in business. But these careers are at the heart of the capacity to master the processes of involvement of the citizen in planning his future. They are more attuned to the society's estimate of priorities than to those of business. The business schools probably are not attracting the needed share of these future-minded students. In contrast, the number of students applying to the nation's law schools was five times greater in 1971 than it was in 1961.[22]

Since the business school reports, the schools have toughened up the curricula largely through greater emphasis upon the use of quantitative techniques in solving business problems. But, unfortunately, values cannot necessarily be quantified. Matrix decision making may show the quantitative contribution but not necessarily final judgments.

it will take more than tools

The updaters of the business school reports might find that although the work of the late 1950s added to the quality and stature of schools of business, it also tended to simplify as seemed best fitted to help the student manage the manageable. But if the world is as we seem to think it is and will be, complex, interrelated, inter-

[20] Willard Wirtz in Julius Rosenthal lectures, Northwestern University, 1, 2, 3 March 1972.
[21] *The U.S. Economy in 1980*, Bulletin 1673 and Manpower Report of the President, 1970.

[22] Robert W. Meserve, "We Are Flooded," *Illinois Bar Journal*, May 1972, p. 772.

dependent, and extremely difficult to manage, the student will need more than tools. More than his predecessors, he will need the psychological capacity (temperament) to manage in an atmosphere of uncertainty, unpredictability, and conflict. The limits of his control will be sharply constrained and his need to accommodate ambiguity and to negotiate arrangements with other sectors of society will be apparent even before he can apply his knowledge and his tools. For the business school administrator this suggests implications not merely respecting curriculum but respecting admissions as well.

For example, administration of a large public hospital system, of which the United States has many and will have many more, requires not only medical and managerial expertise, but also the capacity to manage under stress and conflict arising out of opposing values, expectations, and priorities of the various publics and pressure groups which have an interest in such a system. No one group has free rein to impose its priorities, not even the administration. The political skill to resolve these conflicts in priorities and expectations will be fully as important a requirement of the medical administrator as is his skill as a doctor or his talents as an administrator.

This model of administration is more likely than not to become the rule in the private sector as well, as it strives for a viable existence in the inner cities, and as more and more firms become indebted to government or become government subcontractors or partners in public–private corporations.

a matter of managerial genetics

The updaters of the business school reports might conclude that the next step forward

in the management of a multiracial society of immense diversity would be not the imposition of a business curriculum upon the solving of problems which span both the public and private sectors, but the evolution of a generic school of management which by its nature involves people with diverse interests both in the learning and teaching processes. Such educational arrangements would enable the participants to learn early about the nature of values and priorities and the differences among people in this regard.

Planning and management would be learned under varying conditions: where profit is the regulator, where the logic of economic development is the regulator, where the logic of human development is the regulator, where political strength is the regulator. There are common denominators of management in each, but each has its unique distinctions, too. Thus education for management is not to blend into one what are important differences, but rather to show how the processes are specific to the needs of institutions. It is to demonstrate how as institutions blend or take over one another's functions this alters the decision-making process and even remakes it to respond to new hybrid institutions.

Planning and management would entail not only the method of arriving at the plans to be achieved but also the process for achieving them, which also may include the political process. This is not an uncommon activity of institutions today, especially public sector organizations where program planning budgeting has taken hold. These planning needs will influence the curriculum for both the public and private sector.

The central role of management and planning, as suggested in the beginning of this article, is to aid people and institutions to make decisions: to decide what is important, necessary, too costly, necessary even if too costly, useful or useless either in the context of competition or community decision making. Its role will increase as the free competition sector shrinks; a means for valuing goods and services must be maintained no matter what the competitive condition.

7. a more rational approach to health care delivery
John T. Gentry

Rational is defined as "having reason or of relating to reason." For the purpose of this article, the rationalization of health care delivery is defined as the process of attempting to increase the level of "reason" that prevails, e.g., matching available health services with community health service requirements. Rationalization is also illustrated by efforts to achieve recommended levels of quality and make effective and efficient use of scarce and costly resources. The objectives of this article are to examine: (1) Various approaches to making the delivery of health services more rational; (2) the nature of the forces that are influencing change within the health system; and (3) how well health planning is serving as an integrating and rationalizing force. Attention is directed to the importance of proposed changes as they relate to responsibilities of health care providers and their relationships with other organizations and practitioners.

The levels of rationality inherent in certain health care delivery systems, and the impact of rationalizing forces on these systems, can be examined in several ways. One approach, used in this article, is to identify both the distinguishing characteristics of the health care delivery system with which one is dealing, and the methods by which levels of rationality can be assessed. This approach provides a frame of reference for the selection of specific indicators of rationality and assessment criteria. One can then identify and assess rationality aspects of specific health care delivery issues, e.g., accessibility of services, and evaluate the potential impact of specific proposals for problem resolution. The specific steps of this approach are described under respective section headings. Levels of "reason" imputed by the writer represent value judgments that may not be shared by readers. Examples should, therefore, be viewed as illustrations of principles or concepts and not as absolute values per se.

health care delivery systems

It is assumed that the primary objective of a health care delivery system is to provide health services necessary to sustain or improve the health status of the population it serves. It is also assumed that a health delivery system is comparable to the health care "complex" described by the Program Area Committee on Medical Care Administration of the American Public Health Association.[1] In this characteriza-

Reprinted from *Hospital Progress*, 54, No. 8 (August 1973), pp. 94–103, with permission of the publisher.

[1] The Program Area Committee on Medical Care Administration, *A Guide to Medical Care Administration*, Vol. 1: Concepts and Principles, American Public Health Association, 1965.

tion, health care is described as involving three components: (1) providers of health services, (2) consumers of health services, and (3) organized arrangements to facilitate the provision of services.

The services provided by a health care delivery system can similarly be described according to: (1) types of provider categories involved; (2) consumer groups or categorical health needs for which services are provided; and (3) services characterized by special organizational or financial provisions. For example, provider-oriented service categories include those associated with licensed and non-licensed practitioners; agency- and facility-sponsored services, e.g., those provided by community hospitals; and those providing miscellaneous, supportive materials and services. The latter include suppliers of drugs and equipment, manufacturers of prosthetic devices, and diagnostic laboratories. Third-party funding sources are in this support category.

Consumer groups include mothers and children, the employed adult, the handicapped, and the poor. Services associated with categorical needs can be illustrated by rehabilitation-type activities, mental health services, and communicable disease control activities. Special organizational or financial provisions include home health services, emergency medical services, health maintenance organizations, and neighborhood health centers.

It is also possible to categorize health services according to certain functional objectives and activity goals. Health promotional activities, preventive measures, diagnostic and treatment services, and rehabilitation-type activities constitute one sequence of designated service objectives. Repair and maintenance represent alternate terminology that can be used for designating comparable objectives. Case-finding, patient care planning, referral, information exchange, surveillance, and follow-up services illustrate a more

detailed sequence of activity areas applicable to specific program goals, e.g., reducing the incidence of invasive cancer of the cervix.

Enumeration of the multiple components of the health system and the manner in which functional objectives and activity goals can be described is helpful for several reasons. One area of value is the portrayal of the extensiveness of the system with which one is dealing, and the complex interdependencies of its many parts. A second value is the identification of the numerous opportunities for quantitative and qualitative imbalances that affect directly the level of rationality with which delivery systems undertake the provision of health services. For example, a low level of rationality may be imputed to the management of certain health problems if available service resources are relatively more heavily weighted, quantitatively, in the direction of diagnosis and treatment of acute episodic conditions rather than preventive or rehabilitation measures.

The use of various classification schemes for identification of the nature and/or resolution of specific rationalization issues is illustrated in subsequent sections.

methods of assessment

Assessment of the level of rationality that prevails within a health care delivery system depends on two data sources. One consists of information concerning the health services required to prevent or alleviate community health problems, i.e., the service objectives toward which a community would strive if all constraints were removed. The second pertains to the level at which specific health services and activities are actually provided and utilized.

Analysis of the quantitative differences between required and available services provides one estimate of the relative level of rationality achieved. Additional analyses require assessment criteria that can help interpret the importance of the presence or absence of specific services or support activities. For example, the presence or absence of certain types of services, e.g., predischarge planning, can result in different levels of quality as measured by health service outcomes and health status. Four assessment criteria are used in this article: (1) comprehensiveness, (2) continuity, (3) quality, and (4) economy. Definitions of these criteria and a description of the analytic methods with which they are used are provided elsewhere.

Identification of the nature and extensiveness of the services required to prevent or alleviate community health problems can only be determined after existing health problems are identified and measured. Identification and measurement of the amount of disability and premature death within given populations are the concern of numerous agencies, including the National Center for Health Statistics. Identification and measurement methods include interview and examination, surveys, vital records, and health care records. An extensive literature is available concerning the usefulness and limitations of available methods and representative findings.[2]

Approaches to estimating health services and the service resources necessary to prevent or alleviate specific health problems also constitute an extensive literature. The work of Lee and Jones represents an early effort to estimate the number of physicians required to provide health services for a specific population.[3] More recent work by Falk and Schonfeld

has refined and expanded these efforts, which now include dentistry and pediatrics.[4] The specificity of this work is illustrated by documentation of the time in minutes required by dentists and dental auxiliaries to perform initial dental examinations. Additional efforts to quantify the time required to perform service tasks and to outline specific manpower task delegations are illustrated by the work of Ast, in children's dentistry,[5] and Yankauer, in pediatrics.[6]

Work has also been undertaken by Sparer and Alderman to estimate the total service staffing requirements necessary to fulfill the comprehensive health care responsibilities of neighborhood health centers.[7] Service multipliers, specific for age and sex, were developed for estimating the number of annual medical and dental encounters necessary to meet service requirements for target populations. Annual productivity data applicable to

---

[4] I. S. Falk *et al.*, "The Development of Standards for the Audit and Planning of Medical Care I. Concepts, Research Design, and the Content of Primary Physician's Care," *American Journal of Public Health*, July, 1967, pp. 1,118–1,136; H. K. Schonfeld *et al.*, "The Development of Standards for the Audit and Planning of Medical Care: Good Pediatric Care—Program Content and Method of Estimating Needed Personnel." *American Journal of Public Health*, November, 1968, pp. 2,097–2,110; H. K. Schonfeld *et al.*, "The Content of Good Dental Care: Methodology in a Formulation for Clinical Standards and Audits, and Preliminary Findings," *American Journal of Public Health*, July, 1967, pp. 1,137–1,146.

[5] David B. Ast *et al.*, "Time and Cost Factors To Provide Regular, Periodic Dental Care for Children in a Fluoridated and Non-fluoridated Area," *American Journal of Public Health*, June, 1965, pp. 811–820.

[6] Alfred Yankauer *et al.*, "Task Performance and Task Delegation in Pediatric Office Practice," *American Journal of Public Health*, July, 1969, pp. 1,104–1,117.

[7] Gerald Sparer and Anne Alderman, "Data Needs for Planning Neighborhood Health Centers," *American Journal of Public Health*, April, 1971, pp. 796–806.

---

[2] National Center for Health Statistics, *Vital and Health Statistics Series*, April, 1972.

[3] Roger I. Lee and Lewis W. Jones, *The Fundamentals of Good Medical Care*, Chicago, University of Chicago Press, 1933.

specific categories of practitioners were then used to estimate health manpower requirements.

Despite numerous limitations, these data sources illustrate the service standards and guidelines against which the adequacy of community health services must currently be evaluated. The actual level of health services that are available within a specific study community is usually obtained through an inventory of both community health service providers and the nature and extensiveness of the services they provide.

The four assessment criteria previously cited are useful because they apply to frequently identified problems, e.g., lack of comprehensiveness and continuity of available services, inadequate quality levels, and inefficient use of scarce and costly resources. Definitions of these criteria and more explicit illustrations of the rationale for their use follow.

Comprehensiveness is defined as the extent to which all of the health service requirements of an individual, or target population, can be met. For example, dental problems are usually responsible for an important component of health service requirements. The services provided by a comprehensive health center will, therefore, be more comprehensive if they include dental services than if they exclude dental services. Dental services, per se, will be more comprehensive if they include a complete spectrum of preventive and restorative services and if available service resources can provide, quantitatively, the amount of services required.

Continuity can be described as the extent to which required services are provided with minimum delays or interruption of services that are imposed by avoidable changes of personnel and location, or lags in receipt of care. For example, health care delivery systems may have family health workers who can provide follow-up services in the home. Systems with these types of resources have a greater capacity for assuring continuity of necessary care than those delivery systems that either do not have family health workers, or confine them to the site of institutional facilities. The rationale for including continuity is illustrated by Williamson's outcome approach to assuring the quality of health services.[8] Williamson's findings revealed a doubling of the expected mortality of hypertensive patients because of inadequate referral, information exchange, outreach, and follow-up activities.

At the process level, *quality* is defined as the extent to which services are provided in accordance with recommended standards and guidelines. The relative use of recommended x-rays and laboratory tests for diagnostic purposes is illustrative. At an outcome level, quality is impaired when services are not comprehensive or continuous, and economical use is not made of available resources.

Economy is defined as the extent to which services are provided with the most efficient use of resources, especially costly and scarce resources. For example, it is more economical to use a nurse practitioner for providing certain services than to use the physician. Quality is adversely affected by the inefficient use of limited resources because individuals may thereby be deprived of the receipt of necessary health services that otherwise could be provided.

The manner in which assessment criteria can be integrated with quality-related concepts of structure, process, and outcome is illustrated in Figures 1 and 2. Figure 1 provides more explicit definitions of terms, including "effectiveness" and "efficiency" of health services. Figure 2 illustrates the manner in which assessment criteria are operationalized. The use of an

[8] John W. Williamson, "Evaluating Quality of Patient Care: A Strategy Relating Outcome and Process Assessment," *Journal of the American Medical Association*, Oct. 25, 1971.

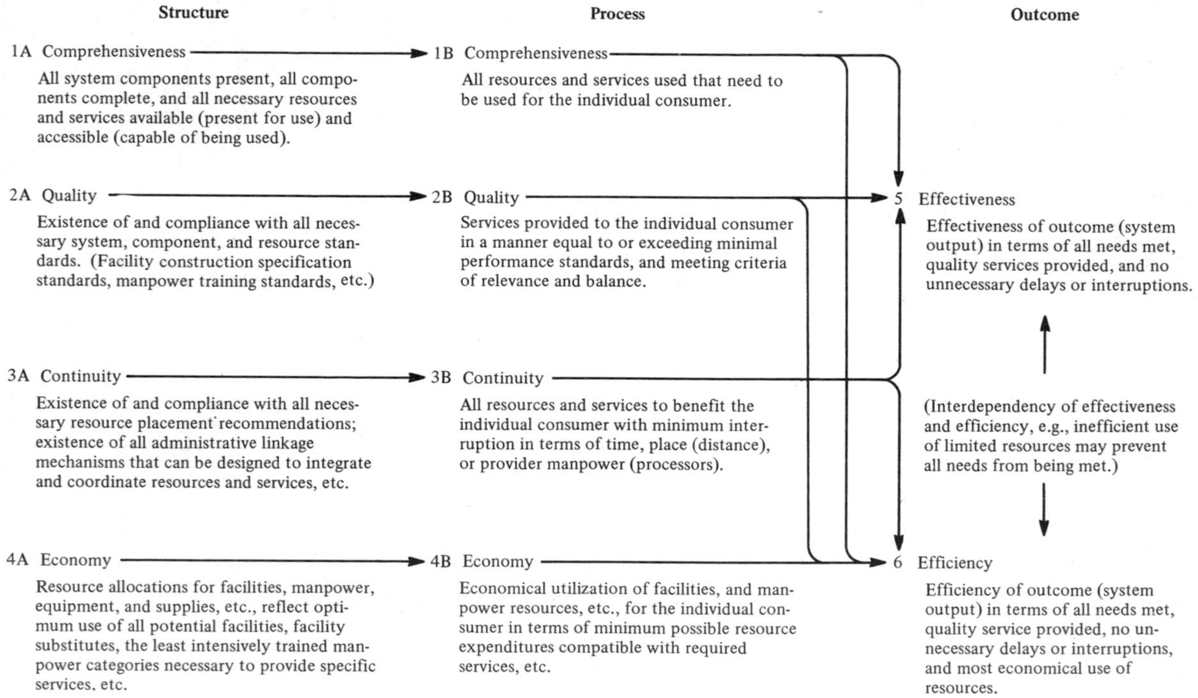
Structure
Process
Outcome
1A Comprehensiveness
All system components present, all components complete, and all necessary resources and services available (present for use) and accessible (capable of being used).
1B Comprehensiveness
All resources and services used that need to be used for the individual consumer.
2A Quality
Existence of and compliance with all necessary system, component, and resource standards. (Facility construction specification standards, manpower training standards, etc.)
2B Quality
Services provided to the individual consumer in a manner equal to or exceeding minimal performance standards, and meeting criteria of relevance and balance.
5 Effectiveness
Effectiveness of outcome (system output) in terms of all needs met, quality services provided, and no unnecessary delays or interruptions.
3A Continuity
Existence of and compliance with all necessary resource placement recommendations; existence of all administrative linkage mechanisms that can be designed to integrate and coordinate resources and services, etc.
3B Continuity
All resources and services to benefit the individual consumer with minimum interruption in terms of time, place (distance), or provider manpower (processors).
(Interdependency of effectiveness and efficiency, e.g., inefficient use of limited resources may prevent all needs from being met.)
4A Economy
Resource allocations for facilities, manpower, equipment, and supplies, etc., reflect optimum use of all potential facilities, facility substitutes, the least intensively trained manpower categories necessary to provide specific services, etc.
4B Economy
Economical utilization of facilities, and manpower resources, etc., for the individual consumer in terms of minimum possible resource expenditures compatible with required services, etc.
6 Efficiency
Efficiency of outcome (system output) in terms of all needs met, quality service provided, no unnecessary delays or interruptions, and most economical use of resources.

Figure 1. Planning and Evaluating Health Systems. A conceptual model utilizing system output assessment criteria of comprehensiveness, quality, continuity, and economy: Definition and relationships.

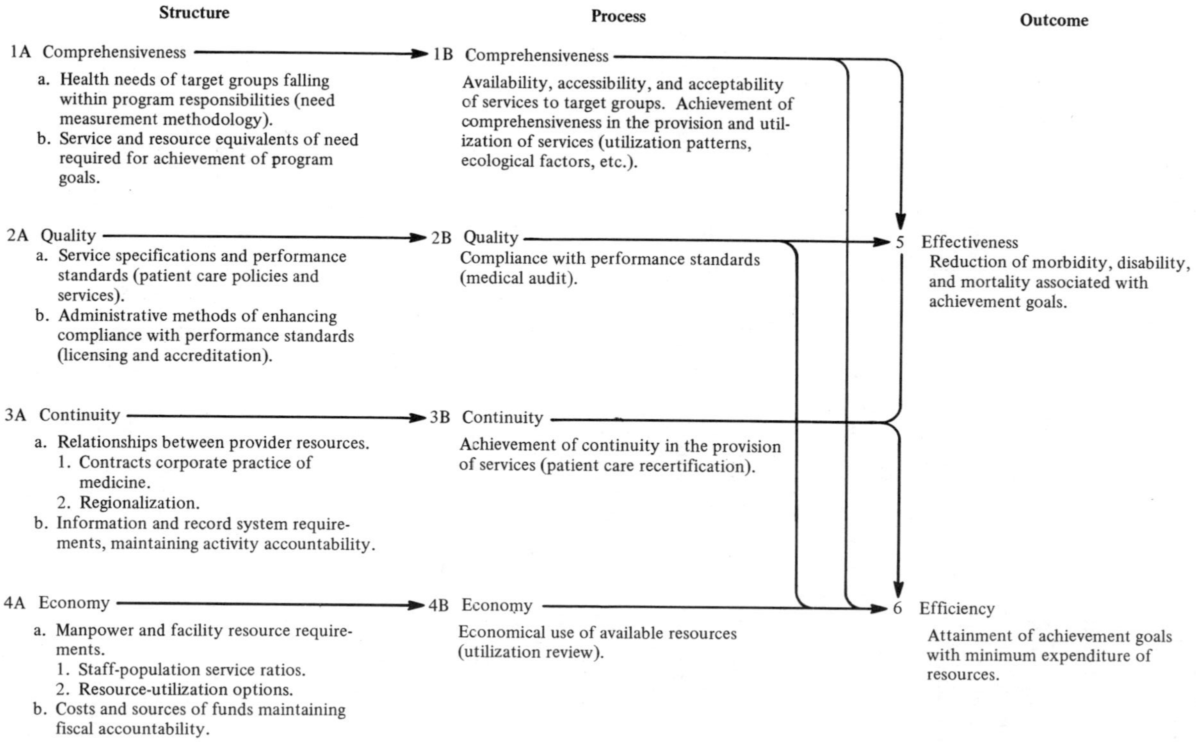
Structure
Process
Outcome
1A Comprehensiveness
a. Health needs of target groups falling within program responsibilities (need measurement methodology).
b. Service and resource equivalents of need required for achievement of program goals.
1B Comprehensiveness
Availability, accessibility, and acceptability of services to target groups. Achievement of comprehensiveness in the provision and utilization of services (utilization patterns, ecological factors, etc.).
2A Quality
a. Service specifications and performance standards (patient care policies and services).
b. Administrative methods of enhancing compliance with performance standards (licensing and accreditation).
2B Quality
Compliance with performance standards (medical audit).
5 Effectiveness
Reduction of morbidity, disability, and mortality associated with achievement goals.
3A Continuity
a. Relationships between provider resources.
1. Contracts corporate practice of medicine.
2. Regionalization.
b. Information and record system requirements, maintaining activity accountability.
3B Continuity
Achievement of continuity in the provision of services (patient care recertification).
4A Economy
a. Manpower and facility resource requirements.
1. Staff-population service ratios.
2. Resource-utilization options.
b. Costs and sources of funds maintaining fiscal accountability.
4B Economy
Economical use of available resources (utilization review).
6 Efficiency
Attainment of achievement goals with minimum expenditure of resources.

Figure 2. Planning and Evaluation of Health Systems. A conceptual model utilizing system output assessment criteria of comprehensiveness, quality, continuity, and economy: Operationalizing assessment categories.

analytic systems framework permits the incorporation of all related components and analyses, including medical audit and utilization review activities.

problems and issues

Crises of the United States health system reflect the level of rationality of the system and include: (1) imbalances between health problems and health services; (2) limited accessibility and acceptability of services; and (3) rapidly rising costs. Problems and factors contributing to the creation and continuation of these problems are described under respective headings.

1. *Imbalances Between Health Problems and Health Services.* As previously noted, imbalances between health problems and the services necessary for the prevention or alleviation of these problems result in an inadequate level of "comprehensiveness" of required services. Under these circumstances, "continuity," "quality," and "economy" are also adversely affected. Illustrations have included the more adequate allocation of service resources for the diagnosis and treatment of acute conditions than for health promotional activities, preventive services, and rehabilitation-type activities. Imbalances may also be illustrated by relatively more attention being directed to physical problems than to the social and emotional needs of individual patients.

Limited provision of services falling within rehabilitation categories is illustrated by data from a national survey of acute short-term hospitals. The levels at which study hospitals have implemented various services have also been summarized.[9] Whereas 68 per cent of all

[9] J. T. Gentry *et al., The Provision of Health Services by Hospitals in the United States: A National Sample,* Chapel Hill, University of North Carolina, 1972.

hospitals provide physical therapy services, only 32 per cent have occupational therapy services, and only 28 per cent provide speech and hearing therapy services. In addition, only 38 per cent have adopted routine nursing orders, e.g., the use of foot boards for positioning stroke patients, and only 21 per cent routinely screen patients for rehabilitation needs.

It can be assumed that 100 per cent of the respondent hospitals will admit patients that require some form of rehabilitation services. Theoretically, each hospital should have appropriate screening mechanisms to identify such individuals and have standing orders for the routine management of certain conditions. In addition, optimum rationality calls for each hospital to either provide specific services, e.g., physical therapy, or refer patients to another community resource where such services can be obtained. In contrast, 40 per cent of the hospitals without physical therapy service provisions did not have patient referral arrangements with other community resources providing these services.

Factors contributing to health service imbalances include health manpower education practices, the decision-making authority of certain practitioners, and financing and payment mechanisms. For example, the medical education model focuses primarily on the diagnosis and treatment of the acutely ill hospitalized patient. Because of this model, the provision of comprehensive rehabilitation services has not been an integral part of many medical students' initial learning experience, or their subsequent practice behavior. The attitude and behavior of physicians are particularly noteworthy because of traditional vesting of patient care responsibility in the hands of the physician. Under usual circumstances, rehabilitation services will not be provided unless referred by the physician.

The relatively low priority with which

many physicians view rehabilitation services further reinforces attitudes and perceptions of hospital administrators developed during their own educational preparation. The education of the administrator has focused primarily on institutional management, not patient care services. As a result, the administrator may not be well-grounded regarding the rationale for rehabilitation services. Study data suggest that some administrators confuse occupational therapy services with vocational training or recreational therapy.[10]

Third-party funding benefits have included payment for physical therapy services if they are carried out on an inpatient, but not on an outpatient, basis. Compensation for occupational therapy and speech and hearing therapy services is not usually provided regardless of where services are provided.[11]

2. *Limited Accessibility and Acceptability of Services*, particularly for the poor, are associated with: (a) financial barriers; (b) limited skill in coping with the system; (c) limited transportation or child care resources; and (d) miscellaneous administrative practice illustrated by the absence of patient appointment systems.

Factors contributing to the problem areas cited include: (a) limited population coverage by social insurance health benefits; (b) limited insurance coverage of the health care expenditures incurred by individual patients, e.g., only one-third of health care costs is usually covered by health insurance; (c) a general failure to include the cost of non-institutional support services as part of the cost of providing services; and (d) management of health care delivery systems with little

in the way of consumer participation in the formulation of administrative policies.

3. *Rapidly Rising Costs* can be illustrated, in part, by escalating health manpower costs and their impact on facility expenditures. Factors contributing to this phenomenon include the market mechanism under which the health system operates; conflicts of interest, especially in the use of provider-controlled fiscal intermediaries; and the general ineffectiveness of cost containment endeavors.

The contributing factors cited primarily reflect the nature of the market mechanisms that govern the behavior of the health industry, and secondarily reflect the absence of effective planning and coordinating mechanisms. For example, dysfunctional aspects of existing financing and payment practices persist because of competitive market mechanisms. Also the relatively unrestricted freedom of the market is inconsistent with the level of rationality required by planning and coordinating mechanisms for problem resolution, i.e., free market is incompatible with extensive capacity for implementation of "rational" plans.

approaches to problem solving

One indicator of the general level of rationality inherent in the health care system is how adequate some approaches are in resolving health care delivery problems, e.g., will a specific proposal actually increase the comprehensiveness of health services? This level of analysis is also helpful in assessing the general likelihood of success of rationalization efforts, i.e., is the system as a whole making any progress in becoming more rational? It is helpful to include in these analyses the problem areas for which proposed solutions have not been forthcoming and/or alternate approaches to a specific problem that have not been completely articulated.

---

[10] J. T. Gentry *et al.*, "Attitudes and Perceptions of Health Service Providers: Implications for Implementation and Delivery of Community Health Services," *American Journal of Public Health* (in press).

[11] *Ibid.*

The latter can be illustrated by failure to consider the use of capitation payment mechanisms in other than group practice settings, e.g., with the solo practitioner.

Approaches to problem solving and making health care delivery systems more rational have included three major areas: (1) financing and delivery, (2) health manpower, and (3) planning and regulation. An assessment of the relative level of rationality of specific approaches follows under respective headings.

1. *Financing and Delivery.* Four overlapping areas are important: (a) national health insurance; (b) cost containment; (c) models for the delivery of services; e.g., the HMO, and (d) quality assurance.

a. *National Health Insurance.* The level of rationality in national health insurance proposals can be illustrated, in part, by examining medicare experience data. Medicare is noteworthy because of its goals to increase the financial accessibility to the elderly of certain health services; to expand service benefits beyond the range of traditional health insurance coverage, e.g., include skilled nursing facilities and home health benefits; and to assure important quality criteria as a prerequisite for vendor payment, e.g., conditions of participation. Despite these efforts, financial accessibility and the comprehensiveness of service benefits are still grossly deficient. Whereas health insurance benefits have covered approximately 33 per cent of health care costs, medicare benefits have covered only 45 per cent of such costs. Furthermore, increased charges to medicare recipients have resulted in a net benefit to the recipient of only 15 per cent over prior noninsurance expenditures, i.e., reduction of "out-of-pocket" costs.[12]

Utilization of skilled nursing facilities and home health agency services are permitted only after three days of hospitalization in an acute, short-term facility.

This practice has resulted in "very little use of the post-hospital alternatives."[13] For 1967, 6.5 per cent of total medicare expenditures were for skilled nursing facilities, one per cent for outpatient hospital services, and one per cent for home health services. This low level of use has persisted. An early recommendation by the Health Insurance Benefits Advisory Committee that the three-day hospitalization requirement for home health benefits be eliminated has not been adopted.[14] Medicare experience data thus suggest that rationalization efforts to increase comprehensiveness and continuity of services, and to make more effective and efficient use of costly resources, have achieved very limited success. A question that has not been asked is what is the level of savings that could be accrued by more extensive use of hospital alternatives? Also what increase in the comprehensiveness of services could be achieved by the use of these savings for other necessary health care services?

The plethora of national health insurance proposals generated since the passage of medicare are equally noteworthy because of the continued difficulty of their sponsors to: (1) equate proposed benefits with health service requirements; (2) distinguish program costs as an integral portion of total health care expenditures; and (3) differentiate social insurance from private insurance.[15] Also, the potential use of national health insurance as an approach to resolve the numerous deficiencies associated with Workmen's Compensation funded health services has not been articulated.[16]

---

[12] Howard West, "Five Years of Medicare —A Statistical Review," *Social Security Bulletin*, U.S. Dept. of HEW, December, 1971.

[13] *Ibid.*

[14] Health Insurance Benefits Advisory Committee, *Annual Report on Medicare*, Dept. of HEW, covering the period July 1, 1966–Dec. 31, 1967. Mimeographed report of 71 pages.

[15] Health Insurance Association of America, *Program for Healthcare in the 1970's*, 1970.

[16] Center for Rehabilitation Services, *New York University Workmen's Compensation Study*, New York University, 1961.

Experience data also suggest that the private health insurance industry is perpetuating dysfunctional benefit practices because of the industry's inability to undertake self-directed rationalizing efforts.[17] For example, insurance carriers are currently reacting within a competitive market to the service benefit specifications resulting from collective bargaining between consumer groups and their employers. Whereas insurance industry representatives will point out the need for a national health policy mandating minimum benefit standards, proposed government regulation of the health insurance industry has been addressed primarily to cost containment measures.

b. *Cost Containment.* Concerns with the rising costs of health services have resulted in numerous cost containment efforts. These efforts have been directed especially to medicaid expenditures. For example, the early history of the California Medical Assistance Program is replete with cost containment endeavors.[18] For the most part, these efforts were undertaken without regard for initial program objectives. Levels of rationality are illustrated by the fact that the formal objectives for which the program was initiated, i.e., comprehensive services of high quality, were negated by initial policy planning decisions concerning provider compensation levels.[19] Only physician practitioners and hospital facilities were compensated at usual and customary fees, and at reasonable costs. Continuation of inadequate levels of compensation for all other providers resulted in the same low levels of participation by these providers that the program was intended to correct.

A limited number of incentive reimbursement experiments have been sponsored by the Social Security Administration.[20] These experiments were initiated for the purpose of testing whether alternate payment mechanisms could lead to lower costs. One industrial engineering project was directed to increasing the efficiency of operational units within the hospital, e.g., reducing laundry costs per pound. Another experiment has dealt with prospective budget estimates in which the facility is rewarded if expenditures are less than anticipated.

Little attention has been directed to eliminating the financial penalties to which hospitals are subjected, i.e., no income for unoccupied beds, and that are primarily responsible for dysfunctional behavior.[21] It can be assumed that if hospitals are compensated for all fixed costs regardless of bed occupancy status, hospital administrators and trustees would be less motivated to maintain a high bed census. "Reason" dictates that maintenance of a high bed census, regardless of patient care needs, is counterproductive to cost containment objectives, i.e., increased use of less costly skilled nursing facilities and home health services.

c. *The Delivery of Health Services.* Models for the delivery of services include the HMO; the health care corporation endorsed by the American Hospital Association; health components of model cities programs; and comprehensive health service projects such as neighborhood health centers.

---

[17] Gentry, "Attitudes and Perceptions."

[18] Acton W. Barnes, "A Description of the Organization and Administration of the California Medical Assistance Program: Title XIX," Chapel Hill, Department of Health Administration, School of Public Health, University of North Carolina, July 1, 1968.

[19] J. T. Gentry and M. Schaefer, "The Impact of State and Federal Policy Planning Decisions on the Implementation and Functional Adequacy of Title XIX Health Care Programs," *Medical Care*, March–April, 1969.

[20] U.S. Dept. of HEW, *Guidelines for Incentive Reimbursement Experiments Under the Medicare, Medicaid, and Maternal and Child Health Programs*, Washington, D.C., March, 1968.

[21] Leon Bernstein, personal communication, December, 1972.

The HMO has been promoted, in part, for its cost containment potential. In addition, HMOs have been described as enhancing quality and encouraging increased attention to preventive measures and the "maintenance" of health.[22]

Analysis of HMO proposals indicates that potential accomplishments fall short of correcting or alleviating major health care crises. There may be little or no increase in comprehensiveness or continuity of services. There also may be little change in the accessibility of services. Equally important, there appears to be little potential for enhancing the adequacy of planning and coordinating mechanisms.[23]

Contrary to expectations, there are financial disincentives for undertaking certain preventive measures, e.g., cervical cytology screening. Until the incidence of invasive uterine cancer begins to be reduced, cytology screening will cost HMOs more, not less, money. In recognition of this phenomenon, the Health Insurance Plan of Greater New York supplements the capitation payment of participating groups of physicians in proportion to the per cent of eligible women included in their cytology screening activities.[24] Supplementary compensation is provided at the end of the contract year after performance levels are reviewed retrospectively.

The Kaiser-Permanente HMO model is characterized by ownership of hospital facilities. This feature has resulted in newly proposed HMOs seeking to obtain their own facilities. Whereas the construction of additional hospital beds may be indicated in some communities, in others there may already be a surplus of acute care beds. In the latter circumstances, "reason" dictates that existing hospital resources and newly created HMOs collaborate and adapt, administratively and procedurally, to a shared use of available beds. In contrast, advocates are concerned that certificate of need legislation that attempts to match numbers of beds to community requirements will interfere with new HMO development, i.e., restrict market entry.[25]

d. *Quality Assurance.* Approaches to assuring the quality of health services are demonstrating increasing rationality. The Williamson strategy relating outcomes and process assessment has already been cited. Process variables are assessed when final outcomes do not meet accepted standards. For example, a one-year follow-up study of 98 patients with heart failure management needs revealed that mortality was double that of "accepted standards." Examination of process variables indicated that numerous patients were neither under a physician's care nor taking needed medication. Furthermore, many individuals were under the care of private physicians, but were not receiving required medication for hypertension or heart failure. Similar outcome studies by Brook

[22] P. M. Ellwood, Jr., "The Health Maintenance Strategy." Institute for Interdisciplinary Studies. Mimeographed, 19 pages, March 9, 1970. Revised Oct. 7, 1970.

[23] J. T. Gentry, "The Health Maintenance Organization Strategy: How Effectively Will It Meet the Health Care 'Crisis'?" *Proceeding of the Annual Meeting of the American Physical Therapy Association*, Boston, June 30, 1971.

[24] Health Insurance Plan of Greater New York, *Information for Physicians Interested in a Prepaid Group Partnership Practice with HIP Affiliation.* Publication 123-7C, February, 1971, 35 pp.

[25] Rick J. Carison and Patrick O'Donoghue, "Health Maintenance Organizations and Health Planning," paper presented at the Conference on Health Planning, Certificates of Need, and Market Entry, Washington, D.C., June 15–16, 1972; William J. Curran and Frances Glessner Lee, "National Survey and Analysis of State Certificates of Need Legislation for Health Care Facilities," paper presented at the Conference on Health Planning, Certificates of Need, and Market Entry, Washington, D.C., June 15–16, 1972.

have reaffirmed the importance of patient referral, information exchange, outreach, surveillance, and follow-up activities.[26]

The efficacy of the medical record for assessing the quality of care has also come under scrutiny. Fessel and Van Brunt have demonstrated disparities between documentation of results and outcomes.[27] Goldberg and his associates from the Division of Medical Care Standards of the Health Services and Mental Health Administration have also concluded that random chart-by-chart reviews do not produce meaningful results. As a result, Medical Care Evaluation Studies have been introduced as an alternate for fulfilling medicare requirements.[28]

2. *Health Manpower.* From one perspective, the preparation and task delegation of health manpower are becoming increasingly rational. Task analysis and task delegation are resulting in a more comprehensive range of services, e.g., outreach services by neighborhood health workers, and, in more effective use of scarce and costly resources, e.g., the use of the nurse practitioner for medical encounters. The neighborhood health worker's role brings with it the capacity to make certain services more accessible and acceptable to target populations. The nurse practitioner and the physician's assistant illustrate "rational" alternatives to presumed physician "shortages." Additional examples include less categorical and more generic educational preparation of the health administrator and planner.

Yet difficulties persist in efforts to achieve effective health manpower "teams" and to make full use of the nurse practitioner and the physician's assistant. These difficulties reflect traditional role perceptions and competitive market mechanisms involving practitioner compensation on a fee-for-service basis.

In fact, some observers of the health system view over-all manpower development as a process having little rationality.[29] These observers note that the health system now has 125 recognized health occupations and 250 secondary specialist descriptions. Job categories and training programs are described as "chaotic." The system is further described as setting worker against worker, and skill against skill. For example, the nurse practitioner is described as vying with the physician's assistant for status, autonomy, and upward mobility.

3. *Planning and Regulation.* Continuing efforts to increase the rationalization of health care delivery are exemplified by comprehensive health planning, hospital franchising, and certificate-of-need legislation. Despite initial expectations, analysis of available experience data suggest that the activities of many planning agencies have been of limited effectiveness in achieving stated objectives. The issues faced by decision makers are frequently political in nature. Furthermore, the information-gathering activities of planners are often irrelevant to the decisions that must be made.[30]

Study data also indicate that not all health agency planners are attempting to match available health services with

[26] Robert H. Brook and Robert L. Stevenson, "Effectiveness of Patient Care in an Emergency Room," *New England Journal of Medicine*, Oct. 22, 1970, pp. 904–907.

[27] W. J. Fessel and E. E. Van Brunt, "Assessing Quality of Care from the Medical Record," *New England Journal of Medicine*, Jan. 20, 1972.

[28] George A. Goldberg *et al.*, "Medical Care Evaluation Studies: A Utilization Review Requirement," *Journal of the American Medical Association*, April 17, 1972.

[29] Health-PAC, "Fragmentation of Workers: An Anti-Personnel Weapon," *Health-PAC Bulletin*, November, 1972.

[30] Jerome Hallan, "Use of Information in Health Planning," Chapel Hill, School of Public Health, University of North Carolina. Unpublished doctoral dissertation, December, 1971.

community health service requirements.[31] Furthermore, these planners do not regard the identification and measurement of over-all community health problems as an appropriate agency function. Instead, they have concerned themselves primarily with a series of well-circumscribed projects, often with specific follow-up and implementation responsibilities. For example, over 60 per cent of study respondents did not know whether cervical cytology screening services were provided within their respective jurisdictions.

One can conclude that there are different perceptions concerning appropriate roles for health planning agencies. Although there are many notable exceptions, one can also conclude that health planning has had a limited impact as an integrating and rationalizing force.

discussion and summary

Examination of the level of rationality inherent in health care delivery systems indicates that the level of rationality is low, and that approaches to making the delivery of health services more rational have not been very effective. Whereas it can be assumed that most health service providers perform their individual tasks well, some service requirements may not be provided at all. Major problems stem from the absence of effective planning and integrating mechanisms. This deficiency is a manifestation of health care delivery systems as a whole, and their inability to assure individuals that necessary health services will be received. Inability to deal effectively with performance requirements of the complete system thus appears to underlie most of the problem areas cited, e.g., manpower, facilities, and third-party benefit provisions. These problems result in inadequacies in the comprehensiveness and continuity of services, low quality

levels, and ineffective use of scarce and costly resources. These findings raise two questions. First, why does the health system operate at such a low level of rationality? Second, is it feasible to strive for a higher level of rationality? If the answer to the second question is affirmative, there is a need to identify approaches to increasing rationality that are more effective than those that have been identified.

The first question can be answered, in part, by an examination of the extensive literature dealing with planning processes in general and administration of human services in particular. Three interpretations have evolved to explain observed phenomena. An early interpretation viewed planning and administration as a rational-legal ordering of relationships with clear separation of functional roles.[32] This view has been discarded as invalid. The second interpretation considers administration as a continuing political process within which there are rationalized mechanisms for problem solving.[33] This view is considered applicable primarily to the management of smaller or more circumscribed organizations and subsystems, e.g., the acute short-term hospital. The third interpretation regards rationalization efforts as severely limited by the existence of multiple, competing organizations, by the openness of decision processes, and by man's inherent limitations and his reluctance to view issues comprehensively and undertake rational problem solving. This third, or "market" interpretation, is generally acknowledged as the most accurate description of behavior of the health industry as a whole.

---

[31] Gentry, "Attitudes and Perceptions."

[32] L. Gulick and L. Urwick, *Papers on the Science of Administration*, New York, Columbia University, Institute of Public Administration, 1937.

[33] P. H. Appleby, *Policy and Administration*, Tuscaloosa, University of Alabama Press, 1949.

The strongest advocate of the market interpretation is Lindblom.[34] Lindblom suggests that social policy problems are dealt with through political mechanisms that closely resemble the economist's view of the free market. This model describes continuing conflict and struggle, in which the ratifying and registering of a series of decisions represent successive points of equilibrium in conflicts between different interest groups. Lindblom rejects the notion that major development processes can involve comprehensive data, identification of alternatives, and the rational evaluation of available choices. Instead, he concludes that problem resolution tends to be "fragmented, remedial, sequential, and subject to incremental changes" in direction and objectives. He suggests that there are difficulties in distinguishing means from ends, and that there is a high degree of interaction between means and ends.

The accuracy with which Lindblom's market model describes the health system is relevant to the second question, i.e., can the level of the rationality be increased? Major policy questions concerning methods of providing financial compensation to large practitioner groups, e.g., physicians, certainly will continue to be resolved as equilibrium points in continuing conflicts and struggles. Also secondary issues that are perceived as bearing on these same major questions will tend to be immersed in similar conflicts. Experience data suggest, however, that many proposals for problem resolution are sound and that certain conflicts can be avoided. Success in conflict resolution appears to depend on the care that is taken to clarify issues and reassure involved individuals

and organizations that their interests are being protected.

Facilitating activities designed to minimize resistance to proposed change thus illustrate an important component of approaches to the achievement of increased rationality. An extensive behavioral science literature dealing with innovation and change bears directly on this subject.[35] Investigators in this field are attempting to identify social, psychological, and economic factors that facilitate or impede the provision and utilization of various types of health services.[36] Study findings are of value for the identification of specific activities or "interventions" that can accelerate the acceptance and utilization of individual services and support activities. Examples of interventions are: (1) the use of new or more complete information concerning the rationale for a specific proposal; (2) financial incentives, e.g., expansion of health insurance service benefits; and (3) group process activities

[34] E. Lindblom and R. A. Dahl, *Politics, Economics, and Welfare*, New York, Harper and Row, 1953; E. C. Lindblom and D. Braybrooke, *A Strategy of Decisions*, New York, Macmillan Publishing Co., Inc., 1963.

[35] Jerald Hage, "A System's Perspective on Organizational Program Change," paper presented at seminar on Innovation in Health Care Organizations: An Issue in Organization Change, Chapel Hill, School of Public Health, University of North Carolina, May 18–19, 1972; A. D. Kaluzny and Jane B. Sprague, "Innovation in Health and Welfare Organizations: A Review and Critique of Current Theory and Research," paper presented at seminar on Innovation in Health Care Organizations: An Issue in Organization Change, Chapel Hill, School of Public Health, University of North Carolina, May 18–19, 1972; Gerald Gordon et al., "Organizational Structure and Hospital Adaptation to Environmental Demands," paper presented at seminar on Innovation in Health Care Organizations: An Issue in Organization Change, Chapel Hill, School of Public Health, University of North Carolina, May 18–19, 1972.

[36] J. T. Gentry et al., "Determinants of Components of the Health Care System," funded by the Health Services Research Center of the University of North Carolina through Research Grant HS-00239 from the National Center for Health Services Research and Development.

designed to facilitate decision making and conflict resolution. Successful interventions provide opportunities to manipulate components of the health system, e.g., increase, quantitatively, previously deficient services. Through these efforts, health services can theoretically be made to match more adequately the health service requirements of the target populations under consideration.

The extent to which rationality can be increased depends on a number of variables. These variables include the attributes of the services or activities under consideration, e.g., compatibility with existing organizational goals. Another variable is the potential impact of a specific innovation for increasing rationality, i.e., relatively low or relatively high impact. For example, the sequence of case-finding, patient planning, referral, information exchange, outreach and surveillance-type services, and support activities is considered to have high potential impact for rationality. Furthermore, the implementation and utilization of these types of services and activities are relative-

ly low. Only 40 per cent of the acute short-term hospitals in the United States have instituted pre-discharge planning activities, and only 36 per cent provide routine screening services for the detection of cervical cancer.[37] Interventions of potential relevance for these types of services can be illustrated by the use of information to: (1) increase cognitive knowledge concerning the nature and objectives of specific services and activities, and (2) increase the level of value or worth with which health service providers perceive these measures for increasing the over-all quality of health services. The linkage and coordinating nature of these particular service examples are noteworthy for health providers concerned with their relationships with other organizations and practitioners. Whereas new and more extensive relations with other organizations and practitioners are required, acceptance and utilization of these mechanisms will permit providers to stop being part of the problem and become part of the solution.

[37] Gentry, *Provisions*.

8. international management of tomorrow: a new frontier of administrative thought

Narendra K. Sethi

Management is the image of the changing socio-economic, political, and cultural patterns of the world. It represents the *totality* of human behavior inasmuch as it voices the industrial development of the

Reprinted from *S.A.M. Advanced Management Journal*, 35, No. 3 (July 1970), pp. 38–42, with permission of the publisher.

world as well as the welfare of the people resulting from such growth. Therefore, it is the proverbial mirror of the society, for it is through the varying concepts of management thought and practice that one can observe the changing dimensions of modern society, in all its glory and weakness, in all its success and failure, and in its true character and attitude.

It is in this all-embracing character of management that we see its future directions in the years ahead. From Scientific Management to Management Science was but a short span to cover when compared with what it has to reach for in the coming years. It has now to cover a much larger bridge over more turbulent waters: the bridges of cross-cultural relationships, similarities, and differences, ranging over a multitude of nations, in varying degrees of economic development and cultural progress. From a national idea of organization, we have now to move towards an international concept of managerial administration. We are not speaking of traditional internationalism here, but of a newly emerging concept thereof: a cross-cultural addendum of nations, divided not only in geographical distance, but also in their time-realization, and industrial transition.

It is the thesis of this article that the new frontiers which management will face in the years to come are the rapidly changing themes in the body of international administrative practice. Some of the key areas where one will observe the distinction between the traditional and the emergent views on the subject are as follows:

1. The new thinking will evolve around the determination of those concepts of American management which can be transferred with equal applicability and effectiveness in other countries.

2. A new discipline of *Comparative Management* will focus attention on the determination of those criteria of comparative analysis which can properly evaluate the similarity and/or variance in the management practices of the different countries.

3. Attention will focus around the element of "time-overlapping," which characterizes the fact that several countries can operate their industrial mechanism in different "time-zones" simultaneously.

4. Greater attention will be put on the relationship between indigenous and "foreign-based" companies operating in a developing nation.

5. The concept of Economic Development will undergo a modification in terms of being re-interpreted as a dynamic system: one capable of assuming varying degrees of progress and/or retardation, rather than a uniform system which it has been traditionally represented to be.

6. Finally, a new emphasis will be put on the task of developing an optimum management system for each culturally homogeneous *territory* (as distinguished from the traditional idea of nation) within the framework of new internationalism.

These are the major frontiers of management practice in the years to come. They require planning from the outset, even before their overt symptoms have appeared on the surface of conventional administrative wisdom.

The future trends in management practice and accomplishment will make it quite obvious that the totality of American management know-how cannot be transferred to other management systems. The universality of management principles needs to be re-examined in the light of the observation that differing management systems have different action-centers and varying philosophies. They sometimes comprise of sharply variant values and aspirational levels. Therefore, rather than attempt a total transfer of American management, will it not be more advisable and also more effective to isolate those managerial concepts which might be acceptable in a foreign land?

Management practitioners must start to

think in terms of developing suitable criteria for the determination of acceptable management principles (and concepts) in other countries.

One way to develop a model of transference will be to examine the *degree* of socio-economic and cultural awareness in the country, relate the same to its present and projected industrial growth, equate it with the available administrative personnel in the land (and also with those foreign experts whose services can be made available on a short-term basis), and then transfer only those principles (beliefs, norms, and values) of American managerial know-how, which generally fit in the above presented framework.

comparative management

Allied with the idea of transferable managerial values in foreign countries, is the methodology of comparison between two management systems. Managers must pay a great deal of attention towards determining the actual *base of comparison* while comparing two management ideologies. When we compare management in India or in France with that in the United States, what is it that we are actually trying to compare and what is the yardstick in this comparative analysis? Will it be a comparison of efficiency? Then the comparison is one of management-*objectives*. Will it be a comparison of administrative brilliance? Then the comparison is one of management-*leadership*. Or will it be a comparison of the enterprise functions and their growth? This comparison process will indeed generate a lot of scholarly attention and controversy in the coming years.

It will be seen that in all comparative processes, the subjective element of the comparator plays a leading role. Therefore, all purposeful management comparison will be in relation to the management-system of the person performing this comparison. Rather than use only mathematical and statistical indices as comparison bases, it is suggested that qualitative and culturally-oriented variables should be developed with a view towards clearer and sharper comparative analysis.

time-overlap

Managers of today are now beginning to be aware of the element of "time-overlap" in understanding the workings of international management. Many developing countries combine the traditional love of older business values with the innovistic admiration for the newer technological processes and scientific techniques. Thus, they perform in a variety of time-zones concurrently. Their production efforts are directed towards modern techniques; and, their operational philosophy and organizational structures are motivated by tradition-ridden beliefs. Therefore, no international management practice can function properly unless it has taken full note of this overlapping time consciousness in the countries with developing economies.

Another interesting idea in this context which will generate attention is the question of "time-integration" at different *levels* of managerial organization in these developing countries. In the same organization the top, middle, and the junior levels of management operate in different time-zones simultaneously, as regards their response to the same (identical) managerial problem. This practice of different time-consciousness at different levels of administrative hierarchy will raise several new problems and challenges in the years to come, and will require an enlightened understanding by the emerging body of international management people.

duality

In the international business scene, both the local companies as well as the foreign-based (or controlled) companies will play a significant role in shaping the host country's industrial progress. But till now, much attention has not been paid to the relative functions of these two different corporate units; their relationship with one another and with the national government; the areas of competition between them once the rate of economic development has accelerated; and the cultural problems which can (and will) arise for the employees of these two components of the country's industrial life. In the coming years, this duality of corporate structures will feature more and more in the practice and process of management.

It should also be noted that the duality of corporate structure also will manifest itself in an identical duality of business objectives. The indigenous company will function at the level of the country's *own* productivity and human resources; while the foreign based (or controlled) enterprise can take the advantage of obtaining the "best of both worlds" in shaping its managerial programs. The salary structure, status, symbology, human relations conception, and market orientation of the former also will differ substantially from those of the latter. This dichotomy is capable of generating an enormous socio-political controversy which the industrial administrators of both lands and governments will have to consider carefully.

dynamic economic development

Conventional wisdom always has characterized economic development as a static process which continues on its course with a predetermined (or even pre-determinable) rate, affecting the material welfare of the people residing in the country. It is proposed that in the coming years, administrative management will become increasingly conscious of economic development *not* as a mere passive and uniform statistical index, but as a heterogeneous and dynamic indicator of a multitude of things, capable of moving forwards, backwards, and sideways at the same time, and also capable of influencing *every* aspect of mankind, not just their materialistic welfare alone.

The idea of "development" in the future managerial conception will represent the *totality* of progress. No human activity is beyond the scope of managerial action, and hence the idea of development (may it be in recreation or in retirement, in culture or in cuisine, in science or in semantics), is central to the managerial vision of tomorrow.

optimum territory management

Traditionally, it is believed that geographical boundaries are logical limiting areas for individual studies of management systems in international perspective. Future management students will soon realize that geographical boundaries are not very meaningful as far as a conceptual framework of international management is concerned. Homogeneity of cultural values rather than geographical frontiers should be the guide-lines for such demarcations. There also is a possibility that even in the same country, there may not be one management system, but two or more, depending upon the identity of cultural sub-systems within the nation itself. In such an event of plurality, a single national management system of the country will serve no meaningful purpose in a comparative analysis.

To apply human effort for the most productive use, and to consolidate all the available resources for the optimum welfare of the mankind, it will be extremely important for the administrators of to-morrow to develop a cross-national system of management (between such nations which might be culturally homogeneous) and then integrate the managerial energy of each comprising country in such an administrative system. In this way, it will be possible to develop a highly effective management "United Nations." The only exception will be that while the political "United Nations" is an assembly of differing and warring nations, the administrative "United Nations" will be an assembly of cooperating nations, with identical cultural beliefs and motivating levels working jointly for a common purpose.

The task of finding such homogeneous territories and nations which might be culturally identical, not only at a super-ficial level of overt behavior, but at the level of action and thought combined, will be a major frontier before the future managers, and will require extensive research by all participating countries.

conclusion

A major frontier of management today comprises the new area of internationalism which is just opening to its fullest impli-cations and potential, both as a source of optimum human welfare and a concept of cross-cultural integration. The traditional thinking in the area has so far been characterized by a tendency to relate it to a variety of foreign countries only. The new wisdom will develop more challenging areas of socio-economic and cultural synthesis—extending the frontiers of for-eign lands into the unifying consciousness of homogeneous cross-national territories.

We have outlined a few major hy-potheses in this article which constitute significant frontiers of modern administra-tive management. Fortunately, some in-tellectual quest already has started in the direction of some of the points mentioned above but most of these are still in ex-ploratory phases, which further sharpens the frontier-rationale of these propositions.

discussion questions: part I

1. How is a Technology of Man related to a conceptual framework for management?
2. What are some of the most important factors in the development of a conceptual framework for management?
3. Distinguish the differences between the major approaches to management today.
4. Is the contingency theory of management an adequate integrative mechanism for the major approaches to management? Why or why not?
5. Analyze the values that have influenced the average manager two decades ago. Contrast those values with the values that influence the average manager today.
6. Is social responsibility as an organizational concept definable? If so, define it. If not, why is it not definable?
7. Is the concept of a socially responsible management an implementable one? If yes, describe potential ways in which it could be implemented. If no, determine ways in which the term "socially responsible" would have meaning to corporate managements.
8. Differentiate between the major types of organizations that are present in today's society. Indicate any trends in the growth or decline of the various major types of organization.
9. Do you believe that the evolution of "emerging public corporations" is related to changing value structures in American society? Why or why not?

10. Develop a delivery system for one of the following urban problem areas: transportation, education, or public safety (fire and police). In developing your system, be sure to employ at least the following criteria: comprehensiveness, quality of service, continuity, and economy.

11. How would the changing value structure of American society impinge upon international operations of American-based corporations?

12. In the expanding areas of management, what new areas of the economy do you see as developing fields for managers?

selected references: part I

A. *conceptual frameworks for management*

Dutton, John M., and William H. Starbuck, "On Managers and Theories," *Management International Review*, 3, No. 6 (1963), pp. 25–35.

Filley, Alan C., "Common Misconceptions in Business Management," *Business Horizons*, 7, No. 3 (Fall 1964), pp. 87–97.

Flippo, Edwin B., "Integrative Schemes in Management Theory," *Academy of Management Journal*, 11, No. 1 (March 1968), pp. 91–98.

House, Robert J., "Research Criteria and Methods for the Development of Management Theory," *Academy of Management, Proceedings of the 1963 Annual Meeting* (University Park, Pa.: 1964), pp. 7–13.

Koontz, Harold, "The Management Theory Jungle," *Academy of Management Journal*, 4, No. 3 (December 1961), pp. 174–188.

——— (ed.), *Toward a Unified Theory of Management* (New York: McGraw-Hill Book Company, 1964).

Litzinger, William D., and Thomas E. Schaefer, "Management Philosophy Enigma," *Academy of Management Journal*, 9, No. 4 (December 1966), pp. 337–343.

Mockler, Robert J., "Situational Theory of Management," *Harvard Business Review*, 49, No. 3 (May–June 1971), pp. 146–151; 154–155.

Petit, Thomas A., "Systems Approach to Management Theory," *Journal of Systems Management*, 23, No. 7 (July 1972), pp. 32–34.

Sayles, Leonard R., and Margaret K. Chandler, *Managing Large Systems: Organizations for the Future* (New York: Harper & Row, 1971).

Suojanen, Waino, "Management Theory: Functional and Evolutionary," *Academy of Management Journal*, 6, No. 1 (March 1963), pp. 7–18.

Urwick, Lyndall F., "Have We Lost Our Way in the Jungle of Management Theory?" *Personnel*, 42, No. 3 (May–June 1965), pp. 8–18.

B. *changing values and social responsibility in management*

Ackerman, Robert W., "How Companies Respond to Social Demands," *Harvard Business Review*, 51, No. 4 (July–August 1973), pp. 88–98.

Adizes, Ichak, and J. Fred Weston, "Comparative Models of Social Responsibility," *Academy of Management Journal*, 16, No. 1 (March 1973) pp. 112–128.

Bauer, Raymond A., and Dan H. Fenn, Jr., *The Corporate Social Audit* (New York: Russell Sage Foundation, 1972).

DeSalvia, Donald N., and Gary R. Gemmill, "An Exploratory Study of the Personal Value Systems of College Students and Managers," *Academy of Management Journal*, 14, No. 2 (June 1971), pp. 227–238.

Fenn, Jr., Dan H., and Daniel Yankelovich, "Responding to the Employee Voice," *Harvard Business Review*, 50, No. 3 (May–June 1972), pp. 83–91.

Fulmer, Robert M., "Business Ethics: Present and Future," *Personnel Administration*, 34, No. 5 (September–October 1971), pp. 48–56.

Massarik, Fred, "Changing Social Values and Their Impact on Future Management Organization and Picture," *Academy of Management Proceedings, 30th Annual Meeting* (San Diego, Calif.: San Diego State College, 1970), pp. 63–76.

Mazis, Michael, and Robert Green, "Implementing Social Responsibility," *MSU Business Topics*, 19, No. 1 (Winter 1971), pp. 68–76.

Rourke, Daniel L., Ralph Lewis, David Snyder, and Norman C. Dalkey, *Studies in the Quality of Life* (Lexington, Mass.: D. C. Heath and Co., 1972).

Sethi, S. Prakash, "Getting a Handle on the Social Audit," *Business and Society Review/Innovation*, No. 4 (Winter 1972–1973), pp. 31–38.

Steiner, George A., "Social Policies for Business," *California Management Review*, 15, No. 2 (Winter 1972), pp. 17–24.

C. *expanding scope of management: public, health, and international*

Drucker, Peter F., "Global Management," *The Conference Board Record*, 10, No. 3 (March 1973), pp. 48–53.

Gabriel, Peter P., "MNC's in the Third World: Is Conflict Unavoidable?" *Harvard Business Review*, 50, No. 4 (July–August 1972), pp. 93–102.

Georgopoulos, Basil S. (ed.), *Organization Research on Health Institutions* (Ann Arbor: Institute for Social Research, University of Michigan, 1972).

Gottschalk, Shimon S., "The Community-Based Welfare System: An Alternative to Public Welfare," *Journal of Applied Behavioral Science*, 9, Nos. 2/3 (1973), pp. 233–242.

Kuin, Pieter, "The Magic of Multinational Management," *Harvard Business Review*, 50, No. 6 (November–December 1972), pp. 89–97.

Milliken, J. Gordon, and Edward J. Morrison, "Management Methods from Aerospace," *Harvard Business Review*, 51, No. 2 (March–April 1973), pp. 6–22; 158–164.

Nash, Paul, "Authority Relationships in Higher Education," *Journal of Higher Education*, 44, No. 4 (April 1973), pp. 255–271.

Nathan, Harriet (ed.), *The Art and Practice of Public Administration* (Berkeley, Calif.: Institute of Governmental Studies, University of California, 1971).

Rogers, David, *The Management of Big Cities* (Beverly Hills, Calif.: SAGE Publications, 1971).

Schindler-Rainman, Eva, and Ronald Lippitt, *The Volunteer Community* (Washington, D.C.: Center for a Voluntary Society, NTL Institute for Applied Behavioral Science, 1971).

Schollhammer, Hans, "Organization Structures of Multinational Corporations," *Academy of Management Journal*, 14, No. 3 (September 1971), pp. 345–363.

Sweet, David C. (ed.), *Models of Urban Structure* (Lexington, Mass.: D. C. Heath and Co., 1972).

Taylor, Bernard, "The Management of Public Corporations," *Journal of Business Policy*, 3, No. 1 (Autumn 1972), pp. 73–80.

process approaches

part II

In the early part of the twentieth century, scientific management dominated the practice of management in American industry while the process approach[1] influenced management in Europe. Henri Fayol, a French executive in a metallurgical company, developed the process approach. In carrying out certain managerial functions such as planning, organizing, commanding, coordinating, and controlling, he emphasized the importance of top management.[2] While the scientific management school based its approach upon empirical data, the process approach was based primarily upon observations and experience. Unfortunately for the field of management, Fayol's contributions were not translated into English until after his death in 1925, and were not available in the United States until 1949.

As the process approach gained wider acceptance, other writers began to elaborate upon specific managerial functions.[3] In general, it established principles

[1] The process or functional approach is also called the classical approach.

[2] Henri Fayol, *Industrial and General Administration*, trans. J. A. Coubrough (Geneva: International Management Institute, 1929); and Henri Fayol, *General and Industrial Management* (London: Sir Isaac Pitman and Sons, Ltd., 1949).

[3] For example, see R. C. Davis, *The Fundamentals of Top Management* (New York: Harper and Row, 1951); William H. Newman, Charles E. Summer, and E. Kirby Warren, *The Process of Management*, 2nd ed. (Englewood Cliffs, N.J.: Prentice-Hall, Inc., 1967); George Terry, *Principles of Management*, 6th ed. (Homewood, Ill.: Richard D. Irwin, Inc., 1972); Harold Koontz and Cyril O'Donnell, *Principles of Management*, 4th ed. (New York: McGraw-Hill Book Company, Inc., 1968); and Henry H. Albers, *Principles of Organization and Management*, 3rd ed. (New York: John Wiley and Sons, Inc., 1969).

by which the various functions should be carried out. Although most of these principles were based upon managerial experience, a few have been derived from experimental studies. This approach has been utilized in many different types of organizations.

Academic scholars and practitioners have continued to develop the process approach. Over time, organizations have discovered and rediscovered the importance of planning—both short and long range—in their operations.[4] Today new ways of organizing work have been developed which do not support some of the older principles of management. In some organizations, directing has taken on new dimensions through the evolution of innovative decision-making techniques and new concepts of leadership and communication. Control through the development of better feedback systems has improved the capability of managers for rational growth of organizations. Opportunities for the development of additional human resources through manpower planning have substantially improved the organization's efficiency. This part covers some of the recent contributions to the continuing evolution of the process approach.

In the planning section, Bruce N. Baker demonstrates company goals, company planning, and project matrices and emphasizes the importance of integrating short-, medium-, and long-range plans for modern organizations. In the second selection, William K. Hall provides perspectives on the use of strategic planning. He discusses some of the changes which are occuring in corporations including anticipatory decision-making, utilization of systems analysis in planning, innovational planning systems, mathematical models, and evolving internal and external environmental factors.

In modern organizations, many new types of structure are evolving to meet the needs of a constantly changing society. Joseph M. Pastore describes the relationship of functionally designed organization structures to classical organization theory, of project structures to systems theory, and of project structures to groups. He attempts to illustrate the organizational metamorphosis which may occur among project groups designed to generate growth-oriented behavior and to develop a dynamic organizational model to illustrate these relationships. In the next selection, Gordon L. Lippitt analyzes traditional hospital organizational structures and processes and points out that these will be ineffective in the future. Throughout his discussion, he examines the characteristics of future hospital organizations and their implications for the health care field.

Victor H. Vroom points to a new way of looking at managerial decision making as a social process; the important task of a manager is to determine how the problem is to be solved, not the solution to be implemented. In the second selection, Jay Hall cites communication breakdown as the single greatest barrier to organizational excellence. He discusses the relationships between interpersonal styles and a number of corporate dilemmas including communication breakdowns, emotional climates, quality of relationships, and managerial practices.

[4] George A. Steiner, *Top Management Planning* (New York: Macmillan Publishing Co., Inc., 1969).

In the next section, Leonard Sayles outlines several levels of managerial control including: (1) high level, which provides reassurance to organizational sponsors; (2) low level, which closes the feedback loop; and (3) middle level, which provides guidance to subordinates throughout the organization. Through these controls, managers may assess organizational effectiveness. Although most control systems rely on feedback, there frequently are slow reactions to signals of error or deviation. As a result, these deviations persist and continue to cause the organization to incur costs. In the second article, Harold Koontz and Robert W. Bradspies have adapted the principle of feedforward control, which is used in engineering systems, to correct this type of control problem.

Today, organizations have more of an opportunity to use all of the human resources in society than even before. In his article on manpower administration, Frank Cassell stresses the changes in corporate manpower policy as a result of a national manpower policy and its implications for the organization today. Additional manpower resources can be provided from underutilized and under-employed segments in the society such as women, minorities, and the handicapped. Finally, Gopal C. Pati and Patrick E. Fahey discuss some of the problems which organizations face in the implementation of affirmative action programs.

planning

9. improving essential facets of planning integration
Bruce N. Baker

Planning integration is receiving more and more emphasis within industry, the national government, regional areas, states, and municipalities. The reasons for this great interest in integration of plans are clear:

- Traditional patterns of suboptimization are costly, cumbersome, and often mutually contradictory.

- The development of sophisticated management systems makes it possible to achieve integration where it was never feasible before.

- It has been found that the advantages of decentralization can be realized while at the same time centralization of information and coordination of planning can enhance these advantages.

- The public is demanding better planning integration in order to

Reprinted from *Managerial Planning*, 22, No. 2 (September–October 1973), pp. 32–36, and 40, with permission of the publisher.

more effectively use the nation's resources and to achieve better environmental cleanliness and balance.

Although planning integration is an esoteric sounding objective with which most people can agree, the means to accomplish it are often vague and the essential facets of planning integration are not often understood. There is developing a general consensus that we need better planning and that we need better integration of plans. The problem is where to go from there.

Much has already been written regarding "how to plan"—at least within industry.[1] In the few pages that follow, guidelines are set forth to enable planning integration to become more of a reality than a concept.

The problem has three facets, each of which is important to the overall objective of integration of plans.

[1] For example, see George Steiner's *Top Management Planning*.

facet 1—integrating plans among subordinate organizations

Traditionally, the problems of suboptimization have hampered integration of plans among subordinate organizations, e.g., the sales department of an industrial organization often seeks to satisfy their customers by advocating short range planning techniques which emphasize rapid reaction time to customer demands no matter what the costs; the production department advocates short range planning techniques which emphasize smooth production runs with sufficient backlog; and both sales and production may lose sight of intermediate and long range changes necessary to keep the company viable. In addition, the phenomenon of the "isolated loop" is often prevalent. The term "isolated loop" should be distinguished from the term "closed loop." Closed loops are desirable feedback mechanisms in the planning cycle, but the isolated loop, Figure 1, is created when subordinate organizations develop their own planning tools, and their own reporting and control tools in isolation. As a result, the net effect is similar to a series of dogs chasing their own tails. Plans created by subordinate organizations are not comparable, consistent, or compatible with each other. Reports may be distributed to other organizations but may not even be read, let alone digested or used by others in their own planning cycle.

To overcome these traditional problems of planning integration among subordinate organizations, the following practices are recommended:

- Establish compatible objectives and goals through participative planning sessions. These sessions are preferable to the pure top down approach, which may result in lack of commitment to the objectives and goals. They are also preferable to the pure bottoms-up approach which may result in a series of incompatible objectives and goals. A synergetic mixture of both approaches can be achieved through such participative planning sessions, and a total systems approach to establishing the objectives and goals.

- Provide common frameworks for planning by constructing several levels of planning matrices. Three levels of matrices for an industrial organization are depicted in Figure 2. Such matrices provide not only a set of common frameworks for planning, but they also enhance planning communication and integration.

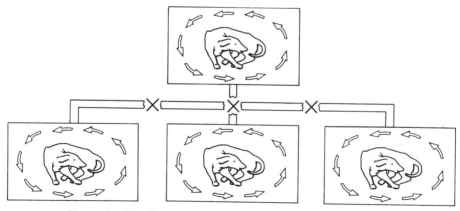

Figure 1. The "Isolated Loop" Approach to Planning and Control.

- Establish project organizations, or principles, if warranted. In some cases no formal changes in organization are required to attain the benefits of project management. Placing people in the same general area or opening new lines of communication through recognized points of liaison is often sufficient to reap some of the benefits of project planning and control principles. Project management has been found to result in better schedule and cost performance

than traditional functional approaches to management.

- Standardize forms and procedures in order that all planning documents will be consistent in format and can be readily machine processed and tabulated, where appropriate. The matrices themselves can often serve a variety of planning purposes, including visual displays for highlighting critical planning areas.

- The project planning matrix can be

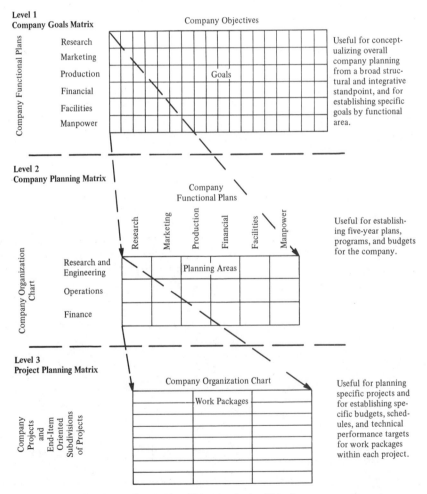

Figure 2. Frameworks for Planning.

used to develop cost estimates, establish budgets and track cost performance. Schedule information and technical performance data can also be highlighted on such a matrix.

- Undertake other general planning improvements such as periodic planning reviews, and better lateral communication. Such improvements tend to reinforce the other improvements outlined above.

facet 2—integrating short range, intermediate range, and long range plans

Traditionally, organizations are so involved with the crises at hand that they have little time to concentrate upon anything more than short range planning, if that. Long range planning, if it exists, is often the function of some staff officer with little power and infrequent interaction with line management. Intermediate range plans often become a "no man's land" in such situations. The result is a complete lack of integration among short, intermediate, and long range plans.

These problems can also be overcome even in the most hectic types of organizations with proper approaches:

- Select a dynamic interactive individual to coordinate the long range planning effort. His main job is to stimulate top line management, including the President of the organization, to think and act today to prepare for five years from today. This is a herculean task, and more art than science, but there are those who can carry it off year after year. Such a man must interact continuously with line management because once he has crawled into his shell, he has lost his utility to the company. Although some writers claim that the planning department does not (or

should not) plan, in practice, they must plan to get the job done. The secret is to plant ideas and see them return as someone else's ideas with appropriate modifications and embellishments.

- Establish a planning cycle which is strictly enforced and which is more than a periodic ritual. Many companies determine when their least hectic times are in the year. One slack period is chosen for formulating short range plans one year ahead. Another slack period is chosen for formulating intermediate and long range plans. Intermediate and long range plans must build upon short range plans (sometimes termed, "forward seeking") and, more important, short range and intermediate range plans must derive from the long range plans in a "backward-seeking" manner. The emphasis is again upon systems thinking and systems approaches. And, since the same people should participate equally in each segment of the planning cycle, consistency is more likely to occur than under traditional patterns.

- Undertake other improvements such as better representation in long range planning departments (or at least better inputs) from research personnel and the principal line organizations. Diagrams and other visual depictions of the planning cycle can greatly facilitate understanding of, and participation in, the planning cycle. As more people become aware of the organization's planning cycle, more planning inputs are introduced for the consideration of management.

facet 3—integrating sets of plans from year to year

There are many traditional problems of integrating sets of plans from year to year.

Generally, the process is dropped for several years due to the departure or transfer of the driving force or disenchantment with a plan that went awry. Even if the cycle is carried out each year, little comparison of accomplishments versus plans is carried out. Too little effort is expended in learning from past mistakes or in building upon past successes. Often, the most striking successes are hardly planned at all and so planning is downgraded in importance. Last, but not least, when operations are going well, there seems to be little need to plan. This complacency is perhaps the most dangerous deterrent to planning. It takes a period similar to the late 1960's and early 1970's to shatter such complacency.

In order to achieve better integration of sets of plans from year to year:

- Arrange for better continuity with respect to record keeping, documentation, and personnel involved with planning. In order to accomplish the mechanical aspects of continuity, periodic reviews and formalized updates of plans are required. Through better attention to such continuity, an organization can gain better perspective upon its strengths and weaknesses.

- Establish a baseline approach to planning. The baseline approach, so necessary for planning and controlling large weapons systems programs, can be used with success in any planning situation involving change. (See Figure 3).

- Change is an inherent part of planning. Change is not bad *per se*. It is bad when it is uncontrolled and undocumented. The important thing is to control change and to communicate it properly and rapidly to the affected parties. This requires a planning change control center responsible for keeping track of changes and communicating them. Such a center can minimize traditional comments such as, "I don't mind changes but I would like to know about them when they occur." By continually updating the plan, a measuring stick against which to judge performance is also assured. One can rarely judge performance against a plan which was prepared years ago and was never updated.

- Plot important internal and external trends. Through trend analyses, better anticipation of developing problems or opportunities can be uncovered in time to plan accordingly.

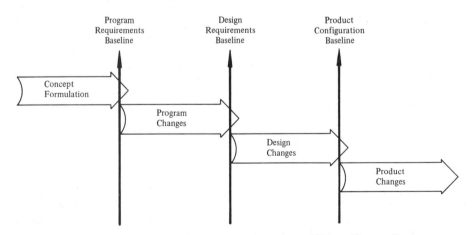

Figure 3.   The Baseline Approach to Planning a Large Weapon System Program.

	Among Subordinate Organizations	Among Short-Intermediate- and Long-Range Plans	Among Sets of Plans from Year to Year
Traditional Problems	Suboptimization. Isolated loops.	Total concentration upon current crises by line management. Long-range planning a staff function with little power or interaction with line management.	Departure or transfer of the planning driving force. No comparison of accomplishments against plans. Complacency leading to downgrading or elimination of planning.
Recommendations	Establish compatible objectives and goals through participative planning sessions. Provide common frameworks for planning by constructing several levels of planning matrices. Establish project organizations, or principles, if warranted. Standardize planning forms and procedures. Establish periodic planning reviews and better lateral communication.	Select a dynamic, interactive individual to coordinate long-range planning. Establish a strictly enforced planning cycle. Seek better representation and inputs to planning, and use diagrams to aid everyone's understanding of the planning cycle.	Arrange for continuity of record keeping, documentation, and personnel. Establish a baseline approach to planning. Plot important internal and external trends.

Figure 4. Improving Planning Integration.

summary

Figure 4 summarizes the principal points of this article. Through adaptation of the principal recommendations for improving planning integration, combined with proper attention to the traditional principles of planning, planning integration can be considerably improved among subordinate organizations, among short, intermediate, and long range plans, and among sets of plans from year to year.

10. corporate strategic planning—some perspectives for the future   William K. Hall

Before embarking on any discussion of corporate planning, it should be recognized that not all corporate managers are

Reprinted from *Michigan Business Review*, 24, No. 1 (January 1972), pp. 16–21, with permission of the publisher, the Graduate School of Business Administration, The University of Michigan.

enamored of the subject of planning. There are those who argue that we shouldn't plan—that "If we take care of the present the future will take care of itself." And there are those who argue that even if we should plan, we can't—that "The future is too complex and difficult to anticipate." And finally there are those who argue that even if we should and can plan, we won't—that "The most significant planning done in corporations today is deciding where to go for lunch and what to have."

The question which must be asked, however, is: What happens to those corporations that don't plan? These firms are likely to get into trouble, as unanticipated unfavorable factors hit them—an outcome that can be avoided by planning for the future? The accelerating pace of change in our society, the growing complexity of the future effects of current decisions, and increasing regulatory and competitive pressures all are contributing to an environment which the business firm must anticipate and influence in order to meet its growth and survival objectives.

At the same time that these factors create an enlarged demand for planning, they will change the philosophies, the techniques, and the horizons of planning. These coming changes are the topic of this paper. The concepts discussed are derived from extensive discussions with corporate planners in banking, utility, and manufacturing corporations. These discussions were conducted as part of a research project designed to ascertain the "state of the art" in corporate strategic planning and to develop research programs to improve the planning process.

anticipatory decision-making

One major change which is already being recognized by progressive firms is an awareness that planning is a *process* of anticipatory decision-making[1]—not a collection of forecasts and unimplemented futuristic studies. While forecasting is a part of this planning process, planning

does not really take place unless forecast predictions form the basis for subsequent *actions* designed to influence the future state of the organization.[2]

It is useful to explore the various facets of this decision-making process in some detail in order to clarify the role of strategic planning within the firm. One conceptualization of these facets is presented as Figure 1. In this figure, strategic (long range) planning is distinguished from tactical (short range) planning by the three factors proposed by Ackoff:

1. Goal formulation as an integral part of strategic planning.
2. Broadness in scope of strategic plans.
3. Enduring (long term) effects of strategic plans.

Of course, in a well-structured planning process, strategic and tactical plans should be highly interdependent; these interdependencies are indicated by the "feedback" arrows in Figure 1.

Strategic planning can be further decomposed into corporate development plan-

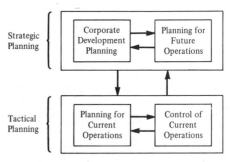

Figure 1. Facets of the Corporate Planning Process.

[1] This definition was first promoted by R. L. Ackoff in *A Concept of Corporate Planning*, Wiley, 1970.

[2] For a further discussion of the relationship between forecasting and planning the reader is referred to an article by R. J. Vogt, "Forecasting as a Management Tool," *Michigan Business Review*, Jan. 1970, pp. 20–24.

ning, which is devoted to the determination of resource selection strategies, and into future operations planning, which is devoted to the determination of resource allocation strategies for future time periods. Here again, a strong inter-dependency exists between these facets.

To complete the taxonomy of Figure 1, tactical planning can be devoted to current operations planning, the determination of resource allocation strategies within the current planning period, and to current operations control, the measurement and sequential improvement of this allocation process. The two-way interactions between operational planning and control form the basis for almost all budgeting and management control policies which are currently implemented in contemporary corporations.

evolving conceptualizations of the planning process

The process of strategic planning can also be usefully decomposed into a set of sequential activities (Figure 2). This process is initiated by an organized search for consensus on long term corporate objectives and alternative means for achieving these objectives. Following this search, planning research must be conducted to determine the technological and organizational feasibility of these alternatives. The results of this research, combined with forecasts of various environmental factors, then lead to an analysis of alternative actions and eventually to consensus on a set of proposed actions. The implementation of these actions then serves as a feedback loop, which iteratively results in the adaptation of the planning decisions to changing conditions and objectives.

This conceptualization of the strategic planning process represents a major change in at least three facets of the tradition philosophy of long range planning:

1. The emphasis is on the process of planning rather than the results of planning. An increasing large number of corporate officials firmly believe that the major benefit of strategic planning lies in the involvement and commitment of employees to the future welfare of the organization and not in a carefully bound document titled "The Five-Year Plan for Company X." Consider, for example, the

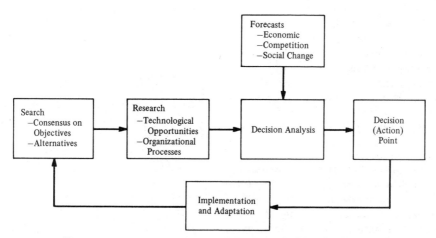

Figure 2. A Conceptualization of the Strategic Planning Process.

following statement made to the present writer by the Financial Vice President of a major multi-national firm: "Once we finish developing our five-year plan, we really don't need to write up the results; most of the benefits have already been derived from the developmental process."

2. The emphasis is on the "research-oriented" nature of planning rather than on the "control-oriented" nature. In fact, there is a growing awareness that the key to successful planning is to encourage and promote innovative thinking, not to develop procedures solely to measure and evaluate performance.

3. The emphasis is on the continuous, adaptive nature of the planning process. This emphasis promotes the idea that strategic decision-making should be on-going activity of corporate employees and not a "special" activity to be conducted only at certain times of the year.

evolving techniques for strategic planning

Associated with the changing philosophies toward planning are new techniques for improving the planning process, involving the employment of systems analysis procedures and mathematical models in the planning process.

Systems analysis is a phrase which is certainly over-used in our society. Nevertheless, the explicit consideration of the interactions among the elements of an organization (the emphasis on the "whole" rather than the "parts") is beginning to yield major benefits in the planning process.

One application of systems analysis has resulted in the implementation of *formal planning systems*—an integrated set of policies and procedures designed to improve the anticipatory decision-making process. While there are many examples of

formal systems in tactical planning (the budgetary system is the most common), there are few examples in strategic planning at the present time. Still, there is no doubt that the tendency to formalize strategic planning will grow. Such formalization is essential to get members of the organization at all levels thinking ahead toward future goals, means, and resources, and in addition, to get the "doers" involved in the planning of their future activities.[3]

A second application of systems analysis will result in *integrated planning and control systems*. As we have seen earlier, there is a growing awareness of the need to build evaluation and adaption into the planning process. Moreover, there is a growing awareness of the need to integrate the planning activities of different levels and of different functional areas within the organization. For example, this concern is resulting in a growing number of "matrix" management-task force approaches to strategic planning and in a tendency toward program-oriented organizational planning structures rather than the traditional functional, product-oriented, geographic structures.

innovational planning systems

A third and exceptionally important application of systems analysis will result in the growth of *innovational planning systems* within the firm. A large number of contemporary firms start the planning search process with an analysis of current goals, resources, and means within the firm. Policies are then developed which project and evolve these sequentially into

[3] A more detailed discussion of formal planning systems is provided by H. W. Henry in "Formal Long Range Planning and Corporation Performance," *Michigan Business Review*, Nov., 1968, pp. 24–31.

the future. The problem with this procedure, of course, is that the planning is necessarily constrained by a tendency to think in terms of present products, markets, and organizational structure. Innovational planning avoids this set of constraints by initiating the process with a search for consensus on what constitutes an "idealized" future for the firm. From this future position, policies are then generated *backward* in time so that current decisions lead toward the desired future rather than perpetuate contemporary practice.

There is little question that innovational planning systems will supplement and perhaps even replace traditional systems in the next twenty years. There are two major reasons for this:

1. In our rapidly changing society more firms are recognizing that the successful implementation of an innovative alternative (a new product, production process, organizational structure, etc.) increases corporate profitability more than a refinement in existing practice.

2. As the rate of change accelerates, past policies, tools and data will become increasingly less useful in developing useful policies for the future. In his recent bestselling book, Toffler[4] makes this point clear in discussing some future trends of society: "There is, however, still another, even more powerfully significant way in which the acceleration of change in society increases the difficulty of coping with life. This stems from the fantastic intrusion of novelty, newness into our existence. . . . The acceleration of change radically alters the balance between novel and familiar situations. Rising rates of change thus compel us not merely to cope with a faster flow, but with more and more situations to which previous experience does not apply."

[4] Alvin Toffler, *Future Shock*, Random House, Inc., 1970.

mathematical models

Mathematical models offer a major new technique, and these are finding increased applications in strategic planning. The idea of abstracting the real world into a simplified set of relations which can be manipulated to aid in anticipating the future effects of current decisions is appealing from a cost, convenience, and intellectual point of view. Various considerations which should be taken into account in applying models to strategic planning have been proposed by many authors,[5] and it would be redundant to repeat these here. Nevertheless, the future role of models in strategic planning will be different from the contemporary role in several important ways:

1. There will be a growing recognition that the process of modeling is equally as important as the ultimate product of this modeling effort. A large number of contemporary planning models have been scrapped recently because (a) conditions have changed since the time of development, thereby affecting model validity, and (b) personnel have changed since the time of development, thereby affecting model credibility and/or implementation. Explicit recognition that the process of model-building is valuable in creating new insights and conceptualizations will increase the utilization of these activities as planning research techniques rather than as research objectives.

2. There will be a growing recognition that large financial simulation models constructed from an extensive statistical analysis of the firm's data system do not offer significant aids in the process of anticipatory decision-making. This recognition will evolve for two reasons. First, more modelers will discover that a model

[5] See, for instance, G. L. Barkdoll, "Using Financial Models to Improve Communications," *Managerial Planning*, May/June, 1971.

developed by using data to associate certain independent variables with other dependent variables can *never* be used to determine how changes in the independent variables *cause* changes in the dependent variables. Since projected cause-effect relationships form the basis for evaluating decisions, these associative models will receive much less emphasis in the future. Second, as was pointed out earlier, the accelerating rate of change in society is making historical data of less use in planning and hence in planning models.

3. There will be a growing tendency to construct models which explicitly incorporate stylistic objectives, the influences of organizational structure on behavior, and other behavioralistic factors. Normative models based upon "idealized" decision making behavior will become less useful as the importance of these intangible factors is recognized and incorporated into the planning process. For instance, consider the statements made by a product planning manager in industrial marketing: " Despite the fantastic rise in mathematical techniques for market planning, our new product sales forecasts still have the same characteristics as they always have. They go up until we decide to 'go' with a product; then, for some reason they always go down!"

evolving environments for strategic planning

As techniques for the conduct of strategic planning change, so will the environments which anticipatory decisions attempt to influence. Four new environments external to the firm will offer growing challenges to the planning process over the next two decades: consumerism, internationalism, governmentalism, and environmentalism.

There is little question that contemporary organizational planning has largely failed to anticipate and influence the current changes in consumer attitudes and demands upon the corporation. Since the behavior of consumers will grow more complex and, simultaneously, since their demands for truth and quality will become stronger, there is a growing awareness that these factors must be taken explicitly into account in the strategic decision-making process.

The threats and opportunities posed by an increasingly international economic environment offer another challenge. Clearly the recent "crisis-oriented" responses to foreign competition must be supplemented with long term plans designed to change both management and products so that this competition can be met and/or joined to promote the firm's welfare. Simultaneously, the opportunities offered by foreign countries with accelerating rates of growth should be anticipated and taken advantage of through the creation of multinational enterprises and new product offerings.

The public sector of our economy is the fastest growing sector, both in terms of size and the range of its activities, and there is no doubt that this trend will continue. The current tendency to react only after governmental intervention and regulation are proposed must be replaced with a long term plan designed to anticipate and favorably influence such actions. One recent example of such long range planning is provided by several public utility companies that are explaining their strategic planning activities to state regulatory agencies in an attempt to educate these agencies as to the enduring effects of current rate and capacity decisions. This type of planning for " governmentalism" will grow rapidly over the next decade.

The recent clamor for reducing the external diseconomies created by private enterprise has been highlighted by demands for increased ecological responsibility. Here again, the corporate tendency to fight back—claiming that these effects are the "price of production"—must be replaced with a long range plan to forecast environmental effects, to determine the real costs of these effects, and to study technologies for alleviating those effects which are truly adverse. An example of such planning is provided by the recent decision of a large manufacturer to build electrostatic precipitators rather than to fight anti-smoke regulation. The result is a new, highly profitable product which will eventually form the basis for a new corporate division.

internal environments

The demands for long range planning also prevail because of changing conditions within the corporation, notably in employee relations and organizational structure.

Since the employee is a consumer of the services and external diseconomies produced by the corporation, his attitudes toward these factors will increasingly influence long range corporate policy. Moreover, long range policies will have to be developed to incorporate evolving employee goals as these change from economic gain toward increases in personal job satisfaction. Simultaneously, plans must be developed to alleviate the personnel problems introduced as the pace of work automation accelerates.

Changes in organizational structure will be necessary to implement these new employee policies and at the same time to implement long range plans directed at other problems. Clearly, improvements in the structure of decision-making offer an area for active planning research. For instance, it is well known that many potentially profitable new product and process alternatives currently "die" at lower levels of the organization because of inadequate support for and commitment to these ideas. The development of purposeful plans for adaptively improving this structure to alleviate such problems obviously has a high payoff in improving organizational performance.

summary

This paper discusses some philosophical, technical, and environmental changes which will affect the future conduct of corporate strategic planning. While some of these changes are speculative, there is no doubt that the majority will occur in those organizations which successfully adapt to a rapidly changing future. Still, it must be observed that at the present time the rate of initiation for these proposals is slow, even in the most progressive contemporary corporations. Two major research efforts are necessary to increase this rate of "planning for planning." First, research must be conducted to improve understanding of the strategic decision-making process within the organization. Normative theories, laboratory experiments, and models have helped in this regard, but significant field research into actual strategic corporate decision-making must be conducted to complete this effort. Second, further research must be conducted to gain insight into the effects of change—especially resistance to change—on people within organizations. Significant interaction and commitment will be necessary between corporations and researchers to successfully conduct these projects, and innovative approaches should be developed soon to initiate these efforts.

organizing

11. organizational metamorphosis: a dynamic model
Joseph M. Pastore

As if it were the only *raison d'être*, rapid growth and consequent complexity of the corporation undoubtedly characterize the contemporary industrial milieu. Scholarly evidence of this growth phenomenon exists in both *a priori* and empirical forms, but, even to the layman, the evolution of massive and still growing corporate forms is quite apparent. Words and phrases such as "conglomerate," "growth company," and "multinational corporation" seem to dominate the pages of most popular and professional journals almost to the point of abuse.

The rationale for this relatively rampant corporate growth is far from dependent upon only a few factors. Rather, a highly complex environment, complete with many interdependent and often ill-defined variables, is responsible for perpetuating growth-oriented behavior among cor-

porate entities. Documentation of these variables is difficult; generalization about them is practically irreverent.[1] It would appear sufficient to say, however, that unprecedented economic and technological development coupled with changing and often perplexing consumer values have been instrumental as environmental change agents.

The behavior of the environmental factors described above has exerted severe pressure for adjustments in corporate policies and procedures. Accountants, for example, have been plagued with the need to formulate accounting methodologies appropriate for the growth oriented firm. Marketers and researchers have been confronted with the problem of keeping

Reprinted from *Marquette Business Review*, 15, No. 1 (Spring 1971), pp. 17–30, with permission of the publisher.

[1] The difficulty of defining the environment in which a corporation operates is aptly described in Francis J. Aguilar, *Scanning the Business Environment*. New York, Macmillan Publishing Co., Inc., 1967, particularly pp. 8–16.

pace with technological innovation in the form of new products and services. And, equally important, organization planners have been confronted with a need for social innovation to the extent that the status and effectiveness of traditional work logic and organization concepts have been challenged. Contemporary research has stressed that the traditional line and staff or functional structure, with its emphasis on organizational control and stability, has failed to provide needed organizational flexibility and design for growth.[2]

Observation of corporate practices, too, offers explicit evidence that corporations have been forced to change their traditional organizational patterns in order to countervail diseconomies of complexity and growth. Particularly evident are those firms intricately involved with defense contracts, such as aerospace, where the pace of technological change and the existence of competitive uncertainties are nearly incomprehensible. Studies witnessing organization change within such firms have described an organizational evolution from functional structures to the emerging "project" or "task" organizations.[3] Such project structures are said to permit a deviation from the control-oriented behavior fostered by classical systems and provide organizational behavior conducive to innovation.

It is the purpose of this paper to explore the organizational consequences of the environmental transformations just described and present a dynamic organizational model designed to cope with environmental change.

the dilemma of organizational theory

The impact upon the study of organizational theory and behavior as a result of the change phenomena described above has manifested itself in the form of a conflict in organizational thought. This polarity of thought, quite familiar to students of management, is easily documented by little more than a superficial search of the literature. The dichotomy is recognized by many labels: formal versus informal, "Theory X" versus "Theory Y," differentiation versus integration, and "mechanistic" versus "organic."[4]

The division in organizational thought represents more than a mere taxonomy. It represents a very active, often academic, and more often futile debate primarily between classical and contemporary organizational notions. What is the essence of this organizational debate?[5] An overview of the argument can be sketched in the form of a dichotomy with the classical or mechanistic model at one extreme versus the contemporary or systems (organic) model at the opposite extreme.

[2] See, for example, Warren G. Bennis, "The Decline of Bureaucracy and Organizations of the Future," in *Changing Organizations*, ed. by Warren G. Bennis. New York, McGraw-Hill Book Co., 1966.

[3] Some prominent investigations are offered by David I. Cleland and William R. King, *Systems Analysis and Project Management.* New York, McGraw-Hill Book Co., 1968; and, Richard Johnson, Fremont Kast, and James E. Rosenzweig, *The Theory and Management of Systems.* New York, McGraw-Hill Book Co., 1967.

[4] Most recognize the terms "Theory X" and "Theory Y" as stemming from the work of Douglas McGregor, *The Human Side of Enterprise.* New York, McGraw-Hill Book Co., 1960; the terms "mechanistic" and "organic" are from Tom Burns and G. M. Stalker, *The Management of Innovation.* London, Tavistock Publications, 1959, pp. 119–22.

[5] It is not the purpose of this paper to offer a thorough treatment of the theory conflict cited above—the literature is well-endowed with such discussions. See, for example, William G. Scott, *Organization Theory.* Homewood, Ill., R. D. Irwin, Inc., 1967, Chaps. 5 and 6.

Generally, the basis of the classical system is that it is oriented toward control and stability, advocating such concepts as: "authority should equal responsibility," "line and staff," "functional division of labor," "unity of command," and "chain of command."

The systems theory, comprising the other half of the dichotomy, is based mostly on an orientation toward change rather than control and stability. Rather than the classical "divisions of labor," this theory stresses the "integration" of knowledge; rather than rigidly defined authority-responsibility relationships, the systems theory imposes a participatory or "bargaining" organizational environment in which one's responsibility may purposefully exceed one's authority.

The question as to which of the two organizational schemes is most appropriate may not be relevant—despite the fact that it has been considered repeatedly for many years. Both systems have been attacked. The classical system is criticized because of its rigidity. The systems notion is challenged on essentially two counts: first, because of what some have characterized as an unrealistic "harmony of interest" theme devoid of organizational conflict,[6] and, secondly, because important neo-classical writers, such as Mayo, conceived the business concern as an integrated and self-contained social system apart from its external environment.[7] In effect, the answer to the question which asks which of the theories is best often must take the form of "it all depends."[8]

[6] Sherman Krupp, *Patterns of Organization Analysis: A Critical Examination.* Philadelphia, Chilton Co., 1961, p. x.
[7] Elton Mayo, *The Human Problems of an Industrial Civilization.* Boston, Harvard Graduate School of Business Administration, 1946, p. 173.
[8] For a somewhat "maverick," but important work regarding this question see Harvey Sherman, *It All Depends.* University, Alabama, 1966.

A discussion of an emerging, "contingent" theory of organization follows in an attempt to quiet the seemingly futile debate between classical and neo-classical ideologies.

a "contingency" theory

In part, this paper attempts to applaud the currently evolving notion that the "proper" organizational perspective is dependent upon the environment with which it is to cope, and is, above all, the one which "works." Empirically, Lawrence and Lorsch have recognized this dependency relationship between organization and environment and have formulated a theory which they have named a "contingency" theory.

These findings suggest a contingency theory of organization ... The basic assumption underlying such a theory ... is that organizational variables are in a complex interrelationship with one another and with conditions in the environment.

This contingency theory of organizations suggests the major relationships that managers should think about as they plan organizations to deal with specific environmental conditions. It clearly indicates that managers can no longer be concerned about the one best way to organize. Rather ... this contingency theory ... provides at least the beginning of a conceptual framework with which to design organizations according to the tasks they are trying to perform.[9]

The "contingency" theory, then, offers a basis for an organizational design which could borrow from *both* classical as well as contemporary organizational concepts. Thus, in an environment where routine processes are stressed, where, perhaps, *production* is the core around which corporate activity revolves, the classical

[9] Paul R. Lawrence and Jay W. Lorsch, *Organization and Environment.* Cambridge, Mass., Harvard University, 1967, pp. 157–58.

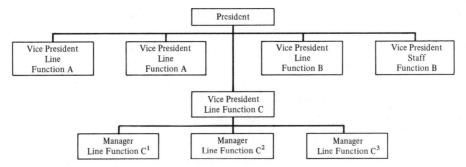

Figure 1. The Functional Structure.

system, with its emphasis on differentiated, control-oriented behavior, may be operable. In an environment characterized by change, where processes are heuristic rather than routine, and where *marketing innovation* is the core around which corporate activity revolves, the organic system's emphasis on integrated, change-oriented behavior appears more appropriate.

structural extensions of each theory

The classical and systems theories of organization each form bases for certain types of organizational designs or structures. Specifically, the classical theory provides the framework for what is often referred to as the "functional" organization structure, while the systems perspective lies at the root of contemporary designs referred to as "project" or "matrix" organizations.

the functional structures

The functional structure follows the tenets of classical organization theory in that it is an essentially hierarchical and differentiated structure consisting of line and staff functions. Figure 1 shows a typical functional design.

the project structure

The project structure is an organizational scheme designed to cut across functional lines of authority and responsibility in an attempt to integrate various functions (e.g., marketing, engineering, etc.) as they might be needed to achieve a certain objective.[10] Thus, while functional designs highlight the classical principle of specialization or differentiation among functions, the project design is an attempt to apply the tenets of systems theory and achieve organizational integration.

Differences in organizational design, however, extend beyond a simple variance between functional and project structures. Differences exist also among project designs themselves. Thus, within a firm organized primarily according to a functional design, there may exist one set of project groups which are highly dependent upon and closely contained by the functional organization and, at the same time, another set of project groups which may be quite autonomous and independent of the functional organization. Of those

[10] For a general description of project management, particularly as it has been used in defense work, see David I. Cleland, "Project Management," in *Systems, Organizations, Analysis, Management: A Book of Readings*, ed. by David I. Cleland and William R. King. New York, McGraw-Hill Book Co., 1969, pp. 281–90.

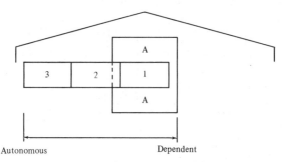

Code: 1, 2, and 3 represent quasi-dependent to autonomous project structures (task
groups), respectively. "A" represents the permanent, functional organization.

Figure 2. A Continuum of Project Structures: Dependent to Autonomous. The firm's external
environment.

highly dependent project groups, the project design is viewed simply as an overlay upon the existing functional structure; those projects possessing relative autonomy, however, are almost entirely divorced from the basic, functional organization and possess independent functional capabilities such as marketing research and production. In a sense, these autonomous units have been referred to as functionally decentralized units.[11]

The differences, then, among project groups may be seen as a continuum ranging from quasi-dependent to autonomous relationships with the parent, functional organization. Figure 2 attempts to illustrate this continuum.[12]

The continuum shown in Figure 2 appears to conform to the observation of

various project management systems by Keith Davis.[13] Davis cites four types of project management of which three are distinct:

1. The project expeditor (coordinator) type.

2. The project confederation type.

3. The project general management type.

A verbal and schematic presentation of each of these project organizations follows:

My experience with manufacturing firms—discloses that there are several types of organization which are sometimes designated "project management" ... The first type has only a *project expeditor*. He does not perform primary management functions ... but he does perform two other activities essential to good management. First, he is supposed to expedite the work by dealing with all persons involved to assure that schedules are met; however, he has no power other than persuasive and reporting back to his superior. This reflects his second function, that of serving as a center of communication to be able instantly to report to general management on the *whole* of the projects and thus relieve

[11] Selwyn W. Becker and Gerald Gordon, "An Entrepreneural Theory of Formal Organizations Part I: Patterns of Formal Organizations," *Administrative Science Quarterly* (December 1966), p. 339.

[12] A similar representation of this relationship was presented in a working paper by Andre L. Delbecq, "Matrix Organization— An Evolution Beyond Bureaucracy," *Proceedings of the 11th Annual Midwest Management Conference*, ed. by Raymond L. Hilgert (St. Louis, Mo.: Washington University, April 5–6, 1968), p. 125.

[13] Keith Davis, "The Role of Project Management in Scientific Manufacturing," in *Systems, Organizations, Analysis, Mangement*, ed. by Cleland and King, pp. 308–14.

general management of the tedious task of keeping up with all the details.[14]

Thus, the first type of project structure is simply a *control-oriented* type with the project "manager" acting as a liaison or staff assistant to a general manager. In a very real sense, this first type of project organization is simply an administrative overlay upon the existing functional organization and may be represented by task group number one in Figure 2.

Schematically, the design of the first type of project structure is represented by Figure 3. Any projects that the functional departments may be working on are monitored by the project "manager." For each project there would be a project expeditor or coordinator primarily to insure that the project meets time and cost constraints.

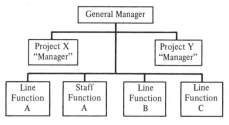

Figure 3. Type 1 Project Structures— Monitoring Authority Only.

The second type of project structure, that which Davis refers to as the "project confederation," is what is generally referred to as the "matrix" organization.

The [second] type of project organization is headed by a manager who actually performs the full range of management functions from planning to controlling the work of others; hence, he may properly be called "manager." However those persons he directs are mostly working in other departments spatially removed from him and are, consequently, not subject to his

[14] *Ibid.*, p. 309.

operating supervision throughout the work day. Though they are assigned to his project, they remain in their permanent departments.[15]

Thus, the second type of project organization is actually based on shared authority and responsibility between project and functional managers. As far as hierarchical relationships are concerned, both project and functional managers are on an equal scale. In effect then, individuals working on the project have two "bosses"— functional head and a project head. The reader will note that such a relationship is contrary to the principle of unity of command advocated by classical theorists.

The matrix organization, then, creates an organizational climate where bargaining and compromise prevail. Bargaining transactions become the mechanism for reconciling conflicts pertaining to such activities as personnel allocation and appraisal. This relationship, it might be noted, is used extensively in defense industries such as aerospace.[16] The matrix organization is shown schematically in Figure 4.

The third and final type of project structure might be viewed as an attempt to reduce the overall functional structure to micro-structures. Each micro-structure is functionally designed but concerned with only one specific activity or project rather than all of the organization's projects. Davis described this third type as follows:

The third type of project organization has the ultimate organizational objective of unity of command, ... Persons are temporarily withdrawn from their departments and wholly assigned to the project under the project manager. He is their chain-of-command manager until they are removed or the project plays out. This

[15] *Ibid.*
[16] For a description of the "matrix" scheme in defense industries see David I. Cleland, "The Deliberate Conflict," *Business Horizons* (February 1968), p. 78–80.

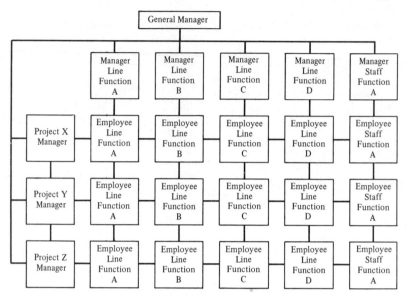

Figure 4. Type 2 Project Structure—"Matrix" Organization.

third type is *project general management.* Its manager directs virtually the complete project. He is in many respects a separate branch manager with profit authority and responsibility, subject to general direction by his superior.[17]

Schematically, the third type of project structure is represented in Figure 5.

a dynamic organizational model

Thus far this paper has shown that functionally designed organization structures conform to classical organization theory, that project structures conform to systems theory, and that project structures vary in type from control-oriented, organizationally dependent groups to planning-oriented, organizationally autonomous groups. Table 1 summarizes these relationships.

This section represents an attempt to illustrate the organizational metamor-

[17] Davis, "The Role of Project Management in Scientific Manufacturing," p. 310.

Table 1.   A Summary of the Relationships Between Organization Theory and Structure

Theory	Structure
Classical	Functional
Systems	Project (Types 1–3)
Contingency	A dynamic structure which incorporates both functional and project designs in response to changes in the environment within which it is to operate

phosis which may occur among project groups designed to generate growth-oriented behavior and results. Growth-oriented behavior is defined, generally, as behavior designed to increase a firm's sales. The manner in which this growth-oriented behavior is expressed may be in terms of activities geared to creating new products which complement existing lines or it may be by generating entirely new directions and businesses for the firm through acquisitions or research and

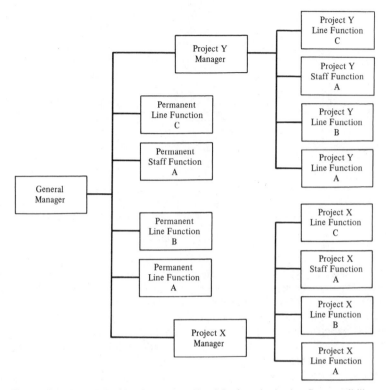

Figure 5. Type 3 Project Structure—Total Project Authority–Responsibility.

development. In practice, these growth-oriented project groups have been referred to as "venture management" or "venture teams." [18]

To explain the organizational metamorphosis growth-oriented project structures may undergo, it might be advisable to identify the metamorphosis which occurs in the environment in which these growth-oriented project groups operate. This is particularly important because, as this paper has indicated, significant evidence exists to show that the nature of an organizational design is, to a great extent, a function of the environment with which it is to cope.

The environment in which growth-oriented project groups must operate is quite familiar to the student and practitioner of management. Generally, it follows the well-known product life cycle shown in Figure 6.[19] Variations of this life cycle have been developed by Hanan and

[18] See, for example, Russell W. Peterson, "New Venture Management in a Large Corporation," *Harvard Business Review* (May–June 1967), pp. 68–76; and, Mack Hanan, "Corporate Growth Through Venture Management," *Harvard Business Review* (January–February 1969), pp. 43–61.

[19] Some readers may question the validity of the product life cycle as an adequate indication of the environmental pattern many products experience. For an empirical verification of the product life cycle see Rolando Polli and Victor Cook, "Validity of the Product Life Cycle," *The Journal of Business* (October 1969), pp. 385–400.

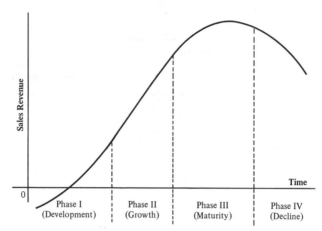

Figure 6.   New Venture Life Cycle.

Kast, particularly as they relate to growth-oriented or venture behavior.[20] Hanan's description of the environment for growth-oriented groups is not as extensive, however, as this paper intends to present this environment. Specifically, Hanan limits his discussion to the first phase (development) of the growth-oriented cycle, while this paper is concerned with an analysis of venture or growth-oriented project structures as they relate to the entire cycle.

A correlation appears to exist between each type of organizational design exhibited by growth-oriented project groups (Types 1–3) and each phase of the new product or new business life cycle. The developmental stage, for example, is marked by an environment characterized by uncertainty. As such, the activities required of a project group operating in such an environment are based on essentially heuristic and planning-oriented behavior. The need for opportunity and customer definition, the need for financial feasibility studies, and the need for technical planning in terms of product and

[20] Hanan, "Corporate Growth Through Venture Management," pp. 51–61; Fremont Kast, "A Dynamic Planning Model," *Business Horizons* (June 1968), pp. 61–68.

production specifications, all characterize the *search* behavior of the first stage. For this reason, the organizational design of the project group required to achieve phase #1 or developmental objectives appears to assume the pattern of the Type 3 project structure described earlier. Evidence to document this relationship between organizational type and new venture phase is provided by the following description of such a venture group at E. I. DuPont de Nemours, Inc.:

After selecting an idea for expanded development effort, the Development Department submits a detailed proposal to the company's Executive Committee . . . to secure approval to set up a development group for launching the new business. If approval is granted the Research and Development Division of the department selects a venture manager. This man is the entrepreneur with responsibility and authority to develop and direct the project.

He [the venture manager] is provided with the necessary dollars, personnel, and facilities to make his group self-sufficient. He and all his people are put full time on the new venture . . .

Skilled people from marketing, manufacturing, and research functions in other company departments are transferred into the new venture groups. These people stay with the venture throughout its growth . . .[21]

Such an organizational scheme is not unique to DuPont. Of the thirty-six companies included in a recent study, twenty reported the use of similar organizational designs for growth-oriented tasks.[22]

The question, now, becomes: Does the organizational design just described change as the environment with which the project must cope changes? In other words, are there, in practice, dynamic organizational models which incorporate both classical and contemporary organizational notions and which exhibit structural changes contingent upon changes in environment? The literature, as well as the

writer's study and experience, seem to indicate that such an organizational metamorphosis does occur.[23]

Table 2 is an attempt to describe the probable organizational change occurring within growth-oriented projects. The reader will note that the behavior of this organizational change closely approximates the project structure continuum presented earlier in Figure 2. Also, this organizational change, as a function of environmental change, it should be noted, relates closely to Lawrence and Lorsch's "contingency" theory findings cited earlier. Thus, growth-oriented project groups

[21] Peterson, "New Venture Management," pp. 70–71.

[22] Joseph M. Pastore, Jr., "A Classification and Analysis of Growth-Oriented Project Groups in Non-Defense Industries" (unpublished doctoral dissertation, St. Louis University, 1969), pp. 41–51.

[23] See, for example, the description of the change in growth-oriented project organizations at DuPont in Peterson, "New Venture Management," pp. 71–72; also, very little exists in the form of empirical research related to organizational growth or change through time and/or environment changes; for an outline of organizational growth and some suggestions for research see Scott, *Organization Theory*, pp. 135–48.

Table 2. The Metamorphosis of Growth-Oriented Project Structures

Growth-Oriented Phase	Phase Environment	Organizational Type
Phase #1 (Development)	Highly uncertain . . . project activity characterized by heuristic behavior in the form of customer identification as well as financial and technical feasibility studies	Type 3 project structure designed to provide project *direction*
Phase #2 (Growth)	Customer and product definition more certain, . . . market penetration accelerating . . . project activities generally involve the establishment of a more complete production and distribution network	Type 3 project structure begins to fade and Type 2 emerges thus easing the transition from *direction-oriented to control-oriented* behavior
Phase #3 (Maturity)	Demand begins to level off . . . project activity characterized by control-oriented market and production maintenance (i.e., "running the business")	Type 2 project structure fades and Type 1 emerges in an attempt to provide project *control*
Phase #4 (Decline)	New product or business begins to lose market appeal . . . project activity characterized by salvaging behavior in the form of promotional gimmicks, for example	Type 1

can be said to exhibit a "contingency" structure.

The effect of the organizational change model described in Table 2 is that it provides an organizational scheme responsive to variations in the organization's tasks. For heuristic tasks, project groups with total task authority and responsibility integrate the necessary functional skills for task achievement. As the venture or project grows and matures to the point where it can be operated according to essentially programmed and routine methodology, the organizational scheme changes from a total project design (Type 3) to an essentially functional structure with a project overlay (Type 1) for limited integration and coordination purposes.

The implication of the model is that as a new venture moves from heuristic to programmed stages, the Type 3 or heuristic project group is freed to move on to venture tasks related, perhaps, to different marketing directions. Not only does the design move on, but significantly, most of the personnel in the project group do also—particularly the venture manager who appears to possess an entrepreneural character profile. It is in this fashion that a company can organize itself to "exploit" its product life cycle such that as an existing product or business in the company begins to decline another product or business venture is researched and developed to take its place.[24]

summary

It should be apparent that the prolonged debate among managerial theorists as to which organizational theory and structure is "best" is both academic and futile. Theories and their applications stem from circumstances—from environments. As such, normative theories and their positive extensions must be related to circumstances and environments. The structural metamorphosis of growth-oriented project groups from heuristic to programmed forms, as the task environment changes from relative uncertainty to certainty, is indicative of the organizational flexibility required for task achievement. Hopefully, this paper has indicated that organizations are beginning to recognize these organizational prerequisites and that managerial theorists have begun to meet them.

[24] An excellent description of this type of marketing behavior is provided by Theodore Levitt, "Exploit the Product Life Cycle," *Harvard Business Review* (November–December 1965), pp. 81–94.

12. hospital organization in the post-industrial society
Gordon L. Lippitt

Many hospital administrators, trustees, physicians, and department heads are wondering if health care institutions can meet the demands of increased and im-

Reprinted from *Hospital Progress*, 54, No. 6 (June 1973), pp. 55–64, with permission of the publisher.

proved delivery of health services in a changing society.

The turbulence faced today by health care institutions is caused both by the increased complexity of their medical-technological functions and by multiple revolutions in contemporary society. In addition, predictable strains are being exerted on hospitals by similar and more dynamic interrelationships and increased interdependence among government agencies (federal, state, and local), industry, communities, and educational institutions. These multiple forces must be met with a process of organization renewal, adaptation, and planning for change.

trends that will influence change

To predict the future of organizational purpose, structure, process, and management, it is necessary to examine the trends that will be affecting such changes. Some of the larger trends will be: the greatly increased standard of living in the U.S. and throughout the world; an increasing gap between the powerful and the rich, and the powerless and poor; a rapid increase in the world population; continued changes in value systems; the greater expectation of people for services in general, but for health care in particular; the increased influence of local, state, and federal governments; an increasing desire for power by minority groups; a continued increase in the influence of mass media; the extensive development of education as it applies to continued growth and development at all ages; a shift from a production to a service economy; a continued increase in technology; an increased confrontation by consumers; the development of new avocations and vocations in society; an increased international interdependence; a continuation of ecological concerns; an increased mobility of people with a lessening of commitment to an organization or community; an increased size of the social systems of mankind so that there will be a greater feeling of powerlessness on the part of members of such institutions; a continued explosion of knowledge; and a

desire for quality, not just quantity, as a goal in life.

These trends are accelerating at an uneven rate, but at a speed that is challenging all the institutions of man, as well as the individual who works within them. This total picture can be described as a shift from the industrial to the post-industrial society, and involves massive changes that are not under control. The dilemma created by these changes is well stated by Eric Trist:

the contemporary environment ... is taking on the quality of a turbulent field. ... This turbulence grossly increases the area of relative uncertainty for individuals and organizations alike. It raises far-reaching problems concerning the limits of human adaptation. Forms of adaptation, both personal and organizational, developed to meet a simpler type of environment, no longer suffice to meet the higher levels of complexity now coming into existence. ... The planner's dilemma ... may be summarized as follows: the greater the degree of change, the greater the need for planning—otherwise precedents of the past could guide the future; but the greater the degree of uncertainty, the greater the likelihood that plans right today will be wrong tomorrow.[1]

industrial vs. post-industrial era

Managers of all institutions, including hospitals, are coping with this transition more slowly than it is occurring. They are still managing with values, organizational structures, and leadership styles of the industrial era. That era adhered strongly to the values and beliefs of the Christian work ethic, economic efficiency, and a dedication to nationalism. The contrasts cited in Table 1 reveal some of the

[1] Eric Trist, "Between Cultures: The Current Crisis of Transition," *Organizational Frontiers and Human Values*, ed. W. Schmidt, Wadsworth Publishing Co., Belmont, Calif., 1970, p. 29.

Table 1.   Changes in Emphasis in the Transition to Post-Industrialism[2]

Type of Change	From	Toward
Cultural values	Achievement	Self-actualization
	Self-control	Self-expression
	Independence	Interdependence
	Endurance of distress	Capacity for joy
Organizational philosophies	Mechanistic forms	Organic forms
	Competitive relations	Collaborative relations
	Separate objectives	Linked objectives
	Own resources regarded as owned absolutely	Own resources regarded also as society's
Organizational practices	Responsive to crisis	Anticipative of crisis
	Specific measures	Comprehensive measures
	Requiring consent	Requiring participation
	Short planning horizon	Long planning horizon
	Damping conflict	Confronting conflict
	Detailed central control	Generalized central control
	Small local units	Enlarged local units
	Standardized administration	Innovative administration
	Separate services	Coordinated services

[2] *Ibid.*, p. 32 (with minor adaptations).

differences between industrial and post-industrial society.

These transitions are now taking place in advanced industrial and urbanized societies like the United States. Change is always difficult, but this shift is particularly painful, complex, and frustrating. Margaret Mead has described this generation as "immigrants in time," as members of the first generation to live in an era when it is not obvious or even plausible that "experience is the best teacher," since the circumstances of today are unlike anything faced by those of middle age. Hospitals and their leaders will be living in this transitional period throughout the 70's and 80's.

The task, then, amounts to reorienting hospitals and other social institutions so that, amoeba-like, they are capable of continuously and consciously undergoing change and renewal. It is no longer sufficient to depend upon remedial splinting of institutional fractures caused by excessive rigidity.

But recognizing that organization renewal and change is required is not equivalent to being able to initiate change. The problem for hospital managements today is whether or not they have the resources and skills to bring about sufficient timely renewal in their organizations to meet the challenges of the only partially known future.

Hospitals have grown in size, but have they matured? Maturation requires adaptability, flexibility, health, and identity, particularly in this era of technological and sociological innovations. Toward what end are hospitals growing? This question is brought into focus by changes wrought not just in medical and managerial technology but in philosophy. These changes include:

- A new concept of *man*, based on increased knowledge of his complex and shifting needs, which replaces an oversimplified, innocent, push-button idea of man.
- A new concept of *power*, based on collaboration and reason, which replaces a model of power based on coercion and threat.
- A new concept of *organization values*, based on humanistic / democratic ideals, which replaces the depersonalized mechanistic value system of bureaucracy.[3]

organization models

These potential changes in philosophy are reflected in the ways organizations are structured and managed. In the past century, many models of organizations have evolved from managerial philosophies, and thereafter were used, although not always successfully, as a guide for specific managerial practices. An attempt to sort out these models may be helpful.

Seven organizational models, distributed along a continuum from autocracy to democracy, have been identified: autocracy (machine model), bureaucracy, systems, decentralization, collegialism, federations, and egalitarianism.[4]

The trend in management is from the autocratic to the democratic side of the continuum in order to meet the changing needs of the post-industrial society. In this context, the models reflect the idea that the practice in organizations is toward greater participation and democracy. It would seem, then, as we examine models

for hospital management, that many of the efforts to change would conform to the described trend; but management practices are not as clear as might be communicated by such listings or terminology. Furthermore, in large hospitals, some segments of the organization may be operating on one basis and other segments on another.

While these multiple approaches to organization management imply that greater value is placed upon participation, it is important to recognize that the organic and growth concepts of organizations imply that at different stages of growth, different kinds of structure and managerial leadership might be appropriate. In the early stages of an organization some degree of autocracy may be appropriate, while it might be inappropriate at the later stages of uniqueness and maturity. It is also relevant to point out that as different crises emerge in an organization and the organization is confronted with a recession, competition, or waning interest in its service, it may need to revert to different styles of management to "see it through" a particular period of its life.

Most attempts to examine organizational dynamics tend to ignore the interplay between environmental forces and organizational responses. Every hospital organization is embedded in a total environment that conditions its forms, its decision-making process, and the way it utilizes its resources. In appropriately responding to situations, an organization should manifest an awareness of its responsibility and compulsion to conform to its larger environment.

[3] Warren Bennis, "Organizations of the Future," *Management of Organization Development*, University of Bradford, United Kingdom, 1971, p. 16.

[4] George Rice and Dean Bishoprick, *Conceptual Models of Organization*, Appleton-Century-Crofts, New York City, 1971.

the hospital in its modern environment

The environments in which hospitals operate today have some unique characteristics. The situation is well stated by Michael Michaelson of the School of Medicine at the University of Pennsylvania:

But what is good health service? Who defines it? Will patients, consumers, citizens make decisions about health and doctors? Or will such people pretend to make medical policy while in fact the medical elite makes it (as, for example, we make military policy with the help and advice of the Pentagon)? These cannot be trivial questions. But the liberal medical establishment has been unable to raise them because it has refused to acknowledge openly what it is doing. ("As to the honor and conscience of doctors," Shaw warned, "they have as much as any other class of men, no more, and no less.")[5]

These issues in health care are now receiving the critical attention of many groups, including the American Hospital Association and the American College of Hospital Administrators. Some of the criticism of health care is strong and far-reaching. The report of the Health Policy Advisory Center is one of the most solid criticisms of American health care now in existence because it is not written to please any power group in the health field, but explains how it feels to be a patient, an orderly, a doctor, a technician, a nurse, and even an administrator in these critical days.[6]

Other reports equally confront the medical profession and modern hospitals. Hospital boards, doctors, and administrators will all have to face the need for new organizational practices. Greenberg comments in a report to the medical profession about the changes that are to

come: "It is not only foolhardy to try to stay the revolution but ... the profession is duty-bound to provide constructive leadership in shaping its course."[7] In the foreword of the report, Robert H. Ebert, MD, the dean of the Harvard Medical School, writes:

Mr. Greenberg provides a panoramic view of the status of health care in this country, and the reader may well be shocked by what he reads. Still he need not despair, for if one reflects for a moment on the intellectual and economic resources of this nation, one cannot but agree that all of the problems catalogued by Mr. Greenberg can be resolved. ....[8]

Dr. Ebert may be optimistic, but much must be done if hospitals are to be appropriately responsive to the new demands they confront. It is necessary to explore the specific implications of the key changes confronting hospitals and their impact on the delivery of health services.

I wish to identify some key characteristics of the hospital of the future that will evolve out of our technological, civil rights, medical, moral, and anti-establishment revolutions that are the locus of the socio-economic forces in modern America. The issues that arise from these forces will create some major changes in the way health care professionals prepare for jobs, the way they manage, and the criteria they use to determine the effectiveness of hospitals.

characteristics of the new organization

The following lists key characteristics of the organization of the future and their implications for management.

[5] Michael Michaelson, "The Medical Elite in the Future of America's Health Care Institutions," *Scientific Institutions of the Future*, ed. Phillip Ritterbush, Acropolis Books, Washington, D.C., 1972, p. 80.
[6] Health Policy Advisory Center, *The American Health Empire: Power, Profits, and Politics*, New York City, 1971.

[7] Selig Greenberg, "The Quality of Mercy, A Report on the Critical Condition of Hospital and Medical Care in America," Atheneum, New York City, 1971, p. 16.
[8] *Ibid.*, p. 5.

1. *Hospitals will require new structures to cope with needed flexibility in health care needs.* Organizations of the future will become increasingly complex in terms of size, financial resources, manpower utilization, and service diversification. Traditional structures will not be adequate. Organizations will need to use "temporary systems." Task forces, project groups, and other such strategies will be required to help a hospital adapt and react to its environment. To permit an organization to be proactive rather than reactive, matrix organization concepts will emerge. This will provide the flexibility to utilize resources wherever they can be found to effectively meet the needs of the hospital. A greater emphasis will be placed on processes and systems within the organization that will permit self-renewing activities and innovation.[9]

We will hear more of various new problem-solving processes. The so-called "matrix" process is a special kind of problem-solving concept, form, and function. It is designed to solve problems that cannot be solved by conventional subsystems, mental processes, and methods. Drawing from the larger, formal, parent organization (and from "outside" sources as well), the men and women, the machines, and the procedures and techniques of diverse social and physical sciences, this process integrates them into a temporary group (force) with the objective of solving a complex problem that formal organization and routine method cannot solve. Upon completion of its task, the special group dissolves and its members return to their normal functional activities. This "matrix" process is already used with cardiac emergency teams in many modern hospitals and is relevant to other medical and nonmedical responses of a hospital.

[9] Gordon L. Lippitt, *Organization Renewal*, Appleton-Century-Crofts, New York City, 1969.

In short, this new process groups together persons of multiple skills and disciplines in order to solve and implement a complex problem that cannot be so handled by conventional means. It is an evolving form responsive to problems of varying complexity and novelty that will emerge in health care. Its chief characteristic at present is "extra-organization," that is, an *ad hoc*, temporary, single-problem-oriented specialist task force that in varying degrees is separated from the parent organization.

We may conjecture that herein lies an evolutionary change in major problem solving; but rather than a "dead branch," the traditional, bureaucratic organization may become an endoskeletal tissue supporting varying matrix form and function as required to cope with the complexity, fluidity, adaptiveness, mobility, and speed of the survival-bound organism. Emergent forms of this problem-solving process already have been employed in various industrial, governmental, educational, social, and scientific enterprises, such as Polaris, Apollo, medical groups (surgical and post-operative teams), college faculties, new products and processes, research and development projects, presidential and congressional reports and studies*, urban planning, technical forecasting, and juries.

There is here the possibility of the evolution of what might be called "Argus man," as contrasted to "Cyclops man." The demand of exceedingly complex, urgent, and total problems has come to require hundred-eyed, problem-solving groups, whose disciplinary membership is of a variety comparable to the problem's variety. This demand cannot be satisfied by cyclopean sensory systems and

* Panels, commissions, committees, and special study groups, however, only partially complete the process: they identify the problem and recommend strategy but they do not *act*; they stop short of total problem solving and hence problems really do not get solved.

philosophical viewpoints of individual man, nor by conventional, monolithic, hierarchical organization or quasi-matrix groups (committees, panels, project groups, task forces, elite "pick-up" teams). *Implications for Administrators.* Hospital administrators must understand and learn to apply the principle of matrix organizations. They will need to recognize that many early theories and assumptions about organizations are obsolete. Hospital management must proceed from the assumption that people can and should be used anywhere in the organization that their talents are required. Focus will be on getting the job done. Systematic efforts will be made to prevent over-emphasis on working through organizational channels which tend to choke and prevent organizational growth and effectiveness.

Administrators must learn to make organization analysis and to interpret the results for the total hospital. They must place greater emphasis on being able to serve as problem-solving links within the organization. Hospital managers must help people become comfortable in the presence of change and to work effectively within organizations characterized by continuous change and *ad hoc* group situations.

2. *Development of all human resources will become a key responsibility of future organizations.* The obsolescence rate of people in the hospital of the future will make it necessary for individuals to cope with change in their own lives, careers, and organizations. People must have second and third careers in order to keep up with the rapid change required in the health care field. The continued rapid growth of a service-oriented society will change the complexity and nature of many organizations and jobs, but will particularly affect hospitals.

In addition, inadequate use of minority group members, such as blacks, Mexicans, Puerto Ricans, women, and older workers, will be a constant challenge in an evolving and changing society. There will be pressure to evolve programs which use the total human resources of the country. Underutilized resources must be recognized at both individual and organizational levels. The middle-class puritan work ethic may be an inappropriate frame of reference for understanding the development problems of persons raised outside of this ethic.

Many believe that the solutions will derive from hospital-sponsored education opportunities for all employes of the hospital. For example:

Time for education will be economically feasible if it results in greater long-term effectiveness. Greater revenue resulting from a higher degree of initiative and innovation can be allocated partly to the educational program. If the organization maintains its vitality and continues to change in keeping with the times, it should sustain a high level of contribution to society to justify a perpetual rebuilding of the educational base of its own employes.

Education might be more effective if it could be properly coordinated with a man's development. This would require a true educational opportunity as a continuing part of the work environment.[10]

The educational program of a hospital must become an integral part of its organizational life.

Implications for Administrators. There must be a better balance between focus on individual and organization development so that the organization may adapt more effectively in meeting its objectives and in utilizing its human resources more creatively.

New methods of training and development will emphasize the need for creativity and innovation. It will become increasingly futile to teach jobs already in existence.

[10] J. W. Forrester, "A New Corporate Design," *Industrial Management Review*, July, 1965, p. 840.

Administrators must develop ways to recognize potential in all persons in the hospital. The role of attitudes must be recognized and techniques developed for minimizing prejudice in the work situation. New ways to interpret and train people for the world of work will be required. This will require an ever-continuing involvement in creating new programs for effectively developing the capabilities of human resources. The administrator will need to be creative and supportive of an ongoing education and development process as part of the way he "manages" the hospital. Implementing organization development and renewal processes will become a key responsibility of management.[11]

In assuming responsibility for organizational and individual diagnosis in the adaptive process, managers will need to develop effectively both line and staff people. In addition, administrators must place greater emphasis on their own development and the professionalism which will be required to face the needs of organizational change.

3. *Mutual confidence, rather than obedience to authority, will provide the basis of work accomplishment.* The organization of the future will base its control and effectiveness on the growth and accomplishment of persons within the organization. The old "command" by authority or even benevolent paternalism will become less viable as a way of managing. Forrester states it well:

If the authoritarian hierarchy with its superior-subordinate pairing is to be removed, it must be replaced by another form of discipline and control. This substitute can be individual self-discipline arising from the self-interest created by a competitive market mechanism.

To depart from the authoritarian hierarchy as the central organizational structure, one must replace the superior-subordinate pair as the fundamental building block of the organization. In the new organization, an individual would not be assigned to a superior. Instead he would negotiate, as a free individual, a continually changing structure of relationships with those with whom he exchanges goods and services. He would accept specific obligations as agreements of limited duration. As these are discharged, he would establish a new pattern of relationships as he finds more satisfying and rewarding situations.[12]

This new kind of relationship is built upon the confidence persons have in one another's integrity, goal orientation, and commitment to a problem-solving process. Such confidence does not need to depend upon authority or status for its success. It derives from some basic trust between the parties without which quality work will be illusory.

Implications for Administrators. Many factors in the traditional organizational pattern caused persons in a hospital to be seen as "doers of work." The task was the first concern of the supervisor. In the new approach, the supervisor sees his major responsibility as the development of others to adult patterns of self-control. He strives to develop effective work functioning and to focus on the "person-centered" needs so as to "release" the potential of others. Fortunately, this kind of supervision fits the job to the person rather than fitting a person to a job description.

To improve performance the manager will create opportunities for the person to set his own "targets" for achievement, work standards, and personal growth. Through the "target-setting" type of experience, the individual meets his task goals in terms of his own drives, standards, and needs linked to clear objectives of the hospital.

4. *Freedom of access to information and*

[11] *Implementing the Organization Renewal Process Program*, Organization Renewal, Inc., Washington, D.C., 1971.

[12] Forrester, p. 824.

two-way communication. The character and climate of an organization can be deduced from the way it extends and withholds information. Effective management should not monopolize information. To possess information is to possess power. Most people in hospitals do not feel they have access to all the information they need to do their job well. Information is the outgrowth of communication, both of which can be stored and retrieved.

The act of communication underlies all we know about ourselves, about other people, and about our world. It underlies all our attempts to work together. In the final analysis all communication is the process that takes place at the individual level. We are concerned with: What is the individual saying? What is he trying to say? What does the individual hear and see? How does he interpret what he hears and sees? Although the policies and standards of an organization and cultural norms enter the communication process, we should consider these only as they affect communication between individuals.

The major revolution in modern communication is that people want to "say it like it is," to have organizations tell them the truth, to be able to influence the situation, and to be "open" in the communication process. This requires managers in hospitals to meet communications situations effectively, not with out-moded Madison Avenue techniques, but through managerial practices which give people access to the information processes and systems of the hospital.

Implications for Administrators. The need for instituting proper management and medical information systems in hospitals is self-evident. New technology in closed-circuit TV, intercommunication warning systems, computer programs, conference phones, etc., are all part of the arsenal of modern information storage and retrieval devices. It does not become communication, however, until it is shared

with those who want and need the information. The effective hospital manager must understand himself and be secure enough to share information, not hide it.

Effective administration needs good communications. It is hard to communicate between generations, among friends, between management and labor, and between departments in a hospital; but without adequate communication, a person cannot be an effective manager.

The two-way process of communication is found in both the formal and informal aspects of organization life. Opportunities to see oneself and the effect of one's supervision are a prime necessity in effective organizational accomplishment. The need for a "feedback" communication system is essential.

An organization, through its policies, philosophy, and management practices, can develop a climate of acceptance which encourages this level of interpersonal and system feedback communication.

5. *Increased interface between state, local, and federal government with other private and public institutions.* Increased interface between the private and public segments of society will create opportunities and problems for hospitals in the future. A better way will be needed to sense and identify the emerging health care problems before they become overwhelming. Opportunities for cross collaboration between health care institutions and government will be required. Interchanging personnel across these organizational systems will increase. More controls of health care at local, state, and national levels will emerge. Codes of ethics and practices will arise from joint commissions. More interdependence will emerge as a regular way of operating institutions.

Implications for Administrators. Hospital managers will move in and out of specific roles and assignments related to cross agency coordination, planning, and problem solving. Managers will need to widen their perspective by working in various types of organizational systems and to develop collaborative skills with organizational systems other than their own. The administrator must learn where to turn to gain the benefits from this kind of interchange. He will need to practice the skills of effective political action. His appropriate use of influence and power will be an important part of his life.

6. *Increased centralization and decentralization of decision-making areas throughout the organization.* The process of involving persons in the decisions which they will implement is an important new aspect of management. Obviously, all persons will not be involved in every decision, even though effective communication about decisions is one level of involvement. The degree of participation will depend on forces in the situation, forces in the leader, and forces in the subordinate groups. Those forces will provide guidelines for the degree to which an organization leader involves members in decision making that is relevant to their competency and experience, and meets the appropriate leader response to a particular situation. Some decisions will be decentralized to specialized units in the hospital. Other decisions on over-all policy in such areas as finance, legal guidelines, and growth rate will be centralized.

In general, however, people will expect to influence the position and role that they perform in the organization. They will want to be part of an organization that is relevant to the problems of the day and to the community. The old methods of inducing people to be loyal to the organization will no longer be appropriate. Individuals will be increasingly concerned with their own self-actualization and will be more loyal to themselves and their profession rather than to organizations.

Organizations must capitalize on this motivation by structuring jobs which allow a greater sense of self-fulfillment and job enrichment. In addition, organizations will be able to secure individual commitment and loyalty only if they prove that the work and organization objectives are relevant to both individual aspirations and social objectives.

Implications for Administrators. They must

- help clarify which decisions will be centralized (system type) and which will be decentralized (human work type).
- help people within the organization to establish targets and to achieve them. This will involve helping people "to do their own thing."
- begin to see the organization as a system designed to release human energy rather than to control human energy.
- realize that organizations, like individuals, pass through levels of maturity, and that very often they get bogged down at the level of maintaining the status quo when they should be growing toward a mastery of change.
- help the over-all organization set targets and objectives, particularly in relation to the development of human resources.

7. *Conflict, confrontation, and stress will continue as a norm of organizational life.* We must begin to recognize that confrontation is not necessarily undesirable, but a way in which people "lay it on the line" and "tell it as it is." Millions of creative ideas have been lost in organizations whose climate does not allow for honest differences in judgments and opinions. Many times pertinent points of view are "filtered out" before they get to

top management. We must strive to avoid a win-lose concept in organizational and societal life and substitute, wherever possible, the concept of win-win. Openness, candor, and frank feedback should not be equated with hostility or obstructionism. Quite the contrary: those who shut off the ideas and contributions of their subordinates are really the obstructionists. We will find an increasing need to use confrontation and conflict in a constructive way. People are no longer ready to accept blindly the judgment or actions of bosses, superiors, or organizational leaders.

Organizations of the future will require the utilization of skills in confrontation by those *inside* an organization. Hospital change can effectively be brought about by internal confrontation of situations, rather than by reacting only to external confrontation by those who may have little concern for long-range maturity of the organization.

Organizations get into trouble because they become blind to their own defects. They cannot solve their problems because they cannot see them.

In using confrontation meetings, employe "rap" sessions, labor negotiations, or other means of dealing with more open communications, there will be a need for an organization in the future to require *confrontation, search,* and *coping.*

We hear a great deal today about confrontation. Youths are confronting organizational management as well as their elders; minority groups are confronting local communities. Patients and others concerned with rising costs confront the hospital. Confrontation today is part and parcel of life. Administrators should expect confrontation to increase rather than subside. On the other hand, this is not undesirable, for confrontation can be a very valuable thing. The management of a hospital cannot change their organization or way of managing unless they con-

front the present inadequacy of the organization and the management's need to improve.

Implications for Administrators. Hospital administrators must help themselves and others learn how to handle conflict and to recognize that confrontation is not simply a technique of "how to fight." As professionals, we must encourage the expressing of convictions and accept other points of view.

Administrators must be willing to confront others with the insistence that clear-cut objectives be identified before any commitment is made to a specific program, budgets, or equipment. They should change the rewards systems in organizations as a means of rewarding new kinds of behavior that contribute to an "open" system. The manager must help the organization determine when confrontation and conflict are appropriate and how they can be used constructively, and when they are not appropriate and could be destructive.

Many hospital managers, however, feel that if they have confronted an organization crisis, their problems are solved and they have coped. This is not necessarily true. It usually is necessary for people to search for ways to work on the process of understanding each other, communicating with each other, solving problems, making decisions, and planning new activities, new programs, and new ways to get people appropriately involved. It is the search for unique and innovative ways to solve organizational problems that will characterize the organization of the future. Search is the key to whether or not coping will take place, because coping means something more than just decision making or problem solving. Coping means confronting a problem and searching for ways of working on it, of learning how to solve similar problems, more problems, and new problems.

8. *Effective face-to-face groups will be*

the key unit of organizational accomplishment. Recent research has recognized the importance of the group as the key unit in the life of the organization. This recognition has been made particularly evident as a result of productivity and morale studies research. Likert comments on the importance of organizational work units:

Each of us seeks to satisfy our desire for a sense of personal worth and importance primarily by the response we get from people we are close to, in whom we are interested, and whose approval and support we are eager to have. The face-to-face groups with whom we spend the bulk of our time are, consequently, the most important to us. Our work group is one of the most important of our face-to-face groups and one from which we are particularly eager to derive a sense of personal worth.[13]

Studies in psychology, sociology, and psychiatry reinforce this statement. It clearly indicates that if an organization is to make the maximum use of the human resources and meet the highest level of man's needs, it will come to function best in situations where the individual relates effectively to those organizational groups of which he is a member and a leader. Such well-knit and effective face-to-face work units will develop out of conditions which provide the trusting relationship between supervisor and members.

As organizations grow more complex and larger, the peer relationship of a work unit is even more crucial. A group can influence the larger system better than the lonely individual.

Implications for Administrators. In the multiple roles in which the administrator finds himself, he must recognize the necessity of taking into account factors of

interdependence with the multiple groups in a hospital. Supervisors must serve as helpers, trainers, consultants, coordinators, and stimulators of their own work unit. The supervisor must exercise his many roles in a sensitive, insightful, and diagnostic manner. Such group skill should be the focus of an enlightened supervisory-training program.

The most frequently advocated organization improvement practice has been the development and building of face-to-face groups (subsystems) of a permanent or temporary nature in the organization. In team-building sessions, the members of these groups are given an opportunity to analyze teamwork factors and to introduce the element of teamwork throughout the organization.

In addition to the top executive group in the organization, it is desirable to create the kind of teamwork that will make it possible for all functional groups to work effectively together, for project groups to relate effectively, and for professional specialists to build a cohesive work unit that will contribute to growth and goals. In other words, a key need in the organization of the future will be to utilize groups effectively.

9. *The utilization and application of general system concepts in organizations.* Another series of activities or processes that will be more evident in organizations of the future will revolve about the systems approach to the organization that should and can affect the total organization.

The concept of socio-technical systems is based on the reality that any production or service system like a hospital requires both a technology and a work-relationship structure that relates human resources to technological resources. In this context, a hospital's total system provides the total set of human activities together with inter-relationships to the techno - physical-financial resources and the process to make and deliver health care services. To

[13] R. Likert, *Developing Patterns of Management*, American Management Association, New York City, No. 182, 1956, p. 7.

think about an organization as a socio-technical system helps make viable the man-machine relationships of the future. Another way of looking at socio-technical systems has been to see them as an energy exchange system:

A more recent way of looking at corporations is to consider them as energy exchange systems in which there is an input of energy from the environment, and a patterned internal activity that transforms the energy into output, which in turn provokes a new energy input. The corporation is thus seen as an open system engaged in constant transactions with its environment, which can be visualized as a system of systems. These systems include the sub-systems within the corporations (divisions, departments) which are constantly engaged in energy exchanges, and the systems operating outside the corporation, but affecting it—other members of the same industry, members of competing industries, suppliers, government institutions, etc. The energy exchanges—transactions—that take place both internally and externally occur in a field of force operating in space/time and made up of all the patterned but individual desires and aspirations of all the people who make up both internal and external environmental systems. This way of looking at a corporation offers a picture that is fairly close to modern physical theory and one which should be capable of expression and measurement in scientific, quantitative terms.[14]

The following three types of systems are sometimes distinguished according to the kind of interaction between the system and its environment: (1) *absolutely closed systems*, where no interaction with the environment is considered; (2) *relatively closed systems*, where little interaction with the environment acts upon the system (inputs) as well as the paths over which the system acts on the environment (outputs) are narrowly defined; (3) *open systems*, where all possible effects of the environment on the system and vice versa are considered.

All organization systems and sub-systems, from the smallest group (a dyad) to the most complex multigroup structure of an international organization, include in their makeup common elements and processes. Without attention to these elements and processes the system cannot function effectively. Attention has been given to improved financial systems, information systems, decision-making systems, and communication processes. *All* of these approaches are essential to hospitals of the future.

Implications for Administrators. The future-oriented hospital administrator will need to be aware, knowledgeable, and skillful in the systems field. Managers will need to interrelate the various operating and human systems.

summary

This list of characteristics of organizations of the future is incomplete and selective. However, a model of the future potential of man's organizations must be developed to elicit action that will be on the frontier of this transitional generation. Table 2 represents characteristics of a future-oriented organization.[15]

The proper approach to hospital renewal no longer considers medical or management technology apart from the human element within the organization or the larger environment. As a result of a historic trend away from the purely mechanistic, the directed development of organizations in the future is now flexibly oriented to specific tasks and values in a known organizational climate.

[14] Don Fabun, "The Corporation as a Creative Environment," *Kaiser Aluminum News*, No. 2, 1967, p. 12.

[15] Adapted from an unpublished paper written by Malcolm Knowles, PhD, Boston University.

Table 2.   **Characteristics of Status vs. Future-Oriented Organizations**

	Characteristics	
Dimensions	*Static Organizations*	*Future-Oriented Organizations*
Structure	Rigid: permanent committees; reverence for constitution & bylaws, tradition Hierarchical: chain of command Role definitions: narrow Property: bound and restricted	Flexible: temporary task force; readiness to change constitution & bylaws, depart from tradition Linking: functional collaboration Role definitions: broad Property: mobile and regional
Atmosphere	Internally competitive Task-centered: reserved Cold, formal: aloof	Goal-oriented People-centered: caring Warm, informal: intimate
Management & Philosophy	Controlling: coercive power Cautious : low risk Errors: to be prevented Emphasis on personnel selection Self-sufficient: closed system re: resources Emphasis on conserving resources Low tolerance for ambiguity	Releasing: supportive power Experimental: high risk Errors: to be learned from Emphasis on personnel development Interdependent: open system re: resources Emphasis on developing and using resources High tolerance for ambiguity
Decision making & Policy making	High participation at top, low at bottom Clear distinction between policy making and execution Decision making by legal mechanisms Decisions treated as final	Relevant participation by all those affected Collaborative policy making and execution Decision making by problem solving Decisions treated as hypotheses to be tested
Communication	Restricted flow: constipated One-way: downward Feelings: repressed or hidden	Open flow: easy access Two-way: upward and downward Feelings: expressed

"Future shock" is neither a disease nor a disaster; it is a dilemma created by too many problems coming too fast from too many directions for traditional problem-solving tools and techniques to handle. It seems that groups of "Argus men," aided by both cybernetics (systems analysis) and electronic computation—as well as by behavioral scientists—are capable of integrating multi-man skills and disciplines into antidotal, discreet problem-solving organic entities of the future. There is an urgent need to develop and perfect this morphology, a new science of man/machine/organization dynamics.

Success starts with awareness. If the hospital managers are not aware of the need for renewal, it is foolish to think that the process will ever be achieved. As Alfred North Whitehead has warned:

The art of free society consists first in the maintenance of the symbolic code, and secondly, in the fearlessness of revision. . . . Those societies which cannot combine reverence to their symbols with freedom of revision must ultimately decay. . . .

Hospital managers in the future may see stagnation and decay as the order of the day unless they develop socio-technical structures and processes that engender resilience, renewal, and a "fearlessness of revision." This is not easy, but it is a necessary task.

directing

13. a new look at managerial decision making

Victor H. Vroom

All managers are decision makers. Furthermore, their effectiveness as managers is largely reflected in their "track record" in making the "right decisions." These "right decisions" in turn largely depend on whether or not the manager has utilized the right person or persons in the right ways in helping him solve the problem.

Our concern in this article is with decision making as a social process. We view the manager's task as determining how the problem is to be solved, not the solution to be adopted. Within that overall framework, we have attempted to answer two broad sets of questions: What decision-making processes should managers use to deal effectively with the problems they encounter in their jobs? What decision-making processes do they use in dealing with these problems and

Reprinted by permission of the publisher from *Organizational Dynamics*, Spring 1973 © 1973 by AMACOM, a division of American Management Associations.

what considerations affect their decisions about how much to share their decision-making power with subordinates?

The reader will recognize the former as a normative or prescriptive question. A rational and analytic answer to it would constitute a normative model of decision making as a social process. The second question is descriptive, since it concerns how managers do, rather than should, behave.

toward a normal model

About four years ago, Philip Yetton, then a graduate student at Carnegie-Mellon University, and I began a major research program in an attempt to answer these normative and descriptive questions.

We began with the normative question. What would be a rational way of deciding on the form and amount of participation in decision making that should be used in different situations? We were tired of debates over the relative merits of Theory X and Theory Y and of the truism that leadership depends upon the situation. We felt that it was time for the behavioral sciences to move beyond such generalities and to attempt to come to grips with the complexities of the phenomena with which they intended to deal.

Our aim was ambitious—to develop a set of ground rules for matching a manager's leadership behavior to the demands of the situation. It was critical that these ground rules be consistent with research evidence concerning the consequences of participation and that the model based on the rules be operational, so that any manager could see it to determine how he should act in any decision-making situation.

Table 1 shows a set of alternative decision processes that we have employed in our research. Each process is represented by a symbol (e.g., AI, CI, GII) that will be used as a convenient method of referring to each process. The first letter in

this symbol signifies the basic properties of the process (A stands for autocratic; C for consultative; and G for group). The Roman numerals that follow the first letter constitute variants on that process. Thus, AI represents the first variant on an autocratic process, and AII the second variant.

conceptual and empirical basis of the model

A model designed to regulate, in some rational way, choices among the decisions processes shown in Table I should be based on sound empirical evidence concerning the likely consequences of the styles. The more complete the empirical base of knowledge, the greater the certainty with which we can develop the model and the greater will be its usefulness. To aid in understanding the conceptual basis of the model, it is important to distinguish among three classes of out-

Table I.   Types of Management Decision Styles

AI	You solve the problem or make the decision yourself, using information available to you at that time
AII	You obtain the necessary information from your subordinate(s), then decide on the solution to the problem yourself. You may or may not tell your subordinates what the problem is in getting the information from them. The role played by your subordinates in making the decision is clearly one of providing the necessary information to you, rather than generating or evaluating alternative solutions
CI	You share the problem with relevant subordinates individually, getting their ideas and suggestions without bringing them together as a group. Then *you* make the decision that may or may not reflect your subordinates' influence
CII	You share the problem with your subordinates as a group, collectively obtaining their ideas and suggestions. Then *you* make the decision that may or may not reflect your subordinates' influence
GII	You share a problem with your subordinates as a group. Together you generate and evaluate alternatives and attempt to reach agreement (consensus) on a solution. Your role is much like that of chairman. You do not try to influence the group to adopt "your" solution and you are willing to accept and implement any solution that has the support of the entire group

(GI is omitted because it applies only to more comprehensive models outside the scope of the article)

comes that bear on the ultimate effectiveness of decisions. These are:

1. The quality or rationality of the decision.
2. The acceptance or commitment on the part of subordinates to execute the decision effectively.
3. The amount of time required to make the decision.

The effects of participation on each of these outcomes or consequences were summed up by the author in *The Handbook of Social Psychology* as follows:

The results suggest that allocating problem solving and decision-making tasks to entire groups requires a greater investment of man hours but produces higher acceptance of decisions and a higher probability that the decision will be executed efficiently. Differences between these two methods in quality of decisions and in elapsed time are inconclusive and probably highly variable . . . It would be naive to think that group decision making is always more "effective" than autocratic decision making, or vice versa; the relative effectiveness of these two extreme methods depends both on the weights attached to quality, acceptance and time variables and on differences in amounts of these outcomes resulting from these methods, neither of which is invariant from one situation to another. The critics and proponents of participative management would do well to direct their efforts toward identifying the properties of situations in which different decision-making approaches are effective rather than wholesale condemnation or deification of one approach.

We have gone on from there to identify the properties of the situation or problem that will be the basic elements in the model. These problem attributes are of two types: (1) Those that specify the importance for a particular problem of quality and acceptance, and (2) those that, on the basis of available evidence, have a high probability of moderating the effects of participation on each of these outcomes. Table II shows the problem attributes used in the present form of the model. For each

Table II. Problem Attributes Used in the Model

Problem Attributes	Diagnostic Questions
A. The importance of the quality of the decision	Is there a quality requirement such that one solution is likely to be more rational than another?
B. The extent to which the leader possesses sufficient information/expertise to make a high-quality decision by himself	Do I have sufficient information to make a high-quality decision?
C. The extent to which the problem is structured.	Is the problem structured?
D. The extent to which acceptance or commitment on the part of subordinates is critical to the effective implementation of the decision	Is acceptance of decision by subordinates critical to effective implementation?
E. The prior probability that the leader's autocratic decision will receive acceptance by subordinates	If you were to make the decision by yourself, is it reasonably certain that it would be accepted by your subordinates?
F. The extent to which subordinates are motivated to attain the organizational goals as represented in the objectives explicit in the statement of the problem	Do subordinates share the organizational goals to be obtained in solving this problem?
G. The extent to which subordinates are likely to be in conflict over preferred solutions	Is conflict among subordinates likely in preferred solutions?

attribute a question is provided that might be used by a leader in diagnosing a particular problem prior to choosing his leadership style.

In phrasing the questions, we have held technical language to a minimum. Furthermore, we have phrased the questions in Yes–No form, translating the continuous variables defined above into dichotomous variables. For example, instead of attempting to determine how important the decision quality is to the effectiveness of the decision (attribute A), the leader is asked in the first question to judge whether there is any quality component to the problem. Similarly, the difficult task of specifying exactly how much information the leader possesses that is relevant to the decision (attribute B) is reduced to a simple judgment by the leader concerning whether or not he has sufficient information to make a high quality decision.

We have found that managers can diagnose a situation quickly and accurately by answering this set of seven questions concerning it. But how can such responses generate a prescription concerning the most effective leadership style or decision process? What kind of normative model of participation in decision making can be built from this set of problem attributes?

Figure 1 shows one such model expressed in the form of a decision tree. It is the seventh version of such a model that we have developed over the last three years. The problem attributes, expressed in question form, are arranged along the top of the figure. To use the model for a particular decision-making situation, one starts at the left-hand side and works toward the right asking oneself the

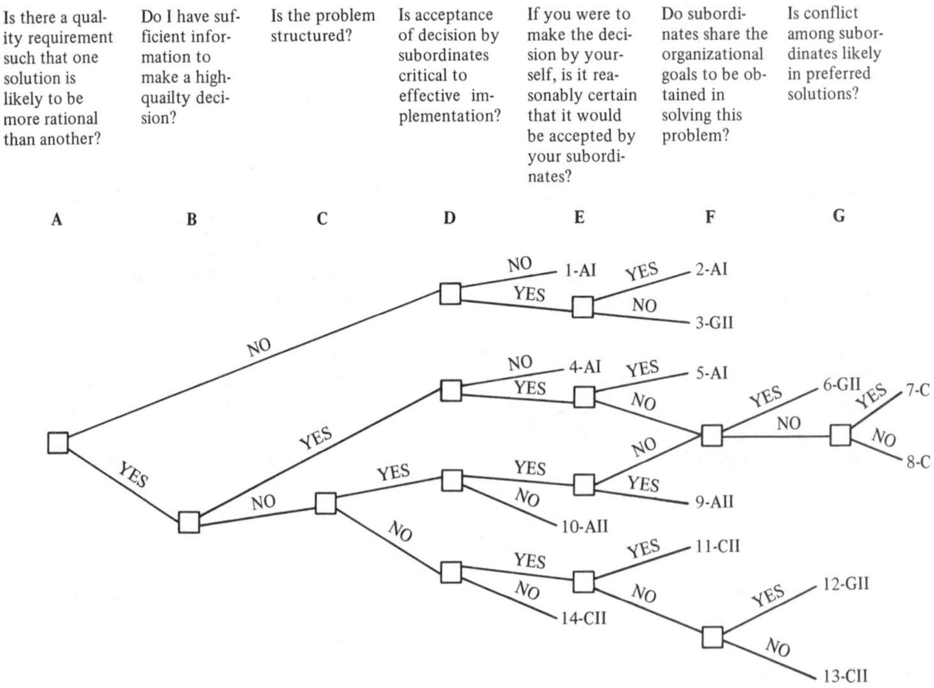
Is there a quality requirement such that one solution is likely to be more rational than another?
Do I have sufficient information to make a high-quailty decision?
Is the problem structured?
Is acceptance of decision by subordinates critical to effective implementation?
If you were to make the decision by yourself, is it reasonably certain that it would be accepted by your subordinates?
Do subordinates share the organizational goals to be obtained in solving this problem?
Is conflict among subordinates likely in preferred solutions?
A
B
C
D
E
F
G
NO
YES
1-AI
2-AI
3-GII
4-AI
5-AI
6-GII
7-C
8-C
9-AII
10-AII
11-CII
12-GII
13-CII
14-CII

Figure 1. Decision Model.

question immediately above any box that is encountered. When a terminal node is reached, a number will be found designating the problem type and one of the decision-making processes appearing in Table I. AI is prescribed for four problem types (1, 2, 4, and 5); AII is prescribed for two problem types (9 and 10); CI is prescribed for only one problem type (8); CII is prescribed for four problem types (7, 11, 13, and 14); and GII is prescribed for three problem types (3, 6, and 12). The relative frequency with which each of the five decision processes would be prescribed for any manager would, of course, depend on the distribution of problem types encountered in his decision making.

Rationale Underlying the Model: The decision processes specified for each problem type are not arbitrary. The model's behavior is governed by a set of principles intended to be consistent with existing evidence concerning the consequences of participation in decision making on organizational effectiveness.

There are two mechanisms underlying the behavior of the model. The first is a set of seven rules that serve to protect the quality and the acceptance of the decision by eliminating alternatives that risk one or the other of these decision outcomes. Once the rules have been applied, a feasible set of decision processes is generated. The second mechanism is a principle for choosing among alternatives in the feasible set where more than one exists.

Let us examine the rules first, because they do much of the work of the model. As previously indicated, the rules are intended to protect both the quality and acceptance of the decision. In the form of the model shown, there are three rules that protect decision quality and four that protect acceptance.

1. *The Information Rule.* If the quality of the decision is important and if the leader does not possess enough informa-

tion or expertise to solve the problem by himself, AI is eliminated from the feasible set. (Its use risks a low-quality decision.)

2. *The Goal Congruence Rule.* If the quality of the decision is important and if the subordinates do not share the organizational goals to be obtained in solving the problem, GII is eliminated from the feasible set. (Alternatives that eliminate the leader's final control over the decision reached may jeopardize the quality of the decision.)

3. *The Unstructured Problem Rule.* In decisions in which the quality of the decision is important, if the leader lacks the necessary information or expertise to solve the problem by himself, and if the problem is unstructured, i.e., he does not know exactly what information is needed and where it is located, the method used must provide not only for him to collect the information but to do so in an efficient and effective manner. Methods that involve interaction among all subordinates with full knowledge of the problem are likely to be both more efficient and more likely to generate a high-quality solution to the problem. Under these conditions, AI, AII, and CI are eliminated from the feasible set. (AI does not provide for him to collect the necessary information, and AII and CI represent more cumbersome, less effective, and less efficient means of bringing the necessary information to bear on the solution of the problem than methods that do permit those with the necessary information to interact.)

4. *The Acceptance Rule.* If the acceptance of the decision by subordinates is critical to effective implementation, and if it is not certain that an autocratic decision made by the leader would receive that acceptance, AI and AII are eliminated from the feasible set. (Neither provides an opportunity for subordinates to participate in the decision and both risk the necessary acceptance.)

5. *The Conflict Rule.* If the acceptance

of the decision is critical, and an autocratic decision is not certain to be accepted, and subordinates are likely to be in conflict or disagreement over the appropriate solution, AI, AII, and CI are eliminated from the feasible set. (The method used in solving the problem should enable those in disagreement to resolve their differences with full knowledge of the problem. Accordingly, under these conditions, AI, AII, and CI, which involve no interaction or only "one-on-one" relationships and therefore provide no opportunity for those in conflict to resolve their differences, are eliminated from the feasible set. Their use runs the risk of leaving some of the subordinates with less than the necessary commitment to the final decision.)

6. *The Fairness Rule.* If the quality of decision is unimportant and if acceptance is critical and not certain to result from an autocratic decision, AI, AII, CI, and CII are eliminated from the feasible set. (The method used should maximize the probability of acceptance as this is the only relevant consideration in determining the effectiveness of the decision. Under these circumstances, AI, AII, CI, and CII, which create less acceptance or commitment than GII, are eliminated from the feasible set. To use them is to run the risk of getting less than the needed acceptance of the decision.)

7. *The Acceptance Priority Rule.* If acceptance is critical, not assured by an autocratic decision, and if subordinates can be trusted, AI, AII, CI, and CII are eliminated from the feasible set. (Methods that provide equal partnership in the decision-making process can provide greater acceptance without risking decision quality. Use of any method other than GII results in an unnecessary risk that the decision will not be fully accepted or receive the necessary commitment on the part of subordinates.)

Once all seven rules have been applied to a given problem, we emerge with a feasible set of decision processes. The feasible set for each of the fourteen problem types is shown in Table III. It can be seen that there are some problem types for which only one method remains in the feasible set, others for which two methods remain feasible, and still others for which five methods remain feasible.

Table III. Problem Types and the Feasible Set of Decision Processes

Problem Type	Acceptable Methods
1	AI, AII, CI, CII, GII
2	AI, AII, CI, CII, GII
3	GII
4	AI, AII, CI, CII, GII*
5	AI, AII, CI, CII, GII*
6	GII
7	CII
8	CI, CII
9	AII, CI, CII, GII*
10	AII, CI, CII, GII*
11	CII, GII*
12	GII
13	CII
14	CII, GII*

*Within the feasible set only when the answer to question F is Yes.

When more than one method remains in the feasible set, there are a number of ways in which one might choose among them. The mechanism we have selected and the principle underlying the choices of the model in Figure 1 utilize the number of man-hours used in solving the problem as the basis for choice. Given a set of methods with equal likelihood of meeting both quality and acceptance requirements for the decision, it chooses that method that requires the least investment in man-hours. On the basis of the empirical evidence summarized earlier, this is deemed to be the method furthest to the left within the feasible set. For example since AI, AII, CI, CII, and GII are all feasible as in Problem Types 1 and 2, AI would be the method chosen.

To illustrate application of the model in actual administrative situations, we will analyze four cases with the help of the model. While we attempt to describe these cases as completely as is necessary to permit the reader to make the judgments required by the model, there may remain some room for subjectivity. The reader may wish after reading the case to analyze it himself using the model and then to compare his analysis with that of the author.

Case I. You are a manufacturing manager in a large electronics plant. The company's management has recently installed new machines and put in a new simplified work system, but to the surprise of everyone, yourself included, the expected increase in productivity was not realized. In fact, production has begun to drop, quality has fallen off, and the number of employee separations has risen.

You do not believe that there is anything wrong with the machines. You have had reports from other companies that are using them and they confirm this opinion. You have also had representatives from the firm that built the machines go over them and they report that they are operating at peak efficiency.

You suspect that some parts of the new work system may be responsible for the change, but this view is not widely shared among your immediate subordinates who are four first-line supervisors, each in charge of a section, and your supply manager. The drop in production has been variously attributed to poor training of the operators, lack of an adequate system of financial incentives, and poor morale. Clearly, this is an issue about which there is considerable depth of feeling within individuals and potential disagreement among your subordinates.

This morning you received a phone call from your division manager. He had just received your production figures for the last six months and was calling to express his concern. He indicated that the problem was yours to solve in any way that you think best, but that he would like to know within a week what steps you plan to take.

You share your division manager's concern with the falling productivity and know that your men are also concerned. The problem is to decide what steps to take to rectify the situation.

Analysis
> Questions—
>> A (Quality?) = Yes
>> B (Managers Information?) = No
>> C (Structured?) = No
>> D (Acceptance?) = Yes
>> E (Prior Probability of Acceptance?) = No
>> F (Goal Congruence?) = Yes
>> G (Conflict?) = Yes
>
> Problem Type—12
> Feasible Set—GII
> Minimum Man-Hours Solution (from Figure 1)—GII
> Rule Violations—
>> AI violates rules 1, 3, 4, 5, 7
>> AII violates rules 3, 4, 5, 7
>> CI violates rules 3, 5, 7
>> CII violates rule 7

Case II. You are general foreman in charge of a large gang laying an oil pipeline and have to estimate your expected rate of progress in order to schedule material deliveries to the next field site.

You know the nature of the terrain you will be traveling and have the historical data needed to compute the mean and variance in the rate of speed over that type of terrain. Given these two variables, it is a simple matter to calculate the earliest and latest times at which materials and support facilities will be needed at the next site. It is important that your estimate be reasonably accurate. Underestimates result in idle foremen and workers, and an overestimate results in tying up materials for a period of time before they are to be used.

Progress has been good and your five foremen and other members of the gang stand to receive substantial bonuses if the project is completed ahead of schedule.

Analysis

Questions—

A (Quality?) = Yes

B (Manager's Information?) = Yes

D (Acceptance?) = No

Problem Type—4

Feasible Set—AI, AII, CI, CII, GII

Minimum Man-Hours Solution (from Figure 1)—AI

Rule Violations—None

Case III. You are supervising the work of 12 engineers. Their formal training and work experience are very similar, permitting you to use them interchangeably on projects. Yesterday your manager informed you that a request had been received from an overseas affiliate for four engineers to go abroad on extended loan for a period of six to eight months. For a number of reasons, he argued and you agreed that this request should be met from your group.

All your engineers are capable of handling this assignment and, from the standpoint of present and future projects, there is no particular reason why anyone should be retained over any other. The problem is somewhat complicated by the fact that the overseas assignment is in what is generally regarded as an undesirable location.

Analysis

Questions—

A (Quality?) = No

D (Acceptance?) = Yes

E (Prior Probability of Acceptance?) = No

G (Conflict?) = Yes

Problem Type—3

Feasible Set—GII

Minimum Man-Hours Solution (from Figure 1)—GII

Rule Violations—

AI and AII violate rules 4, 5, and 6

CI violates rules 5 and 6

CII violates rule 6

Case IV. You are on the division manager's staff and work on a wide variety of problems of both an administrative and technical nature. You have been given the assignment of developing a standard method to be used in each of the five plants in the division for manually reading equipment registers, recording the readings, and transmitting the scorings to a centralized information system.

Until now there has been a high error rate in the reading and/or transmittal of the data. Some locations have considerably higher error rates than others, and the methods used to record and transmit the data vary among plants. It is probable, therefore, that part of the error variance is a function of specific local conditions rather than anything else, and this will complicate the establishment of any system common to all plants. You have the information on error rates but no information on the local practices that generate these errors or on the local conditions that necessitate the different practices.

Everyone would benefit from an improvement in the quality of the data; it is used in a number of important decisions. Your contacts with the plants are through the quality-control supervisors who are responsible for collecting the data. They are a conscientious group committed to doing their jobs well, but are highly sensitive to interference on the part of higher management in their own operations. Any solution that does not receive the active support of the various plant supervisors is unlikely to reduce the error rate significantly.

Analysis

Questions—

    A (Quality?) = Yes

    B (Manager's Information?) = No

    C (Structured?) = No

    D (Acceptance?) = Yes

    E (Prior Probability of Acceptance?) = No

    F (Goal Congruence?) = Yes

Problem Type—12

Feasible Set—GII

Minimum Man-Hours Solution (from Figure 1)—GII

Rule Violations—

    AI violates rules 1, 3, 4, and 7

    AII violates rules 3, 4, and 7

    CI violates rules 3 and 7

    CII violates rule 7

short versus long-term models

The model described above seeks to protect the quality of the decision and to expend the least number of man-hours in the process. Because it focuses on conditions surrounding the making and implementation of a particular decision rather than any long-term considerations, we can term it a short-term model.

It seems likely, however, that the leadership methods that may be optimal for short-term results may be different from those that would be optimal over a longer period of time. Consider a leader, for example, who has been uniformly pursuing an autocratic style (AI or AII) and, perhaps as a consequence, has subordinates who might be termed "yes men" (attribute E) but who also cannot be trusted to pursue organizational goals (attribute F), largely because the leader has never bothered to explain them.

It appears likely, however, that the manager who used more participative methods would, in time, change the status of these problem attributes so as to develop ultimately a more effective prob-

lem-solving system. A promising approach to the development of a long-term model is one that places less weight on man-hours as the basis for choice of method within the feasible set. Given a long-term orientation, one would be interested in the possibility of a trade-off between man-hours in problem solving and team development, both of which increase with participation. Viewed in these terms, the time-minimizing model places maximum relative weight on man-hours and no weight on development, and hence chooses the style farthest to the left within the feasible set. A model that places less weight on man-hours and more weight on development would, if these assumptions are correct, choose a style further to the right within the feasible set.

We recognize, of course, that the minimum man-hours solution suggested by the model is not always the best solution to every problem. A manager faced, for example, with the problem of handling any one of the four cases previously examined might well choose more time-consuming alternatives on the grounds that the greater time invested would be justified in developing his subordinates. Similar considerations exist in other decision-making situations. For this reason we have come to emphasize the feasible set of decision methods in our work with managers. Faced with considerations not included in the model, the manager should consider any alternative within the feasible set, not opt automatically for the minimum man-hours solution.

As I am writing this, I have in front of me a "black box" that constitutes an electronic version of the normative model discussed on the preceding pages. (The author is indebted to Peter Fuss of Bell Telephone Laboratories for his interest in the model and his skill in developing the "black box.") The box, which is small enough to fit into the palm of one hand, has a set of seven switches, each appropriately labeled with the questions (A through G) used in Figure 1. A manager faced with a concrete problem or decision can "diagnose" that problem by setting each switch in either its "yes" or "no" position. Once the problem has been described, the manager depresses a button that illuminates at least one or as many as five lights, each of which denotes one of the decision processes (AI, AII, etc.). The lights that are illuminated constitute the feasible set of decision processes for the problem as shown in Table III. The lights not illuminated correspond to alternatives that violate one or more of the seven rules previously stated.

In this prototype version of the box, the lights are illuminated in decreasing order of brightness from left to right within the feasible set. The brightest light corresponds to the alternative shown in Figure 1. Thus, if both CII and GII were feasible alternatives, CII would be brighter than GII, since it requires fewer man-hours. However, a manager who was not under any undue time pressure and who wished to invest time in the development of his subordinates might select an alternative corresponding to one of the dimmer lights.

toward a descriptive model of leader behavior

So far we have been concerned with the normative questions defined at the outset. But how do managers really behave? What considerations affect their decision about how much to share their decision-making power with their subordinates? In what respects is their behavior different from or similar to that of the model? These questions are but a few of those that we attempted to answer in a large-scale research program aimed at gaining a greater understanding of the factors that influence managers in their choice of decision processes to fit the demands of

the situation. This research program was financially supported by the McKinsey Foundation, General Electric Foundation, Smith Richardson Foundation, and the Office of Naval Research.

Two different research methods have been utilized in studying these factors. The first investigation utilized a method that we have come to term "recalled problems." Over 500 managers from 11 different countries representing a variety of firms were asked to provide a written description of a problem that they had recently had to solve. These varied in length from one paragraph to several pages and covered virtually every facet of managerial decision making. For each case, the manager was asked to indicate which of the decision processes shown in Table I they used to solve the problem. Finally, each manager was asked to answer the questions shown in Table II corresponding to the problem attributes used in the normative model.

The wealth of data, both qualitative and quantitative, served two purposes. Since each manager had diagnosed a situation that he had encountered in terms that are used in the normative model and had indicated the methods that he had used in dealing with it, it is possible to determine what differences, if any, there were between the model's behavior and his own behavior. Second, the written cases provided the basis for the construction of a standard set of cases used in later research to determine the factors that influence managers to share or retain their decision-making power. Each case depicted a manager faced with a problem to solve or decision to make. The cases spanned a wide range of managerial problems including production scheduling, quality control, portfolio management, personnel allocation, and research and development. In each case, a person could readily assume the role of the manager described and could indicate which of the decision processes he would use if he actually were faced with that situation.

In most of our research, a set of thirty cases has been used and the subjects have been several thousand managers who were participants in management development programs in the United States and abroad. Cases were selected systematically. We desired cases that could not only be coded unambiguously in the terms used in the normative model but that would also permit the assessment of the effects of each of the problem attributes used in the model on the person's behavior. The solution was to select cases in accordance with an experimental design so that they varied in terms of the seven attributes used in the model and variation in each attribute was independent of each other attribute. Several such standardized sets of cases have been developed, and over a thousand managers have now been studied using this approach.

To summarize everything we learned in the course of this research is well beyond the scope of this paper, but it is possible to discuss some of the highlights. Since the results obtained from the two research methods—recalled and standardized problems—are consistent, we can present the major results independent of the method used.

Perhaps the most striking finding is the weakening of the widespread view that participativeness is a general trait that individual managers exhibit in different amounts. To be sure, there were differences *among* managers in their general tendencies to utilize participative methods as opposed to autocratic ones. On the standardized problems, these differences accounted for about 10 percent of the total variance in the decision processes observed. These differences in behavior between managers, however, were small in comparison with differences *within* managers. On the standardized problems, no manager has indicated that he would use the same decision process on all problems or decisions, and most use all five methods under some circumstances.

Some of this variance in behavior within managers can be attributed to widely shared tendencies to respond to some situations by sharing power and others by retaining it. It makes more sense to talk about participative and autocratic situations than it does to talk about participative and autocratic managers. In fact, on the standardized problems, the variance in behavior across problems or cases is about three times as large as the variance across managers!

What are the characteristics of an autocratic as opposed to a participative situation? An answer to this question would constitute a partial descriptive model of this aspect of the decision-making process and has been our goal in much of the research that we have conducted. From our observations of behavior on both recalled problems and on standardized problems, it is clear that the decision-making process employed by a typical manager is influenced by a large number of factors, many of which also show up in the normative model. Following are several conclusions substantiated by the results on both recalled and standardized problems: Managers use decision processes providing less opportunity for participation (1) when they possess all the necessary information than when they lack some of the needed information, (2) when the problem that they face is well-structured rather than unstructured, (3) when their subordinates' acceptance of the decision is not critical for the effective implementation of the decision or when the prior probability of acceptance of an autocratic decision is high, and (4) when the personal goals of their subordinates are *not* congruent with the goals of the organization as manifested in the problem.

So far we have been talking about relatively common or widely shared ways of dealing with organizational problems. Our results strongly suggest that there are ways of "tailoring" one's approach to the situation that distinguish managers from one another. Theoretically, these can be thought of as differences among managers in decision rules that they employ about when to encourage participation. Statistically, they are represented as interactions between situational variables and personal characteristics.

Consider, for example, two managers who have identical distributions of the use of the five decision processes shown in Table I on a set of thirty cases. In a sense, they are equally participative (or autocratic). However, the situations in which they permit or encourage participation in decision making on the part of their subordinates may be very different. One may restrict the participation of his subordinates to decisions without a quality requirement, whereas the other may restrict their participation to problems with a quality requirement. The former would be more inclined to use participative decision processes (like GII) on such decisions as what color the walls should be painted or when the company picnic should be held. The latter would be more likely to encourage participation in decision making on decisions that have a clear and demonstrable impact on the organization's success in achieving its external goals.

Use of the standardized problem set permits the assessment of such differences in decision rules that govern choices among decision-making processes. Since the cases are selected in accordance with an experimental design, they can indicate differences in the behavior of managers attributable not only to the existence of a quality requirement in the problem but also in the effects of acceptance requirements, conflict, information requirements, and the like.

The research using both recalled and standardized problems has also enabled us to examine similarities and differences between the behavior of the normative model and the behavior of a typical manager. Such an analysis reveals, at the very least, what behavioral changes could be expected if managers began using the normative model as the basis for choosing their decision-making processes.

A typical manager says he would (or did) use exactly the same decision process as that shown in Figure 1 in 40 percent of the situations. In two thirds of the situations, his behavior is consistent with the feasible set of methods proposed in the model. In other words, in about one third of the situations his behavior violates at least one of the seven rules underlying the model.

The four rules designed to protect the acceptance or commitment of the decision have substantially higher probabilities of being violated than do the three rules designed to protect the quality or rationality of the decision. One of the acceptance rules, the Fairness Rule (Rule 6) is violated about three quarters of the time that it could have been violated. On the other hand, one of the quality rules, the Information Rule (Rule 1) is violated in only about 3 percent of occasions in which it is applicable. If we assume for the moment that these two sets of rules have equal validity, these findings strongly suggest that the decisions made by typical managers are more likely to prove ineffective due to deficiencies of acceptance by subordinates than due to deficiencies in decision quality.

Another striking difference between the behavior of the model and of the typical manager lies in the fact that the former shows far greater variance with the situation. If a typical manager voluntarily used the model as the basis for choosing his methods of making decisions, he would become both more autocratic and more participative. He would employ autocratic methods more frequently in situations in which his subordinates were unaffected by the decision and participative methods more frequently when his subordinates' cooperation and support were critical and/or their information and expertise were required.

It should be noted that the typical manager to whom we have been referring is merely a statistical average of the several thousand who have been studied over the last three or four years. There is a great deal of variance around that average. As evidenced by their behavior on standardized problems, some managers are already behaving in a manner that is highly consistent with the model, while others' behavior is clearly at variance with it.

a new technology for leadership development

The investigations that have been summarized here were conducted for research purposes to shed some light on the causes and consequences of participation in decision making. In the course of the research, we came to realize, partly because of the value attached to it by the managers themselves, that the data collection procedures, with appropriate additions and modifications, might also serve as a valuable guide to leadership development. From this realization evolved an important by-product of the research activities—a new approach to leadership development based on the concepts in the normative model and the empirical methods of the descriptive research.

This approach is based on the assumption stated previously that one of the critical skills required of all leaders is the ability to adapt their behavior to the demands of the situation and that one component of this skill involves the ability to select the appropriate decision-making process for each problem or decision he confronts.

Managers can derive value from the model by comparing their past or intended behavior in concrete decisions with that prescribed by the model and by seeing what rules, if any, they violate. Used in this way, the model can provide a mechanism for a manager to analyze both the circumstances that he faces and what decisions are feasible under these circumstances.

While use of the model without training is possible, we believe that the manager can derive the maximum value from a systematic examination of his leadership style, and its similarities to and dissimilarities from the model, as part of a formal leadership development program.

During the past two years we have developed such a program. It is not intended to "train" participants in the use of the model, but rather to encourage them to examine their own leadership style and to ask themselves whether the methods they are using are most effective for their own organization. A critical part of the program involves the use of a set of standardized cases, each depicting a leader faced with an administrative problem to solve. Each participant then specifies the decision-making process that he would use if faced with each situation. His responses are processed by computer, which generates a highly detailed analysis of his leadership style. The responses for all participants in the course are typically processed simultaneously, permitting the economical representation of differences between the person and other participants in the same program.

In its present form, a single computer printout for a person consists of three 15″ × 11″ pages, each filled with graphs and tables highlighting different features of his behavior. Understanding the results requires a detailed knowledge of the concepts underlying the model, something already developed in one of the previous phases of the training program. The printout is accompanied by a manual that aids in explaining results and provides suggested steps to be followed in extracting full meaning from the printout.

Following are a few of the questions that the printout answers:

1. How autocratic or participative am I in my dealings with subordinates in comparison with other participants in the program?

2. What decision processes do I use more or less frequently than the average?

3. How close does my behavior come to that of the model? How frequently does my behavior agree with the feasible set? What evidence is there that my leadership style reflects the pressure of time as opposed to a concern with the development of my subordinates? How do I compare in these respects with other participants in the class?

4. What rules do I violate most frequently and least frequently? How does this compare with other participants? On what cases did I violate these rules? Does my leadership style reflect more concern with getting decisions that are high in quality or with getting decisions that are accepted?

5. What circumstances cause me to behave in an autocratic fashion; what circumstances cause me to behave participatively? In what respects is the way in which I attempt to vary my behavior with the demands of the situation similar to that of the model?

When a typical manager receives his printout, he immediately goes to work trying to understand what it tells him about himself. After most of the major results have been understood, he goes back to the set of cases to re-read those on which he has violated rules. Typically, managers show an interest in discussing and comparing their results with others in the program. Gatherings of four to six people comparing their results and their interpretation of them, often for several hours at a stretch, were such a common feature that they have recently been institutionalized as part of the procedure.

We should emphasize that the method of providing feedback to managers on their leadership style is just one part of the total training experience, but it is an important part. The program is sufficiently new so that, to date, no long-term evaluative studies have been undertaken. The short-term results, however, appear quite promising.

conclusion

The efforts reported in this article rest on the conviction that social scientists can be of greater value in solving problems of organizational behavior if their prescriptive statements deal with the complexities involved in the phenomena with which they study. The normative model described in this paper is one step in that direction. Some might argue that it is premature for social scientists to be prescriptive. Our knowledge is too limited and the issues too complex to warrant prescriptions for action, even those that are based on a diagnosis of situational demands. However, organizational problems persist, and managers cannot wait for the behavioral sciences to perfect their disciplines before attempting to cope with them. Is it likely that models that encourage them to deal analytically with the forces impinging upon them would produce less rational choices than those that they now make? We think the reverse is more probable—reflecting on the models will result in decisions that are more rational and more effective. The criterion for social utility is not perfection but improvement over present practice.

14. communication revisited
Jay Hall

High on the diagnostic checklist of corporate health is communication; and the prognosis is less than encouraging. In a recent cross-cultural study,[1] roughly 74 percent of the managers sampled from companies in Japan, Great Britain, and the United States cited communication breakdown as the single greatest barrier to corporate excellence.

Just what constitutes a problem of communication is not easily agreed upon. Some theorists approach the issue from the vantage point of information bits comprising a message; others speak in terms of organizational roles and positions of centrality or peripherality; still others emphasize the directional flows of corporate data. The result is that more and more people are communicating about communication, while the achievement of clarity, understanding, commitment, and creativity—the goals of communication—becomes more and more limited.

More often than not, the communication dilemmas cited by people are not communication problems at all. They are instead *symptoms* of difficulties at more basic and fundamental levels of corporate life. From a dynamic standpoint, problems of communication in organizations frequently reflect dysfunctions at the level of *corporate climate*. The feelings people have about where or with whom they work—feelings of impotence, distrust, resentment, insecurity, social inconsequence, and all the other very human emotions—not only define the climate which prevails

[1] R. R. Blake and Jane S. Mouton, *Corporate Excellence Through Grid Organization Development* (Houston, Texas: Gulf Publishing Co., 1968), p. 4.

but the manner in which communications will be managed. R. R. Blake and Jane S. Mouton[2] have commented upon an oddity of organizational life: when management is effective and relationships are sound, problems of communication tend not to occur. It is only when relationships among members of the organization are unsound and fraught with unarticulated tensions that one hears complaints of communication breakdown. Thus, the quality of relationships in an organization may dictate to a great extent the level of communication effectiveness achieved.

interpersonal styles and the quality of relationships

The critical factor underlying relationship quality in organizations is in need of review. Reduced to its lowest common denominator, the most significant determinant of the quality of relationships is the interpersonal style of the parties to a relationship. The learned, characteristic, and apparently preferred manner in which individuals relate to others in the building of relationships—the manner in which they monitor, control, filter, divert, give and seek the information germane to a given relationship—will dictate over time the quality of relationships which exist among people, the emotional climate which will characterize their interactions, and whether or not there will be problems of communication. In the final analysis, individuals are the human links in the corporate network, and the styles they employ interpersonally are the ultimate determinants of what information goes where and whether it will be distortion-free or masked by interpersonal constraints.

The concept of interpersonal style is not an easy one to define; yet, if it is to serve

[2] *Ibid.*, pp. 3–5.

as the central mechanism underlying the quality of relationships, the nature of corporate climate, managerial effectiveness, and the level of corporate excellence attainable, it is worthy of analysis. Fortunately, Joseph Luft[3] and Harry Ingham—two behavioral scientists with special interests in interpersonal and group processes—have developed a model of social interaction which affords a way of thinking about interpersonal functioning, while handling much of the data encountered in everyday living. The Johari Window, as their model is called, identifies several interpersonal styles, their salient features and consequences, and suggests a basis for interpreting the significance of style for the quality of relationships. An overview of the Johari model should help to sharpen the perception of interpersonal practices among managers and lend credence to the contention of Blake and Mouton that there are few communication problems as such, only unsound relationships. At the same time, a normative statement regarding effective interpersonal functioning and, by extension, the foundations of corporate excellence may be found in the model as well. Finally, the major tenets of the model are testable under practical conditions, and the latter portion of this discussion will be devoted to research on the managerial profile in interpersonal encounters. The author has taken a number of interpretive liberties with the basic provisions of the Johari Awareness model. While it is anticipated that none of these violate the integrity of the model as originally described by Luft, it should be emphasized that many of the inferences and conclusions discussed are those of the author, and Dr. Luft should not be held accountable for any lapses of logic or misapplications of the model in this paper.

[3] Joseph Luft, *Of Human Interaction* (Palo Alto, California: National Press Books, 1969), *passim*.

the johari window: a graphic model of interpersonal processes

As treated here, the Johari Window is essentially an information processing model; interpersonal style and individual effectiveness are assessed in terms of information processing tendencies and the performance consequences thought to be associated with such practices. The model employs a four celled figure as its format and reflects the interaction of two interpersonal sources of information—Self and Others—and the behavioral processes required for utilizing that information. The model, depicted in Figure 1, may be thought of as representing the various kinds of data available for use in the establishment of interpersonal relationships. The squared field, in effect, represents a personal space. This in turn is partitioned into four regions, with each representing a particular combination or mix of relevant information and having special significance for the quality of relationships. To fully appreciate the implications that each informational region has for interpersonal effectiveness, one must consider not only the size and shape of each region but also the reasons for its presence in the interpersonal space. In an attempt to "personalize" the model,

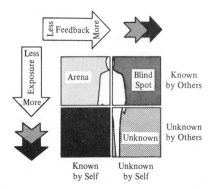

Figure 1. The Johari Window: A Model of Interpersonal Processes.

it is helpful to think of oneself as the *Self* in the relationship for, as will be seen presently, it is what the Self does interpersonally that has the most direct impact on the quality of resulting relationships. In organizational terms, it is how the management-Self behaves that is critical to the quality of corporate relationships.

Figure 1 reveals that the two informational sources, Self and Others, have information which is pertinent to the relationship and, at the same time, each lacks information that is equally germane. Thus, there is relevant and necessary information which is *Known by the Self*, *Unknown by the Self*, *Known by Others* and *Unknown by Others*. The Self/Other combinations of known and unknown information make up the four regions within the interpersonal space and, again, characterize the various types and qualities of relationships possible within the Johari framework.

Region I, for example, constitutes that portion of the total interpersonal space which is devoted to mutually held information. This Known by Self-Known by Others facet of the interpersonal space is thought to be the part of the relationship which, because of its shared data characteristics and implied likelihood of mutual understanding, controls interpersonal productivity. That is, the working assumption is that productivity and interpersonal effectiveness are directly related to the amount of mutually held information in a relationship. Therefore, the larger Region I becomes, the more rewarding, effective, and productive the relationship. As the informational context for interpersonal functioning, Region I is called the "Arena."

Region II, using the double classification approach just described, is that portion of the interpersonal space which holds information Known by Others but Unknown by the Self. Thus, this array of data constitutes an interpersonal handicap

for the Self, since one can hardly understand the behaviors, decisions, or potentials of others if he doesn't have the data upon which these are based. Others have the advantage of knowing their own reactions, feelings, perceptions, and the like while the Self is unaware of these. Region II, an area of hidden unperceived information, is called the "Blindspot." The Blindspot is, of course, a limiting factor with respect to the size of Region I and may be thought of, therefore, as inhibiting interpersonal effectiveness.

Region III may also be considered to inhibit interpersonal effectiveness, but it is due to an imbalance of information which would seem to favor the Self; as the portion of the relationship which is characterized by information Known by the Self but Unknown by Others, Region III constitutes a protective feature of the relationship for the Self. Data which one perceives as potentially prejudicial to a relationship or which he keeps to himself out of fear, desire for power, or whatever, make up the "Facade." This protective front, in turn, serves a defensive function for the Self. The question is not one of whether a Facade is necessary but rather how much Facade is required realistically; this raises the question of how much conscious defensiveness can be tolerated before the Arena becomes too inhibited and interpersonal effectiveness begins to diminish.

Finally, Region IV constitutes that portion of the relationship which is devoted to material neither known by the self nor by other parties to the relationship. The information in this Unknown by Self–Unknown by Others area is thought to reflect psychodynamic data, hidden potential, unconscious idiosyncrasies, and the data-base of creativity. Thus, Region IV is the "Unknown" area which may become known as interpersonal effectiveness increases.

Summarily, it should be said that the

information within all regions can be of any type—feeling data, factual information, assumptions, task skill data, and prejudices—which are relevant to the relationship at hand. Irrelevant data are not the focus of the Johari Window concept: just those pieces of information which have a bearing on the quality and productivity of the relationship should be considered as appropriate targets for the information processing practices prescribed by the model. At the same time, it should be borne in mind that the individuals involved in a relationship, particularly the Self, control what and how information will be processed. Because of this implicit personal control aspect, the model should be viewed as an open system which is *dynamic* and amenable to change as personal decisions regarding interpersonal functioning change.

basic interpersonal processes: exposure and feedback

The dynamic character of the model is critical; for it is the movement capability of the horizontal and vertical lines which partition the interpersonal space into regions which gives individuals control over what their relationships will become. The Self can significantly influence the size of his Arena in relating to others by the behavioral processes he employs in establishing relationships. To the extent that one takes the steps necessary to apprise others of relevant information which he has and they do not, he is enlarging his Arena in a downward direction. Within the framework of the model, this enlargement occurs in concert with a reduction of one's Facade. Thus, if one behaves in a non-defensive, trusting, and possibly risk-taking manner with others, he may be thought of as contributing to increased mutual awareness and sharing of data. The process one employs toward

this end has been called the "Exposure" process. It entails the open and candid disclosure of one's feelings, factual knowledge, wild guesses, and the like in a conscious attempt to share. Frothy, intentionally untrue, diversionary sharing does not constitute exposure; and, as personal experience will attest, it does nothing to help mutual understanding. The Exposure process is under the direct control of the Self and may be used as a mechanism for building trust and for legitimizing mutual exposures.

The need for mutual exposures becomes apparent when one considers the behavioral process required for enlarging the Arena laterally. As a behavior designed to gain reduction in one's Blindspot, the Feedback process entails an active solicitation by the Self of the information he feels others might have which he does not. The active, initiative-taking aspect of this solicitation behavior should be stressed, for again the Self takes the primary role in setting interpersonal norms and in legitimizing certain acts within the relationship. Since the extent to which the Self will actually receive the Feedback he solicits is contingent upon the willingness of others to expose their data, the need for a climate of mutual exposures becomes apparent. Control by the Self of the success of his Feedback-seeking behaviors is less direct therefore than in the case of self-exposure. He will achieve a reduction of his Blindspot only with the cooperation of others; and his own prior willingness to deal openly and candidly may well dictate what level of cooperative and trusting behavior will prevail on the part of other parties to the relationship.

Thus, one can theoretically establish interpersonal relationships characterized by mutual understanding and increased effectiveness (by a dominant Arena) if he will engage in exposing and feedback soliciting behaviors to an optimal degree. This places the determination of productivity and amount of interpersonal reward —and the quality of relationships— directly in the hands of the Self. In theory, this amounts to an issue of interpersonal competence; in practice, it amounts to the conscious and sensitive management of interpersonal processes.

interpersonal styles and managerial impacts

While one can theoretically employ Exposure and Feedback processes not only to a great but to a similar degree as well, individuals typically fail to achieve such an optimal practice. Indeed, they usually display a significant preference for one or the other of the two processes and tend to overuse one while neglecting the other. This tendency promotes a state of imbalance in interpersonal relationships which, in turn, creates disruptive tensions capable of retarding productivity. Figure 2 presents several commonly used approaches to the employment of Exposure and Feedback processes. Each of these may be thought of as reflecting a basic interpersonal style—that is, fairly consistent and preferred ways of behaving

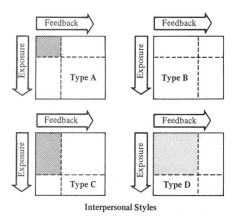

Interpersonal Styles

Figure 2. Interpersonal Styles As Functions of Exposure Use and Feedback Solicitation.

interpersonally. As might be expected, each style has associated with it some fairly predictable consequences.

Type A. This interpersonal style reflects a minimal use of both Exposure and Feedback processes; it is a fairly impersonal approach to interpersonal relationships. The Unknown region dominates under this style; and unrealized potential, untapped creativity, and personal psychodynamics prevail as the salient influences. Such a style would seem to indicate withdrawal and an aversion to risk-taking on the part of its user; interpersonal anxiety and safety-seeking are likely to be prime sources of personal motivation. Persons who characteristically use this style appear to be detached, mechanical, and uncommunicative. They may often be found in bureaucratic highly structured organizations of some type where it is possible, and perhaps profitable, to avoid personal disclosure or involvement. People using this style are likely to be reacted to with more than average hostility, since other parties to the relationship will tend to interpret the lack of Exposure and Feedback solicitation largely according to their own needs and how this interpersonal lack affects need fulfillment.

Subordinates whose manager employs such a style, for example, will often feel that his behavior is consciously aimed at frustrating them in their work. The person in need of support and encouragement will often view a Type A manager as aloof, cold, and indifferent. Another individual in need of firm directions and plenty of order in his work may view the same manager as indecisive and administratively impotent. Yet another person requiring freedom and opportunities to be innovative may see the Type A interpersonal style as hopelessly tradition-bound and as symptomatic of fear and an overriding need for security. The use of Type A behaviors on a large scale in an organization reveals something about the climate and fundamental health of that organization. In many respects, interpersonal relationships founded on Type A uses of exposure and feedback constitute the kind of organizational ennui about which Chris Argyris[4] has written so eloquently. Such practices are, in his opinion, likely to be learned ways of behaving under oppressive policies of the sort which encourage people to act in a submissive and dependent fashion. Organizationally, of course, the result is lack of communication and a loss of human potentials; the Unknown becomes the dominant feature of corporate relationships, and the implications for organizational creativity and growth are obvious.

Type B. Under this approach, there is also an aversion to Exposure, but aversion is coupled with a desire for relationships not found in Type A. Thus, Feedback is the only process left in promoting relationships and it is much overused. An aversion to the use of Exposure may typically be interpreted as a sign of basic mistrust of self and others, and it is therefore not surprising that the Facade is the dominant feature of relationships resulting from neglected Exposure coupled with overused Feedback. The style appears to be a probing supportive interpersonal ploy and, once the Facade becomes apparent, it is likely to result in a reciprocal withdrawal of trust by other parties. This may promote feelings of suspicion on the part of others; such feelings may lead to the manager being treated as a rather superficial person without real substance or as a devious sort with many hidden agenda.

Preference for this interpersonal style among managers seems to be of two types. Some managers committed to a quasi-permissive management may employ Type B behaviors in an attempt to avoid appearing directive. Such an approach

[4] C. Argyris, *Interpersonal Competence and Organizational Effectiveness* (Homewood, Illinois: Dorsey, 1962), *passim*.

results in the manager's personal resources never being fully revealed or his opinions being expressed. In contrast—but subject to many of the same inadequacies—is the use of Type B behaviors in an attempt to gain or maintain one's personal power in relationships. Many managers build a facade to maintain personal control and an outward appearance of confidence. As the Johari model would suggest, however, persons who employ such practices tend to become isolated from their subordinates and colleagues alike. Lack of trust predominates and consolidation of power and promotion of an image of confidence may be the least likely results of Type B use in organizations. Very likely, the seeds of distrust and conditions for covert competitiveness—with all the implications for organizational teamwork—will follow from widespread use of Type B interpersonal practices.

Type C. Based on an overuse of Exposure to the neglect of Feedback, this interpersonal style may reflect ego-striving and/or distrust of others' competence. The person who uses this style usually feels quite confident of his own opinions and is likely to value compliance from others. The fact that he is often unaware of his impact or of the potential of others' contributions is reflected in the dominant Blindspot which results from this style. Others are likely to feel disenfranchised by one who uses this style; they often feel that he has little use for their contributions or concern for their feelings. As a result, this style often triggers feelings of hostility, insecurity, and resentment on the part of others. Frequently, others will learn to perpetuate the manager's Blindspot by withholding important information or giving only selected feedback; as such, this is a reflection of the passive-aggressiveness and unarticulated hostility which this style can cause. Labor-management relations frequently reflect such Blindspot dynamics.

The Type C interpersonal style is probably what has prompted so much interest in "listening" programs around the country. As the Johari model makes apparent, however, the Type C over-use of Exposure and neglect of Feedback is just one of several interpersonal tendencies that may disrupt communications. While hierarchical organizational structure or centrality in communication nets and the like may certainly facilitate the use of individual Type C behaviors, so can fear of failure, authoritarianism, need for control, and over-confidence in one's own opinions; such traits vary from person to person and limit the utility of communication panaceas. Managers who rely on this style often do so to demonstrate competence; many corporate cultures require that the manager be *the* planner, director, and controller and many managers behave accordingly to protect their corporate images. Many others are simply trying to be helpful in a paternalistic kind of way; others are, of course, purely dictatorial. Whatever the reason, those who employ the Type C style have one thing in common: their relationships will be dominated by Blindspots and they are destined for surprise whenever people get enough and decide to force feedback on them, solicited or not.

Type D. Balanced Exposure and Feedback processes are used to a great extent in this style; candor, openness, and a sensitivity to others' needs to participate are the salient features of the style. The Arena is the dominant characteristic, and productivity increases. In initial stages, this style may promote some defensiveness on the part of others who are not familiar with honest and trusting relationships; but perseverance will tend to promote a norm of reciprocal candor over time in which creative potential can be realized.

Among managers, Type D practices constitute an ideal state from the standpoint of organizational effectiveness. Healthy and creative climates result from its widespread use, and the conditions for growth and corporate excellence may be created through the use of constructive Exposure and Feedback exchanges. Type D practices do not give license to "clobber," as some detractors might claim; and, for optimal results, the data explored should be germane to the relationships and problems at hand, rather than random intimacies designed to overcome self-consciousness. Trust is slowly built, and managers who experiment with Type D processes should be prepared to be patient and flexible in their relationships. Some managers, as they tentatively try out Type D strategies, encounter reluctance and distrust on the part of others, with the result that they frequently give up too soon, assuming that the style doesn't work. The reluctance of others should be assessed against the backdrop of previous management practices and the level of prior trust which characterizes the culture. Other managers may try candor only to discover that they have opened a Pandora's box from which a barrage of hostility and complaints emerges. The temptation of the naive manager is to put the lid back on quickly; but the more enlightened manager knows that when communications are opened up after having been closed for a long time, the most emotionally laden issues—ones which have been the greatest source of frustration, anger, or fear—will be the first to be discussed. If management can resist cutting the dialogue short, the diatribe will run its course as the emotion underlying it is drained off, and exchanges will become more problem centered and future oriented. Management intent will have been tested and found worthy of trust, and creative unrestrained interchanges will occur. Organizations built on such practices are those headed for corporate climates and resource utilization of the type necessary for true corporate excellence. The manager's interpersonal style may well be the catalyst for this reaction to occur.

Summarily, the Johari Window model of interpersonal processes suggests that much more is needed to understand communication in an organization than information about its structure or one's position in a network. People make very critical decisions about what information will be processed, irrespective of structural and network considerations. People bring with them to organizational settings propensities for behaving in certain ways interpersonally. They prefer certain interpersonal styles, sharpened and honed by corporate cultures, which significantly influence—if not dictate entirely—the flow of information in organizations. As such, individuals and their preferred styles of relating one to another amount to the synapses in the corporate network which control and coordinate the human system. Central to an understanding of communication in organizations, therefore, is an appreciation of the complexities of those human interfaces which comprise organizations. The work of Luft and Ingham, when brought to bear on management practices and corporate cultures, may lend much needed insight into the constraints unique to organizational life which either hinder or facilitate the processing of corporate data.

research on the managerial profile: the personnel relations survey

As treated here, one of the major tenets of the Johari Window model is that one's use of Exposure and Feedback soliciting processes is a matter of personal decision. Whether consciously or unconsciously, when one employs either process or fails to do so he has decided that such practices somehow serve the goals he has set for himself. Rationales for particular behavior

are likely to be as varied as the goals people seek; they may be in the best sense of honest intent or they may simply represent evasive logic or systems of self-deception. The *purposeful* nature of interpersonal styles remains nevertheless. A manager's style of relating to other members of the organization is never simply a collection of random, unconsidered acts. Whether he realizes it or not, or admits it or denies it, his interpersonal style *has purpose* and is thought to serve either a personal or interpersonal goal in his relationships.

Because of the element of decision and purposeful intent inherent in one's interpersonal style, the individual's inclination to employ Exposure and Feedback processes may be assessed. That is, his decisions to engage in open and candid behaviors or to actively seek out the information that others are thought to have may be sampled, and his Exposure and Feedback tendencies thus measured. Measurements obtained may be used in determining the manager's or the organization's Johari Window configuration and the particular array of interpersonal predilections which underlie it. Thus, the Luft-Ingham model not only provides a way of conceptualizing what is going on interpersonally, but it affords a rationale for actually assessing practices which may, in turn, be coordinated to practical climate and cultural issues.

Hall and Williams have designed a paper-and-pencil instrument for use with managers which reveals their preferences for Exposure and Feedback in their relationships with subordinates, colleagues, and superiors. The *Personnel Relations Survey*,[5] as the instrument is entitled has used extensively by industry as a training aid for providing personal feedback of a type which "per-

[5] J. Hall and Martha S. Williams, *Personnel Relations Survey* (Conroe, Texas: Teleometrics International, 1967).

sonalizes" otherwise didactic theory sessions on the Johari, on one hand, and as a catalyst to evaluation and critique of ongoing relationships, on the other hand. In addition to its essentially training oriented use, however, the *Personnel Relations Survey* has been a basic research tool for assessing current practices among managers. The results obtained from two pieces of research are of particular interest from the standpoint of their implications for corporate climates and managerial styles.

Authority relationships and interpersonal style preferences. Using the *Personnel Relations Survey*, data were collected from 1000 managers. These managers represent a cross-section of those found in organizations today; levels of management ranging from company president to just above first-line supervisor were sampled from all over the United States. Major manufacturers and petroleum and food producers contributed to the research, as well as a major airline, state and federal governmental agencies, and non-profit service organizations.

Since the *Personnel Relations Survey* addresses the manner in which Exposure and Feedback processes are employed in one's relationships with his subordinates, colleagues, and superiors, the data from the 1000 managers sampled reveal some patterns which prevail in organizations in terms of downward, horizontal, and upward communications. In addition, the shifting and changing of interpersonal tactics as one moves from one authority relationship to another is noteworthy from the standpoint of power dynamics underlying organizational life. A summary of the average tendencies obtained from managers is presented graphically in Figure 3.

Of perhaps the greatest significance for organizational climates is the finding regarding the typical manager's use of Exposure. As Figure 3 indicates, one's

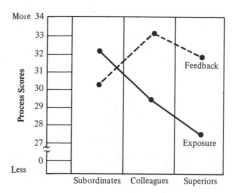

Figure 3. Score Plots on Exposure and Feedback for the "Average" Manager from a Sample of 1,000 Managers in the United States.

tendency to deal openly and candidly with others is directly influenced by the amount of power he possesses relative to other parties to the relationship. Moving from relationships with subordinates in which the manager obviously enjoys greater formal authority, through colleague relationships characterized by equal authority positions, to relationships with superiors in which the manager is least powerful, the plots of Exposure use steadily decline. Indeed, a straight linear relationship is suggested between amount of authority possessed by the average manager and his use of candor in relationships.

While there are obvious exceptions to this depiction, the average managerial profile on Exposure reveals the most commonly found practices in organizations which, when taken diagnostically, suggest that the average manager in today's organizations has a number of "hang-ups" around authority issues which seriously curtail his interpersonal effectiveness. Consistent with other findings from communication research, these data point to power differences among parties to relationships as a major disruptive influence on the flow of information in organizations. A more accurate interpretation, however, seems to be that it is not power differences as such which impede communication, but the way people *feel* about these differences and begin to monitor, filter, and control their contributions in response to their own feelings and apprehensions.

Implications for overall corporate climate may become more obvious when the data from the Exposure process are considered with those reflecting the average manager's reliance on Feedback acquisition. As Figure 3 reveals, Feedback solicitation proceeds differently. As might be expected, there is less use of the Feedback process in relationships with subordinates than there is of the Exposure process. This variation on the Type C interpersonal style, reflecting an overuse of Exposure to some neglect of Feedback, very likely contributes to subordinate feelings of resentment, lack of social worth, and frustration. These feelings—which are certain to manifest themselves in the *quality* of subordinate performance if not in production quantity—will likely remain as hidden facets of corporate climate, for a major feature of downward communication revealed in Figure 3 is that of managerial Blindspot.

Relationships at the colleague level appear to be of a different sort with a set of dynamics all their own. As reference to the score plots in Figure 3 will show, the typical manager reports a significant preference for Feedback seeking behaviors over Exposure in his relationships with his fellow managers. A quick interpretation of the data obtained would be that, at the colleague level, everyone is seeking information but very few are willing to expose any. These findings may bear on a unique feature of organizational life—one which has serious implications for climate among corporate peers. Most research on power and authority relationships suggests that there is the greatest openness and trust among people under conditions of

equal power. Since colleague relationships might best be considered to reflect equal if not shared distributions of power, maximum openness coupled with maximum solicitation of others' information might be expected to characterize relationships among management co-workers. The fact that a fairly pure Type B interpersonal style prevails suggests noise in the system. The dominant Facade which results from reported practices with colleagues signifies a lack of trust of the sort which could seriously limit the success of collaborative or cooperative ventures among colleagues. The climate implications of mistrust are obvious, and the present data may shed some light on teamwork difficulties as well as problems of horizontal communication so often encountered during inter-departmental or inter-group contacts.

Interviews with a number of managers revealed that their tendencies to become closed in encounters with colleagues could be traced to a competitive ethic which prevailed in their organizations. The fact was a simple one: "You don't confide in your 'buddies' because they are bucking for the same job you are! Any worthwhile information you've got, you keep to yourself until a time when it might come in handy." To the extent that this climate prevails in organizations, it is to be expected that more effort goes into facade building and maintenance than is expended on the projects at hand where colleague relationships are concerned.

Superiors are the targets of practices yielding the smallest, and therefore least productive, Arena of the three relationships assessed in the survey. The average manager reports a significant reluctance to deal openly and candidly with his superior while favoring the Feedback process as his major interpersonal gambit; even the use of Feedback, however, is subdued relative to that employed with colleagues. The view from on high in organizations is very likely colored by the interpersonal styles addressed to them; and, based on the data obtained, it would not be surprising if many members of top management felt that lower level management was submissive, in need of direction, and had few creative suggestions of their own. Quite aside from the obvious effect such an expectation might have on performance reviews, a characteristic reaction to the essentially Type B style directed at superiors is, on their part, to invoke Type C behaviors. Thus, the data obtained call attention to what may be the seeds of a self-reinforcing cycle of authority-obedience-authority. The long-range consequences of such a cycle, in terms of relationship quality and interpersonal style, has been found to be corporate-wide adoption of Type A behaviors which serve to depersonalize work and diminish an organization's human resources.

Thus, based on the present research at least, a number of interpersonal practices seem to characterize organizational life which limit not only the effectiveness of communication within, but the attainment of realistic levels of corporate excellence without. As we will see, which style will prevail very much depends upon the individual manager.

Interpersonal practices and managerial styles. In commenting upon the first of their two major concerns in programs of organization development, Blake and Mouton[6] have stated: "The underlying causes of communication difficulties are to be found in the character of supervision. ... The solution to the problem of communication is for men to manage by achieving production and excellence through sound utilization of people." To the extent that management style is an important ingredient in the communication process, a second piece of research employing the Johari Window and Mana-

gerial Grid models in tandem may be of some interest to those concerned with corporate excellence. Of the 1000 managers sampled in the *Personnel Relations Survey*, 384 also completed a second instrument, the *Styles of Management Inventory*,[7] based on the Managerial Grid (a two-dimensional model of management styles).[8] Five "anchor" styles are identified relative to one's concern for production vis-a-vis people, and these are expressed in grid notation as follows: 9,9 reflects a high production concern coupled with high people concern; 5,5 reflects a moderate concern for each; 9,1 denotes high production coupled with low people concerns, while 1,9 denotes the opposite orientation; 1,1 reflects a minimal concern for both dimensions. In an attempt to discover the significance of one's interpersonal practices for his overall approach to management, the forty individuals scoring highest on each style of management were selected for an analysis of their interpersonal styles. Thus, 200 managers—forty each who were identified as having dominant managerial styles of either 9,9; 5,5; 9,1; 1,9; or 1,1— were studied relative to their tendencies to employ Exposure and Feedback processes in relationships with their subordinates. The research question addressed was: How do individuals who prefer a given managerial style differ in terms of their interpersonal orientations from other individuals preferring other managerial approaches?

The data were subjected to a discriminant function analysis and statistically significant differences were revealed in terms of the manner in which managers employing a given dominant managerial

---

[6] R. R. Blake and Jane S. Mouton, *op. cit.*, p. 5.

[7] J. Hall, J. B. Harvey, and Martha S. Williams, *Styles of Management Inventory* (Conroe, Texas: Teleometrics International, 1963).

[8] R. R. Blake and Jane S. Mouton, *The Managerial Grid* (Houston, Texas: Gulf Publishing Co., 1964), *passim*.

style also employed the Exposure and Feedback processes. The results of the research findings are presented graphically in Figure 4. As the bar graph of Exposure and Feedback scores reveals, those managers identified by a dominant management style of 9,9 displayed the strongest tendencies to employ both Exposure and Feedback in their relationships with subordinates. In addition, the Arena which would result from a Johari plotting of their scores would be in a fairly good state of balance, reflecting about as much use of one process as of the other. The data suggest that the 9,9 style of management—typically described as one which achieves effective production through the sound utilization of people—also entails the sound utilization of personal resources in establishing relationships. The Type D interpersonal style which seems to be associated with the 9,9 management style is fully consistent with the open and unobstructed communication which Blake and Mouton view as essential to the creative resolution of differences and sound relationships.

The 5,5 style of management appears, from the standpoint of Exposure and Feedback employment, to be a truncated version of the 9,9 approach. While the

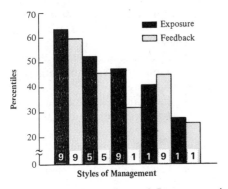

Figure 4. A Comparison of Exposure and Feedback Use Among Managers with Different Dominant Managerial Styles.

reported scores for both processes hover around the fiftieth percentile, there is a noteworthy preference for Exposure over Feedback. Although a Johari plotting of these scores might also approach a Type D profile, the Arena is less balanced and accounts for only 25 percent of the data available for use in a relationship. Again, such an interpersonal style seems consistent with a managerial approach based on expediency and a search for the middle ground.

As might be expected, the 9,1 managers in the study displayed a marked preference for Exposure over Feedback in their relationships with subordinates. This suggests that managers who are maximally concerned with production issues also are given to an overuse of Exposure—albeit not maximum Exposure—and this is very likely to maintain personal control. In general, a Type C interpersonal style seems to underlie the 9,1 approach to management; and it is important that such managerial practices may be sustained by enlarged Blindspots.

Considering the opposing dominant concerns of the 1,9 manager as compared to the 9,1, it is not too surprising to find that the major interpersonal process of these managers is Feedback solicitation. As with the 9,1 style, the resulting Arena for 1,9 managers is not balanced; but the resulting tension likely stems from less than desired Exposure, leading to relationships in which the managerial Facade is the dominant feature. The Type B interpersonal style may be said to characterize the 1,9 approach to management, with its attendant effects on corporate climate.

Finally, the use of Exposure and Feedback processes reported by those managers identified as dominantly 1,1 is minimal. A mechanical impersonal approach to interpersonal relationships which is consistent with the low profile approach to management depicted under 1,1 is suggested. The Unknown region apparently dominates relationships, and hidden potential and untapped resources prevail. The consequences of such practices for the quality of relationships, climates, and communication effectiveness have already been described in the discussion of Type A interpersonal behaviors.

In summary, it appears that one's interpersonal style is a critical ingredient in his approach to management. While the uses of Exposure and Feedback reported by managers identified according to management style seem to be quite consistent with what one might expect, it is worthy to mention that the test items comprising the *Personnel Relations Survey* have very little, if anything, to do with production versus people concerns. Rather, one's willingness to engage in risk-taking disclosures of feelings, impressions, and observations coupled with his sensitivity to others' participative needs and a felt responsibility to help them become involved via Feedback solicitation were assessed. The fact that such purposive behaviors coincide with one's treatment of more specific context-bound issues like production and people would seem to raise the question: Which comes first, interpersonal or managerial style? The question is researchable, and management practices and information flow might both be enhanced by the results obtained.

corporate climate and personal decision

The major thesis of this article has been that interpersonal styles are at the core of a number of corporate dilemmas: communication breakdowns, emotional climates, the quality of relationships, and even managerial practices have been linked to some fairly simple dynamics between people. The fact that the dynamics are simple should not be taken to mean that their management is easy—far from it.

But, at the same time, the fact that individuals can and do change their interpersonal style—and thereby set in motion a whole chain of events with corporate significance—should be emphasized. A mere description of one's interpersonal practices has only limited utility, if that is as far as it goes. The value of the Johari Window model lies not so much with its utility for assessing what is but, rather, in its inherent statement of what might be.

Although most people select their interpersonal styles as a *reaction* to what they anticipate from other parties, the key to effective relationships lies in "pro-action"; each manager can be a norm setter in his relationships if he will but honestly review his own interpersonal goals and undertake the risks necessary to their attainment. Organizations can criticize their policies—both formal and unwritten—in search for provisions which serve to punish candor and reward evasiveness while equating solicitation of data from others with personal weakness. In short, the culture of an organization and the personal and corporate philosophies which underlie it may be thought of as little more than a *decision product* of the human system. The quality of this decision will directly reflect the quality of the relationships existing among those who fashion it.

If the model and its derivations make sense, then corporate relationships and managerial practices based on candor and trust, openness and spontaneity, and optimal utilization of interpersonal resources are available options to every member of an organizational family. As we have seen, power distributions among people may adversely influence their interpersonal choices. Management styles apparently constrain individuals, but the choice is still there. Type A practices require breaking away from the corporate womb into which one has retreated; personal experiments with greater Exposure and Feedback, however anxiety producing, may be found in the long-run to be their own greatest reward. For the manager locked into Type B behaviors, the task is more simple; he already solicits Feedback to an excellent degree. Needed is enough additional trust in others—whether genuine or forced—to allow a few experiences with Exposure. Others may be found to be less fragile or reactionary than one imagined. Learning to listen is but part of the task confronting managers inclined toward Type C styles; they must learn to seek out and encourage the exposures of others. This new attention to the Feedback process should not be at the expense of Exposure, however. Revamping Type C does not mean adopting Type B. These are all forms of low-risk high-potential-yield personal experiments. Whether they will ever be undertaken and their effects on corporate excellence determined depends upon the individual; the matter is one of personal decision.

controlling

15. the many dimensions of control

Leonard Sayles

The subject of management controls is one of the oldest in the field of administration. No matter which theory or system of management one favors or practices, controls inevitably turn up as a central element—and properly so. After all, controls are the techniques by which the manager decides how to expand his most valuable asset, his time. Be they formal or informal, it is through controls that he knows where things are going badly that require his intervention—and where and when he can relax because things are going well. All managers from presidents to foremen make use of controls, some more effectively than others.

We have recently finished a review of the management of the National Aeronautics and Space Agency, extending from first-line technical managers and project

Reprinted by permission of the publisher from *Organizational Dynamics*, Summer 1972 © 1972 by the American Management Associations, Inc.

managers up to the top of the agency. Although NASA has many special complications that wouldn't be found in most companies, its experience in the use of controls has direct relevance to any organization, public or private. Therefore, what follows is a general discussion of the use of management controls, with examples drawn from the space program.

Perhaps more problems are created by the manager's failure to recognize differences among types of control than by anything else. As we begin to look more closely at the functioning of any large organization, we observe four quite distinct types of control that perform very different functions for the manager.

1. *Reassurance to sponsors.* Higher management and sources of funds and support need reassurance that the major objectives are likely to be met efficiently and on time.

2. "*Closing the loop.*" The manager seeks to prove that technical and legal requirements have been met, and therefore

that neither he nor the program is vulnerable to obvious omissions.

3. *Guidance to subordinates from managers.* The subjects their superiors pay attention to, as demonstrated by both written documents and informal observations, give guidance to subordinates as to what is important and what they should concentrate on.

4. *Guidance to lower-level managers by higher management.* Perhaps the most important function of controls is to direct the attention and energies of managers to subjects and locations where accomplishment is lagging and management action is required.

We shall term number 1 high-level controls, number 2 low-level controls, and numbers 3 and 4 middle-level controls, the last being both the most important and the most easily neglected.

high-level controls

In a large organization, top management needs to be convinced that any individual program is reasonably efficient in moving toward its major goals. At the simplest level, this might mean showing the percentage of the total program completed in a given fiscal year. If possible, it is always useful to show that either the rate of completion or the rate of accomplishment per dollar of expenditure is improving.

The distinctive feature of these high-level measures is that they are intended to reassure those who are not sufficiently close to the scene to be able to see any of the detailed activities or to evaluate them. If properly done, they may ward off investigatory activities and provide sponsors and top management with ammunition to counter skeptics and the opposition. These measures, therefore, have a public relations quality about them, and it is unfortunate that a good deal of internal effort may have to be expended

to accumulate statistical information to support pre-established contentions. Nevertheless, in any large organization, public or private, the higher echelons are sufficiently far removed so that they require this type of reassurance.

The business enterprise has the advantage of a slightly less arbitrary system called profit accounting, but its limitations in measuring managerial performance are also well known. Changes in inventory evaluation, decisions as to which costs will be capitalized and which will be expensed, formulas for "distributing" overhead, and similar accounting decisions can influence profitability by a modest factor of 100 percent or more. Even the general public is beginning to realize that profits are rather arbitrary numbers that can be manipulated within a wide range.

High-level controls are not controls in the usual management sense of the term. However, in complex endeavors necessitating substantial expenditures to complete high-risk programs that require many years to show results, it is necessary to provide some regularized feedback to those whose dollars or reputations are involved. The measures that are used demonstrate but do not prove efficiency, nor do they provide adequate bases for continuing supervision.

By this we mean simply that these reports demonstrate that managers are trying to improve performance, but they are not adequate measures of real performance. We are reminded, by analogy, of consulting firms installing new incentive plans that cut labor costs by 25 percent or even 40 percent. The reports made to top management appear to more than justify the investment in heavy installation costs. What the reports don't disclose is the increasing number of grievances over standards and the time and money involved in their settlement, the growing foreman-worker antipathy over the incentive program, and the costs of the continuing industrial engineering needed to update standards as jobs and technology change, as well as the growing resistance to technological change caused by the constant need to negotiate new standards. Added together, as they rarely are, these may show quite a different "profit" on the new incentive plan!

low-level controls

Low-level controls are checking procedures established to insure that neither financial nor technical decisions are taken without adequate review, and that no necessary step has been omitted. Such procedures as these are typical examples:

- All expenditures over $500 have to be approved by the controller's office.
- When "off-standard" temperature prevails for more than five minutes, written authorization from the chief engineer is required to continue processing procedures.
- Storage of flammables within 50 feet of Building 209 requires the permission of the safety officer.
- Any substitution of materials must be approved by the subsystem engineer, the functional manager, and a representative of the project office.

These are old hat in classical scientific management, but they present recurring problems. Perhaps the most obvious problem is the predecision as distinct from a postdecision position of these controls. Nervous managers want to know before, of course, but every advance check is a potential delay; when there are many such checks, gaining the required authorizations, permissions, and what have you can hold up work on a specific problem for weeks or even months.

Important decisions are often subject to before-the-fact review by a number of people. Thus, in a technical program, a design decision by an engineer may be reviewed by his functional manager, a technical specialist in the project office, the project manager, and then the program office. In addition, parallel system managers may also be involved. Such "sign offs" are time-consuming both for the project and for those who must review the technical details. When there are a great number of these to be made, there is a temptation for each echelon to give just a cursory glance.

Many after-the-fact checks are done on a sampling basis to assure functional managers that adequate technical expertise is being utilized and existing organizational policies are being upheld.

One of the most serious defects of these low-level controls is that they divert energy from critical problems to those where someone is checking up. It is the "numbers game" with which every experienced manager is familiar. Efforts are diverted to making oneself and one's department look good at the expense of larger goals and often at the expense of other managers.

The manager of the "frame and mechanics" unit, for example, was approached by the manager responsible for final assembly, who asked whether he would put some re-engineering efforts into reducing frame weight. It was clear that weight was an increasing problem and the total system would not get through final acceptance tests at the rate that the weight was increasing. The frame manager nodded agreement, but he knew he would do nothing. In the history of these projects, he knew that weight was always a problem, and furthermore one to which many managers contributed. The problem wouldn't get critical until the final tests, at which point it would be a problem for everyone—he wouldn't be blamed. On the other hand, if he diverted engineering effort now, a subsystem test next week might be in trouble, and those test results were watched closely by his boss. This manager minimized his potential losses by ensuring that a problem that involved him personally wouldn't occur next week and risking minor trouble a few months from now when the overweight problem would come up.

Many observers have noted what game theorists have called the "minimax" solution to individual efforts to cope with win-lose situations. The manager consistently chooses a decision by which he is guaranteed to minimize his losses, rather than seeking a large payoff at the risk of a big loss.

One all-too-common expression of the playing-it-safe syndrome is making sure that all rules, procedures, and orders are followed and that easily measured quantitative benchmarks are met. Then, if a problem emerges, it can be argued that it is the "other guy's fault" because everything specified was done, as proved by the check results. Naturally, this hinders responsiveness to larger system interests, to facilitating the work of groups who may need your collaboration or modifications in your procedures, and who are dependent on your being flexible. The controls introduce rigidities that can become a serious problem whenever the work is not routine, the technology has intrinsic uncertainties, and the employee is not simply doing the same thing over and over again repeatedly.

Evidence of management concern in most organizations over these control-induced rigidities shows itself in the extent to which middle and upper management seek to see what is really happening, as distinct from what the controls tell them. Even relatively high-level managers, particularly when dealing with advanced technologies, seek to gain a feel for the raw technical data. They are not content to look at staff summary or exception reports. Nor is their concern misplaced. Evidence suggests that this immersion in technical detail is necessary to keep abreast

and knowledgeable. Some even insist on sampling all the original correspondence concerning project progress and problems. Of course, this raises the obvious question of whether technically unsophisticated managers can properly serve in these posts.

Typical of this point of view is the following remark made by a project office engineer:

There is just no substitute for having the technical sophistication and willingness to go into the other guy's shop and look around. In R&D you've got to find out what he is not willing to tell you. The estimates, the test reports, and the progress reports tend to be too optimistic, and you'll go under every time if you take them at face value. The designers are always optimistic about future performance, and the project people naturally cover up their problems, so you've got to be their technical equal and get into the real data to know where you stand.

Of course, this effort also represents what we have called middle-level controls —that is, assessing the organizational effectiveness of various contributors to the system and seeking to predict where breakdowns are likely to occur.

middle-level controls

Middle-level controls are signals that guide managers to act in ways that contribute to overall systems effectiveness, not to paper "wins" or immediate payoffs. They concentrate on what is necessary to keep the organization functioning. As techniques for keeping in touch with the progress of the dispersed parts of the program, assessing information received, and responding to a variety of information inputs, they are vital to any project manager. The project manager here is no different from any manager; handling middle-level controls is the heart of his job, because it determines where and when he must go into action.

Much of traditional management literature dealing with delegation and controls stresses the autonomy that must be given to subordinates for motivational reasons. The superior waits to intervene until the subordinate has manifestly failed; otherwise he stays out of the process.

This is a luxury that the manager and the organization can't afford. In the NASA launch control procedure, there are numerous engineers whose job it is to call a halt to the countdown if the pressure or temperature they are watching goes beyond some precisely defined limits. However, they can't afford to wait until the limit is exceeded; they must seek to predict if it is likely to go out, particularly during the later stages of the countdown. Of course, this takes more judgment and has greater elements of risk, responsibility, and personal stress than simply waiting for a clear signal of trouble.

Obviously, in highly costly programs, even the subordinates can't afford to wait for a technical process to go "out of limits." Failures must be prevented at all costs. NASA managers appear to suffer no ill effect from having their actions reviewed with substantial regularity, even when there is no evidence of failure. They speak with some pride about having developed "over-the-shoulders management" in which the superior endeavors to guarantee success, not to wait for failure. When everyone knows the costs of failure and everyone is committed to the same goal—and not to individual goals, such as the numerical scores so characteristic of low-level controls—there is acceptance of the need for constant review in the most critical areas. Engineers are not distressed because their superiors are watching their actions, ready to step in should the system show signs of breaking down—they appreciate the need, and even welcome the possibility of intervention.

sizing up the other organization

Whether the work is being done by a contractor, within another functional group, by one's own employees, or in another part of the organization not immediately accessible to the project manager, there is the constant problem of predicting the likelihood of successful completion. In complex projects, managers learn to expect the unexpected; they realize that what looks good today may be in deep trouble tomorrow, and that highly effective improvisation may be necessary to overcome very serious problems. Thus it becomes important to assess the capability of the organizations that are dealing with the various subsystems, their leadership, diligence, and competence; to ask what those people are like and how they are really performing.

To find out, the project manager and the coordinators reporting to him seek to build a network of contacts within the various organizations whose work will be vital to the completion of his responsibilities. He seeks contacts at sufficiently low levels to provide him with firsthand information instead of information that is highly filtered and refined, and thus deservedly suspect. Many of these contacts will be "worked" daily during critical periods or when the relationships are being established.

information assessed

The project manager obviously needs information on schedules and budgets, but he must also collect information on the organization itself. These are the principal questions posed: How energetic and qualified are the managers and their key technical people? How much priority do they assign to this project, compared with other work that may be in process or in prospect? How effectively do they work together, and what kind of support do they usually receive from upper management and service groups?

The frequency of checking can have a strong effect on the amount of information collected. When a manager is concerned about how the work of a subordinate or a contractor is progressing, or when the participants are strangers to each other, he will tend to increase the frequency of checking. From the point of view of the man or group being checked upon, a high frequency of checking communicates lack of trust, and it may also be a material handicap because of the time consumed responding to initiations and filling out reports. Moreover, when an individual detects that information will be used against him he tends to be circumspect about what is revealed. It is easy to get into a position in which the person being controlled restrains the flow of information and the controller is required to keep increasing the pressure required to extract valid progress reports. A dangerous spiral of administrative costs and conflicts can ensue.

This process shows itself most acutely when cutbacks are required, and it is necessary to calculate alternative costs and the impact of various budget amounts on existing programs. Lower echelons have a variety of ways of protecting certain programs by "proving" that any cutback will strike at the heart of their favorites.

With trust on both sides, the respondent is more candid, and less time and effort are required to obtain information.

what is *significant* trouble? He is concerned primarily with the kinds of difficulties that the other organization seems incapable of handling with its normal problem-handling apparatus. Put another way, the project manager is endeavoring to assess their reaction to stress situations.

Most managers make the mistake of using "absolutes" as signals of trouble—or its absence. A quality problem emerges—that means trouble; a test is passed—we have no problems. Outside of routine organizations, there are always going to be such signals of trouble or success, but they are not very meaningful. Many times everything looks good, but the roof is about to cave in because something no one thought about—and for which there is no rule, procedure, or test—has been neglected. The specifics of such problems cannot be predicted, but they are often signaled in advance by changes in the organizational system: Managers spend less time on the project; minor problems proliferate; friction in the relationships between adjacent work groups of departments increases; verbal progress reports become overly glib—or overly reticent; changes occur in the *rate* at which certain events happen, not in whether or not they happen. And *they* are monitored by random probes into the organization—seeing how things are going.

In addition, of course, the manager assesses the normal statistical reports on manpower, performance, cost, etc., checks PERT charts, and notes any significant deviations.

sensitivity to signals

Anyone experienced in R&D work learns not to jump at the first sign of trouble; troubles are endemic to these non-routinized, one-of-a-kind activities. The question the manager must always ask is,

further evaluation of signals: when to proceed

The project manager has to decide what signals that suggest potential trouble spots are worth following up by further probes. As we have already suggested, a probe is costly in terms of both the time and energy expended on the probe itself and the lost opportunity of pursuing an alternative probe. All leads can't be followed up.

The information he has is usually combined with other information to determine this decision: previous experience with this particular organization, its reputation, rumors in the field, and other data that may be available—labor problems, materials shortages, pending or recently completed negotiations, and the like. Another element in the manager's decision to act or not are the potential losses in future rapport and the drying up of reliable information once privileged information is revealed.

preliminary steps

If it seems clear that a real problem is emerging, the manager who has made the evaluation may do one or more of the following:

1. Alert higher levels within his own management. Frequently the man who makes the observation is a technical coordinator who must decide when the project office is to be alerted.

2. Alert higher levels within management of the group in trouble. Many coordinators have told us that they observe things that local management hasn't learned, and it often takes a good deal of effort to persuade the organization that they have a problem.

3. Undertake further explorations and probings.

4. Alert other subsystems or stages that may be affected if the problem continues. Timing here is important. Doing this too soon can provide a signal to relax to the other units, and may reduce everyone's effort, particularly when it appears as though the schedule will be changed because of someone else's problems.

next steps

So far the manager has contented himself with alerting the various parties affected by the problem—higher levels of his own management, higher levels in the management of the group in trouble and in interrelated subsystems. If the group in trouble seems unable to resolve the problem, the manager has several options: He may increase the pressure on local management; he may urge local management to take specific measures that he believes will resolve the problem; finally, he may attempt to work around the problem by changing the master plan and allowing stage three to begin, even though stage two has not been completed successfully, or he may authorize another and different method for doing stage two in the hopes that one or the other method will work. Both methods involve increased risks and sharply higher costs, but they may save the schedule.

If these efforts fail and the situation still is not "turning around," then the next step is to consider structural changes. Administrative action is apparently not sufficiently drastic to solve the problem.

Structural changes include evaluating other sources of supply, changing managers, renegotiating certain parts of the contract to reflect changes in requirements or capability, modifications of the specifications, and so forth. More modest examples include providing direct assistance to the troubled unit by sending in specialists from the headquarters organization, requiring more or less subcontracting, and the like.

Structural changes should never be contemplated lightly. Most of these actions involve significant changes in cost; they endanger personal relationships, have wide and sometimes unpredictable impacts, and require substantial effort to implement. A prime test of the effective manager is his ability to anticipate most of the potential ramifications involved in any such drastic action.

assessing organizational effectiveness

Another way of viewing these middle-level controls is that they seek to assess how the organizational system is functioning as a system. They assume that organizational malfunctioning precedes technical malfunctioning; failures in the former are a good predictor of failures in the latter. Let us look at some examples of both the kinds of organizational relationships that can be monitored and their predictive value.

Workflow responsiveness: Organizationally, this means that managers responsible for adjacent workflow stages be willing to engage in some give and take and be responsive to each other's needs so that there can be swift resolution of difficulties that span two or more jurisdictions.

Unfortunately, it is quite easy for any group to refuse to consider alternatives, unless "bribed" excessively, by mustering a number of reasonable technical arguments. Evidence that a given manager consistently responds to the project office or other adjacent groups with flat refusals is a sign that upper management should give the manager its concentrated attention and intervene directly whenever it becomes necessary.

The generalization is true for any large-scale organization: Waiting to look at results guarantees a kind of "crisis management" characterized by turmoil and high costs in both material and human resources. Every organization increasingly needs good middle-level controls, which by continuously measuring the degree to which the organization is holding together as an organization can pinpoint potential trouble spots before they become serious.

Finally, these middle-level controls, because they concentrate on the total system, concern themselves with integra-tion and coordination. This means that they assess the ability of subordinates, managers, and work groups to coordinate their activities, make mutually satisfying trade-offs, and get the total job done. By doing so, they contribute to breaking down departmental boundaries and help to unify the organization.

Polarization of issues: Human groups obtain major satisfactions and facilitate their own cohesiveness by sharing in a common dislike or even hatred. In highly integrated systems, work-related groups cannot afford the luxury of these polarizations.

This happens in any organization. For example, marketing and production are at each other's throats over their relative balance of power. No matter what problem comes up—even if it is only a trivial request by marketing for an advance copy of production's next month's schedule—becomes part of the struggle: "Do they want that schedule early to use it with top management to hang us? In some way or other are they trying to show us that they have the power to get us to change our reporting system, to show that we have to defer to them?" Polarization means that everything is evaluated in terms of a power struggle and that divisiveness dominates all decisions.

Monitoring headquarters-field relationships: Typically, the program and project manager have a somewhat blurred division of labor. It is easy for the program manager to be either too assertive in project affairs or too distant.

In the division of labor between field and headquarters, it is important for the program manager to act as a buffer between the field-level technical staff and external demands. He should be the one who responds to the questions, criticisms, and pressures of other headquarters' functional and program people, as well as to external political, technical, and economic pressures.

There are several reasons for this: A reasonable amount of risk-taking is essential if innovative solutions to both the predicted and unanticipated technical barriers are to be found. An excessively "safe" approach can lead to high costs, delayed schedules, cumbersome redundancy, and uninspired design. This is not to say that field personnel should make imprudent changes, but that long-run success is probably a function of a somewhat protected development environment in which every step does not have to be justified immediately.

This also represents a functional division of labor. Headquarters personnel should have more time; more experience; supplementary resources, such as readily available advisory services; and greater skill in coping with external initiations. Field personnel need all the time they can get for technical coordination, monitoring, and development efforts.

Finally, we have a good deal of evidence that a durable field-headquarters relationship, as is true of most leadership situations, requires the higher-status "partner" to prove to those dependent upon him that he has the willingness, the power, and the skill to represent them and protect them from external threats. Lacking this, the headquarters manager will find it increasingly difficult to communicate to field personnel and get the responses he is seeking.

conclusion

There is an old theme in economics about bad money driving out good, and social scientists have noted an analogous tendency for easily quantified measures to drive out more subjective ones. The problem in the control area of management is that it is easier to give numerical scores to what we have called high-level and low-level performance. The result is that the manager is induced—or seduced—into doing things that make him and his unit look good, often at the expense of larger organizational goals and the larger system.

This is not to deny the usefulness of high- and low-level controls that try to measure accomplishments by comparing cost, schedule, and performance to date with what was predicted or budgeted. Equally important, however, is what these controls fail to do and fail to show. They are misleading as a measure of performance because they assume rigid plans and unified responsibilities, a misconception that is particularly dangerous in an organization in which the nature of the projects insures that unanticipated obstacles will become expected problems on an almost daily basis.

16. managing through feedforward control

Harold Koontz and Robert W. Bradspies

Managers have long been frustrated by making the occasional discovery—*too late*—that actual accomplishments are missing desired goals. Anyone responsible for an enterprise or any department of it has suffered the discomfiture of realizing that typical control reports merely inform him what has already happened and that most control analyses are really post-mortems. It does, indeed, do little good to find out late in December that inventory levels were too high at the end of November because of something that happened weeks or months before. Nor is it helpful to learn that a program is behind schedule or incurring excessive costs because of past events.

Most current control systems rely on some form of feedback. Unfortunately, a feedback loop must sense some error or deviation from desired performance before it can initiate a correction. This is, of course, after the fact. Moreover, since correction takes some time to become effective, the deviation tends to persist. The costs incurred, in many cases, increase directly with the duration of the error.

For example, the costs of holding excessive inventory are proportional to the time the excess inventory is held. The time slippage in a program may continue until correction is applied, and the costs of making up for the time lost usually seem to rise at an increasing rate. It is not surprising, therefore, that most managers consider the problem of control to be one of early recognition of deviations so that correction can be applied promptly. Although many managers have solved this

problem to some extent through careful planning, simulative techniques, and network systems of control (PERT/CPM), truly effective control has rarely been achieved.

To achieve more effective control, it is necessary to reduce the magnitude of the error. To avoid the problems inherent in the response time of a feedback system, deviations should be anticipated. The only way to do this, short of using a crystal ball, is to monitor the critical inputs to a program. If we watch changes in inputs, we can determine whether these would eventually cause failure to achieve desired goals. Time will then be available to take corrective action.

At first glance, it may seem that such a method would be difficult to use in practice. Fortunately, there is now available an approach to effective managerial control through adapting the principles of feed-forward control. This form of control is increasingly being used in systems engineering.

the process of control

Although planning and control are closely related, most managers see planning as the establishment of objectives or goals and the selection of rational means of reaching them, and regard control as the measurement of activities accompanied by action to correct deviations from planned events. It may thus be perceived that the function of managerial control is to make sure that plans succeed.

It is obvious that any system of controls requires plans, and the more complete, integrated, and clear they are, the better control can be. This simple truth arises from the fact that there is no way one can know whether he is going where he wants to go—the task of control—unless he first knows where he wants to go—the task of planning.

Control also requires an organization structure that is complete, integrated, and clear. The purpose of control is to detect and correct deviations in events; this must necessarily be done through people responsible for them. It does little good for a manager to be aware of variances but not know where in the organization structure the responsibility for them lies.

Given these prerequisites, any type of control and any control technique fundamentally involves the same basic process. *First*, standards must exist. While an entire plan can be used as the standard of control, the inability to watch everything usually forces a manager to select relatively few critical points that will reasonably measure how planned accomplishments are proceeding. *Second*, the logic of control requires measurement of performance against standards. *Third*, the process calls for taking action to correct deviations from plan.

shortcomings and needs

Control is really not this simple in practice, however, especially in management. Its basic features should be regarded as a cybernetic system as outlined in Figure 1. These steps represent the kind of feedback system that is involved in the simple room thermostat or the myriad of other control devices that one finds in mechanical and electrical control systems. But it dramatizes what every manager knows so well and many feedback engineers do not consider when they attempt to apply their thinking to management problems.

Simple feedback is not enough. Even the much-heralded ability of electronic data processing specialists to furnish information in real time, that is, as events are happening, is seldom good enough for management control. The fastest possible information may measure actual performance, may often be able to compare this measurement against standards, and may even be able to identify deviations. But analysis of deviations and the development and implementation of programs for correction normally take weeks or months, if the correction can be made at all. Moreover, during this time lag, variances often continue to grow.

An inventory above desired levels may take months to analyze and correct. A cost overrun on a project may not even be correctible. A delay in an aspect of engineering or production, if recoverable at all, may be remedied only by an expensive crash program. Feedback is not much more than a post-mortem, and no one has found a way to change the past.

need for future-directed control

Intelligent and alert managers have recognized that the only problems they can solve are those they see, and the only way they can exercise control effectively is to

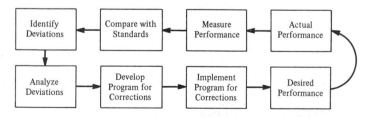

Figure 1. Management Control As a Cybernetic System.

see the problems coming in time to do something about them. In 1956, the senior author of this article identified future-directed control as one of the major principles of managerial control: "Since the past cannot be changed, effective control should be aimed at preventing present and future deviations from plans."[1] At this time it was emphasized that control, like planning, must be forward-directed and that it is fallacious to regard planning as looking ahead and control as looking back.

The simple principle of future-directed control is largely disregarded in practice, mainly because managers have been so dependent on accounting and statistical data instead of forecasts of future events. They have been too preoccupied with decimal accuracy, which can only be attained—if at all—from history. In the absence of any means to look forward, reference to history, on the assumption that what is past is prologue, is admittedly better than not looking at all. But no manager attempting to do an adequate job of control should be satisfied with using historical records, adequate as they are for tax collection and reporting on stewardship of assets to stockholders.

As a matter of fact, Norbert Wiener, the father of cybernetics, recognized the deficiencies of common feedback. He pointed out that, where there are lags in a system, corrections (the "compensator") must predict, or anticipate, errors. Thus, what he referred to as "anticipatory feedback" is often needed, particularly in human and animal systems. However, judging by the slowness in developing future-directed controls or anticipatory feedback in management control systems, there is little evidence that this variation of feedback has had the impact on thinking

[1] Harold Koontz, "A Preliminary Statement of Principles of Planning and Control," *Academy of Management Journal*, I (April, 1958), pp. 45–61.

and practice that might have been expected.

techniques of future-directed control

Relatively few techniques of future-directed control have been devised. Perhaps the most widely used is the continual development and revision of various kinds of forecasts, utilizing current expectancies to forecast probable results, comparing these with performance desired, and then developing programs to avoid undesired forecast events. Many managers, for example, after realistically working out their sales forecasts may be disappointed with the anticipated results; they then may review their programs of product development or marketing to see where changes can be made.

Cash forecasts are also a widely employed kind of future-directed control. Because banks do not normally honor checks without funds in an account, companies seldom can risk waiting until late November to find out whether they had adequate bank balances for checks written in October; instead, they engage in future-directed control by assuring that cash balances will be adequate to absorb charges.

One of the best approaches to future-directed control in use today is the formalized technique of network planning, which is exemplified by PERT networks. In PERT/TIME the discrete events required to accomplish a given program result are depicted in network form (since few programs ever are linear in the sense that one portion of it is sequentially followed by another), and the time required to finish each event is contained in the network. As will be recalled, when this is done, the planner can determine which series of events will have the least slack time.

The simple PERT network shown in

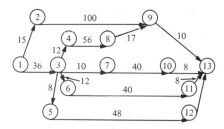

Circled numbers are measurable or verifiable events, and numbers on arrows are estimates of days required to complete an event.

Figure 2. Simple PERT Network.

Figure 2 will illustrate this long-used technique and how the most critical path—the one with the least slack—can be identified. A major advantage of this tool is that, through careful planning and measurement of progress in each event, any time slippage becomes evident long before the program is finished. The time available to finish the remaining events is one of the inputs to those events; if it is less than the minimum desired time, steps can be taken to accelerate any event along the critical path that lends itself to speed-up at minimum cost.

If, for example, there is no slack time on the critical path of events "1-3-4-8-9-13" (in other words, if delivery has been promised in 131 days), the manager knows that if event "3" is ten days late the entire project will be late unless something is done now. Although PERT has tended to become so complex in practice that its use for actual managerial control has declined, it is basically the best single device of future-directed control that has yet been put into practice.

feedforward in engineering

As early as 1928, U.S. Patent No. 1,686,792 was issued to H. S. Black on a "Translating System," which incorporated the principle of feedforward control in en-

gineering systems. However, the application of feedforward in electrical and process systems did not come into common use until a few years ago.[2]

In its essence, engineering feedforward control aims at meeting the problem of delay in feedback systems by monitoring inputs and predicting their effects on outcome variables. In doing so, action is taken, either automatically or by manipulation, to bring the system output into consonance with a desired standard before measurement of the output discloses deviation from standard. Thus, while feedback control relies on detecting errors in controlled variables as system outputs, feedforward is based on detecting and measuring system disturbances, and correcting for these before the system output change occurs. The basic concept of a feedforward and feedback system is outlined in Figure 3.

Feedforward has had wide application in the chemical and petroleum processing industries. It has been found particularly valuable where constant temperatures of material flow, exact mixtures, and various forms of chemical reactions require the precision that ordinary feedback, with its normal cycling, cannot achieve.

Perhaps the simplest form of feedforward control is contained in a system to maintain a fixed temperature of hot water leaving a heat exchanger where cool

[2] See, for example, L. F. Lind and J. C. C. Nelson, "Feed Forward: Concept in Control System Design," *Control & Instrumentation* (April, 1970), pp. 39–40; F. G. Shinskey, *Process Control Systems* (New York: McGraw-Hill Book Company, 1967), Chapter 8; F. G. Shinskey, "Feedforward Control of pH," *Instrumentation Technology* (June, 1968), pp. 69ff.; J. A. Miller, P. W. Murrill, and C. L. Smith, "How to Apply Feedforward Control," *Hydrocarbon Processing* (July, 1969), pp. 165–72.

A review of engineering literature discloses a few references to feedforward control early in the 1960's, but the real volume of writing has occurred since 1967.

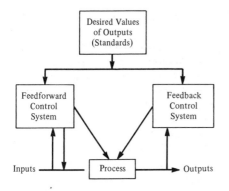

In a feedback system, corrections of outputs are fed back into the process. In a feedforward system, undesired variations of inputs are fed into the input stream for correction or into the process before outputs occur.

Figure 3. Comparison of Feedback and Feedforward Control Systems.

water inputs are heated by steam inputs. A thermostat on the water outlet would hardly be adequate, particularly with intermittent and variable uses of hot water; sudden changes in water output would probably cause bursts of cold water and steam inputs with resultant cycling of the water temperature.

To solve this problem, a systems design would provide a controller that would adjust the opening of the steam valve slightly. As the hot water usage starts to increase, the steam will be on its way into the tank before the water temperature drops below standard. A second feedforward loop might monitor the steam temperature and increase the rate of steam usage if its temperature should fall, in order to maintain the same heat input. By typing mathematical calculations into a computer that translates information to the input control valves, the oscillations characteristic of simple feedback systems can be reduced or entirely avoided.

However, even the most enthusiastic proponents of feedforward control admit that, if input variables are not known or unmeasurable, the system will not work. Therefore, for the best control, the use of feedback for output variables is also suggested.

feedforward in human systems

The feedforward applications one finds in everyday life are far simpler than engineering applications. A motorist who wishes to maintain a certain speed does not usually wait until he notes that his speedometer has fallen below this speed as he goes up a hill. Instead, knowing that the incline represents a disturbing variable in the system of which he is a part, the driver is likely to start correcting for the expected decrease in speed by accelerating in advance.

Similarly, the average person does not wait until a rainstorm actually feeds back to him the need for an umbrella before he carries one. Nor would a successful hunter aim his gun directly at a flying bird; he would "lead" it to correct for the delay in his own system, his reactions, the gun, and the shot velocity.

It is, therefore, surprising that more thorough and conscious feedforward techniques have not been developed in management, particularly since the delay factors in ordinary feedback correction are so long. As mentioned previously in this article, this has been done by such means as forecasting end results and PERT/CPM networks. But a little analysis and ingenuity could result in much wider use of effective controls and even the future-directed controls now in existence could be greatly improved.

A number of illustrations of how the principles of feedforward might be used in management may be given. Many require development of mathematical models of the system so as to provide managers information of forthcoming trouble in time for correction, but space does not permit the display of such models here. The approach of feedforward can be shown by several simple schematic models. For this purpose, the cases of control of cash, inventories, and new product development will be presented.

feedforward in cash planning

Since cash forecasting lies at the base of cash planning and control, this widely used technique of control is one of the best for revealing the application of feedforward to management. The basic inputs and construction of a cash control system may be seen in Figure 4. As can be noted, a number of input variables account for a desired future cash level. This model, representing a fairly simplified prototype of reality, shows that if any of the input variables differ from those premised when the cash plan was made, the desired cash level for the future will be affected.

As can be seen, many of these variables can have either a negative or positive effect on cash flow and the desired cash level at a given time in the future. It is readily

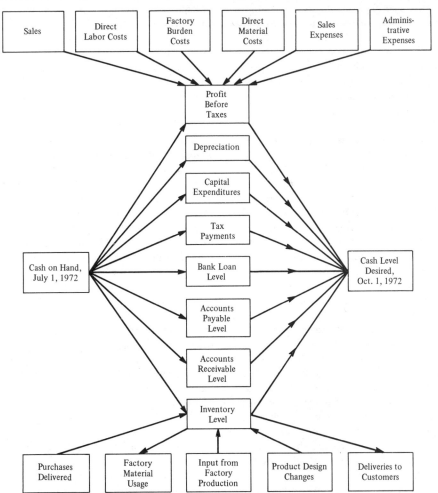

Figure 4. Input Variables for a Cash Plan.

apparent that normal feedback techniques are not adequate, and constant monitoring of the various input variables, with a feed-forward of their influence on cash, is necessary for careful cash control. Of course, one way to avoid the problem of shortages is to have available a ready bank line of credit. But what is likely to happen in this case is that the enterprise will keep unnecessarily high balances of cash, with resultant avoidable interest costs or loss in investment income.

It is also clear from cursory examination of this feedforward system that a mathematical model programmed to a computer can readily trace the influences of changes of input variables on cash flow and availability. Neither this nor careful monitoring of input variables should be very difficult to do in practice.

feedforward in inventory control

One of the most difficult problems in business is the proper control of inventories. Many enterprises incur large and often unexpected cost increases, as well as sizable demands for cash, because of inadequate control of inventories. Moreover, as experience continually teaches us, an inventory discovered to be out of control on the high side is extremely difficult to get under control except, of course, through that most costly of all solutions—writing off excess stocks.

Also, the costs of carrying inventory, due to expenses from handling and storage, interest, property taxes, and possible obsolescence, are higher than generally assumed; 25 percent of inventory value per year is often regarded as a reasonable estimate. Nor should it be overlooked that inventory shortages often have high costs because of missed sales or lost customers.

In recent years, operations researchers have presented a vast array of mathe-

matical inventory models and refinements. There can be no question that they have contributed greatly to effective planning and control of inventories, and many can be used as the basis for effective feed-forward in inventory control. The difficulty with many models is that they tend to concentrate unduly on such matters as economic order quantities and safety stock levels. These may be appropriate for a mass production operation, but may not take into account the many other input variables, such as obsolescence or property taxes, that make effective inventory control so difficult and important.

Any company will do well to develop its own inventory model, using, of course, the many standard algorithms and techniques available, but taking into account as many as possible of the variables that may influence actual inventory accumulation.

The schematic diagram shown in Figure 5 reveals the complexity of inventory control. Once a desired inventory level is established in a way that minimizes costs in the light of demands for adequate inventory, the total (whether expressed in dollars or days of sales) tends to be used as a standard. Actual results are compared to it through feedback with little or no monitoring of the input variables on which the desired level was determined.

The attempt is normally made to maintain the inventory within desired limits by using only reorder point, economic order quantity, and maximum inventory level. In the simplest manual system, when a withdrawal is noted on a stock record, the balance is compared with the reorder quantity. When the balance on hand falls below this level, a purchase order is issued. All of this may take place without considering the predictive changes of the original inputs.

The effect of such action may be to allow inventory to go out of control and raise costs. For example, if the rate of sales

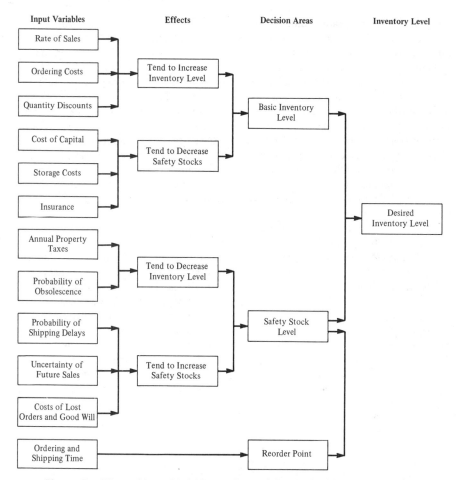

Figure 5. Effect of Input Variables on Determining Desired Inventory Level.

increased for a particular item, a company could find itself reordering too frequently or even running out of stock, thus increasing costs unnecessarily. Conversely, if sales decrease, a company could find that it was wasting cash by holding excess inventory. If sales declined further and a company continued reordering, it could find itself with a large obsolete stock.

If, instead, a company regularly monitored input variables, inventory levels could be adjusted by feedforward control by following the original decision paths and adjusting inventory purchases. In a company that used a manual inventory control system, for example, a simple monitoring system could be devised. It need only consider significant changes in input.

However, it must be admitted that a more sophisticated computer-controlled inventory system would be able to adjust more accurately for the effects of smaller changes in input variables and thereby reduce over-all operating costs by keeping inventory under control.

In reviewing the various input variables, it can easily be seen that different departments within the company would have to be responsible for feeding information (probably into a central inventory planning and control unit) on the variables within its field of knowledge. For example, ordering costs, economic order quantity, and quantity discounts are usually best known by the purchasing department; shipping time and unscheduled delays in shipping are data that could be regularly expected from the traffic department.

Given a recognition of the types of input variables and a system for regularly collecting information on them, it should be easy to anticipate what is likely to happen in inventory. In feeding forward this information, it should be practicable to develop a kind of inventory control that is truly future directed.

feedforward in new product development

The typical new product development program is, in the first instance, a system of interlocking contributory programs, as shown in Figure 6. It can be readily seen that this is similar to a PERT planning and control network. If times and costs are estimated for each program event in the network, the accomplishment of each subsidiary program becomes an input variable by which it is possible to feedforward the probable delays and costs of the completion of the program.

Moreover, each of the major programs in this network can be further broken down into a system of input variables so that completion of the total program can be forecast. Action can be taken in time to make necessary corrections and keep it under control. For example, within the product research program, there will normally be a number of subsidiary programs or events. These may include establishment of design definition and specifications; preliminary design of the product; development of a breadboard model; and testing the model.

Each of the other programs can be broken down into a number of subsidiary

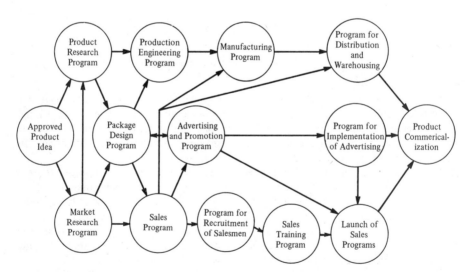

Figure 6. Feedforward Through a System of Interlocking Contributory Programs of a New Product Program.

events or programs. These, in turn, constitute input variables to the individual programs necessary for the completion of a total product development program; their monitoring can feedforward both time and cost factors against the standards desired for the total program.

In addition, analysis can disclose a number of other possible, and usually unplanned, input variables that may affect a desired end result. There are likely to be many of these, including such influences as delay in obtaining needed parts; failure of some part in a test; illness or departure of a key engineer; interference of a higher priority program; or change in a customer's desired specification. While not all of these can be carefully estimated in advance, and some may even be unforeseen, feedforward control can recognize the impact of such disturbances and provide for action in time to avoid program failure.

change of goals

In feedforward control systems in engineering, the systems are almost inevitably designed to correct input variables so that a given standard or goal may be achieved. In its application to managerial problems, the same approach can be used, but it should not be overlooked that the system may lead to changes in goals.

By placing emphasis on input variables, both those foreseen as a part of the program and those unforeseen, feedforward applications can furnish a means of regularly reviewing program goals themselves. A material change in interest rates, for example, may make a review of inventory goals desirable. Or a new development in product technology or market tastes may require a reevaluation of a product program. Managers must always keep in mind that goals and programs may become obsolete.

feedforward control guidelines

Although many other examples of application of feedforward to management control might be given, it is hoped that the transfer of engineering principles to management situations will be clear enough to help open the way toward the systematic application of feedforward in many areas. This can be done more easily than it may first appear. But in doing so several guidelines should be kept in mind.

1. *Thorough planning and analysis is required.* As in all instances of management control, thorough and careful planning is a primary prerequisite. But, especially in applying feedforward, this planning must be as thorough as feasible. Input variables should not only be identified but seen in their relationship and impact on desired end results.

2. *Careful discrimination must be applied in selecting input variables.* Since not all variables that *may* have some effect on output can be identified and monitored in typical management systems, it is essential that only the more critical variables be selected for watching. This is, of course, one of the key requirements of the managerial art—to identify those elements that make a material difference in the operation of a plan.

3. *The feedforward system must be kept dynamic.* There is always the danger that input variables will be identified in the analysis stage and only these will be monitored. The alert manager will, of course, watch for new influences, either within or outside the control system, which might seriously effect a desired output. New technology, unexpected changes in loan rates and availability, changes in customer tastes, and even unanticipated changes in social or political pressures are examples of input variables that may not have been foreseen.

4. *A model of the control system should be developed.* Clearly, if a feedforward

system is to be utilized, the area in which such control is desired must be defined, with the various significant input variables identified and their effects on desired goals analyzed.

This model may be a simple schematic drawing. It is far better, of course, to use an appropriate mathematical model that can be programmed in a computer. This way, the manager can take into account a larger number of input variables, more accurately calculate their impact on program goals, and be able more quickly and accurately to take corrective action.

5. *Data on input variables must be regularly collected.* Feedforward control is, of course, not possible without regular collection of pertinent data concerning the input variables so that the impact of this information can be carefully weighed. It is in this area that fast information availability is highly desirable and real-time information could have much meaning for control.

6. *Data on input variables must be regularly assessed.* No purpose can be served if input data are not regularly and carefully assessed to ascertain their influence on future program results. Barring unforeseen and unprogrammed variables, a computerized system can deliver this assessment quickly. However,

for many feedforward systems, the experienced eye and judgment of a top analyst may be good enough to point toward future deviations from planned results.

7. *Feedforward control requires action.* Few, if any, techniques or systems of management control are self-activating. All the system can do is to surface information that indicates future troubles, hopefully in time for something to be done to avoid them. This, of course, requires action. But if the system can be designed with enough lead time for a manager to take action, that is all that can be expected. And astute managers ask for nothing more than to be able to see their problems in time to do something about them.

There can be no doubt that feedforward is largely an attitude toward the analysis and solution of problems. It is the recognition that feedback information is just not adequate for management control and that a shift must be made away from emphasis on quickly available data on final results to quickly available data on those input variables that lead to final results. It is a means of seeing problems as they develop and not looking back— always too late—to see why a planning target was missed.

staffing

17. manpower administration: a new role in corporate management
Frank H. Cassell

Human Resource Policy seems to have grown out of a desire to:

1. Enlarge the national labor supply through training, a concept reaching beyond mere training to do a job or to improve performance on the job.
2. Give all Americans open and equal access to the job market.
3. Work towards assurance that entrants into a job or the labor market will be able to hold their job, once they get it.

To accomplish this requires a series of adjustments within the labor market and between the labor market and employers. These include:

1. Varying of techniques and quantity of recruiting efforts.

Reprinted from *Personnel Administration*, 34, No. 6 (November–December 1971), pp. 33–37, with permission of the publisher.

2. Alteration of hiring standards.
3. Adjustments of screening procedures.
4. Changes in salary levels.
5. Changes in the quantity and quality of training procedures.
6. Adjustment of machinery, work methods, and technology.
7. Changing or increasing the number of places where people can enter the job structure of the firm.
8. Changes in the size and characteristics of the labor supply.

internal labor market

The employer operates a kind of internal labor market which includes placement and training of the worker and the mobility of the worker once he is employed. In placement and training, the amount and type of training offered to workers inside the company allows the employer to vary both the skill level and quality required for entrance into the company. Training enables lower qualified labor to substitute for qualified, scarce labor. Training also removes a constraint upon the introduction of new machinery, new methods and corporate expansion because the firm does not have to rely exclusively upon the availability of particular skills in the external market.

Introduction of training procedures at a time when the unemployment rate drops to four percent or less may prevent plant productivity from dropping, thus compensating to some extent for the lack of skill or good work habits of those still available in the external labor market. The cost of training can buy a stable level of productivity, if not an increase.

To increase the internal supply as the external supply shrinks in numbers and quality, job ladders may have to be modified, transfers made easier, intermediate skill jobs created to facilitate training and upgrading.

There are barriers which limit internal job mobility and restrict the internal labor supply; they arise out of adjustment of such factors as corporate organization and collective bargaining. Because removal of these barriers can be complicated, resort is often made to the external market first.

The firm is, in effect, attempting to solve a set of simultaneous equations. At present these are largely a series of separate decisions.

new conceptual notions

To change this and to enable the equation to be solved, new conceptual and organization notions are evolving. These include:

 A. *Manpower Planning:* a process which translates corporate objectives and operational needs and plans into future requirements and provides plans to fulfill these requirements through the efficient utilization of manpower. Fundamental to man-

power planning is the need for linkage and integration with other functions of the corporation, including economic and market forecasting, research and development planning, and investment and systems planning.

B. *Manpower Forecasting:* this includes (1) assessment of current manpower needs as to numbers, skill and occupational mix, (2) assessment of the manpower resources already in the organization, i.e. their ability, productivity, mobility, capacity to be upgraded, retrained, reassigned and made adaptable and responsive to the firm's manpower needs, and (3) knowledge and assessment of the impact of investment and facilities plans on the manpower or occupational mix.

The forecast needs are related to the internal labor market, i.e. all the people working for the company wherever they may be located geographically. This is then related to the external market.

Intelligence about the supply of manpower at a given time and place can, and often does, affect the timing of corporate investments. Availability or lack of availability of skills may influence the location of facilities. It is not unknown to have shortages of special skills hold back technological advancement and corporate growth. Facilities planning can, in turn, supply information as to skills needed and lead time available to manpower administration to provide the required work force. In other words, manpower planning can help assure efficient use of capital whether in the public or private sectors.

C. *Manpower Utilization:* this concerns the effective use of manpower at its current level of development, i.e. training, skills and adaptability. Effective utilization requires a free and fast flow of information about jobs and people and minimal restrictions of the movement of people among jobs and around the organization, so that manpower resources can be made available wherever and whenever they are needed. Utilization involves continuous retraining, so that members of the work force can keep pace with technological change. Furthermore, it demands managerial understanding of complex motivational factors, both monetary and non-monetary, individual and group, in achieving high productivity through effective deployment of the work force.

D. Human Resource Development: this function interacts with manpower utilization by enlarging the labor supply; this is done by (1) raising the skills of the work force, (2) increasing its versatility and adaptability, (3) lifting its productivity and (4) attracting workers who see in human resource development a personal opportunity factor in the employment relationship. This may reduce dependence upon the outside labor market but it can also make available to the company a higher quality of manpower which can be more quickly and easily trained.

interaction needed

Inherent in this model is provision for interaction between the planners and policy makers so that corporate goals, timing, availability of product, readiness and the availability of manpower can interact with economic and market forecasts, facilities and investment plans, and thus provide the basis for establishing manpower requirements.

A manpower planning operation can, therefore, consist of a sequence of corporate policy, corporate planning, and manpower requirements and forecasts, utilization of the work force and developing it to meet current and future needs and to help in "make or buy" decisions. It is an interaction between the planners, and the policy makers so that corporate goals, timing of investments, availability of products and facilities, financial resources, the state of the technology, and avail-

ability of manpower interact with economic forecasts, facilities plans, investment plans, and thereby establish the basis for manpower requirements. This then is translated into budgets and goals for the organization. (See Figure 1.)

At this point, it is a matter of solving a simultaneous equation. This involves the utilization function which in turn involves placement of the man on the job, effective leadership, cooperative work relationships; effective organizational arrangements, wage and salary structure, training, and reward systems to the ends of both high productivity and work force flexibility and mobility.

In providing for the future, a sound relationship needs to be established between the cost of providing the needed labor supply from within or without. This involves the advantages and disadvantages of particular hiring criteria, i.e. the wage level, the cost of hiring and training, the search cost, the quality of manpower needed, and the shop rules on promotion, transfer or intake.

These factors are not usually thought of as interacting, but rather as individual actions relating to a particular function, such as employment, training, or wage and salary administration. But they are not separate, and they cost money. Rarely are these alternate costs quantified; machinery to do so is often not available. We do not know whether we are making the best or the worst choice. These options can be quantified and should be. Management must learn whether it is more costly to recruit or to train.

interdependent variables

Manpower administration can be effective here. While a corporation may only see one side of the issue, that of performance and cost, it can be shown how these measures can be applied to personnel and manpower

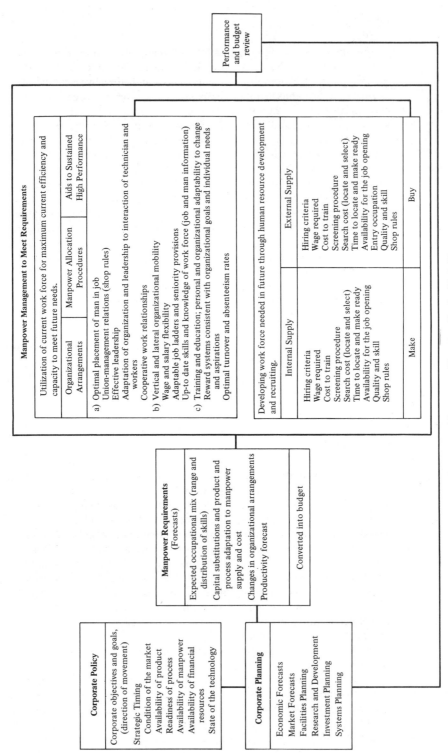

Figure 1. Corporate Manpower Planning Cycle (Detail).

Corporate Policy

Corporate objectives and goals, (direction of movement)
Strategic Timing
Condition of the market
Availability of product
Readiness of process
Availability of manpower
Availability of financial resources
State of the technology

Corporate Planning

Economic Forecasts
Market Forecasts
Facilities Planning
Research and Development
Investment Planning
Systems Planning

Manpower Requirements
(Forecasts)

Expected occupational mix (range and distribution of skills)
Capital substitutions and product and process adaptation to manpower supply and cost
Changes in organizational arrangements
Productivity forecast

Converted into budget

Manpower Management to Meet Requirements

Utilization of current work force for maximum current efficiency and capacity to meet future needs.

Organizational Arrangements	Manpower Allocation Procedures	Aids to Sustained High Performance

a) Optimal placement of man in job
   Union-management relations (shop rules)
   Effective leadership
   Adaptation of organization and leadership to interaction of technician and workers
   Cooperative work relationships
b) Vertical and lateral organizational mobility
   Wage and salary flexibility
   Adaptable job ladders and seniority provisions
   Up-to date skills and knowledge of work force (job and man information)
c) Training and education; personal and organizational adaptability to change
   Reward systems consistent with organizational goals and individual needs and aspirations
   Optimal turnover and absenteeism rates

Developing work force needed in future through human resource development and recruiting.

Internal Supply	External Supply
Hiring criteria	Hiring criteria
Wage required	Wage required
Cost to train	Cost to train
Screening procedure	Screening procedure
Search cost (locate and select)	Search cost (locate and select)
Time to locate and make ready	Time to locate and make ready
Availability for the job opening	Availability for the job opening
Quality and skill	Entry occupation
Shop rules	Quality and skill
	Shop rules
Make	Buy

Performance and budget review

actions as well. In other words, this is a system which encompasses interdependent variables; it can be altered according to the needs of the organization, the condition of the labor markets and the cost of the type of manpower needed to do the job.

The impact of manpower administration upon organization is likely to be considerable.

First, the independent variables cannot become interdependent unless they are so arranged organizationally.

Second, each of the traditional functions of wage and salary administration (i.e. wage and salary supplements, benefits and incentives) will need to be visualized as to how they contribute to manpower planning, utilization, human resource development, recruiting and employment. Each of these functions will need to develop an appreciation of the impact of their actions on the mobility of the internal work force, as well as on the firm's access to the external labor force.

Third, planning and policy development should become the prime function of manpower administration, with goals and performance evaluation as a main part of its work.

Finally, day-to-day administration of personnel needs to be returned to the work place. We may be at a time in the history of our nation when people of all kinds are unhappy with their inability to influence events, especially those that directly affect them. This is true of people who work in large organizations; they have a feeling of remoteness from the place where decisions are made and a belief that, in the minds of leadership, the organization takes precedence over the individual.

Managements, especially middle-level management, often appear to sympathize with these feelings; they give voice to the view that decisions should be made at the lowest levels of the organization. They are especially articulate when it comes to urging decentralization.

gap between promise and performance

However, studies of business organizations show that final actions are often contrary to previous assertions. Personnel and labor relations decisions are really quite centralized.* As such decisions are made by fewer people, and at higher levels of the organization, personnel departments have become, in the eyes of the workers, little more than "way stations" on the journey in or out of the organization.

A centralized personnel department can keep records of absenteeism but it cannot cope by mere exhortation. It cannot affect productivity even if the charts show a need for action, because other people will take those actions. The department cannot prevent high labor turnover because the volume processing function of the "way station" will take precedence; the root causes lie most likely in the work place itself.

action at the grassroots

The planning of manpower administration makes possible the development of the analytical framework needed to strengthen worker and supervisory performance in the work place, but it is only at the grassroots of an organization that meaningful action can be taken to reduce absenteeism or labor turnover, or to increase productivity. It is in the work place that teaching

* Decisions on investment are made at top management levels and at the board level and these decisions supply the constraints for the lower level managers and for the personnel people.

and learning occur. One is forced to the conclusion that the necessary organizational move is to remove the personnel function from the central office and locate it in the work place where it is accessible to the individual, relevant to what occurs; it should be supported by an overall manpower administration in planning, goal setting and evaluation of performance.

Finally, if manpower administration is to be an effective support to the organization, it must have information (much more information than required by traditional personnel administration) about the external labor market as well as the internal market. The concept of a corporate-wide or institutional labor market requires that both the employer and the employees have a knowledge of the job opportunities in the market wherever they may exist, and that the employers have clear knowledge of the capacities and resources of the work force, its availability and its mobility.

leadership needed

Manpower management in the corporation has yet to measure up to the contributions and influence of the finance function. It has tended to react rather than to lead. Staff departments such as finance, systems planning and long range planning have asserted themselves and increased their influence to the extent of bending the line organization to their plans. Yet the manpower and labor relations people have waited at the other end of the telephone, to be called.

Consequently the field of manpower in private industry has attracted far too few of the nation's talented managers. The function has been starved financially, for nobody has seen why it should have more money. The day it claims and earns a position leadership as has the finance function, it will get that money; it can attract better talent and the better students will be attracted to the field.

18. affirmative action program: its realities and challenges Gopal C. Pati and Patrick E. Fahey

Managers in many business organizations are increasingly feeling the impact of public policy in many functional areas of management.[1] This has created an unusual fermentation of mixed feelings of hope and frustrations. It has been further compounded by the complexities and inept-

Reprinted from *Labor Law Journal*, 24, No. 6 (June 1973), pp. 351–361, with permission of the publisher.

[1] Leon C. Megginson, *Personnel; A Behavioral Approach to Administration.* Homewood, Illinois, Richard D. Irwin, Inc., 1972, pp. 244–245.

ness of the technological society which has demanded an unprecedented emphasis on human resource utilization and development.[2] As a matter of fact, in the last several years it has been the area of manpower planning and development in general, and equal employment opportunities in particular, where the role of government has been increasingly ob-

[2] Elmer H. Burack and Gopal C. Pati, "Technology and Managerial Obsolescence," *MSU Business Topics*, Spring, 1970, Vol. 18, pp. 49–56.

served.[3] Many government-initiated and supported programs to ameliorate poverty, unemployment and wastage of human resources have generated numerous kinds of anxieties, debate and bewilderment among educators and practitioners. The affirmative action program is that part of the public policy which has induced many organizations to undertake a more vigorous approach to reach out for members of the minority groups, who have been traditionally left out as a consequence of socio-economic deprivation. More specifically the objective here has been to provide them with training, jobs and an opportunity to share the fruits of our economic system, thereby enabling them to assimilate themselves better in the greater participating democracy.

The experience of the last several years in the area of affirmative action program has been characterized by learning, re-learning, and adjusting to things unheard of before, and clearly indicates the ineptness of many approaches to meet the great challenge. This has also required tremendous change in internal organization, values, climate and many organizational adjustments that were not thought of before. Consequently, the objective of this paper is not only to point out these changes and challenges, but also to point out the bumpy roads and detours that have been encountered by managers within the last several years. The issues to be examined will not only have implications for traditional personnel functions and practices but also for an unprecedented philosophical change that a corporation will have to undertake in order to keep up its commitment to the government and society.

legal requirements in perspective

On July 2, 1965, Title VII of the Civil Rights Act of 1964 became effective. Title VII "Equal Employment Opportunity" covers companies, labor organizations, and employment agencies. It *prohibits* discrimination because of race, color, religion, sex or national origin. During the 1971 Fiscal Year, the Equal Employment Opportunity Commission (EEOC), established by Title VII as the primary federal enforcement agency for the Civil Rights Acts, received 22,920 new charges. This was a substantial increase over the 14,129 charges received during the previous fiscal year.[4]

Under the 1964 law, the EEOC was limited to "informal methods of conference, conciliation and persuasion" unless the Department of Justice concluded that a person or practice of resistance to Title VII was involved. If the employers refused to accept the conciliation conditions, it was the individual victim of discrimination who carried the burden of obtaining an enforceable court order.

Under the recently signed "Equal Employment Act of 1972," the EEOC, if unable to secure an acceptable agreement within thirty (30) days, may bring action in a U.S. District Court. In addition to the above, other provisions of the "Equal Employment Act of 1972" include: coverage of state and local government agencies, coverage of educational institutions, coverage of employers of fifteen (15) or more persons and labor unions with fifteen (15) or more members. The latter coverage is effective March 24, 1973.

[3] Robert A. Gordon, *Toward a Manpower Policy*, New York, John Wiley and Sons, Inc., 1967; also see Garth L. Mangum, *The Emergence of Manpower Policy*, New York, Holt, Rinehart and Winston, Inc., 1968, Elmer H. Burack, *Strategies for Manpower Planning and Programing*, New Jersey, General Learning Press, 1972.

[4] Equal Employment Opportunity Commission, *6th Annual Report*, CCH, Chicago, June, 1972, p. 25.

The changes enacted by the "Equal Employment Act of 1972" will make increasingly stringent demands on employers in the future.

The other federal agency with jurisdiction in the field of employment discrimination is the Office of Federal Contract Compliance (OFCC). The authority of the OFCC is derived from Presidential Orders 11246 and 11375. These orders resulted from the government's decision to use its immense purchasing and regulatory powers to enforce equal employment opportunity.

A federal contractor, which term includes virtually every employer with a contractual, financial, or regulatory relationship with the federal government, is required to go beyond the prohibition to discriminate under the Civil Rights Act. The contractor must take "affirmative action," that is, results-oriented activities, not mere passive compliance.

The Office of Federal Contract Compliance has shifted the burden of proof from the government to the contractor and made eligibility for government contracts, services, financing, etc., dependent on compliance with OFCC guidelines.

Previously "Order #4" and currently "Order #14" set forth the components of an acceptable written affirmative action program, the basis for the compliance review.

An acceptable affirmative action program must include an analysis of minority and female participation in all levels of the organization to determine if minorities or women are being underutilized. Underutilization is defined as "having fewer minorities or women in a particular job category than would be reasonably expected by their availability."[5] Once the deficiencies are identified, the contractor must set goals and timetables to which

[5] *Federal Register*, Section 60-2.11, Vol. 36, No. 234, October 4, 1971.

good-faith efforts will be directed to increase the utilization of minorities and women at all levels where deficiencies exist.

Despite the confusion caused by President Nixon's declaration against quotas in his renomination speech on August 24, 1972, it is improbable that the current method of goal setting will be abandoned. Though the difference between goal and quota might be subtle, it is generally accepted that a goal is a reasonable objective based on the availability of qualified people and a quota would restrict employment opportunities to members of a specific group without regard to qualification.

emerging trend

The above material provides a framework and perspective for understanding the role of government in the personnel decisions and suggests the kind of direction a manager will have to take in reexamining his own values and then reconciling these with those of corporate philosophy and posture in the area of manpower planning and development. Furthermore, it definitely indicates the emergence of more stringent rules and regulations as an answer to the partial failure of many organizations in achieving the result-oriented goals of the affirmative action program. The spirit and the realities of the regulations require that it is not just the personnel manager or department that has to carry the burden, but line and operating managers will also have to do their share to achieve the company objectives. In other words, it does affect the whole organization.

More specifically, this means that the operating manager will have to do things that he has never done before and yet his organization is demanding that he: (1) modify his recruitment, selection and testing policies; (2) vigorously and systematically reassess his training needs and criteria; (3) rechannel his training and developmental facilities and faculty; (4) become involved in better manpower inventory, manpower audit and control. He is further responsible for doing these things within the limitation of budget, without duplicating effort and coordinating better with the federal and state program without annihilating organizational climate. This requires not only broadening the knowledge base of individual managers, but also a serious effort in defrosting old ideas, relearning new developments and refreezing this newly learned knowledge to be useful in organizational growth. Thus, this challenge can only be met by more aggressive consolidation of managerial expertise supplemented by a strong corporate commitment.

recruitment

The immediate impact of AAP and the EEOC regulations has necessitated broadening the base of manpower supply. The basic objective of a traditional recruitment and selection policy has been to get the most qualified people at the least cost from those traditional sources which would be consistent with the organizational way of life in meeting the needs of the available job openings. The frequently used external sources have been (1) employee referrals, (2) private employment agencies, (3) walk-in recruiting, (4) newspaper ads., (5) major senior colleges and universities, (6) (to a lesser extent) vocational and correspondence schools. The traditional internal sources have been (1) transfer, (2) promotion, (3) job upgrading, without giving much attention to the potential of minority manpower within the organization.

Indeed, these sources once served their purpose in the past and still are doing so; however, in light of the developments in the area of reaching new elements of manpower these traditional sources may not be adequate. Consequently, the following sources are emerging as the kind of places that the employers are increasingly contacting to find people as required by the law:

1. Urban league offices,
2. Individual ministers and local religious organizations,
3. Minority-oriented media,
4. Senior and junior colleges with large minority populations,
5. Schools in the inner cities,
6. Local Spanish-American organizations,
7. Trade schools (more vigorously used now),
8. Women's organizations,*
9. Agencies dealing with correctional manpower.

As a consequence of this enlargement of the recruitment base, companies are definitely seeing more people to meet legal requirements as well as corporate ethic.

However, the rejection rate is usually high which can lead to many uneasy moments during a compliance review.

One company provided the following information which illustrates the difficulties that might arise as organizations appeal to minority-oriented agencies to fulfill their affirmative action commitments. During the effective period of an affirmative action program, the rejection rate for black female hourly applicants was 80 per cent while the rejection rate for white female hourly applicants was 68 per cent.

* For example, National Organization for Women, Professional Women's Caucus, Talent Bank from Business and Professional Women.

Though it certainly does not account for the entire disparity in rejection rates between black and white applicants, one statistic does give some insight into the depth of the problem employers are currently facing. In job categories for which a typing test meets the OFCC requirements for testing, the average black female applicants ($N = 70$) typed 30 WPM—approximately 25 per cent below the average typing speed of the remainder of the applicant population.

Furthermore, many agencies do refer people without any skills who miserably fail to meet even the minimum requirements of the company. When qualified individuals are available, frequent lack of transportation to a suburban plant location may prevent them from even appearing for an interview. In addition, many agencies are often speculative about their knowledge of job availability and send applicants to plants without any job openings, creating frustration for many individuals. Needless to say, there is a steep competition among the companies themselves to attract the best qualified personnel available. Consequently, some companies in the area are facing difficulty even in gaining entrance to an organization or institution which might have qualified minority manpower.

Confrontation with the new types of manpower and the sources has also caused reconsideration of the qualification of company recruiters. Today, a recruiter has to be a person who understands the minority culture; if not, at least make an attempt to understand and be sensitive to the needs of divergent groups. Several examples will clarify this point. In one instance a company representative went to a Spanish-American organization meeting to recruit. Ironically, no one spoke English and the entire meeting was conducted in Spanish. The recruiter could not communicate with the prospects and he returned to his office, of course, without

recruiting anyone. The second example is of the case of a recruiter who went to a prominent black educational institution only to be asked "what the hell are you doing here?"* In another instance at a female dominated institution, a recruiter was asked about the real intention of the company for recruiting females. More specifically, a question such as, "Why, Honey, suddenly are you interested in us?" baffled the recruiter.

The implications of these examples are crucial. There exists a tremendous amount of mistrust about the real intent of the corporation in hiring minority groups. They are not sure about their future in these organizations where organizational posture of active recruitment is being considered as the ultimate consequence of severe government prodding and pressure rather than a genuine attempt by the organizations to hire them on an equal basis in any real sense. Accordingly, it is imperative that a recruiter know the sensitiveness of the issue, understand the dilemma, and is prepared to represent the corporation and carry on its objectives in spite of the realities of complex attitudinal crisis.

employment testing

One employment procedure that has come under close scrutiny since the 1966 EEOC published guidelines is employment testing.

The field of industrial testing has grown substantially since World War II. Far too often, testing programs have been incorporated in the selection process based only on the "professional judgment" of personnel executives with little or no expertise, or on the recommendation of consultants motivated more by their fee than by the service they provide to industry.

* Descriptive adjectives have been omitted in the interest of scholarship.

Though the professionals in the field have for decades been recommending validation of personnel tests for their intended purpose, the widespread failure to establish criterion-related validity has resulted not only in the denial of employment to minorities but also in a waste of money. Contrary to generally accepted business practices, top corporate executives have been approving expenditures for testing programs that screen out people who would be productive employees and select people who will be marginal employees at best. Funds are allocated to production, advertising, research, etc., only if a reasonable return is anticipated but this requirement is lacking in the allocation of funds to personnel department testing programs in most cases.

In the U.S. Supreme Court decision *Griggs v. Duke Power Company*,[6] the Court adopted the interpretative guidelines of the EEOC that tests must fairly measure the knowledge or skills required in a job in order not to unfairly discriminate against minorities.

"Nothing in the Act precludes the use of testing or measuring procedures; obviously they are useful. What Congress has forbidden is giving these devices and mechanisms controlling force unless they are demonstrably a reasonable measure of job performance."[6a]

The Supreme Court decision in upholding the EEOC guidelines settled much of the confusion centered around test usage. A test can be used only if professionally developed and validated against job performance in accordance with the standards found in *Standards for Educational and Psychological Tests and Manuals*[7]

[6] "*Griggs v. Duke Power Company*," Labor Law Reports, Commerce Clearing House, Inc., p. 15, 1971. (39 U.S.I., W., 4317.)
[6a] Ibid.
[7] *Standards for Education and Psychological Tests and Manuals*, Washington, D.C., American Psychological Association, 1966.

and the burden of proof is placed on the employer in the area of business necessity.

Government contractors subject to the Rules and Regulations of Order #14 are required to provide an analysis of testing practices used in the past six months to determine if equal employment opportunity is being offered in all job categories. This will include the number of men and women acceptable on the test, the number of men and women not acceptable on the test, the same information for Negroes and Spanish-surnamed Americans, American Indians, Orientals and others when the group constitutes 2 per cent or more of the labor market or recruiting area for non-minority men and women. If there is a disparate rejection rate the test must be validated in accordance with the OFCC Testing Order (except for language arising from different legal authority, this order is the same as the EEOC guidelines).

Test validation will not bring about equal employment opportunity but will allow the employer to determine the relationship between the test and job performance and determine the significance of the test as a predictor of job performance for racial, sex or national origin groups. A test that has been validated against job performance, used with other selection or assessment tools, can significantly aid in the development and maintenance of an efficient work force. Such a test does not violate the civil rights law nor is it forbidden by the executive orders.

At this point it seems appropriate to discuss the validation study recently completed by one industrial organization.

A test battery was administered to 165 applicants over a four-month period. Though the battery included five short, professionally-developed tests, and the tests were chosen only after a thorough job analysis by an individual with a graduate degree and experience in both job analysis and testing, only one of the battery met the requirements for test usage.

The job is an inspection job that requires a background in electrical circuitry. The applicants selected for employment are enrolled in a company training school program for eleven days prior to actually starting on the job. During this period each employee is paid approximately $300.00. The selection tools used prior to the test validation study were considered unsatisfactory and the company considered it necessary to find additional tools to reduce the failures in the training school and the turnover on the job. (It should be noted that the training school evaluation was also validated against subsequent job performance by the Pearson product moment coefficient method with a coefficient of .4965.) The sample size was sixty-seven and the coefficient .4965 is significant at the 1 per cent level and satisfies the requirements of both the EEOC and OFCC.

The test was one of the Purdue Vocational Tests with two forms. In the study, Form B was used and Form A would be available for retesting purposes. Though the test carries a twenty-five minute time limit, this was disregarded and it was considered a work limit test.

The above clearly indicates that the classes projected by Title VII are adversely affected, that is, 48 per cent of Caucasians tested were subsequently enrolled in the training program but only 32 per cent of Negroes and 36 per cent of Spanish-Americans. As there is a disparate rejection rate, the test must be validated. The related criteria considered were (1) training school evaluation and (2) job performance criteria.

The training school evaluation consists of four paper and pencil tests on the subject matter taught during the eleven-day program. As noted previously the correlation coefficient between Training School Evaluation and job performance criteria is .4965.

I. validity—test correlated to training school evaluation

N = 67
Mean = 39.7
Standard Deviation = 10.2
Correlation Coefficient = .4877

The Pearson product moment method results in a .4877 coefficient which is significant at the 1 per cent level and satisfies the testing requirements.

II. validity—test correlated with job performance criteria

In this case the performance criteria consisted of a thirteen-week average percentage of a standard set by the Time-study Department.

N = 38
Mean = 41.2
Standard Deviation = 10.05
Correlation Coefficient = .3788 which is significant at the 5 per cent level and satisfies the requirements of the order and the guideline.

Number Tested	Mean Score	Race	Enrolled in Training School
108	38.75	Caucasian	52
41	24.92	Negro	13
1	—	Oriental	1
1	—	American Indian	0
14	29.53	Spanish-American	5

Therefore, it is considered that the above meets the requirements set by the OFCC and EEOC. The authors are aware of the issues not considered above, that is, differential validity, etc. These were part of the study but not noted here.

III. reliability

The method chosen was the split half estimate. The number in the sample was 158, none of which were retests. The scores of the odd number items were correlated against the even number items by the Pearson product moment correlation coefficient. The resultant correlation coefficient .857 was corrected by the Spearmen Brown formula to correct the reliability coefficient for the full length test to .9229, certainly in the acceptable area for continued test usage.

The test was validated in a period of economic downturn as clearly indicated by the number who successfully completed the training school (59) and the number included in the efficiency study (38). Nineteen employees were transferred out of the inspection group prior to the time meaningful proficiency data was available.

In view of the above, expectancy charts were constructed but a cut-off score was not determined until a later date and was based on "need" for inspectors as well as test score.

Though a complete explanation of the statistical data is not included here, it is obvious that the efforts generated to validate the test will not only reduce costs of failure and turnover, it will also be a more objective evaluation of prospective employees which is expected to increase the chances of minority group members to be selected.

There was not a disparate rejection rate for female applicants and the test validity study did not report validity correlation coefficients by sex.

promotion

Promotional opportunities for minorities and women has been thus far a neglected subject primarily because of the initial emphasis on economic opportunities and its delivery system rather than vertical mobility within the organizational structure. Since some progress has been made in the employment opportunity area, the promotional aspect becomes the next logical step. This is a recent phenomenon and has been effectively dramatized in those organizations with a large population of female employees. An example of this was the recent EEOC charge against the Bell system for lack of females in management level jobs.[8] As a result of this charge and consequent negotiations, Illinois Bell has agreed to promote 2,500 women employees by 1974. On the national level, the AT&T system has agreed to promote 50,000 women into higher paying jobs, including 10 per cent into management posts. Furthermore, 6,600 members of the minority groups will be promoted into higher paying jobs, 12 per cent of them into management. Before specifying the regulations for government contractors in this section, one must pause to consider the significance of the AT&T agreement. If it took eight long months for AT&T to conclude an agreement such as this, other organizations traditionally less committed to equal employment opportunity must now recognize that they cannot ignore this enormous responsibility they are charged with.

The emerging government regulations require government contractors to insure that minority and female employees are given equal opportunity for promotion. Suggestions for achieving this result include: (1) post or announce promotional opportunities, (2) take inventory of

[8] *Chicago Sun-Times*, Thursday, September 21, 1972.

current minority and female employees to determine academic skill and experience level of individual employees, (3) initiate remedial training and work study programs, (4) develop and implement formal employee evaluation programs, when apparently qualified minority or female employees are passed over for upgrading and require supervisory personnel to submit written justification, (5) establish formal counseling programs and hold supervision responsible for having qualified and promotable minority or female employees in their organization.

The question of promotional opportunity is a twofold question.

One, minorities have been historically hired in the least desirable jobs, if hired at all. It appears that recruiting minorities for supervisory, technical and clerical jobs is a step in the right direction. It will only be after qualified minorities are on the payroll that the question of promotion will occur. Promotions of minorities must be made on the basis of qualification and potential, not on how well they measure up to some undefined profile that has no proven relationship to job performance. The problem in this area is also related to the structural condition of the economy and the labor market in particular. During recent years there has been little turnover in managerial jobs and new jobs have not been created as anticipated. This has been further compounded by the lack of manpower planning and developmental efforts within organizations and the lack of consideration for people with potential within the organizational reservoir, particularly women and minorities.

Two, qualified women have always been hired but often not on jobs that truly utilize their abilities. To alleviate this problem organizations must open up their training program for females with management potential. Failure to open the facilities to women or minorities will invite stringent rules and regulations imposed by governmental authorities. This means that the burden of proof will not only affect personnel people but other line personnel who will be required to spend a great deal of time in manpower inventory and audit. This will be an additional burden to the line organizational personnel who will have to spend more time and energy in developing human resources, a task for which they are seldom trained.

supervisory and corporate attitude

Perhaps it is the preoccupation with our own frustrations that emotionally isolates us from one another. This is particularly true for many supervisors and foremen who are frustrated because they feel that they are being "left-out" from some of the action of the great society. Affirmative action programs are a traumatic experience for them. To them government pressure signals the practice of dual standard; company commitment appears phony in view of his usual assumption of the role of responsibility without accompanied authority. His own values and his inability to understand the motivation of youth, women and black employees; his own changing neighborhood, his own employer's emphasis upon his reeducation for organizational mobility or survival; increasing economic demand on him to make any significant headway in the inflationary economy—all these baffle him and place him in a very defensive mood. Thus, when the personnel department tries to select people *in*, the foreman seems to select them *out*. The supervisory groups just do not believe that "equal employment opportunity" is really happening and do not believe that the company is serious.

An unprecedented amount of attitudinal modification on the part of the top as well as supervisory groups is necessary if this program has to succeed. A strong support system within the organization is a necessity if any significant progress is intended to be made. And that support system can be developed if,

1. A vigorous organizational renewal program is pursued (at least partially),
2. an organizational development effort is seriously launched,
3. company reassurance of supervisory job security is strengthened,
4. 100 per cent company commitment is demonstrated, and
5. reward is given to the supervisory and various support personnel for their cooperation in an effort to create a better organizational climate.

If the above-mentioned is not being done (and in most cases that we studied it is not), then we should not be surprised about the dubious impact of the action-oriented affirmative action program. First line supervisors in most instances do not know what it takes to make a good worker and performer out of an individual. Under this condition it is very unlikely that a person without training and previous work experience will survive in an organization once hired.

implications

One, increasingly stringent goals and timetables as well as increased pressure from municipal Human Relations Commissions will emerge in the future. Only with specific goals derived from factual analysis will a company be able to carry the burden of proof against the OFCC and sell the program internally to non-persuaded upper management.

Two, the proposed regulations to re-quire federal contractors to keep records of employees' religious and ethnic background will eventually be adopted in spite of protests from groups that consider such regulations an invasion of privacy.

Three, federal contractors will find it necessary to appoint a full-time Compliance Officer. An effective affirmative action program requires a strong results-oriented executive, not the average impotent personnel executive nor the unqualified token minority, too often administering programs at present.

Four, a considerable amount of money has been spent in recent years to fund neighborhood agencies to train and assist minority group members to secure employment. Many of these organizations have failed miserably. In the future, business organizations must take an interest, both financially and with their training expertise, to ensure that qualified applicants are available from the sources an affirmative action program requires companies to contact.

Five, this indeed is a very sensitive area and will continue to be a serious problem for those organizations who are passive. A strong corporate commitment supplemented by an internal support system will have to be undertaken to live up to the real spirit of the equal employment practices.

Six, in light of our experience in the Midwest it is very clear that recruiting a few warm bodies to meet the legal requirements is not enough. The real spirit of the law requires reevaluation of corporate philosophy, changes in traditional personnel practices, modification of attitude of the operating managers and a type of complete involvement which will help minorities to retain a job and grow within the organization. Otherwise, more interesting laws will be forthcoming.

And finally, with regard to continued progress by minorities in all job categories, comparative data for about 31 million employees covered by 1970 EEO-1 employment reports indicate that since 1966, Negro employment as a proportion of total employment is up 1.9 per cent in total employment, 1.0 per cent among officials and managers, 1.2 per cent in professional category, 2.1 per cent among technicians, 1.9 per cent among sales workers and 3.7 per cent in office and clerical category. Spanish-surnamed Americans and women also showed increases in each of these job categories. While it can be assumed that the percentage gains would have been higher in a more dynamic economy, that is, minorities remain in a great many cases "last in," "first out;" our conclusion is that minorities remain grossly underrepresented in the more desirable jobs in industry in spite of law and moral suasion. Furthermore, if we are to use our human resources to their potential, organizations must make total commitments to expend time, money, energy and expertise at least to the extent imparted to the other factors of production, for example, finance, plant acquisitions, technology, etc. If this is not done, the chances of living up to the real spirit of the burgeoning laws is very slim.

discussion questions: part II

1. What role should top management play in long-range planning? Why?
2. Discuss the function of short-, intermediate-, and long-range plans for organizations. Are there differences between these types of plans? If so, what are they? If not, why not?
3. Distinguish the differences between strategic and tactical planning. How are strategic and tactical planning related to short-, intermediate-, and long-range planning?
4. Develop an integrated diagrammatic model for short-, intermediate-, and long-range planning.
5. What is project management? In what types of organization could such a concept be employed? Why?
6. After analyzing the characteristics of the organization of the future, apply those characteristics to some present-day organization (excluding hospitals) and discuss the implications of those characteristics for the organization.
7. How soon do you think we will see future-oriented organizations as opposed to static organizations? Why?
8. Would you be able to utilize the Vroom model of decision making in a military organization? Why or why not?
9. Describe the Johari Window. How would you use it if you were a middle manager?
10. What major problem areas in leadership need to be researched today? Why?
11. Differentiate between high, middle, and low levels of controls in an organization. Note the similarities between each type of control.
12. If you were attempting to assess the effectiveness of control in the organization, what criteria would you use? What methods would you utilize?
13. What is feedforward control? In what ways could it be used in the organization?
14. How would you implement feedforward control in an organization which previously had a feedback control system which was ineffectual?
15. In staffing the organization, what are some of the crucial questions to be asked?
16. Describe several techniques whereby an organization could maximize the use of human resources both internal and external to the organization.
17. What is an affirmative action program? How is it related to the utilization of human resources in the corporation?

selected references: part II

A. *planning*

Ackoff, Russell L., *A Concept of Corporate Planning* (New York: Wiley-Interscience, 1970).

Davisdon, Arthur B., "New Concepts and Problems in Urban Inner-City Planning," *Managerial Planning*, 21, No. 2 (September–October 1972), pp. 21–26.

Glaser, Edward M., "Outline for Long-range Corporate Planning," *S.AM. Advanced Management Journal*, 36, No. 1 (January 1971), pp. 51–56.

Levine, Robert A., *Public Planning: Failure and Redirection* (New York: Basic Books, Inc., 1972).

Litschert, Robert J., "The Structure of Long-range Planning Groups," *Academy of Management Journal*, 14, No. 1 (March 1971), pp. 33–43.

Makowski, Robert J., "Hospital Planning—Synthesis and Restatement," *Hospital Progress*, 54, No. 4 (April 1973), pp. 24–28, 38.

Mayer, Robert R., *Social Planning and Social Change* (Englewood Cliffs, N.J.: Prentice-Hall, Inc., 1972).

Miller, Ernest C., "Advanced Techniques for Strategic Planning," *AMA Research Study 104* (New York: American Management Association, 1971).

Reimnitz, Charles A., "Testing a Planning and Control Model in Nonprofit Organizations," *Academy of Management Journal*, 15, No. 1 (March 1972), pp. 77–87.

Steiner, George A., *Top Management Planning* (New York: Macmillan Publishing Co., Inc., 1969).

B. *organizing*

Famularo, Joseph J., *Organization Planning Manual* (New York: American Management Association, 1971).

Grimes, A. J., S. M. Klein, and F. A. Shull, "Matrix Model: A Selective Empirical Test," *Academy of Management Journal*, 15, No. 1 (March 1972), pp. 9–31.

Mace, Myles L., "The President and the Board of Directors," *Harvard Business Review*, 51, No. 2 (March–April 1972), pp. 37–49.

Newman, William H., "Strategy and Management Structure," *Academy of Management Proceedings, 31st Annual Meeting* (Boston: Northwestern University, 1972), pp. 8–24.

Sexton, William P., "Patterns of Reorganization for Renewal." *Hospital Progress*, 52, No. 10 (October 1971), pp. 38–44.

Simon, Herbert A., "Applying Information Technology to Organization Design," *Public Administration Review*, 33, No. 3 (May–June 1973), pp. 268–278.

Vance, Stanley C., *Managers in the Conglomerate Era* (New York: John Wiley and Sons, Inc., 1971).

C. *directing*

Carne, E. Bryan, "Telecommunications: Its Impact on Business." *Harvard Business Review*, 50, No. 4 (July–August 1972), pp. 125–133.

Fiedler, Fred E., "How Do You Make Leaders More Effective? New Answers to an Old Puzzle," *Organizational Dynamics*, 1, No. 2 (Autumn 1972), pp. 2–18.

Hollander, Edwin P., "Style, Structure, and Setting in Organizational Leadership," *Administrative Science Quarterly*, 16, No. 1 (March 1971), pp. 1–9.

Meier, Richard L., "Communications Stress—Threats and Remedies," *Organizational Dynamics*, 1, No. 3 (Winter 1973), pp. 69–80.

Owens, James, "The Uses of Leadership Theory," *Michigan Business Review*, 25, No. 1 (January 1973), pp. 13–19.

Tannenbaum, Robert, and Warren H. Schmidt, "How to Choose a Leadership Pattern," *Harvard Business Review*, 51, No. 3 (May–June 1973), pp. 162–180.

Valentine, Raymond F., *Initiative and Managerial Power* (New York: AMACOM, 1973).

D. controlling

Fleming, John E., "The Spectrum of Management Control," *S.A.M. Advanced Management Journal*, 37, No. 2 (April 1972), pp. 54–61.

Graziano, Vincent J., "Integrated Logistics Planning and Control," *Management Controls*, 19, No. 2 (February 1972), pp. 26–32.

Livingston, John L., "Management Controls and Organizational Performance," *Personnel Administration*, 28, No. 1 (January–February 1965), pp. 37–43.

McGregor, Douglas, "Do Management Control Systems Achieve Their Purpose?" *Management Review*, 56, No. 2 (February 1967), pp. 4–18.

McMahon, J. Timothy, and G. W. Perritt, "The Control Structure of Organizations: An Empirical Examination," *Academy of Management Journal*, 14, No. 3 (September 1971), pp. 327–340.

Murdick, Robert G., "Managerial Control: Concepts and Practice," *S.A.M. Advanced Management Journal*, 35, No. 1 (January 1970), pp. 48–52.

Vancil, Richard F., "What Kind of Management Control Do You Need?" *Harvard Business Review*, 51, No. 2 (March–April 1973), pp. 75–86.

E. staffing

Boyle, Barbara M., "Equal Opportunity for Women Is Smart Business," *Harvard Business Review*, 51, No. 3 (May–June 1973), pp. 85–95.

Jones, Edward W., "What It's Like to Be a Black Manager," *Harvard Business Review*, 51, No. 4 (July–August 1973), pp. 108–116.

McConnell, John J., and Treadway C. Parker, "An Assessment Center Program for Multi-Organizational Use," *Training and Development Journal*, 26, No. 3 (March 1972), pp. 6–14.

Miner, John B., "Personnel Strategies in the Small Business Organizations," *Journal of Small Business Management*, 11 (July 1973), pp. 13–16.

Mintzberg, Henry, *The Nature of Managerial Work* (New York: Harper & Row, Publishers, 1973).

Stroh, Thomas F., *Managing the New Generation in Business* (New York: McGraw-Hill Book Company, Inc., 1971).

Walker, James, W., "Models in Manpower Planning," *Business Horizons*, 14, No. 2 (April 1971), pp. 87–94.

Wortman, Jr., Max S., "A Conceptual Framework for a Macro-Manpower System," *Academy of Management Proceedings, Thirty-Second Annual Meeting, Minneapolis, Minnesota, August 13–16, 1972* (Vancouver, British Columbia: University of British Columbia, 1973), pp. 229–230.

behavioral approaches

part III

The initial impetus for utilizing behavioral approaches in management began with the extensive studies of human behavior in organizations at the Western Electric Company in the 1920s.[1] Using sociological and psychological research techniques to examine first-line management problems, the researchers concluded that the contribution of social and human factors to productivity is frequently more important than the physical environment in which work is carried out. For the past fifty years, research into human behavior in organizations has been accelerating. Many different aspects of individual and group behavior have been tested experimentally. The impact of group norms, factors contributing to job satisfaction, the effect of informal groups and leaders within organizations, and the roles of status and power are just a few of the topics studied.

As the research efforts have intensified, the behavioral science approach to management slowly has become better defined. In 1962, Wilmar F. Bernthal defined the behavioral science approach as one which explains the behavior of individuals in a given social system which is designed to achieve particular objectives through cooperative effort.[2] This approach involved (1) the analysis

[1] For discussion of these experiments, see F. J. Roethlisberger and William J. Dickson, *Management and the Worker* (Cambridge, Mass.: Harvard University Press, 1939). For a later evaluation, see Henry A. Landsberger, *Hawthorne Revisited* (Ithaca, N.Y.: Cornell University Press, 1958).

[2] Wilmar F. Bernthal, "Contributions of the Behavioral Science Approach," *Academy of Management, Proceedings of the 1962 Annual Meeting* (University Park, Pa.: 1963), p. 22.

of the environmental setting within which the individual and group behavior occurs, by historians, economists, political scientists, and anthropologists; and (2) the examination of individual and group behavior within that environmental setting by psychologists, sociologists, social psychologists, and applied anthropologists.[3] Although a few of the research and conceptual efforts in the behavioral approach to management have been interdisciplinary, many of them have been initiated within one discipline.[4]

Several major contributions to management have been made by the behavioral sciences including (1) *conceptual*, the formulation of concepts and explanations about individual and group behavior in the organization; (2) *methodological*, the empirical testing of these concepts in many different experimental and field settings;[5] and (3) *operational*, the establishment of actual managerial policies and decisions based on these conceptual and methodological frameworks. Since behavioral approaches have become widely disseminated throughout the management literature, there has been an increasing acceptance of the behavioral approach by management.[6] For example, the behavioral scientists have been examining such problems as the factors, including salary, which determine the levels of motivation and performance in organizations;[7] the integration of minority groups into the structure of an organization;[8] the impact of the manager upon the organization;[9] and the environmental constraints upon individual, group, and organizational behavior.[10] Indirectly, the behavioral approach has forced managers to examine some of the ethical questions which are related to human behavior in the organization.[11]

Although the terms "organization theory,"[12] "organization behavior,"[13] and "organization development,"[14] are not always clearly defined nor agreed upon in the literature, this part of the book focuses upon some of the conceptual, methodological, and operational issues involved in the behavioral approaches to management.

[3] Bernthal, p. 22.

[4] William G. Scott, *Organization Theory: A Behavioral Analysis for Management* (Homewood, Ill.: Richard D. Irwin, Inc., 1967), p. 3. For a typology of behavioral science research, see A. B. Cherns, "Can Behavioral Scientists Help Managers Improve Their Organizations?" *Organizational Dynamics*, 1, No. 3 (Winter 1973), pp. 51–67.

[5] Scott, p. 4.

[6] For other reasons why the behavioral approach is achieving more influence in management today, see Scott, pp. 17–18; Bernthal, pp. 21–28; and Cherns, pp. 52–67.

[7] For example, see Lyman W. Porter and Edward E. Lawler, III, *Managerial Attitudes and Performance* (Homewood, Ill.: Richard D. Irwin, Inc., 1968).

[8] See Elmer H. Burack, *Strategies for Manpower Planning and Programming* (Morristown, N.J.: General Learning Press, 1972), pp. 195–213.

[9] See Jay Hall, "Communication Revisited," *California Management Review*, 15, No. 3 (Spring 1973), pp. 56–67.

[10] Stahrl Edmunds and John Letey, *Environmental Administration* (New York: McGraw-Hill Book Company, 1973).

[11] Bernthal, p. 28.

[12] D. S. Pugh, "Modern Organization Theory: A Psychological and Sociological Study," *Psychological Bulletin*, 66, No. 4 (October 1966), pp. 235–251.

[13] Cherns, pp. 52–54.

[14] Wendell L. French and Cecil H. Bell, "A Definition and History of Organization Development," *Academy of Management Proceedings, Thirty-First Annual Meeting* (Boston: Northeastern University, 1972), pp. 146–153.

In the first section, Y. K. Shetty and Howard M. Carlisle examine three current models of organizations—classical, behavioral, and organic—and postulate a new contingency model of organization design. The second reading, by Forest W. Horton, clearly demonstrates the expansion of administrative science into the public sector by his analysis of task forces and project management as viable forms of organization. In his discussion, he succinctly defines several terms which have been intimately related to the project management concept.

In developing his behavioral model of organization, Ralph M. Stogdill attempts to account for the formal as well as extraformal aspects of an organization. Throughout the development of the model, he continually has shown his awareness of its relationship to the real world. Dorothy A. Seese attempts to show how the classical representations of organizations are not always accurate and to indicate the ways in which the work group concept should replace traditional organizational formats. In the third selection, Fred Luthans and Robert Ottemann suggest the use of a new technique—organizational behavior modification—to predict and direct individual behavior within the organization. They feel that the approach is simpler and more direct than employing traditional content motivational methods.

A rapidly expanding area in behavioral approaches to management is that of organization development. Alan D. Bauerschmidt and Richard W. Brunson attempt to define "organization development," explain its origin, analyze the methods used, and describe the modes of delivery in a hospital setting. The concluding article is another approach to the development of organizations through improved utilization of human resources. Robert M. Ford analyzes the ways in which American Telephone and Telegraph Company has pioneered in the field of job enrichment of both routine white-collar and blue-collar jobs, including a new approach—the "nesting" of related jobs—which goes beyond individual job enrichment.

organization theory

19. a contingency model of organization design
Y. K. Shetty and Howard M. Carlisle

Organizations have played an important role in the history of mankind, but attempts to analyze and understand them have progressed very slowly and perceptions about them are often elusive. However, the last decade witnessed a new direction in the study of organizations. Evidence from recent research indicates that there is no one best way to organize an enterprise as was once thought. An organization is not an independent entity, but rather an interdependent system—a result of complex interaction between itself and the environment. A consistent organization style is no virtue if it prevents an organization from coping effectively

© 1972 by The Regents of the University of California. Reprinted from *California Management Review*, Vol. 15, No. 1, pp. 38–45, by permission of The Regents.

The authors wish to express sincere thanks and deep gratitude to Dr. S. B. Prasad of Ohio University, College of Business Administration for his comments on the first draft of this paper.

with its problems and opportunities. The type of organization most suitable in a particular setting depends on its internal and external environment. Basically, this approach is leading to the development of the "contingency model" of organization design. The optimal organization pattern is contingent on the managerial situation. To put it differently, organizational designs appropriate to one technological and market environment may not be appropriate for another. It must be tailor-made for the firm.

This article will examine some of the recent research findings on organizations and suggest a scheme for understanding how different organizational patterns may develop in response to specific combinations of elements in the internal and external environment. Before pursuing this, a brief review of the theories of organization will help provide a suitable background.

Classical Model. Early in the twentieth

century the great German sociologist Max Weber, noting common elements in different types of organizations (business, government, and military), called this form of organization, bureaucracy. In his bureaucratic system, Weber placed very heavy emphasis on a hierarchical structure, position, authority, and rules for solving repetitive problems. Functionaries with specialized training learn their tasks better by practice. "Precision, speed, unambiguity, knowledge of the files, continuity, discretion, unity, strict subordination, reduction of friction and of material and personal costs—these are raised to the optimum point in the strictly bureaucratic administration, and in its monocratic form."[1] It could be said that Weber tried to promote efficiency through technical proficiency, a disregard for personal feelings, and governance by rules and regulations. As bureaucracy develops towards perfection, the more it is dehumanized and the more completely it succeeds in eliminating from official business all purely personal, irrational and emotional elements. Weber said that bureaucracy was succeeding because of its machine-like qualities.

Around the same time, Frederick W. Taylor popularized "scientific management" in which man is thought of as mechanical and motivated by economic considerations. Though Taylor was primarily concerned with the production aspects of an organization, some of his proposals, such as functional foremanship and separation of planning and doing, had indirect implications to organization structure. The classical organization theory was further developed and refined by Mooney and Reiley, Fayol, Gulick, Urwick and others. They based their theory of departmentalization on the assumption that an organization, given an overall mission, will be able to identify the required tasks, allocate and coordinate these tasks by giving jobs to sections, place the section within units, unite the units within departments and coordinate departments under a board, all in the most economic manner. They thought of an organization as a rational instrument for implementing objectives and policies.

The classical organization theory met with widespread acceptance among many managers and some writers in management. But in recent years the theory has encountered growing criticism. A major criticism is that the classical organization principles are too broad to provide much help in the actual work of designing organizations. The principle of specialization, for example, does not tell the organizer how the tasks should be divided, and to say that an organization needs coordination is merely to state the obvious. It is also claimed that some of the principles contradict others and that, therefore, it is impossible to observe them all. Herbert A. Simon agrees that unity of command is incompatible with the principle of specialization. He concludes that some of the other classical principles are "no more than proverbs," and that administrative theory must be concerned with the weights that should be given to each of the various principles in any concrete situation.[2] Simply stated, this criticism implies that the classical theory is simplistic, contains contradictory principles, and is "normative" rather than "empirical," (it says what ought to be rather than what is).

The most insistent criticism leveled against the classical organization theory comes from behavioral scientists. They

[1] H. H. Gerth and C. Wright Mills (eds.), *From Max Weber: Essays in Sociology* (Fair Lawn, N.J.: Oxford University Press, 1958) p. 214.

[2] Herbert Simon, *Administrative Behavior* (New York: Macmillan Publishing Co., Inc., 1957), p. 44.

claim the classical theory is too mechanistic and thus ignores major facets of human nature. The rational model has been attacked as an abstraction that overlooks human behavior, the non-rational elements in human conduct and their implications for operators. Some even claim that the theory is incompatible with human nature. This is a serious omission for formal structures are designed solely for the purpose of enabling people to work effectively together for a common goal.

Of late, bureaucracy has been attacked on another count. It is argued that "bureaucracy thrives in a highly competitive, undifferentiated and stable environment ... A pyramidal structure and authority, with power concentrated in the hands of few with the knowledge and resources to control an entire enterprise was, and is, an eminently suitable social arrangement for routinized tasks. However, the environment has changed ... which makes the mechanism most problematic."[3]

Behavioral Model. The behavioral theory reacts to the excessive mechanistic structure and argues that an industrial organization should be viewed as a social system with at least two objectives: producing the product and generating and distributing satisfaction among employees (achieving both economic effectiveness and job satisfaction). Hence, an organization should be considered a social system which has both economic and social dimensions.

Behavioralists argue that effectiveness is achieved by arranging matters so that people feel that they count, that they belong, and that work can be made meaningful. The behavioralists do not necessarily reject the classical doctrine, but they feel that more goes into an organization design than rules, regula-

[3] Warren Bennis, "Beyond Bureaucracy," *Trans-Actions* (July–August 1965), pp. 31–35.

tions and strict rationality. For instance, every member of any organization is unique to some degree, and all actions are not necessarily explained rationally. There is the element of subjectivity to an individual's actions: they are based on his perception and personal value system.

Behavioralists, at least the earlier ones, do not necessarily prescribe any one form of organization structure but believe it can be improved by modifying it in accordance with informal structure—through less narrow specialization and less emphasis on hierarchy, by permitting more participation in decision-making on the part of the lower ranks, and by a more democratic attitude on the part of the managers at all levels.

Organic Model. Recent years have seen the development of a form of organization structure based on behavioral theories called the organic organization—a structure in which there is a minimum of formal division of duties. According to this view, organizations should be composed of temporary task forces in which membership will shift as needs and problems change. Warren Bennis argues that bureaucracy (the classical structure) is too rigid to be serviceable in the time of rapid technological change and that it will therefore be replaced by the task-force type of organization. He says:

First of all, the key word will be temporary. Organizations will become adaptive, rapidly changing temporary systems. Second, they will be organized around problems-to-be-solved. Third, these problems will be solved by relative groups of strangers who represent a diverse set of professional skills. Fourth, given the requirements of coordinating the various projects, articulating points or "linking pin" personnel will be necessary who can speak the diverse language of research and who can relay and mediate between the various project groups. Fifth, the groups will be conducted on organic rather than on mechanical lines; they will emerge and adapt to the problems, and leadership and influence will fall to those who seem most able to solve the problems rather than the programmed role expectations. People will be differentiated, not according to rank or roles, but according to skills and training. ... Though no catchy phrase comes to mind, it might be called an organic-adaptive structure.[4]

organization patterns

The literature on organization shows that organizations can be characterized in various ways, but the degree of specificity of role prescription and its obverse, the range of discretion, seem most appropriate. The resulting dichotomy can be represented by these distinctions: closed system v. open system, formal v. flexible, programmed v. non-programmed, mechanistic v. organic (or organismic), habit v. problem solving, and structured v. unstructured.[5] The mechanistic structure is likely to be less open, more formalized, and so on, while the organic structure is likely to be open and less formalized.

Thus organization patterns can be portrayed on a scale with mechanistic at one end and organic-adaptive at the other. Organic organizations are characterized by less formalized definitions of jobs, by more stress on flexibility and adaptability and by communication networks involving more consultation than command. Mechanistic organizations are characterized by rigid specialized functionalization, and in general define the opposite pole from an organic-adaptive continuum. In between the poles are various patterns which an organization can display. In general terms, functional organization falls closer to mechanical structure and project organization comes closer to organic structure.

[4] Warren Bennis, "Organizational Developments and the Fate of Bureaucracy," *Industrial Management Review* (Spring 1966), p. 52.
[5] D. J. Hickson, "A Convergence in Organization Theory," *Administrative Science Quarterly* (September 1966), pp. 224–237.

Most organizations are formed through evolutionary processes rather than by design. At certain stages, design or re-design takes place, by codification or modification of the results of the evolution or by reaction to environmental forces. An adequate framework for developing organization theory should make it possible to increase the role of a conscious design process in the development of an organization. Hopefully, the suggested model would provide such a framework. The question of organization design can fruitfully be explored by identifying the diverse forces influencing the structure. Then the question is: What factors or forces should be considered in deciding how to design an organization structure? These are of particular importance:

- forces in the manager,
- forces in the task,
- forces in the environment, and
- forces in the subordinates.

The following is a brief analysis of these elements which would indicate how they might influence a company's actions in designing an organization. The strength of each will, of course, vary from instance to instance, but management which is sensitive to them can better assess the problems which face it and determine which mode of organizational pattern is most appropriate for it.

Forces in the Managers. The design of an organization in any instance will be influenced greatly by the many forces operating within managers' personalities. Managers, of course, perceive their organizational problems in a unique way based on their background, knowledge, experience and values.

Management, particularly top management, may be the most important influence in shaping organization structure. They decide initially what industry the organization will enter, how it will compete (for example, price, quality, diversity of product line, service, and so on), where it will be located, the kind of organization it will be, who will be the top managers, and who will directly influence the organization structure. All these decisions have to be made in the context of the relationship between the environment and the managerial philosophy of the entrepreneurs involved. As R. M. Cyert and J. G. March point out, "Organizations do not have objectives; only people do."[6]

Alfred Chandler has clearly shown the relationship between the strategy a business adopts, consciously or otherwise, and the structure of its organization.[7] According to him, different types of organizations will necessarily cope effectively with different managerial strategies. The choice of corporate purpose and the design and administration of organizational process for accomplishing purposes are by no means impersonal procedures, unaffected by the characteristics of the manager.

How strongly the manager feels that individuals should have freedom and autonomy in their own sphere of work will have an important influence in organizational design. Douglas McGregor[8] identified the bedrock assumptions about human nature which support markedly different approaches to organization and management—the theories X and Y. The organization structure emerging from the managerial value system implied by the view that man is inherently lazy and pursues goals contrary to the interests of the company is not the same as that which emerges from the obverse image of human nature. The implicitly held management value system manifests itself in contrasting

organizational designs. The manner in which work is organized and decision-making authority is distributed, the span of control, the shape of the organization, and so forth—all depend upon the underlying value system of managers. A theory X value system might lead to a more mechanistic organization, while a theory Y value system might lead to a more organic structure.

Managers' assumptions about the external environment and its relations with the organization will influence the organization structure. If the managers believe that organizations could function effectively by being able merely to adjust to external environmental conditions, then the structural model will be closer to bureaucracy. This is basically a process of equilibrium, rather than change. When managers believe that an organization could not only respond to change but could be an agent of change, then the structure will be closer to organic-adaptive.

Forces in the Task. The task element in an organization situation is the central point of concern in any type of organization design and analysis. The nature of the task will have important influence on how the organization is designed.

Significant empirical literature is emerging relating technology to various organization variables. Joan Woodward, Charles Perrow, James D. Thompson and several others consider technology to be a major determinant of organization structure.[9] In her study, Joan Woodward reveals some interesting insights into the relationship between technology and organization structure. She found that organization

---

[6] R. M. Cyert and J. G. March, *A Behavioral Theory of the Firm* (Englewood Cliffs: Prentice-Hall, Inc., 1963).

[7] Alfred D. Chandler, *Strategy and Structure* (Cambridge, Mass.: MIT Press, 1962).

[8] Douglas McGregor, *The Human Side of Enterprise* (New York: McGraw-Hill, 1960).

[9] See Joan Woodward, *Industrial Organization: Theory and Practice* (Fair Lawn, N.J.: Oxford University Press, 1965); also Charles Perrow, "A Framework for the Comparative Analysis of Organization," *American Sociological Review* (April 1967), pp. 194–208; and James D. Thompson, *Organizations in Action* (New York: McGraw-Hill, 1967).

structure varied according to the type of technology. Let us examine some of the technological variables influencing the structure.

The production technology limits the amount of discretion which subordinates can be given and, hence, influences organization structure. Woodward found that the organization structure varied depending upon the type of technology— different technologies seem to have varying degrees of "management content." Management content is substantially higher in continuous-process technology than in the unit-production technology. Fewer managers supervise more people in unit production than in mass-production or continuous-process technologies. Since unit production technologies have the fewest managers and supervisors in relation to subordinates, it would mean that these technologies also have the wider span of control or "flat" organization structure. If technology can dictate the ratio of managerial personnel it may, therefore, limit the amount of freedom which subordinates can be given.

Also, under unit-production technology, relatively higher levels of skills may be necessary at the worker level in terms of technical knowledge of the job, methods, tools, knowledge about operating errors, inspection skills and control. Under these conditions the employees are more likely to perform effectively when they are given more freedom on the job. Research suggests that skilled workers feel more involved in their jobs and are more anxious for an opportunity to participate in making decisions relating to it than are unskilled workers. This makes it possible to delegate more authority to lower levels in the organization.

Technology may determine the extent to which the job may be programmed, that is, employee behaviors may be precisely specified. The kind of organization required in a low task structure is not the same as that required in a high task structure. It is meaningless to talk of permitting exercise of discretion to assembly line workers; the very nature of technology tends to develop unique interests. While the organic type of work organization has a relatively autonomous task, each member of the group feels responsible for the entire organization. Under such circumstances competent internal coordination and group responsibility develop. In situations where cooperation arises spontaneously out of the structure of the work it is far easier to adopt more flexible structure compared to a highly structured arrangement, where coordination is not so spontaneous.

One of the elements of technology which is also related to the organization pattern is the nature of work flow. The amount of discretion given to subordinates seems to vary according to the type of specialization. Parallel specialization occurs where work flow is organized to minimize the amount of coordination required, that is, the work flow among individuals and departments is at a minimum. Interdependence specialization occurs where the activities of one individual or department are closely dependent on other individuals or departments. Unit production technology is one of the examples of parallel specialization and mass production technology is an example of interdependent specialization.

Interdependent specialization is characterized by lateral relationship in order to obtain effective coordination between specialized groups. At the same time, under this type of specialization, the subordinates have a vested interest in their own typical point of view or approach to problems and are unable to see the impact of their actions on others. Only the personnel at the top would have the interest of the total organization and, thus, be able to see the overall picture and integrate the efforts of the different parts in order to achieve the overall organizational goals.

Under unit-production, employees see themselves as responsible for a total process, something with an observable output, and are able to see the total efforts rather than a part. For these reasons, under parallel specialization, a more organic type of organization may be appropriate, but interdependent specialization may call for a less organic type of structure and a decreasing delegation of authority to the lower levels.

The size of an organization influences its coordination, direction, control, and reporting systems and, hence, the organization structure. Where an organization is small, interaction is confined to a relatively small group, communication is simpler, less information is required for decision-making and there is less need for formal organization aspects.

Forces in the Environment. The environment in which an organization as a whole functions—its product and supply markets, the field of relevant technical knowledge, its political and socio-cultural environments—has a strong influence on the organization. Recent studies suggest that the most effective pattern of organization structure is the one which enables an organization to adjust to the requirements of its environment.[10] It is argued that the pattern of these environmental requirements over time, particularly with respect to their variability, may create different

levels of uncertainty with which the organization has to cope through its structural arrangements. These different environments will tend to require different structural accommodation.

The market environment that an organization chooses to enter substantially influences the design of an organization. The market environment includes the availability of resources, the type of products or services provided by the company, the nature of competition, the predictability or unpredictability of demand, product innovation, and change, to mention a few. The characteristics of the product or service pervasively influence the entire organization and its component parts.

Lawrence and Lorsch[11] found that organizations operating effectively in different environments had different patterns of differentiation, and had developed different organizational mechanisms to achieve the differentiation and integration required by their environments. They found (from their research of ten firms in three distinct industrial environments) that the environments of uncertainty and rapid rates of market and technological change place different requirements on the organizational design than do stable conditions. They also found that the degree of differentiation among the functional units of the organization was related to the relative certainty of the parts of the environment and their resulting diversity or homogeneity.

The managers in the functional departments of the most dynamic environments had developed a high degree of differentiation in thought and pattern. In the most stable environments there was less differentiation in pattern and thought. Also, for firms in these environments to be effective, they must have developed the

[10] See Paul R. Lawrence and Jay W. Lorsch, *Organization and Environment* (Boston: Harvard Business School, 1967); also, T. Burns and G. M. Stalker, *The Management of Innovation* (London: Tavistock, 1961); also, F. E. Emery and E. L. Trist, "The Casual Texture of Organizational Environment," *Human Relations* (February 1965), pp. 21–32; and Jay R. Galbraith, "Environmental and Technological Determinants of Organization Design," *Studies in Organization Design* (Homewood, Ill.: Richard D. Irwin, 1970), pp. 113–139.

[11] Paul R. Lawrence and J. W. Lorsch, *op. cit.*

required state of interdepartmental integration. A firm's departments must function in unique ways to fulfill their individual purposes, but must also coordinate to be completely effective. Their study strongly indicates that organizations with less formal structure and widely shared influence (organic) are best able to cope with uncertain and heterogeneous environmental conditions. Conversely, highly structured (mechanistic) organizations will be more effective in stable environments.

According to Burns and Stalker[12], in the science-based industries such as electronics, where innovation is a constant demand, the organic type of organization is appropriate. Lacking a frozen structure, an organic organization grows around the point of innovating success. Studies of communication reinforce the point that the optimal conditions for innovation are non-hierarchical. In an organization not primarily concerned with technological innovation but preoccupied with production problems, however, a mechanistic type of structure is needed to facilitate coordination.

Jay Galbraith[13] used data collected at the Boeing Company to substantiate a similar point. He describes conditions prior to 1964 and then the changes which occurred in the environment in which Boeing was operating. There was an increased demand due to increased air traffic, and there was a very significant change in the market in which Boeing was operating. Their response was mainly to increase coordination. There was more uncertainty in decisions and plans. Boeing had to become much more functional to maintain its position. A liaison group was developed between product and process design to reduce uncertainties. Another coordination device was the task

force which provided additional interfunctional coordination. Task force members worked full time as long as the task existed. This was a temporary structure change which modified the authority relationship during the periods of high uncertainty. In this case, organizational change followed an environmental change and Galbraith treats the uncertainty of the task as the basic independent variable influencing the design of the organization. On the whole, considerable research has indicated that organizations with low degrees of formal structure could more profitably cope with changing environments than those which have a higher degree of formal structure.

Forces in the Subordinates. There is some research evidence suggesting that a major contribution to organizational effectiveness will derive from adapting the structure to accommodate more adequately the psychological needs of organizational members. Chris Argyris, Frederick Herzberg[14] and others have drawn attention to the conflict which is likely to prevail between a traditional definition of formal organization structure and the needs of psychologically mature individuals. Herzberg has developed a two-factor theory of employee motivation which suggests specific structural adaptation to provide the "job enrichment" to enhance motivation and performance. Therefore, before designing an organization structure, it is necessary to consider a number of forces affecting the subordinate's behavior and performance. The subordinate's desire for independence, skill and motivation for assuming responsibility, need for a sense of achievement, and so forth, will greatly influence the organization structure. Research suggests that, compared to

---

[12] T. Burns and G. M. Stalker, *op. cit.*
[13] J. R. Galbraith, *op. cit.*

[14] See Chris Argyris, *Integrating the Individual and the Organization* (New York: Wiley, 1964); also Frederick Herzberg, *Work and Nature of Man* (New York: The World Publishing Company, 1966).

unskilled workers, skilled workers and professional personnel are more involved in their jobs and are more anxious for an opportunity to have a high degree of autonomy on the job and an opportunity to participate in making decisions relating to it.[15] Studies consistently show that scientists as well as professional employees want autonomy and job freedom. They prefer not to be commanded in the same way as other employees in the organization.

There is also research evidence to suggest that some workers have positive attitudes toward work and can be called "motivation seekers," while others, who seem relatively unaffected by the same conditions, can be called "maintenance seekers." Perhaps the significant difference is that maintenance reaches a state of relative fulfillment at the primary needs level, whereas motivation seekers continue to be motivated by the need for higher level of social acceptance.[16] This implies that certain forces in the subordinates will have substantial influence in designing an organization structure.

a contingency model

The organization structure is a product of many forces: the forces in the managers, the forces in the technology and environment, and the forces in the subordinates. The structure evolves through a complex and dynamic interaction between these forces which can be depicted graphically (see Figure 1).

These simultaneously interacting forces shape the pattern of organization chosen by companies. Every organization is in

[15] Howard Vollmer, *Employment Rights and the Employment Relationship* (Berkeley: University of California Press, 1960).
[16] M. Scott Myers, "Who Are Your Motivated Workers?" *Harvard Business Review* (January–February 1964), pp. 73–88.

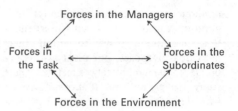

Figure 1. Interacting Forces in Which Organization Structure Evolves

the middle of varying and complex pressures. They react to the many pressures and demands of environment. The successful organization is one that takes into account the forces suggested above and which is sensitive to individual situational needs. Once a firm adopts this contingency framework, it will begin to look more closely at and analyze more thoroughly the relevant variables. It is a company which identifies the kinds of conditions which enhance a particular pattern of structure in some situations and impedes its effectiveness in others. It is neither a bureaucracy nor a complete organic-adaptive model, but rather maintains a balance determined by the particular situation in question. The consistent and effective practices of an organization at one level may be of little use in another department having different technological considerations. The organization appropriate in one market-technology environment may be irrelevant or even dysfunctional in another environment. A firm producing a standardized product sold in a stable market may require a pattern of organization altogether different from a company manufacturing a highly technical product for a more dynamic market. There is no one pattern of organization style that is universally appropriate.

conclusion

Organization theory has increased in importance as organizations themselves have become more complex. The production-centered classical theory stressed strict compliance to rules and regulations. The behavioral theory was people-centered and behavioral scientists stressed the worth of the individual, his needs, and the functioning of social groups. Today, the organic approach is gaining strength in a number of technologically advanced firms. Generally speaking, whereas the classical model tended to hold in more stable environments, the organic model is more appropriate to dynamic environments.

A contingency theory is developed which puts the stress of organizing on a number of variables. The theory supports the idea that there is no one best way in which to organize. The design is conditional. An effective organization, it was found, must be designed to fit its managers, market environment, technology and its subordinates. The need to understand the theoretical aspects stems from the need to solve what, at first sight, seem to be low-level operational problems but which on closer examination may turn out to be organizational problems of a higher order.

20. organization and management techniques in the federal government

Forest W. Horton, Jr.

The population, knowledge and technology explosions which have taken place primarily since the end of World War II have had a profound effect on many of the fundamental assumptions and doctrines underlying traditional organization and management theory.

For example:

- Bureaucracy as we know it is becoming obsolete as a social system effective in organizing the efforts of human and other resources to achieve stated goals.
- Classic organization and management theories, such as span of control formulas prescribing "optimal" ratios of supervisors-to-workers, are

Reprinted from *S.A.M. Advanced Management Journal*, 35, No. 1 (January 1970), pp. 66–77, with permission of the publisher.

proving to be either incorrect or no longer valid.

- The emergence of a new discipline—Behavioral Science—is bringing with it a new concept of the relationship of man to his environment; a concept based on increased knowledge of his complex and changing needs which replaces the oversimplified, innocent push-button idea of man.

From a managerial standpoint, then, a key dimension to the problem of modern organizational structure is the *temporal dimension*. That is, the need for organizations to become more adaptive and responsive to rapidly changing environments, problems, and objectives.

This article discusses one possible solution to this problem—the use of "task forces" and project managers as techniques in improving problem-solving and goal achievement as well as in motivating people to higher productivity and job satisfaction.

While some authors have argued that highly flexible and adaptive organic structures will eventually become the *only* viable form of organization, that thesis goes beyond the scope of this article. It will be my contention that task forces and project managers are useful management techniques even in the highly functionally-oriented, traditionally-structured organizations that characterize most of industry and government today.

some conclusions

1. The Task Force and Project Manager Concepts are very effective approaches to contemporary problem-solving and goal achievement in large and complex modern organizations.

2. The Task Force and Project Manager Concepts are more rewarding and productive approaches to the ego-satisfaction and motivation needs of human behavior in modern organizational settings than are the more traditional approaches based on classic organizational theory.

3. As a first general rule, the larger and more complex an organization and the more specialized and diversified its product lines, services and objectives, the greater the utility of these approaches.

4. As a second general rule, the larger the number of individual skill categories needed to produce a product or service or accomplish an objective, the greater the utility of these approaches.

5. As a third general rule, the larger the number of organizational sub-elements (i.e., the greater the compartmentalization), the greater the utility of these approaches.

6. The Task Force and Project Manager concepts are most useful in organizational settings wherein top management is committed to that set of values embodied essentially by the late Douglas McGregor's Theory Y.[1]

7. The Task Force and Project Manager concepts are more useful in organizations with large numbers of professional personnel than in organizations with primarily semi-skilled or unskilled personnel.

8. Even in organizations with primarily semi-skilled and unskilled personnel, these modern approaches will find increasing utility as the pressures of leisure time create increasing emotional needs for a higher order of job satisfaction.

background

There is fairly widespread agreement of the concepts of the Task Forces and Project Management (use of Project Managers) developed as a new method of management during World War II in both the military establishment and in industry.

A number of different terms have been applied to what is essentially the same basic concept. They are:

- *"Project Management"* which is the term given to the concept as it originated primarily in the Defense Department. The aerospace industry-government relationship in World War II had developed a tendency toward greater use of *ad hoc* offices concerned exclusively with the managerial integration of a single major weapon. The head of the office re-

[1] McGregor, Douglas, *The Human Side of Enterprise*, McGraw-Hill Book Company, 1960.

sponsible for the effort was generally called the Project Manager (or sometimes and more specifically, for example, the Weapons Systems Manager).

- *"Product Management"* was the more or less equivalent term introduced in industry. As new products began to appear with increasing frequency than ever before, and tended to be discounted after a shorter stay on the market, the idea of a Product Manager who could coordinate the traditional functions of engineering, manufacturing, purchasing, quality, sales and the other functions, came into being.

- *"Program Management"* was the term introduced in the non-defense side of the government establishment, as well as in other forms of organizations outside of the private industry, such as non-profit foundations. In these kinds of organizations, the "program" was the discrete task that cut across organizational boundaries and required coordination among the various functional departments.

- *"Task Force"* is a more general-purpose term used extensively even before World War II to describe the technique of bringing together a variety of specialists to perform a specific task. One connotation of this concept that has persisted over the years is the notion of the task itself having to be one of very high priority and having a relatively short or "tight" deadline for accomplishment.

- *"Matrix Management"* is perhaps the most recent title given to what is still essentially the same concept. It has won favor with the behavioral scientists particularly. Its focus is on the vertical, horizontal and diagonal relationships between and among staff and line managers. It emphasizes

the critical importance of the coordination function and process as opposed to traditional chain of command, span of control, and similar notions.

The device of the "committee" also deserves attention in this context. While it, too, fits the basic criteria of a temporary organizational approach to problem-solving, through the years it has taken on some unfortunate negative connotations that probably account for its exclusion from the family of terms described above. For one thing, committees have often deliberately been used as a means of delaying or deferring problem-solving rather than promoting it. For another, committees have gained the reputation, perhaps undeservedly, of "producing a camel from what is essentially a horse!" In government circles particularly, the comment is often heard that if one doesn't know what else to do with a problem, then one should turn it over to a committee! That, such cynics contend, will be sure to kill it!

Notwithstanding the cynics, the device of the committee does have its place and is perhaps used at least as widely as are task forces. There are some key differences, however.

First, committees are more formal than task forces and their very formality tends to run counter to some of the underlying purposes of task forces. Task forces thrive on informality, easy interpersonal relationships and the absence of rigid sets of rules that prescribe the modes and norms of "acceptable" behavior and procedure. The task force leader or project manager does not have to rely on a *Robert's Rules of Order* or other parliamentary conventions to achieve his goals and carry out his assigned tasks. Other aspects of the formality variable that differentiate these two approaches include the need for formal agendas, formal written periodic reports, "hearings," etc. Usually none of these are required of task forces and project managers.

Second, committees tend to be convened to deal with chronic and longstanding major policy and organizational problems that often have significant legal, legislative, or other "external" environmental aspects that may involve the interests, rights or obligations of diverse groups, whereas, task forces tend to be organized to deal with special, critical and sensitive high priority problems that have cropped up rather suddenly and which can be "solved" rather than just "studied."

I think a final word is necessary to distinguish the task force concept from the project management concept since I have chosen both as my subjects and have thus far referred to them in the text as if they were virtually synonymous in concept, purpose, and application.

They are in fact very closely related. The essential difference is that task forces are usually organized to deal with *problems* rather than monitor "from birth to death" a project or product. The project manager and his project office staff are dealing with a more tangible item—the project or product. But both are temporary, composed of specialists brought together because of their unique skills and abilities to contribute to the overall task, and are built upon the same fundamental assumptions about the nature of man and his needs espoused by McGregor and the modern behavioral scientists.

Therefore, for the balance of this article I will deal with them interchangeably— essentially as one concept, but recognizing that strictly and technically speaking they are in reality two very closely related species belonging to the same family.

Because the problems encountered in the defense industry have, in respect to the need to adjust to drastic and accelerated change, been perhaps more crucial than in other industries, it is not surprising that this industry has been in the forefront of the development of the task force concept.

Among those names most prominently mentioned in the literature as being on the leading edge in the use of this technique have been such groups as the RAND Corporation, Stanford Research Institute, Research Analysis Corporation (RAC), Systems Development Corporation (SDC), The Jet Propulsion Laboratory, Rocketdyne, Thomson-Ramo-Wolridge (TRW), Boeing Aircraft, Martin-Marietta Company, Lockheed Corporation and International Business Machines. Nearly all are members of the Aerospace and defense-related industries. Nearly all have reputations of "progressive" management philosophies; have felt keenly the competitive pressures of needing to act decisively in a very limited time frame in order to complete a proposal or respond to a bid; have felt the severe pressures of competing in very limited human resource markets for scarce skills such as electronic engineers, data processing systems analysts, physicists, mathematicians, etc.; and have been at the forefront in developing new technologies in the very exciting and challenging creative areas of satellites, missiles, high energy physics, nuclear reactors, atomic energy and others. In other words, these are the firms that have marched at the front of the modern technological revolution.

On the government side, as one might suspect, those government organizations and agencies which have been associated with the modern technological revolution also have experimented the most with this technique. Among these agencies, those most generally acknowledged to be the leaders have been such agencies as the Department of Defense, Atomic Energy Commission, National Aeronautics and Space Agency, Central Intelligence Agency and the Office of Economic Opportunity.

NASA

NASA's experience is perhaps the most instructive and in many ways the most typical of the agencies cited. Furthermore, its experiences have tended to meld the use of this technique as between government and industry. For these reasons, I think it would be useful to look at their experience a little more closely.

NASA's James E. Webb[2] recently said, "We are seeing increasing use of organizational concepts like product management and project management in which the responsibility for the development and marketing of a product or for the completion of an important project are put in the hands of one individual who has all of the required elements of command over all the resources he needs. What characterizes these new kinds of organizational structures is that they cut across the traditional proverbs used to express concepts of authority and responsibility. They utilize, rather than accept as limits, the differences of functional discipline or the division of work into bits and pieces. At NASA, for example, whenever possible, even while exercising very broad authority associated with his responsibility for performance, cost and schedule, an individual is left attached to the laboratory or technical group or department within his technical competence, where his skill was demonstrated and where the forward thrust of current research keeps him up to date. This also gives him easy access to colleagues who know how to wring out the facts needed for the difficult trade-off decisions."

Another idea advanced by Mr. Webb is that as organizations become more complex and their challenges more interdisciplinary in character, it is becoming

[2] Webb, James E., "New Challenges for Organization," *Harvard Business School Bulletin*, March/April, 1967.

increasingly apparent that there is nothing sacred about the notion of a single chief executive. Accordingly, he points out, there has been an increasing tendency to experiment with the idea of the "multiple executive," usually in the form of an "office of the president" concept.

Although Mr. Webb alluded to the context of the "multiple executives" in the context of NASA's *permanent* organizational structure, he was also drawing a parallel to the purpose and utility of such an arrangement within the context of the task force concept which embodies a *temporary* organizational structure. Underlying the multiple executive idea is the more fundamental notion beginning to take hold in both modern organizational and behavioral science theory that the leadership function can often be shared. Some research is even beginning to indicate that under certain conditions sharing the leadership function among the members of a group can be more effective than vesting the functions in a single individual.

This is not to say necessarily that the "chairmanship should rotate" among members or that sub-tasks should be divided up so that each man bosses his own piece of the pie; but rather that the atmosphere, structure, and values personified by the task force concept are more conducive to a participative approach to the leadership function than are traditional concepts.

Mr. Webb summarized his experiences using this technique saying that "in the complex challenge that we are talking about, it is rarely possible to attribute the solution or an achievement to one individual. In this kind of effort, the boundaries between disciplines are all but erased. The skills of individuals fuse with one another. It is virtually impossible to identify who has contributed some key elements to the final outcome."

Of course, what Mr. Webb leaves implicit is recognition that under such a system personal job satisfaction and reward come equally from feelings of being a member of an effective and competent *team* and from feelings of individual accomplishment, not solely from the latter.

project managers

Cleland[3] points out that forerunners of the project manager are designated as "project expeditors;" they do not perform line functions but rather informally motivate those persons doing the work. The project expeditor is mainly concerned with schedules and relies upon his personal diplomacy and persuasive abilities to remove bottlenecks in the management process. He is perhaps the earliest kind of project manager; ranked slightly above him in terms of time and responsibility is the "project coordinator" who has a more formal role in the organization and who is concerned with the synchronization of organizational activities directed toward a specific objective in the overall functional activities. His limited independence is reflected in his freedom to make decisions within the framework of the overall project objectives; he does not actively enter into the management functions outside of his particular organization. The project coordinator has specific functional authority in certain areas such as budgeting, release of funds, and release of authority to act as in the dispatching function in the production control environment.

The difference, then, between the early beginnings of the project management concept and today's stage of evolution of the concept is that today's project manager is *in every sense a manager*. He actively participates in the organic functions of

[3] Cleland, D. I., "Why Project Management," *Business Horizons*, Winter 1964, Vol. 7, No. 4.

planning, organizing, directing, and controlling the organization of the specific project. The project manager usually accomplishes the management process through other managers. Many of those feel the force of his leadership in the departments and organizations separate from the project manager's parent unit. Since these people are not subject to his operating supervision and owe their fidelity to a superior line manager, a unique set of conflicts of purpose and tenure (job seniority and rank) arise. The project manager has real and explicit authority but only over major considerations involved in the project plan. One of the project manager's biggest problems (which I shall examine in more detail later) is how to get full support when the functional people are responsible to someone else for pay raises, promotion, and the other expected line superior-subordinate relationships.

discussion and analysis

First, I want to summarize some key assumptions which I think are crucial to any discussion and analysis of the concept of task forces and project management. They are:

- The need for organizations to react quickly and effectively to risks and opportunities before either the risk becomes seriously threatening or the opportunity is lost.

- The need for organizations to utilize a wide variety of skills and expertise to solve problems, meet risks and take advantage of opportunities. Often many disciplines, experts in highly specialized fields and persons with broad experience backgrounds, must be brought together quickly. Rarely can all of the people "assigned" to any given standing functional unit solve a given problem.

- The need for organizations to create conditions in a working environment wherein people from different "cultures" and "subcultures" can come together with maximum interpersonal and intergroup effectiveness; where conflict is constructively channeled; and where there is a rapid and intense involvement with a minimum of cross-cultural "wasted motion."

- The recognition that problems and objectives are constantly in a state of flux; old ones are being resolved and new ones are being created. Rarely is the organization faced with long-standing, chronic and unresolved issues. (If it is, it will often go bankrupt or otherwise decay.)

- The hierarchal, traditional concept of authority is becoming increasingly less useful in solving modern organizational problems because more and more of these problems are cutting across jurisdictional lines within the organization. Therefore, all units that have an interest in the problem have virtually equal status and must work together without any particular one being considered the "boss" and thus having preemptive influence or authority over the others. Voluntary cooperation, therefore, becomes the only viable means of cohesiveness.

- The emphasis that bureaucracy places on structural maintenance leads to sanctification of procedure and to domineering attitudes of officials. Although apparently quite unlike, these two structural pathologies have one thing in common: the frequent failure of bureaucratic functionaries to separate means from ends. Procedures which are means become ends for the functionary who is imbued with the sanctity of impersonal application of abstract rules. This is not in the interests of problem-solving and goal achievement.

My contention in this article has been that task forces and project management offer a great deal of promise to organizations faced with the kinds of problems that stem from the foregoing assumptions.

The concept offers this promise by placing a premium on the conditions under which motivation, communication, goal-setting, decision-making, problem-solving, and performance evaluation can best take place. Rewards and punishments are geared to constructive group effort, not to the traditional measures of reward such as status, position, rank, pay, title, size of office, thickness of carpet on the floor and size of desk.

That is not to say that these considerations are entirely "missing" from the rewards and punishments system; but rather that they are given *secondary* rather than primary emphasis. Status, rank, pay, and similar considerations must always enter the motivation process. But if rewards and punishments are largely (if not entirely) based on *just* those kinds of considerations, then I would contend that in the long run productive, collaborative group effort will suffer and progressively deteriorate.

Now let us examine more closely some of the specific problems and issues which have given rise to these new theories.

First, recognition of the fact that people are basically different in makeup. Their values, attitudes, behavior, etc. vary widely. Janger[4] points out in studies he has made that project managers themselves feel that not all people fit into their project organization. There are some people who can't stand the informality.

[4] Janger, A. R., "Anatomy of the Project Organization," *Business Management Record*, November 1963.

If two people have demands made on them, they feel that they have two bosses which to them is intolerable. There are people who want their work laid out for them precisely and who feel insecure without established procedures. Then there are people who misuse freedom of communication to go over their superior's head. Unless these people learn to work together as "responsible professionals" they don't stay on a team for long! Generally those groups which do not adapt as well to this permissive environment are in the less-skilled, lower-paid, and more security-conscious job categories such as those characterized by large numbers of blue collar, assembly-line workers in minimal competition industries and organizations.

Second, shifting people from project to project leaves them in a constant state of flux. Some people have more tolerance for such a state than others. Shifting people from project to project may disrupt the training of new employees and specialists, interfering with the growth and maturation of specialists within the fields of specialization. Furthermore, the long-term capability and effectiveness of an organization may be further impaired if project-team members fear they may not have their jobs when the project is over.

To offset this fear, some companies heavily involved with project work attempt to stabilize employment in a number of ways: (1) by seeking enough new business to keep people working; (2) by avoiding, insofar as possible, projects that may go through periods of unpredictable delay or show likelihood of being cancelled; (3) by scheduling projects so that several do not begin or end at the same time; and (4) by scheduling the work in several projects so that, as specialists finish work on one project, they may be moved smoothly to another, cutting the likelihood of shortages or surpluses in particular specialties.

Third, since in the event of disagreements with the head of functional units project managers have only one "technically feasible," authoritative recourse, namely to go to their common superior to get what they want, how does the project manager really continue to get things done if he has "used up his currency" with the top common superior by going to him too often? The answer, of course, as has been implied above, is that the real key to the project management is to establish and maintain good, mutually helpful relationships with functional managers. The operative words here are consultation, involvement, participation, cooperation, collaboration and trying to develop and attain shared goals.

Fourth, in recognition of the immediately preceding point, does it necessarily follow that all managers make good project managers? Gaddis[5] thinks not. He says that a project manager is not a superman. He cannot be expected to double as a member of an executive committee and as a scientist or some other kind of expert or professional as well. Being a little of both, he is different from both. And it is, according to Gaddis, precisely this quality which makes him so valuable. In his own right he does what neither the front office executive nor the specialist can do: accomplish the aims of his corporate management, while serving as a perpetual buffer so that the engineers, scientists, and other technical and specialist personnel can meet the technological objectives that only they can define and only their output can meet.

Fifth, even if we wanted to, the pure functional approach cannot be applied when the task at hand involves the coordinated effort of hundreds of organizational elements and the coordinated efforts of hundreds of people. A combat

[5] Gaddis, P. O., "The Project Manager," *Harvard Business Review*, Vol. 37, No. 3, May/June 1959.

aircraft, for example, is developed and produced through the coordinated efforts of literally dozens of industrial and governmental units. Certain advanced, functionally-oriented, management methods have been invented to help alleviate this problem of coordinating the efforts of so many elements and individuals—such as PERT. But even these, by themselves, cannot "automatically" coordinate the management of the totality of the efforts involved. The sheer magnitude is simply too great.

handling the problems

Recognizing these problems, then, how does the project manager deal with them? Here, the perspectives and points of view of the three major groups or schools of management theorists—the "structuralists," the "functionalists" and the "behavioralists" all differ somewhat. Therefore, I think it would be useful to examine their various arguments.

First, the structuralists, such as Likert,[6] would argue that the project manager, as a unifying agent, integrates the parochial interests of autonomous organizational elements toward a common objective. Traditional lines of authority and responsibility are altered by the prerogatives of the project manager who possesses influence and power necessary to ensure unanimity of objective for all organizations involved in the project. More narrowly looked at from the commerical organization's point of view, the project organization offers an alternative to a functionally organized company or division that is big enough and complex enough to require some standard organization for product emphasis, but that cannot divisionalize along product lines.

Second, the functionalists such as Johnson et al,[7] would argue that project management is in reality simply the application of the systems concept to organization problems, given the recognition of the need for the breakdown of traditional functional specialization geared to optimizing performance of particular departments (which they allege is really sub-optimizing the overall organizational goals). The systems concept calls for integration, into a separate "organizational system," of activities related to particular projects or programs. The business organization, this school of thought contends, can no longer be thought of as a functional division of activities such as sales, finance, production, and personnel. Its breakdown into separate functional areas has been an artificial organizational device. Management science techniques, computer simulation approaches, and information-decision systems are just a few of the tools which will make it possible for management to visualize the firm as a total system.

Finally, the behavioralists such as Bennis[8] see the task force as organized around problems (not just products, programs, projects, or tasks, for example). They are, he says, often composed of groups of strangers who represent diverse sets of professional skills. They will, he contends, be arranged on an organic, rather than a mechanical model. The "executive" thus becomes a coordinator or "linking pin" between various task forces or projects. The task force leader or project manager must be a man, Bennis says, who can speak the diverse languages of research, with skills to relay information and to mediate between

[6] Likert, R., *The Human Organization: Its Management and Value*, McGraw-Hill, 1967.

[7] Johnson et al., *Theory and Management of Systems*, McGraw-Hill, 1963, Part IV, "The Future."

[8] Bennis, Warren G., "Changing Organizations," *The Technology Review*, Vol. 68, No. 6, April 1966.

groups. People will be differentiated not vertically according to rank and status, but flexibly and functionally according to skill and professional training. This is the organizational form that will gradually replace bureaucracy as we know it. Bennis calls this form the "organic-adaptive" structure.

What is interesting, it seems to me, is that these three essentially disparate perspectives could come together on the utility of the task force as a useful device in group problem-solving situations. It is indeed rare (I know of only one or two other areas) where these schools of theorists agree! It would seem to be a strong argument, therefore, that the task force and project management concept should be given very serious attention as a useful approach to organizational problem-solving.

While companies and other organizations are reluctant as yet to go so far as to make explicit (in the form of stated policy, for example) their attitudes on this question, one cannot deny that pragmatic expediency, if nothing else, is causing more and more of them to experiment with the use of task forces and project management.

Let's look at some evidence.

First, Scott[9] points out that more and more companies are becoming international in character. There are, therefore, at least three major dimensions to the modern multinational company's problems—a geographic dimension, a product line dimension and a functional dimension. An increasing number of problems—in trying to find the location for a new plant, in trying to decide what new markets to enter, in deciding what new products to manufacture and which to discontinue—

all of these kinds of problems cut across the organizational boundaries of compartmentalized elements.

Second, recognition of the hard and perhaps brutal fact that the official given the task of solving such problems doesn't last very long if he takes the position that he cannot tolerate the environmental and interpersonal ambiguity of reporting to more than one boss. Litterer[10] emphasizes that the official is finding that somehow he must acquire the interpersonal skills that will permit him to deal effectively with, for example, the engineering vice president, the head of the eastern division, and the chief of the advanced product line.

Third, Carzo[11] mentions that competition between companies and organizations is getting fiercer on a global scale every day. It has been predicted that the number of international firms doing business on a global scale will be reduced to 300 large multinational organizations by 1980. The organization which is not quick and effective in responding to problems of where to market, what to produce, how to finance, etc., will lose out to its competitors. This is not the prophet of doom—but the realization of the hard facts that are already staring many large corporations squarely in the face. Only through the use of the modern management technology, including modern organizational and structural approaches to problem-solving, can the organization survive.

In summary, I think the research evidence coming from management science in all three areas of endeavor—structure, technology, and behavioral science—clearly demonstrates that task forces and

[10] Litterer, J. A., "Program Management: Organizing for Stability and Flexibility," *Personnel*, Vol. 40, No. 5, September/October, 1963.
[11] Carzo, R., and Yanouzas, J. N., *Formal Organization—A Systems Approach*, Richard D. Irwin, Inc., 1967.

[9] Scott, W. G., *Organization Theory: A Behavioral Analysis for Management*, Richard D. Irwin, 1967.

project management as organizational approaches are useful to problem-solving in organizational contexts.

conclusions

1. The Task Force and Project Management concepts are very effective approaches to modern problem-solving and goal achievement problems in large and complex modern organizations. While not useful to all forms of organizations or all kinds of problems, they are becoming increasingly useful as organizations themselves become more complex in terms of products or services, markets, and specialization. They embody the fundamental assumption that compartmentalization, specialization and increasing technological sophistication are the "givens" of this last half of the twentieth century.

2. The Task Force and Project Management concepts are more rewarding and productive approaches to the ego-satisfaction and motivation aspects of human behavior in modern organizational settings than are traditional approaches based on classic organizational theory. There is a harmony between the educated individual's need for meaningful, satisfactory and creative tasks and a flexible organizational structure. Greiner[12] points out that skills in human interaction will become more important, due to the growing needs for collaboration in complex tasks. There is a danger, however, that there may be reduced commitment to work groups, because these groups are transient and changing and not all people will be able to develop quick and intense relationships on the job and learn to bear the loss of more enduring work relationships.

3. As a first general rule, the larger and more complex an organization, the more specialized and diversified its product lines, services, and objectives, the greater the utility of these approaches. Organizations are, in fact, growing larger, more complex and more compartmentalized. No longer are small, "lean groups of a dozen or so old friends" able to come together to solve problems, except in very small organizations. In smaller organizations where personal relationships are closer simply by virtue of long-standing friendships, physical proximity of tasks performed and simplicity of functions to be performed, the task force approach will have minimal application.

4. As a second general rule, the larger the number of individual skill categories needed to produce a product or service or to accomplish an objective, the greater the utility of this approach. The greatest number of applications will continue to be in such industries as the aerospace and defense-related industries which will continue to be at the forefront of the technological revolution. For example, the production of a nuclear reactor or missile, which requires the close synchronization of the work of hundreds of different kinds of skills will make better use of this technique than will, for example, the production of relatively simple items of capital equipment such as a bus, motorboat, bulldozer or steam boiler.

5. As a third general rule, the larger the number of organizational sub-elements (i.e., the greater the compartmentalization), the greater the utility of this approach. For example, as Schultze[13] has indicated, in government there is a need for a single Federal manager to coordinate the various grant programs that may involve 25 or 30 different Federal Government agencies, all fifty states, perhaps

[12] Greiner, Larry E., "Successful Organization Change," *Harvard Business Review,* May–June 1967.

[13] Schultze, Charles L., Statement before the Subcommittee on Executive Reorganization on the Senate Committee on Government Operations on the Federal Role in Urban Affairs, June 28, 1967.

several thousand counties, and tens of thousands of cities. Literally, such an overall manager must coordinate the work of hundreds or even thousands of managers vertically, horizontally, and diagonally.

6. The task force concept and approach are most useful in organizational settings wherein top management is committed to that set of values embodied by the late Douglas McGregor's Theory Y.

7. The task force approach and concept are more useful in organizations with large numbers of professional personnel than in organizations with primarily semi-skilled and unskilled personnel. For example, in general the approach is more useful in industrial settings than agricultural settings; in research and development organizations rather than production and assembly-line settings; in "white-collar" settings rather than "blue-collar" settings; and in specialty product/service organizations rather than in staple good industries with little competition—or publicly regulated industries such as public utility companies.

8. Even in organizations with primarily semi-skilled and unskilled personnel, the task force concept will find increasing utility as the pressures of leisure time create increasing emotional needs for greater job satisfaction and motivation. Bennis, for example, does not agree with those who emphasize a New Utopianism, in which leisure, not work, becomes the emotional-creative sphere of life. "Jobs," he contends, "should become more rather than less involving; man is a problem-solving animal and the tasks of the future guarantee a full agenda of problems."

organizational behavior

21. a behavioral model of organization

Ralph M. Stogdill

Formal organizations that appoint new members to established positions tend to shortcut many of the interactional and behavioral exchanges that occur in newly formed groups that are beginning to organize. Status structures, roles, and norms in the latter emerge from the reinforcement of intermember expectations in the process of interaction. Status structures, role specifications, and certain norms may be determined in highly formalized organizations by published charts and manuals. But the specifications contained in such documents are translated into member behavior through processes that are similar to those that occur in the newly formed group. New members acquire norms and definition of status and role through interaction with previously established members. The translation of

Reprinted from *Proceedings of the Eastern Academy of Management, Tenth Annual Meeting, May 10–12, 1973, Philadelphia,* 10 pp., with permission of the publisher and the author.

printed specifications into member performance is seldom complete. As a result of changing task demands, interactions, and mutual reinforcement of expectations, members develop norms and patterns of task performance that were not specified by the organization. Such informal norms may become more potent than formal roles in determining various aspects of member response to the organization.

Whether one's ultimate interest is in formal organizations or in emergent groups, it will be found that both are to be understood in terms of the same basic processes. In other words, the processes that give rise to role structure and norms in spontaneously created groups operate in formal organizations (1) to transmit to new members a set of previously defined norms and role specifications and (2) to develop norms and patterns of role performance that are not formally specified by the organization. Traditional theories of organization have been concerned primarily with the former set of considerations—member compliance with formal specifications. Behavioral theorists have emphasized the importance of the latter set of considerations—the emergence of norms and structures that differ from those of the formal organization in their impact on member satisfaction and performance.

A theory of organization should be capable of accounting for the formal as well as the extra-formal aspects of organization. Such an integrative theory was presented [Stogdill, 1959] as a set of hypotheses. The purpose of the present paper is to reformulate the theory in terms of a mathematical model. A theory is usually regarded as a definitive statement of a set of relationships, whereas a model may be granted a more transitory status. Since numerous revisions have been made and others are anticipated, the present formulation should be regarded as a model rather than as a finalized theory.

As a basis for the model, a group was defined as a social interaction system, and an organization as an interaction system that has become structured in terms of the mutually reinforced expectations of the members regarding the role that each is to play. The additional assumption was made that an organization can be represented as an input-processing-output system.

input variables

The outcomes that can be generated by a model depend entirely upon the nature of the input variables. The author has been influenced by Parsons [1951] and Homans [1950], who based their theories on *actions, interactions,* and *sentiments* as input variables. If no physical or monetary inputs are being operated on, the structure and processes of a group or social system can be explained in terms of actions, interactions, and sentiments considered as inputs. In order to generate the outcomes required for the present model, there is need for a more closely defined set of input variables than those of the Parsons and Homans theories. The variables are *performances, interactions,* and *expectations.* Performances and expectations are characteristics of individual members, while interactions are interpersonal variables.

Performance is defined as any action by an individual that identifies him as a member of a group. Performance may consist of working alone or cooperatively on a task, sitting at a desk, talking with other members, wearing a uniform, paying dues, and the like.

Interaction is regarded as an action-reaction system such that if a is an action of A and b is an action of B, then the sequence of their mutual reactions can be represented as $I = a_1, b_1, a_2, b_2, \ldots, a_n, b_n$. Interaction implies that two or more members are responding to each other.

Expectation is defined as an individual's readiness for reinforcement. As such, it is a function of the estimated probability of an outcome, the estimated value of the outcome, and orientation toward the outcome.

The above inputs are all behavioral in nature. For many groups such as discussion groups and committees, these may be the only inputs. Other groups utilize various sorts of physical task materials as inputs.

It is necessary to assume that individual characteristics are transformed into group characteristics. In other words, the group members, through their individual and cooperative performances, interactions with each other, and reinforcement of each others' expectations, generate effects that are characteristic of the group as a whole. If an organization consists of numerous subgroups, the scores of the members of each subgroup may be summed and averaged in order to obtain scores for the subgroup. The subgroup scores may then be intercorrelated in order to gain insight into the effects generated by the interaction of variables for the organization as a whole. In other words, it is regarded as legitimate to add the scores of individuals in order to obtain measures for subgroups and for the organization.

If individual characteristics are transformed into group characteristics, we need some method for distinguishing between the two sets of characteristics. Let

P = Performances of a group member
I = Interactions of a member with other members
E = Expectations of a group member

Then, for each member of a group there exists

$$P = p_1, p_2, p_3, \ldots, p_n$$
$$I = i_1, i_2, i_3, \ldots, i_n$$
$$E = e_1, e_2, e_3, \ldots, e_n$$

which are inputs to the group. Inputs P, I, and E are characteristics of individual members. If the scores of individual members can be summed, then it will be assumed that for all the members $(a, b, c, \ldots, n)$ combined of a subgroup there exists.

$$\sum P = P' = P_a + P_b + P_c + \cdots P_n$$
$$\sum I = I' = I_a + I_b + I_c + \cdots I_n$$
$$\sum E = E' = E_a + E_b + E_c + \cdots E_n$$
$$\sum S = S' = S_a + S_b + S_c + \cdots S_n$$

which are characteristics of a subgroup of the organization. The symbols, P', I', E', and S' will be used instead of $\sum P$, $\sum I$, $\sum E$, and $\sum S$ in the equations to follow, primarily for the sake of simplicity and neatness.

decomposition of the input variables

Performances, interactions, and expectations are extremely complex. Each of these concepts needs to be broken down into a set of useful and relevant components. The author has been guided by the results of empirical research in attempting to arrive at sets of variables that account for important relationships involved in the study of groups and organizations [Stogdill, 1959, 1965]. The resulting list of variables is shown in Table 1, page 216.

Performance is broken down into task performances, specialized performances, and nontask-related performances. For some purposes, task-related performances should be broken down in detail, and the same should be done for nontask-related performances.

Interactions are broken down into task-related, nontask-related, and reciprocated interactions, and interactions that tend to bypass immediate superiors. This analysis seems adequate for the present purpose. However, in the study of large departmentalized organizations, it is often useful to subdivide them into interactions within own work group, interactions with members outside own work group, interactions with members one echelon above (and below) one's own, and so on.

Expectation is here shown to be far more complex than performance or interaction. It is broken down into expectation regarding task performances, nontask performances, task urgency, goal attainment values, status position, freedom of action, freedom of interaction, contributions, returns, liking, reference group support, and discontinuity of membership.

Satisfaction, although a characteristic of individuals, is not an input. It varies as a result of reinforcement or nonreinforcement, and should be regarded as a subtype of mediating variable that can feed back as an input as the group progresses in its activities. It is divided into satisfaction with contributions, returns, status, organization, and freedom of action.

Table 1. Decomposition of the Group Input Variables

Performances

P'_n = Nontask performances
P'_t = Task performances
P'_q = Specialized performances

Interactions

I'_m = Mutual (reciprocated) interactions
I'_n = Nontask related interactions
I'_t = Task-related interactions
I'_x = Interactions that bypass immediate superiors

Expectations

E'_b = Expectations regarding contributions to be made
E'_f = Expectations regarding freedom to act and decide
E'_g = Expectations regarding goal (outcome) values
E'_i = Expectations regarding freedom to interact
E'_j = Expectations regarding discontinuity of membership
E'_m = Expectations regarding mutual liking
E'_n = Expectations regarding nontask performances
E'_q = Expectations regarding task specialization
E'_r = Expectations regarding returns from the organization
E'_t = Expectations regarding task performance
E'_u = Expectations regarding task urgency
E'_w = Expectations regarding reference group support

Mediators (Resultants of Reinforcement)

S'_a = Satisfaction with status
S'_b = Satisfaction with contributions to organization
S'_f = Satisfaction with freedom of action
S'_k = Satisfaction with organization and supervision
S'_r = Satisfaction with returns from the organization

the mediating and processing variables

After identifying the inputs, the next step is to determine some method that will account for a set of mediating variables. Here, it is assumed that the three inputs operate on each other as the members perform, interact, and reinforce each other's expectations to generate a set of mediators. A large body of research on experimental groups indicates that newly formed groups with tasks to perform, quickly develop role structures. The work of the operations researchers calls attention to the fact that organizations engage in operations: that is, processes and procedures for getting work done. Thus far, we have identified two important mediating variables—*structure* and *operations*. These were included in the 1959 formulation. They fail to account for another important set of variables—member satisfactions and the exchange relationships between member and member, as well as between each member and the organization. In a later publication [Stogdill, 1966], this set of variables was identified as *interpersonnel*. It accounts for a large segment of interpersonal relations, reinforced expectations, and satisfactions, that can be easily differentiated from structure and operations.

Operations may be defined as the sum of

all the members' performances in processing the task materials of the group (i.e., executing the group task). Task materials may consist of words, ideas, and plans, as well as physical materials.

Interpersonnel is defined as the psychosocial exchange system that develops between member and member as well as between members and the organization.

Structure is defined as the differentiated role system that results from the mutually reinforced expectations of the members regarding the part each is to play in the group and the pattern of interactions he is to exhibit.

The three sets of processing and mediating variables are regarded as characteristics of organization. It is assumed that the processors interact with each other and act back on the input variables to generate a set of outputs.

the structure of the mediating variables

The sums of scores of individual members will be used to account for the mediating and processing variables. The equation for organizational operations is as follows:

$$O = P'_t \times E'_t \times \frac{I'_t}{I'_m} \qquad (1)$$

Group operations (O) is shown to be essentially a function of the task performances (P'_t) and expectations (E'_t) of all group members who are operating on the task materials utilized by the group. The formula suggests that operations will be conducted more actively when task-related interactions (I'_t) are high and reciprocated interactions (I'_m) are low.

The input variables needed to account for interpersonnel are as follows:

$$L = P'_n \times E'_n \times I'_n \qquad (2)$$

Interpersonnel (L) is shown to be a function of nontask interactions (I'_n),

performances (P'_n), and expectations (E'_n). In other words, personal relations and exchanges will be more congenial when the members are engaged in nontask performances and interactions.

Group structure (Z) is essentially a function of performances and expectations involving task specialization.

$$Z = P'_q \times E'_q \times \frac{I'_m}{I'_x} \qquad (3)$$

Structure will be high when specialized task performances (P'_q) and expectations (E'_q) are high, and when reciprocated interactions (I'_m) are high in relation to interactions that bypass superiors (I'_x).

Performances, interactions, and expectations are involved in all three of the mediating variables. Operations is heavily weighted with task performances and task materials, as it should be. Interpersonnel has a heavy core of nontask interactions and performances, as it should have. Structure is explained primarily in terms of role specialization.

structure of the output variables

Considering the complex nature of the inputs, one would expect a group to generate a complex set of outputs. Stogdill [1959] identified productivity, drive, and cohesiveness as outputs. Tuckman [1965] analyzed some sixty studies of developmental trends in groups engaged in therapy, training, problem solving, and experimental study. After the initial development of role structure, groups exhibit *storming* (drive), then *norming* (cohesiveness), and finally *performing* (productivity). Hood, Showell, and Stewart [1967] factor analyzed the intercorrelations between items used by members to describe group performance. The factors were identified as general affiliation (cohesiveness), task orientation (productivity), and task motivation (drive). It is not argued that productivity, drive, and cohesiveness are the only outputs produced by a group. However, these are well identified aspects of group performance.

Productivity is defined as change in expectancy value resulting from group operations. If a group does not operate upon any physical or monetary inputs, its productivity can be regarded as a change in expectancy value. The product of a game of chess is the player's success or failure in confirming the expectation of winning. However, for many kinds of organizations, there are more tangible products that can be identified. A school may evaluate its productivity in terms of the number of students it trains and aids to achieve success. The product for a social agency may be the number of clients it serves. A retail store may measure its productivity in terms of volume of sales, while a manufacturing firm may count, or determine the monetary value of the units of output it produces.

Drive is defined as degree of group arousal. Mutually reinforced expectations define an area of freedom for the group and determine to a large degree the objective or objectives toward which drive will be directed. Under conditions of high commitment to group goals and freedom from restraint, drive is likely to be expended in effort toward goal achievement. However, under high restraint, drive may become directed toward the reduction of restraint as a secondary objective. Drive can be measured in terms of the degree of enthusiasm, esprit, or forceful behavior exhibited by a group.

Cohesiveness is defined as the capacity of a group to maintain its structural integrity. The cohesiveness of work groups can be measured in terms of the extent to which its members mutually prefer to interact with each other, support each other, and get along together harmoniously. The cohesiveness of an organization

as a whole can be measured in terms of degree of member loyalty and willingness to support the organization under conditions of emergency and stress.

It is assumed that the mediating variables, operating back on the inputs, generate a set of outputs. Equation 4 accounts for the productivity of an organization.

$$K = O \times (E'_g + E'_b) \times \frac{E'_u + E'_j}{S'_a + S'_b} \quad (4)$$

The productivity (K) of an organized group is shown to be essentially a function of group operations (O) evaluated in terms of goal expectancy values (E'_g) and expectations regarding contributions (E'_b). Productivity will be high when these variables are high, and when expectations relative to task urgency (E'_u) and discontinuity of membership (E'_j) are high in relation to satisfaction with status (S'_a) and contributions (S'_b).

Organizational drive (D) is a function of interpersonnel (L), expectations of task freedom (E'_f), expectations of freedom to interact (E'_u), and satisfaction with freedom of action (S'_f).

$$D = L \times (E'_f + E'_u + S'_f) \times \frac{E'_b + E'_r}{S'_b + S'_r} \quad (5)$$

Drive will be high when these three variables are high, and when expectations regarding contributions (E'_b) and returns (E'_r) are high in relation to satisfaction with contributions (S'_b) and returns (S'_r).

The formula for organizational cohesiveness is as follows:

$$C = Z \times (S'_a + E'_m) \times \frac{E'_w + S'_k}{E'_u + E'_j} \quad (6)$$

Cohesiveness (C) is shown to be a function of structure (Z), satisfaction with status (S'_a), and expectations of mutual liking (E'_m). Cohesiveness will be high when these variables are high, and when expectations of reference group support (E'_w) and satisfaction with organization (S'_k) are high in comparison with expectations regarding discontinuity of membership (E'_j) and task urgency (E'_u).

Although oversimplified, these formulations appear to exhibit some degree of common sense logic. We should expect productivity to be high under intensified operations and motivational expectancies. Drive should be high under high degrees of freedom of action and when expectation exceeds satisfaction. Cohesiveness should be high when the group members expect to like each other and when expectations of reference group support exceed expectations of losing membership in the organization.

It is generally recognized that operations is the decisive variable of organization that leads to productivity. However, it may not be equally clear that interpersonnel is a major contributor to drive, or that structure plays a major part in cohesiveness. The rationale in regards to drive is as follows: Drive is released by inter-member stimulation. Some actions on the part of certain group members, particularly supervisors, may arouse high degrees of drive. Other actions induce discouragement and listlessness. Despite the fact that individuals carry their own motivations with them into the organization, the general drive level of work group is determined to a high degree by inter-personnel relations within the group. Our research [Stogdill, 1965] has shown that the considerateness of supervisors is related to worker satisfaction with freedom on the job and to group drive.

With respect to cohesiveness, we have defined it as the maintenance of structure. Thus, cohesiveness and structure are related by definition. Our research [Stogdill, 1965] lends further support to the assumption that they are related. It was found that the structuring behavior of supervisors is related positively to the satisfaction of workers with the organization and to measures of work group cohesiveness. The equations for drive and cohesiveness are derived from logical considerations. In addition, we find research evidence to support the formulations.

For an exact description of the realities of organizations, it is probable that the equations for productivity, drive, and cohesiveness would not assume exactly the same form. In plotting the relationships between the output variables for several industrial organizations, some degree of curvilinearity was observed. However, in no case was there a statistically significant departure from linearity. As empirical data become available it may be possible to develop more sophisticated equations than those presented here. How critical one may feel about these formulations depends upon the particular logic of organization that is applied in evaluating them. An attempt has been made to reconcile different theories in so far as possible. But the primary aim has been to satisfy a logic that is imposed by experimental findings.

summary and discussion

A model has been developed that incorporates many of the variables encountered in behavioral theories of organization. Various aspects of member performance, interaction, and expectation are treated as inputs. Input variables interact to generate group operations, interpersonnel, and structure. These three mediating variables interact with each other and with various input variables to generate a set of outputs—productivity, drive, and cohesiveness.

The model makes no attempt to account in detail for the multiplicity of inputs and outputs that are to be observed in any specific class of organization. Its aim is to explain organizations in general regardless of size, objectives, and operational characteristics. The model is capable of accounting for the major variables that behavioral theories seek to explain.

While recognizing that an organization engages in exchange relationships with its environment at the input, processing, and output stages, the model does not attempt to account for these relationships. Additional concepts could be incorporated to take these factors into account. But in the interest of simplicity and understandability, the model is confined to events that take place within the organization.

The model is regarded as a tentative formulation that needs repeated testings in real life situations. If empirical research shows it to be valid, it should provide new insights into the variables that generate group drive and cohesiveness. Wheeler [1972] tested one version of the model in two industrial firms. His results aided in the revision of the model presented in this paper.

references

Homans, G. C. *The Human Group*. New York: Harcourt, Brace, 1950.

Hood, P. D., Showel, M., and Stewart, E. C. *Evaluation of Three Experimental Systems for Noncommissioned Officer Training*. Washington, Human Resource Office, George Washington University, 1967.

Parsons, T. *The Social System*. Glencoe, Ill.: Free Press, 1951.

Stogdill, R. M. *Individual Behavior and Group Achievement*. New York: Oxford University Press, 1959.

Stogdill, R. M. *Managers, Employees, Organizations*. Columbus: The Ohio State University, Bureau of Business Research, 1965.

Stogdill, R. M. Dimensions of Organization Theory. In J. D. Thompson (ed.), *Approaches to Organizational Design*. Pittsburgh: University of Pittsburgh Press, 1966.

Tuckman, B. W. Developmental Sequence in Small Groups. *Psychological Bulletin*, 1965, *63*, 384–399.

Wheeler, W. R. A Field Test of Stogdill's Mathematical Model of Group Achievement. Doctoral Dissertation, The Ohio State University, 1972.

22. the management of work   Dorothy A. Seese

The classic representation of an organization is a structured drawing called an organization chart. This representation usually is depicted by the hanging tree of boxes, showing relative positions of

Reprinted from *Journal of Systems Management*, 22, No. 9 (September 1971), pp. 36–41, with permission of the publisher.

persons and departments in relation to the chief executive; the other form is the pyramid, with the chief executive placed at the top and other relationships as boxes on shelves of the pyramid. The assumption is inherent, but not always valid, that these persons and functions exist because they are necessary to the execution of the business and that they provide vital work in the accomplishment of the company's objectives.

But, such representations do not always accurately depict an organization. There are two obvious faults and one which is not so obvious. These are:

1. The positions on the organization chart seldom reflect the actual power centers or channels of information and direction in everyday company business functions.

2. The structured organization chart is usually related to the company's legal positions and tends to group persons and departments in a "status bloc" with respect to their proximity to the chief executive.

3. The organization chart never depicts functions which are related to objectives because it is static while the organization is dynamic. Roles, relevance, and accomplishments change daily. Therefore in the work-objective relationship, the organization chart imposes a status rigidity which is totally irrelevant to, and actually damaging to the setting of objectives and the staffing of the functions with the persons best qualified to perform the work. Thus the members of top management cannot consider themselves as members of work groups and actually participate in work groups by contributing their specialty; they are literally "boxed in."

The organization must have objectives or it could not accomplish anything. Accomplishment demands both a cause and an effect. Objectives trigger work, and there exists a cycle in the work-objective relationship which all organizations act upon, although they may be actually unaware of what contributions any par-

ticular function makes to the accomplishment. By spelling out the work-objective cycle, it is possible to understand both what is happening when objectives are established, and how things can be directly related so that once the cycle is understood, it can be managed, which is the *Management of Work.*

Once a set of objectives is determined by a company, it must then get the work done. Functions are activities performed by one or more persons. They must accomplish all or a portion of one or more objectives. The objectives create the need for the work to be performed. If it is necessary to sell, a sales function will be created. If it is necessary to keep books, an accounting function will be created. If it is necessary to make the product to sell, a production function will be created. Thus a company can state an objective: "To make 10,000 units of XYZ product per month, to sell them at a 15% gross profit, and to make a net profit for the year of 12% of gross profit." Breaking down the objectives, it is obvious that production, sales and accounting are necessary. But, where is the the best place to sell? A sub-function may then lead to the creation of a market research group to accomplish part of the work of sales or to make sales more efficient. And similar breakdowns of production will lead to the creation of sub-functions. All must have a direct and measureable result on the accomplishment of the major objectives, although each function or sub-function may have individual objectives stemming from the major objective.

functions define assignments

If the function of sales is to sell, then someone has to do the sales work, whether it is in person, by creating direct mail or other advertising copy, or by telephone. Once a function is created, the analysis of the function itself will begin to define assignments. However, the contribution of each assignment must be judged by its impact on the objective, which could be the overall objective or the objective of a sub-function. One of the duties of proper organization is to correctly assess the assignment which the function defines, and assign a proper impact factor or "weight" to such assignment. The factor can be temporary or permanent.

If objectives create functions, and functions define assignments, then assignments, in order to be effective in relationship to the objectives, must be measured to determine (a) whether the function was correctly defined in relation to the objective; and (b) whether the individual or individuals performing the work are doing an adequate job. Generally, there are five broad categories of true measurement: Productivity; Cost; Efficiency; Accuracy and Net Result. Almost all other data which is generated in the form of measurement data really supports one or more of the measurement categories. All individuals who perform a role in a function can be measured against the objectives of that function via these measurements as can the function as a whole. Without adequate measurements, it will never be possible to offer more than a subjective evaluation of whether a group is doing its job. A person can work and contribute little or nothing if he neither understands his objectives, knows why the function was created, nor has a yardstick to gauge his measure of accomplishment. Yet many companies do not measure the impact or results of departments or functions, with the net result that they are gauged by opinion, often conflicting, and are rewarded or punished on the basis of what they seem to be.

The word "control" has fallen into disrepute among companies because of its association with regimentation, but correctly applied controls geared toward measuring results allow more freedom. They give the individual, and the group, a sense of direction based on measurements. Controls are generated by reporting systems on the five key measurement areas (and any others which may be needed for differing companies or circumstances). Each assignment within a function can be assessed as to its objective and reported on through a system which permits the leader of the function to know what is taking place and to apply immediate corrective action or guidance when needed. Further, by the entire function reporting accomplishments and activities (including costs, results, productivity, etc.) it is possible for the leader of a function to take group action or to demonstrate to his people what they have done, the probable causes, and the best known methods of correction. Rewards are handled in the same manner.

Proper controls will permit measurement of work performed against minor objectives, and collectively against major objectives. It is essential to take corrective action whenever and wherever any functional segment is not contributing properly, accurately, or effectively. The organization is a composite of the functions it generates; therefore if a function is not working properly or effectively, the objectives can and will not be met unless the difficulty is quickly corrected.

Perhaps one individual is responsible; perhaps incorrect reporting procedures have been devised; perhaps the function was not correctly divided into the proper functional assignments. An investigation, conducted with the assistance of the function's leader, should result in uncovering the causes and correcting the situation. However, the cyclical effect of the Work-Objective relationship has to be understood by the persons concerned, or an attempt to "cover up" will inevitably result. That is why measurements, and their requisite controls, need to be implemented for every function. It is difficult to cover up the facts when the objectives, functions, assignments and measurements are there. In fact, the controls which report activity against objectives serve as a dual-purpose instrument. When they are not properly utilized, or are ignored, that in itself constitutes a control because it shows something is wrong. The completed cycle (see Figure 1) constitutes the Work-Objective relationship which is the basis for the management of work.

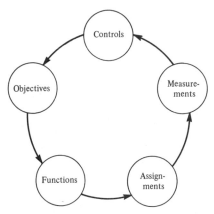

Figure 1. The Work-Objective Cycle.

the work group concept

All work is performed by individuals, but not all individuals can do some or all of the work to be done. It is historically an ancient process to divide the work to be done, and then assign the people to do various aspects of the work. Here, the work is represented by objectives to be accomplished; division of the work is accomplished by establishing functions and their sub-functions or smaller components to actually execute tasks or perform work. Specific assignments are then made so that a task is equal to an individual's ability to perform a segment of the work. Measurements are adopted to determine the success or lack of success of each function and each assignment. Then controls are instituted so that the measurements can be established upon reported facts and substantiated with as much information as needed to determine underlying causes, to assist in defining problems, and to indicate appropriate corrective action.

The "Work Group Concept" sums up the nature of work: All groups assigned to do anything consist of identical elements regardless of the simplicity, complexity, duration or scope of the work to be performed. The work group always consists of a leader, specialists to perform the primary assignments, and support staffs to assist with specific duties to support the primary assignments.

The major difference in operating a business under the work group concept is that all work groups derive their relevance from the major objectives through a series of minor objectives down to individual tasks without respect to a formalized organization chart. The objectives, broken down into functions, dictate the specialties needed to perform the work. Although everybody reports, for some length of time, to a "permanent" leader, the emphasis is on determining the capabilities of each individual and relating them to priority-ranked objectives and functions so that every individual can undertake assignments as a leader, a specialist, or a support staff member as required to accomplish the objectives of the company, because its members perform work, and need to be measured in exactly the same manner as any other individuals performing work.

There are differences between management by committee and the work group. While both committees and work groups have a leader and objectives, a committee consists of individuals who represent diverse interests and attempt to establish some common result, such as a report, an agreement, or a plan. A work group, while composed of individuals who may be recruited from diverse places, not only has objectives and functions, but a common goal which unites the interest of each member of the work group because measurements and controls are applied to measure each one's effectiveness. The committee member is independent and represents his interest-group. The work group represents people who must subordinate their interests to the function or there will be no benefit to any member or to the company. This is Management by System, or more accurately, Organization by Function. The work group achieves both results because it is not organized around a personality, but around a function and its objective.

All work groups (see Figure 2) are identical in composition regardless of the work to be accomplished or the size of the work group. The division of labor and specialization is accomplished as follows:

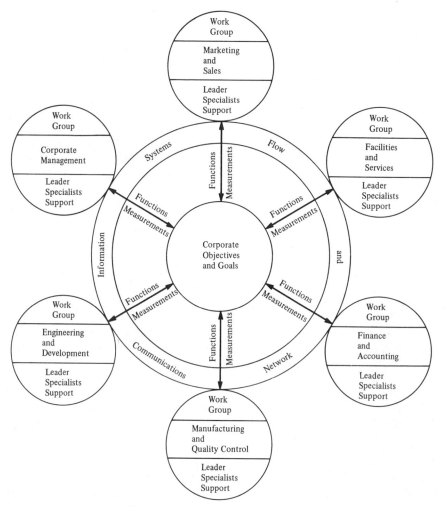

Figure 2.   The Work Group "Wheel."

1. The leader is responsible for the results of the work group and for knowing its objectives, functions, assignments, key measurement areas and control procedures. He is responsible for knowing the time elements allotted for accomplishing segments of the work or, in the case of specific short-term projects, all the work. He must know the relationship of his work group to other work groups, and the effects which his output has in relation to the output of other work groups. He must comprehend the measurements and be able to communicate results. He must take corrective action and make changes as required by changes in objectives, emphasis shifts in functions, the need to split or combine work groups, etc. He must actually manage the work.

2. The specialists execute the assignments or tasks. They are primarily responsible for either doing the work personally or delegating the work in such a way that they control the results. They must combine their own efforts with the efforts of others, as needed, to accomplish the work.

3. Support staff members may be members assigned to the work group or recruited, on a temporary basis, to accomplish specific tasks. They may support the leader or any specialist or group of specialists. They are measured by their ability to execute specific tasks with relation to the objectives of *each* work group for whom they perform tasks.

Most people will belong to a relatively permanent work group. However, it is part of the total work group concept that any individual, at any time, may simultaneously be the leader of one work group, a specialist in another, and from time to time offer support services to others.

assigning individuals to work groups

In the organizational phase of the work group concept, that is, initial implementation, work groups are generally organized (see Figure 3) as a result of examining the objectives of existing departments, sections, groups, etc. After the objectives and functions are matched, work group leaders are assigned to the relatively permanent work groups and generally, previous heads of functions are assigned as the work group leaders. It is then their responsibility to divide large areas into smaller work groups as necessary and dictated by a thorough study of objectives and functions. Thereafter, all work groups must be created by splitting or combining existing work groups even though the actual jobs to be done may require hiring people to become members of such work groups. Only in the case of the acquisition of an existing company could an entirely new work group come into being. Even then it is imperative that such a work group be defined, and as far as possible, merged into existing work groups or reorganized to perform to the objectives and measurements of the acquiring company.

It is not only possible but likely that each person will become a part of more than one work group. While this is not as apt to be true for production workers as it is for specialists such as engineers, accountants, analytical specialists and other professional staff specialists, it could be true in instances where R&D or pilot production work groups required a full complement of people for a specific project. Even the president of the company, who is the leader of a work group at all times, may be a consulting specialist on another work group and even a support specialist to other work groups.

Studying the positive effects, four specific areas which firmly establish the work group concept can be briefly expanded

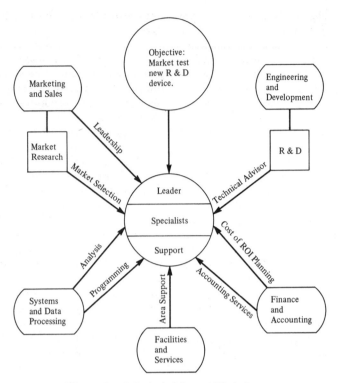

Figure 3. A Project-Oriented Work Group.

upon, because they are based on human and business principles fundamental to the behavior of organizations:

1. *Division of Labor and Specialization.* The work group concept allows for the fullest expression of this basic principle of business or organizational efficiency. Every member of a work group is a specialist whose effort is directed toward the accomplishment of predetermined objectives. The leader's responsibility for correctly and adequately staffing his work group by dividing the objectives into respective functions, assignments and tasks is his own measure of accomplishment, in addition to managing the work itself.

2. *Organization Flexibility Without Displacement Shock.* In the structured organization which tries to live up to the

organization chart, the movement of one individual from a certain position to another, unless it is an obvious promotion, causes displacement shock. It is tacitly assumed, if by no one other than the individual concerned, that he was not performing adequately in the former position.

Since individual relevance in the work group concept is placed on performance or the accomplishment of objectives, it does not matter where one participates. As long as the specialist is gaining exposure and recognition for the contribution made, the human need is satisfied if it is work-oriented.

3. *The Development of the Individual.* Numerous methods have been tried by companies in order to encourage indi-

vidual development. There are three key elements provided by the work group concept. First, status is self-contained in the professionalism attributed to the job no matter what it is. Rewards for good work are built into the entire concept. The work group member can see immediate results of any self-improvement attempt, either via company training or individually initiated schooling.

Second, work groups derived from the progressive subdividing of company objectives into sub-objectives, function, sub-functions, assignments and tasks keep each member from being treated as a "number" or "badge code." Work groups are always small enough for each individual to be known to all other members of the group. Where members of a work group are scattered, periodic meetings, telephone discussions, memorandums, or a combination of these serves to bridge the gap.

Third, the feeling of relevance is a by-product of the objective-measurement cycle which is an end-item in itself. But being constantly exposed to measurements, the individual gains the ability to self-measure in relation to what is to be accomplished, thus further equipping himself to perform more effectively as a leader. Thus the very act of participation stimulates training while work is being accomplished so that productivity and potential are developed as an additional concomitant of utilizing, effectively, the work group concept.

4. *The Development of the Organization.* The employment of the work group concept also expresses three key elements in the development of the organization which are as much in demand of satisfaction as individual needs. The first is the principle of participation which is used to its fullest extent.

Second, the organization benefits because of the maximum exposure and participation of individuals to as many situations as possible. This creates a continually developing, mobile, contributing work force, which through the use of work groups conquers the challenge of change. Many people see multiple facets of the company's operations. The more aggressive people contribute more actively by mobility.

Third, the cycle of objectives-functions-assignments-measurements-controls leads back to the creation of new objectives or the expansion of the scope of existing ones as work is accomplished. All work is not only meaningful and measurable, but both individuals and the company grow by the enforcement of a growth plan to accommodate a system which is designed to accomplish work rather than spread it around to keep people busy.

conclusion

While simple in theory, the work group concept is not yet an accepted method of accomplishing the management of the work of the future. But two things are known: management must change its structured concepts to meet both the human and organizational needs of the future; and a logical progression from history indicates a continuation of the trend of individual contribution and recognition as the fundamental key to the continued growth of the socio-economic environment. The centerpoint is need, not want. Yet, is it not basically true that wants stem from needs, elaborate upon them, and become irrelevant only when objectives fail to place needs and wants into meaningful perspective? The emphasis is the study of needs, the translation of needs into objectives, and the execution of their accomplishment via a technique which satisfies these elements.

This is what the Work Group Concept can be used to do. If it is a tool of organization, then it is not of company organization alone, but of human organization also. This is why it is a valuable tool for any company looking to the future. It is based on maturity. So is the survival of the human organism itself. Therefore what seems most difficult is especially the more elemental in its basic nature and application.

23. motivation versus learning approaches to organization behavior

Fred Luthans and Robert Ottemann

Motivation theory has played the dominant role in the emerging field of organizational behavior. Both content and process theories of motivation have been considered. Initially, content theories, such as Maslow's hierarchy of needs and Herzberg's two-factor approach, were widely accepted by management scholars and practitioners.

These two well-known theories attempted to identify specific variables which would energize or motivate organizational behavior. The Maslow theory inferred that esteem and self-actualization would motivate organizational participants; Herzberg's motivators included recognition, advancement, responsibility, growth, and achievement. Unfortunately, neither of these content theories has been satisfactorily substantiated by research or practice.

the process approach

In search of alternatives to the simplistic content theories, many management scholars have begun to develop and test more

Reprinted from *Business Horizons*, 16, No. 6 (December 1973). Copyright, 1973 by the Foundation for the School of Business at Indiana University. Reprinted by permission.

complex process theories of motivation. These theories attempt to explain the process of how organizational behavior is activated, directed, sustained, and extinguished. The two major approaches are oriented toward drive and expectancy. Drive theory has its roots in hedonism and Thorndike's classic law of effect, but its modern development starts with the work of Clark Hull. In the 1940s and 1950s he identified the variables of drive strength, habit stength, and incentive, which he said combined in multiple ways to produce behavior.

Similar to this past-oriented drive approach but of more direct relevance to understanding organizational behavior are the "forward oriented" expectancy theories of the motivational process. The expectancy theories of Victor Vroom and of Lyman Porter and Edward Lawler are becoming increasingly accepted. Vroom postulates that motivation is a function of the interactions among effort-performance expectations, performance-outcome instrumentalities, and outcome valences.

Porter and Lawler have a somewhat more elaborate expectancy model that relates the nine variables of value of reward, perceived effort-reward, effort, abilities and traits, role perceptions, performance, intrinsic rewards and extrinsic rewards, perceived equitable rewards, and satisfaction. The expectancy motivation theories have stimulated numerous research questions and have begun to provide an explanatory framework for organizational behavior. To date, research has generally supported expectancy motivation models.[1]

The process approach to motivation seems to hold much more promise for understanding organizational behavior than the simplistic content approach. For example, expectancy models now are providing explanations of how expectancies and instrumentalities are acquired and modified.[2] To the degree that these motivational processes affect subsequent behavior, investigation of the interaction between the organizational environment and individual perceptions will contribute to the understanding of organizational behavior. Yet practitioners still subscribe primarily to content models of motivation. There is a great deal of surface logic to the content approach, and it can be easily adapted to practical applications.

Even though the expectancy models of motivation are similar to operant models when operationalized in actual practice, operant learning as a theoretical base for organizational behavior has been almost completely ignored. In the behavioral sciences as a whole, however, the new, exciting breakthroughs in understanding, predicting, and controlling human behavior are based on learning, not motivation theory. The dramatic impact that behavior modification techniques derived from operant learning theory have had on the mental health and education fields is a case in point. Is it possible to use the same theoretical framework in the field of organizational behavior? It is the authors' contention that operant learning theory can add a necessary dimension to the process theories of motivation in understanding organizational behavior.

In particular, the authors feel that the operant model and behavior modification techniques may prove to be more successful in predicting and controlling organizational behavior than have been the content motivational models and techniques. The term O.B. Mod. (organizational behavior modification) is used to represent this operant approach to the management of human resources.[3]

motivation as hypothetical construct

Motivation is a basic psychological process which involves needs (deprivations) that set up drives (deprivations with direction) to accomplish goals (alleviation of needs). In this process, needs stem from within the person and drive him to search for goals that will satisfy his needs. This "motivated" behavior is purposive and means-ends oriented. It must be remembered, however, that no one has ever actually observed this motivational process. It is merely a hypothetical construct or intervening variable or "black box" concept that is used by all sciences to explain the unexplainable. The term "motivation" refers to unobservables which are inferred from observable behavior.

A motive can be thought of as an intervening variable or hypothetical construct that is often inferred from observable behavior. When motivation is used to explain organizational behavior, there is always the risk of using a given motive as

[1] Charles N. Greene, "The Satisfaction-Performance Controversy," *Business Horizons*, XV, No. 5 (October 1972), pp. 31–41.
[2] George S. Graen, "Instrumentality Theory of Work Motivation: Some Experimental Results and Suggested Modifications," *Journal of Applied Psychology Monograph*, LIII, No. 2 (1969), pp. 1–25.

[3] Fred Luthans, *Organizational Behavior* (New York: McGraw-Hill Book Company, 1973), pp. 521–23.

an explanation of the observed organizational behavior from which it was inferred. For example, when a worker is highly productive or a manager works diligently on a project, it is easy to explain this behavior by inferring that the person has a motive, for example, a high need for achievement.

Although this may be descriptive of the behavior, it certainly does not explain the causes of the productive or diligent behavior. It cannot automatically be assumed that the worker or manager has a high need for achievement. The same observable behavior may be produced by controlling the environment.

Operant learning theory emphasizes that behavior is greatly influenced by environmental consequences, not just by unobservable inner states such as achievement motivation. Most behavior, including achievement motivated organizational behavior, can be considered to be a function of its consequences and not merely a hypothetical construct called motivation.

deprivation, satiation, and reinforcers

Obviously, not all motivated behavior can be explained by its consequences. For example, deprivation and satiation have two major effects on behavior which cannot be fully explained by learning alone. First, primary or unconditioned reinforcers such as food, water, sex or sleep will be reinforcing only if the person has been deprived of them. Deprivation increases the relative value of these reinforcers while satiation diminishes their value. A second major effect of deprivation-satiation involves purposive means-end behavior. As deprivation of a need increases, the person will exhibit those behaviors that have in the past led to reinforcement. The deprived person is purposive and efficient in his reward-seeking behavior while the satiated person tends to be nonpurposive and inefficient.

The deprivation-satiation of primary reinforcers have been a central concern of traditional motivation theorists in psychology. However, in organizations these primary needs and drives have little relevance to more complex human behavior. Of greater importance to organizational behavior are the conditioned or secondary reinforcers. Conditioned reinforcers acquire their rewarding value as a result of learning or experience. Objects or events which were initially neutral in value acquire rewarding properties by being paired with other reinforcers. In addition, most conditioned reinforcers become discriminative and generalized. A conditioned reinforcer may serve as the means to the end of an unconditioned reinforcer or another conditioned reinforcer.

Some conditioned reinforcers, because they have been paired with many other reinforcers and because they have served as a means to many other ends, often become ends in themselves. Conditioned reinforcers, such as money, social approval, attention, praise, and responsibility, probably fit this latter category for most organizational participants.

Because of their almost universal reinforcing properties, these generalized conditioned reinforcers have often been assumed to be subject to the same deprivation-satiation effects as the primary reinforcers. This assumption has led to explanations of complex human behavior in terms of various underlying constructs such as motivation, attitudes, and other internal states that are difficult if not impossible to observe, measure, and operationally define. These vague explanations have tended to discourage the active search for antecedent (stimulus conditions) and consequent (reinforcers) factors in organizational behavior.

The motivational construct still has a

definite place in understanding human behavior as a whole. For example, deprivation and satiation determine the relative reward value of primary or unconditioned reinforcers. On the other hand, it is not these primary reinforcers that are most important and relevant to the prediction and control of organizational behavior. The organizational environment factors which act as positive or negative reinforcements for participants are mainly conditioned or secondary reinforcers. For example, an increase, in responsiblity, a salary raise, or praise from the boss acquire rewarding value from past learning or experience.

These conditioned reinforcers are not subject to the same deprivation-satiation effects as the primary reinforcers. Complex organizational behavior is much more concerned with conditioned than with primary reinforcers. Therefore, consequences of behavior and the administration of this consequent behavior through schedules of reinforcement, timing of reinforcement, and the determination of reward value of reinforcement become relatively more important than deprivation-satiation in understanding, predicting, and controlling organizational behavior.

application of O.B. mod. approach

One learning theorist has bluntly stated that "all of the phenomena that have been called motivational can be translated, without loss, into phenomena of reinforcement" and the result is that "what can be said in the language of motivation can be said as well in the language of reinforcement."[4]

This proposed importance of reinforcement is justified on the basis that ob-

[4] Robert C. Bolles, *Theory of Motivation* (New York: Harper and Row, 1967), p. 434.

servable stimuli control and reinforce behavior, whereas motivations merely explain behavior in terms of unobservable inner states. Reinforcement, or more specifically O.B. Mod., attempts to name, without reference to unobservable intervening variables, the conditions and the processes by which the environment controls human behavior. The behavior itself is always dealt with directly.

A motivational approach to organizational behavior infers that the practicing manager should attempt to define and manipulate such vague internal states as desire, satisfaction, and attitude. Under the O.B. Mod. approach, the manager determines the organizational goals he wants participant behavior to accomplish, the organizational stimuli available to control the behavior, and the types and schedules of reinforcement that can be applied to the consequent behavior. In other words, under O.B. Mod., organizational behavior is subjected to *observable* analysis so that the stimulus conditions and reinforcing events can be determined and administered by management.

stimulus control

Organizational stimulus control is derived from observable analysis made by management. Such control is accomplished when a certain response is reinforced in the presence of a discriminative stimulus, and this response is not reinforced when the stimulus is changed or absent. A specific organizational example can be found in a stamping mill. The operator must occasionally stop the mill to sharpen and reset the dies. If the operator is consistently reinforced for stopping the process and resetting the dies when the product is off-standard, then the presence of the defect will control the occurrence of the chosen response. This chosen response (resetting the press) will occur when the discriminative stimulus (defect) is present, but not when the discriminative stimulus is changed or absent.

In this example, stimulus control has been achieved. Adams and Scott note that, "A supervisor could either implement an avoidance procedure in which a negative reinforcer such as criticism or a threat is made contingent upon not stopping the press and cleaning the dies in the presence of the defect, or he could make a positive reinforcer contingent upon stopping the press and cleaning the die. The end result will be the same in that the defect will come to evoke the ... behavior, but the relationship between the supervisor and the operator may be quite different."[5]

punishment

Managers and supervisors typically depend upon various forms of threat or punishment in attempting to change subordinates' behavior. Learning experts acknowledge that punishment does have an immediate effect on stopping an undesired response. On the other hand, they are careful to point out that punishment also has several undesirable side-effects. Most prominent is the fact that, although punishment will suppress an undesired response, it does not normally extinguish it. When the punishing agent is removed or the punishment discontinued, the behavior is likely to recur.

An additional negative effect of punishment occurs if no acceptable alternative to the punished response is provided. Punishment only leads to the suppression of one response and leaves the punished person in a conflicting state between habit and inhibition. Unless the punished person

[5] Everette E. Adams and William E. Scott, "The Application of Behavioral Conditioning Procedures to the Problems of Quality Control," *Academy of Management Journal*, XIV, No. 2 (June 1971), p. 184.

is given an alternative response to the situation, he does not know what to do the next time he is in the situation where his previous response was punished. A third possible negative effect is that the punished response may not be made under conditions deemed more appropriate. For example, a project manager may assume additional responsibility on a project that he is heading. This behavior may be punished by his boss who feels the manager is overstepping his bounds. The punishment may generalize to the point where his initiative to assume additional responsibility may be inhibited in all cases, even those projects where his boss feels he should assume more responsibility.

Finally, the administration of the punishment may become associated through conditioning with the punishment itself and take on accompanying negative properties. Since the punisher is also most often the source of reinforcement, the two roles become incompatible, and there is a loss of effectiveness as either a punisher or a rewarder.

positive reinforcement

A vital task for management is to learn to use O.B. Mod. techniques which do not have the negative side-effects of punishment. Positive reinforcement should be used whenever possible. Positive reinforcement in O.B. Mod. is operationally defined as a response followed by a reward, which will increase the probability that the response will be repeated. In other words, behavior is a function of its consequences.

Positive reinforcement has wide generality and great practical significance to the practice of management. For instance, positive reinforcement principles can be applied to job and organizational design, wage and salary administration, training, supervisory techniques, and overall organizational development. However, it is not easy to readily identify specific events that are rewarding to organizational participants. Since human behavior is so highly dependent upon positive reinforcement, the key for the prediction and control of organizational behavior is to find the conditions or contingencies of reinforcement. Learning principles such as the one developed by David Premack would seem to be especially valuable in this effort.

the premack principle

The Premack principle of reinforcement is an accepted part of operant learning knowledge. The principle simply states that the opportunity to perform a response of high probability can be used to reinforce less probable responses. Stated more precisely, the Premack principle says that one event is capable of reinforcing another event if the reinforcing event has a higher probability of occurrence and its occurrence is made contingent upon emission of a lower probability behavior. Any response A will reinforce any other response B as long as the independent response rate of A is greater than that of B.

Thus far, concepts from learning theory like the Premack principle have not been applied to the theory of practice of management. Yet if organizational behavior is largely controlled by its consequences (ranging from pay to a pat on the back), then concepts like the one proposed by Premack seem directly applicable. In modern organizations with participants who are not physiologically deprived, traditional reinforcers tend to lose their reward value. This means that either organizational participants have simply lost their capacity to be reinforced or that they no longer value the normal reinforcers provided by management. Man-

agement could analyze this situation by providing employees with a wide variety of different possible reinforcers. Then by using the Premack principle management could determine which of these reinforcers are truly reinforcing.

The first step would be to determine the participants' independent rates of response for the various possibilities and then rank the responses in terms of frequency. Since reinforcement is relative rather than absolute, the more frequent responses of the set will reinforce all other lower responses. By the same token, the least probable responses will not reinforce any of the other higher response rates in the set. In other words, the reinforcing properties of the various responses will depend upon the responses to which they are paired. Based upon the Premack principle, the guideline would be that, to have reinforcing properties, a response must be more probable than that of the response to be reinforced.

concluding comments

The content motivational approach to the management of human resources has primarily relied upon job enrichment, which will presumably lead to increased performance and goal attainment. The approach is based on the assumption that the feelings of responsibility or achievement will affect job satisfaction, which in turn will improve job performance. This explanation is in terms of internal, non-observable states. The operant-based O.B. Mod. approach suggests that a simpler and more direct alternative explanation for improved performance is possible. Job enrichment increases the number, type, and variety of tasks available to the employee. This increased set of tasks can serve as potential reinforcers for the employee.

Since each task has an independent rate

of response, Premack's principle suggests that a task with a higher rate of response will reinforce a task with a lower rate of response. Thus, the impact from job enrichment can be better explained in terms of the greater number of reinforcers and how they are sequenced rather than by unobservable motivational changes on the part of the employee. From the viewpoint of the O.B. Mod., the organization is a potential source of a great many positive reinforcers, including job enrichment.

There seem to be many direct applications of learning concepts, such as the Premack principle, to the management of human resources. For example, the first step in job design would be to determine the independent rates for several of the employee's responses and rank them in terms of frequency. This procedure would result in a reinforcement "menu." Generally, such a menu contains many possible reinforcers which were not even considered. Also of great significance to cost conscious management is the fact that most of these reinforcers are nonfinancial. Since the employee is able to select his own reinforcers, the most effective ones are immediately programmed into his work environment. This helps to ensure that the consequences of his behavior will in fact increase the frequency of desired behavior (for example, productive performance and goal attainment).

After the activities the employee wants and does not want to do are determined, management should permit him to do the desired activities, provided he first performs the less desired but necessary activities. All employees like or dislike particular aspects of their jobs. A salesman may like to travel in a certain part of his territory. According to this approach, he would first be required to travel in a less desirable part of his territory or he might be required to demonstrate proficiency in a tedious training exercise. Another example would be an assembler on a production line who performs a single, monotonous operation all day. This job could be made self-rewarding by increasing the number of tasks the assembler performs and then making the performance of the tasks with the higher response rate contingent upon the performance of the task with the lower response rate.

This type of job design would seem to be mutually beneficial to both employee and organization. The employee is being continually reinforced by natural reinforcers in the immediate work environment, and the organization is getting needed tasks performed at a minimum cost. With this approach, there is no need to explore the underlying motives of the employee. Management simply asks the employee what parts of his job he prefers and then schedules the work accordingly.

The Premack principle represents only one tool in the O.B. Mod. approach that can be used by management in today's complex organizations. Even punishment, if properly administered and the negative side-effects are avoided, can be effectively used.[6] O.B. Mod. has been taught to and successfully applied by supervisors in managing their workers. The authors, along with David Lyman, conducted an O.B. Mod. program for a medium-sized human relations training, the group of supervisors were trained to manage their workers contingently.[7] The trainers served as supervisory behavior models and contingently reinforced the desired behavior with valued rewards. As a consequence, the supervisors learned to use

[6] Fred Luthans and Robert Kreitner, "The Role of Punishment in Organizational Behavior Modification: (O.B. Mod.)," *Public Personnel Management*, II, No. 3 (May–June 1973), pp. 156–61.

[7] Fred Luthans and David Lyman, "Training Supervisors to Use Organizational Behavior Modification (O.B. Mod.)," *Personnel* (September–October 1973).

the principles of O.B. Mod. to analyze and solve human performance problems in their departments.

The approach was basically to identify behavioral events that need to be changed, measure the frequencies of behavior to be changed, perform functional analysis by examining antecedents and consequences, develop intervention strategies that stress positive reinforcement, apply the strategy contingently, and evaluate. In the area of sales training, Edward Feeney, then of Emery Air Freight, developed a program utilizing operant conditioning in the training of supervisors. Evidence indicated that new salesmen who participated in the program were more effective and comfortable in developing client relationships.

In addition to the examples cited, there seems to be a natural alliance between an O.B. Mod. approach and the currently popular job enrichment and management by objectives approaches to organizational development. A strict motivational approach to the understanding, prediction, and control of organizational behavior has not proved to be sufficient. With operant learning theory serving as the base, what has been termed here as O.B. Mod. may prove to be a much needed new dimension to the understanding and, even more important, to the prediction and control of organizational behavior.

organization development

24. organization development

Alan D. Bauerschmidt and Richard W. Brunson

Programs which carry the identifying initials OD are quickly becoming the fashion among American business corporations. OD (Organization Development) is successfully furthering profit and service objectives, while providing the opportunity for increased individual satisfaction and growth. This promise of increased effectiveness is possible for enterprises which have an organizational format of specialized activities linked by a common goal. Because hospitals fit these criteria, it is the purpose of this article to review the various aspects of organization development as they pertain to the hospital setting.

Earlier writings have explored particular organization development applications in hospitals.[1] It is not the purpose of this article to consider such applications in detail but, rather, to concentrate upon the concept of organization development itself in its broader framework, and to provide some insight into the origins of the organization development technique and its relationship to other techniques which promise similar improvements in organizational efficiency and effectiveness.

Before proceeding to these issues, however, it would be well to dispel the notion that OD is just another transient management technique. OD has been designed to incorporate the discrete contributions of the various behavioral and administrative sciences into a single framework. It is a culmination of an evolutionary process directed toward making these sciences relevant to the management of organizations. OD demands the full com-

Reprinted from *Hospital Progress*, 54, No. 9 (September 1973), pp. 62–68, with permission of the publisher.

[1] Robert G. Holloway and Wallace G. Lonergan, "A Survey Program for Management and Organization Development," *Hospitals*, August, 1968, pp. 59–65; and W. J. Reddin, "Managing Organizational Change," *Hospital Administration*, Winter, 1970, pp. 79–86.

mitment of management and cannot be delegated to a staff training function. It becomes a way of life to every group and individual within the organization and, in its insidious way, affects the very being of man within the organization.

the imperative for OD

OD is considered by many to be the solution to management's desperate problem of adapting to fast-breaking changes in technology. Most of the writings of the leading proponents are marked by a moral fervor in regard to the need for organizational renewal and revitalization in the broad reaches of social and economic enterprises. In justification of this imperative for changing organizations, they note a continuing inability of various forms of enterprise to adjust to changing social and individual values and beliefs. Further, they detect the growing inability of traditional forms of organization to cope with problems in a manner which is both effective and efficient.[2]

The stature of these writers is enough to dispel the notion that these preambles to OD concepts are being advanced as a technique of salesmanship. Evidence of increased ability to adapt through OD is mounting. Many corporate specialists across the nation credit OD with increasing the effectiveness of their organizations.[3] Warnings about the impact of

social change upon the ability of managed organizations to respond in time-proven ways have become a part of the more general literature.[4] This need to preface OD concepts with an imperative for change has even resulted in the evolution of a body of literature which considers this topic for separate treatment, parallel to the writings about OD itself.[5]

Most managers and administrators recognize the inadequacy of traditional organizational remedies to solve their problems. As managers of organizations, they are well aware that the classical responses of individuals to the organizational phenomena no longer pertain if they had any original relevancy beyond their theoretical construction. At best, the critique of classical organizational concepts within the framework of changing social values and beliefs provides insight into the need for new forms of response to the efforts of managers who must accomplish their tasks in archaic or otherwise inappropriate structures of organization.

Managers and administrators need organization. Specialization of tasks creates the need for coordination and integration, which is the role of the manager. On the other hand, organization is a tool of the manager as well as the

---

[2] See Warren Bennis, *Organization Development: Its Nature, Origins, and Prospects*, Addison-Wesley Publishing Co., Reading, Mass., 1969; and Chris Argyris, *Intervention Theory and Method: A Behavioral Science View*, Addison-Wesley Publishing Co., Reading, Mass., 1970.

[3] Five cases of increased effectiveness are documented by Richard Beckhard in *Organization Development: Strategies and Models*, Addison-Wesley Publishing Co., Reading, Mass., 1969. Many corporations have been implementing OD as presented by Robert R.

Blake and Jane S. Mouton in *Building a Dynamic Corporation Through Grid Organization Development*, Addison-Wesley Publishing Co., Reading, Mass., 1969.

[4] Studious attempts to spread this message of social change are characteristic of such works as: Marshall McLuhan, *Understanding Media: The Extensions of Man*, McGraw-Hill Book Co., New York City, 1964; and more recently Alvin Toffler, *Future Shock*, Random House, New York City, 1970.

[5] Such recent concern with the large social critique underlying organization development is well represented by Warren H. Schmidt, ed., *Organizational Frontiers and Human Values*, Wadsworth Publishing Co., Belmont, Calif., 1970.

cause of his creation. Tasks are differentiated to permit the administrator-manager to carry out his responsibility: the efficient and effective accomplishment of the objectives of the enterprise. Organization provides the basis for communication and, therefore, decision making in complex, differentiated structures. In sum, the fact of organization provides the administrative problem as well as the route to its solution.

Hospital administrators need not be reminded of these facts about organization. Most administrators react to their situation in a way that indicates their awareness of the discrepancy between organization as a problem and as a solution. The administrator who resolves to bring order out of chaos must first catalog the structural problems which usually defeat all attempts to solve a full range of problems. This catalog of structural problems then becomes either the cause of immediate concern through the remedies which are suggested, or the stock of explanations for future failure as the remedies fail to produce improvement. Admonitions about the "dry rot" which infests organizations,[6] or the "changing realities" of organizational existence,[7] bring nods of understanding from knowledgeable administrators but lend little in the way of new information. A study of these root causes of the organizational problem, however, may be necessary to gain acceptance for many of the radical solutions which are a part of the OD package.

the origin of the OD concept

One should not misunderstand the prefatory remarks contained in OD writings. They are not meant to imply, in most cases, that the origin of OD rests in some

new aspect of the organization or social phenomena. Improvement changes and the search for enterprise stability have always been a part of the historical perspective. Rather, the evolution of OD as a unique technique for the improvement of organizational performance can be traced to the confluence of various trends and contributions within behavioral science with insights provided by systems thinking and analysis.

The basic proposition of OD is directed toward the concept that changes in individual and group behavior resulting in improved levels of organizational effectiveness depend upon the pattern and mode of interrelationships, existing among the organization's individuals and groups. Only when the structure and method of interrelationships among the component parts of the organization are favorable to a specific improvement in human behavior will attempts to change such behavior have a reasonable chance for success. OD, therefore, is concerned with behavioral change which is appropriate to the structure of relationships that exist and, more positively, with changing the nature of relationships to support more effective behavior.

The heavy emphasis upon change in behavior and the nature of interrelationships helps explain why many of the early exponents of the development concept labeled the process as organizational change, although it is also possible to view the companion concepts of OD and organization change as reflecting the somewhat separate focus of the applied psychologist and sociologist.[8] As each of

[8] An excellent collection of earlier and later works which reflect the emphasis of social change processes and the growing maturity of the sociological contribution within the behavioral sciences is: Warren G. Bennis, Kenneth D. Benne, and Robert Chin, eds., *The Planning of Change: First and Second Editions*, Holt, Rinehart, and Winston, Inc., New York City, 1961 and 1969.

[6] Argyris, *Intervention Theory*, p. 2.
[7] Bennis, *Organization Development*, p. 19.

these separate disciplines within the behavioral sciences come to rely more upon the systems analysis of organizational problems and to broaden or narrow their domains of interest as the case may be, the discrepancy between the two approaches in practice tends to disappear. At the present time the term "organization development" appears to be in ascendancy in the United States, although important contributions to the underlying theory continue to appear under the "change" label.

Any theoretical discrepancy which might still exist between the two approaches would be important only to the hospital which is trying to decide between a consultant and a packaged program for hospital OD. The term "development" in OD is, undoubtedly, an outgrowth of earlier approaches to segmented personnel training. It is possible that more traditional management or employee development programs are being marketed under the disguise of the OD label. Whatever the benefits of such programs might be, they have the tendency to speak to, rather than to treat, the nature of systematic interrelationships in organizations. An administrator reviewing such a program should consider it on its own merits rather than under the endorsement of OD where the entire organization is dealt with through its essential interrelationships.

At the other extreme of bias, an administrator might wish to determine whether the particular approach to OD which he is considering for his hospital is unduly focused upon the rectification of structural discrepancies responsible for the prevention of some level of optimal performance. The poor over-all results which often accrue to employee development programs have their parallel in programs of reorganization which failed to consider fully the human factor. To a large extent, the more comprehensive organization programs tend to deemphasize reorganization. This is particularly true where management is satisfied that the present structural pattern is compatible with the technology of the enterprise and that it provides the membership of the organization with differentiated tasks that have sufficient scope to be potentially attractive and personally satisfying.

In summary, the origin of OD can be viewed as the result of the integration of concepts and techniques from various behavioral and administrative science fields with pragmatic and comprehensive programs for the renewal and revitalization of existing, purposeful organizations. A hallmark of OD programs is their individual design to fit the needs of the particular organization, although the concept recognizes that similar patterns of problems exist in all organizations. These common problems confront the organization in terms of the nature of its internal interrelationships among groups and individuals and of the methods by which the organization attempts to adjust to its external environment. Through systematic analysis, the ways in which these common problems manifest themselves in a particular organization can be isolated and used as a basis for a designed solution or set of solutions. The solutions themselves consist largely of more traditional training and educative methods combined with individual and group introspection. Because these needed methods are derived from a comprehensive analysis of the entire pattern of organizational relationships, they will necessarily involve the entire organization.

the modes of OD

An organization will consider an OD program only after it senses that the organization is underachieving. Individual managers and administrators will have different views regarding maximum effectiveness. Comparison with similar organizations may only reflect the variety of criteria under which these organizations operate. In hospitals, such comparison of effectiveness might reveal only a generalized malaise which infects the entire industry, and the often commented upon phenomena of indecisiveness brought about by multiple objectives and the lack of clear-cut criteria for evaluation.

As mentioned before, the more probable trigger to consideration of OD is the awareness, over a period of time, that well-recommended techniques for improvement fail in actual operation. The chief executive comes to the realization on his own, or upon accepted advice, that the failures in method or technique are not inherent in themselves but, rather, are the common result of his faulty and ineffectual basic organizational workbench. Adoption of OD will then be contingent upon the chief executive's awareness of the availability of OD as a solution and the willingness to accept a painful remedy.

OD emphasizes the role of the change agent. Obviously, such a comprehensive approach requires individuals who are well-versed in the behavioral science skills. Because such programs are tailored to the particular organization and its problems, the design must be predicated upon extensive evaluation and diagnosis of that organization's present condition.

While the title of change agent can be applied to any individual who meets these criteria and who can perform this function, an outside consulting role usually is recommended. This form of relationship between an organization and an individual or group independent of the organization has considerable merit. Outside consultation provides a degree of objectivity which often is unavailable to the person immersed in day-to-day affairs. Because of his transient relationship with many organizations, the consultant should be able to amass considerable experience in applying the techniques of his specialty. Unlike an insider, an outside consultant would be free of the temptation to enhance his own position within the organization. Consultation is further recommended because of the need to provide a catalyst to bring about a reapproach among individuals while remaining removed from the interrelationship process itself. This latter benefit is based upon a noted need for the improved relationship to continue after the subtraction of the change agent as a third party to the arrangement; if the change agent is a part of the permanent organization, it may prove difficult to divorce him from the continuing exchange between the primary parties whose behavior in interrelationship has been modified.

For these reasons the recommended readings in OD largely favor the consulting role.[9] Most of these writers, however, are OD pioneers and, therefore, reflect the uncertainty associated with its earliest applications. From their knowledge of the behavioral sciences, they can anticipate problems in the initial phase of organizational analysis. A still more poignant comment on the utilization of outside consultants in OD is the considerable cost to the organization from the fees involved. OD is a protracted process and the caliber of persons accomplished in its achievement are of the highest order. Both of these factors lead to bid estimates which are sometimes astronomical. Some organizations may have a broader base upon which to spread the cost of consultants because their problems often

[9] The organization development program reported by Holloway and Lonergan, "A Survey Program," appears to deemphasize the outside consulting role, although training assistance is provided externally and analysis of organizational problems is remotely accomplished by experts external to the organization.

can be compartmentalized and geographically isolated. A hospital, however, is an integrated whole and must be dealt with as one unit. The complexity of hospital organization does not permit a reduction of the extended time associated with OD, in spite of the relatively small size of hospitals as compared with more complex organizations. These factors may help explain why the practice of OD has made only limited intrusion into the hospital industry.

The theory and practice of OD have reached a level of maturity which will permit new forms of application that are within the financial reach of the hospital industry. Such applications are enhanced by the commonality of problems associated with hospital administration and the centralized nature of training and education for hospital occupations. Hospitals are much alike in their organizational dimensions because they constantly adopt changes in the prevalent technology,

as well as employ professionals in groups. Hospital employees are also more aware of the human dimension in organization because of the problems they face in a labor-intensive industry and because of the nature of the personal service they render. The education of the administrator and the dominant employee group, nurses, has continued to emphasize the lore of the behavioral sciences, and, while the depth of understanding thus provided could never hope to match that of the accomplished OD consultant, it may be sufficient to support a well-designed program for OD that would deemphasize the consulting role and be economically feasible for the average hospital.[10]

[10] The authors are presently developing an organization development program package for hospitals based upon these premises. This program will be a product of the Educational Resources Foundation, 2712 Millwood Ave., Columbia, S.C. 29205.

25. job enrichment lessons from AT&T

Robert M. Ford

There is a mounting problem in the land, the concern of employed persons with their work life. Blue-collar workers are increasingly expressing unhappiness over the monotony of the production line. White-collar workers want to barter less of their life for bread. More professional groups are unionizing to fight back at somebody.

The annual reports of many companies

Reprinted from *Harvard Business Review*, 51, No. 1 (January–February 1973), pp. 96–106, with permission of the publisher. © 1973 by the President and Fellows of Harvard College; all rights reserved.

frequently proclaim, "Our employees are our most important resource." Is this a statement of conviction or is it mere rhetoric? If it represents conviction, then I think it is only fair to conclude that many business organizations are un-unwittingly squandering their resources.

The enormous economic gains that sprang from the thinking of the scientific management school of the early 1900's— the time-and-motion study analysts, the creators of production lines—may have ended insofar as they depend on utilizing human beings more efficiently. Without discarding these older insights, we need to consider more recent evidence showing that the tasks themselves can be changed to give workers a feeling of accomplishment.

The growing pressure for a four-day workweek is not necessarily evidence that people do not care about their work; they may be rejecting their work in the form that confronts them. To ask employees to repeat one small task all day, at higher and higher rates of speed, is no way to reduce the pressure for a shorter workweek nor is it any longer a key to rising productivity in America. Work need not be so frequently a betrayal of one's education and ability.

From 1965 to 1968 a group of researchers at AT&T conducted 19 formal field experiments in job enrichment. The success of these studies has led to many company projects since then. From this work and the studies of others (many of them discussed previously in HBR), we have learned that the "lifesaving" portion of many jobs can be expanded. Conversely, the boring and unchallenging aspects can be reduced—not to say eliminated.

Furthermore, the "nesting" of related, already enriched jobs—a new concept— may constitute another big step toward better utilization of "our most important resource."

First in this article I shall break down the job enrichment strategy into three steps. Then I shall demonstrate what we at AT&T have been doing for seven years in organizing the work beyond enrichment of individual jobs. In the course of my discussion, I shall use no illustrations that were not clearly successful from the viewpoint of both employees and the company.

While obviously the functions described in the illustrations differ superficially from those in most other companies, they are still similar enough to production and service tasks in other organizations to permit meaningful comparison. It is important to examine the nature of the work itself, rather than the external aspects of the functions.

Moreover, in considering ways to enrich jobs, I am not talking about those elements that serve only to "maintain" employees: wages, fringe benefits, clean restrooms, a pleasant atmosphere, and so on. Any organization must meet the market in these respects or its employees will go elsewhere.

No, employees are saying more than "treat me well." They are also saying "use me well." The former is the maintenance side of the coin; the latter is the work motivation side.

anatomy of enrichment

In talking about job enrichment, it is necessary to go beyond such high-level concepts as "self-actualization," "need for achievement," and "psychological growth." It is necessary to specify the steps to be taken. The strategy can be broken down into these aspects—improving work through systematic changes in (a) the module of work, (b) control of the module, and (c) the feedback signaling whether something has been accomplished. I shall discuss each of these aspects in turn.

work module

Through changing the work modules, Indiana Bell Telephone Company scored a striking success in job enrichment within the space of two years. In Indianapolis, 33 employees, most of them at the lowest clerical wage level, compiled all telephone directories for the state. The processing from clerk to clerk was laid out in 21 steps, many of which were merely for verification. The steps included manuscript reception, manuscript verification, keypunch, keypunch verification, ad copy reception, ad copy verification, and so on —a production line as real as any in Detroit. Each book is issued yearly to the customers named in it, and the printing schedule calls for the appearance of about one different directory per week.

In 1968, the year previous to the start of our study, 28 new hires were required to keep the clerical force at the 33-employee level. Obviously, such turnover had bad consequences. From every operating angle, management was dissatisfied.

In a workshop, the supervisors concluded that the lengthy verification routine, calling for confirmation of one's work by other clerks, was not solving the basic problem, which was employee indifference toward the tasks. Traditional "solutions" were ineffective. They included retraining, supervisor complaints to the employees, and "communicating" with them on the importance to customers of error-free listing of their names and places of business in the directories. As any employee smart enough to be hired knows, an incorrect listing will remain monumentally wrong for a whole year.

The supervisors came up with many ideas for enriching the job. The first step was to identify the most competent employees, and then ask them, one by one, if they felt they could do error-free work, so that having others check the work would be pointless. Would they check their own work if no one else did it?

Yes, they said they could do error-free work. With this simple step the module dropped from 21 slices of clerical work to 14.

Next the supervisory family decided to take a really big step. In the case of the thinner books, they asked certain employees whether they would like to "own" their own books and perform all 14 remaining steps with no verification unless they themselves arranged it with other clerks—as good stenographers do when in doubt about a difficult piece of paperwork.

Now the module included every step (except keytape, a minor one).

Then the supervisors turned their attention to a thick book, the Indianapolis directory, which requires many hands and heads. They simply assigned letters of the alphabet to individuals and let them complete all 14 steps for each block of letters.

In the past, new entries to all directories had moved from clerk to clerk; now all paperwork connected with an entry belonging to a clerk stayed with that clerk. For example, the clerk prepared the daily addenda and issued them to the information or directory assistance operators. The system became so efficient that most of the clerks who handled the smaller directories had charge of more than one.

Delimiting the Module. In an interview one of the clerks said, "It's a book of my own." That is the way they felt about the books. Although not all modules are physically so distinct, the idea for a good module is usually there. Ideally, it is a slice of work that gives an employee a "thing of my own." At AT&T I have heard good modules described with pride in various ways:

- "A piece of turf" (especially a geographic responsibility).
- "My real estate" (by engineers responsible for a group of central offices).
- "Our cradle-to-grave modem line" (a vastly improved Western Electric switching-device production line).
- "Our mission impossible team" (a framemen's team, Long Lines Department).

The trouble with so much work processing is that no one is clearly responsible for a total unit that fails. In Indianapolis, by contrast, when a name in a directory is misspelled or omitted, the clerk knows where the responsibility lies.

Delimiting the module is not usually difficult when the tasks are in production, or at least physically defined. It is more difficult in service tasks, such as handling a telephone call. But modules make sense here, too, if the employee has been prepared for the work so that nobody else need be involved—in other words, when it is not necessary to say to the caller, "Let me connect you with my supervisor about that, please" or "May I give you our billing department, please?"

It is not always true that any one employee can handle a complete service. But our studies show that we consistently erred in forming the module; we tended to "underwhelm" employees. Eventually we learned that the worker can do more, especially as his or her experience builds. We do not have even one example from our business where job enrichment resulted in a *smaller* slice of work.

In defining modules that give each employee a natural area of responsibility, we try to accumulate horizontal slices of work until we have created (or recreated) one of these three entities for him or her:

1. A customer (usually someone outside the business).
2. A client (usually someone inside the business, helping the employee serve the customer).
3. A task (in the manufacturing end of the business, for example, where, ideally, individual employees produce complete items).

Any one of these three can make a meaningful slice of work. (In actuality, they are not separated; obviously, an employee can be working on a task for a *customer*.) Modules more difficult to differentiate are those in which the "wholeness" of the job is less clear—that is, control is not complete. They include cases where—

. . . the employee is merely one of many engaged in providing the ultimate service or item;

. . . the employee's customer is really the boss (or, worse yet, the boss's boss) who tells him what to do;

. . . the job is to help someone who tells the employee what is to be done.

While jobs like these are harder to enrich, it is worth trying.

control of the module

As an employee gains experience, the supervisor should continue to turn over responsibility until the employee is handling the work completely. The reader may infer that supervisors are treating employees unequally. But it is not so; ultimately, they may all have the complete job if they can handle it. In the directory-compilation case cited—which was a typical assembly-line procedure, although the capital investment was low—the supervisors found that they could safely permit the employee to say when sales of advertisements in the yellow pages must stop if the ads were to reach the printer on time.

Employees of South Central Bell Telephone Company, who set their own cutoff dates for the New Orleans, Monroeville, and Shreveport phone books, consistently gave themselves less time than management had previously allowed. As a result, the sale of space in the yellow pages one year continued for three additional weeks, producing more than $100,000 in extra revenue.

But that was only one element in the total module and its control. The directory clerks talked *directly* to salesmen, to the printer, to supervisors in other departments about production problems, to service representatives, and to each other as the books moved through the production stages.

There are obvious risks on the supervisors' side as they give their jobs away, piece by piece, to selected employees. We have been through it enough to advise, "Don't worry." Be assured that supervisors who try it will say, as many in the Bell System have said, "Now, at last, I feel like a manager. Before I was merely chief clerk around here."

In other studies we have made, control has been handed by the supervisor to a person when the employee is given the authority to perform such tasks as these:

- Set credit ratings for customers.
- Ask for, and determine the size of, a deposit.
- Cut off service for nonpayment.
- Make his or her own budget, subject to negotiation.
- Perform work other than that on the order sheet after negotiating it with the customer.
- Reject a run or supply of material because of poor quality.
- Make free use of small tools or supplies within a budget negotiated with the supervisor.
- Talk to anyone at any organizational level when the employee's work is concerned.
- Call directly and negotiate for outside repairmen or suppliers (within the budget) to remedy a condition handicapping the employee's performance.

feedback

Definition of the module and control of it are futile unless the results of the employee's effort are discernible. Moreover, knowledge of the results should go directly to where it will nurture motivation—that is, to the employee. People have a great capacity for mid-flight correction when they know where they stand.

One control responsibility given to excellent employees in AT&T studies is self-monitoring; it lets them record their own "qualities and quantities." For example, one employee who had only a grade-school education was taught to keep a quality control chart in which the two identical parts of a dry-reed switch were not to vary more than .005 from an ideal dimension. She found that for some reason too many switches were failing.

She proved that the trouble occurred when one reed that was off by .005 met another reed that was off by .005. The sum, .010, was too much in the combined component and it failed. On her own initiative, she recommended and saw to it that the machine dies were changed when the reeds being stamped out started to vary by .003 from the ideal. A total variance of .006 would not be too much, she reasoned. Thus the feedback she got showed her she was doing well at her job.

This example shows all three factors at work—the module, its control, and feedback. She and two men, a die maker and a machine operator, had the complete responsibility for producing each day more than 100,000 of these tiny parts, which are not unlike two paper matches, but much smaller. How can one make a life out of this? Well, they did. The six stamping machines and expensive photometric test equipment were "theirs." A forklift truck had been dedicated to them (no waiting for someone else to bring or remove supplies). They ordered rolls of wire for stamping machines when they estimated they would need it. They would ship a roll back when they had difficulty controlling it.

Compared with workers at a plant organized along traditional lines, with batches of the reeds moving from shop to shop, these three employees were producing at a fourfold rate. Such a mini-group, where each person plays a complementary part, is radically different psychologically from the traditional group of workers, where each is doing what the others do.

(In the future, when now undreamed-of computer capacities have been reached, management must improve its techniques of feeding performance results directly to the employee responsible. And preferably it should be done *before* the boss knows about it.)

improving the system

When a certain job in the Bell System is being enriched, we ask the supervisory family, "Who or what is the customer client/task in this job?" Also, "How often can the module be improved?" And then, "How often can control or feedback be improved? Can we improve all three at once?"

These are good questions to ask in general. My comments at this stage of our knowledge must be impressionistic.

The modules of most jobs can be improved, we have concluded. Responsibilities or tasks that exist elsewhere in the shop or in some other shop or department need to be combined with the job under review. This horizontal loading is necessary until the base of the job is right. However, I have not yet seen a job whose base was too broad.

At levels higher than entrance grade, and especially in management positions, many responsibilities can be moved to lower grade levels, usually to the advantage of every job involved. This vertical loading is especially important in mature organizations.

In the Indianapolis directory office, 21 piece-meal tasks were combined into a single, meaningful, natural task. There are counterparts in other industries, such as

the assembly of an entire dashboard of an automobile by two workers.

We have evidence that two jobs—such as the telephone installer's job and the telephone repairman's job—often can make one excellent "combinationman"'s job. But there are some jobs in which the work module is already a good one. One of these is the service representative, the highly trained clerk to whom a customer speaks when he wants to have a telephone installed, moved, or disconnected, or when he questions his telephone bill. This is sometimes a high-turnover job, and when a service representative quits because of work or task dissatisfaction, there goes $3,450 in training. In fact, much of the impetus for job enrichment came through efforts to reduce these costs.

In this instance the slice of work was well enough conceived; nevertheless, we obtained excellent results from the procedures of job enrichment. Improvements in the turnover situation were as great as 50%. Why? Because we could improve the control and feedback.

It should be recognized that moving the work module to a lower level is not the same as moving the control down. If the supervisor decides that a customer's account is too long overdue and tells the service representative what to do, then both the module and the control rest with the supervisor. When, under job enrichment procedures, the service representative makes the decision that a customer must be contacted, but checks it first with the supervisor, control remains in the supervisor's hands. Under full job enrichment, however, the service representative has control.

Exhibit I shows in schematic form the steps to be taken when improving a job. To increase control, responsibility must be obtained from higher levels; I have yet to see an instance where control is moved upward to enrich a job. It must be acknowledged, however, that not every

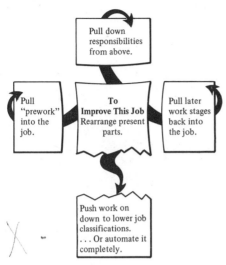

Exhibit I. Steps in Improving a Job.

for. An exception is the small group of mutually supporting, complementary workers, but even in this case each individual needs knowledge of his or her own results.

These generalizations cannot be said to be based on an unbiased sample of all jobs in all locations. Usually, the study or project locations were not in deep trouble, nor were they the best operating units. The units in deep trouble cannot stand still long enough to figure out what is wrong, and the top performers need no help. Therefore, the hard-nosed, scientifically trained manager can rightfully say that the jury is still out as to whether job enrichment can help in all work situations. But it has helped repeatedly and consistently on many jobs in the Bell System.

employee is ready to handle more control. That is especially true of new employees.

Moreover, changing the control of a job is more threatening to supervisors than is changing the module. In rejecting a job enrichment proposal, one department head said to us, "When you have this thing proved 100%, let me know and we'll try it."

As far as feedback is concerned, it is usually improvable, but not until the module and control of it are in top condition. If the supervisory family cannot come up with good ways for telling the employee how he or she is doing, the problem lies almost surely in a bad module. That is, the employee's work is submerged in a total unit and he or she has no distinct customer/client/task.

When the module is right, you get feedback "for free"; it comes directly from the customer/client/task. During the learning period, however, the supervisor or teacher should provide the feedback.

When supervisors use the performance of all employees as a goad to individual employees, they thwart the internalization of motivation that job enrichment strives

job "nesting"

Having established to its satisfaction that job enrichment works, management at AT&T is studying ways to go beyond the enriching of individual jobs. A technique that offers great promise is that of "nesting" several jobs to improve morale and upgrade performance.

By way of illustration I shall describe how a family of supervisors of service representatives in a unit of Southwestern Bell Telephone Company improved its service indexes, productivity, collection of overdue bills, and virtually every other index of performance. In two years they moved their Ferguson District (adjacent to St. Louis) from near the bottom to near the top in results among all districts in the St. Louis area.

Before the job enrichment effort started, the service representatives' office was laid out as it appears in Exhibit II. The exhibit shows their desks in the standard, in-line arrangement fronted by the desks of their supervisors, who exercised close control of the employees.

As part of the total job enrichment

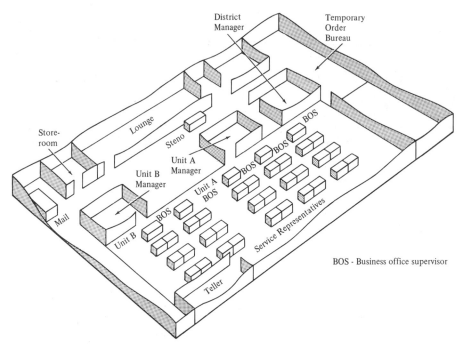

Exhibit II. Ferguson District Service Representatives' Office Layout Before Job Enrichment.

effort, each service rep group was given a geographical locality of its own, with a set of customers to take care of, rather than just "the next customer who calls in" from anywhere in the district. Some service reps—most of them more experienced —were detached to form a unit handling only the businesses in the district.

Then the service representatives and their business office supervisors (BOS) were moved to form a "wagon train" layout. As Exhibit III shows, they were gathered into a more-or-less circular shape and were no longer directly facing the desks of the business office supervisors and unit managers. (The office of the district manager was further removed too.)

Now all was going well with the service representatives' job, but another function in the room was in trouble. This was the entry-level job of service order typist. These typists transmit the orders to the

telephone installers and the billing and other departments. They and the service order reviewers—a higher-classification job—had been located previously in a separate room that was soundproofed and air-conditioned because the TWX machines they used were noisy and hot. When its equipment was converted to the silent, computer-operated cathode ray tubes (CRTs), the unit was moved to a corner of the service reps' room (see Exhibit III).

But six of the eight typists quit in a matter of months after the move. Meanwhile, the percentage of service orders typed "on time" fell below 50%, then below 40%.

The reasons given by the six typists who quit were varied, but all appeared to be rationalizations. The managers who looked at the situation, and at the $25,000 investment in the layout, could see that the feeling of physical isolation and the

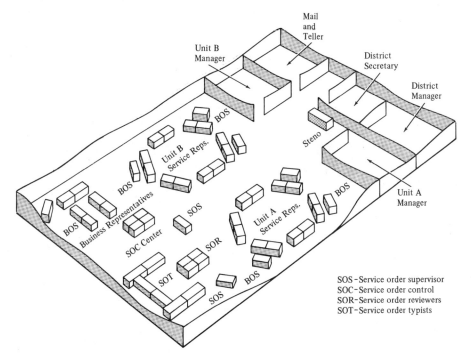

Exhibit III. Service Representatives' Office Layout After Job Enrichment Program Was Implemented.

feeling of having no "thing" of their own were doubtless the real prime factors. As the arrangement existed, any service order typist could be called on to type an order for any service representative. On its face, this seems logical; but we have learned that an employee who belongs to everybody belongs to nobody.

An instantly acceptable idea was broached: assign certain typists to each service rep team serving a locality. "And while we're at it," someone said, "why not move the CRTs right into the group? Let's have a wagon train with the women and kids in the middle." This was done (over the protest of the budget control officer, I should add).

The new layout appears in Exhibit IV. Three persons are located in the station in the middle of each unit. The distinction between service order typist and service order reviewer has been abolished, with the former upgraded to the scale of the latter. (Lack of space has precluded arranging the business customer unit in the same wagon-train fashion. But that unit's service order review and typing desks are close to the representatives' desks.)

Before the changes were started, processing a service request involved ten steps—and sometimes as many persons—not counting implementation of the order in the Plan Department. Now the procedure is thought of in terms of people, and only three touch a service order on its way through the office. (See Exhibit V.) At this writing, the Ferguson managers hope to eliminate even the service order completion clerk as a specialized position.

Has the new arrangement worked? Just before the typists moved into the wagon train, they were issuing only 27% of the orders on time. Within 30 days after the

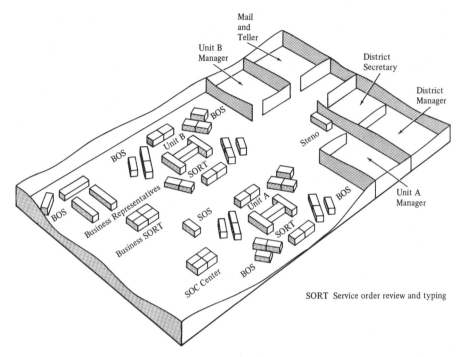

Exhibit IV.   Office Layout After Service Order Typists Were "Nested."

switch to assigned responsibility, 90% of the orders were going out on time. Half a year later, in one particular month, the figure even reached 100%.

These results were obtained with a 21% jump in work load—comparing a typical quarter after "nesting" with one before—being performed with a net drop of 22 worker-weeks during the quarter. On a yearly basis it is entirely reasonable to expect the elimination of 88 weeks of unnecessary work (conservatively, $1\frac{1}{2}$ full-time employees). Unneeded messenger service has been dispensed with, and one of two service order supervisor positions has been eliminated. The entire cost has been recovered already.

The service order accuracy measurement, so important in computerization, has already attained the stringent objectives set by the employees themselves, which exceeded the level supervisors would have set. Why are there fewer errors? Because now employees can lean across the area and talk to each other about a service order with a problem or hand-writing that is unclear. During the course of a year this will probably eliminate the hand preparation of a thousand "query" slips, with a thousand written replies, in this one district.

And what of the human situation? When on-time order issuance was at its ebb, a supervisor suggested having a picnic for the service representatives and the typists. They did, but not a single typist showed up. Later, when the on-time order rate had climbed over 90%, I remarked, "Now's the time for another picnic." To which the supervisor replied facetiously, "Now we don't need a picnic!"

The turnover among typists for job reasons has virtually ceased. Some are asking now for the job of service repre-

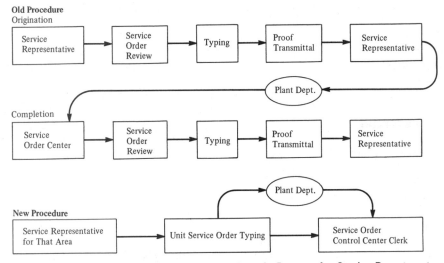

Exhibit V.   Old and New Processing Procedures in Request-for-Service Department.

sentative, which is more demanding, more skilled, and better paid. Now, when the CRTs or the computer is shut down for some reason, or if the service order typist runs out of work supervisors report that typists voluntarily help the service reps with filing and other matters. They are soaking up information about the higher-rated jobs. These occurrences did not happen when the typists were 100 feet away; then they just sat doing nothing when the work flow ceased. (Because of this two-way flow of information, incidentally, training time for the job of service representative may drop as much as 50%.)

As the state general manager remarked when the results were first reported, "This is a fantastic performance. It's not enough to enrich just one job in a situation. We must learn how to put them together."

different configuration

While the Ferguson District supervisory family was making a minigroup out of the service reps and their CRT typists, a

strikingly different minigroup was in formation in the Northern Virginia Area of the Chesapeake and Potomac Telephone Company. There the family hit on the idea of funneling to selected order typists only those orders connected with a given central office, such as the Lewinsville frame. Soon the typists and the framemen—those who actually make the changes as a result of service orders—became acquainted. The typists even visited "their" framerooms. Now some questions could be quickly resolved that previously called for formal interdepartmental interrogations through supervisors.

At the end of the first eight months of 1972, these 9 CRT typists were producing service order pages at a rate one third higher than the 51 service order typists in the comparison group. The absence rate in the experimental unit was 0.6%, compared with 2.5% for the others, and the errors per 100 orders amounted to 2.9 as against 4.6 in the comparison group.

The flow of service orders is from (a) service rep to (b) service order typist to (c) the frameroom. The Ferguson District enjoyed success when it linked (a) and (b), while productivity for the Lewinsville frame improved when (b) and (c) were linked. Obviously, the next step is to link (a), (b), and (c). We are now selecting trial locations to test this larger nesting approach.

lessons learned

In summary fashion, at the end of seven years of effort to improve the work itself, it is fair to say that:

1. Enriching existing jobs pays off. To give an extreme example, consider the fact that Illinois Bell Telephone Company's directory compilation effort reduced the work force from 120 persons to 74. Enriching the job started a series of moves; it was not the only ingredient, but it was the precipitating one.

2. Job enrichment requires a big change in managerial style. It calls for increasing modules, moving control downward, and dreaming up new feedback ideas. There is nothing easy about a successful job enrichment effort.

3. The nesting or configuring of related tasks—we call it "work organization"—may be the next big step forward after the enrichment of single jobs in the proper utilization of human beings.

It seems to produce a multiplier effect rather than merely a simple sum. In the Ferguson District case the job modules were not changed; the service representatives were not asked to type their own orders on the cathode ray tubes, nor were the typists asked to take over the duties of the service representatives. The results came from enriching other aspects (control and feedback) and, more important, from laying out the work area differently to facilitate interaction among responsible people.

4. While continuing job enrichment efforts, it is important not to neglect "maintenance" factors. In extending our work with job nesting, for example, we plan to experiment with "office landscaping," so called. The furniture, dividers, planters, and acoustical treatment, all must add to the feeling of work dedication. By this I mean we will dedicate site, equipment, and jobs to the employees, with the expectation that they will find it easier to dedicate themselves to customer/client/task. Especially in new installations, this total work environmental approach seems a good idea for experimentation. We will not be doing it merely to offset pain or boredom in work. The aim is to facilitate work.

5. A "pool" of employees with one job (typing pool, reproduction pool, calculating pool, and so on) is at the opposite extreme from the team or "minigroup" which I have described. A minigroup is a set of mutually supporting employees, each of whom has a meaningful module or part in meeting the needs of customer/client/task. What is "meaningful" is, like a love affair, in the eye of the beholder; at this stage, we have difficulty in describing it further.

A minigroup can have several service representatives or typists; one of each is not basic to the idea. The purpose is to set up a group of employees so that a natural, mutual dependence can grow in providing a service or finishing a task. It marks the end of processing from person to person or group to group, in separate locations or departments and with many different supervisors.

The minigroup concept, however, still leaves room for specialists. In certain Scandinavian auto plants, for example, one or two specialists fabricate the entire assembly of the exhaust pollution control system or the electrical system. Eventually, a group of workers may turn out a whole engine. In the United States, Chrysler has given similar trial efforts a high priority. The idea is to fix authority at the lowest level possible.

6. Experience to date indicates that unions welcome the kind of effort described in our studies. Trouble can be expected, of course, if the economics of increases in productivity are not shared equitably. In the majority of cases, the economics can be handled even under existing contracts, since they usually permit establishment of new jobs and appropriate wage grades between dates of contract negotiation.

An employee who takes the entire responsibility for preparing a whole telephone directory, for example, ought to be paid more, although a new clerical rating must be established. Job enrichment is not in lieu of cash; good jobs and good maintenance are two sides of the same coin.

7. New technology, such as the cathode ray tube, should enable us to break free of old work arrangements. When the Ferguson District service order typists were using the TRX machines, nesting their jobs was impractical because the equipment would have driven everybody to distraction. Installation of the high-technology CRTs gave the planners the opportunity to move together those employees whose modules of work were naturally related. This opportunity was at first overlooked.

Everyone accepts .the obvious notion that new technology can and must eliminate dumb-dumb jobs. However, it probably creates more, rather than fewer, fragments of work. Managers should observe the new module and the work organization of the modules. This effort calls for new knowledge and skills, such as laying out work so attractively that the average employee will stay longer and work more effectively than under the previous arrangement.

Moreover, technology tends to make human beings adjuncts of machines. As we move toward computerized production of all listings in the white pages of the phone books, for example, the risk of an employee's losing "his" or "her" own directories is very great indeed. (Two AT&T companies, South Central Bell and Pacific Northwest Bell, are at this stage, and we must be certain the planned changes do not undermine jobs.) Making sure that machines remain the adjunct of human beings is a frontier problem which few managers have yet grappled with.

8. Managers in mature organizations are likely to have difficulty convincing another department to make pilot runs of any new kind of work organization, especially one that will cause the department to lose people, budget, or size. Individual job enrichment does not often get into interdepartmental tangles, but the nesting of jobs will almost surely create problems of autonomy. This will call for real leadership.

9. When the work is right, employee attitudes are right. That is the job enrichment strategy—get the work right.

discussion questions : part III

1. Describe the basic models of organization. Compare each model to the contingency model.
2. What is the relationship between task forces and project management? What is the role of the project manager?
3. Why are task forces and project management used? Delineate several types of organizations in which such managers could be easily used.
4. In the behavioral model of organization, do you agree with the inputs and outputs of the model? Should there have been additional inputs and outputs or fewer? Why or why not?

5. How could a behavioral model of organizations be employed by a practicing manager?

6. Clearly differentiate between the classic representation of an organization and the new work group representation. Why is this not a widely accepted method of management at the present time?

7. What is organization behavior modification? What utility would it have in the modern corporation? Why?

8. How can organization development be used in organizations? Why is it used?

9. What is a change agent? Why are change agents needed in organizations? What difficulties are encountered with change agents in some organizations?

10. Analyze the method of job enrichment. Is it a feasible solution to the cries of job dissatisfaction by workers on the assembly line? Why or why not?

11. Describe "job nesting." How can this method be used to improve working conditions for blue-collar workers? For white-collar workers? Could it be used to improve working conditions for managers? Professionals? Why or why not?

selected references : part III

A. *organization theory*

Argyris, Chris, "Personality and Organization Theory, Revisited," *Administrative Science Quarterly*, 18, No. 2 (June 1973), pp. 141–167.

————, "Some Limits of Rational Man Organization Theory," *Public Administration Review*, 33, No. 3 (May–June 1973), pp. 253–267.

Gibson, James, "Organization Theory and the Nature of Man," *Academy of Management Journal*, 9, No. 3 (September 1966), pp. 233–245.

Greiner, Larry E., "Evolution and Revolution As Organizations Grow," *Harvard Business Review*, 50, No. 4 (July–August 1972), pp. 37–46.

Ingham, Geoffrey K., "Size of Industrial Organization and Worker Behavior," *Cambridge Papers in Sociology 1* (Cambridge, England: Cambridge University Press, 1970).

Litterer, Joseph A., *The Analysis of Organizations*, 2nd ed. (New York: John Wiley and Sons, Inc., 1973).

Miner, John B., *Management Theory* (New York: Macmillan Publishing Co., Inc., 1971).

Oberg, Winston, "Charisma, Commitment and Contemporary Organization Theory," *MSU Business Topics*, 20, No. 2 (Spring 1972), pp. 18–32.

Pugh, D. S., "The Measurement of Organization Structures," *Organizational Dynamics*, 1, No. 4 (Spring 1973), pp. 19–34.

————, "Modern Organization Theory: A Psychological and Sociological Study," *Psychological Bulletin*, 66, No. 4 (October 1966), pp. 235–251.

Rice, George H., and Dean W. Bishoprick, *Conceptual Models of Organization* (New York: Appleton-Century-Crofts, 1971).

Urwick, Lyndall F., "Theory Z," *S.A.M. Advanced Management Journal*, 35, No. 1 (January 1970), pp. 14–21.

B. *organizational behavior*

Cherns, A. B., "Can Behavioral Scientists Help Managers Improve Their Organizations?" *Organizational Dynamics*, 1, No. 3 (Winter 1973), pp. 51–67.

Eddy, William B., W. W. Burke, Vladimir A. Dupré, and Oron P. South (eds.),

Behavioral Science and the Manager's Role (Washington, D.C.: NTL Institute for Applied Behavioral Science, 1969).

Emshoff, James R., *Analysis of Behavioral Systems* (New York: Macmillan Publishing Co., Inc., 1971).

Fitzgerald, Thomas H., "Why Motivation Theory Doesn't Work," *Harvard Business Review*, 49, No. 4 (July–August 1971), pp. 37–44.

Huber, George P., and André Delbecq, "Guidelines for Combining the Judgments of Individual Members in Decision Conferences," *Academy of Management Journal*, 15, No. 2 (June 1972), pp. 161–174.

Kaplan, H. Roy, Curt Tausky, and Bhopinder S. Bolaria, "The Human Relations View of Motivation; Fact or Fantasy?" *Organizational Dynamics*, 1, No. 2 (Autumn 1972), pp. 68–80.

Levinson, Harry, "Asinine Attitudes Toward Motivation," *Harvard Business Review*, 51, No. 1 (January–February 1973), pp. 70–76.

Likert, Rensis, "Human Organizational Measurements: Key to Financial Success," *Michigan Business Review*, 23, No. 3 (May 1971), pp. 1–5.

Powell, Reed M., and John L. Schlacter, "Participative Management: A Panacea?" *Academy of Management Journal*, 14, No. 2 (June 1971), pp. 165–173.

Schein, Edgar H., *Organizational Psychology*, 2nd ed. (Englewood Cliffs, N.J.: Prentice-Hall, Inc., 1970).

Thompson, James D., and Donald R. Van Houten, *The Behavioral Sciences: An Interpretation* (Reading, Mass.: Addison-Wesley Publishing Co., Inc., 1970).

C. organization development

Argyris, Chris, "The CEO's Behavior: Key to Organizational Development," *Harvard Business Review*, 51, No. 2 (March–April 1973), pp. 55–64.

Baldridge, J. Victor, "Organizational Change: The Human Relations Perspective Versus the Political Systems Perspective," *Educational Researcher*, 1, No. 2 (February 1972), pp. 4–10, 15.

Beckhard, Richard, *Organization Development: Strategies and Models* (Reading, Mass.: Addison-Wesley Publishing Co., 1969).

Blake, Robert R., and Jane S. Mouton, "Change by Design, Not by Default," *S.A.M. Advanced Management Journal*, 35, No. 2 (April 1970), pp. 29–34.

French, Wendell L., and Cecil H. Bell, Jr., *Organization Development* (Englewood Cliffs, N.J.: Prentice-Hall, Inc., 1973).

Golembiewski, Robert T., and Robert Munzenrider, "Persistence and Change: A Note on the Long-Term Effects of an Organization Development Program," *Academy of Management Journal*, 16, No. 1 (March 1973), pp. 149–153.

Greene, Charles N., "The Satisfaction–Performance Controversy," *Business Horizons*, 15, No. 5 (October 1972), pp. 31–41.

Huse, Edgar F., and Michael Beer, "Eclectic Approach to Organizational Development," *Harvard Business Review*, 49, No. 5 (September–October 1971), pp. 103–112.

Kegan, Daniel L., "Organization Development: Description, Issues, and Some Research Results," *Academy of Management Journal*, 14, No. 4 (December 1971), pp. 453–464.

Lawrence, Paul R., and Jay W. Lorsch, *Developing Organizations: Diagnosis and Action* (Reading, Mass.: Addison-Wesley Publishing Co., 1969).

Strauss, George, "Organizational Development: Credits and Debits," *Organizational Dynamics*, 1, No. 3 (Winter 1973), pp. 2–19.

quantitative approaches
part IV

The newest approaches to management appear to have evolved from mathematics. During World War II, many quantitative methods were developed to solve military problems (e.g., the assignment of millions of military personnel and the deployment of submarines). Following the war, some managers began to use these mathematical techniques and develop models for decision making. Problems which previously had been solved by managerial intuition and experience were now analyzed by operations research and management science techniques. During the past twenty-five years, mathematical solutions to complex problems have become increasingly common—partly owing to increasingly sophisticated techniques and partly owing to the increased capacities of computers. In many instances, these new methods provided several good alternatives which were ranked on a priority basis as contrasted to the older methods which frequently provided one or two alternatives which may not have been optimal.[1]

Techniques of the quantitative approaches have radically changed the decision-making tools available to the practicing executive. Many of these techniques are concerned with problems in which an executive is faced (1) with too many choices to observe readily the consequences of each alternative; (2) with limited courses of action which are difficult to predict; and (3) with multiple objectives

---

[1] Kenneth S. Brown, "Management Science—Its Role in the Organization," *Managerial Planning*, 21, No. 1 (July–August 1972), pp. 6–10, 38; and Patrick Rivett, "The Art of Operations Research," *Organizational Dynamics*, 1, No. 1 (Summer 1972), pp. 32–42.

and unsureness as to the ways in which to reconcile them.[2] These quantitative techniques have generated numerous new analytical devices including (1) physical models; (2) pictorial models; (3) mathematical programming—gaming models, input-output models, and linear programming models; (4) queuing models; (5) critical path models—PERT, CPM, and PEP; and (6) simulation models.[3] Through such techniques, managers have had more and better alternatives for dealing with complex operating problems. Although the tools of the quantitative approaches may not offer optimal solutions to all of the problems of management, they certainly have aided in pinpointing the problems and assisted in resolving them.[4]

In this part, the selections have been chosen to outline clearly what the nature of the quantitative approaches to management are, to discuss some of the newly evolving analytical techniques in organizational decision making, and to demonstrate the valuable contributions of simulation and modeling methods in management.

In the first article of the first section, authored by the Operations Research Society of America's Committee on Professional Standards, the history of operations research, the practice and spirit of operations research, and the uses of operations research in different administrative settings are examined. In the second article, Elmer Burack and Robert B. D. Batlivala analyze the growth of operations research personnel in organizations through the shifts in educational qualifications of operations research personnel, the exposure of top management to information technology, the relationship of top management to operations researchers, the sponsorship of the operations research group, and the relationship of operations research to the decision-making process.

In the next section, Richard Tersine synthesizes decision theory in organizations. His article succinctly covers the establishment of objectives in the organization, the types of decision making available to meet these objectives, and general types of decision models which can be used by managers. Robert M. Fulmer describes the use of one new analytical technique—the Delphi Technique—which is used to forecast the future. This tool is now widely utilized throughout industry and the government.

During the past decade, computers have become increasingly useful in providing the capability to solve large-scale problems in organizations. Today, they may handle problems ranging from production scheduling to manpower forecasting to market simulation problems. In the third section, James B. Boulden describes an on-line management planning and control system and additionally provides an analysis of a major corporate simulator which allows the user to

[2] Rivett, p. 32.

[3] William G. Browne, "Techniques of Operations Research," *Journal of Systems Management*, 23, No. 9 (September 1972), pp. 8–13.

[4] For additional information on quantitative methods in management, see Arthur F. Veinott, Jr. (ed.), *Mathematical Studies in Management Science* (New York: Macmillan Publishing Co., Inc., 1965); Browne, pp. 8–13; and William H. Gruber and John S. Niles, "Problems in the Utilization of Management Science/Operations Research: A State of the Art Survey," *Interfaces*, 2, No. 1 (November 1971), pp. 12–19.

explore the impact of certain variables upon the company trading position. In the final article, Vincent R. LoCascio examines the use of a simulation model for colleges and universities and hypothesizes several major uses for the SEARCH model.

operations management

26. the nature of operations research

ORSA Committee on Professional Standards

the science of operations research

Operations research is an experimental and applied science devoted to observing, understanding, and predicting the behavior of purposeful man-machine systems; and operations-research workers are actively engaged in applying this knowledge to practical problems in business, government, and society.

Thus operations-research workers are engaged in three classical aspects of science:

- Describing the behavior of these systems.
- Analyzing this behavior by constructing theories (frequently called 'models') that account for the observed phenomena.

Reprinted from *Operations Research*, 19, No. 5 (September 1971), pp. 1138–1148, with permission of the publisher.

- Using these theories to predict future behavior, that is, the effects that will be produced by changes in the systems or in their methods of operation.

Since the operating systems studied by operations-research workers arise in a wide variety of practical, industrial, military, and governmental environments, it follows that the results of their research frequently make important contributions to the solution of problems of choice, policy, and planning that arise in these environments; these contributions are characteristically made by presenting the research findings directly to the executives responsible for the operations or systems studied.

history of operations research

Today there are thousands of scientists engaged in operations research, and their work is making increasingly important contributions. The *Operations Research Society of America* helps serve the professional needs of these operations-research scientists through a variety of activities.

In the United States, interest in operations research was born in military problems and flowered first during the war-time years of 1942–45, but by 1952, activities had spread to enough other contexts to warrant founding the *Operations Research Society of America*. In 1953 a similar society, *The Institute of Management Sciences*, was founded to advance the science of management.*

By the mid-1960's, there were large bodies of theory (such as linear and dynamic programming, queuing theory, game theory, network analysis, replacement and inventory theories, scheduling, simulation, and so on), an accumulation of successful applications in many arenas (military operations, manufacturing, transportation, communications, construction, health care, banking, and many others), and graduate programs leading to advanced degrees in operations research at many universities.

Too, by the mid-1960's, operations research had not only achieved a position of important influence in industrial operations and national, state, and local governmental activities, it had also contributed importantly to their planning and policy choices.

In this latter area, OR played a leading role in developing a planning framework

---

* Management Science is a term closely related to operations research. The Institute of Management Sciences has as its objective "to identify, extend, and unify scientific knowledge that contributes to the understanding and practice of management." Also closely related is systems analysis, which can be defined as "a systematic attempt to provide decision makers with a full, accurate, and meaningful summary of the information relevant to clearly defined issues and alternatives."

(called in the U.S. National government the "planning-programming-budgeting system") that relates input resources to output results for major programs over their lifetimes, thus facilitating the quantitative analyses and comparisons of competing programs, and supporting rational choices of preferred programs. This framework was extended to the entire federal government in 1965.

Simultaneously, as this approach was spreading to U.S., state and local governments, similar outlooks and methods were being used in industrial planning and decision making.

As we enter the 1970's, only a quarter of a century after the beginnings of operations research as a coherent activity, this new style of formulating and analyzing planning and policy choices, with operations research at its core, is exercising a pervasive and seminal influence in many governmental and industrial circles.

Thus, in 1970 there are not only very substantial bodies of theory, but also a great many arenas of applications, with many workers devoting attention to each.

the practice of operations research

In the early days of operations research, all of the work was new and, therefore, most of it could be thought of as research in the scientific sense. However, now that a substantial body of knowledge exists, it may happen that a problem can be solved by a reasonably routine application of known theory in a pattern standardized by previous applications to similar problems. In general, however, a client may not even know he has a problem that can be solved by OR techniques. In a typical case, a client, individual, or organization has a problem, he asks operations-research workers (perhaps in a team with workers with other technical skills) to address themselves to it, the OR workers and their colleagues do so and develop a proposed solution or ameliorative course of action, which they then present to the client. In order that the proposed solutions be useful to the client, the OR work must be highly relevant to the client's operations. Since in general the science of OR requires an abstraction from practical operations, compromises are invariably made in the generation of the OR theory. The client is made aware of these shortcomings. Frequently, when the client adopts the proposal, the OR worker assists its implementation or assesses its effects.

The practice of operations research will vary from the detailed application of an existing mathematical tool to a problem, defined by the client, to the definition and isolation of a new problem, defined by the OR workers, and the generation of new OR theory in its solution. Such work may contribute to the science of operations research by describing a new context scientifically and identifying its stabilities, by developing a new theory, or by reporting on the successful predictions of a theory in a new context. In many practical situations, because of the desire to save research time and costs, the client is willing to accept applications of existing theory but not to sponsor extensive forays into the unknown. Thus it is natural that new scientific advances cannot be made frequently in situations of practice.

Specific developments in the science of operations research and applications of operations research to specific problems must be judged differently with respect to their technical competence, accuracy, and relevance. In developing the science of operations research, the principle of careful review is honored by the classic device of having papers proposed for publication in technical journals subjected to a careful refereeing process. In applying the science, however, where a confidential relation between analyst and client frequently exists, the quality of the work must, of necessity, be governed by the competence, standards, and conscience of the analyst, reinforced, perhaps, by the standards and review procedures of the research organization of which he may be a part.

Thus, at a time when the practice of operations research is growing rapidly, it is desirable to develop standards and principles that can serve two purposes: as a checklist for analysts, and as a useful guide to clients—and thus as a common ground for both.

Since operations research is a science and the practice of OR is to be carried out in a scientific spirit, we shall present the relevant characteristics of science. We turn to a description given by an eminent systems analyst:

First, the method of science is open, explicit, ... self-correcting ... [and the results] verifiable. It combines logic and empirical evidence. The method and tradition of science require that scientific results be openly arrived at, so that any other scientist can retrace the same steps and get the same result ... all observations, calculations, assumptions, empirical data, and judgments ... [must] be described in the analysis in such a way that they can be subjected to checking, testing, criticism, debate, discussion, and possible refutation.

Second, scientific method is objective. Although personalities doubtless play an important part in the life of the ... profession, the science itself does not depend upon personalities or vested interests. The truth of a scientific proposition is established by logical and empirical methods common to the profession as a whole. The young and inexperienced scientist can challenge the results of an older and more experienced one, or an obscure scientist can challenge the findings of a Nobel Prize winner, and the profession ... [should] evaluate the results on the basis of methods quite independent of the authority of the contenders, and ... [should] establish what is the correct conclusion. In other words, the result is established on the objective quality ... and not on the reputations of the persons involved. Doubtless, some would scoff at the challenger, and the odds would favor the Nobel Prize winner. But, the ... profession is not likely to harbor incorrect hypotheses for long just because of the authority of their originators.[1]

This at least is the goal.

Third, in scientific method in the broadest sense, each hypothesis is tested and verified by methods appropriate to it. Some are tested and verified logically, some experimentally, some historically, and some in still other ways. Some sciences, of course, lend themselves to inexpensive experimentation and, where this is so, experiments tend to be emphasized. This is notably the case with the physical sciences. In others, particularly some branches of medicine and the social sciences, one cannot experiment as readily, and detailed analysis of available historical data may be more appropriate.

Fourth, quantitative aspects are treated quantitatively ... Nonquantitative judgment is simply not enough ... Where a quantitative matter is being discussed, the greatest clarity of thought is achieved by using numbers, not by avoiding them, *even when uncertainties are present*. This is not to rule out judgment and insight, ... which need, like everything else, to be expressed with clarity if they are to be useful.

systems analysis

As operations-research workers have built up their understandings of the operations of the organizations they have been working with—industrial, governmental, and military—it is natural that they should be called on to illuminate, by use of their knowledge and techniques, the major problems of choice and policy faced by

these organizations. Since these problems are frequently both very important and very complicated, the resulting analyses frequently emerge as major undertakings, and involve the cooperation of many contributing disciplines in addition to operations research. Since the choices frequently lie between competing operating-system possibilities, the analysis of their relative merits has been called *systems analysis*, a term that now extends to all such analyses, whether dealing specifically with systems or not. For the purposes of this discussion, systems analysis can be characterized as

a systematic approach to helping a decision maker choose a course of action by investigating his full problem, searching out objectives and alternatives, and comparing them in the light of their consequences, using an appropriate framework —insofar as possible analytic—to bring expert judgment and intuition to bear on the problem. ... The idea of an analysis to provide advice is not new and, in concept, what needs to be done is simple and rather obvious. One strives to look at the entire problem, as a whole, in context, and to compare alternative choices in the light of their possible outcomes. Three sorts of enquiry are required, any of which can modify the others as the work proceeds. There is a need, first of all, for a systematic investigation of the decision maker's objectives and of the relevant criteria for deciding among the alternatives that promise to achieve these objectives. Next, the alternatives need to be identified, examined for feasibility, and then compared in terms of their effectiveness and cost, taking time and risk into account. Finally, an attempt must be made to design better alternatives and select other goals if those previously examined are found wanting.[2]

To achieve this essence, five major elements usually contribute: objectives, alternatives, costs, the model, and criteria.

---

[1] Alain Enthoven, "Systems Analysis and the Navy," p. 278 of *Planning Programming Budgeting: A Systems Approach to Management*, Fremont J. Lyden and Ernest G. Miller (eds.), Markham Publishing Co., Chicago, 1967.

[2] E. S. Quade and W. I. Boucher (eds.), *System Analysis and Policy Planning Applications in Defense*, pp. 1–11, American Elsevier Publishing Co., New York, N.Y., 1968.

It does not follow that a systems analysis invariably results in unequivocal conclusions as to the best course to follow. In many vitally important future-oriented problems, there is insufficient knowledge of future value systems, future environmental factors, future technical capabilities, and costs to permit a valid conclusion to be drawn that one specific course of action promises to be best in all respects. When this is the case, a competent systems analysis will provide the range of possible outcomes associated with each of the courses of action considered and will discuss their implications.

As we have seen above, systems analysis is closely related to operations research and each is considered by some to be a subset of the other. In this paper, we will assume that the term operations research covers both fields. Likewise some persons performing OR-type studies may not call themselves operations analysts. Our term "analyst" will refer to all persons performing operations research.

operations research—progress and problems

As operations research has tackled more difficult and significant problems, it has followed that:

- The analysis teams and the staffs they serve need to work very closely together at every stage, from evolving the problem and designing the alternatives to interpreting and applying the results.
- Since the problems are both more important and more complicated, it is more difficult to interpret the findings, while at the same time these results are more important—and, probably, more controversial—than ever.

- As the problems get larger, it becomes ever more costly in time and money to give them adequate study.

Thus, there is an important need for the producers and consumers of such studies to have a universally accepted common meeting place, with agreement on the respective roles of each, a common vocabulary of words and concepts, and an understanding and mutual respect for the roles of each.

client and analyst relations

The client is entitled to receive timely, relevant, competent analyses from the analysts he retains. The client requires analyses that will provide him with expert quantitative illumination of the consequences of the alternative courses of action that are open to him. He must cooperate with the analyst to ensure that the analyst can formulate a proper description of the situation to be studied, that he has access to all appropriate data that are required, and that he has frequent opportunities to discuss his progress, problems, and results with the client.

The client must endeavor to ensure that the statement of the problem his analyst works on is correct and that data are complete and accurate. Lack of candor by the client robs the analysis of its validity, hence its value.

Similarly, the analyst must respect the confidence of his client and guard proprietary information from improper disclosure. He must be certain that the client is aware of any limitations that must be placed on his work. Finally, he must understand that in many complex situations his analysis may only illuminate a portion (albeit a significant one) of the total problem being studied. Accordingly, the conclusions reached by the client may not necessarily coincide in all respects with the analyst's conclusions. The client is responsible for the ultimate decisions that he makes, with due regard for all facets of the problem. The client must consider the quantitative (scientific, technical, logistic, economic) aspects as well as the nonquantifiable (social, political, philosophical) aspects of the problem.

The analyst, *as analyst*, must restrict his analysis to the quantifiable and logically structural aspects of the problem only. In complex problems, perhaps the most valuable thing the analyst can do is to point out to his client that there are uncertainties inherent in his analyses and their conclusions, uncertainties deriving from such factors as:

- Lack of agreement on means of evaluating the worth of complex systems.
- Uncertainty about the technical capabilities and costs of systems yet unbuilt.
- Uncertainty about environmental and operational factors that influence performance.
- Uncertainty about the future capabilities or intentions of possible opposition.

The analyst should be prepared to engage in dialogue with the client and other advisors to consider how other value systems, assumptions, and conditions might influence conclusions. In other words, we must avoid and reject the idea that there is a single directed sequence: define—analyze—report. The analyst's job, especially in tough policy questions, is to analyze and help illuminate, and this means having qualities of humility and openness necessary to participate in open dialogue with the client and other advisors.

influencing governmental decisions

Decision making goes on continually, within all living organisms, and at all levels of society. Man is distinguished from other animals in part, we believe, by his self-awareness in the decision-making process. Man possesses the ability to consider the possible outcomes of future courses of actions, and to decide which course of action he prefers, presumably (when acting rationally) because he has concluded that its outcome will be the most favorable.

Operations researchers attempt to influence decisions *in their roles as analysts* by conducting scientific and logical objective studies as described above so as to illuminate the quantitative aspects and logical structure of the problem area as much as possible. Properly accomplished, such a study should play a major role in influencing the decision reached by the decision maker.

In our complex, partly hierarchical, partly competitive society, however, decision-making is not a simple, one-step process. One man's decision maker is often another's staff advisor, and that staff advisor may typically compete with other staff advisors for the allocation of scarce resources to the programs they have recommended. This is true from the lowest to the highest level and even through all governmental levels.

At the highest governmental levels, where the most important issues are debated and decided upon, the decision process is extremely complex and protracted. The United States Constitution has established a balance of powers among the Executive, Legislative, and Judicial branches of our government to ensure that deliberate, thorough, comprehensive consideration is employed in the governing of our country. To this end research, expert judgment, and testimony are sought by the Executive agencies of our government, as well as by the Congress and the Judiciary. When an analyst prepares a study for a manager, he must expect to protect the confidences of that level; for example, certain detailed information may have to be protected. He must recognize the responsibility of the manager to arrive at his own recommendations. If these recommendations conflict with the analyst's conclusions, the analyst must weigh carefully his confidential relation with, and responsibility to, the manager vs. the analyst's sense of the interest of the larger body.

The Executive Departments, notably the Department of Defense, have established agencies to provide them with the benefits of advice based on operations research. The military services, for example, obtain these capabilities through in-house staffs as well as from consultant organizations. It is well known that the individual services may undertake or have undertaken studies in their interest, studies that may or may not be advanced to higher levels in support of the service point of view. Likewise, an Executive Department may have many studies made, of which very few will be advanced in support of a particular proposal and subjected to public criticism. The recommendations that the services forward to the Defense Department on such matters as force levels and compositions, procurements, logistics, etc., frequently have been arrived at after useful study of relevant operations research and systems analyses. The Defense Department itself, in its Office of the Assistant Secretary for Systems Analysis, has a formidable capacity to review the work of the component services, or to accomplish its own analyses as well.

The Congress, at present, is not as well and uniformly staffed to obtain support from operations research as is the Executive Branch. The Library of Congress and the Government Accounting Office provide invaluable assistance to the Congress, and various Committees, Subcommittees, or individual Members of Congress have access to some operations researchers. To a degree, therefore, the decisions that the

Congress reaches, as embodied by the legislation it enacts, are influenced by operations researchers. Of course, their decisions are based on many other considerations as well—all the nonquantified matters that experienced legislators find are essential in producing a sound body of legislation. In reaching their decisions, the Congress seeks and obtains expert advice on a wide gamut of technical and nontechnical matters. Persons trained in systems analysis and operations research are among the experts whose testimony may be advanced in support of a proposal to a Congressional Committee concerning the action Congress should take.

the adversary process

The adversary process is a decision-making process that is successfully used in our civilization. In a sense, it is a decision-making process that may compete with OR, since there is no compulsion for it to use the scientific method. However, operations research is, in general, carried on as part of an adversary process. It is desirable therefore to highlight some aspects of this process that are somewhat foreign to the scientific spirit.

In the adversary process, once a party to a debate has decided what his position is, preferably through careful and objective consideration of the facts in relation to his objectives, he is under no obligation to present his whole analysis with all its strengths and weaknesses to the forum, or to expose it to his adversaries. What he says should be true, at least as far as he is reasonably able to determine, but it does not by any means have to be the whole truth. While he is expected to quote his adversaries accurately, he is under no obligation to take extreme care to quote them in context. He can say as much or as little as he wants in support of his position. Unsupported allegations are not a violation of standards of the process. It is up to the adversary to tear down his opponent's case, to point out the existence of unsupported allegations, to identify the lack of basis for certain reported facts, and to indicate where quotations have been taken out of context. Thus, when one is preparing a position to put forward in an adversary process, one foresees such review, tries to anticipate the counterthrusts of the opposition, and prepares a case that is reasonably resistant to these.

A person putting forward a position in an adversary process is not constrained from using any theories, models, or techniques that he may wish to use to sustain his line of argument. These need not be the most advanced methods of analysis, or even accepted methods. In using them, the party to a controversy does so in the belief that they will support his case and be relatively defensible against the attack of his adversaries. The person does have an obligation to support his conclusions, if requested, by a full and honest explanation of the process by which his conclusions, estimates, or findings were reached.

The adversary process in reality permeates our entire life. Whenever someone does not approve of certain recommended courses of action, it is natural for him to seek weak points in the argument leading to the recommendations. If these recommendations are based upon conclusions of an operations-research study, the basis for the analysis may be subject to great scrutiny. One way of doing this is to start from widely different premises and even use a different logical train of thought. Hence, in order to defend his conclusions, the operations analyst may find himself in an adversary process unexpectedly. In these cases, he may put forward what he considers to be a reasonable argument based upon his own set of values. The opponent may present an entirely different set of values and/or a completely independent argument.

In an adversary process the debate is usually complex. It may range over areas where one party or the other considers his own case weak, or considers the issues discussed to be irrelevant. Even so, the parties will generally conclude that they must test the strength of the opposition's position in each quarter even if they consider that element of his position irrelevant. The senator who may want to kill a program on the ground it is fiscally irresponsible may argue against it on ethical grounds if this is the best way to win his point, even though he himself may not have any particular ethical reservations about the program. His objective is not to convince himself but to find the issues that will be most effective in convincing the forum of the validity of his own position, or casting doubt on the position of his opposition.

Analysts participate in these adversary processes, and they express judgments in public and private that influence decisions. Since analysts are human, they are subject to all the limitations of human behavior. Their judgments may be formed on the basis of little information, poorly evaluated, reported in a biased fashion, and in a way that makes them difficult to check or refute. They may pretend implicitly or explicitly to have an expertise in the subject that they do not actually possess. They may quote their opponents out of context and abuse them in *ad hominem* attacks that are scarcely veiled, if not thoroughly overt. Moreover, as citizens, they have every constitutional right to express themselves in this fashion on any subject whatsoever. However, *in their role as analysts*, representing to decision makers or to the public that these judgments are based on relevant professional qualifications and the methods of science, they are under an obligation to meet the standards of professional practice that are outlined here. *In fact, these guidelines are essential because the cut and thrust of advocacy make them all too easy to ignore.*

27. operations research: recent changes and future expectations in business organizations
Elmer Burack and Robert B. D. Batlivala

Operations research (OR) is concerned with providing optimum solutions to the problems of a given system. Some of its important characteristics are as follows: researching and optimizing operations of an organization for short and long range benefits, synthesis and further development of older management science techniques plus exploring the applications of the latest scientific methods and analytical models, conducting experimental research and integrating various disciplines to formulate solutions for complex operational problems.

The history of OR, however, is relatively short in spite of the importance it now occupies within business organizations. It began as an organized form of research only a few years before World War II. Professor P. M. S. Blackett of the University of Manchester was one of the earliest names associated with the literature of operational research. He and a group of scientists called "Blackett's Circus" conducted operational research for military purposes.[1] During and after the war years there was a rapid development of OR as a military enterprise. In the postwar era its nonmilitary usage began to increase and was eventually incorporated within the U.S. industry.[2]

Since its initial entry into the U.S. industrial scene over 20 years ago, OR has undergone significant organizational development. Up to 1951 there were hardly any OR activities in U.S. industry, and only 10 companies were represented at the founding meeting of Operations Research Society of America (ORSA) in 1952. By 1954, there were about 25 companies carrying on OR activities, and there were an estimated 200 or 300 OR analysts in industry.[3] Since then many changes have taken place at an accelerated rate with a number of new companies coming in and old companies dropping out of the OR scene.

a new survey

Trends noted in a 1971 survey of OR suggest that the pattern of organizational development characteristic of the 1950's and 1960's may be shifting significantly.

An earlier analysis of OR role and trends in 1966, by one of the writers, identified and elaborated on those elements of company organization and

Reprinted from *Business Perspectives*, 9, No. 1 (Fall 1972), pp. 15–22, with permission of the publisher.

[1] See: J. G. Crowther and R. Whiddington, *Science at War* (New York: The Philosophical Library, 1948). Professor Blackett's two papers, "Scientists at Operational Level" (1941) and "A Note on Certain Aspects of the Methodology of Operational Research" (1943) have been published as addenda to his article "Operational Research," which appeared in *The Advancement of Science*, Vol. 5, No. 17 (April, 1948).

[2] For an overview of the earlier history and development of OR see: Florence H. Trefethen, "A History of Operations Research," in *Operations Research for Management*. Joseph F. McCloskey and Florence H. Trefethen (eds.), (Baltimore: The Johns Hopkins Press, 1954), pp. 3–36. C. H. Waddington, "Operational Research," *Nature* Vol. 161, No. 4089 (13 March, 1948).

[3] David B. Hertz, "Progress of Industrial Operations Research in the U.S.," *Proceedings of the First International Conference on OR* (1957).

operation which encourage the emergence of OR, support its growth, and utilize its contributions for better performance and decision making. The five factors found to be of major importance in the success or demise of OR groups were— (1) management attitudes and objectives regarding contributions from support functions; (2) operational characteristics of the decision system such as the number of problem-solving projects which confront an organization in a given period of time, and the technical complexity in solving business-type problems where the solution depends upon scientific, mathematical, or systems concepts; (3) shifts in the locus of power and decision making which sometimes pose implied or real threats to the existing structure of managerial responsibilities; (4) acceptance based upon managerial background and experience, with OR groups enjoying top management support reflecting wider-felt influence in several key management processes such as planning and evaluation; and (5) the economic and competitive environment where continuing high levels of business activity usually provide a context for generating sufficient funds and organizational optimism conducive to the undertaking of OR related projects.[4]

This study visualized limited growth possibilities for OR as a functional research group but projected a rapid growth in the computer supported methodologies associated with the OR effort. Educational programs designed to up-date the background and use of advanced techniques for decision makers along with broader orientation of OR practitioners to the "facts of organizational life" were seen as necessary outcomes to close the communications gap which frequently existed between these groups. The study also anticipated an increasing incorporation of both the computer and more powerful analytical approaches in the operative, administrative, and planning bases for decisions by existing support groups such as production control, planning, and accounting. Where functional groups existed, this increasing reliance on more powerful and computer oriented analytical techniques was expected to necessitate, in some cases, a reassessment of responsibilities and roles within the organization's decision system.

From the information acquired in the most recent study, it appears that the more recent experience in OR growth reflects a blunting of development both as a functional group and within the broad notion of research for executive support. However, progress continues to be made in the integration of OR systems into systems of related functions for improving organizational performance and profit potential.

Also, there has been a notable change in the "methodologies" commonly ascribed to OR relative to their use in management type problems. The significant methodologies of yesteryears have become more routine in ordinary business applications and newer, more sophisticated models have started to move into OR activities. As largely anticipated in the 1966 research, key changes have included the increasing use of more powerful analytical techniques built around the computer in existing support groups including production control, planning and cost analysis as well as improved approaches in operating, administrative, and planning bases for making business decisions.

In some cases, OR groups have made important inroads into organizational decision systems. Newfound analytical techniques or approaches have radically shortened the decision making cycle and

[4] Elmer H. Burack, "OR: Its Future Place in Business Organization," *Business Perspectives* (Winter 1969).

a significant shift is occurring in the further computerization of routine decisions. This shift in decision making bases is expected to accelerate at an even faster rate with far-reaching consequences on the future OR related activities as well as on institutional participants.

This paper probes and examines some of these OR related changes, and evaluates their impact on the current and emergent role of OR in business organizations including decision systems.

basis for analysis

The information gained from a 1971 survey of OR practitioners, consultants, academicians, and top management of major U.S. corporations is supported by information and insights gleaned from recent OR related studies reported in literature[5] and our research investigations

in several hundred companies spanning a six year period.[6] Data from the recent OR study was developed from mailed questionnaires and detailed follow-up interviews in one-fifth of the firms included. Aside from some top management officials, most of the respondents were members of the two principal Operations Research societies, the Institute of Management Services (TIMS) and Operations Research Society of America (ORSA).

Specifically, the questionnaire respondents consisted of OR and managerial personnel of 49 major U.S. corporations, 12 industrial consultants engaged in OR related work, and 34 academicians with OR interests. The study incorporated most of the respondents who had participated in the 1966 survey with the exception of those who had moved on to other positions, and additionally it included personnel and institutions with emerging OR developments. Almost 10 per cent of the participants included in the 1966 survey had moved out of OR related activities, and some 20 per cent of the 1971 respondents had only recently moved into the OR field. This reflected that the rate of OR development in industry is greater than its rate of demise.

The follow-up interviews conducted in 7 major corporations, and 4 smaller firms, involved OR analysts and managers plus top management officials within the organizations. Survey and interview data represent an attempt to achieve a balanced sample of views and developments relative to OR, and statistical results quoted in

---

[5] For the purposes of this paper, relevant papers include: H. F. R. Catherwood, "Management View of Operational Research," *Operations Research Quarterly Special Conference Issue* (July, 1971); Malcolm M. Jones and E. R. McLean, "Management Problems in Large-Scale Software Development Projects," *Industrial Management Review*, Vol. II, No. 3 (Spring, 1970); K. E. Knight, "Evolving Computer Performance, 1963–1967," *Datamation*, Vol. 14, No. 5 (January, 1968); Philip Kotler, "Operations Research in Marketing," *Harvard Business Review* (Jan.–Feb., 1967); Sidney I. Lirtzman, "Overcoming Managerial Reluctance to Computer-Aided Planning," *Computer Operations*, Vol. III, No. 1 (Jan.–Feb., 1969); Karel Montor, "Computer-Aided Instruction for Industry and Management," *Computer Operations*, Vol. III, No. 1 (Jan.–Feb., 1969); Richard de Neufville, "System Analysis—A Decision Process," *Industrial Management Review*, Vol. II, No. 3 (Spring, 1970); John F. Rockart, "Model-Based Systems Analysis: A Methodology Case Study," *Industrial Management Review*, Vol. II, No. 3 (Spring, 1970); Albert H. Rubenstein and others, "Some Organizational Factors Related to the Effectiveness of Management Science Groups

in Industry," *Management Science* (April, 1967); John E. Walsh, "International Operations Research Activities," *Operations Research*, Vol. 16, No. 6 (July, 1968).

[6] Some of these results appear in *Administrative Science Quarterly* (December, 1967); *The Business Quarterly* (Spring, 1966); *Academy of Management Journal* (March, 1966; September, 1967; September, 1969).

this paper, unless otherwise indicated, stem from this survey.

The analyses and discussion in this paper are presented as follows: first, the continuing influence of institutional features on OR development are presented; next, changes in the role of OR plus varying views as to its meaning within particular institutional frameworks are explored, and finally there is a detailed examination of the course of development of OR and future possibilities as a functional unit in organization.

impact of institutional features on OR

The existence of OR as a formal group appears to depend primarily upon the largeness of the firms themselves with decentralization lending a secondary support. This was also confirmed in a recent survey made by the American Federation of Information Processing Societies (AFIPS), in which three-fourths of the respondents working in OR related fields were concentrated in firms with 1000 or more employees.[7] In the survey presented in this paper, firms without formal OR groups were essentially characterized by the relative smallness of their size.

More than one-half of the responding firms with formal OR groups had more than 25 physically decentralized units dealing in either production or distribution. This observation strengthens the previous findings which indicated that industrial companies with OR activities tend to be large, decentralized firms containing rather elaborate production or distribution systems. While the data indicated that a great majority of the responding companies (which were divi-

sions of larger companies) had formal OR groups (over 90 per cent), the conglomerates included in the sample all possessed OR groups. Independents possessed a somewhat smaller number with about three-fourths having a formal OR group.

The use of consultants continues to be closely tied in with the general need and financial capability of a firm. Almost one-half of those companies using consultants for their OR related activities were characterized by 10 or less operating units. Modest financial resources and/or infrequent need for complex problem solving were set out as the justification for use of consultants, yet, surprisingly, about one-third of these firms indicated plans to incorporate resident OR groups in the near future. The major reason given was the growing frequency of complex decision problems arising out of production and/or distribution configurations. Also, rapid growth and increase in size plus a favorable outlook for the future were advanced as consideration in introducing OR groups. The move to formalization of an OR function was supported by a great influx of younger, middle-level managers who were better versed in information technology. The following case study of a chemical-fertilizer manufacturing company illustrates this:

The vice-president of the company felt that it was "most essential" for his company to incorporate a resident OR group to help "manage" the tremendous growth they had experienced in the past decade. The growing business and operations had made it impractical to continue the use of consultants for OR activities. This need for formal OR was frequently brought up at top management policy making conferences by younger and relatively newer executives who indicated a great willingness to initiate and participate in such a project. Very serious consideration was expected to be given to the proposal at the next annual planning and budget meeting.

[7] "The AFIPS Information Processing Personnel Survey," *Computer Group News*, Vol. 2, No, 11 (September, 1969).

The 1966 survey prediction of increasing use of OR in production planning, product-mix distribution, and marketing strategies was borne out in this selection of firms. Nine out of every ten firms which produced in excess of 500 differentiated items had formal OR groups. Similarly, nine out of every ten firms producing 100 or more products from common equipment groupings had resident OR activities. Firms which had indicated commitments to adopting the OR function appeared to have followed through on their plans.

In general, the factors of company features and product mix should continue to play an important role in determining OR formation and growth. Complex organizations, where there are numerous decision options, present several possibilities for uses of OR function or methodology.

changing views concerning operations research

Commonly held views of OR derived from the literature include systems, research, and methodological. The essence of these views include the following key ideas:

1. *Systems.* A view of the business as a system or collection of interrelated functions, where OR activities are concerned with system relationships and an attempt to improve the overall level of the system.

2. *Research.* OR as a specialized research type of activity to undertake selective studies to improve organizational performance. This is similar to the product "research and development" efforts which often treat impersonal product related problems.

3. *Methodological.* This view identifies OR with the application of advanced methodological, analytical, and statistical models for the resolution of significant optional problems or to reinforce on-going management processes such as planning.

This approach emphasizes quantification techniques but may incorporate scientific evaluation of qualitative factors. (See glossary for a brief description of important OR methodologies.)

Among the industrial practitioners, private consultants, and academicians, the "methodological" view was consistently favored as in the 1966 survey, with some one-half of the respondents indicating this choice. However, the composition of the set of methodologies has been rapidly changing. Of those identified closely with OR in the mid 1960's, some have assumed more common usage in routine business processes. This is illustrated by the experiences of a major chemical corporation.

Around 1966, OR utilized some simple Mathematical Statistics to determine Economic Order Quantity for production and inventory control systems. In 1971, these quantitative techniques had become routinized and the set of methodologies identified with OR included advanced Linear Programming models, Simulation, Queuing, and Game Theory—all of which had little acceptance in 1966 and were considered highly theoretical.

Among the more sophisticated methodologies entering into OR related activities would be advanced forms of Linear Programming, Simulation, and Queuing Theory. Those finding moderate acceptance now, but seen as exhibiting future possibilities, are Sequencing, Servo-Mechanism Theory, the modern Utility Concept, Game Theory, and Decision Theory. However, it is unrealistic to assume that all techniques are useful to all companies or that there is an overwhelming flood of these newer methodologies in OR related activities. This change of use in methodologies is part of the progress towards a more enlightened approach to complex decision problems and processes. It is evident mostly among the older established corporations already possessing mature OR groups. It is not related to the acceptance and use of OR but refers only to the changes in methodologies experienced by advanced users of OR.

The increasing importance of the "systems" approach anticipated in the 1966 study appears to have materialized but with a less favorable view in evidence toward OR as a functional research group. The "systems" notion approximated the outlook of almost one-third of the respondents (versus one in ten previously), while the "research" view receded in importance (from one-third previously) and accounted for only one-sixth of the participants. This shift in viewpoints may be a reflection of OR's inability to demonstrate a quick pay off. There are some indications that the OR activities incorporated within research oriented groups would, in the future, be systematically blended into "systems" or "methodological" orientations.

Differences existed in the outlook of officials and practitioners regarding the significance and mission or OR. This analysis, which only included industrial respondents, showed that the preferences among industrial practitioners of OR fell into patterns similar to those already described; thus, over one-half of them preferred the "methodological" view with "systems" and "research" as their second and third choices respectively. The views of the general management officials, however, were strikingly different from those of OR practitioners! "Research" was ranked first by about one-half, "methodology" next with one-third, and "systems" the balance. This gap between the outlook of practitioners and management is a matter of major concern and is discussed more fully in the following section. The short run outlook of respondents in general differed little from that of today, suggesting the possibility for a period of maturity in OR development.

organizational factors and growth

Educational Needs. A significant shift has been occurring among the OR analyst population. The shortage of qualified personnel with OR aptitude is over, and manpower forecasts indicate that the past shortage of technical specialists will turn into a surplus in the 1970's with the colleges graduating some 10,000 trained OR personnel a year.[8] However, the types of personnel the companies are currently seeking as OR analysts falls short of qualifications projected for the immediate future. The current preferences for the M.S./M.B.A. expressed by about one-third of the companies as a minimum entry requirement is expected to increase to one-half. The bachelor degree viewed as currently adequate by one-half of the respondents is expected to diminish; only one-third see this degree as adequate for the near-term future. The remaining one-sixth of the respondents will continue to view their current requirement of some post graduate work as being adequate in the immediate future.

The majority of the respondents indicated mathematics and statistics as the most important areas of study for OR analysts. The near-term projection retains this preference but also gives computer science equal importance. These indicated future requirements are consistent with the companies' efforts to find more qualified personnel and strengthen the contribution of OR. Compared to previous findings, much greater emphasis was given to broader managerial or professional training. This notion of a better balanced professional is highlighted by the new approaches adopted by an oil company.

[8] Robert F. Vandell, "Management Evolution in the Quantitative World," *Harvard Business Review* (Jan.–Feb., 1970).

For several years this large petroleum producer, which was a pioneer in OR activities, had emphasized mathematics and statistics as major areas of study and as a qualifying requirement for its OR staff. However, in recent years, the company felt a distinct lag in coping with suggested techniques, models, and approaches introduced and used by the parent corporation and a very progressive sister division. A study which was initiated to pinpoint more closely the nature of the problems indicated a greater need for broader professional as well as managerial talents within the OR group. The subsequent changes incorporating professional talents with broader training have led to a remarkable improvement in OR operations and have reinstated its innovative mood. This company expects to continue its emphasis in this direction.

Top Management Exposure to Information Technology. An important requirement for wider-spread successful management science activities has been that of giving management exposure and education in the management science area. The degree of such exposure, which ranged fairly low in the early and middle 1960's, has changed over recent years especially since the widespread utilization of computers in the management information systems. About three-fourths of the industrial practitioners noted the computer literacy of their top and middle management to be average or above, with nine out of ten giving their supervisory and staff support groups similar ratings.

In most of the interviewed companies with formal OR groups, the top management had within the past year attended either computer literacy seminars or programs devoted to the applications of computer and/or management science in business decision making and control. In many cases, top management was relying upon their own staff of management science personnel or outside consultants to give them exposure to recently developing ideas. An example of the educational

approach pursued by these companies is derived from the experiences of another oil company.

Short OR/MS seminars for subsidiary OR managers are periodically organized and conducted by a well-trained corporate staff and well known academicians to discuss and examine future projects amenable to OR approaches. These projects are further developed by the subsidiary managers and their staff, and upon completion presented at the general divisional management meetings for further considerations. In recent years, it has also become increasingly common to find members of top divisional management participating in conferences where they are representing their division's progress in information technology to the corporate decision makers.

In many instances, the acceptance of OR is directly related to the background and experience of managers and officials. This factor determines the degree of receptivity of incumbent management officials to proposals for the creation of new groups and the extent of their understanding and use of information provided by existing OR groups. Increasing amounts of top management exposure to information technology in recent years has increased management willingness to accept OR, produced a better understanding of OR activities, and resulted in a faster growth of OR within business organizations.

Top Management Relations. The success of the OR related activities, its growth as well as degree of influence within the firm, is clearly related to the involvement of, access to, and support from top management. The disinterest of the recent past has given way in many instances to keen interest and sponsorship. In one-third of the companies, senior management was directly responsible for all OR activities in sharp contrast to previous findings where ranking officials were only occasionally involved in such matters. Also, discussions with practitioners and managerial personnel indicated that the low level of awareness and interest among top management concerning OR/MS in the recent past had given way to considerable enthusiasm regarding the matter. For example,

The Director of the Management Information Systems of a medium-large corporation in the building construction industry related the following incident: His boss, the Vice-President of General Administration, had recently experienced a keen interest in the future planning of the corporate OR activities, whereas just a few years ago he was only routinely interested in such matters. Now substantial portions of their meetings are devoted to OR planning and development. The result has been an increase in budget allocation for this activity and an expansion of the OR group and activities.

However, a sharp difference exists between the views of top management and OR practitioners regarding the future growth of OR. Although about three-fourths of the practitioners forecasted growth, only about one-fourth of top management gave such a prediction. This disparity may be the result of different interpretations by each group of what would constitute growth and maturity. Top management may be prone to think of maturity in the organizational, location, and stability sense, whereas the practitioners may view growth only as increased OR activities within the organization. This diagnosis will be further confirmed in a discussion of OR activities in relation to location and future status within the formal organization.

Project Sponsorship. Survey data continues to support the observation that, among firms where projects were initiated by top management, considerable expansion could be predicted. The role of OR in solving problems and decision making differed considerably between companies in which management actively endorsed, initiated, and supported OR projects and those in which management was indifferent to OR activities.

This point is well illustrated by results of interviews conducted in two chemical companies of similar size, resources, and OR groups. In the company where management non-participation was evident, routine OR work was the predominant activity, and repeated failures were encountered in newer innovative projects. However, OR had a wider felt influence in a variety of key management processes, such as planning and evaluation, in the company where it had top management participation and support. Also, within this company, there was much speculative OR work being done with expectations for future benefits.

The adaptation process of OR projects with management sponsorship and participation sharply contrasts with the system of management non-participation. In the latter, OR related decisions are made within the limited framework of a single department, subject to severe budget constraints, and often fail to innovate or be of value to user departments. The former, however, usually consists of a series of relevant interactions between an OR coordinator, user department, functional and operating key personnel of the company, OR analysts, and members of top management. The management officials are increasingly being grouped into "Management Information Systems Coordinating Committees," which consist of key senior management members. Besides leading to successful project adaptation and implementation, this process also offers improved departmental interactions and efficient use of organizational manpower and resources.

OR and the Decision System. OR is beginning to make important contributions to the resolution of complex decision problems. The rapid integration of the more sophisticated methodologies previously referred to has shortened the decision cycle, enabling management to explore larger sets of alternatives under a wider variety of circumstances. Of course, various organizational circumstances better the chances for the utilization of OR in decision systems. Burack identified three important conditions encouraging OR efforts—(a) a larger number of problem-solving projects confronting an organization, (b) the technical complexity of these projects with the solution depending upon the applied scientific, mathematical, or systems concepts, and (c) the relatively larger proposition of the problems requiring mathematical or statistical approaches along with computer support for their solution.[9]

Survey results indicate that, in many cases, existing OR groups have been reassessed in terms of their decision role. Where new methodologies and analytical techniques have been accepted and top management support is evident, a significant shift is occurring in the decision process. In several instances, routine decisions are already being handled by the computer processes and the more sophisticated analytical techniques of OR are directed at presenting management with criteria for making complex decisions.

Respondents from all the functional groups agreed that the role of OR in decision making has increased in the past and is expected to increase in the future. This is evident in the greater use of OR in making complex decisions regarding corporate planning, production, finance, and marketing. Table 1 summarizes these responses regarding the future role of OR in decision making responsibilities.

The strongest support came from top management and the staff groups with all respondents in both categories projecting an increase of OR in the decision

[9] Burack, op. cit.

making role. A weaker support came from the OR analysts who were split evenly on their projections of the decision making role of OR increasing or staying the same within organizations. Again, this divergence of views is evaluated as being imbedded in the different interpretations of the functional groups of organizational processes.

Formal Status and Location of OR Activities. Authority level and functional location of a company's OR activities is related to the mission they perform. In the early 1950's, the OR/MS activities were concentrated to a large extent in R & D, engineering, manufacturing, and financial areas. After this initial expansion in the late 1950's and early 1960's, a significant concentration of OR/MS took place in financial areas and concomitantly R & D, engineering and manufacturing failed to establish themselves as logical points for assigning major OR/MS activities. By the mid 1960's, the financial area demonstrated sustained and substantial expansion to become the major location of OR/MS activities in U.S. business organizations. The lodging of OR in the financial area importantly reflected critical information needs and the possession of these, along with computer capabilities in the controller's area, was responsible for the shift.

Survey data indicates that an important change appears to be in the offing for the 1970's and this development may once again change mission-location relationships. Many companies have removed their OR/MS systems from the controller's or financial areas, and have established independent management information departments to coordinate information inputs-outputs of their computer methodologies. In many instances these newer departments are being administered by vice-presidents or directors of management information services who are directly responsible to senior officers

Table 1.   Responses of the Functional Groups Regarding the Future Role of OR in Decision-Making Responsibilities

Functional Group	Decision-Making Responsibilities		
	Increase (per cent)	Stay the Same (per cent)	Decrease (per cent)
OR Analysts	50	50	0
Staff Groups	100	0	0
Middle Management	80	15	5
Top Management	100	0	0

Note: Numbers rounded to nearest zero per cent.

or the president. Thus only one-fifth of the industrial respondents listed OR activities as being directly or indirectly controlled by either the controller or the financial management. This new independence of the OR groups from one functional area's domination has improved their ability to operate more easily over a wider expanse of the firm's activities.

Application areas of OR methodologies are rapidly expanding. The contributions of OR to corporate planning, which were of minor importance previously, have grown considerably in their significance over the past five years. Marketing, which utilized OR but little a few years ago, is now expanding considerably the use of OR with greater progress expected in this area during the early 1970's. Similarly, there is a resurgence of OR usage in production and maintenance. Only research appears to have been not too greatly affected and expects to maintain its rate of OR use. Figure 1 illustrates the current and expected short run use of OR ("two years from now") in various functional areas.

The results point to an increasing use of OR in all the major business activities, with marketing, accounting, and maintenance registering the largest increases. This diffusion of OR is well illustrated by the experiences of the marketing department of a petroleum company.

In the mid 1960's, the marketing department was still shying away from using OR in its sales forecasting, analyses for pricing policies, or general marketing strategies. With the incorporation of OR techniques in the late 1960's, a phenomenal progress was registered in the successful initiation and development of several marketing projects. The use of OR and computer oriented analytical techniques by the marketing department was expected to double in a three year period.

Concurrently with these changes in patterns of OR usage have occurred shifts in the missions or the nature of the project portfolios being pursued by the various OR activities. In the early 1960's companies tended to shy away from "long-run" project missions where activities are devoted to major long range, broader scoped problems generally dealing with overall corporate matters. The emphasis was shifting to "short-run" project missions involving limited, smaller problems. This resulted in a substantial death and decline of OR in some locations, especially R & D, and its emergence in financial areas. The mission-location relationship has been changing again since the late 1960's and is expected to continue the new trend in the 1970's. Although most of the managements interviewed still indicated a desire to stay away from the earlier "optimizing" concept and move toward a more "balanced" concept, they pointed out the re-emergence of larger,

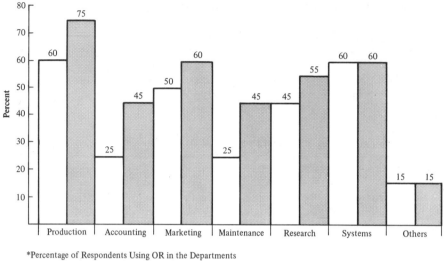

*Percentage of Respondents Using OR in the Departments
Shown on the Horizontal Axis

☐ Current Use   ▨ Short-run Expectations

Figure 1. Current and Expected Areas of OR Usage.

longer range planning projects. This has emerged from the transfer of OR operations to areas of top management, corporate planning, and even marketing. This is illustrated in the following case study.

A steel manufacturing company's OR group started out under the controller's umbrella in the late 1950's and soon undertook major long range R & D and some financial planning projects. In the early 1960's, the emphasis was switched to short run projects, OR still being controlled by the financial area. In the late 1960's, the control moved up to top management with a senior vice-president of administration in charge of all OR activities and reporting directly to the president of the corporation. The OR related activities now consist of "balanced" missions for manufacturing, marketing, R & D, and "long range" projects for corporate planning and financing.

Operations research is starting to more generally approximate a mature state in a number of organizations, although this achievement is not always recognized by principal groups in the firms. The process of "diffusion" and changes in OR related project portfolios reflect practical applications of current concepts of management science approaches. Although the desire for power and control may be a reason in the attempts of functional and divisional groups to have their own OR and information technology, the recognition of the value of modern management approaches is a fundamental factor.

This diffusion and its broader acceptance marks the emergence of the "maturity" phase for OR in business organizations. Top management seems to recognize this maturing, as indicated by three-fourths of them endorsing that concept in the survey. In contrast, the majority of the staff groups and middle management viewed OR as still in a state of continuing growth, and it appears that these groups do not grasp or understand this stability which OR is beginning to enjoy within formal organizations. The

OR analysts seem to have a better sense of this development with one-half of them viewing OR in the maturity phase.

summary and conclusions

Of continuing importance in the success or decline of OR groups are those elements of internal organization which permit the emergence of OR, support its growth, and employ its output for greater organizational health.

OR's limited growth in recent years as a functional group and within the broad notion of research for executive support is expected to diminish even further. Very rapid growth will continue to occur in computer supported OR methodologies, accelerated by the expected infusion of adequate supply of qualified technicians. This will further improve OR's integration into systems of related functions for improving organizational performance and profit potential.

Management's computer literacy is expected to grow and will be interrelated with a greater role for OR in the decision making processes. Decision makers should be able to explore larger sets of alternatives under a wider variety of circumstances via techniques such as simulation.

OR has shaken loose from under the umbrella of finance and is rapidly diffusing into various important locations within the organization. Its application is expected to grow at a very rapid rate in corporate planning and marketing, along with a resurgence in manufacturing and production activities, but declining use is expected within R & D. Although there is some reemphasis on "long range" missions, a balancing of bread and butter projects plus "long range" missions dominate OR related activities. This has been accompanied, in many instances, by the formation of autonomous management information groupings, responsible

directly to the highest level of management, which direct the OR functions. Increasing top management literacy with OR functions and purposes is resulting in more effective utilization along with beneficial results derived from management sponsorship and participation in OR activities.

The substantial gap which existed between OR practitioners and management groups has been diminishing through more enlightened educational processes. However, a clear need still exists for a better relationship between OR practitioners and management groups and a clearer understanding of the mission-location relationship to foster the spirit of inquiry and interaction. Although this type of development may take some years, the increased management computer literacy, broader professionalism, OR's rapid diffusion into different locations, and the general "maturity" it is achieving within the organization will assist this process.

glossary of OR methodologies

Mathematical Statistics. In most operations research problems, a mathematical model (certainty) or a probability model (uncertainty) could be constructed to represent the conditions of operations under study. The model provides a quantitative conceptualization of the problem and the ideal solution which would optimize the final results of the process.

Economic Order Quantity. In its simplest form, it is an equation which minimizes the sum of inventory-carrying and setup costs where the demand is known and constant. More complex procedures are available for situations where there is uncertainty of demand which has to consider the optimum buffer stock to protect against shortages. Specific models have been developed for applications to a hierarchy of storage point, the effect of quantity discounts on purchase quantities, and the imposition of constraints due to limited facilities, time, or money.

Linear Programming. Consists of various techniques for solving optimization problems which deal with the interaction of several variables subject to given restraining conditions. The restraining conditions stem from various sources such as legal restrictions, financial and capacity constraints, etc. The solution finds the course of action that maximizes some linear objective function and is an optimal measure of effectiveness such as production costs and quantities, rate of returns or profits. Some of the most commonly used linear programming methods are the simplex, the transportation, and the assignment techniques.

Simulation. May be defined as the technique of evaluating the merits of alternative courses of action through experimentation performed on a mathematical model which represents the actual decision-making situation. The mathematical model reveals the functional relationships among the variables being investigated and gives the consequences of adopting alternative policies affecting these variables. A simulation model uses statistical experimentation and is distinguished from optimization which solves a mathematical model analytically rather than experimentally.

Queuing Theory (waiting-line theory). Uses relatively complex mathematics to solve problems where units which either require service or which are available for providing service stand idle or wait. Queuing problems involve arrivals which are randomly spaced with service time of random duration. The solutions determine the optimum arrival rate and/or the optimal number of service facilities.

Sequencing. Model is concerned with the sequence in which service is provided to available units by a series of service points. The solution is geared to schedule the arrivals or sequence the jobs such that the sum of the pertinent costs is minimized. Two techniques developed to handle a variation of the sequencing problem that occurs in planning a construction job or a research and development program are called PERT and Critical-Path Method (CPM).

Servo-Mechanism Theory. Deals with the dynamic inventory problem which takes into account the effect of a decision in the current period on subsequent periods. The method utilizes some form of feed-back to adjust production or purchases to changing demand. Statistical control charts or discrete distributions of demand and inventory may be utilized to minimize inventory balance variances under given constraints.

The Modern Utility Concept. John Von Neumann and Osker Morgenstern developed the probabilistic theory of utility, and their N-M utility index is intended to be used for making predictions. The index is a cardinal measure which arithmetically calculates an individual's ranking of alternative choices. The validity of N-M predictions rest on a set of psychological assumptions which consider it much more appropriate to maximize expected utilities than expected value of the rewards. The modern cardinal utility concept is carried over in the development of game theory.

Game Theory. Deals with conflicts which are external to the organization, such as competition, and deduces a rival's most profitable counterstrategy to one's own "best" moves for formulating appropriate defensive measures. It analyzes problems which involve risk with the aid of utility theory (N-M utility) and makes that decision whose expected utility is highest. There are several strategies which a firm can apply such as "maximin" strategy where it seeks maximum among the minimum payoffs or "maximax" strategy where the firm chooses the best of the pessimistic payoffs. The theory deals with constant-sum games where the behavior of the players has no effect on their combined pay off and non-constant-sum games where certain information or cooperation can increase the total gains.

Decision Theory. Deals with problems of decision-making under uncertainty, where the probability figures needed for utility calculations are not available. Quite a bit of the game theory spills over into decision theory. The former has a major element of predictability in the behavior of the opponent, whereas the latter deals with an unpredictable environment. This is because strictly speaking in decision theory there is not even an opponent and the decision problems are called games against "nature", which cannot be counted upon to do anything in particular.

b analytical techniques

28. organization decision theory— a synthesis

Richard Tersine

introduction

While every rational being is an individual decision making mechanism, very little is known about what initiates this mechanism into action and how it operates. Decision making has been an integral part of the management literature for more than three decades. However, because of the emphasis on decision making as a hierarchical right, explorations of the behavioral aspects of the decision process were at a minimum for much of the time. It was not until the early 1950's that developments in decision theory gained a noticeable momentum. During this period, there emerged more powerful and sophisticated tools of mathematics and statistics as well as increased interest in the behavioral sciences. These influences have set the

Reprinted from *Managerial Planning*, 21, No. 1 (July–August 1972), pp. 18–26, 40, with permission of the publisher.

intellectual base for many of the current contributions on the subject.

The most significant aspect of the literature on decision making is what it does not contain. There are few, if any, systematic empirically based longitudinal studies on the decision process. There are relatively few articles classified as research although the literature abounds with limited and partial theories. Many of the theories have been developed by mathematicians and they are modifications of a completely rational man. Such theories in general ignore the psychological characteristics of men or the social environment in which they live.

Organizations per se do not make decisions, people and groups do. In many instances, the decisions made are compromise decisions. The decision maker as an individual, a member of the formal organization, and a member of an informal organization with his own philosophy and perception of the organization, selects solutions for optimizing value within organizational constraints. The organization has objectives, policies, and standards which must be balanced with technology, attitudes, and resources.

Professor Ansoff [2, pp. 5–6] cuts organizational decisions into three categories:

1. Strategic Decisions—are primarily concerned with external rather than internal problems of the firm and specifically with the selection of the product mix which the firm will produce and the markets to which it will sell.
2. Administrative Decisions—are concerned with structuring the firm's resources to create maximum performance potential. These can be subdivided into:
   a. Organization Structure—involves structuring of authority and responsibility relationships, work flows, information flow, distribution channels, and location of facilities.
   b. Resource Acquisition and Development—involves the development of raw-material sources, personnel training, personnel development, financing, acquisition of facilities, and equipment.
3. Operating Decisions—are primarily concerned with the maximizing profitability of current operations. The key decisions involve pricing, establishing market strategy, setting production schedules and inventory levels, and deciding on the relative expenditures in support of R & D, marketing, and operations.

The process of management is fundamentally a process of decision making. The functions of management (planning, organizing, motivating, and controlling) all involve the process of evaluating, selecting, and initiating courses of action.

Decision making is at the center of the functions comprising the management process. The manager makes decisions in establishing objectives; he makes planning decisions, organizing decisions, motivating decisions, and control decisions. In this sense modern decision theory is a logical extension of the management process school. In addition, decision theory enters both the quantitative and behavioral domains.

Alexis and Wilson [1, p. 4] have specified three major approaches to organizational analysis which are:

1. Structural Approaches—traced to early writings of Frederick Taylor, Henri Fayol, and Max Weber. (Line/staff, division of labor, coordination, scalar authority, span of control, unity of command, etc.)
2. Behavioral Approaches—stress human variables. (Hawthorne studies and later behavioral research.)
3. Decision Making Approaches—stress human variables and technology. They view the organization from the locations of the actual decision makers.

One acting in the capacity of a manager or executive must make choices among various plans, policies, and strategies. These choices are made with varying degrees of information. Decision theory gives structure to the different conditions under which decisions are made. The decision making process used by management is becoming more organized and systematic than the intuitive process of the past.

Dahl and Lindblom [4] have suggested four broad influencing factors on the decision making processes in organizations:

1. Hierarchical—leaders are influenced by the structure of the hierarchy itself.
2. Democratic—leaders are influenced by nonleaders through such devices as nomination and election.
3. Bargaining—leaders are to some degree independent of each other and exercise reciprocal controls over each other. (labor vs. management)

4. Pricing System—leaders are influenced by the market place.

Basically, a decision must be made when the organization faces a problem, when it is dissatisfied with existing conditions, or when it is given a choice. A considerable amount of managerial activity precedes the actual decision. In large organizations these activities may be carried on by people other than the decision maker. Staff people and others in the line organization discover problems, define them, and prepare the alternatives for decision. The actual decision is only the conclusion of a process. The process in a broad sense includes (1) the activities of discovering and defining things to decide, (2) determining the objective of the organization, and (3) the enumeration and preparation of the alternative ways of making the decision [3, p. 269].

There is no unified agreement upon structure for decision theory. This paper will add some structure to decision theory and also explore some of its dimensions.

features of organizational decision making

setting of objectives

The establishment and definition of the broad organizational goals of the firm is the basic requirement to all subsequent decisions to be made on a lesser level. From these broad objectives, strategies and departmental goals can be set to provide the framework for decision making at lower managerial levels. Even after organizational goals are set, other problems still exist such as:

1. Multiple Objectives—decision making is complicated by the existence of many diversified objectives. A number of objectives may be difficult to characterize quantitatively. These goals reflect subjective values rather than objective values. Typical objectives involve growth, diversification, industry position, profit maximization, sales maximization, social responsibility, personnel development, employee attitudes, etc.

2. Conflicting Objectives—any comprehensive list of organizational objectives will have areas of conflict. Social responsibility such as pollution control projects may adversely affect profit margins. Product diversification may initially stultify the return on investment during the introductory period.

3. Hierarchy of Objectives—objectives of organizational units must be consistent with the objectives of higher organizational units. This means there are objectives within objectives, within objectives. If the cascade of organization objectives is not consistent, it results in suboptimization. Suboptimization occurs where a departmental level maximizes its own objectives, but in doing so it subverts the overall objectives of the firm. (Sales manager-large inventories; production manager-large production runs; warehouse manager-minimum inventory; purchasing agent-large lot purchases; etc.)

planning horizons

Decision making at various levels of management is concerned with varying degrees of futurity. Top management decisions involve longer time periods than lower level management decisions. Planning horizons precipitate the problem of temporal suboptimization.

sequential/interrelated decision making

Sequential decision making is the process of successively solving interrelated subproblems comprising a large complex problem. Because many managerial problems are extremely complex, organizations resort to specialization of labor or breaking the problem into many subproblems. Consider the problem of production where it is broken down into separate departments: procurement, scheduling, operations, quality control, shipping, etc.

dynamic decision making

Dynamic decision making emphasizes that management's decisions are not usually a one-time event, but are successive over a time frame. Future management decisions are to some degree influenced by past decisions.

programmed/nonprogrammed decision making

Programmed decisions are those that are repetitive and routine. Organizations usually establish definite procedures for making them. In contrast, the nonprogrammed decisions are unstructured and novel; there is no set pattern for handling them. Higher levels of management are associated with the unstructured, nonprogrammed decisions.

cost of decision making

Decision making has a cost, particularly the search process that precedes the decision. Management must determine if the cost of the search process is worth the reduced uncertainty. The cost of the search process should not exceed the benefits of improving the decision.

decision models

One of the primary functions of management is to make decisions that determine

the future course of action for the organization over the short and long term. There are two general types of broad decision models now in use; they can be classified as normative or descriptive. The normative framework describes the classical situation where a decision maker faces a known set of alternatives and selects a course of action by a rational selection process. The descriptive framework incorporates adaptive or learning features and the act of choice spans many dimensions of behavior, rational as well as nonrational.

There are at least six elements common to all decisions:

1. The decision maker—refers to the individual or group making a choice from the available strategies.
2. Goals or ends to be served—are objectives the decision maker seeks to obtain by his actions.
3. The preference or value system— refers to the criteria that the decision maker uses in making his choice. It could include maximization of income, utility, minimum cost, etc.
4. Strategies of the decision maker—are the different alternative courses of action from which the decision maker can choose. Strategies are based on resources under the control of the decision maker.
5. States of nature—are factors that are not under the control of the decision maker. They are aspects of the decision maker's environment affecting his choice of strategy.
6. The outcome—represents the resultant from a given strategy and a given state of nature. When the outcome is expressed in numerical terms, it is called a payoff. (The prediction of payoffs in a matrix is usually assumed to be perfect.)

normative decision models

At the center of this framework is the concept of rationality. The normative models show how a consistent decision maker should act to be successful. Decision procedures are followed that will optimize something, usually output, income, revenue, costs, utility, etc. The ideal rational man makes a choice on the basis of: [1, p. 150]

1. A known set of relevant alternatives with corresponding outcomes.
2. An established rule or set of relations that produces a preference ordering or the alternatives.
3. The maximization of something such as money, goods, or some form of utility.

The major features of a typical decision structure are the strategies of the decision maker, the states of nature, and the outcomes. A typical decision matrix is as follows:

Strategies	States of Nature			
	N_1	N_2	. .	N_m
S_1	O_{11}	O_{12}	. .	O_m
S_2	O_{21}	O_{22}	. .	O_{2m}
.	.	.	. .	.
.	.	.	. .	.
.	.	.	. .	.
S_n	O_{n1}	O_{n2}	. .	O_{nm}

The matrix formulation of a decision problem permits recognition and identification of four distinct kinds of decision situations. The classification is based on what the decision maker knows about occurrence of the various states of nature. They are decision making under certainty, under conflict, under risk, and under uncertainty. Figure 1 illustrates a rational decision theory continuum.

decision making under certainty

Decision making under certainty is the simplest form of decision making. The outcome resulting from the selection of a particular strategy is known. There is just one state of nature for each strategy. Prediction is involved, but prediction is assumed to be perfect. There is complete and accurate knowledge of the consequence of each choice. The decision maker has perfect knowledge of the future and outcome. Certainty implies a state of awareness on the part of the decision maker that seldom exists. The probability that a certain state of nature exists is assumed to be one. The decision maker simply selects the strategy whose payoff is the best.

Examples of decision making under certainty are the simplex method of linear programming, the transportation method of linear programming, basic inventory models, breakeven analysis, etc.

decision making under conflict or competition

The states of nature are subject to the control of an adverse intellect such as might be the case in competitive situations, bargaining, or war. The techniques for handling this type of a situation constitute the subject matter of game theory [13]. The states of nature of the decision maker are the strategies of the opponent. The decision maker is in conflict with intelligent rational opponents whose interests are opposed to his own.

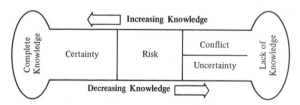

Figure 1.   Rational Decision Theory Continuum.

Games are usually classified according to the degree of conflict of interest, the relationship between opponents, and the number of opponents. When one opponent gains at the loss of the other, it is called zero-sum games. A zero-sum game involves a complete conflict of interest. Games with less than complete conflict of interest are termed nonzero-sum games. In nonzero-sum games, the gains of one competitor are not completely at the expense of the other competitors. The majority of business competitive actions involve nonzero-sum games. The simplest type of game is the two-person zero-sum game.

The Two-Person Zero-Sum Game. The players, X and Y, are equal in intelligence and ability. Each has a choice of two strategies. Each knows the outcome for every possible combination of strategies. The term "zero sum" is used because the sum of gains exactly equals the sum of losses. The four individual payoff possibilities are expressed as numbers; a positive number indicates a payoff to the player who plays the rows (X) and a negative number indicates a payoff to the player who plays the columns (Y). Each player desires to win or to minimize his losses, if he can not win. An example matrix is as follows:

	Player Y	
	Strategy Q	Strategy R
Player X	q_1	q_2
p_1 Strategy M	X wins 2	X wins 3
p_2 Strategy N	X wins 4	Y wins 2

$$\text{Y} \\ \text{or X} \begin{pmatrix} 2 & 3 \\ 4 & 2 \end{pmatrix}$$

A pure strategy exists if there is one strategy for player X and one strategy for player Y that will be played each time. The payoff which is obtained when each player plays his pure strategy is called a saddle point. The saddle point is the value of the game in which each player has a pure strategy. The saddle point represents an equilibrium condition that is optimum

for both competitors. The Wald criterion, which is a variant of decision making under uncertainty, is a useful technique to determine if a pure strategy exists. A saddle point can be recognized because it is both the smallest numerical value in its row and largest numerical value in its column. Not all two-person zero-sum games have a saddle-point. When a saddle point is present, complex calculations to determine optimum strategies and game value are unnecessary. The following two examples illustrate how to determine if a saddle point exists:

Example 1:

	row min	
(2 3)	2	Strategies: X,1: Y,1
(1 -2)	-2	Game Value: $+2$
Column Max.		
2 3		Saddle Point

Example 2:

	row min	
$(-7$ 7 8)	-7	Strategies: X,2; Y,1
$(-4$ -3 $-2)$	-4	Game Value: -4
Column Max.		
-4 7 8		Saddle Point

When a pure strategy does not exist, a fundamental theorem of game theory states that the optimum can be found by using a mixed strategy. In a mixed strategy, each competitor randomly selects the strategy to employ according to previously determined probability of usage for each strategy. Using a mixed strategy involves making a selection each time period by tossing a coin, selecting a number from a table of random numbers, or by using some probabilistic process.

By referring to the originally stated matrix we will determine its mixed strategy. If p_1 and p_2 are the probabilities for Player X strategies, and q_1 and q_2 are the probabilities for Player Y strategies, we can find their values in the following manner:

Expected Value if Q occurs $= 2_{p_1} + 4_{p_2}$
Expected Value if R occurs $= 3_{p_1} - 2_{p_2}$

These two expected values must be equal. Therefore:

$$2_{p_1} + 4_{p_2} = 3_{p_1} - 2_{p_2}$$
$$p_1 = 6_{p_2}$$
$$\text{since } p_1 + p_2 = 1$$
$$6_{p_2} + p_2 = 1$$
$$p_2 = \tfrac{1}{7}; \; p_1 = \tfrac{6}{7}$$

Under these conditions Player X would play strategy M six-sevenths of the time and strategy N one-seventh of the time. In a similar manner, it can be shown that Player Y will play strategy Q five-sevenths of the time and strategy R two-sevenths of the time. If Player X uses a chance process with the derived probabilities, his expected benefit will be the same regardless of Player Y's strategy.

If strategy Q:
expected value $= \tfrac{6}{7}(2) + \tfrac{1}{7}(1) = \tfrac{16}{7}$
If strategy R:
expected value $= \tfrac{6}{7}(3) + \tfrac{1}{7}(-2) = \tfrac{16}{7}$

If Player Y uses a chance process with the desired probabilities, his expected benefit will also be the same regardless of Player X's strategy. (Note signs of values in the matrix change when player Y's choices are considered.)

If strategy M:
expected value $= \tfrac{5}{7}(-2) + \tfrac{2}{7}(-3) = -\tfrac{16}{7}$
If strategy N:
expected value $= \tfrac{5}{7}(-4) + \tfrac{2}{7}(2) = -\tfrac{16}{7}$

As is always the case in the zero-sum game, Player X's gain is Player Y's loss and vice versa. The same procedure can be followed when a greater than two-by-two matrix exists, but it is usually easier to obtain the probabilities by using the simplex method of linear programming. When more than two competitors exist, various kinds of coalitions, treaties, and agreements can develop. The best example of zero-sum games are in problems of the military and various types of athletic competition (football, basketball, hockey, etc.).

The Nonzero-Sum Game. The nonzero-sum games are closer to the actual problems that arise in everyday life and do not lend themselves to straightforward solutions. In most complex games there is no universally accepted solution for there is no single strategy that is clearly preferable to the others. Games with cooperative and competitive elements are usually more complex. Nonzero-sum games require that the payoffs be given for each player since the payoff of one player can no longer be deduced from the payoff of the other, as in zero-sum games. It is no longer true that a player can only benefit from the loss of his opponent. The outcome of the game is influenced by communication, the order of play, imperfect information, threats, agreements, side payments, personalities of the player, behavioral patterns, etc.

Although game models are not of particular value in their present form, they do provide a significant conceptional framework for analysis. They offer a meaningful guide for better decision making by focusing on pertinent problems that are prevalent in our everyday lives. They have found application in product development, product pricing, collective bargaining, athletic competition, war strategy, arbitration, foreign policy decisions, voting block coalitions, contract bidding, oligopolistic and monopolistic market conditions.

decision making under risk

Under this form the various states of nature can be enumerated and the long-run relative frequency of their occurrence is assumed to be known. The information about the states of nature is probabilistic. Knowing the probability distribution of the states of nature, the best decision is to select the strategy which has the highest expected value.

The following is an illustrative example of decision making under risk.

An organization is determining what size plant to build to produce a new product. Three different size plants are under consideration—small (S_1), large (S_2), and very large (S_3). The best plant size is dependent on the level of product demand—low (N_1), medium (N_2), and high (N_3). The possible payoffs and the probabilities of each state of nature obtained from market research are listed on the following matrix:

	States of Nature		
	N_1	N_2	N_3
Strategy	½	¼	¼
S_1	50	-8	0
S_2	-10	64	12
S_3	-20	12	80

S_1 expected value
$$= \tfrac{1}{2}(50) + \tfrac{1}{4}(-8) + \tfrac{1}{4}(0) = 23$$
S_2 expected value
$$= \tfrac{1}{2}(-10) + \tfrac{1}{4}(64) + \tfrac{1}{4}(12) = 14$$
S_3 expected value
$$= \tfrac{1}{2}(-20) + \tfrac{1}{4}(12) + \tfrac{1}{4}(80) = 13$$

The best strategy with the highest expected value is S_1. Using this approach, a small plant would be built to manufacture the new product.

Examples of decision making under risk can be found in queuing theory, statistical quality control, acceptance sampling, program evaluation and review technique (PERT), etc.

decision making under uncertainty

In this case you either don't know the probabilities associated with the states of nature or you don't know the states of nature. If you do not know the states of nature, additional research must be conducted before the problem can be approached. If you do not know the probabilities associated with the states of nature, you can use numerous techniques

in arriving at a strategy. There is no one best criterion for selecting a strategy for a number of different criteria exist. The choice among the criteria depends upon the decision maker and the attitude or value system that he embraces [9, pp. 85-92]. Examples of the applications of decision making under uncertainty are similar to those listed under decision making under conflict. (See Figure 2.)

Subjective Probabilities. This approach assigns probabilities to the states of nature and reduces the problem to decision making under risk. Objective probability flows from the law of large numbers which asserts that the probability of any specified departure from the expected relative frequency of an event becomes smaller and smaller as the number of events considered becomes larger and larger. Objective or *a priori* probability of an event can be defined as the relative frequency with which an event would take place, given a large but finite number of observations. Unlike objective probability, subjective probability is heavily behavioral in its approach and it interprets likelihoods in terms of personal perception. A decision maker's experience about a situation is, in reality, his probability distribution, and his objectives and values constitute his objective function about a given situation. Objective probability does become suspect on one of a kind or nonrecurring decisions. Bayes' theorem enables a decision maker to start with prior probabilities (which can be subjective) and by taking into account additional observational information to emerge with posterior probabilities, i.e., the revised probabilities as modified by the additional information.

Principle of Insufficient Reason (Laplace Criterion). This approach assigns equal probabilities to each state of nature and treats it as decision making under risk. This method selects the strategy with the highest expected value.

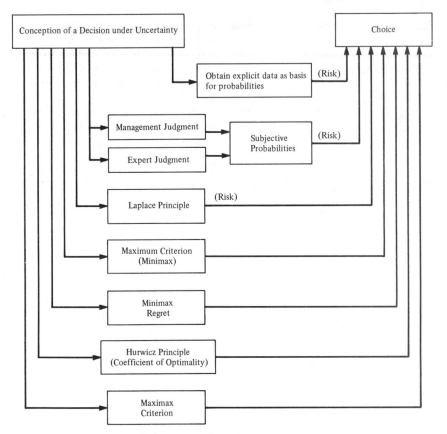

Figure 2.

Using this approach with the example given earlier of plant size, the probability of demand would be one-third for each state of nature. This method would select the very large plant size (S_3) since it has the highest expected value. The calculations are as follows:

Expected value of S_1
$$= \tfrac{1}{3}(50) + \tfrac{1}{3}(-8) + \tfrac{1}{3}(0) = 14$$
Expected value of S_2
$$= \tfrac{1}{3}(-10) + \tfrac{1}{3}(64) + \tfrac{1}{3}(12) = 22$$
Expected value of S_3
$$= \tfrac{1}{3}(-20) + \tfrac{1}{3}(12) + \tfrac{1}{3}(80) = 24$$

Maximin Criterion (Wald Criterion). This approach assumes the worst will happen and it selects the strategy that maximizes the minimum gain (or minimizes the maximum loss). Observing the

smallest gain that could be achieved for each strategy, the strategy with the largest is selected. This criterion assures the decision maker of a payoff at least as large as the maximin payoff. The payoff will never be less than the maximin payoff.

Using this approach with the example given earlier of plant size, the small plant (S_1) would be selected. The strategy with the largest minimum value is S_1 as shown below:

$$S_1 = -8$$
$$S_2 = -10$$
$$S_3 = -20$$

Minimax Regret (Savage Criterion) [10]. An opportunity cost payoff matrix (regret matrix) is established. The decision maker attempts to minimize the regret he may experience. Regret is measured as the difference between the actual and possible payoff he could have received if he knew what state of nature was going to occur. The largest number in each column is subtracted from each other number in the same column. The strategy that minimizes the maximum regret is chosen.

Using this approach with the example given earlier of plant size, the large plant (S_2) would be selected as shown in the regret matrix below:

	N_1	N_2	N_3	Maximum Regret
S_1	0	72	80	80
S_2	60	0	68	68
S_3	70	52	0	70

Coefficient of Optimality (Hurwicz Criterion). The coefficient of optimality is a means by which the decision maker can consider both the largest and smallest payoff, and weight their importance in the decision by his feeling of optimism. A probability is assigned to the largest payoff and also to the smallest payoff; the sum of these two probabilities equals one. The payoffs other than the maximum and minimum are neglected. The probabilities assigned tend to be subjective in nature and reflect how optimistic the decision maker is about the situation. The calculations are straightforward and the selection is determined by the strategy with the largest expected value. If the coefficient of optimality is one, the decision is the same as in the maximax criterion. If the coefficient is zero, the decision is the same as in maximin criterion.

Using this approach with the example given earlier of plant size with the coefficient of optimality equal to .6, the very large plant (S_3) would be selected as shown below:

S_1 expected value
$$= .6(50) + .4(-8) = 26.8$$

S_2 expected value
$$= .6(64) + .4(-10) = 34.4$$
S_3 expected value
$$= .6(80) + .4(-20) = 40$$

Maximax Criteria. This approach is one of complete optimism. The decision maker assumes the very best outcome will occur, and he selects the strategy with the most optimum outcome, largest payoff.

Using this approach with the example given earlier of plant size, the very large plant (S_3) would be selected. The large plant had the largest payoff (80) of all the strategies.

descriptive decision models

In the normative decision model, a few dimensions of the decision environment were admitted into the decision process and the decision maker was assumed to be a logical, methodical optimizer. The descriptive decision model is continually influenced by its total environment and it also influences the environment. It is concerned with how decisions are actually made. The decision maker is influenced by his personal values, the time available for decision, uncertainty, the importance of of the decision, bounded rationality, satisfying behavior, etc.

The descriptive decision model is based on behavioral foundations and the decision maker is considered a complex mixture of many elements, including his culture, his personality, and his aspirations. The decision maker's behavior reflects his perceptions of people, roles, and organizations in addition to his own values and emotions. The whole collection of experiences and expectations, developed from recurring and nonrecurring situations, forms the premises for individual decisions.

An organization has the task of channeling person-centered behavior toward group-defined ends. Organizational structures provide status systems with defined roles. These become premises for individual decisions and hence behavior. The organization provides experiences and information through training and communication. These also are premises for decisions and can become powerful means of influencing individuals toward organizational goals [11, pp. 123–5]. March and Simon offered a satisficing model in contrast to the classical economic rationality model. Their principle of bounded rationality stated that human beings seldom make any effort to find the optimum strategy in a decision problem. Instead, they select a number of possible outcomes of their available strategies which would be good enough [7]. Then they select a strategy that is likely to

achieve one of the good-enough outcomes.

In the descriptive model, the decision maker can be characterized as passing through three time periods as shown in Figure 3 [1, p. 16], [6, pp. 333–78].

Period 1: The individual starts out with an idealized goal structure. He defines one or more action goals as a first approximation to the "ideal goal" in the structure. The action goals may be considered as representative of the decision maker's "aspiration level."

Period 2: The individual engages in search activity and defines a limited number of outcomes and alternatives. He does not attempt to establish the relations rigorously. His analysis proceeds from loosely defined rules of approximation. The alternatives discovered establish a starting point for further search toward a solution.

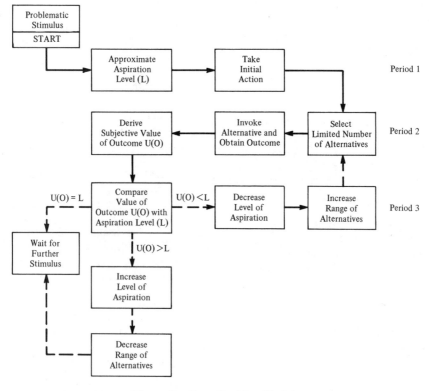

Figure 3. Open Decision Model.

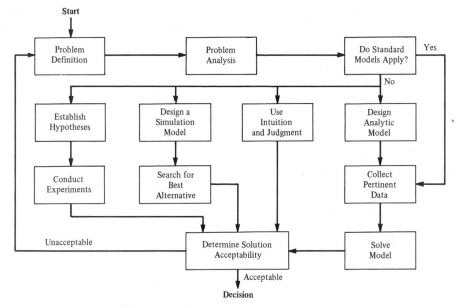

Figure 4. Decision-Making Approaches.

Period 3: Search among the limited alternatives is undertaken to find a satisfactory solution, as contrasted with an optimal one. "Satisfactory" is defined in terms of the aspiration level or action goals.

Differences between normative and descriptive decision models are: [1, p. 161].

1. Predetermined goals are replaced by some unidentified structure which is approximated by an aspiration level.
2. All alternatives and outcomes are not predetermined; neither are the relationships between specific alternatives and outcomes always defined.
3. The ordering of all alternatives is replaced by a search routine which considers fewer than all alternatives.
4. The individual does not maximize but seeks to find a solution to "satisfy" an aspiration level.

Descriptive decision models add realism to the decision making framework. The human capacities of the decision maker are given some measure of recognition.

They bring to bear the totality of forces—external and internal to the decision maker—influencing a decision. The normative decision models are the most valuable on recurring decisions which have a historical background; the descriptive decision models are the most significant on one-time, nonrecurring decisions. Figure 4 outlines basic approaches to decision making that can be used by organizational members in problem solving situations. The specific approach selected for problem solving will depend upon the given conditions, temporal relationships, and value system of the decision maker as modified by environmental restraints.

conclusion

A framework for organizational decision theory has been outlined which includes normative and descriptive models as well as other pertinent dimensions. Decisions are made with varying degrees of information, and decision theory gives structural and rationale to the different possible environmental conditions.

The manager selects one strategy over others based on some criteria such as utility, maximum sales, minimum cost, or rate of return. The specific criterion or combination of goals is not entirely the managers, for the value system is usually modified by groups with special interests such as stockholders, creditors, employers, unions, government, etc. In determining feasible strategies, many strategies can be omitted when they are dominated by a previously stated strategy. A decision is made by selecting one or reducing the number of strategies to one.

Frequently, the best strategy is that with the minimum disutility or the maximum expected utility. Utility tends to be consistent for a given individual, but for groups of individuals there tends to be inconsistence. The relationship between money and utility is complex and a doubling of profits usually does not double utility. Indifference curves are often used to forego the utility measurement in risk problems. The decision maker chooses a strategy that provides an acceptable combination of expected payoff and risk which is usually measured as the variance of return [8]. Indifference curves usually only consider two dimensions of the decision problem and they really have utility built into them. The development of indifference curves exhibit some of the same difficulties as utility indexes.

It is essential to an organization that its management develop rational decision making procedures and strive to improve their decision making capabilities. This can best be accomplished by analyzing their decisions and obtaining a better understanding of decision theory. An aim of decision theory is to better understand the decision process. Decisions are influenced by internal and external environmental factors; these factors have temporal variation which emphasize the dynamic nature of the decision process.

references

1. Alexis, Marcus and Charles Z. Wilson. *Organization Decision Making*. Englewood Cliffs, New Jersey: Prentice-Hall, Inc., 1967.
2. Ansoff, H. Igor. *Corporate Strategy.* New York: McGraw-Hill Book Co. Inc., 1965.
3. Archer, Stephen H. "The Structure of Management Decision Theory," *Academy of Management Journal,* Vol. 7 (December 1964), pp. 269–86.
4. Dahl, Robert A. and Charles E. Lindblom. *Politics, Economics, and Welfare.* New York: Harper & Row, 1953.
5. Hurwicz, Leonid, *Optimality, Criteria for Decision Making Under Ignorance.* Cowles Commission mimeographed discussion paper, Statistics No. 370, 1951.
6. Levin, Kurt, *et al.*, "Level of Aspiration," *Personality Disorders.* J. McV. Hunt, ed. New York: The Ronald Press, 1944, pp. 333–78.
7. March, J. G., and Herbert A. Simon. *Organizations.* New York: John Wiley & Sons, Inc., 1958.
8. Markowitz, Harry M. *Portfolio Selection.* New York: John Wiley & Sons, Inc., 1959.
9. Miller, David W. and Martin K. Starr. *Executive Decisions and Operations Research.* Englewood Cliffs, New Jersey: Prentice-Hall, Inc., 1960.
10. Savage, Leonard J. *The Foundation of Statistics.* New York: John Wiley & Sons, Inc., 1954.
11. Simon, Herbert A. *Administrative Behavior.* New York: Macmillan Publishing Co., Inc., 1957.

12. Simon, Herbert A. *The New Science of Management Decision.* New York: Harper and Bros., 1960.
13. Von Neumann, John and Oskar Morgenstern. *Theory of Games and Economic Behavior.* Princeton, New Jersey: Princeton University Press, 1953.

29. forecasting the future Robert M. Fulmer

"The future of the future is in the present!" In this striking phrase, author John McHale emphasizes the long term implications of decisions made today. Without question, actions undertaken today determine the kind of future we will experience. In the so-called "era of ecology" we are becoming acutely aware that man has to reap the harvest of actions taken without consideration of their long-term consequences.

Most executives have long recognized the importance of planning. But planning a one-year budget is different from probing the outer reaches of 1984 or 2000 A.D. Looking several years into the future is more difficult and requires a different set of skills. Still, the planner actually has a greater chance of shaping the distant future than the next fiscal year.

forecasting the future

Since Henri Fayol's pioneering treatise on management in 1914, planning (or prevoyance as he called it) has involved two considerations: (1) assessing the future and (2) making provisions for it. All planning, whether for the next day or for the next century, should include these factors. Decisions about future activities

Reprinted from *Managerial Planning*, 21, No. 1 (July–August 1972), pp. 1–5, with permission of the publisher.

can be no better than the assumptions or premises upon which those decisions are made.

For the short-range future it is sometimes possible to assume that the future will be very much like the past. Thus, plans may be built on the implied assumption that the economy, political environment, employee attitudes, membership motivations and a host of other variables will remain almost constant. For considerations beyond one year, this can be a very dangerous assumption.

It is becoming quite common for companies and organizations to form long-range planning departments or committees. The existence of such groups is evidence that astute managers are concerned about strategies for survival and growth in a complex, changing future. Unfortunately, there is no way for this concern to be met with complete knowledge about what the future holds for any organization or individual. The reliability with which the future can be predicted is a matter of degree. In planning the day's activities, we are accustomed to predicting the next 24 hours with a reasonable degree of certainty. Although forecasts with a more distant horizon have a noticeable degree of uncertainty, families, firms, and other groups frequently plan as far as a year ahead. In fact, only the most primitive organizations do not attempt to project activities and expenditures for twelve-month periods. Although an unexpectedly sluggish economy may occasionally cause income to run below the original estimate, the annual forecast or budget still has a powerful impact on regulating activities of any group.

Forecasting between one and five years comes under the scope of long-range planning. Currently, most long-range planners rely upon an extrapolation of the recent past and a knowledge of current activities in their attempt to regain reliable results. The past and the present are necessary parts of all planning. It is, however, a grave mistake to assume that change will continue to take place at the same rate that it has during the past. In other words, the simple projection of current trends may cause the planner to overlook the impact of developments which are not evident in any of the trends usually considered.

The problem of considering an anticipated development is especially important in planning beyond the five year period. In this time frame, planning becomes futuristic and new techniques must be considered.

inventing the future

Recently, a small but growing group of individuals, often known as futurists, have advanced the idea that man has the unique ability not merely to guess what the future holds but to make the future what he wants it to become. To exercise this responsibility, scientists in future-oriented organizations such as the RAND Corporation, Hudson Institute, and World Future Society have been developing and refining techniques to anticipate future developments and to assess the consequences of these developments. Usually, a futurist sees himself as far more than a prophet or sooth-sayer. His *end* is not to predict the future in terms of specific

events and innovations, although he may use scientific methods of forecasting. Rather, he prefers to analyze an assortment of possible futures to decide on the policies he prefers and what chance happenings could make each particular future come true. In the long run, accuracy of the forecast is trivial compared with its importance on *making* the future.

According to sociologist Anthony Weiner who heads the Hudson Institute, "trying to anticipate the future serves the same purpose as stowing a spare tire in the trunk of your car. It prepares you to respond to contingencies."

There are other sound reasons for looking far into the future. Inventor Charles Kettering suggested several years ago, "I am interested in the future because I plan to spend the rest of my life there." The same is equally true for each person and group.

future shock

The need for penetrating beyond the next few years is more urgent today than ever. Change comes at us so quickly that unless we have deliberated beforehand on alternatives, we may be overwhelmed. In a new best-seller, *Future Shock*, Alvin Toffler documents a psychological phenomenon which may be the most important disease of tomorrow. A parallel concept, "culture shock," accounts for the bewilderment, frustration, and disorientation which plagues Americans suddenly placed in a totally foreign society. Culture shock typically causes a breakdown in communications, a misreading of reality and an inability to cope. Yet, culture shock is mild in comparison with a much more serious malady, "future shock." The peace corps volunteer who suffers from culture shock has the comforting knowledge that the culture he left behind will be there to return to. The victim of future shock does not.

According to Toffler, future shock is a dizzying disorientation brought on by the premature arrival of the future. Unless he prepares carefully for what tomorrow has in store for him, man will simply not be able to keep up with rapid technological changes as well as their social ramifications.

As the ability to assess the future has become more sophisticated, the spectre of what lies ahead has added fuel to the desire to know and plan for the next generation. Glen Seaborg, chairman of the U.S. Atomic Energy Commission says, "Perhaps the greatest impetus to futurism is the revelation that we cannot continue the way we are going without disastrous consequences."

Another impetus identified by IBM's *Think* magazine is the almost mystical confluence of milestone dates: the 200th anniversary of the United States; 1984, the setting for George Orwell's oppressive big-brother society; and the year 2000. The fear and concern with which we view the coming millennium is not unlike the situation ten centuries ago. History records that the approach of the year 1000 was accompanied by great turmoil and many problems. Europe was being scourged by Slavs and Saracens. St. Peter's in Rome had burned. Famine was wide-spread and many sages were foretelling the end of the world. Although our challenges (or problems) are great, today's futurists are optimistic about their ability to cope with the problems of the coming millennium and the possibility of creating a livable future.

on a clear day you can foresee forever

Futurists focus their vision 5-to-50 years ahead. Immediate problems they leave to the budget-maker and other planners. Beyond 50 years is still the domain of science fiction writers. The critical period in between a time frame in which power will shift from our generation to our children—may become a popular hunting ground for scientists in both government, industry, and associations.

At least 100 major corporations have turned to futurist consultants or set up their own groups to consider the future well beyond their usual planning span. Charles Darling of the National Industrial Conference Board and one of the founders of the Institute for the Future, says that the actual number may be larger because some companies are so excited about their adventures into futurism they are keeping quiet about their exploration.

In early 1970, the Hudson Institute began to seek support for a comprehensive study of "The Corporate Environment: 1975–1985" which was to include the impact of technological innovations, changes in life styles, and the role of multinational and international companies. They reported no difficulty in collecting $720,000 for the first phase of the study which is due for completion in March, 1971.

In Washington, a special inter-agency Federal committee meets regularly to discuss future-oriented research. In 1969, President Nixon created, by executive order, the National Goals Research Staff. This group is part of the White House staff and is charged with search for new ideas to master change. The group has been involved with assessing the long-range consequences of social trends and is preparing a report on the goals of economic growth in terms of quality of life in the U.S.

The supporters of futuristic forecasting are careful not to oversell its precision. "If I were a biologist studying evolution," explains Harvard's Daniel Bell, "I could probably predict the ganglia and skeleton of an emerging species, but not its facial expression."

Norman Dalkey, Rand mathematician and one of the men chiefly responsible for refining the Delphi Technique, adds, "by collecting judgements, we simply push expert opinion a little closer to hard fact."

the delphi technique

As the need for more sophisticated long-range forecasting has become evident, the search for systematic approaches that will yield reliable information about future events has intensified. One of the purposes of this article is to describe and to recommend that associations consider the use of a new but proven approach to long-range forecasting—the Delphi Technique. This technique has been developed, tested, and found to be an extremely effective method of forecasting future events in both business and governmental organizations.

The Delphi Technique was first developed as a means of integrating the opinions of experts without sacrificing or compromising individual suggestions and ideas—as is so often the case when committees are assigned the task of compiling a long-range forecast. Originally used by military to answer questions as, "What would be the effect of a nuclear attack on major U.S. cities?" this technique has since been adapted to deal with the topics relating to product lines, cultural constraints on business enterprises in foreign countries, possible educational innovations, scientific breakthroughs, population control, automation, space progress, and many other topics.

Delphi forecasting makes use of a process which might be called "cybernetic arbitration." Delphi is a method to systematically solicit, collect, evaluate, and tabulate expert opinions. According to the man most responsible for its development, Olaf Helmer, it is "applicable whenever policies and plans have to be based on informed judgment . . . thus to some extent, virtually to any decision-making process."

Instead of using the traditional approach of achieving a consensus by open discussion, the Delphi technique eliminates committee activity in order to reduce the influence of certain psychological factors such as the unwillingness to abandon publicly expressed opinions, persuasive power of an articulate, powerful or loud advocate, and the band-wagon effect of majority opinion. This technique replaces direct debate by a carefully designed program of sequential individual interrogations (best conducted by a series of questionnaires) interspersed with information and feedback or results gained from earlier parts of the program.

illustration of delphi

To illustrate the process, a specific example will be cited. In an inquiry into the future of automation, each member of a panel selected by the RAND Corporation was asked to estimate the year when a machine would become available that could comprehend standard IQ tests and score above 150 (this is slightly above the genius level). Initial response consisted of a set of estimates spread between 1975 and 2000. In the follow-up questionnaire, a summary of the distribution of responses was given to each respondent by stating the median (average) and, as an indication of the spread of opinions, the inter-quartile range (that is, the interval containing the middle 50% of the responses). Each respondent was then asked to reconsider his previous answer and revise it if he wanted to. If his estimated answer was outside the inter-quartile range, he was asked to state briefly why he thought the answer should be that much lower or higher than the majority of opinions.

The effect of replacing the responsibility

for justifying extreme positions had the effect of causing a respondent without reasons or strong convictions to move their estimates closer to the median. Those who felt they had a good argument for a "deviant" opinion tended to keep their original estimate and defend it.

In the third round, the responses which are now spread over a smaller interval, were summarized again and respondents were given a concise summary of reasons presented in support of the extreme positions. They were then asked to revise their second round responses after taking the suggested information into consideration. The respondent whose answer was still outside the new range was required to explain why he was unconvinced by the opposing argument. In the fourth and final round, criticisms of the reasons previously offered were resubmitted to the respondents so that they would have one last chance to revise their estimate in view of counter arguments. The average (median) of these final responses was taken to represent an estimate of group consensus. In the case of the high-IQ machine, the median turned out to be the year 1990 with the final inter-quartile range being from 1985 to 2000. In this instance, the procedure caused the median to move to a much earlier date than was generated in the first round, presumably under the influence of convincing arguments. It also caused inter-quartile range to shrink considerably.

This convergence of opinion has been observed in the majority of cases when the Delphi technique has been used. To be sure that there was not merely a desire to conform with the majority, tests have even been conducted where respondents were asked to reflect upon their answer and to rethink the decision without receiving a report on group response. Even in these cases, estimates in the second round are closer together than they were in the original statement. In other words, both the opportunity to reflect on a previous answer and information about what other people think serve to bring estimates together. In those cases where consensus has not evolved, opinions seem to polarize around two distinct answers. Thus two schools of thought emerge which indicate that opinions are based on different sets of the same data. In this case, the Delphi technique serves its purpose by crystallizing the reasoning process while identifying and clarifying the major alternatives.

the role of organizations in futuristic research

Trade and professional organizations have a unique opportunity to utilize futuristic research. First, there should be a self-directed concern for knowledge about the future and survival. A study currently being considered by the American Society of Association Executive Foundation would help members of their organization plan for the future by identifying the likelihood that potential development will occur and the probability of their taking place by specific dates. In this way, the entire organization would have access to systematically collected and quantified intuitive judgements about the future of organizations. (A graphic model of this project is presented in Exhibit I.)

Additionally, organizations can provide innovative service to their members in the area of long-range forecasting. Many individual and corporate association members are not able to finance the specialized research necessary to probe into the far reaches of the future of organizations. There is, however, a natural responsibility for organizations which represent an entire industry or profession to conduct research concerning the future of their group. The kind of information generated by long-range forecasting should not be viewed as strategic or confidential. According to mathematician Olaf Helmer, who recently left RAND to become President of the Institute of the Future, the pooling of ideas about the future, even among business rivals is likely to be very common. He points out that companies can afford to share a good deal of hard-won knowledge since any competitive advantages will come from how well they manage to provide for the likely contingencies indicated by futuristic research.

Although few firms have sponsored futuristic studies at this time, the next five years is likely to see a large number of major industrial and professional organizations as well as corporations and government agencies sponsoring research of this type. It goes without saying that these will be the most progressive, service-oriented part of the business world.

For each individual and each organiza-tion, the most perplexing question about the future is, "What is my role?" or "Is there a place for me?". As Harvard philosopher Alfred North Whitehead once commented, "It is the business of the future to be dangerous." This comment seems particularly appropriate when con-sidered in reference to the possibility that many of the organizations in existence today will not survive to see the 1980's. Executives in all types of organizations must be prepared for the continuing challenge of change which are to confront them during the last three decades of the 20th century. There may be problems, difficulties and dangers on the horizon but as Marshall McLuhan comments, "There is absolutely no inevitability as long as there is a willingness to contemplate what is happening."

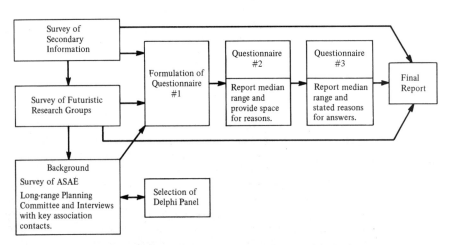

Exhibit I.   Research Model for ASAE Foundation Project.

simulation methods

30. a systems approach to corporate modeling
James B. Boulden

Computerized corporate models have been around for a long time, but the number of successful installations is still small in comparison to the potential applications. Many of the past failures can be traced to the piecemeal approach taken by specialists intent on protecting their professional pride and/or corporate subsidies.

The basic premise here is that a model cannot be developed in isolation from the numerous feeder and user systems. Marketing models must be integrated with capacity models and financial models. Moreover, the total modeling sub-system must be integrated with the accounting, costing, reporting and human systems. The concept of corporate modeling must be expanded to encompass an integrated "Executive Data Service."

Reprinted from *Journal of Systems Management*, 24, No. 6 (June 1973), pp. 14–20, with permission of the publisher.

system specifications

The specifications for computerized corporate modeling systems are derived from the planning and control processes as practised by each individual company. This means that each modeling system is somewhat unique, and that a "canned" or generalized model is of little value.

The characteristics of the system, moreover, vary greatly between the growth plan, the annual estimate and the operational reports (Figure 1). The growth plan requires a small amount of data manipulated by logic of moderate complexity. This model is quick and inexpensive to build, but requires an extended facility for interaction because of the uncertainty involved. The growth plan models need not be linked to other systems, but must have the capacity to run forward from input assumptions and backward from objectives. These models are heavily used by policy level management where per-

Characteristic	Growth Plan	Annual Estimate	Operational Reports
Focus	Policy Level	Major Profit Centers	Line Management
Time Frame	5–20 Years	12 Months	Hourly to Monthly
Frequency of Run	Quarterly	Monthly	Daily to Monthly
Probability	Uncertainty	Less Uncertainty	Certainty
Interactive	Medium	High	None
Logic	Moderate	Complex	Simple
Data	Maximum Ten Thousand	Maximum Hundred Thousand	Millions
Direction of Run	*Backwards and Forwards	Forwards-Backwards	Forwards
Outputs	Small	Medium	Large
Minimum Time for Systems Development	1 Month	4 Months	1 Year
Minimum Cost to Install (Exclusive of Programming)	$10,000	$40,000	$100,000+
Computer	Timesharing	Timesharing or Remote Batch	Batch

* Backwards from objectives to inputs; forwards from inputs to outputs.

Figure 1. Systems Characteristics.

spective rather than detail and precision is required.

The detailed operation reporting system, in contrast, requires no interaction because it deals only with actual information. Large computer power is necessary to handle the extensive data used for control purposes. Linkage to the data base is important, as is an elaborate report generation facility. The system is costly and time-consuming to install.

The annual estimate models must have the capabilities of both the growth plan and the operational reporting systems. Runs are made frequently to analyze performance as compared to plan and to simulate alternative operating tactics. The annual planning system is a decision tool used extensively by management over a broad range of applications. A fully integrated system will, typically, consist initially of 10 to 30 models. Provision must be made for linking these models, not merely summing them up. The tech-

nical problems of accommodating the diverse, customized requirements are immediately apparent. An indispensable element is a *General Purpose Operating System*.

the general purpose operating system

The manager or planner accesses the computer through a remote terminal, as in Figure 2. The computer contains a system of models, the company data, and a General Purpose Operating System (GPOS).[1] The simulation models consist of algebraic equations (called logic) representing the accounting practices and operational inter-relationships of the firm. This symbolic logic manipulates the data according to the commands of

[1] Not to be confused with the computer operating system.

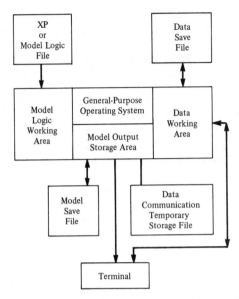

Figure 2. On-Line Management Planning and Control System (Simplified).

the user operating through the GPOS.[2] It is important that the data files be kept separate from the logic for flexibility in changing models and to permit various alternative combinations. For example, the Van Gelder system (Holland) simu-

lates 30 paper machines using one logic set calling up 30 data sets individually.

The housekeeping functions of the system are performed by the General Purpose Operating System, which accomplishes user interaction, computation and report generation as detailed in Figure 3. The conversational portion of the GPOS establishes user communication with the computer, while the computational portion manipulates the data utilizing a

[2] For a detailed discussion of the on-line concept, see "Corporate Models: On-Line, Real-Time Systems," James B. Boulden and Elwood S. Buffa, *Harvard Business Review*, July/August 1970.

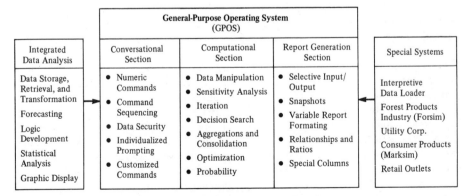

Figure 3. General Purpose Operating System.

broad range of tools for quantitative analysis and handling time relationships. The report generation portion of the program is capable of producing selective outputs in formats specified by management.

Dr. Alistair Carruthers of Unilever developed the matrix in Figure 4 to classify the various software systems used for corporate modeling. He rightly noted that flexibility is the prime criterion for evaluating these systems, and that the full modeling system is highly flexible in both logic and input/output. Thus the GPOS (type 1) is differentiated from report generators (type 2), project evaluation systems (type 3) and fully predefined systems (type 4).

Input/ Output	Logic	
	Highly Flexible	Limited or No Flexibility
Highly Flexible	Type 1	Type 2
Little or No Flexibility	Type 3	Type 4

Figure 4. Software Classification Matrix.

The GPOS system must have the capability to access external files, thus avoiding restriction on the size of the models as well as permitting linkage to an external data base and other modeling systems. Further, the GPOS should encompass an integrated data analysis facility for developing the model logic, forecasting the arrays, graphic display and statistical analysis.

The system should be fairly machine-independent and capable of running in various modes including batch, remote job entry or time-sharing, according to the tasks to be performed and facilities available.

Because of its very nature, a general

purpose operating system must operate using high level generalized commands. Such commands, while very useful for the model builder, often do not provide enough detail for the model user, who may be inexperienced in the actual structure of the general purpose system or the particular model. In addition, the commands of the generalized system are often basic elemental commands; whereas, a particular user will usually structure a particular operation utilizing a series or a string of commands. Because of this, two additions must be made to the general purpose operating system. These capabilities are the use of command files or command strings to chain together the generalized commands, and a user mode capability to structure the input command system so that a map to the data base and systems commands may be tailored to the individual user. Let us examine these in more detail.

The command files facility provides a convenient way of cataloging frequently repeated series of GPOS commands, enabling the entire sequence to be called up by one instruction. In order to provide a framework for this facility, the *input stream* concept is used to handle an ordered sequence of messages containing input for GPOS. This tool is particularly powerful in guiding the untrained user through a complex planning sequence and can be used to standardize procedures such as investment analysis.

Using the capabilities of the user modes and the command files in combination, the modeler can construct an English language system customized to his specific requirements. Further, this system will tutor the unskilled user and lead him through a complex systems run. Not only is this system unique to each company, but it runs very efficiently on the computer as contrasted to generalized English language systems.

Interpretive data loaders are being

installed in most modern systems to assure rapid, accurate updating of the files. These loaders allow off-line loading of data by untrained personnel. The data loader performs the diagnostics to check the data for errors, permits on-line editing, and then loads the corrected data into the proper files. It is significant that much of the data received from operating sources contains extensive arithmetical or mechanical errors.

In those instances where a computerized data base is available, file editors are written to assemble information in the proper form and load it into the GPOS on command. This is particularly important for in-house installations linking the corporate models to the data base.

The new decision packages allow a broad range of quantitative tools for the user. The Unilever installation described in a future section, for example, links the corporate simulation system to a true linear program which optimizes the loading of the refineries as well as linking to a "simulated linear program" to determine the lowest cost formulation of the products.

Decision search tools are still somewhat rudimentary in the interactive systems, and are used less than the new parametric analysis routines. The user can specify up to 10 variables with a range for each and incremental steps to be taken. He can further set up a filter for the system to reject answers outside a stated range. This routine allows the planner to examine a large number of alternatives very quickly to determine strategies which meet his objectives.

Computerized planning and control systems are almost exclusively deterministic. The probabilistic models, which are so dear to the theorist, have found little utility for operating personnel because of difficulty in explaining the logic, impossibility of validation, and problems in assigning probability values. For many problems parametric analysis seems a much more straightforward way of handling problems of uncertainty.

Closely related to parametric analysis is the frequently used "sensitivity analysis," whereby the user studies the *relative* movements of inputs and outputs. For example, what absolute and percentage change in profits will result from a 10% increase in prices?

Another extremely useful routine is the "iteration," which allows the planner to assign a value to any output and search for the input value which will accomplish this objective. As an example, after the planner has performed an analysis to determine the impact of a wage increase on his profits, he then uses the iteration to determine the increased volume necessary to offset this wage increase.

An example of an integrated on-line system is the one developed at Van den Berghs & Jurgens Ltd., a subsidiary of Unilever, which utilizes an advanced General Purpose Operating System. The system is described by Mr. John B. Cooper, Planning Manager, and Mr. Peter L. K. Jones, Corporate Systems Manager, of that organization.

VANGUARD* is a corporate simulator which allows the user to explore the effect on the company trading position of changes in the whole range of variables applicable to the operation, for example:

a. total market sizes and market shares;
b. brand sales values;
c. raw material prices;
d. product formulations;
e. refinery capacities;
f. personnel costs;
g. taxation rates;
h. working capital requirements etc.

"The system consists of a set of 15 interrelated models, each relevant to a separate aspect of the company operation.

* VANGUARD: Van den Berghs' General Utility for the Allocation of Resources and Development.

These models operate within the framework of the General Purpose Operating System." (The overall VANGUARD system structure is shown in Figure 5.)

The Brand Model may be regarded as the heart of the system. Basically it is used to examine the margin statement for any brand up to the level of profit before fixed expenses. All necessary data is stored on the Brand Data File, but any element of this may be changed by direct input from the terminal: this change may be either to provide a new value or, alternatively, the current values may be inflated from a given year by a desired percentage.

Apart from looking at an individual brand, the model is used to aggregate brand data to the level of the company divisions. Very powerful data handling capabilities are provided within the model to cater for this. The fixed aggregations of brands corresponding to the company profit reporting hierarchy are stored within the model, but any other desired aggregation may be selected by the user to generate new hierarchies on-line; a new aggregation created in this way may be needed only once, but if desired can be stored for future use. The system allows an unlimited number of hierarchies.

A maximum of five complete sets of data corresponding to alternative possible

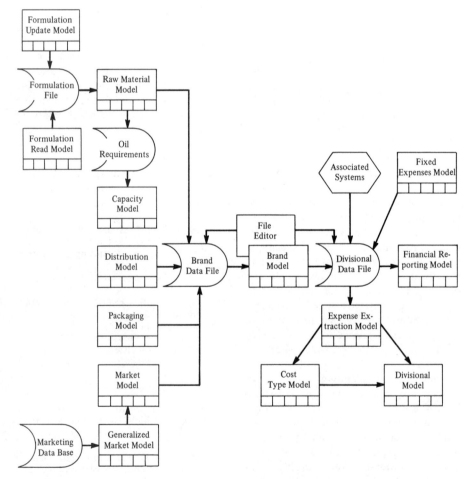

Figure 5. Van den Berghs & Jurgens Ltd. (Unilever) Profit Planning System.

strategies may be stored for each brand. The aggregation facility allows the user to specify for each brand the strategy selected when aggregating.

Any given aggregation can be passed to the Divisional Data File as the basis for a given divisional strategy. Each division may also have as many as five individually specified strategies.

The Fixed Expenses model is then used to enter appropriate divisional expenses for each strategy, and to aggregate divisions to sub-totals and finally the company total, with the same degree of flexibility as at the brand level. Thus the five-year company forward plan may be generated adaptively, with as many changes to values as desired, simulating the effects of combining various strategies for each operating division and each business unit or product group within the division.

The total company source and use of funds is examined in the Financial Reporting model, which is based on selected Divisional Strategies projected to the level of trading profit, and leading to the calculation of operational cash flow.

The actual costs and expenses forming any version of the plan may be examined in greater detail using the Cost Type and Divisional models to break each expense down into categories (personnel, accommodation, etc.); any cost type may be changed with new values or by compound inflation rates (e.g. inflate personnel expenditure by 10% compound from 1972). The model then applies the desired changes to the expenses, and recalculates and prints the divisional or company statement.

(Refer again to Figure 5.) The Brand Data needed by the Brand Model may be input directly using the File Editor. The scope of the system is vastly increased by using the various elemental models (Packaging, Distribution, etc.) to generate Brand Data.

Real time linkage to the data base is provided when desired through file editors. The system operates on an external time shared system for policy simulations, as well as on a compatible in-house system for report generation. An example of a decision sequence using the conversational facility is shown in Figure 6. The system

was designed, coded and validated by six men in five calendar months.

systems integration

One out of three on-line management planning systems is a great success, another third is satisfactory and a final third fails. The primary problems are:

1. Defining objectives of the modeling system, and

2. Integrating the modeling system with the other systems of the organization.

The objective of the system can only be established by constructing a formal study to answer the following questions:

• What are the legitimate areas of application for a computerized planning system?

• What are the relative priorities for development?

• Who will use the system? For what purposes? Definition of "What If?" interrogation requirements.

• What will be the costs of the system? The benefits?

• Who will build, maintain and modify the system?

• How will the interactive system integrate with existing systems and models?

• What is the availability and quality of data?

• How much detail is required in the models?

• What will be the technological structure? Capabilities? Constraints?

Assuming that the computerized planning and control system has been properly designed to meet these objectives, it still cannot function effectively unless it is

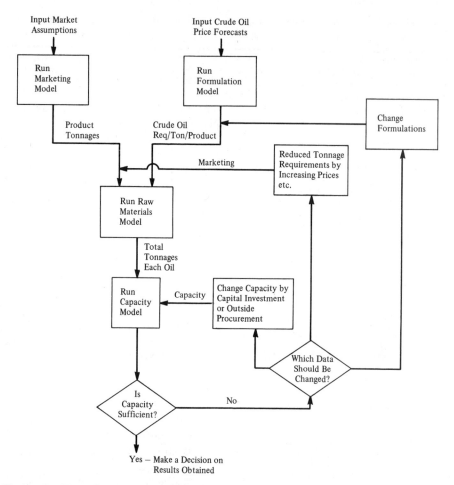

Figure 6. Flow Chart Showing Interrelationships Between the Marketing, Raw Materials, Formulations, and Capacity Models.

properly linked to the following supporting systems: the costing system, so that the correct logical relationships are used and the output of the model is consistent with accounting results; the accounting system, so that the models are continually fed accurate data; purchasing and marketing, so that they receive up-to-date and accurate input assumptions; and the organizational structure, to reflect current profit center accountability. The opportunities for mismatch are large.

conclusion

The on-line system will not survive unless designed with properly defined objectives in mind, and subsequently integrated into the general systems framework of the company. That this is possible is indicated by the following quote from Ken Griggy, Vice President and Director of Operations, Ralston Purina's Consumer Products Group.

Before implementing our on-line planning system, the time needed to help answer a question or develop profit plans puts limitation on the number of alternative plans which could possibly be assessed.

For example, a series of price changes might be required if the commodity price of corn were to increase by $10 per ton. Corn is used in various amounts with various processing yields in over twenty of our products.

Evaluating the cost and profit impact of this change by product, and subsequent analysis of the pricing/volume tradeoffs, would be a time-consuming effort.

This past year, shortly after the completion of our computerized planning system, commodity price revisions came from our buyers, not only for corn, but for many other commodities. We had available to management the full impact of those revisions by product within a couple of hours.

Our profit planning capabilities have improved because we have the ability to see the impact of alternative estimates of volumes, costs, promotion plans or prices.

As well, we can rapidly consolidate forecasts at any of our organizational levels. This means that, as we develop and change budgets to meet the sometimes differing objectives of product, division and corporate management, we can move more quickly and on the basis of hard numbers.

The on-line planning system helps our budget/profit planning activity become an even more dynamic tool . . . as well as an effective control mechanism for the management of the Consumer Products Group.

We will not refer to the comments of those many disillusioned managers who have been the victims of systems myopia. Unfortunately there are all too many dissatisfied sponsors of ill-considered systems.

31. a computerized simulation model for colleges and universities Vincent R. LoCascio

Higher education has become a focal point for insistent demands for change— for new or improved programs aimed at eliminating social problems confronting the community and providing quality education. But while such programs usually have the effect of increasing the complexity and cost of operations, operating revenues are becoming more and more difficult to obtain. The result has been that administrators are being asked —indeed compelled—to make more effective use of available resources.

Reprinted from *Management Controls*, 20, No. 8 (August 1973), pp. 195–200, with permission of the publisher, Peat, Marwick, Mitchell, and Co.

Each problem taken by itself is difficult enough to cope with, but in combination they present an unbelievably complex situation which is complicated even further by the difficulty in measuring or even defining results. Clearly, administrators must find more effective tools to plan college or university operations— tools that allow them to evaluate quickly how planned actions will affect resources both now and in the future—resources not only for the specific item in question, but for all related activities affected by a potential course of action. In this article I will describe a computer-assisted planning model designed to facilitate the task of long-range planning, which we shall refer to by the acronym SEARCH—System for Exploring Alternative Resource Commitments in Higher Education.

a planning tool

SEARCH is a generalized simulation of a college or university. It encompasses students, programs, faculty, facilities and finances, functionally relating each of these aspects to the others, so that it can simulate the behavior of a college as an operating system. Beginning with the actual present state of the institution, it simulates its future state by yearly intervals for up to five years, based upon whatever forecasted environment and potential policy changes the planner wishes to explore. The model is sufficiently flexible and broad in scope to encompass the characteristics and planning information needs of institutions ranging from a private liberal arts college with an enrollment of a few hundred students, to a university with graduate and professional schools and enrollment in the thousands. The number of variables involved in each implementation, therefore, can vary widely, depending upon the characteristics of the institution and the level of detail that administrators wish to employ in planning.

The planning process is one of establishing objectives, taking actions to achieve these objectives, and evaluating the effectiveness of the actions taken. The desire for improved performance and the necessity of responding to new environmental factors and unexpected occurrences require continual review and revision of both objectives and planned action, thus making planning a demanding and time-consuming activity. The SEARCH model enables the administrator to establish realistic goals and make more effective decisions in pursuit of these goals by providing him with a tool that in-

stantaneously considers the major cause-and-effect relationships at play in the institution. More specifically, it can help administrators to:

1. *Identify the Timing and Magnitude of Future Resource Needs*

- How many new faculty members will be required over the next five years? in what disciplines? at what levels?
- What new facilities—dormitories, cafeterias, libraries, laboratories, classrooms, etc.—will be needed? When? What are the capacity requirements for each?
- What will be the level of total expenditures in each of the next five years? the estimated income? the net current fund balance?

2. *Determine How Changes in Policy Will Affect Resource Requirements*

- What will be the effect on facilities, staff and finances of reducing the average section sizes from twenty to sixteen?
- What will be the impact on resources if incoming freshmen having less than the necessary minimum reading skill are required to take remedial reading?
- What will be the long-term impact of an increase in the number of students receiving financial aid, and in the average amount of aid per student?

3. *Test Alternatives for Meeting Resource Needs*

- If more teaching space is needed, should existing space be remodeled; should the number of periods per day be increased; should a new building be built?

- For a given total salary cost, should we rely on more full professors teaching larger sections or more instructors teaching smaller sections?

4. *Design Contingent Plans*

- What if open enrollment legislation is passed in a nearby city or state? How will the added enrollment and changed freshman profile affect teaching load, class size, student services, facilities needs etc.?
- What if the new classroom building, scheduled for September, is not ready on time?

The answers to such questions are needed for the smooth, organized management of a college. How, then, do those responsible for policy-setting and decision-making go about utilizing the data available to them in order to answer such questions? It should be evident that a computer planning model is not the sole answer. No one expects to press a button and have his thinking done for him. On the other hand, the substantial commitment of time and energy to the task of making the seemingly interminable calculations that good budgeting and planning require is often prohibitive in a completely manual system. Mainly, but not solely, because of the time and manpower savings which it affords, the SEARCH model facilitates the planning process.

a delicately balanced system

The single most important consideration in the design of a model is probably the sorting out of those tasks and functions assignable to the machine, and those that are best accomplished by man. The entire process should be a delicately balanced man-machine system. Let us assume, for

example, that a college plans to add a new program in fine arts. Here are some of the major questions to be considered:

- *Students.* How many students will enroll? Will there be resulting reductions in other program enrollments?
- *Program.* What courses will be offered? Which of them will be required? How many sections of each course? What reduction, if any, should be made in other courses and sections?
- *Faculty.* Can any present faculty members be used to teach the new program and, if so, who? How many additional faculty members will be required? At what ranks?
- *Facilities.* Will new facilities be required? Of what kind and how much?
- *Finances.* What will be the added cost of faculty, instructional materials, supplies, facilities, administration? Will there be any offsetting savings?

Except for deciding which courses to offer and what instructional materials to use, a technically complete model could be developed to deal with each of these questions, utilizing a minimum of user inputs and many internal assumptions. However, this would not be the most effective way to approach the problem. Thus, while it is possible, for example, to have a complete current data base to provide the background of every faculty member and to make teaching assignment schedules on this basis, this should be the product of an administrator's judgmental decision based on discussions with department chairmen, rather than output from a computer. Indeed, for the most part, the model should mainly serve as a reminder of all the decisions that must be made, and should readily calculate the quantitative consequences of such deci-sions but the decisions themselves should be made by the responsible administra-tors. Let us now see how this interaction takes place.

how the model works

A model, in general, is any symbolic representation of a real system or process which abstracts from that system its important aspects, thus simplifying it and making it easier to understand. A map is a good example of a model, for it symbolic-ally represents a geographical area. But a map is a static model since it shows the system at only one point in time.

A simulation model such as SEARCH shows how a system changes over time. To do that, such a model, as illustrated in Exhibit 1, must include not only the current state of the system, but also consider environmental and other forces, and show how they work to change the system over time. If we wanted to make the map a simulation model, we would have to add all the influences that shape

the geography—weather, earthquakes, meteors, population shifts, etc.—and then project symbolically (perhaps through the use of overlays) how the area will look five, ten, fifty or one hundred years from now. Some of these influences are controllable while others are not; all, however, will interact with the current set of circumstances to produce a different set of circumstances each year into the future.

The SEARCH model, however, must do more than merely indicate the general nature of the interrelationships between the components of the educational system; the relationships must be precise. Know-ing that Los Angeles is south of San Francisco and New York is east of it does not give much information to the traveler who wishes to evaluate both trips in terms of duration, expense, provisions required, etc. Similarly, any administra-tor knows that an increase in student body will result in increased facility and faculty requirements, increased tuition income and educational expense, larger class sizes or more sections, etc., ad infinitum. What he needs, however, is a specific *measure* of the effect that the increased student

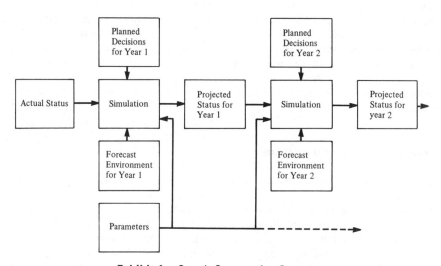

Exhibit 1. Search Computation Sequence.

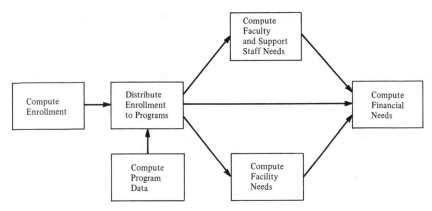

Exhibit 2. Simplified Logic Flow of Model.

body will have, and an indication of the decisions he can make to best accommodate the situation. More than likely, he will want to experiment with various alternatives, and the model, being a symbolic representation of the real system, provides a convenient means for performing this experimentation without having to commit personnel or dollars to the task.

SEARCH, therefore, conceptualizes the college or university as consisting of five major, highly interrelated components—students, program, faculty, facilities, and finances. Organizationally, the college employs resources—faculty, staff, facilities and finances—to support programs for students. Taken together, the five components, or *modules* of the model, form the model's framework. In Exhibit 2, which illustrates this framework, we use arrows to show the primary causal relationships among the modules. As can be seen, students and programs "drive" the other modules; that is, they are the primary determinants of resource needs.

To identify educational system needs, the model must incorporate *quantitative data* concerning students and programs as well as faculty, staff, facilities and finances. The data will, of necessity, be of a summary nature, detailed only to the extent required for significant planning decisions. Relating only to the most crucial planning considerations, the data must therefore exclude information that is only tangentially related to planning. For example, individual students receive widely varying amounts of student aid, but the average amount per student is all that is needed for most planning decisions. In broad terms, then, the types of information needed for each of the modules should include the following:

- *Students.* Enrollment by division and level; average course load.
- *Programs.* Number of courses and sections; section sizes.
- *Faculty.* Number of teachers by rank and department; faculty workload.
- *Facilities.* Number of buildings; number and size of teaching stations; operating hours per day; facility utilization.
- *Finances.* Salaries, supplies, and other expenditures, by department; revenues.

The student module will provide information on average course load and on enrollment by division and level. This information, combined with the number of courses and sections offered (provided in the program module), determines enrollment distribution and section sizes. Then, given current workload and facility policies, administrators can measure teacher and facility requirements. In this way, the model indicates *additional* staff and facility requirements, and then calculates financial needs based on decisions to meet staff needs (salaries, instructional supplies, new hires, etc.), facility needs (construction, remodelling, maintenance, operations, etc.), and direct student and program considerations (instructional materials, direct Federal or state funding, etc.).

Although different processes take place in each of the five modules, they consist of the same basic types of items—variables, relationships and parameters. Variables are those elements of the model that vary over time, such as number of students, revenues, and faculty pay scale. Relationships combine these variables into mathematical expressions that describe how changes in one variable produce changes in others. Parameters tailor the generalized variables and relationships to reflect the specific characteristics of a given institution. The meaning and use of these simulation elements will now be elaborated upon.

variables

There are three types of variables: *state variables*—those that reflect the status of the educational system; *decision variables* —those that change the system's status and are controllable by administrators; and *environmental variables*—those that change the system but cannot be controlled by administrators.

A state variable reflects the *state* of affairs at a point in time (or, less frequently, during a period of time) of a resource of a policy. Examples of *resource*

state variables are enrollment, number of courses, size of faculty, teachers' salaries, and faculty utilization. Policy state variables refer to any rules or guidelines that govern the manner in which resources are used. Examples of *policy* state variables are average student course load, average teacher workload, desired section size, and number of class hours per day.

A decision variable is used to effect a *change* in a state variable, either resource or policy, at a future point in time. Decision variables that change resource levels to *meet* resource requirements at a point in time are called *ad hoc* decisions, as for example, changes in number of teachers, teachers' salaries, or number of buildings. Policy decisions have a broader effect than ad hoc decisions in that they *change* resource requirements from what they would have been if no policy change were made. For example, a change in number of periods per day changes classroom utilization; a change in desired section size changes demand for teachers and classrooms. The user may store in the computer a number of different sets of decisions that constitute plans for different contingencies.

Environmental variables are variables that are largely, if not entirely, beyond one's control, but that still have an impact on the educational system. Some examples are rate of inflation, expected gifts from alumni, voluntary student attrition rate, and number of applicants for admission. Like decision variables, environmental variables should be kept in a number of different sets to provide for contingencies. Thus, the administrator might be saying: "If this set of circumstances presents itself, we will make these decisions. If, however, this other set of circumstances arises, we will most likely counter with this other plan (set of decisions)."

The SEARCH model is set up so that the user must input the environmental forecast for the planning period as well as his anticipated decisions and the independent starting (first year) state variables. All future state variables are then projected on the basis of relationships built into the model.

relationships

We have thus far concentrated on identifying the variables included in the model. We have mentioned only in passing that these variables relate inextricably to each other so that a change in one has primary and secondary effects on many of the others through a network of relationships and interrelationships. Yet, it is this mathematical connection of all the variables into an integrated system that makes the model a model, rather than simply an information system. Without relationships, the data discussed heretofore are not fully useful for planning purposes.

The model uses two basic types of relationships—those that project the future value of a state variable from a knowledge of its own current value and the decision and/or environmental variables acting upon it (inter-temporal relationships); and those that calculate the value of one state variable (dependent variable) from a knowledge of the values of other related state variables within a given year (inter-variable relationships). An inter-temporal relationship exists for each state variable inputted by the user (independent). The enrollment projection serves as a good example. The model will automatically "promote" freshmen to sophomores, sophomores to juniors, etc., taking account of such factors as voluntary and academic attrition rates and transfers from other schools. Incoming freshman enrollment is projected on the basis of number of applicants, number of applicants accepted, "no-show" proba-

bility of accepted students, and desired enrollment levels.

Once the model projects the future value for all independent state variables, inter-variable relationships then calculate the value of the dependent state variables for each year in the planning period. For example: student-faculty ratio (1972) = enrollment (1972) divided by size of faculty (1972); and total revenues (1972) = gifts from alumni (1972) plus revenues from government sources (1972) plus revenues from endowment funds (1972) plus other income (1972).

parameters

Parameters "tailor" the generalized variables and relationships to a college's specific characteristics and information needs, and are of two types—type 1 parameters tailor variables, and type 2 parameters tailor relationships. Type 1 parameters identify and control the level of detail in the breakdown categories used in describing variables. For example, two of the major breakdown categories for enrollment are division and level. One implementing college may define six divisions (liberal arts, business, graduate school, etc.) with four levels (freshman, junior, etc.) for each division except graduate school. Another college may use three divisions to define regular session, night school, and summer session, and perhaps treat the latter as having only one level since it is not crucial for planning purposes. Through the use of parameters, these two colleges can use the same generalized model.

Type 2 parameters identify significant characteristics of each breakdown category to determine whether to include them in a particular relationship. For example, in determining the availability of dormitory space, all divisions should be included which contribute to this demand while excluding others that do not. For example, summer school enrollment which makes a demand for these facilities at a different time should be excluded from this relationship.

using the model for decision-making

Since planning models are merely tools in the overall man-machine planning process, what tasks in that process does SEARCH perform? What is the proper balance between user inputs and internal calculations and assumptions? Having decided on the general level of user inputs and internal calculations, which variables should one treat as independent and which as dependent? These questions are highly interrelated. There are a number of ways in which a model could deal with them. At one extreme, a model might attempt to accept as input the number of incoming students and project everything else internally. Such a model would require many internal assumptions concerning the cause-and-effect relationships at play in the educational system. At the other extreme, a model might be nothing more than a complete data base (information system) from which to obtain key data, but having very little, if any, internal logic to guide the decision-making process.

In our view, neither extreme is desirable. In the one case, the danger is that the model virtually takes over the decision-making process. In the second case, it does not provide as much assistance as an effective administrator would like to have.

In using the SEARCH model, an increase in enrollment would automatically result in an increase in student aid—a natural consequence—but would not make decisions concerning hiring of teachers, facilities planning, etc. How, then, would the user of SEARCH be guided in the various program, faculty, and facility decisions he would have to make? Basically, the model reflects the impact of added students on such variables as average class size, student-faculty ratio, and classroom utilization. It does not automatically add sections, teachers and classrooms because any one of a large number of alternative decisions can deal with the problem, and the choice among them is a policy consideration best left to the planners. Even if, for example, it is obvious that added faculty are required, questions still remain: at what rank, and in which departments? By displaying student-faculty ratio by department and faculty size, by rank (full professor, associate, etc.), the planner is guided to the proper decisions based on his policy preferences. He also has the flexibility of experimenting with the various decision alternatives to see the effects of each.

While SEARCH is a simulation model designed to aid the decision-making process, it does not make decisions; rather, it displays the impact of decisions so that users can see the implications of their plans and make appropriate modifications to them. This man-machine interaction is enhanced because SEARCH is implemented in a timesharing mode by use of a remote computer terminal. Therefore, users can engage in a virtual dialogue with the computer to receive answers that would in many cases require weeks of analysis in a manual system. Thus, SEARCH provides the planner with an inexpensive means of greatly expanding the range of quickly available and informed alternative approaches to resource allocation.

discussion questions : part IV

1. What is operations research? What is management science? How are the two terms related?
2. How are quantitative approaches being used in organizations today?
3. In what ways are quantitative methods personnel being used today that they were not a decade ago? Why?
4. Are analytical techniques useful in all decision problems? Why or why not?
5. How are mathematical models used in solving managerial problems? List the chief advantages and disadvantages in using mathematical models to solve management problems.
6. Compare the major types of decision models. How are they similar? How are they different?
7. Describe the Delphi Technique. What are its primary uses? Develop a Delphi model for determining the future of the urban core community.
8. Describe simulation. In what ways can simulation techniques be used to solve organizational problems?
9. Why are on-line systems developed for managers? How are such systems useful?
10. What is SEARCH? Could such a simulated model be expanded to cover larger parts of the educational system? Why or why not?
11. How does a computer modify the structure of an organization? In the future, what impact will the computer have upon industry? What problems will probably occur as the result of increased usage of computers throughout industry?
12. How is the computer related to the quantitative approach to management?

selected references : part IV

A. *operations management*

Brown, Kenneth S., "Management Science: Its Role in the Organization," *Managerial Planning*, 21, No. 1 (July–August 1972), pp. 6–10, 38.

Browne, William G., "Techniques of Operations Research," *Journal of Systems Management*, 23, No. 9 (September 1972), pp. 8–13.

Dearden, John, and John Lastavica, "New Directions in Operations Research," *Financial Executive*, 38, No. 10 (October 1970), pp. 24–33.

Grayson, C. Jackson, "Management Science and Business Practice," *Harvard Business Review*, 51, No. 4 (July–August 1973), pp. 41–48.

Gruber, William H., and John S. Niles, "Problems in the Utilization of Management Science/Operations Research: A State of The Art Survey," *Interfaces*, 2, No. 1 (November 1971), pp. 12–19.

Kassouf, Sheen, *Normative Decision Making* (Englewood Cliffs, N.J.: Prentice-Hall, Inc., 1970).

Rivett, Patrick, "The Art of Operations Research," *Organizational Dynamics*, 1, No. 1 (Summer 1972), pp. 32–42.

Veinott, Arthur F., Jr. (ed.), *Mathematical Studies in Management Science* (New York: Macmillan Publishing Co., Inc., 1965).

Wagner, Harvey M., *Principles of Operations Research* (Englewood Cliffs, N.J.: Prentice-Hall, Inc., 1969).

Ziegler, Raymond J., "Opportunities in Production Management," *S.A.M. Advanced Management Journal*, 31, No. 3 (July 1970), pp. 27–35.

B. *analytical techniques*

Clayton, Edward R., and Laurence J. Moore, "PERT vs. GERT," *Journal of Systems Management*, 23, No. 2 (February 1972), pp. 11–19.

Fertakis, John, and John Moss, "An Introduction to PERT and PERT/Cost Systems," *Managerial Planning*, 19, No. 4 (January–February 1971), pp. 24–31.

Fourre, James P., *Quantitative Business Planning Techniques* (New York: American Management Association, 1970).

Fusfeld, Alan R., and Richard N. Foster, "The Delphi Technique: Survey and Comment," *Business Horizons*, 14, No. 3 (June 1971), pp. 63–74.

Hall, William K., "Forecasting Techniques for Use in the Corporate Planning Process," *Managerial Planning*, 21, No. 3 (November–December 1972), pp. 5–10.

Karson, Marvin J., and William J. Wrobleski, "A Manager's Guide to Probability Modeling," *Michigan Business Review*, 24, No. 3 (May 1972), pp. 23–30.

Mali, Paul, "Management Climbs the Decision Tree," *Administrative Management*, 34, No. 1 (January 1973), pp. 63–66.

Nielsen, Gordon L., "A Linear Programming Application," *Arizona Business Bulletin*, 16, No. 1 (January 1969), pp. 3–11.

Pattillo, James W., and José G. Secunza, "Mathematical Models: How Helpful Now to the Business World?" *Business Perspectives*, 7, No. 4 (Summer 1971), pp. 20–25.

C. *simulation methods*

Boulden, James B., "Interactive Decision Simulation: A Revolution in Management," *Academy of Management Proceedings, 30th Annual Meeting* (San Diego, Calif.: San Diego State College, 1970), pp. 345–354.

Green, Thad B., and William H. Holley, Jr., "Film Based Simulation Evaluation: An Assessment Technique for Personnel Selection and Promotion," *Business Perspectives*, 9, No. 2 (Winter 1973), pp. 9–13.

Irwin, Neal A., and R. Andrew McNally, "Simulation Models in Regional Planning," *Management Controls*, 19, No. 8 (August 1972), pp. 181–191.

McDougall, John, and Peter F. Oehm, "Simulation in Regional Planning," *Management Controls*, 18, No. 12 (December 1971), pp. 256–264.

Montgomery, Douglas C., and Daniel Sipper, "Probability Zones in Stochastic Project Networks," *Journal of Systems Management*, 23, No. 8 (August 1971), pp. 36–42.

Philippakis, Andreas S., "A Simulation Study of Decentralized Decision Making," *Decision Sciences*, 3, No. 3 (July 1972), pp. 59–73.

Shaw, Robert J., "Simulation of Inventory Policies," *Management Controls*, 18, No. 8 (August 1971), pp. 169–172.

Van Horn, Richard L., "Validation of Simulation Results," *Management Science*, 17, No. 5 (January 1971), pp. 247–258.

systems approaches

part V

Although the process, behavioral, and quantitative approaches have been widely adopted, a growing group of practitioners and academicians have felt that another approach—the systems approach—would encompass the subsystems emanating from the other approaches.[1] Indeed, systems analysts have begun to realize that the modern organization is now fragmented into many specialized systems such as management information systems, wage and salary systems, electronic surveillance systems, and accounting systems.[2] Moreover, highly generalized systems have been developed including philosophical systems, value systems, and mathematical systems. From these specialized and generalized efforts, several major steps have been taken to strengthen both general systems and management systems concepts.

"Systems analysis is the selection of elements, relationships, and procedures to achieve a specific purpose."[3] In other words, such a definition covers many

---

[1] For example, see Thomas A. Petit, "Systems Approach to Management Theory," *Journal of Systems Management*, 23, No. 7 (July 1972), pp. 32–34; Jay W. Forrester, *Industrial Dynamics* (Cambridge, Mass.: The M.I.T. Press, 1961); Richard A. Johnson, Fremont E. Kast, and James E. Rosenzweig, *The Theory and Management of Systems*, 3rd ed. (New York: McGraw-Hill Book Company, Inc., 1973); Stanley Young, *Management: A Systems Analysis* (Glenview, Ill.: Scott, Foresman and Co., 1966); Van C. Hare, Jr., *Systems Analysis: A Diagnostic Approach* (New York: Harcourt, Brace and World, Inc., 1967).

[2] Hare, p. ix.

[3] Ibid.

different possible concepts. The works of Ludwig von Bertalanffy and Kenneth Boulding began to lay the modern foundation for general systems theory.[4] Such a theory is concerned with the development of a systematic theoretical framework for the description of general relationships of the empirical world.[5] Upon this foundation, managers and scholars have developed the systems approach to management.

Several authors have defined the systems approach to management. In one definition, Professor Stanley Young stated that "A management system can be defined as that sub-system of the organization whose components consist of a subset of individuals (man to man) whose duties are to receive certain organizational problems (inputs) and thereupon to execute a set of activities (process) which will produce organizational solutions (output) for either increasing the value of return of the total organizational activity (satisficing) or for optimizing some function of the total organizational inputs and outputs."[6] Thus, systems are deliberate, rational human inventions to achieve certain objectives. As time passes, such systems can be modified resulting in even more value to the system users.

In organizations, managers attempt to weld human, technological, and capital resources into an effective, cohesive whole to achieve the objectives of the organization. When an organization is structured using the systems approach, the need for the elemental functions of management is not eliminated. However, there is a change of emphasis. No longer operating as individual functions within the organization, the systems approach demands that these functions be coordinated into a cohesive whole. Any and all operations and functions implemented by employees and machines must be oriented toward the objectives of the organization.[7] This part of the book examines systems concepts, systems analyses, and management information systems.

In the first section on systems concepts, Fremont E. Kast and James E. Rosenzweig discuss some of the key concepts in general systems theory. After analyzing some of the dilemmas in applying general systems theory to organizations, they indicate the need for more sophistication of systems concepts so that a complete understanding of organizations as total systems will be available. In turn, Richard J. Tersine and Max B. Jones present a multiview systems concept which encompasses several models for examining organizations, including systemic environmental model, systemic planning model, systemic functional model, and systemic operational model.

On the basis of the systems concepts which have been developed during the past two decades, many managers have developed specific systems and subsystems within organizations. In the next section, Richard de Neufville defines the nature of systems analysis, the steps taken to define a systems analysis pro-

[4] L. von Bertalanffy, "General System Theory: A New Approach to the Unity of Science," *Human Biology* (December 1951), pp. 303–361; and Kenneth Boulding, "General Systems Theory: The Skeleton of Science," *Management Science*, 2 (April 1956), pp. 197–208.

[5] Richard A. Johnson, Fremont E. Kast, and James E. Rosenzweig, "Systems Theory and Management," *Management Science*, 10, No. 5 (January 1964), pp. 367–384.

[6] Young, p. 15.

[7] Johnson *et al.*, "Systems Theory . . . ," p. 376.

cedure, and the major issues in effective systems analysis. John F. Rockart contrasts model-based systems analysis with traditional methods of systems analysis. To demonstrate the effectiveness of the former, he employs an application of the technique in a large group medical practice. Although many different systems analyses have been used in such areas as transportation, communications, law enforcement, resource management, and education, they are just part of a larger total urban system. In the concluding selection, Jerry L. Pollak and Martin I. Taft propose the use of existing problem-solving models to answer the complexities of total urban planning.

As another specific application of systems concepts, management information systems have gained more and more attention from managers today. In the third section, Paul Siegel explains the nature of these management information systems and the nature of major systems facing the executive. He also analyzes each of the major corporate systems in terms of major decision areas, measures of performance, major system variables, and major cycle characteristics. In the last article, John G. Burch and Felix R. Strater define and classify the types of organizational decisions into three categories: (1) strategical; (2) tactical; and (3) technical. After detailing the ways information is used in making these decisions, they provide a method for tailoring an information system for the manager.

systems concepts

32. general systems theory: applications for organization and management

Fremont E. Kast and James E. Rosenzweig

Biological and social scientists generally have embraced systems concepts. Many organization and management theorists seem anxious to identify with this movement and to contribute to the development of an approach which purports to offer the ultimate—the unification of all science into one grand conceptual model. Who possibly could resist? General systems theory seems to provide a relief from the limitations of more mechanistic approaches and a rationale for rejecting "principles" based on relatively "closed-system" thinking. This theory provides the paradigm for organization and management theorists to "crank into their systems model" all of the diverse knowledge from relevant underlying disciplines. It has become almost mandatory

Reprinted from *Academy of Management Journal*, 15, No. 4 (December 1972), pp. 447–465, with permission of the publisher and the authors.

to have the word "system" in the title of recent articles and books (many of us have compromised and placed it only in the subtitle).*

But where did it all start? This question takes us back into history and brings to mind the long-standing philosophical arguments between mechanistic and organismic models of the 19th and early 20th centuries. As Deutsch says:

Both mechanistic and organismic models were based substantially on experiences and operations known before 1850. Since then, the experience of almost a century of scientific and technological progress has so far not been utilized for any significant new model for the study of organization and in particular of human thought [12, p. 389].

* An entire article could be devoted to a discussion of ingenious ways in which the term "systems approach" has been used in the literature pertinent to organization theory and management practice.

General systems theory even revives the specter of the "vitalists" and their views on "life force" and most certainly brings forth renewed questions of teleological or purposeful behavior of both living and nonliving systems. Phillips and others have suggested that the philosophical roots of general systems theory go back even further, at least to the German philosopher Hegel (1770–1831) [29, p. 56]. Thus, we should recognize that in the adoption of the systems approach for the study of organizations we are not dealing with newly discovered ideas—they have a rich genealogy.

Even in the field of organization and management theory, systems views are not new. Chester Barnard used a basic systems framework.

A cooperative system is a complex of physical, biological, personal, and social components which are in a specific systematic relationship by reason of the cooperation of two or more persons for at least one definite end. Such a system is evidently a subordinate unit of larger systems from one point of view; and itself embraces subsidiary systems—physical, biological, etc.—from another point of view. One of the systems comprised within a cooperative system, the one which is implicit in the phrase "cooperation of two or more persons," is called an "organization" [3, p. 65].

And Barnard was influenced by the "systems views" of Vilfredo Pareto and Talcott Parsons. Certainly this quote (dressed up a bit to give the term "system" more emphasis) could be the introduction to a 1972 book on organizations.

Miller points out that Alexander Bogdanov, the Russian philosopher, developed a theory of tektology or universal organization science in 1912 which foreshadowed general systems theory and used many of the same concepts as modern systems theorists [26, p. 249–250].

However, in spite of a long history of organismic and holistic thinking, the utilization of the systems approach did not become the accepted model for organization and management writers until relatively recently. It is difficult to specify the turning point exactly. The momentum of systems thinking was identified by Scott in 1961 when he described the relationship between general systems theory and organization theory.

The distinctive qualities of modern organization theory are its conceptual-analytical base, its reliance on empirical research data, and above all, its integrating nature. These qualities are framed in a philosophy which accepts the premise that the only meaningful way to study organization is to study it as a system ... Modern organization theory and general system theory are similar in that they look at organization as an integrated whole [33, pp. 15–21].

Scott said explicitly what many in our field had been thinking and/or implying— he helped us put into perspective the important writings of Herbert Simon, James March, Talcott Parsons, George Homans, E. Wight Bakke, Kenneth Boulding, and many others.

But how far have we really advanced over the past decade in applying general systems theory to organizations and their management? Is it still a "skeleton," or have we been able to "put some meat on the bones"? The systems approach has been touted because of its potential usefulness in understanding the complexities of "live" organizations. Has this approach really helped us in this endeavor or has it compounded confusion with chaos? Herbert Simon describes the challenge for the systems approach:

In both science and engineering, the study of "systems" is an increasingly popular activity. Its popularity is more a response to a pressing need for synthesizing and analyzing complexity than it is to any large development of a body of knowledge and technique for dealing with complexity. If this popularity is to be more than a fad, necessity will have to mother invention and provide substance to go with the name [35, p. 114].

In this article we will explore the issue of whether we are providing substance for the term *systems approach* as it relates to the study of organizations and their management. There are many interesting historical and philosophical questions concerning the relationship between the mechanistic and organistic approaches and their applicability to the various fields of science, as well as other interesting digressions into the evolution of systems approaches. However, we will resist those temptations and plunge directly into a discussion of the key concepts of general systems theory, the way in which these ideas have been used by organization theorists, the limitations in their application, and some suggestions for the future.

key concepts of general systems theory

The key concepts of general systems theory have been set forth by many writers [6, 7, 13, 71, 25, 28, 39] and have been used by many organization and management theorists [10, 14, 18, 19, 22, 23, 24, 32]. It is not our purpose here to elaborate on them in great detail because we anticipate that most readers will have been exposed to them in some depth. Figure 1 provides a very brief review of those characteristics of systems which seem to have wide acceptance. The review is far from complete. It is difficult to identify a "complete" list of characteristics derived from general systems theory; moreover, it is merely a first-order classification. There are many derived second- and third-order characteristics which

could be considered. For example, James G. Miller sets forth *165* hypotheses, stemming from open systems theory, which might be applicable to two or more levels of systems [25]. He suggests that they are *general* systems theoretical hypotheses and qualifies them by suggesting that they are propositions applicable to general systems *behavior* theory and would thus exclude nonliving systems. He does not limit these propositions to individual organisms, but considers them appropriate for social systems as well. His hypotheses are related to such issues as structure, process, subsystems, information, growth, and integration. It is obviously impossible to discuss all of these hypotheses; we want only to indicate the extent to which many interesting propositions are being posed which might have relevance to many different types of systems. It will be a very long time (if ever) before most of these hypotheses are validated; however, we are surprised at how many of them can be agreed with intuitively, and we can see their possible verification in studies of social organizations.

We turn now to a closer look at how successful or unsuccessful we have been in utilizing these concepts in the development of "modern organization theory."

a beginning : enthusiastic but incomplete

We have embraced general systems theory but, really, how completely? We could review a vast literature in modern organization theory which has explicitly or implicitly adopted systems theory as a frame of reference, and we have investigated in detail a few representative examples of the literature in assessing the "state of the art" [18, 19, 22, 23, 31, 38]. It was found that most of these books

Subsystems or Components. A system by definition is composed of interrelated parts or elements. This is true for all systems—mechanical, biological, and social. Every system has at least two elements, and these elements are interconnected.

Holism, Synergism, Organicism, and Gestalt. The whole is not just the sum of the parts; the system itself can be explained only as a totality. Holism is the opposite of elementarism, which views the total as the sum of its individual parts.

Open Systems View. Systems can be considered in two ways: (1) closed or (2) open. Open systems exchange information, energy, or material with their environments. Biological and social systems are inherently open systems; mechanical systems may be open or closed. The concepts of open and closed systems are difficult to defend in the absolute. We prefer to think of open-closed as a dimension; that is, systems are relatively open or relatively closed.

Input-Transformation-Output Model. The open system can be viewed as a transformation model. In a dynamic relationship with its environment, it receives various inputs, transforms these inputs in some way, and exports outputs.

System Boundaries. It follows that systems have boundaries which separate them from their environments. The concept of boundaries helps us understand the distinction between open and closed systems. The relatively closed system has rigid, impenetrable boundaries; whereas the open system has permeable boundaries between itself and a broader suprasystem. Boundaries are relatively easily defined in physical and biological systems, but are very difficult to delineate in social systems, such as organizations.

Negative Entropy. Closed, physical systems are subject to the force of entropy which increases until eventually the entire system fails. The tendency toward maximum entropy is a movement to disorder, complete lack of resource transformation, and death. In a closed system, the change in entropy must always be positive; however, in open biological or social systems, entropy can be arrested and may even be transformed into negative entropy—a process of more complete organization and ability to transform resources—because the system imports resources from its environment.

Steady State, Dynamic Equilibrium, and Homeostasis. The concept of steady state is closely related to that of negative entropy. A closed system eventually must attain an equilibrium state with maximum entropy—death or disorganization. However, an open system may attain a state where the system remains in dynamic equilibrium through the continuous inflow of materials, energy, and information.

Feedback. The concept of feedback is important in understanding how a system maintains a steady state. Information concerning the outputs or the process of the system is fed back as an input into the system, perhaps leading to changes in the transformation process and/or future outputs. Feedback can be both positive and negative, although the field of cybernetics is based on negative feedback. Negative feedback is informational input which indicates that the system is deviating from a prescribed course and should readjust to a new steady state.

Hierarchy. A basic concept in systems thinking is that of hierarchical relationships between systems. A system is composed of subsystems of a lower order and is also part of a suprasystem. Thus, there is a hierarchy of the components of the system.

Internal Elaboration. Closed systems move toward entropy and disorganization. In contrast, open systems appear to move in the direction of greater differentiation, elaboration, and a higher level of organization.

Multiple Goal-Seeking. Biological and social systems appear to have multiple goals or purposes. Social organizations seek multiple goals, if for no other reason than that they are composed of individuals and subunits with different values and objectives.

Equifinality of Open Systems. In mechanistic systems there is a direct cause and effect relationship between the initial conditions and the final state. Biological and social systems operate differently. Equifinality suggests that certain results may be achieved with different initial conditions and in different ways. This view suggests that social organizations can accomplish their objectives with diverse inputs and with varying internal activities (conversion processes).

Figure 1.   Key Concepts of General Systems Theory.

professed to utilize general systems theory. Indeed, in the first few chapters, many of them did an excellent job of presenting basic systems concepts and showing their relationship to organizations; however, when they moved further into the discussion of more specific subject matter, they departed substantially from systems theory. The studies appear to use a "partial systems approach" and leave for the reader the problem of integrating the various ideas into a systemic whole. It also appears that many of the authors are unable, because of limitations of knowledge about subsystem relationships, to carry out the task of using general systems theory as a conceptual basis for organization theory.

Furthermore, it is evident that each author had many "good ideas" stemming from the existing body of knowledge or current research on organizations which did not fit neatly into a "systems model." For example, they might discuss leadership from a relatively closed-system point of view and not consider it in relation to organizational technology, structure, or other variables. Our review of the literature suggests that much remains to be done in applying general systems theory to organization theory and management practice.

some dilemmas in applying GST to organizations

Why have writers embracing general systems theory as a basis for studying organizations had so much difficulty in following through? Part of this difficulty may stem from the newness of the paradigm and our inability to operationalize "all we think we know" about this approach. Or it may be because we know too little about the systems under investigation. Both of these possibilities will be covered later, but first we need to look at some of the more specific conceptual problems.

organizations as organisms

One of the basic contributions of general systems theory was the rejection of the traditional closed-system or mechanistic view of social organizations. But, did general systems theory free us from this constraint only to impose another, less obvious one? General systems theory grew out of the organismic views of von Bertalanffy and other biologists; thus, many of the characteristics are relevant to the living organism. It is conceptually easy to draw the analogy between living organisms and social organizations. "There is, after all, an intuitive similarity between the organization of the human body and the kinds of organizations men create. And so, undaunted by the failures of the human-social analogy through time, new theorists try afresh in each epoch" [2, p. 660]. General systems theory would have us accept this analogy between organism and social organization. Yet we have a hard time swallowing it whole. Katz and Kahn warn us of the danger:

There has been no more pervasive, persistent, and futile fallacy handicapping the social sciences than the use of the physical model for the understanding of social structures. The biological metaphor, with its crude comparisons of the physical parts of the body to the parts of the social system, has been replaced by more subtle but equally misleading analogies between biological and social functioning. This figurative type of thinking ignores the essential difference between the socially contrived nature of social systems and the physical structure of the machine or the human organism. So long as writers are committed to a theoretical framework based upon the physical model, they will miss the essential social-psychological facts of the highly variable, loosely articulated character of social systems [19, p. 31].

In spite of this warning, Katz and Kahn do embrace much of the general systems theory concepts which are based on the biological metaphor. We must be very cautious about trying to make this analogy too literal. We agree with Silverman who says, "It may, therefore, be necessary to drop the analogy between an organization and an organism: organizations may be systems but not necessarily *natural* systems" [34, p. 31].

distinction between organization and an organization

General systems theory emphasizes that systems are organized—they are composed of interdependent components in some relationship. The social organization would then follow logically as just another system. But, we are perhaps being caught in circular thinking. It is true that all systems (physical, biological, and social) are by definition organized, but are all systems organizations? Rapoport and Horvath distinguish "organization theory" and "the theory of organizations" as follows:

We see organization theory as dealing with general and abstract organizational principles; it applies to any system exhibiting organized complexity. As such, organization theory is seen as an extension of mathematical physics or, even more generally, of mathematics designed to deal with organized systems. The theory of organizations, on the other hand, purports to be a social science. It puts real human organizations at the center of interest. It may study the social structure of organizations and so can be viewed as a branch of sociology; it can study the behavior of individuals or groups as members of organizations and can be viewed as a part of social psychology; it can study power relations and principles of control in organizations and so fits into political science [30, pp. 74–75].

Why make an issue of this distinction? It seems to us that there is a vital matter involved. All systems may be considered to be organized, and more advanced systems may display differentiation in the activities of component parts—such as the specialization of human organs. However, all systems *do not* have purposeful entities. Can the heart or lungs be considered as purposeful entities in themselves or are they only components of the larger purposeful system, the human body? By contrast, the social organization is composed of two or more purposeful elements. "An organization consists of elements that have and can exercise their own wills" [1, p. 669]. Organisms, the foundation stone of general systems theory, do not contain purposeful elements which exercise their own will. This distinction between the organism and the social organization is of importance. In much of general systems theory, the concern is primarily with the way in which the *organism* responds to environmentally generated inputs. Feedback concepts and the maintenance of a steady state are based on internal adaptations to environmental forces. (This is particularly true of cybernetic models.) But, what about those changes and adaptations which occur from *within* social organizations? Purposeful elements within the social organization may initiate activities and adaptations which are difficult to subsume under feedback and steady state concepts.

opened and closed systems

Another dilemma stemming from general systems theory is the tendency to dichotomize all systems as opened or closed. We have been led to think of physical systems as closed, subject to the laws of entropy, and to think of biological systems as open to their environment and, possibly, becoming negentropic. But applying this strict polarization to social organizations creates many difficulties. In fact, most social organizations and their subsystems are "partially open" and "partially closed." Open and closed are a matter of degree. Unfortunately, there seems to be a widely held view (often more implicit than explicit) that *open-system thinking is good and closed-system thinking is bad.* We have not become sufficiently sophisticated to recognize that both are appropriate under certain conditions. For example, one of the most useful conceptualizations set forth by Thompson is that the social organization *must seek* to use closed-system concepts (particularly at the technical core) to reduce uncertainty and to create more effective performance at this level.

still subsystems thinking

Even though we preach a general systems approach, we often practice subsystems thinking. Each of the academic disciplines and each of us personally have limited perspective of the system we are studying. While proclaiming a broad systems viewpoint, we often dismiss variables outside our interest or competence as being irrelevant, and we only open our system to those inputs which we can handle with our disciplinary bag of tools. We are hampered because each of the academic disciplines has taken a narrow "partial systems view" and find comfort in the relative certainty which this creates. Of course, this is not a problem unique to modern organization theory. Under the more traditional process approach to the study of management, we were able to do an admirable job of delineating and discussing planning, organizing, and controlling as separate activities. We were much less successful in discussing them as integrated and interrelated activities.

how does our knowledge fit?

One of the major problems in utilizing general systems theory is that we know (or think we know) more about certain relationships than we can fit into a general systems model. For example, we are beginning to understand the two-variable relationship between technology and structure. But, when we introduce another variable, say psychosocial relationships, our models become too complex. Consequently, in order to discuss all the things we know about organizations, we depart from a systems approach. Perhaps it is because we know a great deal more about the elements or subsystems of an organization than we do about the interrelationships and interactions between these subsystems. And, general systems theory forces us to consider those relationships about which we know the least—a true dilemma. So we continue to elaborate on those aspects of the organization which we know best—a partial systems view.

failure to delineate a specific system

When the social sciences embraced general systems theory, the total system became the focus of attention and terminology tended toward vagueness. In the utilization of systems theory, we should be more precise in delineating the specific system under consideration. Failure to do this leads to much confusion. As Murray suggests:

I am wary of the word "system" because social scientists use it very frequently without specifying which of several possible different denotations they have in mind; but more particularly because, today, "system" is a highly cathected term, loaded with prestige; hence, we are all strongly tempted to employ it even when we have nothing definite in mind and its only service is to indicate that we subscribe to the general premise respecting the interdependence of things—basic to organismic theory, holism, field theory, interactionism, transactionism, etc. . . . When definitions of the units of a system are lacking, the term stands for no more than an article of faith, and is misleading to boot, insofar as it suggests a condition of affairs that may not actually exist [27, pp. 50–51].

We need to be much more precise in delineating both the boundaries of the system under consideration and the level of our analysis. There is a tendency for current writers in organization theory to accept general systems theory and then to move indiscriminately across systems boundaries and between levels of systems without being very precise (and letting their readers in on what is occurring). James Miller suggests the need for clear delineation of levels in applying systems theory, "It is important to follow one procedural rule in systems theory in order to avoid confusion. Every discussion should begin with an identification of the level of reference, and the discourse should not change to another level without a specific statement that this is occurring" [25, p. 216]. Our field is replete with these confusions about systems levels. For example, when we use the term "organizational behavior" are we talking about the way the organization behaves as a system or are we talking about the behavior of the individual participants? By goals, do we mean the goals of the organization or the goals of the individuals within the organization? In using systems theory we must become more precise in our delineation of systems boundaries and systems levels if we are to prevent confusing conceptual ambiguity.

recognition that organizations are "contrived systems"

We have a vague uneasiness that general systems theory truly does not recognize the "contrived" nature of social organizations. With its predominate emphasis on natural organisms, it may understate some characteristics which are vital for the social organization. Social organizations do not occur naturally in nature; they are contrived by man. They have structure; but it is the structure of events rather than of physical components, and it cannot be separated from the processes of the system. The fact that social organizations are contrived by human beings suggests that they can be established for an infinite variety of purposes and do not follow the same life-cycle patterns of birth, growth, maturity, and death as biological systems. As Katz and Kahn say:

Social structures are essentially contrived systems. They are made of men and are imperfect systems. They can come apart at the seams overnight, but they can also outlast by centuries the biological organisms which originally created them. The cement which holds them together is essentially psychological rather than biological. Social systems are anchored in the attitudes, perceptions, beliefs, motivations, habits, and expectations of human beings [19, p. 33].

Recognizing that the social organization is contrived again cautions us against making an exact analogy between it and physical or biological systems.

questions of systems effectiveness

General systems theory with its biological orientation would appear to have an evolutionary view of system effectiveness. That living system which best adapts to its environment prospers and survives. The primary measure of effectiveness is perpetuation of the organism's species. Teleological behavior is therefore directed toward survival. But, is survival the only criterion of effectiveness of the social system? It is probably an essential but not all-inclusive measure of effectiveness.

General systems theory emphasizes the organism's survival goal and does not fully relate to the question of the effectiveness of the system in its suprasystem—the environment. Parsonian functional-structural views provide a contrast. "The *raison d'etre* of complex organizations, according to this analysis, is mainly to benefit the society in which they belong, and that society is, therefore, the appropriate frame of reference for the evaluation of organizational effectiveness" [41, p. 896].

But, this view seems to go to the opposite extreme from the survival view of general systems theory—the organization exists to serve the society. It seems to us that the truth lies somewhere between these two viewpoints. And it is likely that a systems viewpoint (modified from the species survival view of general systems theory) will be most appropriate. Yuchtman and Seashore suggest:

The organization's success over a period of time in this competition for resources— i.e., its bargaining position in a given environment—is regarded as an expression of its overall effectiveness. Since the resources are of various kinds, and the competitive relationships are multiple, and since there is interchangeability among classes of resources, the assessment of organizational effectiveness must be in terms of any single criterion but of an open-ended multidimensional set of criteria [41, p. 891].

This viewpoint suggests that questions of organizational effectiveness must be concerned with at least three levels of analysis. The level of the environment, the level of the social organization as a system, and the level of the subsystems (human participants) within the organization. Perhaps much of our confusion and ambiguity concerning organizational effectiveness stems from our failure to clearly delineate the level of our analysis and,

even more important, our failure really to understand the relationships among these levels.

Our discussion of some of the problems associated with the application of general systems theory to the study of social organizations might suggest that we completely reject the appropriateness of this model. On the contrary, we see the systems approach as the new paradigm for the study of organizations; but, like all new concepts in the sciences, one which has to be applied, modified, and elaborated to make it as useful as possible.

systems theory provides the new paradigm

We hope the discussion of GST and organizations provides a realistic appraisal. We do not want to promote the value of the systems approach as a matter of faith; however, we do see systems theory as vital to the study of social organizations and as providing the major new paradigm for our field of study.

Thomas Kuhn provides an interesting interpretation of the nature of scientific revolution [20]. He suggests that major changes in all fields of science occur with the development of new conceptual schemes or "paradigms." These new paradigms do not just represent a step-by-step advancement in "normal" science (the science generally accepted and practiced) but, rather, a revolutionary change in the way the scientific field is perceived by the practitioners. Kuhn says:

The historian of science may be tempted to exclaim that when paradigms change, the world itself changes with them. Led by a new paradigm, scientists adopt new instruments and look in new places. Even more important, during revolutions scientists see new and different things when looking with familiar instruments in places they have looked before. It is rather as if the professional community has been suddenly transported to another planet where familiar objects are seen in a different light and are joined by unfamiliar ones as well. . . . Paradigm changes do cause scientists to see the world of their research-engagement differently. Insofar as their only recourse to that world is through what they see and do, we may want to say that after a revolution scientists are responding to a different world [20, p. 110].

New paradigms frequently are rejected by the scientific community. (At first they may seem crude and limited—offering very little more than older paradigms.) They frequently lack the apparent sophistication of the older paradigms which they ultimately replace. They do not display the clarity and certainty of older paradigms which have been refined through years of research and writing. But, a new paradigm does provide for a "new start" and opens up new directions which were not possible under the old. "We must recognize how very limited in both scope and precision a paradigm can be at the time of its first appearance. Paradigms gain their status because they are more successful than their competitors in solving a few problems that the group of practitioners has come to recognize as acute. To be more successful is not, however, to be either completely successful with a single problem or notably successful with any large number" [20, p. 23].

Systems theory does provide a new paradigm for the study of social organizations and their management. At this stage it is obviously crude and lacking in precision. In some ways it may not be much better than older paradigms which have been accepted and used for a long time (such as the management process approach). As in other fields of scientific endeavor, the new paradigm must be applied, clarified, elaborated, and made more precise. But, it does provide a fundamentally different view of the reality of social organizations and can serve as

the basis for major advancements in our field.

We see many exciting examples of the utilization of the new systems paradigm in the field of organization and management. Several of these have been referred to earlier [7, 13, 19, 22, 23, 24, 31, 38], and there have been many others. Burns and Stalker made substantial use of systems views in setting forth their concepts of mechanistic and organic managerial systems [8]. Their studies of the characteristics of these two organization types lack precise definition of the variables and relationships, but their colleagues have used the systems approach to look at the relationship of organizations to their environment and also among the technical, structural, and behavioral characteristics within the organization [24]. Chamberlain used a system view in studying enterprises and their environment, which is substantially different from traditional microeconomics [9]. The emerging field of "environmental sciences" and "environmental administration" has found the systems paradigm vital.

Thus, the systems theory paradigm is being used extensively in the investigating of relationships between subsystems within organizations and in studying the environmental interfaces. But, it still has not advanced sufficiently to meet the needs. One of the major problems is that the practical need to deal with comprehensive systems of relationships is overrunning our ability to fully understand and predict these relationships. *We vitally need the systems paradigm but we are not sufficiently sophisticated to use it appropriately.* This is the dilemma. Do our current failures to fully utilize the systems paradigm suggest that we reject it and return to the older, more traditional, and time-tested paradigms? Or do we work with systems theory to make it more precise, to understand the relationships among subsystems, and to gather the informational inputs which are necessary to make the systems approach really work? We think the latter course offers the best opportunity.

Thus, we prefer to accept current limitations of systems theory, while working to reduce them and to develop more complete and sophisticated approaches for its application. We agree with Rapoport, who says:

The system approach to the study of man can be appreciated as an effort to restore meaning (in terms of intuitively grasped understanding of wholes) while adhering to the principles of *disciplined* generalizations and rigorous deduction. It is, in short, an attempt to make the study of man both scientific and meaningful [7, p. xxii].

We are sympathetic with the second part of Rapoport's comment, the need to apply the systems approach but to make disciplined generalizations and rigorous deductions. This is a vital necessity and yet a major current limitation. We do have some indication that progress (although very slow) is being made.

what do we need now?

Everything is related to everything else— but how? General systems theory provides us with the macro paradigm for the study of social organizations. As Scott and others have pointed out, most sciences go through a macro-micro-macro cycle or sequence of emphasis [33]. Traditional bureaucratic theory provided the first major macro view of organizations. Administrative management theorists concentrated on the development of macro "principles of management" which were applicable to all organizations. When these macro views seemed incomplete (unable to explain important phenomena), attention turned to the micro level—more

detailed analysis of components or parts of the organization, thus the interest in human relations, technology, or structural dimensions.

The systems approach returns us to the macro level with a new paradigm. General systems theory emphasizes a very high level of abstraction. Phillips classifies it as a third-order study [29] that attempts to develop macro concepts appropriate for all types of biological, physical, and social systems.

In our view, we are now ready to move down a level of abstraction to consider second-order systems studies or midrange concepts. These will be based on general systems theory but will be more concrete and will emphasize more specific characteristics and relationships in social organizations. They will operate within the broad paradigm of systems theory but at a less abstract level.

What should we call this new midrange level of analysis? Various authors have referred to it as a "contingency view," a study of "patterns of relationships," or a search for "configurations among subsystems." Lorsch and Lawrence reflect this view:

During the past few years there has been evident a new trend in the study of organizational phenomena. Underlying this new approach is the idea that the internal functioning of organizations must be consistent with the demands of the organization task, technology, or external environment, and the needs of its members if the organization is to be effective. Rather than searching for the panacea of the one best way to organize under all conditions investigators have more and more tended to examine the functioning of organizations in relation to the needs of their particular members and the external pressures facing them. Basically, this approach seems to be leading to the development of a "contingency" theory of organization with the appropriate internal states and processes of the organization contingent upon external requirements and member needs [21, p. 1].

Numerous others have stressed a similar viewpoint. Thompson suggests that the essence of administration lies in understanding basic configurations which exist between the various subsystems and with the environment. "The basic function of administration appears to be co-alignment, not merely of people (in coalitions) but of institutionalized action—of technology and task environment into a viable domain, and of organizational design and structure appropriate to it [38, p. 157].

Bringing these ideas together we can provide a more precise definition of the contingency view:

The contingency view of organizations and their management suggests that an organization is a system composed of subsystems and delineated by identifiable boundaries from its environmental suprasystem. The contingency view seeks to understand the interrelationships within and among subsystems as well as between the organization and its environment and to define patterns of relationships or configurations of variables. It emphasizes the multivariate nature of organizations and attempts to understand how organizations operate under varying conditions and in specific circumstances. Contingency views are ultimately directed toward suggesting organizational designs and managerial systems most appropriate for specific situations.

But, it is not enough to suggest that a "contingency view" based on systems concepts of organizations and their management is more appropriate than the simplistic "principles approach." If organization theory is to advance and make contributions to managerial practice, it must define more explicitly certain patterns of relationships between organizational variables. This is the major challenge facing our field.

Just how do we go about using systems theory to develop these midrange or contingency views. We see no alternative but to engage in intensive comparative investigation of many organizations following the advice of Blau:

A theory of organization, whatever its specific nature, and regardless of how subtle the organizational processes it takes into account, has as its central aim to establish the constellations of characteristics that develop in organizations of various kinds. Comparative studies of many organizations are necessary, not alone to test the hypotheses implied by such a theory, but also to provide a basis for initial exploration and refinement of the theory by indicating the conditions on which relationships, originally assumed to hold universally are contingent. . . . Systematic research on many organizations that provides the data needed to determine the interrelationships between several organizational features is, however, extremely rare [5, p. 332].

Various conceptual designs for the comparative study of organizations and their subsystems are emerging to help in the development of a contingency view. We do not want to impose our model as to what should be considered in looking for these patterns of relationships. However, the tentative matrix shown in Figure 2 suggests this approach. We have used as a starting point the two polar organization types which have been emphasized in the literature—closed/stable/mechanistic and open/adaptive/organic.

We will consider the environmental suprasystem and organizational subsystems (goals and values, technical, structural, psychosocial, and managerial) plus various dimensions or characteristics of each of these systems. By way of illustration we have indicated several specific subcategories under the Environmental Suprasystem as well as the Goals and Values subsystem. This process would have to be completed and extended to all of the subsystems. The next step would be the development of appropriate descriptive language (based on research and conceptualization) for each relevant

Organizational Supra- and Subsystems	Continuum of Organization Types	
	Closed/Stable/Mechanistic	Open/Adaptive/Organic
Environmental relationships		
General nature	Placid	Turbulent
Predictability	Certain, determinate	Uncertain, indeterminate
Boundary relationships	Relatively closed; limited to few participants (sales, purchasing, etc.); fixed and well-defined	Relatively open; many participants have external relationships; varied and not clearly defined
Goals and values		
Organizational goals in general	Efficient performance, stability, maintenance	Effective problem-solving, innovation, growth
Goal set	Single, clear-cut	Multiple, determined by necessity to satisfy a set of constraints
Stability	Stable	Unstable
Technical		
Structural		
Psychosocial		
Managerial		

Figure 2. Matrix of Patterns of Relationships Between Organization Types and Systems Variables.

characteristic across the continuum of organization types. For example, on the "stability" dimensions for Goals and Values we would have High, Medium, and Low at appropriate places on the continuum. If the entire matrix were filled in, it is likely that we would begin to see discernible patterns of relationships among subsystems.

We do not expect this matrix to provide *the* midrange model for everyone. It is highly doubtful that we will be able to follow through with the field work investigations necessary to fill in all the squares. Nevertheless, it does illustrate a possible approach for the translation of more abstract general systems theory and management practice. Frankly, we see this as a major long-term effort on the part of many researchers, investigating a wide variety of organizations. In spite of the difficulties involved in such research, the endeavor has practical significance. Sophistication in the study of organiza-

tions will come when we have a more complete understanding of organizations as total systems (configurations of subsystems) so that we can prescribe more appropriate organizational designs and managerial systems. Ultimately, organization theory should serve as the foundation for more effective management practice.

application of systems concepts to management practice

The study of organizations is an applied science because the resulting knowledge is relevant to problem-solving in on-going institutions. Contributions to organization theory come from many sources. Deductive and inductive research in a variety of disciplines provide a theoretical base of propositions which are useful for understanding organizations and for managing them. Experience gained in management practice is also an important input to organization theory. In short, management is based on the body of knowledge generated by practical experience *and* eclectic scientific research concerning organizations. The body of knowledge developed through theory and research should be translatable into more effective organizational design and managerial practices.

Do systems concepts and contingency views provide a panacea for solving problems in organizations? The answer is an emphatic *no*; this approach does not provide "ten easy steps" to success in management. Such cookbook approaches, while seemingly applicable and easy to grasp, are usually shortsighted, narrow in perspective, and superficial—in short, unrealistic. Fundamental ideas, such as systems concepts and contingency views, are more difficult to comprehend. However, they facilitate more thorough understanding of complex situations and increase the likelihood of appropriate action.

It is important to recognize that many managers have used and will continue to use a systems approach and contingency views intuitively and implicitly. Without much knowledge of the underlying body of organization theory, they have an intuitive "sense of the situation," are flexible diagnosticians, and adjust their actions and decisions accordingly. Thus, systems concepts and contingency views are not new. However, if this approach to organization theory and management practice can be made more explicit, we can facilitate better management and more effective organizations.

Practicing managers in business firms, hospitals, and government agencies continue to function on a day-to-day basis. Therefore, they must use whatever theory is available, they cannot wait for the *ultimate* body of knowledge (there is none!). Practitioners should be included in the search for new knowledge because they control access to an essential ingredient—organizational data—and they are the ones who ultimately put the theory to the test. Mutual understanding among managers, teachers, and researchers will facilitate the development of a relevant body of knowledge.

Simultaneously with the refinement of the body of knowledge, a concerted effort should be directed toward applying what we do know. We need ways of making systems and contingency views more usable. Without oversimplification, we need some relevant guidelines for practicing managers.

The general tenor of the contingency view is somewhere between simplistic, specific principles and complex, vague notions. It is a midrange concept which recognizes the complexity involved in managing modern organizations but uses patterns of relationships and/or configurations of subsystems in order to facilitate improved practice. The art of management depends on a reasonable success rate for actions in a probabilistic environment. Our hope is that systems concepts and contingency views, while continually being refined by scientists/researchers/theorists, will also be made more applicable.

references

1. Ackoff, Russell L., "Towards a System of Systems Concepts," *Management Science* (July 1971).

2. Back, Kurt W., "Biological Models of Social Change," *American Sociological Review* (August 1971).

3. Barnard, Chester I., *The Functions of the Executive* (Cambridge, Mass.: Harvard University Press, 1938).

4. Berrien, F. Kenneth, *General and Social Systems* (New Brunswick, N.J.: Rutgers University Press, 1968).

5. Blau, Peter M., "The Comparative Study of Organizations," *Industrial and Labor Relations Review* (April 1965).

6. Boulding, Kenneth E., "General Systems Theory: The Skeleton of Science," *Management Science* (April 1956).

7. Buckley, Walter, ed., *Modern Systems Research for the Behavioral Scientist* (Chicago: Aldine Publishing Company, 1968).

8. Burns, Tom and G. M. Stalker, *The Management of Innovation* (London: Tavistock Publications, 1961).

9. Chamberlain, Neil W., *Enterprise and Environment: The Firm in Time and Place* (New York: McGraw-Hill Book Company, 1968).

10. Churchman, C. West, *The Systems Approach* (New York: Dell Publishing Company, Inc., 1968).

11. DeGreene, Kenyon, ed., *Systems Psychology* (New York: McGraw-Hill Book Company, 1970).

12. Deutsch, Karl W., "Toward a Cybernetic Model of Man and Society," in Walter Buckley, ed., *Modern Systems Research for the Behavioral Scientist* (Chicago: Aldine Publishing Company, 1968).

13. Easton, David, *A Systems Analysis of Political Life* (New York: John Wiley & Sons, Inc., 1965).

14. Emery, F. E. and E. L. Trist, "Sociotechnical Systems," in C. West Churchman and Michele Verhulst, eds., *Management Sciences: Models and Techniques* (New York: Pergamon, Press, 1960).

15. Emshoff, James R., *Analysis of Behavioral Systems* (New York: Macmillan Publishing Co., Inc., 1971).

16. Gross, Bertram M., "The Coming General Systems Models of Social Systems," *Human Relations* (November 1967).

17. Hall, A. D. and R. E. Eagen, "Definition of System," *General Systems, Yearbook for the Society for the Advancement of General Systems Theory*, Vol. 1 (1956).

18. Kast, Fremont E. and James E. Rosenzweig, *Organization and Management Theory: A Systems Approach* (New York: McGraw-Hill Book Company, 1970).

19. Katz, Daniel and Robert L. Kahn, *The Social Psychology of Organizations* (New York: John Wiley & Sons, Inc., 1966).

20. Kuhn, Thomas S., *The Structure of Scientific Revolutions* (Chicago: University of Chicago Press, 1962).

21. Lorsch, Jay W. and Paul R. Lawrence, *Studies in Organizational Design* (Homewood, Illinois: Irwin-Dorsey, 1970).

22. Litterer, Joseph A., *Organizations: Structure and Behavior*, Vol. 1 (New York: John Wiley & Sons, Inc., 1969).

23. ———, *Organizations: Systems, Control and Adaptation*, Vol. 2 (New York: John Wiley & Sons, Inc., 1969).

24. Miller, E. J. and A. K. Rice, *Systems of Organizations* (London: Tavistock Publications, 1967).

25. Miller, James G., "Living Systems: Basic Concepts," *Behavioral Science* (July 1965).

26. Miller, Robert F., "The New Science of Administration in the USSR," *Administrative Science Quarterly* (September 1971).

27. Murray, Henry A., "Preparation for the Scaffold of a Comprehensive System," in Sigmund Koch, ed., *Psychology: A Study of a Science*, Vol. 3 (New York: McGraw-Hill Book Company, 1959).

28. Parsons, Talcott, *The Social System* (New York: The Free Press of Glencoe, 1951).

29. Phillips, D. C., "Systems Theory—A Discredited Philosophy," in Peter P. Schoderbek, *Management Systems* (New York: John Wiley & Sons, Inc., 1971).

30. Rapoport, Anatol and William J. Horvath, "Thoughts on Organization Theory," in Walter Buckley, ed., *Modern Systems Research for the Behavioral Scientist* (Chicago: Aldine Publishing Company, 1968).

31. Rice, A. K., *The Modern University* (London: Tavistock Publications, 1970).

32. Schein, Edgar, *Organizational Psychology*, rev. ed. (Englewood Cliffs, New Jersey: Prentice-Hall, Inc., 1970).

33. Scott, William G., "Organization Theory: An Overview and an Appraisal," *Academy of Management Journal* (April 1961).

34. Silverman, David, *The Theory of Organizations* (New York: Basic Books, Inc., 1971).

35. Simon, Herbert A., "The Architecture of Complexity," in Joseph A. Litterer, *Organizations: Systems, Control and Adaptation*, Vol. 2 (New York: John Wiley & Sons, Inc., 1969).

36. Springer, Michael, "Social Indicators, Reports, and Accounts: Toward the Management of Society," *The Annals of the American Academy of Political and Social Science* (March 1970).

37. Terreberry, Shirley, "The Evolution of Organizational Environments," *Administrative Science Quarterly* (March 1968).

38. Thompson, James D., *Organizations in Action* (New York: McGraw-Hill Book Company, 1967).

39. Von Bertalanffy, Ludwig, *General System Theory* (New York: George Braziller, 1968).

40. ———, The Theory of Open Systems in Physics and Biology," *Science* (January 13, 1950).

41. Yuchtman, Ephraim and Stanley E. Seashore, "A System Resource Approach to Organizational Effectiveness," *American Sociological Review* (December 1967).

33. models for examining organizations

Richard J. Tersine and Max B. Jones

Management scholars and practitioners are finding it increasingly difficult to relate to their surroundings. There is too much knowledge for any one manager. The result is specialization. Systems theory can provide the necessary link for inte-

Reprinted from *Journal of Systems Management*, 24, No. 9 (September 1973), pp. 32–37, with permission of the publisher.

grating knowledge derived from these splintered subdivisions.

Many disciplines are becoming isolated subdisciplines with nonexistent or tenuous lines of communications. This hinders the total growth of knowledge. The value of a general systems theory lies in spotlighting areas where gaps exist in knowledge.

The systems approach is primarily a point of view and a desirable goal rather than a particular method. It is not something new, but just a change in emphasis that considers internal and external environmental factors. Professors Johnson, Kast, and Rosenzweig demonstrated the application of general systems theory to management practice as early as 1964.[1] Here we will concentrate on *organizational* systems theory as a subset of general systems theory.

The management processes require decision theory to select alternatives. Decision theory utilizes system theory to determine the outcomes of available alternatives. In this manner the requirements for systems analysis are precipitated by the management processes. Organization, a major function in the management process, is found throughout our society. A way of life has evolved that is characterized by the proximity and dependency of people on each other and organizations.

The systems concept is a way of thinking about the job of managing. It provides a framework for relating internal and external environmental factors into an integrated whole. The organization is part of an environment which it influences and in turn is influenced by. It is a man-made system of interrelated parts working in conjunction with each other to accomplish goals.

Systems analysis has resulted from the growing complexity and near unmanageability of modern organizations. It measures efficiency and effectiveness.

a multiview systems concept

The more complicated and realistic a model, the more unwieldy it becomes as a

[1] Richard A. Johnson, Fremont Kast, and James E. Rosenzweig, "Systems Theory and Management," *Management Science*, Vol. 10, No. 2 (January, 1964), pp. 367–384.

tool for analysis. For this reason, simple models that can be solved by analytical techniques are often used. However, the computer, with the aid of quasi-analytical and heuristic search techniques, has increased the probability of finding a near optimum solution to more complex models.

The question is not which version of a model is right or wrong, but whether or not any version is truly explanatory. A conceptual model becomes useful when it assists in making order out of confusing data. Its value lies in allowing experimental pretesting of decisions.

In viewing an organization, no single model is appropriate in depicting the multiplicity of relationships. Numerous models, therefore, must be utilized to convey conceptual and functional relationships. A model is neither true nor false; the standard for comparing models is utility, i.e., adequate description or successful prediction. Let's consider four models that provide different views of an organization. The four models are the Systemic Environmental Model, the Systemic Planning Model, the Systemic Functional Model, and the Systemic Operational Model. The models represent perspectives that move from the very broad to the specific, and from the long-term to the near-term time frame. These models assume a physical product is produced, but are easily adaptable to a service. (See Figure 1.)

It is useful to classify the environments into micro, linking, and macro environments. The micro environment represents the organization itself and its internal affairs; the linking environment represents the interfaces the organization has with the external environment; and the macro environment represents the environment external to the organization.

The Systemic Environmental Model (SEM) and the Systemic Planning Model (SPM) include the three environments:

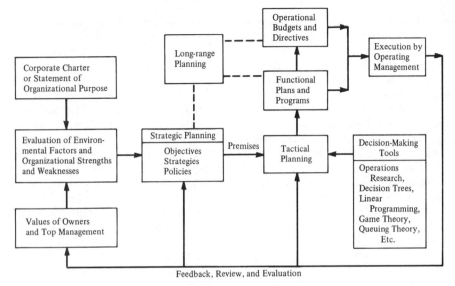

Figure 1.   Systematic Planning Model.

the Systemic Functional Model (SFM) emphasize the linking and micro environments; and the Systemic Operational Model (SOM) puts major emphasis on the micro environment.

systemic environmental model

The SEM model abstracts from all three organizational theories (Classical, Neoclassical and Modern) and contains elements of scientific management, human relations, small group theory, economics and decision making. (See Figure 2.) Each action has a reaction. A change in an input or relationship results in a reorientation of the entire system to some degree. The model does not depict the efficiency of transfers between different sectors, but it does emphasize the path of the flow. The models unite the macro, linking, and micro environments.

The micro environment includes the firm and its internal affairs. The mutual dependency of the formal organization upon the informal organization is depicted by the area of their overlay of the transfor-

mation section. The organization imports inputs which it uses in the transformation operation to produce an output. In economic organizations, the value of the output exceeds the value of the inputs or the firm will eventually go out of business.

The formal organization is an arrangement of tasks or duties so as to efficiently accomplish its goals. The formal organization is impersonal and usually defined by job descriptions and organization charts. Under the concept of division of labor, job activities and relationships are determined by job descriptions and organization charts. After dividing complex jobs into smaller jobs, all operations must be coordinated. This is the function of an information system. The information system provides the input to planning and control so the decision maker can coordinate activities to meet the organizational goals.

The informal organization is a product of the formal organization and is derived from the needs and requirements of people. People have needs and objectives that may or may not be congruent with the organization. The groups provide support and certainty to their members. The formal organization is incapable of coping with these needs.

People who work together often become friends because they presume that people who do the same thing are somewhat similar to themselves. And, people who like each other tend to work well together. From these activities, people develop status and roles that may not be legitimately conferred by the formal organization, but that accommodate the human needs of its members.

linking environment

The linking environment impinges upon the organization in three modes—when inputs are obtained from it (factor market); when output is sold to it (product market); and when the goals, objectives, and methods of the organization are sanctioned by it (societal market). The factor and product markets are well defined by micro economics, but the societal market is less clearly defined. The organization needs certain inputs to meet their goals and objectives. They purchase services and material inputs from the factor market. The output of the organization is sold in the product market. The societal market is where the public places constraints on the organization such as requirements for social security, workman's compensation, and minimum wage.

The linking environment represents the connecting systems between the organization and its external environment. Business decisions that deal with the linking environment fall into functional areas—finance, procurement, personnel, sales, legal and so forth. Unfortunately, many firms have tended to ignore the societal market and they have given more emphasis to economically oriented factor and product markets.

The macro environment represents everything external to the firm. It is difficult to characterize since it can be quite different for any two firms. Generally it is where a firm buys and sells, and can be broad or narrow.

The macro environment can be considered as an interdependent and interrelated complex of political forces, economic forces, social forces and the state of science. All organizations do not have a macro environment of the same consistency. For example, a computer hardware firm may be subject to little governmental influence, while technology could be ultra important; an automobile manufacturer may experience little year-to-year technological change, but be subject to a great deal of governmental influence.

An organization must understand its macro environment for it has tremendous influence on intermediate and long range planning. For example, changes in the macro environment of the tobacco industry via government influence, has modified this industry's long range objectives considerably. As a consequence these firms are now diversifying. The influence of the macro environment through the societal market can have a more pronounced effect than through the factor and product markets.

micro-linking-macro factors

The key factors of the Systemic Environmental Model are balance and reciprocity. Balance refers to the ability of the system to absorb shocks and still survive. The system can be shocked by the process of decay where products become technologically obsolete or by an overheating of the system which results in a constriction of flow to and from the markets. It is imperative that the system be able to take various shocks from both inside and outside the organization and still return to a state of balance. Some examples of shocks are undesirable merger takeover attempts, government ban on the sale of cyclamates, union strikes, acts of God, failure of a new product to be accepted, and so forth.

Reciprocity can be called a means by which different interests are satisfied. Complementing, supplementing and conflicting forces allow the organization to continue its existence because they benefit directly or indirectly from it. The relationships are symbiotic because two or more dissimilar groups receive mutual benefit. An organization must provide mutual benefit to its owners, employees, and the public or its existence will be in jeopardy. Without the factors of balance and reciprocity the organization could not survive over an extended period of time.

The Systemic Planning Model unites the macro and micro environments. An important function of planning is to integrate the knowledge of the existing environments so management can establish premises for the organization. Planning is required to insure the continuing viability of the organization in the midst of changing conditions. The objectives of the organization must be congruent with the needs of society as well as organizational members. The systemic planning model attempts to maintain this congruency while narrowing the boundaries of uncertainty. (See Figure 1.)

The Systemic Functional Model emphasizes to a greater degree the linking and micro environments. (See Figure 2.) The perspective of this model is much narrower than in the systemic environmental model. The concern is for the functions that must be performed by the organizations in getting a successful product to market.

The systemic functional model can be subdivided into five interdependent categories—policy decisions, product decisions, process decisions, plant decisions, and operations decisions. These categories give answers to questions of why make it, what to make, how to make, where to make, and when and how many to make.

Policy decisions begin with the statement of the broad long range objectives of the organization. (Typical examples are growth, market share, sales maximization, market leadership, social responsibility, customer satisfaction, product leadership, survival, return on investment, etc.) These broad objectives are modified to account for internal and external restraints. These restraints are limiting factors such as technology, financial resources, sources of capital, market conditions, size of the firm, competitor's actions, strength and weaknesses of the existing organization, etc. The redefinition of broad objectives to a nearer time-frame in line with the capabilities of the organization, results in strategies. From the objectives, these specific plans are developed to attain the strategies. The plans are inputs to market analysis which helps to determine what goods or services the public wants that are within the framework of organizational plans.

Product decisions begin with general specifications from market analyses which indicate customer requirements. From general specifications, technical specifications are written. They define the product in much greater detail. Technical specifications are the structure for the functional design and include both form and function of the product. The next step is production design—an effort to design the final product so it can be produced for low manufacturing costs. The final release of drawings and specifications of what to make terminates product design.

process decisions

Process decisions determine how to best produce the product. These decisions start with product analysis and use

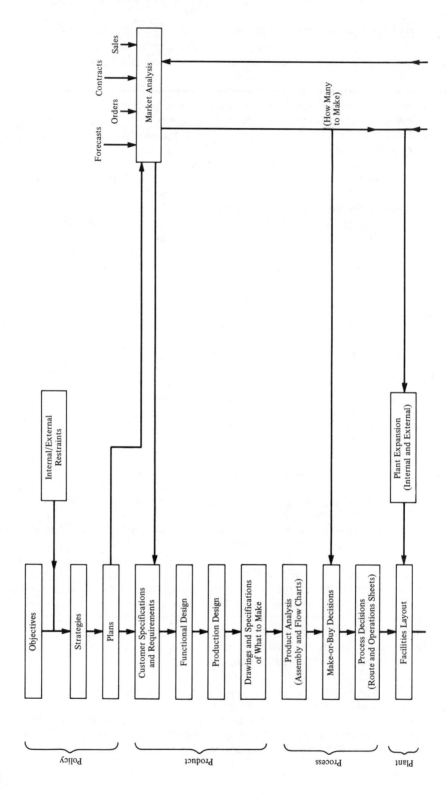

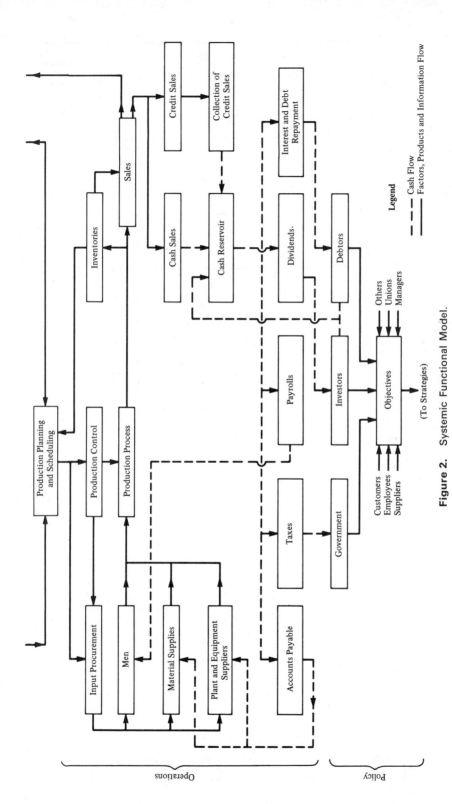

Figure 2. Systemic Functional Model.

343

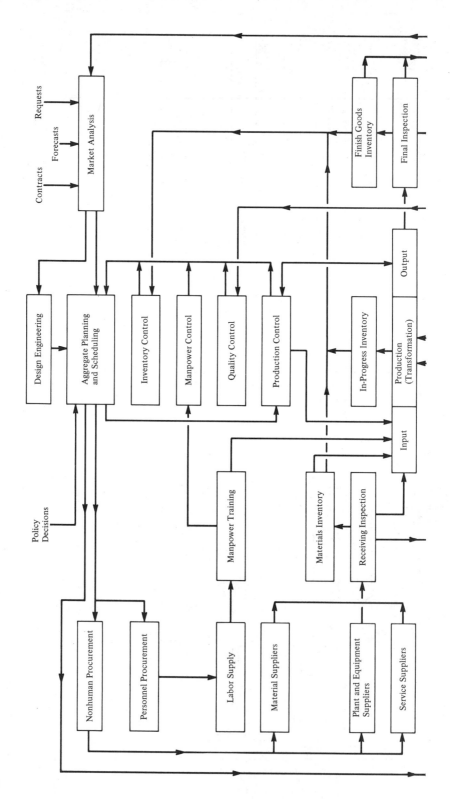

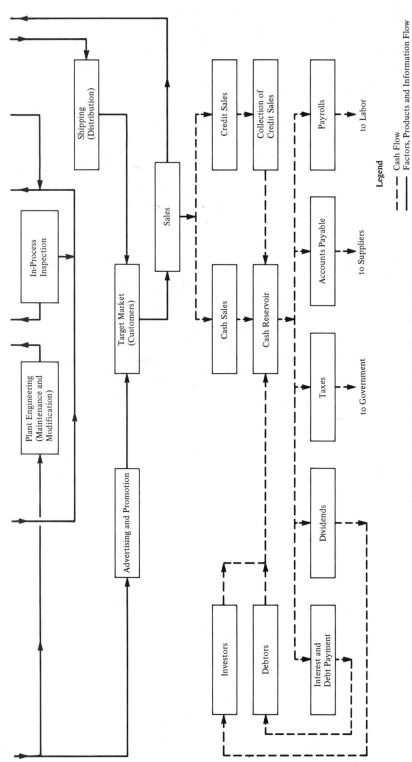

Figure 3. Systemic Operational Model.

assembly and flow charts for analyzing each component. The decision to sub-contract or build in-house is made. Process decisions are made for all in-house work and include a definition of the processes as well as the steps and procedures for each process. Operations sheets then specify in detail how to perform each operation of a process. Finally, route sheets are developed to plan the physical flow of the product through the different operating departments.

Plant decisions begin with a decision to utilize unused capacity, expand existing plant, or build a new plant to accommodate the product. After this decision, the layout of the physical facilities is necessary, including work station design and the selection of materials handling equipment.

Operations decisions decide when and how many units to make. They begin with production planning and scheduling orders for the acquisition of men, materials, plant, and equipment. Activation and organization are achieved during this phase.

Production control concerns itself with the short term scheduling of the resources into the production process. The production process generates inventories of products which, in turn, are depleted by sales. Sales, as well as investors and creditors, generate an inflow into the cash reservoir. Many parties have claims on this reservoir—employees, investors, creditors, government, and so forth.

Objectives are met when these claims are balanced with expectations. Any party able to modify this balance, in turn, influences the objectives of the firm. At this point, the model reflects a full circle return to the objectives in policy decisions.

The Systemic Operational Model places its emphasis on the micro environment (the firm itself) and it is short term in its perspective. (See Figure 3.) It assumes that the plant and personnel are already

in existence. The optimum operation and control of the system is the main consideration. The major decision areas include forecasting, planning and scheduling, procurement, production, plant engineering, sales and control (production control, cost control, and quality control).

The system operates from forecasts and future orders which are transmitted to the "brain center," planning and scheduling. This central decision area determines what must be done to meet the future demand. It established the type and mix of inputs and schedules them for the production process. Procurement obtains the desired mix of human and non-human inputs. Production uses and transforms the inputs into the output product. Plant engineering maintains, modifies, and installs new plant and equipment. The sales function provides the successful interaction of the consumer with the output product. The control areas regulate quantity, quality and cost.

A close examination of the systemic operational model reveals that many long-run decisions are omitted. This model does not give adequate attention to the location of the system, physical facility layout, job design, work measurement, selection of equipment and processes, and so forth. The model concentrates on short term decisions that do not require a longer time perspective. (Should a marginal producer be allowed a line of credit in slack production period?)

conclusion

The models developed (SEM, SPM, SFM, and SOM) have been used to emphasize the inadequacy of any single model for all occasions. Different conditions and situations require an adaptive view that can only be obtained from multi-perspectives. The systems approach spotlights the objectives of the total system rather than a separate department. This more realistic approach reduces suboptimization. (The condition where department optimization is not optimum for the total entity.)

Each organization must be designed as a unique system. Structuring an organization to the systems concept does not eliminate the need for the management functions. There is a change in perspective. All activities revolve around the system with its objectives. The functions are executed only as a service to this end. In this capacity the organization is viewed as a set of flows of information, men, materials, and behavior.

Organizations are combinations of socio-economic-technical systems and any approach which does not give attention to the combination is suboptimal. The systems approach provides management the means with which to recognize the relationships between those elements necessary for a realistic synthesis.

b

systems analyses

34. systems analysis: a decision process

Richard de Neufville

Systems analysis is a coordinated set of procedures which addresses the fundamental issue of how money, men, and materials should be combined to achieve a larger purpose.[1] This resource allocation problem is, in effect, the one element present in all decision-making.

At its simplest, systems analysis is a study of the possible ways to achieve certain goals. More technically, it generally involves the use of such analytic tools as: production functions to represent the combination of supplies; marginal analysis concepts and optimization techniques to determine preferable alternatives; utility and decision theory to define optimally

desirable configurations; and sensitivity analysis to investigate the reliability of conclusions. The use of sophisticated tools does not, however, constitute a systems analysis by itself. A good system analysis— at any level—is one that identifies the important issues and alternatives and relates the several costs and benefits of each alternative in a meaningful way to the persons responsible for making decisions.

At the global policy level, systems analysis may rely on mathematical models and computational techniques which are fairly unsophisticated. The critical issues at that level can often be identified more effectively by an insightful analyst with pencil and paper than by a complex computer model whose assumptions are partially or totally hidden from view.

At the more detailed level, systems analysis is founded on the combination of advanced quantitative techniques and data processing methods. The speed and dexterity with which computers effect the

tion is used throughout government and industry. In computer design, however, systems analysis refers to detailed programming. Attempts to create new words to distinguish between these meanings have led only to further semantic difficulties.

Reprinted from *Industrial Management Review*, 11, No. 3 (Spring 1970), pp. 49–58, with permission of the publisher.

[1] This defini-

348

necessary calculations and process the large number of variables and the masses of data required to describe complex situations are rapidly altering the decision process. The environment now developing frees the decision-maker from many routine calculations so that he can approach more challenging issues.

Systems analysis is an orderly procedure for considering the full spectrum of factors relevant to the decision-making process. Its analytic character imposes a new discipline on the nature and conduct of the search for solution alternatives. The functional characteristics of systems analysis sharpen the decision-maker's awareness of objectives, encourage him to predict the future, and force him to establish strategies and procedures for generating, evaluating, and selecting alternatives.

organizing principle

The shape of the decision process is an essential component of any decision theory. How decisions evolve should be of central concern; the patterns of development will strongly influence the final choice. The nature of the analysis process itself should be as rigorous and self-correcting as possible.

The process of systems analysis, as proposed, is perfectly congruent with the scientific method. In the natural sciences, the scientific method iteratively searches for the most plausible explanation of known natural phenomena through the formation of hypotheses, the verification of these trial explanations through experiment, and their subsequent improvement to take into account test results. In decision-making, systems analysis narrows in on a solution by learning from previous analyses and, over time, from the effects of the implementation of portions of a system under development The decision process is a learning process. In the search

for the best solution, as in the search for a scientific truth, preliminary schemes must be revised in the light of new insights obtained as analysis proceeds or implementation takes place.

In systems analysis, the hypotheses about the behavior of the world are known as models. They must not only describe the interactions between the complex factors of the environment which will load the system, but must also identify the causal dependencies between these factors so that the analyst can correctly perceive the effect of substantial changes introduced by large-scale projects. Because models are the means whereby the decision-maker can trace out the consequences of potential solutions, they are central to the process.

The systematic development of good behavioral models should therefore be an inherent part of large-scale analyses. Following the scientific method, these models should be validated in the usual scientific way. As shown in Figure 1, this

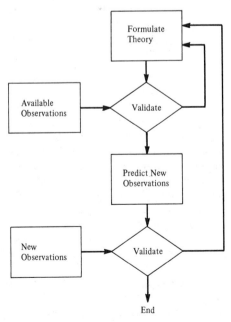

Figure 1. The Scientific Method.

can be visualized as a four-step process: (1) the formulation of a theory or model; (2) initial verification by comparison with available observations; (3) use of the theory to predict results for new situations; and (4) refinement of the model until behavior can confidently be predicted within the margin of error expected from the imprecision of the observations.

To obtain good analytic models, it is important to ensure continuous feedback between the analysis and the implementation phases of system development. In this context, master planning is definitely unscientific insofar as it rigidly adheres to preconceived solutions rather than adapts to newly perceived requirements. Failure to recognize the continuing need for up-to-date representations of the forces that will act upon proposed systems leads to neglect of the crucial feedback loops. Inattentive analysts then find that their work degenerates and the use of the model in the analysis becomes a sterile sequence of mathematical manipulations.

the basic steps

For the purposes of presentation, the systems analysis procedure can be represented in five fundamental steps: (1) definition of objectives, (2) formulation of measures of effectiveness, (3) generation of alternatives, (4) evaluation of alternatives, and (5) selection of preferred alternatives. This breakdown is a useful means of establishing a clear perspective of the process, although a simple summary of this sort cannot fully describe all the elements of a complex analysis. The intent here is to present a perspective—to provide a conceptual framework.

Definition of Objectives. No logical analysis can proceed far without precise, explicit statements of purpose. Any coherent plan entails certain consequences

which imply a system of values. These values are nothing less than an image of the objectives which the analyst may or may not have made clear to himself or anyone else. A man's plans imply his purpose just as thoroughly as his deeds speak for his character. All analyses are based upon some set of objectives, and it seems better by far to define them openly.

If the analyst were working solely for his own edification, it would be of little consequence whether or not his goals were hidden. But he rarely works only for himself; his investigations are generally made for clients who have their own purpose in mind. Before making any decisions, they will want to know what the implications of their objectives are and how the analyst has taken them into account. The analyst has a professional obligation to see that his studies are discussed intelligently and that they serve as the basis for sound decisions. For both reasons, he should be as clear as possible about his assumptions.

Much of the value of systems analysis lies in the identification of objectives and the clarification of issues, not in their concealment. This truism would hardly be worth stating if it were not ignored so frequently. In the systems design courses at MIT, for example, many students initially react to problems in a Pavlovian fashion. "Goals," they say, "Who needs them? Let's just get to work and design!" This kind of response is not limited to neophytes; professionals often express similar feelings.

A major part of the analyst's job is to challenge loosely defined goals and identify the fundamental purpose of a system. Systems analysis, by closely examining objectives, often restates problems in a way which permits substantial economies or increases in efficiency.

The analyst must frequently contend with substantially different kinds of objectives. According to Marglin [3], one can distinguish between the following principal classes of goals: (1) pure economic efficiency measured by return on investment without regard to the recipient or the cost; (2) redistribution of income through the promotion of certain public interests at the expense of others; (3) fulfillment of ends which are not justifiable on economic grounds but which provide other worthwhile benefits.

Each of these objectives has its own merits and must be considered by its own criteria. The designer should, however, always be suspicious of economically unjustifiable goals. While resources are allocated to them each day, all too often the promoters of such projects try to cloak them in "the public interest." It is extremely difficult to distinguish between meritorious and spurious appeals to the public interest, and the analyst should beware.

Formulation of Measures of Effectiveness. The ultimate purpose of the analysis process is to develop an appreciation for the relative effectiveness with which selected alternatives meet stated objectives. Measures of effectiveness must therefore be defined, and care must be taken to ensure that they are appropriate. The choice of measures of effectiveness is crucial because they determine, to a great extent, the final analysis. The merits of each possible configuration of a system may appear different from different points of view. What may seem most advantageous from one standpoint may not be so from another; thus the selection of the preferred decision alternative may hinge on the choice of the measures of effectiveness.

The influence of the effectiveness measures on the final decision can be illustrated by a simple example. Suppose an inexpensive mass transportation system must be designed. How should its costs be measured so that its effectiveness can be evaluated? In terms of dollars per passenger-mile? Dollars per ride? Or perhaps per vehicle-mile? Each of these quantities could be and has been used to measure the efficiency of transportation systems. The cost per passenger-mile measure would favor long, high-density hauls where overhead could be shared over many trips. Use of cost per ride as an index would, on the other hand, lead to the definition of a dense, closely spaced network. Finally, consideration of the costs per vehicle promotes small vehicles. The choice of the measure of effectiveness will, in this case, represent a design decision. It is therefore necessary to give considerable thought to this selection.

Further complexities are introduced into the choice of the measures of effectiveness because of the frequent non-linear relationship between these measures and the values they are intended to represent. Indeed, the utilities associated with each unit of performance or achievement may not be identical. The value of the first plate of food given to a starving man is, for example, clearly far greater than the fourth or fifth. In practical analyses, therefore, limits and ranges will often have to be applied to the measures of effectiveness.

Generation of Alternatives. Since the overall purpose of analysis is the discovery and specification of preferred solutions, it follows that the analyst should devote considerable effort to the exploration of a wide range of possible solutions. The questions are: How shall they be identified? In what order? How many and which ones should be looked at? To what degree?

Except for the most restricted problems for which a closed mathematical formulation is available, it appears neither practical nor reasonable to consider all possibilities. The human mind can always conjure up a new variant beyond any already devised. Even if it were feasible to think of all variations, common sense suggests that the investigation of all alternatives is not worthwhile—some are not sufficiently different to warrant separate treatment and some are clearly dominated by others.

Because of limited resources, the analyst must be discriminating in his choice of alternatives to consider. It is important to determine the sensitivity of an alternative to changes in its major parameters and assumptions. Having done so, the analyst should proceed with a detailed examination of the most attractive alternatives according to the following principles:

1. The major analytical effort should be devoted to those alternatives which have been shown to be most productive.

2. The total effort spent on the analysis should not exceed its expected benefits. Before the analyst can evaluate alternatives, he must be able to generate them. This process involves identification of classes of solutions and examination of solutions in a given class. Leaving aside the semantic issue of what might constitute a class, it is useful to focus on two rather different approaches to search procedures.

The first is a deliberate attempt to stretch one's mind in an effort to identify all relevant kinds of solutions. For instance, if the problem were to ease a housing shortage, it might be desirable to look not only at different forms of housing that might be built, but also at ways to encourage the relocation of people to areas of housing surplus. The need for imagination in the generation of alternatives is explicitly stated here because its lack is a common defect of many analyses.

The second general approach to the generation of alternatives consists of a deliberate definition of possibilities which exhaust the most attractive variations of a particular kind of solution. Extending the illustration of the housing problem, it would be desirable, for example, to consider in detail the advantages of the many possible forms of housing that might be built. This is the kind of task most readily done by computer, which can easily change discrete variables one at a time so that all of the possible combinations are considered.

In closing this important but necessarily intuitive section, it seems useful to state clearly the desirability of considering more rather than fewer alternatives. The development of computers has enormously increased the designer's ability to do this, and has thereby made it possible for analysts to generate comprehensive studies in an effective, orderly fashion. Indeed, a deliberate generation of a wide range of choices is an essential component of systems analysis.

Evaluation of Alternatives. It is necessary to distinguish between the evaluation of each alternative and the selection of a final solution. In practice, this distinction is generally not made and, as a consequence, alternatives are rarely given full consideration in relation to stated objectives.

The evaluation process is simply the identification and measurement, in light of defined goals, of the effects of each alternative. Selection, on the other hand, is an examination of these effects, a comparison of their relative values, and a choice of that alternative which moves the decision-maker closest to his desired ends. As defined here, evaluation is essentially a mechanical process and selection is an exercise of judgment. The distinction highlights the delicate nature of making the final choice.

Selection. Selection is the task of balancing consequences. It applies value judgments to the effects of each alternative as determined in the evaluation process. Selection must consider the distribution of costs and benefits among all groups affected by a decision. Simple, common-sense equality requires that benefits not accrue to one group at the expense of another; the political viability of a decision often depends on an even distribution of costs and benefits. A good assessment of the cost/benefit distribution can often be

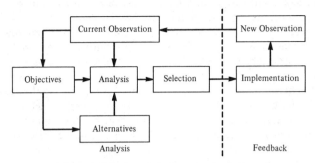

Figure 2. Dynamic Systems Analysis.

made with the use of impact-incidence matrices [1 and 2].

The selection process is not a technical one. The analyst's role is precisely that of strengthening the decision process by removing as many technical uncertainties as possible. Once all issues and alternatives have thus been defined, the decision-maker is free to exercise his selective judgment.

feedback

Feedback mechanisms are fundamental to any process based upon the scientific method. The general procedures presented above represent one phase of a continuing process. Since the time required to implement a large-scale project is usually long and full of uncertainties, the initial analysis results in only a preliminary approximation of the total system to be examined. It is therefore necessary to refine the plan as projects are installed and uncertainties resolved. The planning and execution phases of a project can be seen as parts of the continuous analysis process. Periodic re-analysis is desirable for the same reason that multistage control is required for any continuous production process—it is the only way to obtain optimal results in a changing environment. Viewed another

way, each step in the implementation of a plan is an experiment which, by eliminating some uncertainties, defines a new set of conditions in which to reformulate the analysis.

The role of feedback in systems analysis is shown in Figure 2. The portion on the left represents the five steps of systems analysis already suggested. The portion on the right indicates the dynamic feedback elements. The figure illustrates that the decision-making process can, in a sense, be considered as an ordered information flow. This concept is particularly useful in the structuring of work teams for large-scale analysis and design projects.

issues

The five steps of systems analysis provide a useful way in which to grasp some essential components of the process, but do not by any means describe it in its full complexity. Having submerged many of the difficult issues in order to clarify major concepts, let us now surface them. The questions raised below form the central core of the disagreements that arise over the process of systems analysis. They must be faced directly.

First, we must ask how objectives are established. Is there ever a well-defined set of goals on which consensus exists? To what extent does a client or organization have the technical capability to formulate goals which are relevant to the design of a system? Should the analyst accept objectives as stated? Or does he have a responsibility to question them? And if so, how and to what extent?

Second, what measures of effectiveness are pertinent to any given set of objectives? On what kind of scale should they be measured? How do the selected measures themselves bias the results of an analysis? The choice of criteria for the evaluation is not a trivial exercise, but one that vitally affects the outcome of the analysis.

Third, how does one proceed to generate alternatives efficiently? How can one best organize this search process? Simply varying elements of a system bit by bit will produce several alternatives, but will they be significantly different? Does such an approach use analysis resources effectively? Will it miss desirable possibilities altogether? Most importantly, how can imaginative, innovative approaches be stimulated?

Fourth, what models should we choose to estimate future behavior? How should they be built and how does this construction prejudice the outcome of the analysis? How do simplifying assumptions influence a particular study, and which ones should be made? By what criteria should they be judged and how shall they be refined? The behavior and performance of the models is especially sensitive since it is the heart of an analysis.

Finally, how should the relative importance of the several objectives be weighed, and how should the tradeoffs be made? How shall the differential impacts of the alternatives be represented and by what mechanism shall they be balanced? The selection process, representing the culmination of informed opinion, is always potentially controversial. While many issues on other counts may be amenable to purely theoretical solutions,

many of the factors influencing choice are subjective.

Because a set of alternatives depends upon relatively undefinable values, the final selection process can be quantified and made automatic only at great risk. It is highly improbable that any analyst can accurately foresee—let alone quantify—the relative importance decision-makers will eventually ascribe to each of the several economic, social, and other factors to be considered. It is perhaps best, therefore, for the systems analyst to recognize that his most appropriate function is to present decision-makers with an attractive set of alternatives together with an explicit identification of their consequences rather than with a single solution.

references

1. Hill, M. "A Goals-Achievement Matrix for Evaluating Alternative Plans," *Journal of the American Institute of Planners*, Vol. 34, no. 1 (January 1968), pp. 19–28. Also: Comment by J. E. Brandl and Rejoinder by Hill, Vol. 35, no. 2 (March 1969), pp. 139–142.

2. Manheim, M. L., and Hall, F. "Abstract Representation of Goals—A Method for Making Decisions in Complex Problems." New York Academy of Sciences, *Proceedings, 1967 Transportation Engineering Conference.*

3. Marglin, S. *Approaches to Dynamic Investment Planning.* Amsterdam, North-Holland Publishing Co., 1963.

additional sources

Ackoff, R. L. *Scientific Method: Optimizing Applied Research Decisions.* New York, Wiley, 1962.

de Neufville, R. "Systems Analysis of New York City's Primary Water Supply System." In: *Proceedings, Urban Systems Symposium.* New York, Association for Computing Machinery, October 1969.

Hitch, C. *Decision Making for Defense.* Berkeley, University of California Press, 1965, Lecture 3, pp. 139–142.

Hitch, C., and McKean, R. *The Economics of Defense in the Nuclear Age.* New York, Atheneum, 1965, Chapter 8, pp. 133–158.

Kaplan, A. *The Conduct of Inquiry.* San Francisco, Chandler Publishing Co., 1964.

Manheim, M. L. *Hierarchical Structure: A Model Design and Planning Process.* Cambridge, Mass., MIT Press, 1966.

Optner, S. *Systems Analysis for Business Management.* Englewood Cliffs, N.J., Prentice-Hall, 1968, Chapter 1, pp. 3–20.

Quade, E. *Analysis for Military Decisions.* Chicago, Rand McNally, 1967, Chapter 16, pp. 300–316.

Quade, E. "Cost Effectiveness, an Introduction and Overview," *Transportation Journal,* Vol. 5, no. 4, pp. 5–13.

Simon, H. A. *The Science of the Artificial.* Cambridge, Mass., MIT Press, 1969, Chapter 3.

Torgerson, W. S. *Theory and Methods of Scaling.* New York, Wiley, 1958.

35. model-based systems analysis: a methodology and case study*   John F. Rockart

introduction

In the past fifteen years, the computer industry has seen extraordinary changes for the better in hardware development, operating systems, and programming languages. For example, in the hardware area, new circuitry and other techniques have enabled computer performance at equivalent cost to approximately double every year since 1950 [12, p. 32].[1] Operating systems, virtually non-existent in 1953, are now a way of life; they allow the implementation of many applications which were barely imagined a dozen years ago.

In addition, the move from machine languages and basic assembly languages to higher level languages has reduced considerably the time necessary to translate from human-sensible program specifications to machine-sensible code.

Unfortunately, improvements in the "front end" of the process of converting information systems from manual to machine processing have been almost negligible. This front end, the processes of systems analysis and design, has been rather sadly left without major changes in approach or methodology throughout the years. I state nothing new. Moravec voiced this same complaint in 1965:

Analyzing a corporate data system is still a primitive process. Although the computer has revolutionized data systems in the past decade, there has been no corresponding revolution in the procedures of

Reprinted from *Industrial Management Review*, 11, No. 2 (Winter 1970), pp. 1–14, with permission of the publisher.

* The author thanks Professor David N. Ness for his helpful comments.

[1] See Knight (12), p. 32.

installing and operating them. The rationale for determining what data to analyze and how to go about it and the basic techniques for interviewing, documenting, flow charting, and analyzing have changed little since the advent of the computer. Indeed, they have not changed greatly since the nineteenth century."[2]

More recently, Canning has pointed to the "painfully slow response" to management needs provided by the current techniques of systems analysis and design.[3] Nor are these two alone in their comments. Words like "cumbersome tools" and "the tendency to simply copy the old system over into the new" are sprinkled through the bulk of the literature on the subject.

Today, most of the more common traditional programmed[4] functions of business management, such as payroll and order entry, have been translated into computer processing. To handle new and less well understood functions, which are now of greater interest, the old techniques of systems analysis and design are inadequate. In order for systems analysis and design to perform effectively in these areas, a new framework is necessary. The model-based systems design as espoused by Carroll[5] and others appears to be one key to innovation and greater certainty of results in the fabrication of a new system.

The step preceding the design step in the data processing conversion process is, however, also in need of a new framework. It is this initial systems analysis step (sometimes referred to as the "systems study") with which this paper is concerned. After a discussion of existing conventional systems analysis theory and tools, a three-pronged, model-based, systems analysis theory will be presented.

[2] See (16), p. 127.
[3] See (6), p. 373.
[4] In the sense of programmed versus non-programmed functions as described by Simon (22), p. 5.
[5] See (4), p. 158.

conventional systems analysis

First, let us pause to establish some definitions. In general, the process of converting from a manual system to an automated one has been divided into three steps, systems analysis, system design, and programming. "Analysis . . . is finding out *what* is to be done; design is finding out *how* it should be done; programming is *making* the specified system a reality."[6] In practice, the distinction is not as clear cut. "As we know, the people called systems analysts actually do some of the work called systems design and, in some cases, so do the programmers."[7] There is extensive interaction between phases of the process; however, the analysis function, no matter when performed, is clear. It "is restricted to fact-finding and to examining systems to learn how they work. . . ."[8]

Conventional analysis of information systems is described in varying ways by different authors.[9] They generally agree, however, that the process is a series of steps dominated by interviews of operating personnel and data collection in the area to be studied. Typical of these formulations is a five-step program for the system analyst presented by Gregory and Van Horne. They suggest that the systems analyst should:

First, *obtain facts* by interviewing people and observing activities about the events—their type, volume, and timing—that lead to the origination of documents, maintenance of files, issuance of reports, processing steps done at each work station, and flow of documents between stations.

[6] See Scharf (21), pp. 57–59.
[7] See Scharf (21), p. 59.
[8] See Gregory (10), p. 175.
[9] See, for example: Awad (3), pp. 402–406; Langefors (14), p. 34; Moravec (16), p. 134; Optner (17), p. 52; Withington (24), pp. 115–118.

Second, *collect sample copies* of filled-in documents . . .

Third, *study processing operations* to learn the how and why of every document that each person receives or issues . . .

Fourth, *organize the facts* obtained into flow charts, flow lists or other suitable form to trace the path of data from origin, through each stage of communication and processing, into files, and out of files to reports.

Fifth, *interview each user* of documents and reports to learn what information he uses in his work and what he thinks he needs.[10]

To assist him in studying a system, the information system analyst has conventionally had a limited kit of tools and techniques. In the last few years, this kit has been expanded slightly, primarily by adding the tool of simulation, but the methodology of systems analysis has remained much the same. The system analyst's current tool bag contains the following:

Data Gathering Techniques. Most authors consider *interviews* to be the most "fruitful" form of securing information.[11] Drawbacks in this technique are fully recognized. Instructions on interviewing are usually laden with the language of social and personal psychology. Analysts have been warned that "personal interviews can become confused, redundant, and time-consuming . . . The position and personality of the person being interviewed can inject a pronounced bias. . . ."[12] Despite these drawbacks, and for lack of a better mechanism, interviews have remained the most important tool in systems analysis.

During the past decade and a half, a plethora of special *data collection forms* to assist in systems analysis have been devised and exhibited. In general, these forms present a uniform method for listing the contents of documents worked upon at a particular clerical station and for noting the volume of each document.

One helpful technique which results in a compact portrayal of the data items utilized in a system is the *input-output (I/O) chart*.[13] The use of I/O charts leads to an identification of the significant data items in the particular system being analyzed, and allows the elimination of redundant data item inputs. I/O charts also focus attention on often-used permanent types of information which should be stored on a master file.[14]

It has long been recognized that a relatively few, well-chosen observations will permit inferences to be drawn regarding the total population from which the sample was drawn. In order to reduce system study costs, *statistical sampling techniques* have necessarily been utilized.

As a last resort, where the above techniques have been unsuccessful in gathering data, the analyst often has turned to his data gathering tool of last resort— *estimating*. Not much is written about this tool, but it is often used.

Data Presentation Techniques. Two techniques are used by systems analysts to describe the logical flow of the procedures that have been studied. The most widespread is *flow charting*. The other major technique utilized by systems analysts to exhibit procedural flows is the *decision table*. The popularity of decision tables is due to three factors. They are compact. They are an important aid for the programmer since the program logic is neatly laid out. Finally, they can be translated into some machine languages automatically, thus eliminating further programming steps.

The most recent weapon which has been added to the system analyst's limited arsenal is that of *simulation*. Although

---

[10] See (8), pp. 177–178.
[11] For example, see Glans (9), p. 45.
[12] See Optner (17), pp. 53–54.

[13] For an example, see Evans (8), p. 98.
[14] See Evans (8), pp. 92–104.

primarily reported as a tool for systems design,[15] simulation is also valuable in the analysis process. Systems which are not completely understood can be simulated using the data obtained in the system study. If the parts as analyzed can be synthesized into an accurate working simulation of the system, the inference can be drawn that the analyst has succeeded in the comprehension of the system.

model-based systems analysis

For nearly two decades, the above tools and techniques have been used to answer the question, "How does one go about the process of information systems analysis." Their weakness, however, is that the significant questions in the systems study field are not begun with the interrogative "how" but rather with "what." The truly serious questions for the systems analyst are "*What* should I look at?" and "*What* is the best approach to understanding this system?"

These questions are best answered by turning to model-based systems analysis. The analyst who has a clear model of the area he is researching will do a faster and more effective job of systems analysis. The importance of this approach has been suggested by Pounds.[16] Concerned with the question of how managers determine which problems they must act upon, he postulates that managers have models which they compare with the existing real world situation at a particular time. The manager notes the existence of a problem when significant differences are seen between the actual situation and the model Pounds suggests that four major types of models are used by managers: historical models, planning models, other people's models, and extraorganizational models.

[15] See Carroll (4) and Kriebal (13), p. 385.
[16] See Pounds (18).

A simple example of a planning model is the budget. If a manager finds that he has spent $100,000 for direct labor in a period during which only $80,000 was budgeted, he notes the existence of a problem.

The system study is, to a great degree, a problem-finding process. The goals of the process (the design of a more effective and efficient system) are best served if the primary view is that of a Poundsian problem-finding approach. Where the study is merely seen as "finding out how the current system can best be computerized," important dimensions of the process can be overlooked. Model-based, problem-finding, systems analysis assists in ensuring (1) that no important areas of the system are overlooked, (2) that deficiencies in the current process are identified and improved, and (3) that the information system is designed to be able to adjust to and take advantage of improvements in the basic process as they are carried out.

Traditional Use of Same-Application Models. Although not formally labeled as such, same-application models have provided the framework for much traditional systems analysis. These models have been introduced into the analysis-design-programming continuum in one or more of the following ways:

1. A computer equipment salesman has provided documentation of the same application as performed in a similar company.

2. An application program has been investigated to ascertain the logic used, to "look for good ideas," and to ensure that no vital area or benefit of computerizing the system has been overlooked.

3. The systems men have visited other installations to see a similar application and to question the methodology used in designing the system.

4. The manufacturer's systems engi-

neers or consultants with experience in the same application area have been called upon to assist in the analysis and design process.

Each of these steps makes use of a model of the same application area. The systems analysis, as well as the design, process followed by a company has often been significantly altered through contact with these models.

Use of "Internalized" Models in the Marketing Area. Systems analysis in marketing differs significantly from applications in other areas. Until recently, the necessary data to aid marketing management were uncertain and the systems required to process them in more than rudimentary form had not yet been designed. With the exception of some retrospective sales analysis reports, little had been done to aid the marketing manager. The pioneers in the field had to develop new approaches. One of these was model-based. Using the *internalized* market models of top managers as a starting point, and simulation as a tool, Amstutz and his co-workers were able to perform effective systems analysis in a highly unstructured area.[17]

Model-Based Systems Analysis in Newer Application Areas. Yet a third model-based approach can be utilized for other application areas which are not well defined—especially those outside the traditional scope of industrial applications. Models of similar processes which have been thoroughly researched and developed in the industrial sphere can be applied to similar processes in the increasingly important sectors of medicine, education, and government.

In areas where little attention has been given to the management process in the past, a suitable perspective on the process

[17] See Amstutz (1).

is often lacking. Appropriate models, which are after all only structures from which to view a particular situation, can provide this perspective. Their greatest strength lies in assisting the systems man to stand back from the process he is analyzing and gain perspective on *all* important aspects.[18] The tendency merely to automate the current system can thus be countered.

There are subsidiary reasons for the systems analyst to study all possible perspective-giving normative models before analyzing an area. Models assist in developing:

1. Some insight into the most efficient overall plan for the study.
2. Better initial communication with personnel within the department(s) studied.
3. An ability to ensure that parts of the system which are highlighted in the models are not overlooked. In effect, a "check list" of activities which should be studied is developed.
4. Possible structures to guide the design process when the emphasis is shifted from systems analysis to systems design.

the case study

The model-based, problem-finding, system analysis technique was used at the Lahey Clinic in Boston to study the patient appointment scheduling system. The Lahey is a distinguished group medical practice of approximately 100 doctors. Its primary service is an "out-patient" or ambulatory

[18] Langefors (14), p. 49, implicitly recognizes this need for additional frames of reference: "People tend to neglect the importance or the existence of things they are not able to see or perceive." Zannetos (25), p. 21, has also suggested that normative models be given greater importance in management systems determination.

practice which is, in effect, a collection of doctors' offices together with the necessary facilities to perform medical tests.

The area investigated was that of reserving time for patients. This function, which fits into Anthony's category of an operational control system,[19] is performed primarily by a department called the Central Appointment Office (CAO). A group of 25 secretaries schedules appointments for the clinic's physicians and for a few major medical tests. An attempt is made to schedule patients for all the physicians whom the secretary believes the patient should see. The choice of departments and doctors is dictated by a set of rules developed by clinic medical management.

The scheduling of tests by the CAO is quite limited. In general, only a half dozen major, time-consuming tests, such as electrocardiograms, electroencephalograms, and intravenous pyelograms are scheduled. The scheduling of doctors is, however, extensive. Not only does the CAO schedule patients to one or more of the 12 major departments (e.g., general surgery, neurosurgery, urology, internal medicine), but it also attempts to schedule the patient to the appropriate subspecialty within a department (e.g., within internal medicine, to sub-specialties such as cardiac, vascular). Furthermore, an effort is made to steer specific patients to particular sub-subspecialists who are interested and expert in one disease or particular area.

In all cases, the appointment secretary must select from an inventory of available doctors and test times a feasible and hopefully optimal series of appointments for a patient.[20] The clinic's management originally viewed the problem as akin to

[19] See Anthony (2).
[20] The schedule should be "optimal" in terms of choosing the correct doctors and tests while minimizing the patient's time spent at the clinic in the diagnostic process.

the airlines reservation process, and the initial systems effort was in these terms.

The Problem in Brief. It became clear early in the feasibility study that the problem was quite complex. Each patient who enters the clinic has a unique problem which requires a particular set of specialists and a specific set of test facilities. The problem of determining exactly which physicians and major tests should be scheduled, *and* in which order these should be scheduled, appears to be a very difficult task for a group of lay secretaries. Yet the secretaries *were* able to build a schedule for each patient.

In making these choices, the appointment secretaries faced a major dilemma. On the one hand, if the secretary scheduled the patient to see more doctors than he required, there was a high probability that the first doctor to see the patient would cancel the excess appointments, and that the suddenly released doctor time would not be used by other patients. There is no backlog of patients waiting to be moved up automatically in the queue for a doctor if another patient's appointment is cancelled. On the other horn of the dilemma, if the patient is scheduled to see fewer doctors than necessary, it is quite possible that the *additional* doctors for whom the patient should have been scheduled will be booked completely on the day the patient enters the clinic. If the patient is from out of town, he may have to extend his stay in a hotel; if he is a local patient, he may have to make another trip to the clinic.

The initial model, a simple reservations system, appeared too limited to deal with what was, in effect, a major scheduling problem. Two other models appeared to be more applicable on an a priori basis. The first was of the traditional type—a composite model drawn from the study of systems utilized by other group practices. The second was an industrial job shop scheduling model.

The "Other Clinic" Simple Scheduling

Model. On the surface, the process of scheduling patients through a multiple-specialist medical practice appears to be fraught with uncertainty. "In the general case involving a new patient, a nervous and perhaps somewhat embarrassed prospective patient attempts to explain often vague symptoms over the telephone to a secretary who has had minimal, if any, medical training. The secretary must then translate this dubious evidence into a series of appointments for the patient with the correct specialists for the correct amount of time for each visit."[21] These evident inherent difficulties in scheduling doctors have led most multi-specialist clinics to make the decision that uncertainties are not to be dealt with at the clerical level. The result has been a straightforward scheduling model utilized at most other clinics. The patient arrives at the clinic scheduled to see an initial physician. The remainder of the routing is performed by the first doctor whom the patient sees. The routing is done only after the patient has been given a complete physical examination by the doctor. As a result, the doctor is the scheduler. And the scheduling is done on the day that the patient arrives at the clinic. Since there is no need for one group of secretaries to have access to all the appointment cards (so that they can preschedule patients to all necessary physicians), most appointment cards are kept in each physician's location—on a *decentralized* basis.

The Job Shop Model. The process of looking at other clinic appointment systems (i.e., the use of same-industry models) has been hallowed by tradition. The utility of the industrial model chosen, the job shop model, is not as clearly evident. However, upon comparison, the job shop scheduling model appeared to be a good match to the clinical reservation system, now regarded as a scheduling

system. The systems are alike in basic structure. Each is characterized by a set of *facilities* which perform work; a *routing* procedure to direct a set of *items* through the facilities; *precedence relationships* which provide a necessary ordering of facility visits; unique *service times* for the items undergoing processing at a particular facility; *waiting time* during which the item is inactive; and a *basic scheduling point* from which the item's "loading" to the various facilities is offset. Furthermore, both the job shop and clinical scheduling systems have two scheduling modes with regard to time: *static scheduling*, a loading of facilities to some preset limit before the actual day of operation; and *dynamic scheduling*, a continuous rescheduling of facilities which takes into account the latest events and conditions up to the moment each segment of the schedule is executed. Finally, each system has a criterion function, by which its output may be judged.

In order to validate that the job shop model was at least roughly equivalent to the patient scheduling system, some additional comparisons were made for each of these dimensions.

In the job shop, the facilities are a set of machines encompassing various subsets or machine groups. All the machines in a machine group have the same general performance characteristics. In addition, the groups are usually further subdivided. For instance, within a machine group of boring tools, there may be a subgroup of automatic borers, with a setup time that makes them efficient for long runs but not for short jobs. For any operation, one type of machine, not specifically designed for that operation, may be substituted for the specialized machine, with some loss in efficiency.

The facilities in the clinic are basically of two types. They consist of physicians and test facilities. The doctors in a group practice are most often highly specialized.

[21] See Rockart (19), p. 24.

Like the machines of the job shop, there are usually several available with similar specialties; that is, there are "physician groups" just as there are machine groups. In medical practice, physicians are divided among approximately a dozen major specialties, such as orthopedic surgery, internal medicine, urology.

As in the job shop, there are subgroups within these general groups. A notable example is internal medicine, which has such well-recognized subspecialties as cardiac, vascular, hematologic, and thyroid. In addition, however, there are often sub-subspecialists, such as a hematologist particularly concerned with leukemia. Although physicians are somewhat interchangeable, there is some loss in efficiency when a doctor whose prime field is allergy, for example, sees a patient with a thyroid condition—*if the thyroid condition is definite or highly probable.*

The items in the job shop are products that must be developed during their travels through the various machines. The items in the clinic are, quite simply, patients. Just as there is a routing schedule, which moves a product through a machine shop, so there is an appointment schedule, which moves a patient through the clinic. For each patient, there is a given set of doctors whom the patient should see and a preferred series of tests that should be performed on the patient.

The routing procedure in the job shop usually includes rather tightly defined precedence relationships (a product must first be bored, before it can be reamed, before . . ., etc.). There are also many definite precedence relations in the clinic scheduling problem. For example, an appointment with the orthopedic department must be arranged before a barium swallow test is given if both are to take place on the same day. (The reason is that the orthopedic specialist may order roentgenograms that might be obscured by previously ingested barium.)

In the job shop, production time is the time spent at each facility while the product is worked upon. Waiting time is the "dead" time caused by delays due to the unavailability of a machine, the lack of availability of material, or poor scheduling. In general, waiting time involves a cost to the shop without visible progress in the movement of the product toward its completion.

In the clinic, production time is the time spent with each doctor or during the actual performance of each test. Waiting time occurs when the patient is not involved in either of the activities listed under production time. In general, the cost of this time to the clinic is minimal as long as the waiting is kept below a certain threshold. Above that threshold, the cost may rise dramatically as patients become bored, nervous, unhappy and, ultimately, walk out of the clinic.

In the job shop, the due date is usually the basic scheduling point, at least for the original schedule. The facilities are usually scheduled in reverse order to that on the routing sheet, taking into account the production time necessary at each facility and the availability of each facility.[22] In the clinic, the basic scheduling point is usually the entry time. The routing determined for the patient is scheduled forward from this entry time. As with due dates in the job shop, this basic scheduling point can be negotiated.

To date, most formal job shop scheduling has been static scheduling, primarily the loading of machines by means of Gantt charts. Recently, computers have made centralized dynamic scheduling possible. Factors such as machine breakdowns, poor materials, and defective items that test as unacceptable, render the current shop schedule no longer optimal— and possibly not feasible. For these reasons, which reflect the uncertainties in

[22] See Emery (7).

production, schedules must be reassessed dynamically.

Like the job shop, patient scheduling has static and dynamic versions. At the present time, almost all patient scheduling is of the static variety. However, the need for dynamic rescheduling is also present. Static schedules quickly decay because of service-time variations, patient no-shows, physicians' lateness, and other factors.

The criterion function in the job shop varies from shop to shop. In general it includes weights for such factors as job tardiness, inventory costs, costs of hiring and firing, overtime costs, and other factors. There is also a criterion function for the patient scheduling problem. It is a combination of several variables with the weighting of each differing with diverse managers. The prime variables for the clinic criterion function are doctor idle time, patient waiting time, and the cost of the scheduling system.

problem finding

An analysis of possible problem areas at the clinic, detected by comparing the two models with the actual system, revealed some significant potential problems. Pounds states that "... the word 'problem' is associated with the difference between some existing situation and some desired situation."[23] This definition can be broadened to suggest that even if it is not certain that another specific situation is "desired," the search for problems can fruitfully take place when differences are noted between an existing and a desired situation. The difference between the systems portrayed by the two models and the Lahey Clinic system were numerous.

Three major differences were noted between the "other clinic" model and the Lahey Clinic system. First, the "other clinic" model did not incorporate multiple-appointment clerical routing of patients; the Lahey system included extensive clerical routing through a series of carefully chosen specialists. Second, the "other clinic" clerical scheduling system was decentralized, while the Lahey system was based on a centralized CAO. Finally, the scheduling rules in the other system, because of its nature, were simple and straightforward; in the Lahey system, they were extremely complex.

The differences between the Lahey scheduling system and the job shop model were more extensive, primarily because in the medical situation we are dealing with human beings, not machinery and raw materials. One difference existed in the routing area. In the job shop, the routing of a product through machines is fairly easily determined. In the medical case, the routing was seen to be very uncertain and heavily dependent upon good communication of symptoms by the patient and efficient interpretation of those symptoms by the scheduler.

Another apparent major difference existed in the area of scheduling production time. In general, a machine or class of machines can be expected to perform its assigned tasks at a certain rate. The complex relationship between physician and patient, however, appeared to make scheduling the correct amount of "production" time for each patient appointment very uncertain.

A third difference appeared in the handling of clerical work. An increasing number of industrial organizations are now performing job shop scheduling by computer. As Emery has pointed out, even Gantt chart-like, computer-assisted static scheduling in the manufacturing area helps to avoid infeasible loads, decreases clerical errors, and increases the ability to manipulate extensive data files.[24] In addition, a dynamic computer scheduling

---

[23] See (18), p. 5.

[24] See Emery (7).

system in an on-line real-time configuration has the ability to monitor the current situation on the shop floor as well as to react to unpredictable stochastic occurrences, such as machine breakdowns. Rescheduling can take the *current* situation into account. The Lahey scheduling system, however, was a manual system incapable of reacting to dynamic situations.

Problem-Finding Results. At the conclusion of the systems study, the conventional volume figures had been gathered and data flows recorded. More importantly, 17 major reasons why the actual scheduling system at the Lahey Clinic was less than optimal had been identified. Of these, 13 had been indicated directly by the comparison of the models and the Lahey system. The problems indicated in the static scheduling system by the models/clinic comparison were the need for better definition of service time per patient, the less than optimal routing of patients, the desirability of both centralized and decentralized (from the physician's office) access to the scheduling records, the difficulty of rearranging schedules and the inaccessability of the data base with a manual system, the presence of clerical error, and the incompleteness of current scheduling rules.

In addition, the job shop model had suggested the need to search for stochastic disruptions of the dynamic scheduling system. Among problems found in this area were patient "no-show," physician lateness, patient lateness, late cancellations, and the randomness of patient time with the physician (even assuming better service time projections). The job shop model had also suggested that there could be problems in the area of "visibility" from one service area to another. In the medical setting, this is the problem of determining whether required specialists are available (and which specialist is *most* available) for a necessary additional consultation.

Four problems were not indicated by the models/clinic system comparison. These four were exposed only in the conventional system study. These problems were (1) the distinct differences in the routing of various classes of patients (patients from a distance versus local patients, etc.), (2) the lack of feedback to the appointment secretaries on their scheduling performance, (3) the effect upon the scheduling system of the failure of such other clerical systems as medical record routing, and (4) the uncertainty in the schedules of the time to be allowed for test results to be reported before additional appointments could be scheduled.

conclusions

A model-based, problem-finding, systems analysis technique has been presented which allows the analyst to uncover the major problems in the current system. This technique assists in structuring the environment in which the analyst will work and in avoiding the all too common problem of merely "automating the current misinformation system."

Would all the problems that were indicated by the models have been found if the models had not been utilized? Possibly. If the conventional systems analysis had been approached with imagination, and the signals from the environment correctly evaluated, the same specifications *might* have resulted. However, more than two-thirds of the problems were suggested by the models, and the model-based approach allowed a *much faster* zeroing in on the major problem areas. It provided, in effect, a check-list for the analyst of *what* areas should be investigated. The uncovering of problem areas is therefore made more automatic, less dependent on the talents of a particular analyst. The technique helps to ensure (1) that no important areas of the system are overlooked, (2) that deficiencies in the current process are identified, and (3) that the system is designed to incorporate improvements in the basic process as deficiencies are corrected in each problem area.

references

1. Amstutz, A. E. *Computer Simulation of Competitive Market Response.* Cambridge, Mass., MIT Press, 1967.

2. Anthony, R. *Planning and Control Systems: A Framework for Analysis.* Boston, Harvard Business School Division of Research, 1965.

3. *Business Data Processing.* Englewood Cliffs, N.J., Prentice-Hall, 1968.

4. Carroll, D. C. "Implications of On-line, Real-time Systems." In: C. A. Myers (ed.), *The Impact of Computers on Management*, pp. 140–167. Cambridge, Mass., MIT Press, 1967.

5. Carroll, D. C. "On the Structure of Operational Control Systems." In: J. F. Pierce (ed.), *Operations Research and the Design of Management Information Systems*, pp. 391–415. New York, Technical Association of the Pulp and Paper Industry, 1967.

6. Canning, R. G. "Coming Changes in System Analysis and Design," *Proceedings of 21st National Conference, Association for Computing Machinery*, Washington, D.C., Thompson Book Company, 1966.

7. Emery, J. C. "An Approach to Job Shop Scheduling Using a Large-Scale Computer," *Industrial Management Review*, Vol. 3, no. 1 (Fall 1961), pp. 78–96.

8. Evans, M. K., and Hague, L. R. "Master Plan for Information Systems," *Harvard Business Review*, Vol. 40, no. 1 (January–February 1962), pp. 92–104.

9. Glans, T. B., *et al. Management Systems.* New York, Holt, Rinehart & Winston, 1968.

10. Gregory, R. H., and Van Horne, R. L. *Automatic Data-Processing Systems.* Belmont, Calif., Wadsworth Publishing Co., 1963.

11. IBM. "*Data Collection at Barnes Drill Company.*" IBM Application Brief, Form K20-0006; White Plains, N.Y., IBM Data Processing Division.

12. Knight, K. E. "Evolving Computer Performance 1963–67," *Datamation*, Vol. 14, no. 1 (January 1968), pp. 31–35.

13. Kriebel, C. H. "Operations Research in the Design of Management Information Systems." In: J. F. Pierce (ed.), *Operations Research and the Design of Management Information Systems*, pp. 375–390. New York, Technical Association of the Pulp and Paper Industry, 1967.

14. Langefors, B. *Theoretical Analysis of Information Systems*, Vol. I. Lund, Studentlitteratir, 1966.

15. Malcolm, D. R. "Real Time Management Control in a Large Scale Man-Machine System," *Industrial Engineering*, Vol. 11 (March–April 1960), pp. 103–110.

16. Moravec, A. F. "Basic Concepts for Designing a Fundamental Information System." In: P. P. Schoederbeck (ed.), *Management Systems: A Book of Readings*, pp. 127–136. New York, John Wiley & Sons, 1967.

17. Optner, S. L. *System Analysis for Business Management.* Englewood Cliffs, N.J., Prentice-Hall, 1968.

18. Pounds, W. F. "The Process of Problem Finding," *Industrial Management Review*, Vol. 11, no. 1 (Fall 1969), pp. 1–19.

19. Rockart, J. F. "The Medic Center." Unpublished paper; Cambridge,

Mass., MIT Sloan School of Management, 1965.

20. Rockart, J. F., *et al.* "A Symptom Scoring System for Subspecialty Classifications," *Proceedings of the Annual Conference on Engineering in Medicine and Biology*, Houston, 1968.

21. Scharf, T. "Management and the New Software," *Datamation*, Vol. 14, no. 4 (April 1968), pp. 52–59.

22. Simon, H. A. *The New Science of*

Management Decision. New York, Harper and Row, 1960.

23. Sprague, R. E. *Electronic Business Systems*. New York, Ronald Press, 1962.

24. Withington, F. G. *The Use of Computers in Business Organizations*. Reading, Mass., Addison-Wesley, 1966.

25. Zannetos, Z. "Toward Intelligent Management Information Systems," *Industrial Management Review*, Vol. 9, no. 3 (Spring 1968), pp. 21–39.

36. urban planning: ripe for systems analysis
Jerry L. Pollak and Martin I. Taft

Although considerable work has been done on the analysis of transportation, communication, production, law enforcement, resource management, and educational systems, these are but subsystems of the typical urban system. The systems analyst is faced with a complex total system which poses some unique problems. Some of these major problems are:

1. There is no general understanding of what the significant problems are in urban planning.

2. Responsibility and authority are diffused among many planning organizations hindering good communications and cooperation.

3. Independent and reliable criteria for evaluating alternative solutions are hard to establish because of the conflicting interests of the various organizations.

4. Much demographic and other statistical data is in existence but it is often not available when needed.

5. The relationships between variable segments of urban systems are hard to define because of the long periods of time and extraordinarily large sums of money required for testing and verification.

6. Simulation models for urban systems tend to be so large and complex that few organizations have the resources for their development and maintenance. There is also a shortage of trained people who can effectively utilize such models and interpret the results to others.

7. There are as yet no generalized approaches to systematic planning which have found wide acceptance among all interested parties.

Reprinted from *Journal of Systems Management*, 22, No. 1 (January 1971), pp. 12–17, with permission of the publisher.

The following is an overview of the analytical tools and areas in which systems development work must be done.

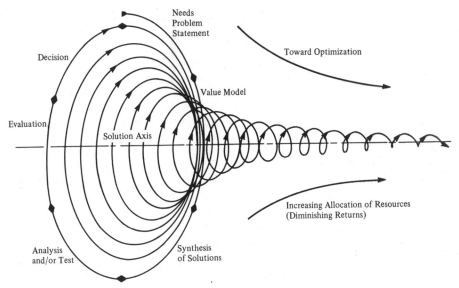

Figure 1. The Problem-Solving Spiral Model.

a general problem-solving model

The process of solving any type of problem may be shown by means of the spiral model (Figure 1). The solution of the problem lies somewhere on the axis of the spiral. The process of solving the problem involves proceeding along the spiral path toward a solution. The solution axis is also a "time" axis. As the spiral converges on the axis in an exponential manner, the ideal solution occurs at an infinite time in the future. Thus, the ideal solution can be reached, providing that the resources and time do not run out. In the real world, one works with limited amounts of money, time, and other resources. So the model indicates that there are "diminishing returns" in the refinement of the solution. Initially great progress is made toward the solution but with each succeeding loop the improvements become smaller and smaller. At some point, it becomes more prudent to allocate resources to a new problem rather than to try to refine the present solution another few percentage points.

The structure of the problem-solving process is often called the "morphology" of the process with every loop of the spiral being characterized by a number of distinct steps. These steps, or activities, are depicted in Figure 2 and are commonly called the "anatomy" of the problem-solving process. Although activities may be traversed in a sequential manner (as shown by the double-lined arrows), it is possible to proceed from any activity to any other activity at any instant in time. The single lines in the diagram indicate some of the alternative paths that may be taken between activities.

the systems design procedure

Figure 3 represents a highly aggregated schematic of the processes involved in the design or redesign of socio-economic systems. This design procedure is an outgrowth of well-established methodologies in the engineering design of complex physical systems. If the system must be designed in its entirety, then the starting point may be as shown in Figure 3. However, in the modification or in the redesign

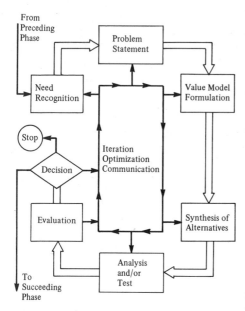

Figure 2. A General Model of the Anatomy (Horizontal Structure) of the Problem-Solving Process.

of an existing system, it is possible to start at any other point in the loop.

In defining the objective functions of the urban system (Step 3) one could maximize the economic value of land in a given sub-section, in relation to the availability of manpower, financial capability of local industry, time and budget allocated for planning, and so forth. Or, for some other problem, given the planning of a low-income neighborhood, the analyst may attempt to minimize the average walking distance covered by the local residents in their everyday activities, such as shopping, schooling, and recreation.

The problem of defining the objective functions is a very difficult one, especially at the beginning of an analysis. This is often due to the lack of the pertinent information. However, tentative generalizations can be made and be refined as the analysis proceeds. The usual procedure is to find one single major objective and

optimize its subject to a series of lesser constraints.

The descriptive model of the system usually consists of a series of generalized block and flow diagrams (Step 6). The block diagrams delineate the control volumes that will be used in the analysis. Each control volume usually represents a subsystem of the entire system; in this case the entire system may be a city and subsystems may be a residential neighborhood, industrial parks, shopping centers, civic monuments, municipal parks, and other kinds of operational entities within the city.

The control volumes represent highly aggregated levels of the system. The control volumes or subsystems measure and control the quantities of people, automobiles, raw materials, and so forth which enter or leave these subsystems, over finite periods of time. Flow diagrams are used to show all of the flows and their interrelationships.

Once the total picture in terms of control volumes is reached, the analyst has an initial concept of all the interrelationships, the questions as to whether the properties of the various flows can be measured in such a way to determine whether the system is achieving its objectives. At this point, chances are that measurement of the quantities which are necessary for the kind of analysis outlined will be unavailable. Therefore, the system switches to a Control Mass Analysis by observing the interactions of a single citizen or a group of citizens within the environment. Theoretically, the answers gained from Control Mass Analysis should be identical to those received from a Control Volumes Analysis. However, the difference in perspective gives a great deal more information and ability to measure things. Ability, for instance, to measure income levels, employment opportunities, average walking or riding distances, or accessibility of recreative facilities.

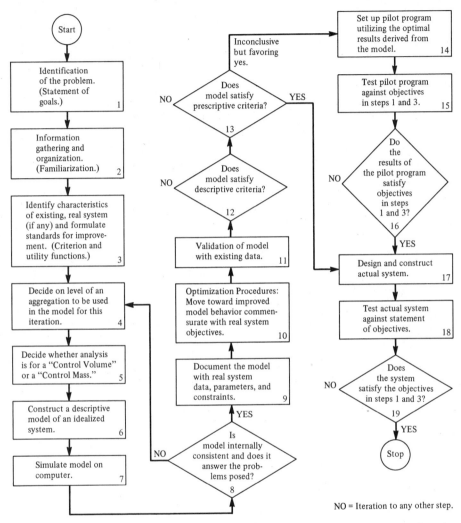

Figure 3. Generalized Systems Design Procedure: A Schematic Representation of the Iterative Process.

If the measurements enable the analyst to set up standards for achieving the objective functions, then he would proceed to the next step in the systems analysis. If not, he returns to the Control Volumes Analysis and deaggregates. The deaggregation process involves breaking down into more and more elemental components each of the subsystems that have already been delineated. Having reached a level of aggregation at which the variables in question cannot only be quantified but also be measured, the analyst is now in the position to develop a mathematical or a computer-based model of the system.

a program planning and evaluation model

The solution of a given problem (Figure 4) begins with a recognition of a need which must be satisfied. There may be a need for new policies, new procedures, replacement of roads or sewers, improved information, or more money. The "need statement" recognizes the problem. The problem definition involves stating what the problem is, who will do it, when it must be completed, and the resources to be allocated to the solution of the problem. The next step, namely the specification of a value system, is often left largely to the imagination.

The long-range goals represent the

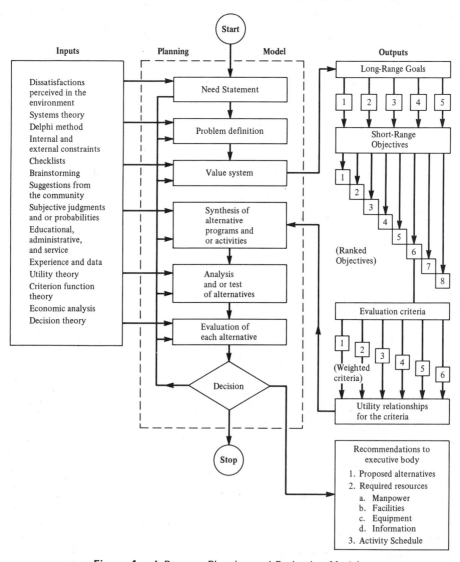

Figure 4. A Program Planning and Evaluation Model.

"directions"; the short-range objectives represent specific steps that must be taken in order to move in the directions of the goals. Usually it is possible to write the objectives in their relative order of importance with respect to achieving the goals. An objective is an activity, a task, or a project which must be completed within a given amount of time with a given set of resources such as manpower facilities, equipment, and information. Some objectives may be achieved sequentially through time while others may be achieved simultaneously or in parallel with each other. The objectives may be thought of as milestones against which progress toward the goals can be measured.

It is important to develop a set of evaluation criteria for each of the short-range objectives. Criteria, such as cost, effectiveness, reliability, attractiveness, and so forth, make it possible to evaluate the relative merits or value of each of the potential solutions to the problem. Since not all of the criteria are equally important in terms of the goals and objectives of the problem solver, they must be weighed relative to each other. For instance, the utility of a freeway may vary inversely as to its costs but directly as to its effectiveness. Furthermore, the relationships between utility and the criteria are usually nonlinear. It is essential to develop such utility relationships and to make them explicit.

Once the value system has been established it is then desirable to consider as many alternative solutions to the problem as possible. The usual tendency is to select one alternative solution and then proceed to carry it out after much work. If this solution proves to be inadequate, another one is attempted. Such a procedure is usually very inefficient. It is suggested that many different alternatives be considered and the ones that are most obviously the least compatible with the long-range goals, objectives, constraints, and avail-

able resources be rejected. Thus it is possible to reduce a large number of alternatives to a small number of realistic ones. Each of these potential solutions may then be analyzed or tested to determine its properties. The important properties are those represented by the evaluation criteria. A rating for each criterion may be obtained by computation, empirical testing, or by utilizing the subjective judgments of one or more individuals.

The evaluation phase of this problem-solving model involves converting each of the ratings into a corresponding utility number and summing[1] all of the utility numbers for a given alternative solution to obtain its total utility to the problem solver. The relative overall utilities of the various solutions may then be compared and the alternative having the highest utility may be selected. In some problems, resources are allocated in direct proportion to the utility of the given project, program or activity.

In Figure 4 it can be seen that the decision-making process offers three major alternatives. First, it is possible that more information is needed before continuing on to another phase of the problem or to another problem, resulting in an iteration to any of the preceding steps. On the other hand, the analyst may decide that all of the work done so far has led to unacceptable alternatives and that the project should be ended. Hence, "stop."

Finally, the analyst may consider that the problem under consideration has been satisfactorily solved, and would submit a set of recommendations to some higher authority or make the required decision. This above set of recommendations typically includes a set of conclusions

---

[1] This procedure requires that the criteria selected be relatively independent of each other. To the extent that they are independent, the additivity concept holds; otherwise it must be considered as a good first approximation.

regarding the alternative solutions that were considered, a detailed projection of the resources required to implement the recommended solution, and a tentative schedule of forthcoming activities.

conclusion

It has been shown that some of the existing problem-solving models of systems analysis can be readily applied in the field of urban planning. What is urgently needed is an intensive continuous dialogue between systems analysts, operations researchers, computer technologists, political scientists, sociologists, economists, architects, educators, and urban planners. Such a dialogue is already occurring on large-scale urban projects, but day-to-day interaction between professionals in diverse fields is yet to come.

management information systems

37. management information system planning for the executive
Paul Siegel

This is the age of specialization. Within the corporation each specialist sees the corporation from his own narrow viewpoint. The production man sees a continuous process from the receipt of materials to the output of products for sale. The marketing man sees an organization in constant competition with other organizations in supplying customer wants and needs. The research and development engineer sees an organization adapting itself through technological innovation. The cost accountant believes that careful control of the cost of all elements contributing to development and sale of a product is a sine qua non of good management. Other managers place their faith in organization charts, systems and procedures, system analyses, models, schedules, PERT charts, and scores of other techniques.

Reprinted from *Managerial Planning*, 19, No. 6 (May–June 1971), pp. 5–14, with permission of the publisher.

All these different people want information systems to help them make decisions. This is why almost all present information systems are application oriented.

To break away from this trend, to rid himself from this fractured approach, and to enable him to see the corporation as an organic whole, the executive must think of the corporation as a business system. To enable him to understand the nature of the corporation so that he can influence the direction of its development, he must study the business system in a manner similar to the way the scientist studies a natural system.

The scientist uses the scientific method. He assumes a hypothesis relating the variables in the system, gathers data about the variables and analyzes them in an attempt to prove or disprove the hypothesis. Though the hypothesis is most often wrong, the scientific investigator learns enough to enable him to modify the hypothesis, repeat the procedure and obtain improved results. He reiterates many times, and with each reiteration he comes a little closer to the truth.

What the scientist can do with a natural system, the executive can do with a business system. Considering the knowledge he has of the corporation, the executive assumes a hypothesis—often called a model—which explains the relationship among variables in the business system. Once he has done this, he needs to arrange to record events and to measure success due to the hypothesis. Success, in this case, means improvement in the executive's control and planning capability. Though the executive may fare no better, and probably worse, than the scientist he still may learn enough to enable him to improve the hypothesis. With enough iterations he may eventually reach the point where he has a dependable rule for decision making. The executive thus has a means of making the business system improve with time.

A good management information system is one which aids the executive in his "experimentation" with the business system. It stores hypotheses, monitors many types of events on various timetables, aggregates the data collected in many ways and compares actual results with those deduced from the hypotheses. This it does at the same time that it aids current decision making with the partially satisfactory hypothesis.

The planning of the management information system must be done by the executive, since he understands the business system best and knows better than anyone how he wants the system to develop. The detailed design of the management information system, however, requires the services of scientists, mathematicians, programmers and system analysts. But these technologists follow the executive's plan, not the other way around.

In what follows, the above thesis of management information system planning is developed in greater detail under the following headings:

1. Nature of Systems.
2. Major Systems of Concern to the Executive.
3. The Business Information System.
4. "Experimental" Technique.
5. Planning and Design.

nature of systems

During the early days of chemistry, chemists studied individual chemical reactions. Progress was slow until Mendeleev uncovered a system: he showed how all the basic elements of matter are related by means of the table of periodic elements. With the aid of this system, chemists discovered many chemical laws. The result has been a proliferation of chemicals, synthetic materials and medicines useful for manufacturing and for the well being of man.

During the early days of astronomy, astronomers made observations of the sun, the moon and the planets. Again, progress was slow until a system was developed: the solar system. Using the solar system, which is based on Kepler's Laws, astronomers were able to learn enough to form a solid foundation for our space program.

As the above two examples show, thinking of systems simplifies generalizations, which in turn improves understanding. This is true, providing we realize that the system is not what is being studied, but that it is a model of the reality under investigation. The solar system does not physically exist. It is an artifact enabling us to see broad relationships among bodies in space.

If we can design a system which is a model of natural phenomena, why not a system which is a model of a task to be executed? Thus, the Apollo engineers have designed a method of landing men on the moon by thinking of a space transportation system. This system is so complex it consists of launching, orbiting, communication, environmental control and many other subsystems.

If we can design a system which is a model of a task to be executed, why not a system which is a model of an organization concerned with accomplishing a task? Thus, we may have a business system, and it too may consist of many subsystems.

Since a system is a model, it must be judged by its usefulness. In science, usefulness of the system is judged by its ability to aid the investigator in discovering natural laws. In engineering, usefulness of the system is judged by its ability to aid the engineer in accomplishing the task. In business, usefulness of the system is judged by its ability to aid the executive in accommodating the business to a changing environment.

A business system is different from other systems in the following three major ways:

1. *The Business System Is Open, Not Closed.* A closed system is one which may be considered to be an entity within itself, without regard to its environment. An open system accepts inputs from its environment, executes a process or group of processes, which produce outputs returned to the environment (Figure 1a). All businesses, except for perhaps some rare monopolies, are definitely open.
2. *The Business System Is Dynamic, Not Static.* In a static system, inputs are received and outputs returned to the environment; there's no relationship between input and output. In a dynamic system there is feedback: outputs are returned and become inputs. This feedback is shown by the bold control loop in Figure 1b. An example of control is quality control: tests are made at the end of a production line to see if the product meets specifications; if it does not, it

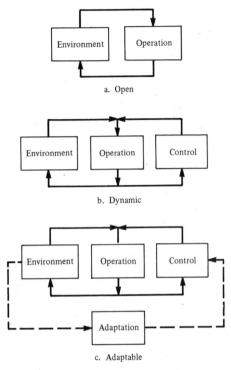

Figure 1. Types of Systems.

is returned and becomes an input for reprocessing.
3. *The Business System Is Adaptable.* Though it may possess feedback for keeping operations under control, the non-adaptable system does not change as its environment changes; after a while it becomes an obsolete dinosaur-type system. An adaptable system studies its environment, predicts the future environment and then tries to make changes, especially to the control loop, which will cause the system to meet the requirements of the future as well as it meets those of the present (Figure 1c).

major systems of concern to the executive

Since a business system is open, dynamic and adaptable it may be represented by the three loops shown in Figure 2: operation, control and adaptability. Because of

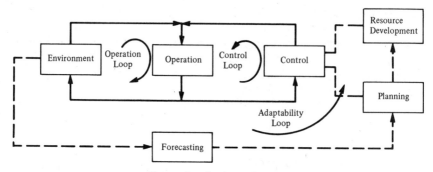

Figure 2. Business System.

its importance, the adaptability box has been expanded into three boxes: forecasting, planning and resource development. Each of the three loops of the business system describes the entire corporation, but each from a different point of view. Contrast this with the boxes on an organization chart which show unrelated pieces of the total organization. Because we are concerned with studying the business system as a viable whole, the three loops make excellent subsystems. In addition, the adaptability system may be expanded into three subsystems, each concerned with one of the major functions comprising adaptability. Thus, the five major subsystems of a business system are:

> Operation.
> Control.
> Forecasting.
> Planning.
> Resource Development.

Each of these is discussed, in turn, as an open, dynamic and adaptable system.

operation system

The Operation System executes all the basic functions of the business system. Some of these functions are primarily concerned with maintaining openness. Among them are purchasing, marketing and distribution. Other functions, such as production and quality control, are concerned with the actual processes performed and in the direct control necessary to keep them going. A third group of functions, such as maintenance and engineering is concerned with improving the Operation System.

Two aspects of the Operation System may be distinguished: the immediate and the long range (Figure 3). The immediate accepts material, supplies, services and money as inputs, and produces outputs in the form of products and services. Resources, such as personnel, equipment, data and finance may be considered as long range inputs and outputs. They contribute to the processes, but over the long run.

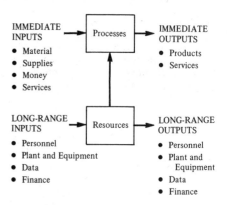

Figure 3. Operation System.

control system

Control consists of monitoring the outputs of the Operation System and then altering its variables to improve Operation System performance. From the broad point of view the Control System includes much more than management. Included in the system are the data gathering by operating personnel and machines. This data is then aggregated into measures of performance of all types in order to determine whether preestablished goals have been met. The Control System also includes analysis of status information to decide upon action and determine if the control loop is operating properly and adapting to new conditions. Communicating decisions and achieving action based upon these decisions are in the control loop too.

forecasting system

The first step in adapting to future contingencies is to forecast the future characteristics of the environment with which the business system will interact. This is the task of the Forecasting System. Again, this system is not as specialized as appears on the surface. As part of the loop there are operating personnel interacting with the environment, such as salesmen and maintenance personnel; engineers studying advanced technology; finance and legal officers involved in government taxation and regulation. People gather data, execute statistical analyses, make forecasts, judge how close to reality the forecasts are, keep the forecasting loop under control in terms of daily needs, and make sure the forecasts improve with time.

planning system

Because of the complexity of the modern business system and because of the rapidity of environmental change, a formalized Planning System is becoming a necessity. Based upon what the Forecasting System tells him of the future, and based on the knowledge he has on how other systems within the business system operate, the planner can define achievable objectives and then decide upon the best strategy for reaching these objectives. To aid him in this task he needs system analysts, operations research people, mathematicians, programmers and other technologists.

Many detailed plans must be designed and executed in order to assure success of the strategic plan. This means that the high level strategic planner must work closely with men at all rungs of the ladder. A properly designed hierarchy of plans has many elements at its lowest level which are specific goals which can be monitored by the Control System. The long range objectives, however, need to be monitored, and the results analyzed at times determined by the planner's judgment. As part of this analysis, he should decide if the planning loop is functioning properly.

resource development system

The most action-oriented subsystem in the adaptability system is the Resource Development System. The Resource Development System takes the long range plans as inputs and develops the resources that the business system needs to meet them.

As previously mentioned, the major resources of the business system are:

> Personnel.
> Plant and Equipment.
> Data.
> Finance.

To meet future personnel needs, it develops hiring, incentive and training programs. To meet future plant and capital equipment needs, it makes investments, merger and divestment decisions. To build its fund of technical data about processes, it does research and development. To improve the business system's capability for accomplishing the previous tasks, it develops a sound financial base.

None of these tasks is more important than the other. They must all be done together or Resource Development will lag.

As with the other systems, Resource Development includes the data gathering, analysis and decision making required to keep it dynamic and adaptable to new circumstances.

business information system

The above five systems taken together comprise the Business System. The Business System itself is embedded within the Environment System; in other words, the Business System serves the needs of the Environment System (Figure 4). In a similar manner, there is a Business Information System embedded within the Business System; it serves the needs of the Business System.

Stated another way, the Business Information System provides for each of the five systems comprising the Business System all the data that must be collected, aggregated and compared; all the alternatives that must be analyzed and evaluated; and all the decisions that must be made and acted upon. In effect, it is the one point where all the systems within the Business System meet, and is therefore the place where the global view of the corporation can be found.

Practically everyone in the Business System interacts with the Business Information System, some as members of one of the major subsystems, others as members of several. To best serve the needs of the Business System, the Business Information System must be dynamic (under a control loop) and adaptable (modifiable) to serve changing system needs. Figure 4 shows another system—the Technological System—as serving the needs of the Business Information System. This Technological System consists of computer and communication hardware and software. The executive need not concern himself with these aspects at all.

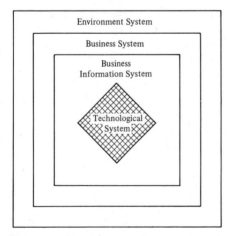

Figure 4. The Information System As Part of Business System.

summary

To summarize, the six major systems of concern to the executive are:

1. *Operation System*—which executes basic functions upon inputs from the environment.
2. *Control System*—which sees that the Operation System functions properly.
3. *Forecasting System*—which forecasts the future state of the Environment System.
4. *Planning System*—which sets objectives and goals to meet the forecasted environment.

5. *Resource Development System*— which develops organizational resources to enable the Business System to adapt to the forecasted environment.

6. *Business Information System*—which models the other five systems in terms of data and procedures necessary to study them.

the business information system

Like the Business System that it serves, the Business Information System may be subdivided, as shown in Figure 5. The part of the Business Information System serving the needs of the Operation System, executes specific data processing tasks. In other words, it is applications oriented. The remainder serves the needs of management in the control and adaptability systems. That is why it is often called the Management Information System (M.I.S.) Because the Control System is less variable and more predefined than the Adaptability System, the portion of the M.I.S. serving its needs is called the Programmed M.I.S. whereas the portion serving the Adapt-ability System is called the Non-programmed M.I.S.

applications information system

The general process flow for a corporation that engineers and produces custom made technical products may be given as in Figure 6. Not all functions are shown. But it can be seen that there is a loop between the environment (*customers*) and the steps in the process executed by the Operation System, and that they are linked by inputs (orders) and outputs (*products and services*).

It is possible to build a specialized data processing system for each of the boxes shown. Thus, there may be an information system to improve sales, to aid design, to automate production, and to determine the best distribution technique. The form these systems take varies greatly depending upon specific process variables. Though these systems are extremely useful in providing the backbone to the M.I.S., by themselves they do not help the manager obtain a better understanding of the overall Business System.

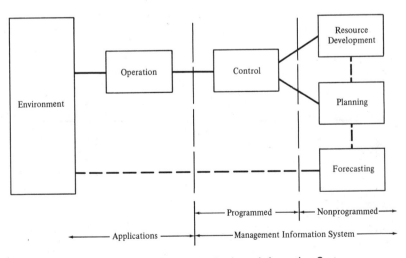

Figure 5. Major Divisions of the Business Information System.

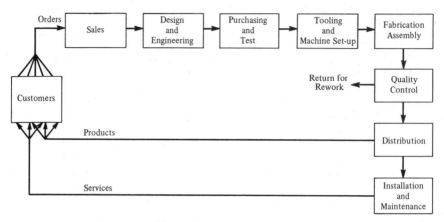

Figure 6. Process Flow.

programmed M.I.S.

The Programmed M.I.S. serves the Control System, the system which represents corporate reality, as it is understood today. In other words, it serves as a yardstick. As such, it should not change too rapidly, for this would make periodic comparisons of progress difficult. On the other hand, it should not be entirely unchangeable, for this implies there could be no improvement in the Control System with time.

A simplified block diagram of the Programmed M.I.S., as it relates to the process in the Operation System, is shown in Figure 7. Within the process are data collection points. Data collected may be with reference to material flow, units made, personnel tasks executed, quality assurance.

Data may be collected automatically by machine, semi-automatically by inserting cards or manually. Data may also be obtained from an application information system.

After the data is collected, it is used to update files concerned with such things as personnel, inventory, purchase orders, projects, accounts payable and accounts receivable. This is followed by data aggregation. Fixed cost is an aggregation of cost of capital equipment and cost of overhead. Variable cost is an aggregation of cost of labor and cost of material. Cost of sales is a higher level aggregation, since it is the sum of fixed costs, variable costs and expenses.

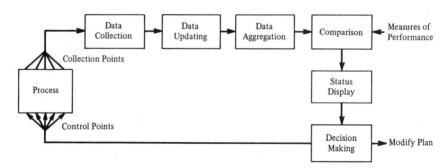

Figure 7. Programmed M.I.S.

Some higher level aggregated values, such as profit, capital turnover, and return on investment, are considered to be measures of performance. The values of these measures are compared with the values previously planned, and the resultant status is displayed.

The status display may be a report preprogrammed to be produced periodically, or upon occurrence of an alarm situation. On the other hand, the status display may be a message returned to a manager in response to a query.

The display is presented in a manner which aids decision-making. For this purpose, tables are better than text; bar charts and trend lines are better than tables.

After analysis of status data, the decision-maker may decide to modify control points in the Operation System. For example, if the manager finds that the cost of production of product A is too high, he may request data on the elements comprising the cost of production:

Material Cost.
Personnel Cost.
Machine Breakdowns.
Number of Rejects.

If he finds that machine breakdowns are too high, the manager may decide to go to the capital equipment control point and order a new machine.

If improvement is not readily available by a simple modification of a control point, the manager may refer the problem to the Adaptability System. For instance, if new machines are available which operate in a radically new way, the Adaptability System needs to evaluate the long term effects on the Business System of purchasing such a machine.

Although the Programmed M.I.S. follows a specific loop, it may be altered in two ways. The first is by the planner who enters measures of performance against which comparisons are to be made, and

who takes the problem when the control loop can not handle it.

This is part of normal operation. The second is the result of improved knowledge resulting from system "experimentation." When a hypothesis has been proven, the control loop may be modified accordingly by changing data collection points and control points, as well as the manner and frequency of collection, update and display.

non-programmed M.I.S.

The Non-programmed M.I.S. serves mainly the needs of the forecasting, planning and resource development subsystems of the Adaptability System.

Since these systems are not structured, the information system consists of a flexible data base upon which many types of procedures can be performed, as shown in Figure 8. Data entry can be achieved from data processed by the Programmed M.I.S., as well as from data gleaned manually from the environment. In addition to being able to enter data from various sources, the user should be able to construct many types of statistical tables.

Once the data is stored in the form it is most convenient for the problem at hand, many tasks need to be executed upon the data. A user should be able to probe in order to find relationships among diverse data elements; he should be able to test the degree of sensitivity of a parameter as a part of a model; he should be able to evaluate several alternative courses of action with reference to a given guide line; he should be able to compare values and trends of important measures of performance. In addition, the user should be able to execute special sophisticated techniques, such as linear programming, modeling and simulation. Another important function of the system is to improve communication for selling of

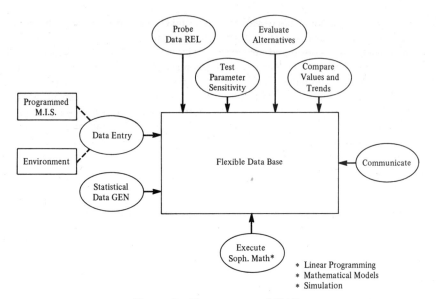

Figure 8.   Nonprogrammed M.I.S.

plans to management, for training personnel in new approaches, and to aid execution of decisions.

"experimental" technique

The executive uses the basic "experimental" technique shown in Figure 9.

The assumption is made that the Programmed M.I.S. is based upon the Control System. The executive develops a hypothesis compromising elements from forecasting, planning and resource development. He then applies the hypothesis to solve business problems. After some period of time he evaluates and analyzes

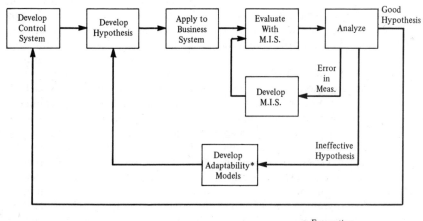

Figure 9.   Evolution from Hypothesis to Central Model.

results, using the M.I.S. If he finds the adaptability models are at fault, he modifies them before revising his hypothesis and reiterating. If he finds the Programmed M.I.S. at fault since it has introduced errors in measurement, he improves the M.I.S. before continuing. After many such iterations he finds that the hypothesis becomes good enough to be considered a rule for decision-making. He then tries to incorporate the basic principle of the hypothesis within the Control System.

This is the general iterative procedure. However, developing the hypothesis, developing adaptability models, and developing the Programmed M.I.S. are iterative procedures in themselves.

hypothesis development

The steps in hypothesis development, as given in Figure 10, are:

1. *Define New Hypothesis.* A new hypothesis is formed, which relates variables in forecasting, planning and resource development models to variables in the Control System. The procedure for doing this is simplified if the Non-programmed M.I.S. has a data base which facilitates finding relationships and statistical correlations among diverse data items.
2. *Gather Data.* Data is gathered from the Programmed M.I.S. Some of it is raw data, some have been processed. Data is also gathered from external sources. These include data on population trends, technological changes, governmental regulation, taxes, competition, planning techniques, new training methods, R and D Processes, investment opportunities, company threats, stock market trends and much more. As part of the data gathering task, the Non-programmed M.I.S. is used to prepare tables which show the relationship among internal and external data.
3. *Test Hypothesis.* Measures of performance are applied to the above historical data, as a dry run of the hypothesis. If the test is passed, the next step is followed. If not, a new hypothesis is defined.
4. *Apply Hypothesis to Business.* The Non-programmed M.I.S. is used to apply the hypothesis to solve business problems. Since no better method is known for the solution of these problems, results are accepted, but modified by human judgment.
5. *Evaluate and Analyze.* The Non-programmed M.I.S. is used to perform statistical and other analysis, in order to determine whether the hypothesis is:
   Bad—It does not aid control or adaptability.
   Faulty—It's good; but it requires changes in detail to make it more useful.
   Good—Proven, it can be relied upon to provide useful decisions.
   If it is bad, a new hypothesis is defined; if faulty, the hypothesis is

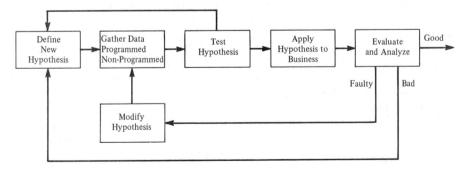

Figure 10. Hypothesis Development.

modified; if good, the Control System is improved.

6. *Modify Hypothesis.* Viewed as an isolated step, this may be considered to be the point where a slight change is made to one or more variables in the hypothesis. Viewed in toto, however, what is needed is to design a statistical experiment so that many variables may be varied according to a defined pattern encompassing many iterations of the loop. This procedure may require a sophisticated program using the Non-programmed M.I.S.

adaptability model development

At the same time that a hypothesis is being developed and evaluated, models upon which the hypothesis is based are running through similar iterative loops in the Non-programmed M.I.S.

In forecasting, we define a statistical model, or an econometric model using simultaneous equations, Gross National Product, Input-Output Technique, or Flow of Funds Technique. Time series and other statistical data are gathered upon which the model is tested. After this the model is used as a basis for a forecast.

At a future time, actual occurrences are compared with forecasted variables. Based upon the results, the forecasting model is modified and another iteration of the loop is executed.

Planning is much more complex than forecasting, since a complete hierarchy must be produced, from strategic plans which embody long range objectives, to tactical plans which specify specific goals. At the lowest level, some goals are monitored by the Control System. Other plans provide goals for the Resource Development System.

In planning, many types of models have been used, among them being:

1. Trade-off Curves.
2. Linear Programming.

3. Expected Value Cash Flow Model.[1]
4. Monte Carlo Simulation[2].
5. Industrial Dynamics Model[3].

After using the Non-programmed M.I.S. tools to do extensive study of the Business System, a planning model is developed. Historical data is gathered in order to test the model. If it is found appropriate a plan is defined which is based on this model, as well as upon a forecast. Here is a lot of hit and miss in planning in the sense that sound plans are first created, then compared in order to choose the best. At a future time, actual outputs of the Business System are compared against the plan. At that point it is extremely important to be able to separate the results due to improper forecasting and to improper implementation, from those due to the faults of the planning model. Again, improvement in planning is achieved by many iterations of the loop.

After a plan is made to raise given resources of the Business System to a specific level, Resource Development goes about achieving this goal. Specifically, Resource Development is concerned with such things as:

1. Preparing a Plant Building Program.
2. Securing Advanced Capital Equipment.
3. Developing a Personnel Hiring and Upgrading Program.
4. Executing a Research and Development Program.
5. Executing a Financial Development Program.

Though it is more action-oriented than the others, Resource Development also

[1] Goetz, *Quantitative Methods*, McGraw-Hill Book Co., N.Y., 1965.
[2] Evans, Wallace and Sutherland, *Simulation Using Digital Computers*, Prentice-Hall, Englewood Cliffs, N.J., 1967.
[3] Forrester, *Industrial Dynamics*, MIT Press, Cambridge, Mass., 1961.

follows an iterative procedure. A model is developed, and data gathered to test it. After this the model is used to execute specific tasks. At a future time, results are evaluated and analyzed, and another iteration of the loop is initiated.

programmed M.I.S. development

When results achieved by the Business System are not quite as expected, one cause may lie in an Adaptability System model, as was stated. However, another cause may be errors of measurement by the Programmed M.I.S. In other words, the Programmed M.I.S. may not be obtaining the correct status information, or it may not be measuring an important variable at all, or it may not be measuring the variable at the appropriate time or with the appropriate frequency.

This is why Programmed M.I.S. development must follow a similar iterative cycle. The Programmed M.I.S. defines the Control System which is used to keep tabs on the health of the Business System. At the same time that it does this, it gathers statistics to determine whether it's doing it's basic job properly. These statistics are analyzed to determine whether changes should be made in the Programmed M.I.S. As time goes on, the Programmed M.I.S. becomes better and better.

planning and design

A Management Information System stores within it representations of the four non-operation systems comprising the Business System, as well as data and procedure related to the "experimental" technique for assessing hypotheses.

The first major step in planning an information system is to thoroughly study all five corporate systems, not only as they are today, but how they may be expected to develop in the future. The second step is to develop an "experimental" plan which provides means for defining, testing, evaluating and analyzing a range of hypotheses. The last step is to integrate the above requirements into a unified Management Information System.

The result is a plan of the Management Information System. This is forwarded to the EDP technologist for quantitative design. Several iterations of the planning-design loop are needed before a viable Management Information System evolves.

the five corporate systems

Each of the five systems is studied from at least the following points of view:

1. Major Decision Areas.
2. Measures of Performance.
3. Major System Variables.
4. Major Cycle Characteristics.

First is the Operation System. The study can be aided by drawing process flow charts. These can point out application areas for information systems. But more important, they can delineate data collection points and control points for the Control System.

The Control System represents the "known" part of the universe and is the major yardstick for testing hypotheses. An important tool for assuring a well integrated, tight system for performance measurement, is the hierarchical data chart. An example of such a data hierarchy is given in Figure 11. This chart is from a financial standpoint only. Similar charts may be prepared which include qualitative as well as quantitative variables.

Some important control cycle characteristics to be studied are:

1. Frequency of collection, updating, aggregation, display.

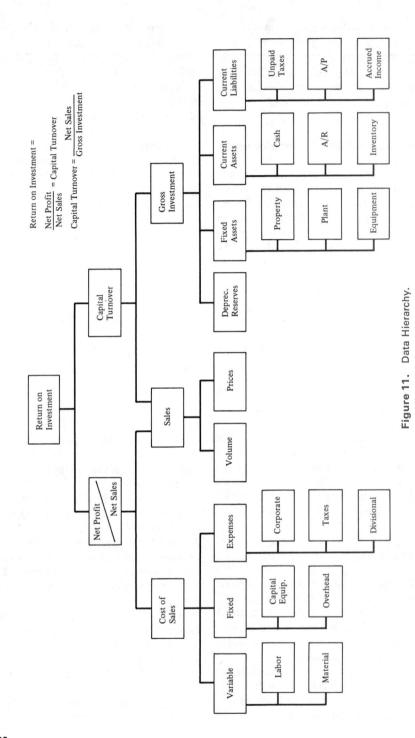

Return on Investment =

$$\frac{\text{Net Profit}}{\text{Net Sales}} = \text{Capital Turnover}$$

$$\text{Capital Turnover} = \frac{\text{Net Sales}}{\text{Gross Investment}}$$

Figure 11. Data Hierarchy.

2. Reliability in terms of data accuracy, completeness, significance.

3. Responsiveness in terms of speed, ease of use and flexibility.

The Forecasting, Planning and Resource Development Systems are the "known" part of the universe. These should be studied with the idea of determining a range of hypotheses. Since these hypotheses relate forecasting, planning and resource development models to the Control System, the study can be aided by studying technological and modeling trends, as well as trends in corporate organization, social change, governmental control, education and finance.

"experimental" plan

The basis for the "experimental" plan is the range of hypothesis to be evaluated. Based on order of priority and upon the necessity for evaluating a fundamental idea before considering an idea derived from it, a sequence of "experiments" to be executed over a long range of time is prepared.

The sequence of "experiments" serves as a guide to the next step: defining data and procedure needed to execute these "experiments." Means must be provided to store the hypotheses and to execute these relationships at appropriate times. Means must be provided to store measures of performance as well as data for comparison in a statistically appropriate fashion. Means must be provided to execute the sophisticated analyses which determine which variables to modify for the next iteration.

planning vs. design

Formulation of the plan consists of integrating these data and procedure requirements into a Programmed M.I.S. and a Non-programmed M.I.S. The first handles the Control System plus basic measurements. It should include means for making modifications after a hypothesis has been proven, as well as means of improving the information system itself. The second handles all processes concerned with development, use, evaluation and modification of hypotheses. As with the Programmed M.I.S. means must be included for improvement of the Non-programmed M.I.S. with time.

Two activities may aid in the integration process:

1. *Defining Data Standards.* Name and define all raw data items, data aggregations and measures of performance. Use the same standard means and definitions throughout the information system. Place a data base manager in control of these data standards.

2. *Define Communication Standards.* Define the language and rules for communication between decision-makers and other decision-makers, and between decision-makers and data stored.

Because a Management Information System reflects an executive's philosophy of management, no cookbook approach can be given for preparation of the plan. However, the above guidelines may help.

Not so with the M.I.S. design. Design is quantitative and is based upon the work of a system analyst who studies objectives, procedures, forms and information flow in excruciating detail according to well-developed techniques.[4] In addition, some sophisticated mathematical, statistical and modeling techniques may need to be incorporated. When the executive receives the tentative design of the M.I.S., he knows that it is based upon his business concepts and plans. He need not under-

[4] Glans, Grad, Holstein, Meyers and Schmidt, *Management Systems*, Holt, Rinehart and Winston Inc., N.Y., 1968.

stand all the technological details of the design; only their effect upon his yardstick and upon his "experimental" plan. After he makes further changes in the plan, he is

well on the way toward development of a Management Information System which will keep his Business System dynamic and adaptable.

38. tailoring the information system

John G. Burch and Felix R. Strater

In any kind of management system, there are different classifications of decision making with which the manager must deal. The decisions can range from the very routine, perfunctory kind of decisions to the complex ones. For definition and classification, the types of decisions can be put into three categories: (1) strategical, (2) tactical, and (3) technical.

Even if it were technically and economically feasible to have an omnipotent information system, the concern here is with ways to make information systems produce timely information which is pertinent and applicable to a particular decision maker. A decision maker needs an array of information that is tailored to his activities and decision making level.

There is no great accomplishment when a system is developed to store, manipulate, and integrate large masses of data, if the system design has failed to provide adequate and pertinent information to tactical and strategical decision makers. If systems are designed to process voluminous quantities of data routinely and without specific objectives, then such systems are overloaded with data. The resulting information is inadequate in terms of the accessibility, comprehensiveness, appro-

priateness, timeliness, and clarity of the information produced. Systems that are designed to process data without meeting informational requirements flood decision makers with data and not information.

the three levels

If the management function is divided into two activities of planning and controlling, it can be seen that decisions made at the strategical level require a great deal of planning. Strategical decisions, characterized by a great deal of uncertainty, are future oriented. These decisions establish long range policies which affect the entire organization. The goals of the organization are stated and a range of strategies are made which may entail, for example, plant expansion, determination of product lines, mergers, diversification into other areas, capital expenditures, or the sale of the organization.

Tactical decision making pertains to short term activities and the allocation of resources for the attainment of the objectives. This kind of decision making concerns formulation of budgets, funds flow analysis, deciding on plant layout, personnel problems, product improvement, and research and development. Whereas strategical decision making entails largely a planning activity, tactical decision

Reprinted from *Journal of Systems Management*, 24, No. 2 (February 1973), pp. 34–38, with permission of the publisher.

making requires a fairly equal mix of planning and controlling activities.

The technical level of decision making is a process of ensuring that specific tasks are implemented in an effective and efficient manner. This kind of decision making requires specific commands to be given which control specific operations. The primary management function involved is that of control with planning performed on a rather limited scale. Examples of this kind of decision making involve acceptance or rejection of credit, process control, scheduling, receiving, shipping, inventory control, and allocating workers.

informational requirements

Different kinds of decision making require different informational requirements. The higher the level of the decision maker, the more data he needs about external conditions (see Figure 1). The lines in Figure 1 cannot be precisely delineated. In a practicable situation, the lines between categories of decision making are blurred and tend to overlap. Analysts must, however, be aware of these types of decision

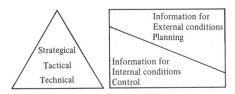

Figure 1. Kind of Information Required for Various Classifications of Decision Making.

making and how the information system can be designed to meet differing requirements because the information which is produced by the information system is dependent upon these requirements. The characteristics of information which meet these needs are listed in Figure 2.

All organizations have some kind of information system that is supposed to meet informational requirements and reduce the probability of making poor decisions. However, many information systems are incapable of providing relevant information for strategical decision making, and to some degree, tactical decision making. It is imperative that for strategical decision making, information systems will have to be designed to grasp the realities of the environment. This would include

Strategical Information	1. External Information
	   a. competitive actions
	   b. customer actions
	   c. availability of resources
	   d. demographic studies
	   e. government actions
	2. Predictive Information (Long-term trends)
	3. Simulated-What If Information

Tactical Information	1. Descriptive-Historical Information 2. Performance-Current Information 3. Prediction-Future Information (Short-term) 4. Simulated-What If Information
Technical Information	1. Descriptive-Historical Information 2. Performance-Current Information

Figure 2. Characteristics of Information Which Meets the Requirements of Different Kinds of Decision Making.

reporting actions of competitors; economical, social, and political trends; situations in foreign countries; technological developments.

The information system must be designed to satisfy all three classes of decision making. In many organizations many strategical and tactical decisions are made more on the basis of intuition, heuristics, and interpretation than on relevant information from the formal information system. Implementation of strategical type information processed by the information systems will be valuable to ones who make these decisions. However, a formal information system is limited in how effective it can be in producing relevant information for the three kinds of decision making. This is based on the concepts illustrated in Figure 3.

Each of these schematics represents general concepts which are subject to

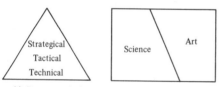

(a) Degree to which decision making is an art/science.

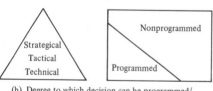

(b) Degree to which decision can be programmed/nonprogrammed.

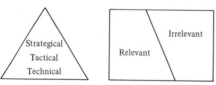

(c) Degree to which information produced by the formal information system is relevant/irrelevant.

Figure 3. Concepts Which Show the Degree of Effectiveness a Formal Information System Can Have on Decision Making.

modification. These illustrations show the potential effectiveness of the formal information system and the probable limitations. Each organization and its decision making processes have to be considered in individual situations.

relationship of classifications

A matrix, in Figure 4, relates major classifications of information to the three categories of decision making. The nature of the information requirements can be related to the decision making process. For each decision making activity, the manager should determine what information he needs for planning, controlling, organizing, implementing of assignments, and so forth. Both the analyst and the user should consider the scope of coverage, degree of detail, contents of reports, frequency of reporting, period of time to be covered, and distribution and communication methods.

The principal user of the information should be given considerable leeway in determining his information requirements and the conditions of processing and communication. Because the information system is costly and is designed on the basis of information requirements which are to be met, it is important that each user request only the information he will use.

For example, as shown in Figure 4, the amount of information required online for strategical level decision making would normally be moderate, if not nil. Picturephone units and CRT's could be installed in top management offices to display information in conjunction with normal voice communication. This would make available such facts as actual sales to date compared with sales targets, prior year's actual sales, income after taxes year to date of Division A, and so forth.

All of this information is vitally important, but strategical decisions of any con-

| | Categories of Decision Making | | |
Classification of Information	Technical	Tactical	Strategical
Dependence on External Information	Very Low	Moderate	Very High
Dependence on Internal Information	Very High	High	Moderate
Information Online	Very High	High	Moderate
Information in Real Time	Very High	Very High	Very High
Information Reported Periodically	Very High	Very High	Very High
Information That Is Descriptive-Historical in Nature	High	High	Low
Information That Is Performance-Current in Nature	Very High	High	Moderate
Information That Is Predictive-Future in Nature	Low	High	Very High
Information That Is Simulated-What If in Nature	Low	High	Very High

Figure 4. Classification of Information Which Meets the Requirements of the Three Categories of Decision Making.

sequence normally require days, weeks, or months of thought. Instantaneous decisions to complex problems cannot be made quickly. Secondly, even when online information, such as schedule trips of top executives, stock exchange information, political news, and foreign exchange rates, is available the cost of providing this kind of information via online facilities may far exceed the effectiveness of such a system. The same information is often available from other, less elaborate sources at lower costs.

There are methods which can streamline the information producing process. The Management Science Method is one. Data processing systems developed for routine tasks make up the major portion of information systems. Such systems have data bases which may be adequate for information conversion methods such as management science techniques. The data base alone, however, has a very low utility in strategical and tactical decision making situations, since the characteristic of information required for technical operations differs significantly from that required in strategical and tactical decision making.

If designed properly, the information system, with its data collection storage, processing, and communication capabilities, can provide meaningful information. Strategical and tactical decision making can be facilitated by applying various management science techniques to the data to identify objectives and courses of action.

An ABC Analysis of inventory items, for example, may provide important insights to a company which is considering reducing its product line. A material yield analysis available on demand may provide important information concerning the attractiveness of a new raw material. Various queuing models can assist management in deciding upon production schedules, personnel assignments and/or shipping priorities. These and other management science techniques can provide valuable information to all levels of management.

filtering method

The major portion of input from all sources may, at the time of entry, be irrelevant to a particular decision maker. But, if the systems are designed properly, some portion of that data will be relevant at some time. It is, therefore, necessary to design the information system to filter certain data elements from the data base to give the decision maker a level of detail applicable to his needs. The alternative is for the decision maker to filter the data himself. This takes too much of his time.

The degree of filtering depends on who is making the decision. For example, strategical decision makers usually can comprehend more detail than a technical decision maker. The analyst must be aware of this difference within each category of decision making. Some decision makers can operate better with a lot of detail, while others are overwhelmed by it.

interrogative method

Filtering manipulates and summarizes data in order to tailor it and make it more appropriate to a particular decision maker's needs. An interrogative method is a micro, interactive concept which is applicable to a specific user who wants a specific response based upon a specific interrogation of the data base. This method is supported by online fast response devices which are designed to give the overburdened manager rapid access to pertinent bits of information.

The challenge to implementing this method as well as other methods is to determine: (1) what data to capture, (2) when and where to capture it, (3) where and in what form to store it, and (4) when and on whose initiative to give access to it. The proper aim is to have in the data base data stored and organized in a manner where a variety of users can get access to different data elements as needed. Often the manager is ineffective by not having a specific piece of information at the time

he needs it. The interrogative method sets up an interactive system between the user and the computer.

This kind of method helps to alleviate the controversy about centralization and decentralization of decision making by permitting independent access to a common data base. Whatever his level of responsibility, the decision maker can be accommodated by providing direct access to the common data base. Modification of the organizational structure is neither demanded nor precluded by utilization of the interrogative method. The users are able to retrieve timely and unbiased responses by by-passing hierarchical levels and breaking through functional lines.

The interrogative method allows the manager to go as deep into the data base as authorized and retrieve as much detail as he needs. It does not counter or conflict with the filtering method; it simply provides the decision maker with another dimension of information communications; it allows different decision makers who may have different detail thresholds to get quick, pertinent responses to simple queries, and it provides added flexibility necessary to find and use information as general or as detailed as needed.

Financial data can be stored regarding closings and financial planning. Orders entered for a specific time period, sales billed, and income after taxes to date can be displayed instantaneously. Sales managers can interrogate sales statistics files to access information pertaining to market participation, product performance, salesmen performance, customer activity, and up to date forecasting information.

This method can also aid plant management by placing the burden of programmed decision making on the computer. For example, a production employee can get his next work assignment by asking the computer via a teletype or CRT. He simply identifies himself and his work station and requests his next job assignment. A message is displayed to the employee telling him the next job order number and operation, the location of the material and manufacturing information, and a list of tools he needs and their location.

In addition, employees use these terminals to record their attendance and overtime, job requests, job completions, materials and tool receipt and issues, shift-end accomplishments of each employee as he leaves for the day, and all inspections. In return, the plant manager, in addition to other managers, can retrieve via their own terminals a broad spectrum of information including [2, p. 20]:

1. Long-term backlog behind critical facilities.
2. Short-term backlog behind each facility and work station.
3. Up-to-the-minute status of every order in work.
4. Promised dates on all orders.
5. Location of all tools in the plant.
6. Status of all purchase orders.
7. Complete inspection and quality control information.
8. Status of work-in-process as to percentage completion.

exception method

Implementation of feedback procedures in the information system will provide a means by which the exception method can be utilized. This is a method which directs management's attention only to that performance which has deviated beyond established criteria or predetermined standards. Only that information which is deemed significant is reported. With exception reporting, the volume of information flowing to the decision makers will

be greatly reduced because on-target performance can proceed without continuous monitoring by the decision maker. His attention is thus freed for complex, ill-structured problems involving organization philosophy, planning, budgeting, research, personnel evaluation and training, and other management areas where human talents are needed.

Information is communicated to those who have the authority and responsibility for performance of certain tasks or projects. Standards or performance criteria are established against which product quality, material usage, labor usage, overhead usage, different costs, and completion time are measured. Evaluation procedures are developed for comparing actual performance against standards. The entire operation is continually monitored by a feedback system that reports to the manager significant deviations, who in turn makes decisions and gives commands to correct or prevent deviations from planned performance.

external method

There is information in the environment which may have particular significance for tactical and strategical decision makers. This information can be gathered from newspapers, trade journals, government reports, demographic studies, marketing studies, and so forth. Facts from these sources are applicable to higher level decision making. There is a limited utility to what can be provided by the computer, by the computer affiliated data base, and even by the application of management science techniques to satisfy informational requirements at the strategical level.

It is difficult to give a definitive list of external information required to manage the organization properly. However, the analyst can be more effective if he is cognizant of these needs. He can make publications available for quick dissemination through the use of collating, indexing, and document retrieval. He can gather and summarize statistical abstracts from government about legislation directly affecting the organization, e.g., truth in packaging, wage and price control, foreign trade, indicators from GNP, consumer affairs, foreign exchange rates, stock exchange information, and so forth. And, he can make demographic studies to highlight population trends, gather data on research activities, development in the money market, general trading and stock trends, and developing technology.

The previous methods help make the information system more efficient in its operations and more responsive to management's needs. The last method, in addition, embraces external information which pertains to economic, political, social, and competitive factors. This external information has come into the organization on a somewhat spasmodic, informal basis through general reading and occasional studies by management personnel. This informal approach becomes inadequate when organizations grow larger and more complex. A point is reached where this information has to be communicated in a formal manner and less and less through occasional collection and observation by the decision maker himself.

conclusion

Since there are different levels of decision making, there have to be different kinds of information to specifically serve these levels. To a large extent, the strategical decision maker needs filtered, future-oriented, and external information. Formal information systems are severely limited as to how much relevant information they can provide this level of decision making. Information systems are sub-

stantially more effective and serve better tactical and technical decision making although there is still a great potential for analysts to serve the strategical level better than it has been served in the past.

Informational needs at all levels can be met more effectively if the analyst and user will work together to tailor the information output to fit the user's needs. Systems which produce and disseminate volumes of irrelevant data to the users are good data processors, but poor information processors. The information systems analyst can improve the effectiveness of information output by following five basic methods, which include: (1) management science method, (2) filtering method, (3) interrogative method, (4) exception method, and (5) external method.

The management science method utilizes models in which data are manipulated to show optimum alternatives. Filtering of data is a summarization concept where data are buffered to produce that information which is relevant to the user. The interrogative method has a similar purpose; however, it allows the user to interact with the data base and retrieve a specific response based on a specific inquiry. The exception method reports only those deviations from standard which require corrective action from the decision maker. The external method is used to gather information which is primarily external to the organization such as trade journals, government reports, legislation, demographic studies, and competitive statistics.

bibliography

1. Kelly, Joseph F. *Computerized Management Information Systems*. New York: Macmillan Publishing Co., Inc., 1970.
2. LaRoe, T. A. "A Manufacturing Plant Information System," *Proceedings Third Annual Conference*, September 9

and 10, 1971. Denver, Colorado: The Society for Management Information Systems.

3. Schoderbek, Peter P. *Management Systems*. New York: John Wiley and Sons, Inc., 1967.

discussion questions: part V

1. Define the following terms: system, general systems theory, management systems theory. Describe the relationship between a general systems theory and a management systems theory.

2. How are traditional concepts of management related to systems concepts? In what ways could the process, behavioral, and quantitative approaches be integrated into a total management systems approach?

3. What is a multiview systems concept?

4. Differentiate between these models: systemic environmental model, systemic planning model, systemic functional model, and systemic operational model. How are they related? Are they related to the process approach? If so, in what ways? If not, why not?

5. Evaluate the arguments for and against a total systems concept. What position would you take with respect to a total systems concept? Defend your position.

6. How are systems analysis and management planning related? How are systems analysis and management information systems related?

7. What is systems analysis? How is it related to the decision-making process in organizations?

8. Utilize the concept of model-based systems analysis in examining the management of a public agency at the local, state, or federal levels.

9. What is the purpose of a management information system? Why is such a system important? What steps would you take to design a management information system? What impact do you feel an information system has on management? Why?

10. What are the major operational systems within an organization? How can these systems be related to a total management information system?

11. How is a management information system related to strategic, tactical, and technical decision making in the organization? Explain.

12. Consider the possible research problems that could be carried out in the systems concepts and systems analyses areas. Discuss several major problems which you think are the most important and why.

13. After examining the general systems and management systems concepts, outline what you consider to be the major points in each. How would you improve these concepts? Why?

selected references: part V

A. *systems concepts*

Ericson, Richard F., "Visions of Cybernetic Organizations," *Academy of Management Journal*, 15, No. 4 (December 1972), pp. 427–443.

Forrester, Jay W., *Industrial Dynamics* (Cambridge, Mass.: The M.I.T. Press, 1961).

————, *Urban Dynamics* (Cambridge, Mass.: The M.I.T. Press, 1969).

Gullett, C. Ray, "The Systems Concept Revisited," *S.A.M. Advanced Management Journal*, 36, No. 2 (April 1971), pp. 45–48.

Johnson, Richard A., Fremont E. Kast, and James E. Rosenzweig, *The Theory and Management of Systems*, 3rd ed. (New York: McGraw-Hill Book Company, Inc., 1972).

Peery, Jr., Newman S., "General Systems Theory: An Inquiry into Its Social Philosophy," *Academy of Management Journal*, 15, No. 4 (December 1972), pp. 495–510.

Smith, August W., "Toward a Systems Theory of the Firm," *Journal of Systems Management*, 22, No. 2 (February 1971), pp. 10–12.

Von Bertalanffy, Ludwig, "The History and Status of General Systems Theory," *Academy of Management Journal*, 15, No. 4 (December 1972), pp. 407–426.

Woodside, Arch G., "Analysis of General System Theory," *Marquette Business Review*, 13, No. 2 (Summer 1969), pp. 45–64.

B. *systems analyses*

Guthrie, Chester L., "The Place of Small General Purpose Computers in Enterprise," *S.A.M. Advanced Management Journal*, 37, No. 3 (July 1972), pp. 23–29.

Hare, Van C., Jr., *Systems Analysis: A Diagnostic Approach* (New York: Harcourt, Brace, and World, Inc., 1967).

Hodgson, R. N., "Design Considerations in Planning and Control Systems," *Managerial Planning*, 19, No. 3 (November–December 1970), pp. 1–4.

Hudson, Miles H., "A Technique for Systems Analysis and Design," *Journal of Systems Management*, 22, No. 5 (May 1971), pp. 14–19.

Odiorne, George S., "A Systems Approach To Training," *Training Directors Journal*, 19, No. 10 (October 1965), pp. 11–19.

Rossi, Robert C., "Applied Network Logic to Corporate Acquisitions," *S.A.M. Advanced Management Journal*, 36, No. 1 (January 1971), pp. 39–50.

Schmitz, Homer, H., "An Evaluation of a Modular Hospital Information System," *Hospital Progress*, 53, No. 6 (June 1972), pp. 70–76.

Young, Stanley, "Designing a Behavioral System," *Academy of Management, Proceedings of the 1963 Annual Meeting* (University Park, Pa.: 1964), pp. 76–83.

C. *management information systems*

Argyris, Chris, "Management Information Systems: The Challenge to Rationality and Emotionality," *Management Science*, 17, No. 6 (February 1971), pp. B275–B292.

Buckley, John W. "The Empirical Approach to MIS Design," *Organizational Dynamics*, 1, No. 2 (Autumn 1972), pp. 19–30.

Gessford, John E., "Management Information Systems Development: Parts I and II," *Managerial Planning*, 21, No. 4 and No. 5 (January–February and March–April 1973), pp. 15–20 and pp. 1–5, 18.

Gorry, Anthony G., and Michael Scott Morton, "A Framework for Management Information Systems," *Sloan Management Review*, 13, No. 1 (Fall 1971), pp. 55–70.

Harrill, E. Reece, "An Information System for Local Government," *Management Controls*, 19, No. 6 (June 1972), pp. 129–140.

Hurtado, Corydon D., "Establishing a Government IMS," *Journal of Systems Management*, 22, No. 6 (June 1971), pp. 40–43.

McFarlan, F. Warren, "Problems in Planning the Information System," *Harvard Business Review*, 49, No. 2 (March–April 1971), pp. 75–89.

Powell, Reed M., and Paul L. Wilkens, "Design and Implementation of a Human Resource Information System," *MSU Business Topics*, 21, No. 1 (Winter 1973), pp. 21–27.

Powers, Richard F., and Gary W. Dickson, "MIS-Project Management: Myths, Opinions and Reality," *California Management Review*, 15, No. 3 (Spring 1973), pp. 147–156.

Wilkinson, Joseph W., "Classifying Information Systems," *Journal of Systems Management*, 24, No. 4 (April 1973), pp. 28–31.

management in the future

part VI

Throughout this book, an attempt has been made to examine the present and future problem areas in management. Since World War II, the field of management has changed significantly, and it will change even more dramatically in the next twenty-five years. New types of work organizations and new forms of voluntary associations have risen and will continue to grow. Different structural forms of organization such as the matrix form will be initiated during the future. Organizations will continue to dominate, control, and influence us all. Therefore, the critical decisions made by managers will affect the ways in which each and every one of us lives in modern society.

In the future, organizations will have to be extremely flexible to compete in rapidly changing internal and external environments.[1] At the same time, managers will constantly have to be retrained to handle these rapidly changing conditions. New types of conflicts between the individual and the organization, between the individual and groups within the organization, and between groups will arise. New modes of effecting organizational change and organizational development will have to be initiated. Some of the new approaches and techniques will assist managers in solving problems which appeared to be unsolvable.

[1] See Alvin Toffler, *Future Shock* (New York: Bantam Books, Inc., 1970), pp. 124–151; Daniel Bell (ed.), *Toward the Year 2000: Work in Progress* (Boston, Mass.: Beacon Press, 1968); and Richard N. Farmer, *Management in the Future* (Belmont, Calif.: Wadsworth Publishing Co., Inc., 1968).

Amitai Etzioni begins by analyzing the shifts toward new forms of organization in a free society. He stresses the movement toward a third system of organizations—one in which organizations utilize principles emanating from both public and private systems. He also comments on some third sector organizations such as national health insurance, student loan programs, NASA, U.S. Postal Service, and Amtrak. In the concluding selection, James D. Thompson attempts to predict the future in organizations around the year 2000. After making the assumptions that complex organizations will continue to exist, that they are doing more good than harm, and that human desires will not change significantly from the present, he predicts the major shifts in organizations and the significant issues that will be current twenty-five years from now.

39. the third sector and domestic missions*

Amitai Etzioni

What tools are best suited to serve our economic and social needs? This question has been debated for more than a century, usually in the name of the virtue of capitalism, which lauds the market system, and socialism, which favors, in effect, state administration. Each ideological system has sought purity in its guiding principles, despite the fact that they are not mutually exclusive.

Thus, private enterprise plays a significant role in the production and distribution of goods and services in socialist republics, but this activity is considered an exception, a residue, a transitory element, or a concession to the old-fashioned, something to be eliminated later. Similarly, in the United States, the existence of large-scale government business—for example, the Atomic Energy Commission and the Postal Service—is viewed as exceptional, and either undesirable or to be condoned for special purposes, such as security or lack of profitability in a vitally needed service.

Actually, over the years, the private sector has grown in the Soviet Union and government business has expanded in the United States.[1] Nevertheless, this fact is either disregarded or bemoaned by each side as a sure sign of increasing "softness"

—if not outright deterioration—in the respective system. Like many other ideological debates, this one has concealed more truth than it has highlighted and it is particularly unhelpful in providing insight into the dynamics of the societies involved. As several keen analysts already have indicated, the capitalist and socialist systems, contrary to their avowed intentions, are actually moving toward each other.[2]—or, as I see it, they are moving toward a third system, one in which both profit making and administrative principles of organization, production, and distribution are widely used.[3] This is *not* to suggest that the differences will disappear; the state enterprise will surely continue to play a major role in the Soviet Union in the foreseeable future, just as the profit motive will continue to dominate in the United States, but the two systems are becoming ever less "pure," more "mixed," and hence closer to a third type.

Moreover, even this picture—i.e., the notion of a private economy with a public ingredient, and a public economy with a private factor—does not get close enough to the societal reality to allow careful analysis of the main options for economic, social, and domestic efforts, nor does it reveal the proportion or direction that the mixes will change. To achieve this we must move closer to the situation, which we attempt to do by focusing here one country at one state in time—the U.S.A.—at the end of the '60s, early '70s.

Reprinted from *Public Administration Review*, 33, No. 4 (July–August 1973), pp. 314–323, with permission of the publisher and the author.

* The author is indebted to Nancy Castleman who served as a research assistant in preparing this report which is part of a larger work in progress under the auspices of the Center for Policy Research.

[1] For example, see Eli Ginsberg, Dale L. Hiestand, and Beatrice G. Reubens, *The Pluralistic Economy* (New York: McGraw-Hill Book Company, 1965).

[2] For example, see Zbigniew Brzezinski and Samuel P. Huntington, *Political Power: USA/USSR* (New York: The Viking Press, 1964).

[3] For more on the author's views, see Amitai Etzioni, *The Active Society* (New York: The Free Press, 1968), chapters 16–18.

where we are

In the U.S.A. ever since the Republicans returned to the White House in 1969, frequent tribute has been paid to the capitalist, market, profit-making ideology. The expansion of government in any form is seen as evil by the modern conservative ideologists, who suggest that tasks and funds should be shifted from the government to the private sector. One spokesman for this approach, Peter Drucker, professor at the New York University Business School, has called the change "reprivatization"; he has written that the government should act like a conductor in a concert—initiating, guiding, coordinating, but not actually carrying out the missions. That job would be returned to the private sector.[4]

However, in the formative years of the Nixon Administration, the Chief advisor to the President in domestic affairs was a New Deal liberal, Pat Moynihan, not Drucker. And practically all the major programs initiated or advocated by the Nixon Administration have been those that entail increased governmental efforts. Thus, the major anti-poverty, welfare plan of the Nixon Administration has been based not on black capitalism, JOBS (a businessmen-based drive for work to the unemployed), or any other private enterprise approach, but on the federally funded, federally administered, notion of guaranteed annual income, known as the Family Assistance Plan. Nixon's "full-employment" budget attempts to give an added boost to the economy through such measures as expanding the money in circulation, increasing the national debt, and reducing some taxes—all made on the federal level. And Nixon's "revolutionary," "bold," and "most significant" domestic proposal—revenue sharing—only involves

[4] Peter Drucker, *The Age of Discontinuity* (New York: Harper & Row, 1969).

the transference of some monies from Washington to states, cities, and other local governments. But of more consequence than all this, of course, is the setting up of price and wage controls. They will subject to government review and control most aspects of the private sector previously untouched by the state. At least theoretically, all businesses (and especially larger ones) now have a status similar to that heretofore reserved for utilities, which cannot adjust rates, approve raises, or basically change their services without government approval or without adhering to government guidelines.

The major exception to this general trend of increased federal involvement is Nixon's proposed health plan, which calls for a "partnership" between the business community, its employees, and the federal government. (This plan is discussed in greater detail below.) Private insurance companies would administer a plan whereby the business community would have to provide health insurance for employees, who themselves would contribute about one third of the necessary funds for their health care. The federal government would supply the funds for the poor and the unemployed. The proposed national health insurance plan points the way that many new domestic plans might follow.

the third sector

While debate over how to serve our needs has focused on the public versus the private alternative, a third alternative, indeed sector, has grown between the state and market sector. Actually this third sector may well be the most important alternative for the next few decades, *not* by replacing the other two, but by matching and balancing their important roles.

The situation is analogous to the early

days of the capitalist era. Rapid industrial growth "took off" only after a new legal and organizational concept paved its way, namely the limited liability corporation. This allowed for the accumulation of the large amount of capital necessary for industrialization and large-scale marketing —amounts which most families or partnerships could not amass.

In the present era, when society increasingly turns to provide public goods such as education, health, and welfare, *the search is on for appropriate legal and organizational tools.* Of course some public goods are, and will continue to be, provided by the private sector, e.g., production of text-books for schools. And there certainly is no question that the government does and will provide many services, like social security. But increasingly we find missions—such as pollution control—where the profit motive is not great enough and/or costs involved in making the mission profitable seem too high. At the same time, we are ever more tired of the reliance on multiplying, expanding government bureaucracies. A method must be developed to combine "the best of both worlds"—efficiency and expertise from the business world with public interest, accountability, and broader planning from government.

An answer is coming not from theory but from a large variety of experimentations with new forms which are developing to carry out our domestic missions. All of these may be seen as attempts to find the appropriate vehicle through which to conduct the social as well as the economic "business" of mature capitalism. These developing forms are mainly in the *third sector,* which is neither governmental nor private. Some are created out of a mix of private business and governmental elements. Others take the form of voluntary associations (e.g., the Red Cross or the League of Women Voters) and the non-profit corporations (e.g., the Ford Founda-

tion). Not all are successful, not by a long shot; but many seem to do significantly superior work than either the federal or local governments, and they are able to carry out missions which are not profitable enough to attract the private sector. *In fact, the most promising solutions to our domestic problems are among the third sector approaches now evolving.*

It should be noted that there is a semantic difficulty indicative of the ideological confusion and novelty of the development we seek to highlight, which often clouds the debate about different approaches to domestic problems. Usually reference is made to the private vs. the public sector. This, though, hides the fact that the term "public" refers to both governmental and voluntary (or not-for-profit) beings. Moreover, while often the "non-profit" beings are lumped with the government ones, on other occasions they are treated as part of the private sector, e.g., Columbia University is referred to as a "private" university. As the third sector beings differ significantly from both dominant sectors, we suggest reference shall be made to *private* (profit), *governmental* (state), and *public* sectors (not-for-profit, voluntary).

That there is a need for such a concept can be seen by the semantic contortions writers have engaged in to point to the divergent type they recognized but had no category for. Thus, writing about the condition in which the United Kingdom government has a majority or minority holding of the shares of an "undertaking" which remains juristically a "private" company (quotation marks in original), one author uses the term "mixed enterprise," in quotes, to indicate its novelty.[5] No wonder; the author uses the term public corporation to refer to fully nationalized, i.e., state, ones.

[5] J. F. Garner, "Introduction" to W. G. Friedman and J. F. Gerner (ed.), *Government Enterprise* (New York: Columbia University Press, 1970), p. 5.

Professor Hokan Stromberg, discussing the situation in Sweden, tries to play the distinction at hand by referring to two kinds of public corporations: "state-controlled company" and "public institutions."[6]

And, when discussing the Children's Television Workshop, the producer of the world-renowned *Sesame Street*, Linda Francke, writes: "Legally, CTV is a 'public' rather than a 'private', non-profit foundation, the essential difference being that it is not only supported by government, but also gets additional income for the sales of shows . . . ."[7]

third sector bodies

We turn to review the large variety of third sector beings.

health insurance

One major type is the government-private sector partnership. It is illustrated by an idea which so far has not been enacted, the health insurance plan that has already been mentioned.

The national health insurance plan that the Nixon Administration proposed places part of the financial burden on employers, part on the workers. Employees:

. . . would pay 35 percent of the cost on insurance premiums at the start of the program and 25 percent after 1976. . . . [In addition, there is a suggested government contribution of] provisions costing about $1.4 billion for covering the poor with a family health insurance program, increasing the supply of doctors and other health professionals and streamlining the manner

in which medicine has been practiced in the United States.[8]

Nixon's plan requires, in fact depends on, the participation of private health insurance firms in this "governmental" effort. These companies would underwrite the increased employer costs as well as the family health insurance plan (for the poor, unemployed, and self-employed). Nixon recognized the "mix" nature of the plan. He stated in his message to Congress:

Good health care should be readily available to all of our citizens. . . . I believe the public will always be better served by a pluralistic system than by a monolithic one, by a system which creates many effective centers of responsibility— both in public and private—rather than one that concentrates authority in a single governmental source.[9]

He did not suggest that, in effect, a third being, pieced together from private and governmental elements into one system, be generated.

student loans

Another program, similar in basic conception, is already at work in the student loan program. In this plan, the loan is taken by a student. The interest accumulated during the school years is paid by the government. The student repays the loan and the remaining interest after graduation at a rate of 7 per cent. The program is administered differently in different states, with some states guaranteeing a part of the loan against default and other states playing no role whatsoever. However, there are a number of features which are common to all of the loan programs regardless of the specific

---

[6] *Ibid.*, p. 168.

[7] Linda Francke, "The Games People Play on Sesame Street," *New York Magazine*, April 5, 1971, pp. 26–29.

[8] Richard D. Lyons, "Nixon's Health Care Plan Proposes Employers Pay $2.5 Billion More a Year," *New York Times*, February 19, 1971.

[9] "Excerpts from the President's Message Urging a New National Health Strategy,'" *New York Times*, February 19, 1971.

mechanisms of administration: (1) the federal government guarantees the loans against default, death, or disability of the borrower; (2) the family income of the student must be below $15,000 after adjustment for number of dependents and number of dependents in school; (3) the student may use the loan for tuition or for living expenses; (4) the total amount of loans may not exceed $7,500; and (5) the school plays no part in the loan procedures other than to certify the student's good standing.

The growth of the guaranteed loan program has been large and the ambitions held for it yet larger.[10] In 1969 approximately 75,000 students received $670 million, with government financing totalling $71,200,000. In 1970, 923,500 students received loans adding up to $794,241,000, with $114 million of government financing.

It must be pointed out that in comparison to federal fellowships, with their monumental paperwork (announcements, application forms, recommendation letters, transcripts of grades, evaluation, forms, accounting) and high cost to the taxpayer, the student loan program involves little red tape, and the costs to the taxpayer are minor. It should also be noted that the administrative costs of the program are remarkably low. For instance, the appropriation for 1969–70 included $62.4 million for interest subsidies, $10.8 million for default insurance, and only $1.5 million for computer services.

The program is far from perfect; the rates are still too high, and many fear that the funds will soon run out. It is also criticized for not being responsive to the needs of poor and minority group students. The "Survey of Guaranteed Student Loan Accessibility," done by an independent firm (*Chronicle of Higher Education*,

[10] The figures and estimates have been reported in the *Chronicle of Higher Education* based on Office of Education figures.

3/16/70), found this to be true. While 42 per cent of the applicants were female, females accounted for 51 per cent of the refusals. Although 11.7 per cent of the sample was non-white, non-whites accounted for 36.4 per cent of the refusals. The report concluded that "the proportion of females and non-whites not receiving loans was significantly higher than could be explained by chance occurrence." But these shortcomings are being overcome by an increase in the federal contribution and the development of closer cooperation between banks and financial aid officers of universities. By and large, the student loan program provides a fine model for management of federal aid, in which the effects of dollars spent are multiplied many times through the economy.

NASA

Perhaps the most famous of the government-private sector mixes was developed under NASA for project Apollo. The successful completion of the program was made possible by the combination of government facilities and funds, third sector beings, and private corporations. Thus, aeronautical engineers at universities and research foundations worked on government contracts with the businessmen from the aerospace industry to build spacecrafts that were tested and launched on government land. In reporting on their four years of intensive study of NASA, Sayles and Chandler point out that:

NASA, at its peak in the mid-1960s, sought contributions from 20,000 different organizations! ... A scientist may be part of a university, responsible for the design and testing of an experiment to be flown by a NASA spacecraft, serving as a consultant to an industrial contractor that builds equipment for the agency, and a member of an advisory board that helps shape future science policy for NASA and other government agencies.[11]

Sayles and Chandler go on to say:

... thousands of engineers, scientists, technicians, and administrative personnel are employed in laboratory and field-development work, in basic research, in launching and tracking spacecraft, and in a whole host of support activities. While outsiders employed by contractors may comprise 90 percent of the work force, a critical amount of designing, testing, planning, and operating is conducted "in-house" by NASA personnel. Further, NASA believes, with substantial justification, that outsiders cannot be successfully stimulated, managed, or coordinated without a technologically sophisticated internal organization.[12]

Given the successes of NASA, it seems clear that it was able to overcome many difficulties and coordinate the efforts of all these individuals who worked for NASA at different points in time, with different perspectives and training, etc.

The key to making the NASA structure work rests upon creating an effective network of formal and informal communications. ... To be on the safe side, NASA may err in over-communicating upward, laterally, and downward. It engulfs anyone who can conceivably influence or implement the decision. It establishes various "management councils" composed of co-equal associates to share progress and problems on a frequent basis. In an unending effort to exchange information in real-time, it uses telephone, hot lines, executive aircraft, datafax, and long distance conference hook-ups by voice and data display and computer data transmission.[13]

[11] Leonard R. Sayles and Margaret K. Chandler, *Managing Large Systems* (New York: Harper & Row, 1971), p. 6.
[12] *Ibid.*, p. 161.
[13] Albert Siepert, "NASA's Management of the Civilian Space Program," speech prepared for presentation to the Institute for Management Science meeting, March 28, 1969, mimeo.

Most of these networks cut across the sectors and thus help integrate them. The details of this necessarily well-coordinated operation are not important for our discussion. However, it should be remembered that no such approach has been attempted on our domestic problems. Imagine what effective an attack could be made on heroin addiction if government funds, hospital staffs, community groups, and local businesses got together to tackle the program under a well-coordinated and well-financed system! The same holds for pollution control, crime reduction, and consumer protection.

postal service

Sometimes third sector beings are created by governmental fiat. The U.S. Postal Service is an example of such a public corporation. While the pre-1970 Post Office Department was dependent on Congress for rate increases, the new one must become entirely self-supporting. In fact, the last attempt of the old Post Office Department to increase its rate was vetoed by Congress. A year later, the Postal Service increased its rates. According to the Postal Reform Act, increased charges can be levied once the Postal Commission, not Congress, approves them. The enacting legislation requires the Postal Service to do what is necessary to maintain itself as a financially independent corporation.

In order to provide better service, this semi-independent corporation has altered its traditional way of operating. Thus, local postmasters used to have to turn to Washington (or at least regional offices) for every decision; now, the local branches seem to be remarkably free from centralization. For example,

Until a year ago the Baltimore office couldn't pay its own utility bills. ... The bills had to be certified and forwarded to a center in Atlanta for payment. Baltimore and other major post offices have also recently received authority to open small branch offices without higher approval and to make repairs and improvements costing up to $2,000. ... Next fall the Baltimore office will move into a spacious new building filled with modern mail-processing equipment. The budgeting basis will be different, too. For the fiscal year beginning July 1, Postmaster Bloomberg is asking for a budget of about $60 million. Previously, postmasters in big cities had no budget; everything was decided by regional bosses.[14]

Before the Postal Service was formed, postmasters were often outsiders, appointed because of political connections. Now, on the other hand, men and women selected for these jobs are experienced and qualified. Their skills, rather than who they know, get them their jobs; thus, it is much more conceivable that one will go up through the ranks of the new postal system. This must lead to higher morale, if not to greater efficiency on the part of Postal Service employees. Although the average letter writer may not notice any difference, except in the color of the mailboxes, it is inconceivable to me that the new system, which cuts through many of the bureaucratic hassles created by an overly centralized operation, could be doing as poor a job as the old Department did. In fact, according to one source, improvements have been made. The *San Francisco Examiner* repeated a survey it did before the Postal Service was formed. Mailings were sent to over 675 individuals in the U.S., Great Britain, Mexico, and the Orient. People who had complained to the *Examiner* in the past about the postal system were reinterviewed as were postal officials and employees. Post offices were also revisited. The findings of this

survey when compared to the past survey were:

- The public attitude towards mail service has vastly improved.
- More mail (especially packages) is damaged in transit.
- There is less personnel dissatisfaction with pay (workers have had a 39.4 increase all-around) and with working conditions.
- There is less political manipulation.
- There is less overt racism and greater minority participation.
- There is more dissatisfaction in respect to service to and from APO and FPO addresses (service men).
- Special delivery service is almost an utter waste of time and money.
- San Francisco originating complaints (once many and varied) are largely limited to plaintive wishes from the public that "the mailman would show up earlier than he does." (No complaints about hairy or barefoot postmen any longer.)
- Indefinitely worse service between Bay Area cities; some of it incredibly bad.
- Infinitely better service (than in 1963) to and from business and banking firms in the area.[15]

amtrak

Amtrak, the new federally chartered corporation that now runs the intercity passenger trains in this country, is another example of a third sector being created by governmental fiat. The long-range task of the National Railroad Passenger Corporation (Amtrak is its nickname) is "turning a collection of rickety, money-losing

[14] Kenneth H. Bacon, "New Postal Corporation Seeks to Become a Business Rather Than a Bureaucracy," *Wall Street Journal*, February 18, 1971.

[15] Robert Patterson, "Postal Service Found Better in New Study," *San Francisco Examiner*, December 6, 1971.

passenger trains into a swift, modern transportation system that will attract more riders and make a profit—before it goes broke"[16] Amtrak started operations on May 1, 1971. It received $40 million from Congress and an additional $300 million in loans and guarantees.

Amtrak has since taken a number of steps to remodel passenger railroad transportation, not all of which have been well received. Amtrak reduced the number of trains from 300 to 186. And passenger trains are now given the priority—formerly granted to freight trains—to make intercity trips shorter, trains no longer stop in many of the very small towns where trains used to stop. In addition, new train service has been added to heavily travelled routes. Connections have been improved because schedules have been revised.

Amtrak continues to have a number of problems that may have more to do with the recentness of the change than with the third sector approach. Many trains are not filled to capacity or even full enough to allow Amtrak to meet its costs.

Initially, Amtrak was set up as a for-profit corporation. However, it suffered unanticipated financial problems less than six months after it took over the largely unprofitable passenger trains and could not achieve the aim of financial independence from Congress. There are many who see Amtrak as the first step in nationalizing the railroads in this country. Companies like the Penn Central can no longer foot the bills created by their large work crews, the loss of business to trucking firms, and the disappearance of certain markets. "As the government moves toward subsidizing long-haul passenger operations through Amtrak, it's an easy jump to rationalize federal support for short-haul freight operation," an Interstate

Commerce Commission official says.[17] Many railroad officials, Congressmen, and other public spokesmen are opposed to efforts toward nationalization of the railroads, while union members, creditors, and some Congressmen favor this solution. "And though the industry is generally horrified at the thought of government takeover, some railroad executives do see public demand for maintaining maximum rail service as tending to force public ownership."[18]

It is far too early to judge where all this will end. If large deficits will continue to plague the railroads. Amtrak might become little more than a "Department of Railroads," a way to nationalize passenger trains, thus becoming a new *government* arm. If miraculously the trains would be profitable enough to be entirely self-supporting, Amtrak may move toward the *private* sector. Most likely it will continue to be partially subsidized and otherwise mix or bridge the two sectors.

other organizations

There are other branches of our federal government, aside from the postal system, which might be profitably cut off from the bureaucratic maze and made into what the press refers to as semi-private agencies. It has been suggested that since the U.S. Office of Economic Opportunity is becoming mainly a research unit, it would be more effective if it were isolated from political pressures. One way to remove it from direct bureaucratic control would be to set up a public corporation and semi-private agency that would be partially funded by Washington. In an earlier publication, this author suggested a reorganization of the Food and Drug Administration which would be similar to

---

[16] Albert R. Karr, "Government Train Service Is Set to Begin, but Few Improvements Are Likely at First," *Wall Street Journal*, April 27, 1971.

[17] Albert R. Karr, "The Takeover Route," *Wall Street Journal*, January 6, 1972.
[18] *Ibid.*

the one our postal system recently underwent.[19]

The Food and Drug Testing Corporation, as the liberated FDA might be called, would be a public corporation endowed by Congress. Its trustees would be appointed from the scientific community, the National Science Foundation, the consumer protection movement, labor unions, etc. The newly formed non-profit corporation would charge a nominal fee to industries desiring the certification of their products. In this way, some of the costs of testing and research could be covered.

The new organization would be removed from the political pressures which hamper the effective operation of the FDA. Its long-term endowment could insure its semi-independent status and its financial security. Our purpose here is not to review all the recent criticisms of the FDA and to show how our own idea would save the day, but as has already been said, it is inconceivable that the new public corporation could do as bad a job as the old one.

The possibilities of the creation by government of public corporations are tremendous. For example, there is evidence that the public would be willing to try a radically different approach to our welfare problems. According to a poll conducted by the Center for Policy Research in 1969, 48 per cent of Americans would pay an average of $6 a month (or $72 a year) to insure themselves against poverty.[20] Given that about a million Americans fall into poverty each year, the income generated by the premiums would provide all Americans a minimal income

of $1,600 a year. Higher income could be provided if the premiums are raised. Welfare could be handled at least in part through the development of a public corporation that would be in charge of anti-poverty insurance.

Another way to modify anti-poverty programs has been suggested by a bi-partisan group of 98 senators and representatives. They introduced "legislation to create an independent National Legal Services Corporation, which would be funded by Congress and operated by an autonomous board of public and private members."[21]

The suggested National Legal Services Corporation would be much more insulated from the political pressures that have surrounded government-run attempts at providing legal aid for the poor. Like my proposed Food and Drug Testing Corporation, the National Legal Services Corporation would be cut off from the bureaucratic maze of governmental agencies because of its autonomous status as a public corporation.

These governmentally created public corporations *do not* have to be on the national level. In New York City, the massive hospital system has been turned into the New York City Health and Hospitals Corporation. The quality of hospital care was rapidly deteriorating in New York City. If the budget for the Corporation is not cut too drastically, we will be able to see what a difference the third sector approach can make in this area. It is hard to imagine that the newly formed corporation will do nearly as poor a job as the worn out agency did.

There have been other corporations that have been public, third sector *from inception*. The Public Broadcasting Corporation which, though far from an unmiti-

[19] Amitai Etzioni, "Freeing the Food and Drug Administration," *The Conference Board Record*, Vol. 7 (October 1970), pp. 37–39.
[20] Reprints of this unpublished report may be obtained from the Center for Policy Research, Inc., 475 Riverside Drive, New York, New York 10027.

[21] "Bipartisan Group in Congress Urges a Legal Services Corporation for Poor," *New York Times*, March 18, 1971.

gated success, is widely regarded as more effective than governmental agencies in the same business, (e.g., New York City's own TV program on channel 31), or commercial TV, as far as broadcasting public education and information is concerned.

Third sector beings can operate in another fashion. Public nongovernmental authorities can be formed to carry out domestic services. One of the problems we frequently run into in this area is caused by the semantics I discussed earlier. The difference between "public" and "private" often hides the possibilities and the achievements of nongovernmental enterprises. For example, we have public universities, like the New York State Universities, and private ones, like Harvard. The same holds for hospitals—the Veterans Administration Hospitals are viewed as public while hospitals like the Columbia Presbyterian are private.

universities

The *really* "private" sector schools are created for profit. Famous Artists and Career Academy would be examples. And the truly private hospitals are proprietary. Nonprofit hospitals, research organizations, universities and colleges, legal aid societies, abortion referral agencies, etc., differ markedly in organization, accountability, and cost-effectiveness from either governmental *or* private sector beings which produce the same kind of public goods.

Given our present situation, where the private sector has not been sufficiently mobilized to produce public goods on a large scale, the best services and facilities can often be found in the third sector. In the educational system, for instance, the universities most highly thought of are not governmental nor are they commercial (Harvard, MIT, Yale, Princeton, Colum-

bia, etc.). And the state-run universities that are highly respected are treated as if they were in the third sector. Berkeley and the University of Wisconsin would be good examples of these. Interestingly, those whose autonomy from state control is being violated are the ones which are on the decline.

There have been some recent attempts to allow the private sector to be more directly involved in the teaching of children. Thus, private concerns were to be paid only to the degree that they improve the performance of students. "Performance contracting," as it is called, was tried out in at least 16 states at a cost of $6.5 million to the federal government. "On the average, each private contractor must improve students' performance in reading and mathematics by 1.6 grades in order to break even."[22]

Indications so far are that contract teaching does not work. A study carried out for HEW by the Rand Corporation found that the programs run by private contractors produced no overall gains in the performance of the children in most cases, the children progressed at the same rate as those not involved in performance contracting.[23]

hospitals

"Voluntary" hospitals are considered to be the best in our country. Ten experts on hospital care were asked the following question: "If you or your family required major hospital services—diagnosis or treatment—which 25 hospitals in the United States would you select as repre-

---

[22] Jack Rosenthal, "U.S. Plans Test of the Teaching of Pupils by Private Contractors," *New York Times*, July 15, 1970.

[23] See *Science News*, Vol. 100, No. 25 (1972).

sentative of the best?"[24] The following hospitals were the most popular: (1) Massachusetts General, Boston; (2) Johns Hopkins, Baltimore; (3) University of Chicago, Chicago; (4) Columbia Presbyterian, New York; (5) New York Hospital, New York; (6) (tied) Barnes, St. Louis, and Henry Ford, Detroit; (7) Mount Sinai, New York; (8) St. Mary's, Rochester, Minn.; (9) (tied) Palo Alto-Stanford, Palo-Alto, California, and Yale-New Haven, New Haven, Conn.; (10) (tied) University Hospital, Ann Arbor, Mich., and University of Minnesota Hospital, Minneapolis, Minn. All of these hospitals are also non-profit teaching institutions. They are all in the third sector—none are proprietary and none are governmental.

Proprietary medical schools were forced to close down as long ago as 1910 when the American Medical Association began to set new standards for accreditation.[25] Proprietary hospitals in general seem to be of lower quality than third sector ones. Government hospitals do not usually measure up to the third sector ones either. A good example of this would be a comparison of mental hospitals. The state institutions are basically inferior to third sector facilities.

Since July 1, 1970, abortions have been legal in the state of New York. Two different kinds of abortion referral agencies developed. The first kind is offered as a free service by groups like Planned Parenthood, the Family Planning Information Service, the Clergy Consultation Services on Abortion, and other non-profit groups. The other group consists of profit-making firms. These "have found

in the hard-won reform the basis for 'one of the most lucrative businesses of the year.' ... [according to] Stephen E. Mindell, an assistant attorney general in the office of State Attorney General Louis J. Lefkowitz. ..."[26]

The State Attorney General's Office now has an operating injunction against these commercial firms. They found that the profit-making abortion referral agencies were splitting fees with doctors and advertising medicine in a way that was contrary to the common law of the state. The case against Abortion Information Agency, Incorporated, a profit-making firm, is now in the Court of Appeals. (The state won its case in the New York State Supreme Court and the decision was affirmed in the Appellate Division.)

In addition, the New York State Legislature passed a statute which prohibited the operation of for-profit abortion agencies. This statute has been upheld by a panel of three federal judges convened to hear the case.

The non-profit abortion referral agencies, which neither split fees nor advertise specific doctors, may continue to operate. In this case, the merits of the public sector over the private one, for this kind of service, are particularly evident.

These brief comments on relative quality of services may seem gratuitous, especially to those familiar with the complexities of making full-fledged evaluative studies. However, only few such studies have been undertaken, and hence statements which compare the merits of doing things one way or another are necessarily tentative, until more studies are conducted.

Of course, not all third sector beings are superior on all counts, as is illustrated by the New York Triboro Bridge and Tunnel Authority. The Authority is reported to use its monopoly power to

[24] Roul Tunley, "America's 10 Best Hospitals," *Ladies Home Journal*, Vol. 85 (February 1967), pp. 34, 134.

[25] See editorial entitled "Higher Education and the Nation's Health" by John H. Knowles, general director, Massachusetts General Hospital, in *Science*, Vol. 171 (January 1971).

[26] Linda Charlton, "Abortion Brokers Are Under Study," *New York Times*, February 10, 1971.

generate excessive income and keep its facilities in unnecessarily good condition. The New York Port Authority is certainly not known for its efficiency. Maybe the reason is that most of these ineffective bodies, *within* the third sector, are on the less "privatized," more "governmental" side.

two success stories

Those third sector beings which have been relatively more "privatized" seem to be, on balance, much more successful. Two major cases in point are COMSAT and Fannie Mae.

fannie mae

Fannie Mae (or FNMA) which stands for the Federal National Mortgage Association, is reported in the press daily as a high volume stock on the New York Stock Exchange. But it is far from just another stock of a typical corporation. (Even technically it has had a special status which reflects its government support: until April 1971 the "margin" required for it was much lower than for other common stocks; it was closer to that required for government bonds.) Originally a government agency, which issued some *non-voting* stocks to the public, with the balance being funded by the treasury, it was "privatized" in 1968. All the stocks were sold to the public and made into voting stocks which elect up to 10 of the 15 board members (the rest being appointed by the Secretary of HUD).

However, about one-third of Fannie Mae's volatile stock is owned by companies involved in housing-related industries; they are, for the most part, the mortgage bankers with whom Fannie Mae does a major part of its business.

Fannie Mae now ranks as the eighth largest corporation in the United States. Its aim has been to meet the public's need for housing by providing a secondary market for government-insured mortgages.

Investment-wise, Fannie Mae is a unique animal. One reason is the complex nature of its earnings. Despite the fact that there has probably never been a company on which more information was available, the variables are so great that a line-by-line prediction is extremely difficult to make. Management stresses that when one component such as fees goes one way, another element, perhaps the sale of mortgages, will move in the opposite direction.

Skeptics insist that Fannie Mae is a near monopoly, government-sponsored and controlled, which will never be allowed to earn more than a public utility or other regulated companies. If Congress thinks Fannie Mae is making too much money, they say, it could intervene and change the charter of the company. Further, the Secretary of HUD, George Romney, holds the power to narrow or broaden the ratio of debt to equity.[27]

While there are clearly a number of problems like these that potential investors in Fannie Mae must take into account, it is also clear that Fannie Mae has made money available to potential home buyers in a time of tight credit and high interest rates. For example, Fannie Mae's "net new business in 1970 totaled 25 per cent of U.S. residential mortgage credit. Moreover, in 1969 and 1970, Fannie Mae helped boost FHA and VA financed housing starts 140 per cent, while conventional starts declined 7 per cent."[28]

In the last few years, Fannie Mae has been trying to balance its responsibility to the public with its responsibility to achieve stable returns for its stockholders. In the process Fannie Mae has been reorganized in a more efficient manner by *cutting* its staff substantially as the volume of work *rose*.

[27] Robert Lenzner, "What Makes Fannie Run?" *Barrons*, July 12, 1971.
[28] *Ibid.*

comsat

The Communications Satellite Corporation, known as Comsat, was created by the government through a congressional act in 1962. Federal money appropriated for defense and space financed the development of its chief technology—the world-hugging satellites. Civilian use was made possible through a corporation financed half by the public and half by the commercial communications companies. Comsat's board of directors includes representatives of the industries involved, presidential-appointed directors, and public officials. The *Economist* referred to orbiting a world-wide system within seven years, as "magnificent."[29]

[29] *The Economist*, August 9, 1969.

conclusion

Surely other third types, either to be composed of government and business elements or third sector beings from inception, can be identified, and others could be evolved if there were greater experimentation. There is no doubt that we need more information and evaluation on the production of public goods in the various sectors and mixes of sectors. But it seems that enough is known for us to be able to state now that greater reliance on the third sector, both as a way of reducing government on all levels and as a way of involving the private sector in the service of domestic missions, would be significantly more effective than either expanding the federal or other levels of government or dropping them on the private sector.

40. society's frontiers for organizing activities*

James D. Thompson

Predicting the future seems more futile than ever.

Our world contains more variables than ever before. Some of the old ones are capable of wider variation than formerly. And there seems to be nothing which we can take for granted. With so much complexity, we hardly know what to expect next, let alone predict it or bring it about.

Reprinted from *Public Administration Review*, 33, No. 4 (July–August 1973), pp. 327–335, with permission of the publisher and the author.

* The author is indebted to Robert Stern for reactions to an earlier version of this paper.

Yet I think selective perception operates here. Because we are concerned or fearful about the future in times of great social change, we exaggerate the uncertainties and ignore the things which are least problematic. Perhaps if we take stock of those variables which seem least worrisome, we can find ways in which they limit the variation of other things which worry us most. This would not enable us to predict the future with precision, but it might help us anticipate possibilities and reduce the likelihood of surprises.

I will shoot for the year 2000, partly because it is the roundest figure I can find, and I am partial to round figures. But there is another reason for that kind of time perspective. When first invited to prepare this article, I suggested that I shoot for something less than 20 years hence, but as I began to think about preparing for the future I became more aware of the fact that most of us do and must make projections of 30 or more years. Decisions about how to raise our children, or what kinds of environments to expose them to, involve implicit or explicit considerations of what kind of world they will face as mature adults. Decisions to undertake a 30-year mortgage involve 30-year projections. Decisions in revamping our curricula involve projections about the demands which will be placed on our students well into the 21st century.

In crystal-balling about the year 2000 then, I do not feel especially brave or foolhardy; if there is folly in the venture it is in making explicit what we usually are allowed to leave implicit. One reservation, however. Even if I am lucky enough to be thinking in the right direction, the speed of changes is another question, and I hope it is understood that I am thinking of the year 2000 *plus or minus* 10!

I will proceed on the following agenda:

First, I will make two fundamental assumptions, on which the remainder of my argument will hinge. Then I will turn attention to changes which seem to be clearly in the works, with reasons for them. Finally, I will speculate about some of the problems which I believe will be gnawing at us in 2000—plus or minus 10.

hinging assumptions

1. *Complex organizations were invented, have existed, and will continue to exist because they are tools for doing what must be done or what most of us want done, and we judge them to be doing more good than harm.*

This may seem too obvious to make explicit, but I do want to spend a minute

or two on it, for it goes counter to some of the excited chatter which passes for contemporary nonfiction. This chatter says complex organizations have gotten out of hand, that "people" are at the mercy of "organizations," or that "they" are forcing "us" to use goods and services we do not want, or that complex organizations are unwilling to change to meet new conditions and new needs.

I think these complaints are simply wrong.

True, some organizations like some individuals do things which are detrimental to others and to societies. True, some of these harmful consequences are deliberately perpetrated, even if others are the result of ignorance. True, people of modern societies are highly dependent on complex organizations, and the population of Manhattan would have to flee on foot or bicycle or starve if the complex organizations which regularly provide food, water, heat, sewage disposal, and other essentials were suddenly to stop operating. True, complex organizations may need several years to stop doing some things and start doing others—and to the individual who equates eternity with months, these organizations may appear not simply sluggish but incapable of change. True, organizations do not dance to *my* tune—not even the organizations to which I belong—but that does not mean that they do not dance. Anyone who insists—to take one frequent example—that American universities have not changed in the last century, or even in the last 20 years, simply does not know what he is talking about.

When we get right down to fundamentals, organizations are *not "them"* in distinction to "*us*." Complex organizations are you and me and the guy down the street. Just as *we* are the family, the community, and the nation, *we* are in a particular configuration—complex organizations. And my first hinging assumption is that we joined in the particular configurations called complex organizations because we believed it was to our advantage to do so—that our resources could be mobilized and allocated more effectively through such organization than otherwise. And as we learned about some of the difficulties inherent in those organizations, we tinkered with them to gradually improve them. I see no reason to believe that we will forego the advantages in the future, unless our desires change in rather basic ways. This brings me to my second hinging assumption.

2. *Human desires will not be fundamentally different in 2000 than they have been through the 20th century.*

Again, this is going counter to some of the agitated chatter which maintains that fads and fashions and experiments of the year are a preview of the future, and I need to explain why I reject that chatter.

Worldwide, I believe we can say that fundamental human demands associated with biological survival and comfort will continue to claim the attention of large blocs of the world's population. Whether the green revolution will increase food productivity faster than population growth may be debatable. An optimistic view may be that we have the know-how to feed and clothe and shelter the expanding population. An even more optimistic view may be that we will learn how to modify political / economic / religious / cultural factors to at least reduce the discrepancies between the have and have-not components of the world.

Even if we grant for the moment that these states of affairs may be attainable by the year 2000, they can only be attained through the highly organized efforts of many people involved in very many complex organizations and networks of organizations. Affluence does not simply occur; it is produced by the efforts of people, and I believe that in the foreseeable future this will remain true.

Still, even if the discrepancies between have and have-not societies are reduced, it is safe to say that there will be geographic pockets or social segments with economic abundance, for whom food, shelter, clothing, and medical care can be taken for granted. Some of the chatter we hear maintains that the achievements of affluence is killing off desires for more material wealth, that the new young adults have rejected the values of their predecessors and are satisfied with less. But I believe these predictions are the result again of selective perception, that the new generations are just as wise but no wiser than preceding generations, just as altruistic but no more, just as greedy but no more.

I suggest that at each stage of the life cycle certain values become salient while others are latent or disappear. In an affluent period, the young adults can afford to be nonchalant about the acquisition of economic assets and to assert that they will not emulate their predecessors. Because of the baby boom following World War II, the world is proportionately full of young adults, and in the relatively prosperous sectors of that world, they can easily be seen and heard denying the values and motives of the earlier generations. But just as the world in 1970 was "full" of 20-year-olds, the world of 1985 will be "full" of 35-year-olds raising their children, worrying about their health and education and safety and neighborhood influences. And the world of 2000 will be "full" of 50-year-olds worrying about their grandchildren—and beginning to worry about their health and their old age. In short, a world "full" of 50-year-olds is going to look very different than a world "full" of 20-year-olds. To the extent that in 1973 the "values" of the 1940s and 1950s and 1960s have been "rejected," it appears to be temporary rejection with a built-in antidote.

some basis for change

So I am proceeding as if organizations were going to be around, that we will be making more, not less, use of them, and that families are going to interact with complex organizations as both sources of goods and services and as arenas out of which to fashion careers through the life cycle.

One change I foresee, then, is "more." But beyond that, can we see how organizations of 2000 will differ from today's organizations?

I suggest we are in a watershed period, and that in the more developed parts of the world, at least, we are in the process of determining which organizational configurations are viable for new conditions and which are not—just as we can look back now upon the 1940s as the watershed decade which determined that supermarket food stores were viable for United States conditions but the "mom and pop" grocery was not, or that the one-room school house was no longer adequate to the task. In the 1940s both kinds of groceries existed and both kinds of schools existed. But at the time, only some saw what almost all of us now see—that forces already in progress were rendering certain organizational forms invalid.

A decade or two from now I believe we will be able to look back and see that we were—in the 1960s and 1970s—struggling to sort the viable from the decaying forms of organization. Those who are forging the new reality are doing so without the help of us who study and write about organizations, for I believe we academics are still in a conceptual box built for an earlier period, and that being in the box, we are only barely aware of what is happening out there.

crumbling current assumptions

Our conceptual box, I believe, is *formal organization*. Some of us have adopted the term *complex organization* for aesthetic reasons, but for most of us the two terms —formal and complex—have been synonyms. The watershed will, I predict, reveal two realities, one corresponding to theories of formal organization, but another for which the term complex organization may indeed be more appropriate. Let's examine some of the important dimensions of the formal organization conceptual box, and then see what may lie outside.

1. Formal organization theory assumes that each member performs for the organization and no other. Max Weber[1] saw this as a key factor in the development of social rationality, and the assumption probably has been very true in a probability sense. But:

Item: I do not know when the role originated, but as early as 1950 I became aware of "technical representatives" on the U.S. Air Force bases. The "tech reps" lived in the vicinity and worked regular hours at the bases, coordinating their activities to military operations, and in most respects appeared to be "members" of the military organization. Technically, however, they were employees of the manufacturer of the aircraft, and were assigned to work in a liaison capacity between the manufacturer and the customer. They were part of the complex organization of the military, but not part of the formal organization of the military.

Item: In every university of which I have been a member, I have had faculty colleagues who were "obviously" members of my department. They helped prolong the agony of faculty meetings. They took part in curricular revisions. They taught classes, directed dissertations, came to faculty parties. Yet at any time you choose to specify, one or more of them had their salaries paid in whole or

[1] Max Weber, *The Theory of Economic and Social Organization*, A. M. Henderson and Talcott Parsons (trans.) (New York: Free Press, 1947).

in part by funds from governments, foundations, or contracting firms, on grounds that the research they were doing contributed to the mission of the funding agency as well as the mission of the university.

Weber[2] made quite a point of the bureaucratic official being on salary. Neither he nor those of us who quote him may ever have bothered to specify that the salary was paid by that bureaucracy, but I am sure that is what Weber meant. And in the formal organization box, I believe that makes sense. But then what about my universities? Did my faculty colleagues belong to the university—or to another agency? I believe the reality is that they were simultaneously in two systems of complex, coordinated activities which happened to coincide in a particular place and person. Formal organization theory has led us to think they belong to the university (which issued the paycheck) rather than to the agency which supplied the ("soft") funds.

2. Formal organization theory assumes that an organization exists in a delineated and relatively permanent geographic space, to serve a specifiable and delimited clientele.

In the industrial sphere, for example, firms began usually as local or regional firms, and the nationwide firm emerged only when economies of scale combined with transportation in such industries as steel and automobiles. Armies were formed from locally recruited, locally organized, and locally led components. At least in our case, governmental organizations, hospitals, and schools originated as local organizations. The resources put into them originated at home, and the services they were to provide were to local people. But:

Item: Large-scale projects such as building of a major hydro-electric/irrigation

dam or vehicles for space exploration involve networks of formal organizations. Typically the network is built on a configuration of subcontractors around a prime contractor. Any given formal organization involved may be devoting all or a major portion of its resources and energies to a product or service for a clientele it has never before served and at considerable distance from its geographic location. Once the mission has been completed, that organization may never again be involved in the same configuration of formal organizations.

Item: The international consortium brings together large financial institutions, governmental insuring or underwriting agencies, engineering firms, transportation organizations, and perhaps others. They participate in the launching and operation of large developmental projects beyond the scope of any single organization. None of the consortium participants need be solely in this venture, but for all of them it is one of their major undertakings, and serving in this capacity certainly does not fit our usual conceptions of "organization-client relations" or of "market behavior." The delicacy with which such consortia are put together is underscored nicely by Sune Carlson's[3] accounts of the Volta River Project in Ghana and the Liberian American-Swedish Minerals Company in Liberia.

Item: We lack a label for the kind of thing so well described by Burton Clark[4] in analyzing just how the teaching of physical sciences in secondary schools was revitalized. The best phrase I can think of is "organized movement," but it certainly required the coordinated activities—coordinated in the sense of different functions

---

[2] *Ibid.*

[3] Sune Carlson, *International Financial Decisions* (Amsterdam: North-Holland Publishing Co., 1969).

[4] Burton Clark, "Interorganizational Patterns in Education," *Administrative Science Quarterly* (September 1965).

and in the sense of sequences—of a committee of scientists, the National Science Foundation, book publishers, state and local school boards, and others. None of the participants had this as a sole responsibility, but for certain important purposes the organizations involved—or components of those organizations—behaved very much as part of a movement organization.

These three items—the prime-contractor /sub-contractor configuration, the international consortium, and the organized movement—all seem to me to be examples of complexly organized activity. But none is characterized by a permanent geographic location or a delimited and specifiable clientele, as I believe formal organization theory assumes.

3. Formal organization theory assumes that an organization revolves around a unitary authority system. But:

Item: The "war on polio" had most of the earmarks of a complex organization without a unified "chain of command." By Riley's[5] account, it involved the activities of 3,100 local chapters, each of which raised funds through solicitations by volunteers, with 50 per cent of those funds to be retained locally for treatment of local polio victims. But it motivated the pooling of the remaining 50 per cent nationally, both as insurance against local outbreaks which might overrun local funds and for research and education purposes. In 20 years the Foundation spent $315 million on patient care, $55 million on research, and $33 million on fellowships and scholarships to medical students, physicians, researchers, physical therapists, medical social workers, and nurses. In 1938, the science of virology consisted of fewer than 40 individuals; the Foundation helped train 373 researchers,

[5] Edward R. Riley, "Organizational Effectiveness in American Voluntary Health Organizations," unpublished Ph.D. dissertation, Indiana University, 1968.

288 practicing physicians, 2,674 physical therapists, 778 medical social workers, and several thousand other skilled persons.

But while the National Foundation was maintaining its ability to raise funds through volunteers and was stimulating the training of specialists for both therapy and research, it was also devising and directing a research program. This focused especially on prevention rather than care and cure after the fact. The Foundation's program led to a Nobel Prize in 1954 and culminated in the Salk and Sabin vaccines.

Here, it seems to me, we have an example of a sustained and complexly organized activity with virtually no authority relationships involved. Certainly the fund-raising volunteers were not subject to authority as we usually think of it. The training of therapists and of research specialists was not done by a hierarchically organized foundation, but was instead facilitated through scholarship and fellowship grants to individuals and institutions. The significant research was not done "within" the Foundation, even though it was done within the *program* designed by the Foundation.

Item: Although I have not seen documentation, I have heard that the scarcity and indispensibility of powerful nuclear research facilities such as at Argonne and now the new National Accelerator Laboratory in Illinois result in research activities being coordinated by allocating committees of scientists who thereby shape nationwide research programs without exercising "authority" over their participants.

These examples suggest to me that complexly organized activities need not rely on authority as the glue which holds them together. If we look at some of these activities from the social level I believe we see division of labor, coordinated activity, hierarchy (of knowledge or prestige), mobilization, and allocation and reallocation of resources—but not authority.

if trends, why?

So far I have established (to my satisfaction) that some activities can be seen in our contemporary society which correspond to a common sense notion of complicated, coordinated purposeful activity on a large and complicated scale—and yet which do not fit what we think of as formal organization theory. It is necessary to relax one or more of the usual assumptions in order to delineate these complexly organized activities. Are these simply the exceptions which prove the rule?

On the contrary, I believe these are previews of coming attractions, and that there are identifiable reasons to think so.

One of the contributing factors to the changes which I think are already under way is that our *networks of cause/effect are expanding*. Acts which under some conditions are private acts— such as burning of refuse—become public in their consequences as the population becomes denser. As the field in which problems occur becomes larger, locally available resources become inadequate to the challenge, and we organize on a broader scale to solve problems of a wider scale. There can be no doubt of a trend toward wider organization and away from what traditionally we considered local matters for local effort—interstate authorities to deal with water reclamation and population, consolidated school districts to achieve economics of scale and to smooth out inequities growing from local disadvantages, multi-governmental port authorities, and so on. However we feel about it, it becomes clear that "local" no longer can be a synonym for "sacred."

A second contributing factor is the *pace of change*. With the combination of a larger population and rapid communication and transport, interdependence not only covers a wide territory, but events anywhere within that territory can have rapid consequences elsewhere and call for the speedy mobilization and deployment of resources. An epidemic in one locale, or a natural disaster, can have more devastating effects under the new conditions of density and interconnecting networks; but communication and transportation possibilities now permit the marshalling of specialized resources and their redeployment on virtually a worldwide basis. Similarly, a new solution to human needs, or new invention to satisfy human desires, can move through the multi-national organization for rapid dispersion or diffusion throughout the world.

And a third reason for thinking that formal organizations will be less important in relation to complex organizations is that *technology* is becoming increasingly *knowledge-intensive* rather than labor-intensive or capital-intensive. This trend is spotty, of course, many of the developing countries have more than adequate labor supplies but are short both on capital and knowledge; however, it appears that in the relatively developed portions of the world, the routine activities and brute strength activities are being transferred to the machine, with human energies increasingly devoted to the discretionary applications of knowledge. The ease with which knowledge and the people who possesses it can be transported, relative to the transportation of capital goods or large labor forces, is obvious.

If problems no longer remain local, if the pace of change is swift, and if resources are rapidly redeployable, then it seems inevitable that we will learn—and have been learning—to organize our activities into large, non-local configurations, to marshall resources from far and wide and deploy and redeploy them as needs, desires, problems, and knowledge change.

We are learning to hang looser, I think, and we will be doing more of it in the future.

And from the point of view of many

individuals, participation in complexly organized activity is going to require more exercise of discretion, more learning and growth of the individual during a career, more mobility at least in the sense of temporary assignment to varied configurations at various points in space.

Now I hope I have not given the impression that I think all is peaches and cream—that we are moving inevitably toward an organized, coherent, rational society in which beautiful careers are available to all, in which goods are available at the drop of a hat and efficient services are distributed to all. My interpretation of history is much like that of Thornton Wilder—that we get by "by the skin of our teeth." At about the time we get smart enough to solve our pressing problems, it turns out that they are no longer pressing, while others for which we seem to have no solutions are pressing very hard.

issues for 2000, plus or minus 10

While I think the kinds of trends discussed above may be "in the cards," I do not think we will adapt gracefully and easily to them, or that when these trends have reached fruition, we will have reached a millennium. Indeed, I think the trends I anticipate will involve some pretty hectic adaptations, and I would like to consider what some of the issues may be:

1. Evaluation and certification of individuals and of organizations is going to have to be refined.

If resources are to be more mobile, free to be combined in new ways and new places, then we must have ways of knowing which resources are appropriate for new and ad hoc arrangement, and this means closer tolerances in evaluation and certification of readiness or fitness. And while such certification will emphasize capability not for future routine activities

but for the exercise of discretion, there must evolve standardized bases for certification, so that personnel can flow freely irrespective of political boundaries. This, in turn, suggests to me serious pressures in bringing educational programs more closely into alignment throughout the world, so that physicians, for example, trained in one location can apply their skills anywhere. We are already seeing demands for this kind of equivalence of certification in the European Common Market—demands for "harmonization of education" and for "freedom of establishment" whereby educational systems in member nations would be coordinated and the trained person would have the right to practice his occupation or profession in a country other than the one in which he received his education.[6]

Surely these kinds of pressures will expand—but not without internal conflict back in the several "sovereign" nation-states.

2. We are going to have to invent new ways of "accounting"—for keeping track of the contributions of various components in fluid cause/effect fields.

We are great at accounting for the contributions of various resources in routinized kinds of activities where each resource has a fixed relation to all others and there each has one and only one consequence. We have had trouble for several decades with the situation in which technologies are complicated enough to require resources which contribute, simultaneously to several functions; what is the value, for example, of a personnel office or of a vice-chairman of the board in accounting for the various accomplishments of a business firm or university? And we have still more trouble in accounting for the results when we put into one

[6] Robert H. Beck *et al.*, *The Changing Structure of Europe: Economic, Social and Political Trends* (Minneapolis: University of Minnesota Press, 1970).

configuration organizations which perform at different stages in the overall production process; "inter-firm" pricing of goods by one unit and used as inputs by the next has never been satisfactorily settled. Nor have universities ever learned how to acknowledge and compensate the arts college for its contributions to the education of students in professional schools!

But if we are still having trouble in 1973 in accounting for or keeping track of the contributions of resources in these relatively simple configurations, what can we expect if indeed we do move to less permanent, less formal, less local configurations?

3. The administration of complex configuration is going to be a problem.

Although we do not always succeed, I believe we have learned how to build and administer large formal organizations to do very complicated tasks. Our food, clothing, housing, and transportation are provided through very many and intricate arrangements—but for the most part these are hidden from us. True, we can get pretty vexed when it takes a week for the replacement part of a car to be delivered. And we can get frustrated at finding that particular type of cheese at the last minute before a party. But these are minor annoyances compared to the very many instances which we take for granted. And we can do so because formal organizations are administered to absorb complexity. The complexity is there, but it is hidden behind the interface of the organization with the client or customer.

But if activities are to be performed through configurations or formally separate resource units, how is complexity to be absorbed? I suggest we are getting a preview of the general problem in the field of health currently. What we now refer to as a "Health-Care-Delivery-System" involves private practitioners (sometimes in series), clinics, laboratories, nurses, technicians, dietitians, aides and order lies, therapists of various sorts, accountants, third-party-payers, and computer specialists—to say nothing of patients and their families. Unless my experiences have been very unusual, those components operate as reasonably competent components but rather incompetently as elements in a larger system. To the extent that there is coordination among them, it is the patient or patient-representative who must bring it about. It appears to me that each component in his complicated system is telling the client that he/she must worry about the articulation—that it is too complicated for the health care delivery system to handle.

But my guess is that we are going to have to learn how to absorb such complexity into the system, rather than push it off onto the client.

Another version of the problem of administering complex configurations occurs when the component units in the the configuration change frequently. One of the facilitating features of formal organizations is the predictability each component has about the other components with which it must deal. In part this stability is in the "files" and written records, and in part it lies in the personnel who man the offices and know how those files are organized. But with fluid configurations of components, experience becomes less reliable as a guide to predictability.

A preview of this kind of problem lies, perhaps, in the administration of "professional societies." So long as these remain relatively inactive and function primarily as roster-keepers whereby professionals find each other, administration is relatively simple and can perhaps be accomplished by rotating officers elected annually. However, when professional societies take on "missions" such as lobbying in legislatures, crusading for particular uses of their knowledge, or accreditation, then continuity over several years is required and the annual rotation of decision makers does not provide it. Whenever the programs involved span larger periods than the terms of office of officers, I think we see decision making gravitate to some more permanent cadre or secretariat. These problems and these solutions may appear increasingly in relatively modern sectors of society where traditionally we have relied on formal organizations.

4. We are going to have to develop new concepts of "ownership." Now I am not espousing "socialism" or "nationalization" of industries or organizations, because I think those concepts—as well as the concept of "private capitalism"— are going to be less relevant in the future than in the past.

Let me give an example close to home. My university, like many others, is involved in an Urban Renewal Program adjacent to the present, traditional campus. A year or so ago, we were hauled into court on the grounds that the *public* right of eminent domain should not have been exercised on behalf of a *private* university. Now, I want to ask whether the notion of a "private university" makes any sense at all in the contemporary world—let alone the world of 2000 plus or minus 10.

Sure, if you ask the legal question of who holds legal title to the assets, we can point to a board of trustees, and show that this board is legitimated in a different way than is the board of trustees of most or all "public" universities, and we can be quite precise about the legal differences.

But if you ask about sources of resources, the picture is less sharply black and white than it once was, and it probably will be even less sharp before long. My university gets some income from an endowment but none from a legislative, public source at the state or local level. In this sense the public/private distinction seems to hold—until we look in one direction and see "state-aided" private universities, or in the other direction and see universities which have established foundations to hold assets and use the derived income and have, in effect, an endowment. Or we can look at student fees and see that my university charges considerably higher fees than most" public" universities do, and this is a difference. But many fellowships are tenderable at either kind of institution, and then the distinction washes out. And both "public" and "private" universities seek donations, and federal government appropriations or grants, and research contracts.

Or suppose we look at *consequences;* can we say that any universities are now "private"? True, you can argue that my university is used by some selfish or greedy students to enhance their abilities to amass economic wealth, and I would agree, but similar motives propel some to public universities, too. And on both campuses we can find individuals with broader interests and motives. Perhaps the "private" university is distinguishable from the "public" one in some statistical sense by the kinds of career paths their graduates are launched into. But if we ask how complicated modern societies assure themselves of skilled manpower, then the "private" university apparently does its share of meeting the "public" or societal need. And again, if we ask where new ideas are generated which eventuate in solutions to public, social problems, then again the "private" universities play a "public role" just as much as do the "public universities."

Sticking with the formal organization scheme, Vanderbilt has a discernible location in geographic space, it is relatively permanent in that space, and it is "owned." But if we relax the criteria a bit, and look instead for the complex organization involved, it is not at all clear that Vanderbilt University is "private," or that it is "owned." Nor is it clear just who owes "allegiance" to Vanderbilt University, nor who her clienteles are, nor to whom she is ultimately responsible and accountable, nor what kinds of effects she can cause for whom.

5. Problems of the social control of organizations are likely to be even more vexing than now, for the organizational interfaces we experience as consumers will be an even smaller fraction of the complex networks on which we depend, and it seems unlikely to me that we will automatically appreciate these unseen but essential props for our daily lives. Although I am rather likely to take them for granted, I can appreciate my supermarket, service station, department store, and hospital. All of these I come face to face with and I therefore know they serve me. Not perfectly, but I do depend upon them, and therefore I can observe the importance of their personnel. Toward those whom I personally observe at the interface, I can understand the division of labor—that they are doing what they do so that I won't have to. And I can perhaps remind myself that somehow my activities may ultimately contribute to those I meet at the interface.

But if we elongate and intensify technologies, and weave activities into more complicated and round-about networks of interdependence, we become dependent upon those we never see—and in ways we cannot even suspect. We get a glimpse of these unseen supports occasionally, when, through strikes or scarcities, one of them fails us. But mostly, it seems, it is a case of out-of-sight, out-of-mind.

How many layers of dependence can we imagine? And how can we appreciate the contribution of those seven or eight layers behind the interfaces we personally experience?

Some of the problem areas I have suggested above, to the extent that they are solved, may help in this connection. If we learn how to account for costs and con-

tributions in more flexible networks, perhaps this will help us appreciate those unknown others. If we revamp our concepts of "ownership," recognizing perhaps a variety of "public" organizations, then perhaps we will be less ready to distinguish "ours" from "theirs" and to the extent that our career roles in organizations give us more insight into the complexities behind our consumer interfaces, we may be more ready to recognize that "they" are also "us." But my guess is that the gulf between "them" and "us" may seem even wider than now, in 2000 plus or minus 10.

conclusions

In trying to anticipate change it is easy to overlook stabilities. It is time to remind myself that what I have tried to designate as formal organizations will be very much a part of my world in 2000, plus or minus 10. And many of us, or our successors, will hold regular jobs in formal organizations with geographic identities and regularities, with recognized clienteles and functions. Similarly, all of us will likely be doing our shopping and getting many of our services from nearby outlets of formal organizations.

But I believe such things will be routine, taken for granted, unproblematic. Our preoccupations as a society, I believe, will not be in this arena but rather with that which I have tried to designate as *complex organizations* of a much more fluid, ad hoc, flexible form. Perhaps these should not be designated organizations at all, and the emphasis should instead be placed on the administration of temporarily organized activities. One prototype of this may be what I and some of my colleagues once referred to as a *synthetic organization* which we saw emerging in communities hit by natural disasters. There, we said, such notions as formal authority and ownership were relaxed and resources were seeking new applications.[7]

But a characteristic of the synthetic organization, at least as we conceived it, was that ultimately it crumbled from its own success, and resources were withdrawn to old purposes as ownership and authority were reactivated. Finally the synthetic organization disappears.

Society's frontiers for organizing activities in 2000, however, may take a somewhat different form with the development of administration teams or cadres to specialize in a continuous process of synthesizing. Perhaps complex organizations of the future will be known not for their components but by their cadres, with each cadre devoted to mobilizing and deploying resources in shifting configurations, to employ changing technologies to meet changing demands. We may well be seeing the early forms of this in what became identified during the last decade as the *conglomerate* corporation. Clearly many of these were put together too hastily to get accounting and tax advantages rather than for more functional reasons. Whatever the incentives for starting them, however, their problems of survival may result in development of new concepts that will serve us better in the future.

[7] James D. Thompson and Robert W. Hawkes, "Disaster, Community Organization, and Administrative Process," in George W. Baker and Dwight Chapman (eds.), *Man and Society in Disaster* (New York: Basic Books, 1962).

discussion questions : part VI

1. What is the third sector? What types of organizations could you see developing in the future beyond those outlined in the text? Why?

2. If you were attempting to project the future shape of organizations in the year 2000, would you agree with Professor Thompson's assumptions? If yes, why? If not, why not?

3. Establish your own assumptions about the future and predict the shape of organizations in the year 2025.

4. After examining the four major approaches of this book, what type of approach would you take to management in a multinational company? Explain.

5. What are some of the challenges for future managers? What potential solutions do you see for these challenges?

6. Describe several of the major problems facing managers in the next decade (you may use the entire book, not just this section, in answering this question). Establish a set of criteria upon which to judge whether or not the problem is a major problem before you answer the question.

7. Formulate an eclectic approach to management which could be used by executives. Be sure to consider the major approaches to management.

selected references : part VI

management in the future

Bass, Bernard M., "Organizational Life in the 70's and Beyond," *Personnel Psychology*, 25, No. 1 (Spring 1972), pp. 19–30.

Bell, Daniel, "The Coming of Post-Industrial Society," *Business and Society Review/Innovation*, No. 5 (Spring 1973), pp. 5–23.

Farmer, Richard N., "Looking Back at Looking Forward," *Business Horizons*, 16, No. 1 (February 1973), pp. 21–28.

Mee, John F., "Changing Concepts of Management," *S.A.M. Advanced Management Journal*, 37, No. 4 (October 1972), pp. 22–34.

Preston, Paul, "The Future: Prospects and Alternatives for a Business Role," *Business and Society*, 13, No. 2 (Spring 1973), pp. 5–9.

Scott, William G., "The Theory of Significant People," *Public Administration Review*, 33, No. 4 (July–August 1973), pp. 308–313.

Simon, William, "Management in the Future," *The Conference Board Record*, 10, No. 3 (March 1973), pp. 44–47.

Steiner, George A., "The Second Managerial Revolution," *The Conference Board Record*, 10, No. 7 (July 1973), pp. 28–31.

Yankelovich, Daniel, "Business in the '70's: Decade of Crisis," *Michigan Business Review*, 24, No. 5 (November 1972), pp. 27–31.

index

Accountability, public, 48–49
Ackoff, R. L., 90, 327
Adams, Everette E., 232
Administration (*see also* Management)
  defined, 70
  international concept, 73
Administrative theory (*see* Management theory)
Affirmative action program (*see also* Equal employment opportunity), 174–184
  attitudinal modification, 182–183
  corporate commitment, 183
  emerging government regulations, 181
  experience, 175
  implications, 183–184
  legal requirements, 175–177
  minority, 174–184
  objective, 175
  promotion, 181–182
  recruitment, 177–178
  supervisory attitudes, 182–183

  testing, 178–181
  trend, 176–177
  women, 174–184
Ahlbrandt, Roger S., 44–45, 48, 54
Air pollution (*see* Pollution)
Alderman, Anne, 60
Alexis, Marcus, 283, 286, 292
American Association for the Advancement of Science, 47
American College of Hospital Administrators, 110
American Hospital Association, 67, 110
American Public Health Association, 58
American Society of Association Executives, 299–300
American Telephone and Telegraph, 241–253
Analytical techniques, 282–300
Ansoff, H. Igor, 283
Antitrust laws, 41–42, 53
  reformers, 42
Argus man, 111, 119

Argyris, Chris, 140, 199
Authoritarian hierarchy, 113
Authority, 98, 113
    project, 103
    relationships, 143–145
    shared, 101
Auto pollution (*see* Pollution)
Autocracy, 109

Baker, Bruce N., 84–89
Baker, Russell, 46
Barnard, Chester I., 1, 323
Bativala, Robert B. D., 268–281
Bauerschmidt, Alan D., 236–241
Behavioral approaches, 16–18, 21, 189–
    255
Behavioral change, 238
    model, 20–21
Behavioral model, 213–220
    assumptions, 214
    decomposition of input variables, 215–
        216
    input variables, 214–215
    mediating variables, 216–217
    output variables, 217–219
    processing variables, 216–217
Behavioral sciences, 122, 190, 201
Bennis, Warren G., 20, 194–195, 209–
    210
Bertalanffy, Ludwig von, 320–326
Bernthal, Wilmar F., 189–190
Black, H. S., 161
Blake, Robert, 135–136, 145–146
Blau, Peter, 333
Boulden, James B., 301–309
Boulding, Kenneth, 320
Bradspies, Robert W., 158–168
Bremer, Otto A., 22–28
Brook, Robert H., 68
Brunson, Richard W., 236–241
Burack, Elmer, 268–281
Burch, John G., 388–395
Bureaucracy, 20, 109, 193–194, 201
    corporate, 41
    public, 41
    school, 47
Burns, T., 199, 331

Business, new social values, 22–28
Business education, indictments, 53
Business information system (*see also*
    Management information system),
    378–379
Business life cycle, 104
Business schools, 52–58
Business system, 373–388
    concepts, 375
    major subsystems, 375–378
    nature, 374–375

Canning, R. G., 356
Capitalism, theology of, 30
Carlisle, Howard M., 192–201
Carroll, D. C., 356
Carzo, Rocco, 210
Cassell, Frank H., 43–58, 169–174
Centralization, hospital decision making,
    115
Chain of command, 98
Chamberlain, Neil W., 331
Chandler, Alfred, 196
Chandler, Margaret K., 405–406
Change, 88, 97
    organization, 108, 238
    planning, 88
Change agent, 240
Change program, 238–241
Civil Rights Act of 1964, 175
Cleland, David I., 206
Cohesiveness, 218–219
Collegialism, 109
Commanding, 16, 81, 113
Committee for Economic Development
    (CED), 44–45, 48–49, 54
Committee structure, 203–204, 223–224
Communication, 16, 135–148
    breakdown, 135
    dilemmas, 135
    effectiveness, 145
    open, 141
    problems, 135
    process, 114, 116
    two-way, 113–115, 119
Comparative management (*see also* Inter-
    national management), 72–76

leadership, 74
objectives, 74
Computer models, 301–316
Computer simulation (*see also* Systems analysis)
  decision variables, 314–315
  environmental variables, 314–315
  state variables, 314–315
Computer software, classification matrix, 304
Conflict, 115–116
Confrontation, 115–116
Consumer behavior, planning, 94
Consumer group, health care delivery, 59
Consumer protection, 30
Consumerism, 94
Consumers, technology and, 5
Contingency approach, 19, 332–333, 335
Contingency theory, 16–21, 98–99, 105, 192–201, 332
Control, 82–83, 88, 149–168, 222–223
  cash forecasts, 160
  contractor coordination, 153–154
  as cybernetic system, 159
  defined, 158–159
  dimensions, 149–157
  feedforward, 158–168
  forecasts, 160
  future-directed, 159–161
  goal changes, 167
  information, 153–154
  needs, 159
  PERT networks and, 160–161
  problem-solving and, 154–155
  process, 158–161
  review, before-the-fact, 151
  rigidities, 151–152
  shortcomings, 159
  structural changes, 155–156
  systems, 158
  types, 149–150
Controlling, 81, 149–168
Controls, 149–157
  high-level, 150–151
  low-level, 151–152
  managerial performance, 150
  middle-level, 152–153

Coordinating, 81, 153
Coordination and assessing of information, 153–154
Corporate Accountability Research Group, 29
Corporate climate, 135
  interpersonal style, 147–148
Corporate growth, 96–106
Corporate modeling, 301–309
  concept, 301
  establishing objectives, 307
  general purpose operating system, 302–307
  growth plan, 301–302
  linkages, 308
  management planning and control system, 303–304
  problems in systems integration, 307
  profit planning system, 306
  software matrix, 304
  system specifications, 301–309
  system characteristics, 302
  systems integration, 307–308
  VANGUARD, 305–309
Corporate responsibility (*see* Social responsibility)
Corporation
  evolutionary view, 41–42
  nonprofit, 2
  public, 2, 40–58
  public–private, 44–45, 57
  traditional approach, 40–42
Council on Economic Priorities, 29
Council of Social Advisers, 51
Critical Path Method (CPM), 158, 162
Cybernetic system, control, 159
Cybernetics, 160
Cyert, R. M., 196

Dahl, Robert, 283–284
Davis, Keith, 100–102
Decentralization, 19–20, 109, 115
Decision, categories, 388–389
Decision making, 121–134, 282–295
  adversary process, 266–267
  approaches, 293
  cases, 127–129

Decision making (*cont.*)
  categories, 283
  under certainty, 286
  classifications of information, 390–391
  coefficient of optimality, 291
  under competition, 286
  under conflict, 286
  cost, 285
  effectiveness of information system, 390
  features, 284–285
  hospitals, 115, 119
  information required, 389
  maximax criterion, 291
  maximin criterion, 290
  minimax regret, 290–291
  model, 121–134, 285–293
  new process, 52
  nonprogrammed, 285
  normative model, 121–122
  operations research, 275–276
  outcomes, 122–123
  planning horizons, 284
  principle of insufficient reason, 289–290
  private, 48
  process, 133
  programmed, 285
  research methods, 130
  under risk, 288–289
  sequential, 284–285
  setting objectives, 284
  as social process, 121
  strategy selection, 294
  structure, 95
  subjective probabilities, 289
  tasks, 123
  time periods, 292–293
  under uncertainty, 289–291
Decision model, 122–129, 285–294
  descriptive, 291–293
  feasible processes, 126
  long-term, 129–130
  normative, 285–293
  open, 292
  problem attributes, 123
  rationale, 125–127
  rules underlying, 125–126
  short-term, 129–130
  use, 133
Decision processes, 283–284
  alternative, 121
  feasible, 126
  participative, 131–132
Decision theory, 281–295
  continuum, 286
Decision tree, 124
Delphi technique, 298–300
  concept, 298
  development, 298
Deutsch, Karl W., 322
Directing, 16, 82–83, 121–148
Division of labor, 98, 224
Drive, 218–219
Drucker, Peter, 402

Ebert, Robert H., 110
Economic development, 75
Economic theory, 25
Egalitarianism, 109
Employee relations, planning, 95
Energy
  environment, 11–13
  management of, 11–13
  model, 12–13
  national system, 11–12
  needs, 11–13
  nuclear policy, 11
  planning, 11–13
  problems, 11–13
  system, 12–13
  use, 12
Energy exchange system, 118
Environment
  contemporary, 107
  industrial effects, 43
  internal and planning, 95
  international and planning, 94
  pressures, 46–47
  private enterprise planning, 95
  and technology, 4–15, 198–199
Environmental control, 47
  social responsibility and, 32, 34
Environmental Protection Act, 8, 10

Equal employment opportunity (*see* Affirmative action program)
Equal Employment Opportunity Act of 1972, 175
Equal Employment Opportunity Commission (EEOC), 175, 178–181, 183
regulations, 177
Etzioni, Amitai, 401–413
Exception principle, 393
Executive, multiple, 205
Expectation, 214–217
Expenditures, federal, 50

Fabun, Don, 118
Fahey, Patrick E., 174–184
Fayol, Henri, 1, 16, 81, 193, 283, 295
Feedback, 82, 138–148, 158–168
anticipatory, 160
communication, 114
concept, 161–162
job enrichment, 245–246
Feedback loop, 158
Feedback systems, 82, 158–159
Feedforward control, 158–168
action under, 168
cash planning, 163–164
concept, 161–162
in engineering, 161–162
guidelines, 167–168
human systems, 162–163
input variables, 167–168
inventory, 164–166
mathematical models, 162–164
model, 167–168
new product development, 166–167
planning and analysis, 167
Fessel, W. J., 69
Fiedler, Fred, 20–21
Ford, Robert M., 241–253
Forecasting, 295–300
examples, 297–298
Formal organization, 213–220, 339, 416
Fulmer, Robert M., 295–300
Future shock, 296–297
Futuristic research, 295–300
role of organizations, 299–300

Futurists, 296–300
role, 296

Gaddis, P. O., 208
Galbraith, Jay, 199
Galbraith, John Kenneth, 40–43
Game theory, 280, 286–288
nonzero sum game, 288
pure strategy, 287
two-person zero-sum game, 287
General Purpose Operating System, 302–307
General systems theory, 19, 322–338
application dilemmas, 326–330
applications, 322–337
closed systems, 327–328
concepts, 117–118, 324–325
continuum of organizations, 334
defined, 320
history, 322–324
macro approach, 332–334
open systems, 327–328
organizations as contrived systems, 329
relationship to organization theory, 323
subsystems, 328
systems effectiveness, 329–330
variables, 334
Gentry, John T., 58–72
Gilbreth, Frank, 1
Goals
control and change, 167
corporate, 43
social, 28
Goldberg, George A., 69
Gordon–Howell Report, 53–54
Greenberg, Selig, 110
Gregory, R. H., 356–357
Griggs v. Duke Power Company, 179

Hall, Jay, 135–148
Hall, William K., 89–95
Hanan, Mack, 103
Health care
components, 59
needs, 111–112
Health care delivery (*see also* Health care delivery systems), 58–72

Health care delivery (*cont.*)
  assessment criteria, 60–64
  levels of rationality, 58–72
  methods of assessment, 59–63
  rational approach, 58–72
  rationalization defined, 58
Health care delivery systems, 58–72, 106–120
  acceptability of services, 65
  administration defined, 70
  consumer groups, 59
  cost containment, 67
  defined, 58
  delivery, 67–68
  evaluating, 62–63
  financing and delivery, 66–69
  health services, 59
  imbalances, 64–65
  incentive reimbursements, 67
  issues, 64–65
  limited accessibility, 65
  manpower, 69
  national health insurance proposals, 66
  planning, 62–63
  planning agencies, 69–70
  planning and regulations, 69–70
  policy questions, 71–72
  problems, 64–65
  quality assurance, 68–69
  rising costs, 65
  services, 59
Health care status, 110
Health Maintenance Organization
    (HMO), 67–68
Health manpower, 69
Health planning agencies, 69–70
Health services
  estimating approaches, 60
  objectives, 59
  quality, 110
Heilbroner, Robert, 30
Hierarchy of needs, 228
Henning, Joel F., 51
Herzberg, Frederick, 199, 228
Heuristic tasks, 106
Hoffman, Kenneth, 12
Holmes, Oliver Wendell, 39

Homans, G. C., 214
Horton, Forest W., 201–212
Horvath, William J., 327
Hospitals
  change, 116
  communication, 119
  decision making, 119
Hospital administrators, 112–120, 236–241
Hospital organization, 106–120
  interface private institutions, 114–115
  interface public institutions, 114–115
  maturation, 108
  modern environment, 109–110
  new structures, 111–112
  policy making, 119
  total system, 117
Hull, Clark, 228
Human insatiability, 15
Human relations movement, 17
Human resource policy, 169
Human resources development, 112

Industrial era, 107–109
Informal organization, 339
Information, 113–114, 174
  control and, 153–154
Information processing model, 136
Information technology, 274
Ingham, Harry, 136, 142
Institute of Management Sciences
    (TIMS), The, 261, 270
International management, 72–76
  duality, 75
  emergent views, 73
  territory management, 75–76
  time-integration, 73–74
  time-overlap, 73–74
  traditional views, 73
  transference model, 74
Interpersonal processes
  basic, 138–139
  exposure, 138–142, 145–146, 148
  feedback, 138–142, 145–146, 148
Interpersonal relationships
  imbalances, 139
  model, 136

Interpersonal style, 136–137
    authority relationships, 143–145
    corporate climate, 147–148
    defined, 135–136
    managerial impacts, 139–142
    nature, 142
    quality of relations, 136–137
    types of behavior, 139–142, 144–148
Inventory control, 164–166

James, William, 15
Janger, A. R., 207
Job enrichment, 18, 115, 199, 233–234, 241–253
    change in managerial style, 252
    configurations, 251–252
    control of module, 244–245
    delimiting modules, 243–244
    feedback, 245–246
    lessons, 252–253
    maintenance factors, 252
    mini-group concept, 252
    nature, 242–246
    nesting of jobs, 242, 247–251
    self-monitoring, 245
    system improvement, 246–247
    technology and, 253
    unions and, 253
    work module, 242–244
    work organization, 252
Job shop model, 361–363
Johari Window, 136–138, 141–142, 145–147
    blindspot, 137, 140, 144
    concepts, 136–138
    dynamic open system, 138
    Managerial Grid and, 145–146
Johnson, Richard A., 209, 339
Jones, Max B., 337–347

Kahn, Robert L., 326–327, 329
Kast, Fremont E., 19, 104, 322–337, 339
Katz, Daniel, 326–327, 329
Koontz, Harold, 16, 158–168
Kuhn, Thomas, 330–331

Lawler, Edward, 228

Lawrence, Paul R., 19, 98, 105, 198, 332
Leader
    human-relations oriented, 20
    task-directed, 20
Leader behavior, descriptive model, 130–133
Leadership, 16
    effectiveness, 20
    model, 20
Leadership development, new technology for, 133–134
Leading, 16
Leakey, Louis S. B., 47, 56
Likert, Rensis, 117–118, 209
Lindblom, C. E., 71, 283–284
Line–staff, 97–98
Linear programming, 21, 280, 305
Linking pin concept, 209
Lippitt, Gordon L., 106–120
Litterer, Joseph A., 210
LoCascio, Vincent R., 309–316
Long-range planning, 82, 87, 89–95, 295, 309
    concepts, 91–92
    consumerism, 94
    corporate development, 90–91
    departments, 87, 295
    environments, 94–95
    future operations, 91
    governmental, 94
    internationalism, 94
    public sector, 94
    techniques, 92
Lorsch, Jay W., 19, 98, 105, 198, 332
Luft, Joseph, 136, 142
Luthans, Fred, 16–21, 228–235
Lyman, David, 234

McAdam, Terry, 29–39
McGregor, Douglas, 196, 202, 212
McLuhan, Marshall, 300
Man
    concept, 109
    environment, 4
    expectations, 15
    insatiable animal, 14–15
    technology of, 14–15

Management
  application of systems concepts, 334–335
  autocratic, 109
  behavioral approaches, 16–18, 21, 189–255
  cross-national system, 76
  democratic, 109
  expanding areas, 2
  expanding scope, 40–76
  in future (*see* Management in future)
  health, 58–72
  international (*see* International management)
  interpersonal styles, 135–148
  by objectives, 235
  operative values, 28
  philosophy (*see* Philosophy of management)
  principles, 1, 81–82, 193
  process approaches, 81–187
  profession, 1
  public, 40–58
  public–private, 43–58
  quantitative approaches, 16–18, 21, 257–318
  socially responsible (*see also* Social responsibility), 2, 22–39
  systems approaches, 18–19, 21, 273, 319–397
Management approach, generic, 55–56
Management decision styles, 122–130
  autocratic, 122–130
  consultative, 122–130
  group, 122–130
Management decisions, social consequences, 28
Management foundations, 1–79
Management frameworks, 2–3
  conceptual, 4–21
Management functions, 283
Management in future, 72–76, 106–120, 295–300, 401–425
  administration of complex organizations, 421–422
  concepts of ownership, 422–423
  evaluation and certification of individuals and organizations, 420
  issues in year 2000, 420–423
  new ways of accounting, 420–421
  social control of organizations, 423
  trends, 107, 419–425
Management information systems, 339, 373–395
  adaptability model, 384–385
  applications information system, 379
  communication standards, 387
  data standards, 387
  exception method, 393
  experimental technique in programmed, 382–383
  external environment method, 393–394
  filtering method, 391–392
  five corporate systems in, 385–387
  hypothesis development, 383–384
  impact upon decision making, 390
  information requirements, 389–390
  interrogative method, 392–393
  management science method, 391
  nonprogrammed, 381–383
  planning, 373–388
  planning and design, 385, 387
  programmed, 380–381
  programmed development, 385
  strategical decisions, 388–395
  tactical decisions, 388–395
  tailoring, 388–395
  technical decisions, 388–395
Management process, 81–187, 338
  social responsibility in, 37
Management science, 14, 18, 73
  approach, 17
  tools, 15
Management theories, 1, 16
Management theory, 2, 16–17, 201
Management theory jungle, 16–21
Managerial decision making (*see* Decision making)
Managerial ethics (*see also* Social responsibility), 2
Managerial functions, 50, 81
Managerial genetics, 57–58
Managerial grid, 145–146
Managerial style

changes under job enrichment, 252–253
interpersonal practices and, 145–147
Managerial values (*see also* Values), 2
Managers
hospital, 106–120
opportunities, 56
preferences, 56
Manpower, new types, 178
Manpower administration, 169–174
centralized, 173
daily, 173
human resource development, 171
impacts on organization, 173
information use in, 174
interdependent variables, 171–173
internal labor market, 169–170
leadership, 174
manpower planning, 170–172
new concepts, 170–171
planning, 173–174
policy making, 171
Manpower forecasting, 170
Manpower planning, 82, 170–172, 174
cycle, 172
Manpower utilization, 170–171
Manufacturing employment, 56
March, J. G., 196, 292
Marglin, S., 350–351
Maslow, Abraham, 228
Mathematical models, 93–94, 162–164
behavioral, 214–220
Matrix management
defined, 203
task force, 92
Matrix organization, 101, 111
Mayo, Elton, 98
Mead, Margaret, 108
Medicaid, 67
Medicare, 66
Metatechnology (*see also* Technology), 6, 14
age of, 6
building, 11
defined, 6
Michaelson, Michael, 110
Miller, James, 329

Minority group, 112, 116
affirmative action program and, 174–184
Model
administration, 57
behavioral change, 20–21
contingency, 19–20, 192–201
decision, 122–129, 285–293
defined, 374
expectancy, 228–229
first-approximation, 12
leader behavior, 130–133
leadership, 20
mathematical, 17, 93–94, 162–164
normative, 94, 130, 133, 285–293
operations research, 21
organization, 96–106, 109, 337–347
simulation, 93
social interaction, 136
steady-state planning, 12
systems, 97
transference, 74
types of management, 358
Modeling, process of, 93
Monopolist, emerging, 26–28
Moravec, A. F., 355–356
Motivation, 16, 220–228
defined, 229
as hypothetical construct, 229–230
models, 229
Motivators, 220–228
Motive, 229–230
Mouton, Jane S., 135–136, 145–146
Multinational management (*see also* International Management), 210
Murray, Henry A., 328–329
Myers, Charles, 19

Nader, Ralph, 22, 29
National Aeronautics and Space Agency (NASA), 149, 153, 204–205, 405–406
National Center for Health Statistics, 60
National health insurance proposals, 66, 404
Needs, 230, 242
classification, 228, 230

Needs (*cont.*)
  future human, 415
  theory of, 228
de Neufville, Richard, 348–355
Nixon, President Richard M., 43, 176, 402, 404

Objectives, 221, 284
O'Donnell, Cyril, 16
Office of Federal Contract Compliance (OFCC), 176, 179–181, 183
Ombudsman, 28
Operant learning theory, 229–230
Operations management (*see also* Operations research), 260–281
Operations research, 21, 260–281
  adversary process, 266–267
  applications, 261, 277–278
  changes, 268–281
  client–analyst relations, 264–265
  consultants, 271
  defined, 260, 268
  educational needs, 273–274
  expectations in, 268–281
  growth, 273–279
  history, 260–261, 268
  influencing governmental decisions, 265–266
  information technology, 274
  management support, 269, 274–275
  nature, 260–267
  organization of, 271–272, 276–279
  organizational factors, 273–279
  practice, 261–263
  problems, 264
  progress, 264
  relevance to client, 262
  role of advocate, 266–267
  science of, 260
  scientific characteristics, 262–263
  sponsorship, 275
  status, 276–279
  systems analysis, 263–264
  systems approach, 273
  techniques, 17
  terms, 272, 279–280
  theory, 261

  uses, 260, 278
Operations research analyst, 264–265, 273–274
Operations research glossary, 279–280
Operations Research Society of America (ORSA), 260–267, 270
Organization
  assignments, 222–223
  assumptions underlying complex, 414–415
  changes in practices, 108
  classical system, 98–99
  defined, 18
  dynamic model, 96–106
  functions, 221–225
  future, 413–425
  future-oriented, 118–119
  hospital, 106–120
  manpower impacts, 173
  micro-structure, 101
  new characteristics, 110–118
  objectives, 221
  as organism, 326–327
  pace of change, 419
  patterns, 195–200
  project, 97, 99
  synthetic, 423–424
  temporary, 205
  third sector (*see* Third sector organization)
  trend toward larger, 419
  trends, 419–423
Organization analysis, 112
Organization behavior modification, 21–22, 229–235
  application, 231–233
  deprivation, 230–231
  learning concepts, 234
  positive reinforcement, 232
  Premack principle, 233–234
  punishment, 232
  reinforcers, 230–231
  satiation, 230–231
  stimulus control, 231–232
Organization change, 108
Organization chart, 220
  faults, 221

Organization climate, 101, 119
Organization design, 19–20, 104, 199–200
  bureaucratic, 19–20
  differences, 99
  environment and, 105, 198–199
  forces in task, 196–198
  managerial forces, 195–196
  matrix, 20
Organization development, 17, 112–113, 236–253
  administrative views, 239
  concept, 238–239
  hospital use, 241
  modes of, 239–241
  origins of concept, 238–239
  reasons for, 237–238
Organization planning (see Planning)
Organization renewal, 108
Organization structure, 96–106
  bureaucratic, 20, 193
  change, 95, 97
  contingency models, 19, 102–106
  dimensions, 119
  functional, 99
  planning, 96
  theory relationships, 102
Organization theory, 17, 97–98, 192–212, 214, 333
  assumptions, 416–418
  behavioral, 194, 213–220
  classical, 99, 192–194
  dilemma, 97–98
  organic, 194–195
  relationship to general systems theory, 323, 327
  structure relationships, 102
Organizational analysis, 283
Organizational behavior, 213–235
  defined, 17
  problems, 134
Organizational change (see Change and Planned change)
Organizational effectiveness
  assessment (see also Control), 156–157
  levels of analysis, 330

issue polarization, 156
  monitoring relationships, 156–157
  workflow responsiveness, 156
Organizational philosophies, changes, 108
Organizing, 81–83, 96–120

Parsons, Talcott, 214, 323
Participation, 115, 131
Pastore, Joseph M., 96–106
Pati, Gopal C., 174–184
Performance, 214–217
Performance criteria
  community, 51
  in management information systems, 393
Personnel Relations Survey, 142–143, 145, 147
Phillips, D. C., 332
Philosophy of management, 1–2, 119
Pierson Report, 53–54
Pigors, Paul, 19
Planned change, 88
Planning (see also Long-range planning, Short-range planning, and Plans), 12–13, 16, 46, 48–49, 51, 57, 81–82, 84–95, 295
  base-line approach, 88
  challenges to traditional, 46
  change, 88
  change control center, 88
  communication in, 85–89
  corporate, 90–91
  cycle, 87
  decision making in, 90
  defined, 50, 90, 158
  documents, 86
  energy, 12–13
  evolving concepts, 91–92
  facets, 84–95
  frameworks, 85–86
  goals, 85
  government economic, 45, 48, 54
  guidelines, 84–89
  innovative systems, 92–93
  intermediate range, 87
  mathematical models, 93–94
  objectives, 85

Planning (*cont.*)
  participative sessions, 85
  periodic reviews, 87–88
  philosophies, 92
  policies, 92–93
  project matrix, 86–87
  project organizations, 86
  public, 50
  research, 91
  solutions, 85–87
  structures, 92
  trend analyses, 88
  urban, 366–372
Planning integration, 84–89
  closed loop, 85
  facets, 84–89
  guidelines, 84–89
  isolated loop, 85
  problems, 85
  sets of plans, 87–89
Planning process, concepts, 91–92
Planning-programming-budgeting system,
    24, 57, 261
Plans
  continuity, 88
  reasons for integration, 84
  sets, 87–89
  strategic, 90
  subordinate organizations, 85–87
  tactical, 90
  updates, 88
Policy, 147
  energy, 11
  planning, 92–93
Policy making, 119
Pollack, Jerry L., 366–372
Pollution, 6–13, 46–47
  air, 9–11
  auto emissions, 9–11, 13
  emission standards, 9–10
  energy, 11–13
  eutrophication, 6–9, 13
  phosphates, 6–8
  research and development in, 10–13
  technologies, 7–9
  water, 6–9
Porter, Lyman, 228

Post-industrial era, 107–109
Pounds, W. F., 358
Power
  concept, 109
  differences, 143–144
  distributions, 147
  information and, 114
  relationships, 144
Power dynamics, 143
Premack principle, 233–234
Principles of management, 1, 81–82, 193
Private enterprise, 40–41, 43, 44, 47, 49,
    54, 94
Private sector, 45–46, 48–49, 51, 401–
    413
  publicizing, 49
Problem solving
  additional steps in control, 155–156
  control, 154–155
  mathematical solutions, 257
  preliminary steps in control, 155
Process approaches, 16–17, 81–187, 228–
    229
  developed, 81–82
  management, 16–17, 81–187
Product development, 166–167
Product management, 203
Production, 98, 197
Productivity, 218–219
Profit, 51
Profit planning system, 306
Profit system, 51
Profitability, 93
Program Evaluation and Review Tech-
    nique (PERT), 154, 158, 160–162,
    166
  advantage, 161
  control and, 160–161
Program management, 203
Program planning and evaluation model,
    370–372
Project groups, 100, 102, 111
  organizational design, 104
Project management, 86, 201–212
  assumptions, 206–209
  background, 202–204
  concepts, 202, 211–212

defined, 202–204
general, 100–102
NASA, 205–206
problems and issues, 207–209
problem handling, 209–211
project confederation, 100–101
project expeditor, 100–101, 206
rules for using, 202, 211–212
utility of, 210
Project organization, 97, 99
Project structure, 99–102, 105
growth-oriented, 103, 105
Public corporation, 40–58
Public employment law, 43
Public enterprise, 41
Public hospital system, 57
Public institutions, 41
Public interest, 43, 48
Public–private management, 43–58
Public sector, 46, 48–49, 51, 94, 401–413
organizations, 57, 401–425
planning, 94
privatizing, 49

Queuing theory, 280
Quantitative approaches, 16–18, 21, 257–318
decision making, 260–281
defined, 17
operations research, 17, 260–281
techniques, 257–258

Rapoport, Anatol, 327, 332
Research and development, pollution, 10–13
Resource, demand, 14
Resource allocation, social responsibility, 32–33
Resources, exhausting, 12
Responsibility, 98
project, 103
shared, 101
Rewards systems, 116
Rockart, John F., 355–356
Rockefeller, David, 51
Rosenzweig, James E., 19, 322–337, 339

Satisfaction, 215

Sayles, Leonard, 149–157, 405–406
Science, characteristics, 262–263
Scientific management, 17, 73, 81, 151, 193, 241
Scientific method, 262–263, 349–350, 373
steps, 349–350, 373–374
Scott, William E., 232
Scott, William G., 210, 323, 332
Seashore, Stanley E., 330
Seese, Dorothy A., 220–228
Self-actualization, 242
Self-fulfillment, 115
Sensitivity analysis, 305, 348
Sethi, Narendra K., 72–76
Shetty, Y. K., 192–201
Short-range planning, 82, 87
current operations, 91
operations control, 91
Siegel, Paul, 373–388
Silverman, David, 327
Simon, Herbert A., 4–15, 193, 292, 323, 324
Simulation, 280, 357–358
Simulation methods, 301–316
Simulation model, 301–316
colleges and universities, 309–316
SEARCH, 310–316
Situational theory, 18, 131
Social contract, 50–52
Social responsibility, 22–39, 52
analysis, 32–37
approaching, 30–32
chief executive officer, 31
corporate, 29–39
critical activity areas, 36
defined, 22–28
developments, 29–30
flexible approach, 31
ground rules, 31
legislation, 30
line management, 31
major pitfalls, 31–32
new programs, 37
objectives, 36–37
organizational approaches, 39
philosophy, 36

Social responsibility (*cont.*)
  resource allocation decisions, 32–33
  revised programs, 37
  strategy, 36
  values, 27–28
Social responsibility efforts
  officer, 37
  permanent board committee, 38
  permanent management committee, 38
  permanent organization group, 38–39
  task force, 37–38
Social responsibility issues, 29, 32–36
Social responsibility review, 32
Society
  decisions, 48–49
  expectations, 49–50
  impacts of technology, 5–6
  post-industrial, 106–120
  priorities, 49–50, 52
Span-of-control, 201
Sparer, Gerald, 60
Staffing (*see also* Manpower administration), 169–184
  affirmative action programs, 174–184
  barriers, 170
  manpower utilization, 170–171
  sources, 177–178
  testing, 178–181
Staff–line relations (*see* Line–staff relations)
Stalker, G. M., 199, 331
Stogdill, Ralph M., 213–220
Strategic planning (*see* Long-range planning)
Strater, Felix R., 388–395
Stress, 115–116
Styles of Management Inventory, 145
System for Exploring Alternative Resource Commitments
  characteristics, 310–311
  computation sequence, 312
  in higher education (SEARCH), 310–316
  logic flow, 313
  major questions asked, 311–312
  modules, 313–314
  operations, 312–314

  parameters, 315–316
  as planning tool, 310–311
  relationships, 315
  using model, 316
  variables, 314–315
Systemic Environmental Model, 339–341
Systemic Functional Model, 341–346
Systemic Operational Model, 346
Systemic Planning Model, 341
Systems (*see also* Systems analysis), 109
  closed, 19, 118, 195, 322, 326
  energy, 12–13
  feedback, 82
  formal planning, 92
  innovative planning, 92–93
  integrated planning and control, 92
  nature of, 374–375
  open, 19, 118, 138, 195, 324–325
  socio-technical, 117–118, 347
  temporary, 111
Systems analysis, 348–372
  alternative evaluation, 352
  alternative generation, 351–352
  alternative selection, 352–353
  concept of model-based, 358–359
  conventional, 356–358
  data gathering, 357
  data presentation, 357
  as decision process, 348–355
  defined, 92, 263, 319–320, 348–349, 356
  definition of objectives, 350–351
  effectiveness measures, 351
  examples of model-based, 358–359
  feedback, 353
  inadequacy of, 355–356
  issues, 353–354
  job shop model, 361–363
  major elements, 263
  marketing models, 359
  model-based, 355–366
  models, 348
  new applications, 359
  in operations research, 263–264
  organizing principle, 349–350
  problem finding, 363–364
  simple scheduling model, 360–361

simulation, 357–358
steps, 350–353, 356–357
urban planning, 366–372
uses, 348–349
Systems analysts, 319, 350–355, 356–359, 366–372
Systems approaches, 18–19, 21, 273, 319–397
    defined, 18
Systems concepts, 209, 322–347
    entrophy, 19, 325
    equifinality, 19, 325
    feedback, 325
    hierarchy, 325
    homeostasis, 325
    input-transformation-output model, 325
    multiple goal-seeking, 325
    multiview, 338–339
    subsystems, 325
    system boundaries, 325
Systems theory, 322–337
    study of organizations, 330–332

Tactical planning (*see* Short-range planning)
Taft, Martin I., 366–372
Task definition, 20
Task force (*see also* Project management), 111, 194, 201–212
    defined, 203–204
Task goals, 113
Task organization, 97
Taylor, Frederick W., 1, 193, 283
Technologies
    energy, 11
    nuclear, 11
    water pollution, 7–9
Technology, 197–198
    consumers, 5
    defined, 4
    dimensions, 5–6
    and environment, 4–15
    impacts on society, 5–6
    job enrichment and, 253
    knowledge-intensive, 419
    of man, 14–15
    unit-production, 197

Territory management, 75–76
Tersine, Richard, 282–295, 337–347
Theory (*see also* Organization theory)
    bureaucratic, 332
    contingency, 16–21, 98–99, 105
    general systems, 19
    mechanistic, 97, 195
    normative, 95
    organic, 97, 195
    systems, 98
Theory X, 97, 122, 196
Theory Y, 97, 122, 196, 202, 212
Third-sector organizations, 401–413
    Amtrak, 407–408
    Comsat, 413
    concept, 402–404
    defined, 401
    Federal National Mortgage Association, 412–413
    National Aeronautics and Space Agency, 405–406
    national health insurance plan, 404
    potential, 408–410
    student loan program, 404–405
    U.S. Postal Service, 406–407
    universities, 410
Thompson, James D., 196, 328, 333, 413–425
Toffler, Alvin, 296–297
Trist, Eric, 107

United Nations, 76
U.S. Postal Service, 2, 406–407
Unity of command, 98, 101, 193
Urban planning, 366–372
    general problem-solving model, 367
    problems, 366
    program planning and evaluation model, 370–372
    systems design procedure, 367–369

Values
    behavior and, 23
    business, 22–28
    business decisions and, 24
    changing, 22–39, 108
    concept, 109

Values (*cont.*)
  decisions of managers and, 23
  defined, 22–28
  economics, 23, 52
  future, 415
  impact of business, 23
  management, 28
  other institutions, 24
  social, 22–28
Value input sources, 25–26
  traditional, 26
Van Brunt, E. E., 69
Van Horne, R. L., 356–357
Venture behavior, 104
Venture management, 103
Venture teams, 103
Vroom, Victor H., 121–134, 228

Water pollution (*see* Pollution)
Webb, James E., 205

Weber, Max, 193, 283, 416–417
Western Electric Company, 189
Whitehead, Alfred North, 119, 300
Wiener, Norbert, 160
Williams, Martha S., 142
Wilson, Charles Z., 283, 286, 292
Wirtz, Willard, 51, 56
Women, affirmative action and, 174–184
Woodward, Joan, 19, 196–197
Work group, 117, 220–228
  concept, 223–225
  division of labor, 226
  flexibility, 226
  individual assignment, 225–227
  individual development, 226–227
  organization development, 227
Work objective cycle, 223

Young, Stanley, 21
Yuchtman, Ephraim, 330